JOHN CATT'S

Which School? 2024

Orders: please contact Hachette UK Distribution, Hely Hutchinson Centre, Milton Road, Didcot, Oxfordshire, OX11 7HH.
Telephone: +44 (0)1235 827827.
Email: education@hachette.co.uk.
Lines are open from 9 a.m. to 5 p.m., Monday to Friday.

A CIP catalogue record for this book is available from the British Library.

ISBN: 9781036005313

Published in 2023 by
John Catt from Hodder Education,
An Hachette UK Company
15 Riduna Park, Station Road,
Melton, Woodbridge IP12 1QT
Telephone: +44 (0)1394 389850
www.johncatt.com

FSC
www.fsc.org
MIX
Paper | Supporting responsible forestry
FSC™ C104740

A catalogue record for this title is available from the British Library

Contacts

Editor
Phoebe Whybray
Email: Phoebe.Whybray@johncatt.com

Advertising & School Profiles
Tel: +44 (0) 1394 389850
Email: sales@johncatt.com

Contents

How to use this guide

Which School? has been specifically designed with the reader in mind. There are clearly defined sections providing information for anyone looking at independent education in the UK today.

Are you looking for help and advice? Take a look at our editorial section (pages 5-36). Here you will find articles written by experts in their field covering a wide variety of issues you are likely to come across when choosing a school for your child. Each year we try to find a differing range of topics to interest and inform you about the uniqueness of independent education.

Perhaps you are looking for a school or college in a certain geographical region? Then you need to look first in the directories, which begin on page D305. Here you will find basic information about all the schools in each region complete with contact details. From this section you will be directed to more detailed information in the guide where this is available. An example of a typical directory entry is given below.

Are you looking for a certain type of school or college in your local area? Then you will need to look in the directories for your local area (see contents page for a list of all regions). Underneath each school you will find icons that denote the different types of schools or the qualifications that they offer.

Some of you may already be looking for a specific school or college. In which case, if you know the name of the school or college but are unsure of its location, simply go to the index at the back of the guide where you will find all the schools listed alphabetically. Page numbers prefixed with the letter D denote the directory section; those without, a detailed profile.

If, however, you need to find out more information on relevant educational organisations and examinations, then you can look in the appendices where you will find up-to-date information about the examinations and qualifications available (page 403). There is also a section giving basic details about the many varied and useful organisations in the education field (page 423).

The profile and directory information in this guide is also featured on **www.schoolsearch.co.uk**, which also includes social media links, and latest school news.

Key to directory

Key	Example
County	**Wherefordshire**
Name of school or college	**College Academy**
Indicates that this school has a profile	***For further details see p. 12***
Address and contact number	Which Street, Whosville, Wherefordshire AB12 3CD **Tel:** 01000 000000
Head's name	**Head Master:** Dr A Person
Age range	**Age range:** 11–18
Number of pupils. B = boys G = girls VIth = sixth form	**No. of pupils:** 660 B330 G330 VIth 200
Fees per annum. Day = fees for day pupils. WB = fees for weekly boarders. FB = fees for full boarders.	**Fees:** Day £11,000 WB £16,000 FB £20,000

Key to directory icons

Key to symbols:

- Boys' school
- Girls' school
- International school
- Tutorial or sixth form college

Schools offering:

- A levels
- Boarding accommodation
- Bursaries
- Entrance at 16+
- International Baccalaureate
- Learning support
- Vocational qualifications

The questions you should ask

However much a school may appeal on first sight, you still need sound information to form your judgement

Schools attract pupils by their reputations, so most go to considerable lengths to ensure that parents are presented with an attractive image.

Modern marketing techniques try to promote good points and play down (without totally obscuring) bad ones. But every Head knows that, however good the school prospectus is, it only serves to attract parents through the school gates. Thereafter the decision depends on what they see and hear.

When you choose a school for your son or daughter, the key factor is that it will suit them. Many children and their parents are instinctively attracted (or otherwise) to a school on first sight. But even if it passes this test, and 'conforms' to what you are looking for in terms of location and academic, pastoral and extracurricular aspects, you will need to satisfy yourself that the school does measure up to what your instincts tell you.

Research we have carried out over the years suggests that in many cases the most important factor in choosing a school is the impression given by the Head. As well as finding out what goes on in a school, parents need to be reassured by the aura of confidence which they expect from a Head. How they discover the former may help them form their opinion of the latter.

So how a Head answers your questions is important. Based on our research, we have drawn up a list of 24 points on which you may need to be satisfied. The order in which they appear below does not necessarily reflect their degree of importance to each parent, but how the Head answers them may help you draw your own conclusions:

- How accessible is the Head, whose personality is seen by most parents as setting the 'tone' of the school?
- Will your child fit in? What is the overall atmosphere?
- To which organisations does the school belong? How has it been accredited?
- What is the ratio of teachers to pupils?
- What are the qualifications of the teaching staff?
- How often does the school communicate with parents through reports, parent/teacher meetings or other visits?
- What is the school's retention rate? Do larger lower classes and smaller upper classes reflect a school's inability to hang on to pupils?
- What are the school's exam results? What are the criteria for presenting them? Are they consistent over the years?
- How does the school cope with pupils' problems?
- What sort of academic and pastoral advice is available?
- What is the school's attitude to discipline?
- Have there been problems with drugs or sex? How have they been dealt with?
- What positive steps are taken to encourage good manners, behaviour and sportsmanship?
- Is progress accelerated for the academically bright?
- How does the school cope with pupils who do not work?
- What is the attitude to religion?
- What is the attitude to physical fitness and games?
- What sports are offered and what are the facilities?
- What are the extracurricular activities? What cultural or other visits are arranged away from the school?
- What steps are taken to encourage specific talent in music, the arts or sport?
- Where do pupils go when they leave – are they channelled to a few selected destinations?
- What is the uniform? What steps are taken to ensure that pupils take pride in their personal appearance?
- What are the timetable and term dates?
- Is it possible to speak to parents with children at the school to ask them for an opinion?

Endless choices, greater diversification

Tim Head, Deputy Director of Admissions and Teacher of English at Wellington College, believes that an independent education will help your child find their identity

Your child is unique, so perhaps the chief reason for choosing an independent school is to find somewhere that not only recognises that but actively seeks to engage your child as the individual you know they are. When it comes to education, one size certainly doesn't fit all, and the very best schools are able to provide a bespoke learning experience.

At Wellington, for example, we understand that there is no such thing as a single school. The truth is that there are over 1,000 different Wellingtons, as each child builds their own school around them. Take the example of twins who joined over three years ago: now in the Sixth Form, one is studying the IB Diploma with a programme based around their love of humanities and languages; the other is following a rigorous course of A-level sciences. One enjoys team games, the other excels at individual sports. James spends much of his co-curricular time in the music school, Jemima is a dancer who also finds time to pursue her passion for debating. They may go to the same school, but their experience of it could not be more different.

The choices begin the moment children start at their senior school. Beyond the core academic subjects of Maths, English and Science they can choose between French, Spanish, German, Russian, and Mandarin; Greek and Latin, Geography, History or Philosophy; Art, Computer Science, PE, DT, Dance or Drama. The chances of any pupil following the same academic programme are slim indeed, so varied are the permutations.

When it comes to sport the choices are also endless. At Wellington there are over 20 sports to choose from spread over three different terms, and provision for elite athletes as well as those who enjoy a more participatory role. The 21st-century child's physical needs are extensively and imaginatively catered for; gone are the days of shivering on the wing simply so the school can get a team out. Parents may worry about the size of an independent senior school, compared to many preparatory schools, but in truth with size comes greater diversification, and it's the ratio of teachers to children that is the most important metric.

Perhaps the true jewel in a school's crown is the range of co-curricular enrichment activities. Clubs and societies allow children to pursue their own interests, or explore new ones. Model United Nations, Debating, Current Affairs, Creative Writing, Entrepreneurial and Business clubs all broaden horizons, as do Robotics, Engineering and TV and Radio societies. Fancy a career in the media? See yourself as a MasterChef? Imagine what it would be like to design a green-powered racing car? Seek to make a difference through international charity work? The chances are the best independent schools will cater for such dreams and visions, and that so many of these societies are student-led also provide countless and invaluable leadership opportunities.

But the all-important journey towards self can only happen if student wellbeing and rigorous safeguarding are front and centre of a school's provision. Dedicated pastoral teams, a well-regulated tutorial system and frequent reporting and feedback all speak of a school's desire to place the individual at the heart of their education. Adolescence is a time of great opportunity and growth, but it is also a time of confusion and uncertainty. The best schools understand this and provide the space, time and stability all youngsters need if they are to truly grow and flourish.

In short, the very best reason for choosing an independent school is that your child will feel safely empowered to make their own choices on their journey towards true independence.

For more information about Wellington College, see page 256

When it comes to education, one size certainly doesn't fit all, and the very best schools are able to provide a bespoke learning experience.

COLLEGE LIBRARY

Life lessons: the importance of charity in educating our children

With increasing research around the positive impact of charity and acts of kindness on our mood and emotional wellbeing, North Bridge House School explores how making these connections with others is vital in educating children

From raising money for the Royal Free Hospital at Summer and Winter Fair events, to providing gifts for Ukrainian refugees as part of the Rotary Shoebox Scheme, North Bridge House pupils support and often lead on charity initiatives which support causes both close to home and all around the world. In linking formal education to dynamic, community-led projects, the school encourages meaningful connections between pupils as they bond through these group efforts and with members of the wider community. Connecting with others from different age groups and backgrounds in this way is vital to children's character development; building these relationships has been proven to positively impact wellbeing and, at the same time, the school is equipping children with a strong set of core values as they progress into young adulthood.

Sustainability and environmental conservation are essential to our younger generation's future and as such, North Bridge House aims to prepare not just global citizens, but agents of change. Pupils at the school have embarked with enthusiasm on a remarkable initiative to fundraise for 'Just One Tree', starting their very own North Bridge House Forest to aid global reforestation efforts.

Nishi Kapoor, Head of School at North Bridge House Nursery in Hampstead, says:

"Children develop their understanding of global issues through active learning – in engaging our early learners in fundraising events and instilling a can-do attitude from the very beginning of their education, we are equipping them with the empathy, resilience and empowerment to eventually become change makers themselves. Most importantly, we are teaching them that their actions have consequences, not just for themselves or their immediate social circles, but for whole communities – worldwide communities – and this brings a depth of pride and perspective that many other life lessons cannot."

While the school's charitable outlook begins in the Nursery, where a visit from Children in Need's Pudsey Bear is all the motivation the young philanthropists need to do their bit for a greater good, older students at North Bridge House develop key leadership and teamwork skills as a result of their involvement with charity projects.

"The idea is that we are empowering the next generation to take responsibility for both their future and their mental wellbeing; charity is a collaborative effort, connecting young people as they impact something much bigger than themselves, and this creates a heightened sense of capability as well as mood – it provides them with a sense of purpose, which they're probably less likely to find in maths when trying to solve a quadratic equation, for example. With feelings of detachment amongst young people on the rise in this digital age, meaningful connections for a shared cause make all the difference in ensuring pupils feel present and valued," says Headteacher at North Bridge House Senior Hampstead, Christopher Jones.

"The sense of unity created by contributing to a shared cause ignites genuine enthusiasm in pupils, parents and staff alike, at the same time as presenting us with real-world learning opportunities to prepare our pupils for life beyond the school walls," Nishi, Head of the Nursery School adds.

Nurturing strong relationships within an empathetic community is core to the North Bridge House ethos, whether that be through the school's many charity initiatives or prioritising diversity and inclusion within the student, staff and parent body.

The student 'Pride and Diversity Council' is an innovative engine for change at NBH, working to create a whole-school culture of inclusion year-round. For Pride Month in particular, the council launched the student created film, We Are One in assembly; worked with the school's newspaper editorial team on *The History of the Gender Binary* feature and a profile on Alan Turing OBE FRS, who was notoriously persecuted for his homosexuality by the government he helped save; and designed a survey to bring to light and thus eradicate any homophobic, biphobic, or transphobic language used in school.

Whatever the month, however, student voices are championed, as are real-life issues such as Black Lives Matter. While Black History Month inspires all areas of the curriculum, inclusivity is at the forefront of children's education at NBH whatever the time of year, nurturing children's cultural awareness alongside their appreciation of what it truly means to give back and be charitable.

With volunteering linked to lower rates of stress and anxiety due to the positive effects of helping others and the feel-good brain chemical, dopamine, North Bridge House promotes charitable involvement as key to children's personal growth and development. And in a school community where everyone is seen, heard and celebrated, the overall inclusive and holistic approach to every child's wellbeing is arguably just as important as the focus on academic excellence.

For more information about North Bridge House School, see page 152

BUILD
CHALLENGE
Your peers
"YOUR SO GAY."
A Celebration of
LGBTQ
Literary history

Co-curricular opportunities and future careers

Gordon's School explains why co-curricular activities are a fundamental part of school life and how they help equip students with essential skills for the future

No doubting the importance of exam grades and qualifications, but increasingly employers are looking at the soft skills that separate one candidate from another.

And while the classroom will gain students their first job or place at university, it is the character acquired on the games field or in the school play, the team spirit, ability to get on with others as part of a team – a thirst for success, that will sustain them through life.

Gordon's School, a non-selective residential boarding and day school in Surrey and Boarding School of the Year in the TES Schools Awards for 2022, boasts a top five per cent place for progress at A Levels of all schools in England and Wales. Telling that the statistic is for progress as the school places such importance on sport and co-curricular activities.

All students are given opportunities throughout the day to play sport, indulge in a hobby or interest or perhaps set up their own society - with a choice of 128 activities currently on offer! This is carried through to Saturday mornings.

The school also records higher than average numbers of students completing their Duke of Edinburgh's Awards. And in Year 10 every student joins the CCF (Combined Cadet Force), choosing the Army, Navy or Air Force.

Students are also encouraged to apply for leadership posts during their time at Gordon's, whether becoming a Student Governor; Head of House/Prefect or taking on the role of team captain in sports teams or Pipe/Drum Major in the Pipes and Drums. As part of their leadership positions, they are offered the chance to study for industry-recognised qualifications through the ILM (Institute of Leadership and Management).

Careers Lead Augusta Kennedy sees these opportunities as vital not only for their physical and mental wellbeing but for improving transferrable skills and ultimately their chances in whatever they decide to do after leaving school.

"Increasingly employers aren't just looking at exam grades but the additional skills that candidates can bring to the workplace. Duke of Edinburgh Awards for instance, demonstrate commitment, diversity, the ability to handle pressure, time management, a have a go attitude and certainly enhances a student's employability.

"The opportunities that students have access to at Gordon's, which include sport, DofE, CCF, creative arts and the many chances to perform publicly, take students out of their comfort zone. They become more confident through taking part in these disciplines, learn leadership qualities, versatility, perseverance, endurance, teamwork, problem-solving and discover new skills - all necessary qualities for their working life whatever career they choose."

All the major sports are represented at Gordon's as well as equestrian, golf, karting and cycling and there are ample and varied opportunities for creative arts including drama, music, art and LAMDA with many chances to participate in plays, exhibitions and performances.

The new sports hub and additional all-weather sports pitch has enhanced the already extensive sporting facilities at Gordon's and creative arts has benefitted from new art studios with plans for a new performing arts centre.

In September 2020 the school welcomed the first clutch of students on the Harlequins DiSE (Diploma in Sporting Excellence) programme to provide a pathway for 16-18 year olds pursuing a professional career in rugby. Partnerships with Superleague Netball team Surrey Storm and National League Football Team Aldershot Town have followed.

The commitment to sports extends to the school's staff. Many of them have excelled in their fields, ensuring the highest level of coaching and commitment. The impressive line-up includes Pakistan Olympic Hockey player Muhammad Irfan together with former GB hockey player David Mathews; former Wales International and ex-Chelsea player Gareth Hall and three times Olympian cox Alan Inns.

Some students leave Gordon's for American universities on scholarships for golf and football. Others are set to tread a path to becoming a professional sportsman or woman in this country. But all take part in some form of competitive sport, whatever their ability.

Director of Sport Jamie Harrison explained why there is such a strong emphasis on co-curricular options at Gordon's and the importance of encouraging every student to participate.

"The ethos of the school is to develop the whole child and our sporting and creative arts infrastructure provides our students with the best coaching, facilities and experiences. Every student is encouraged to have a go at something.

"The emphasis at Gordon's is very much 'why not?' and we see time and again those that would otherwise not attempt competitive sport or performing in a play, doing so, enjoying and benefitting from it!"

For more information about Gordon's School, see page 210

The benefits of a prep school education

Guy Musson, Headmaster at Orwell Park School, reflects on the enhanced opportunities available at preparatory schools and the importance of a values-driven education

Suffolk-based artist and author Charlie Mackesy's 2019 book *The Boy, the Mole, the Fox and the Horse* is one of the most heart-warming, poignant and welcome publications of our lifetimes. Not since A.A. Milne and E.H. Shepherd's 1926 classic, which might have been entitled 'The Boy, the Bear, the Tiger and the Donkey'*, have we been gifted an illustrated story that transcends all age groups containing such a treasure trove of wise mantras, underpinned by kindness, friendship, vulnerability and resilience. In throwing together a group of similarly unlikely friends (for the cheerful *Tigger* and the grumpy *Eeyore*, read the wary Fox and the greedy *Mole*), Mackesy succeeds in striking a chord with so many of us as we support children (and each other) in embracing the beauty and challenges of the world.**apologies to fans of Piglet, Rabbit, Owl, Kanga and Roo.*

The book and subsequent Oscar-winning animated screenplay have presented school teachers and leaders with a remarkable number of quotes that get right to the heart of so many of the values that schools champion.

- For growth mindset: "When have you been at your strongest?" asked the boy. "When I have dared to show my weakness."
- For kindness: "Nothing beats kindness," said the horse. "It sits quietly beyond all things."
- For ambition and courage: "Most of the old moles I know wish they had listened less to their fears and more to their dreams."
- For valuing every child: "I'm so small," said the mole. "Yes," said the boy, "but you make a huge difference".
- And my personal favourite: "What do you think is the biggest waste of time?" "Comparing yourself to others," said the mole.

You may justifiably be wondering what this all has to do with country prep schools and the answer is the Mole's favourite food: "If at first you don't succeed, have some cake." I like to think of schools as cakes (for the purposes of this article, it is a more helpful metaphor than Pooh's love of honey). All schools share core ingredients and parents have rightly come to expect academic ambition and high standards of teaching and learning, underpinned by dedicated pastoral care to be the first two non-negotiable levels of sponge. Getting the right balance and quality of ingredients is clearly vital as the foundations are laid. When parents choose to invest in an independent education, they are however expecting more than just plain sponge, however good those layers might be.

The icing on the cake is the hugely exciting and varied extra- and co-curricular provision which you will find in a thriving boarding prep school. Not only does this save busy parents from taxiing their children to external sports, drama and dance clubs, but it crucially also enables teachers to gain a deeper understanding of what makes each child tick. Such an offering also presents us with further opportunities to stretch and challenge children, but also support them, laugh with them and pick them up when they fall. In addition to endless sport, music, art and drama, Orwell Park pupils benefit from an outdoor pool, an observatory, sailing, a residential at Mayo College in India, our very own assault course built by an army regiment, bushcraft and camping in our forest and a woodland forest school for the youngest children (often accompanied by our resident deer).

> We must provide them with a wide range of platforms on which they can build their confidence and shine brightly.

Part of a great prep school education is understanding that children will get it wrong sometimes but that this is ultimately the only way in which they will learn and grow. In seeking to develop their passions, we must provide them with a wide range of platforms on which they can build their confidence and shine brightly. I firmly believe that all children are intelligent and all children are special. They have the capacity to do the most amazing things – it is our job and our privilege to help them find their intelligence or talent and to support them in realising their potential. The thicker the layer of icing (in my view it should be as thick as the sponge itself!), the better the chance we have to develop children's characters and set them up for success at their senior schools and beyond.

Today's world requires children to develop an adaptable skillset alongside interpersonal and creative talents and the experience a boarding prep school can offer will only maximise this toolkit. Ultimately, prep school should be fun, memorable and packed with opportunities for children to throw themselves into. We return to 1926 for our final quote: "You can't stay in your corner of the Forest waiting for others to come to you. You have to go to them sometimes."

For more information about Orwell Park School, see page 82

The Musson Family

Choosing a co-ed or single-sex school for your child

Mark Turner, Head of King's House School in Richmond, considers why they decided to transition to co-education

King's House was founded in 1946 as a boys' prep school near Richmond Hill, and is now a thriving school of over 400 children. In 2009 we opened the co-ed nursery, which has since expanded to a busy two-year pre-school of nearly 60 children. In March 2023 we announced that girls would start to join the school from September 2024, as we begin the transition to full co-education. Understandably, some asked why having educated boys for over 75 years, we would decide to move to co-ed. As is probably the case at most single sex schools, it's been a topic of discussion amongst the Senior Management Team and Board for many years. Whilst we decided in 2023 that the time was now right for us to move to co-education, it would have come earlier had it not been for Covid. The pros and cons of co-ed versus single sex have long been discussed; ultimately, these are the reasons that drove our decision to become co-ed.

Early Years

Co-ed throughout the early years encourages the development of social skills at a young age, where children are learning to play and socialise together. Our Nursery has welcomed both boys and girls since it opened, and over the last decade it's been a real shame to see the friendships forged between boys and girls there not be able to continue into Reception. Those key communication and collaboration skills can now continue to grow once the children join the Junior Department (Reception to Year 3). Many of our older pupils move on to co-ed senior schools, and some of those were formerly boys only too. For these pupils, co-ed is representative of the world beyond education and can encourage understanding and respect between genders.

Inclusivity

Co-education can create a more diverse and inclusive environment for children, with the safety to explore their identity and interests. It reflects the diversity of London, broadening children's perspectives and empowering them to learn from and socialise with the other gender. With a more diverse student cohort, the pupils will naturally see children of both genders with different interests. Over the last few years our staff EDI committee has led a review to ensure all ethnicities, religions, and genders were represented in our resources and curriculum. Where many single sex schools must work harder to counter stereotypes, this can be done more naturally in a co-ed environment.

Widening the curriculum

Whilst our curriculum and extra-curricular programme is already focused on being broad and balanced, with much of the focus being beyond the traditional core subjects, the move to co-ed has presented the opportunity to review what we offer. Throughout the 2023-24 school year, dance, gymnastics and cooking will be added as clubs, benefitting our current boys and catering to a wider and more diverse range of interests. Our Director of Music is thrilled about the variety the girls will bring to the many choirs and ensembles in the Senior Department (Year 4 to 8)!

Parent demand

Listening to parental demand and the needs of families is key to being a forward-thinking and modern prep school. Logistically, for many families being able to drop and pick up all their children from the same school, with one set of term dates and events, is vital and often a deciding factor when choosing a school. There are currently no co-ed prep schools in Richmond, and our transition to co-ed gives local families a wider choice when deciding on a school for their child.

Ultimately there is not one right answer, and the choice for parents will differ depending on the needs of their child and family life. For some of our parents that may mean a co-ed prep school and a single sex senior school, or perhaps co-ed throughout their child's education.

Regardless, each school must work to create a respectful and inclusive environment where all students feel comfortable and can thrive academically, socially, and emotionally.

For more information about King's House School, see page 114

Co-education can create a more diverse and inclusive environment for children, with the safety to explore their identity and interests.

To board or not to board? There is another option...

Stephen Mullock, Deputy Head at Ellesmere College, considers the benefits of weekly boarding and why it is often a brilliant alternative

When looking at school options for your children, there only used to be two choices - boarding or not boarding, and these days knowing that your child is getting a consistent, high-quality education regardless of the external environment is crucial for their personal development and educational journey.

Well luckily many boarding schools today offer a number of boarding options, but one option in particular that is becoming increasingly popular with a large number of parents is part-time or weekly boarding - a helpful and viable alternative to, and a bridge between, the world of a day pupil and that of a full-boarder.

The choice can also depend on the distance away from the school – usually the determining factor for many parents in the choice of a school – and so the option to weekly board offers parents a much broader choice for their child as they can board on an ad-hoc basis during the week, and return home at the weekends, or part way through the week as desired using a school bus service or evening collection by parents.

The choice of schools available based on the needs of the child increases dramatically – schools that were considered 'too far away' are now within reach, and journey times on a daily basis through the week are reduced, leaving the drive to and from school only on a Sunday and a Friday.

Flexibility is key

Weekly boarding is also the next logical step for many students after having 'ad-hoc' boarding experiences – a flexible option based on the needs of the child for specific events or family reasons, for geographical reasons, or here and there for academic or co-curricular commitments after school. And if a child weekly boards and usually goes home at the weekend but would like to stay for a fixture or a concert at the weekend, the school should - and usually can - accommodate most requests!

This provides parents with a 'helping-hand', giving them their own flexibility not only in being able to successfully manage their work or personal commitments without the stress of baby-sitters or cost of nannies, but also to control the growth of independence of their child. The child can then maintain a level of consistency, security and familiarity with their academic and co-curricular schedules during the week, and enjoy the many programmes of activities that are on offer in the evenings. It is also a way to break into the field of full boarding perhaps during the Sixth Form years and can be easily aligned with College events and exeats. The step to University or moving away from home also becomes an easier one for both parent and child as the level of independence and confidence grows through the years.

The benefits of weekly boarding for students

Ad-hoc and weekly boarding is a great introduction - a taster! - of what full boarding is really like and gives children a chance to experience what life is like as a boarder as they move through the school, as well as the opportunity to meet students from many other nationalities. It also works really well to ready a child for the move from senior school to college or university where they often live away from home in halls of residence, teaching them valuable lessons in independence and resilience in a safe, familiar and monitored environment. Quite often, after perhaps one or two ad-hoc boarding sessions which offer a brief insight into boarding life, it is the child who then initiates the next step in asking if they can weekly board as they grow older, more confident and need to spend more time with academic studies (Sixth Form for example), or if they are involved in after school co-curricular activities.

Boarders also grow and learn within larger friendship groups, share more experiences together and form life-long relationships and usually provide an opportunity for students to take on roles of responsibility – Head of House for example - and learn to become more independent, whilst developing the skills to work together as a team. Through this many students develop greater self-esteem, confidence and feel better prepared and ready for the next phase of their lives.

Ultimately, weekly boarding is an option in many boarding schools which is going from strength to strength and which many parents, students and staff have seen the benefits for all.

And above all boarding is fun!

And last but not least... boarders of every type have fun! There are usually a huge range of exciting and meaningful activities on offer to weekly and full-boarders; from co-curricular activities such as sport and drama, CCF and Duke of Edinburgh, a round of golf, games in the sports hall or working out in the gyzm or heated pool, evening debating groups, even taking part in twilight catch up lessons. Not to mention the sporting, cultural and retail experiences on offer.

Author

Stephen Mullock is Deputy Head External Relations at Ellesmere College in Shropshire – a co-educational day, weekly and full boarding school for students aged 7-18 years old.

For more information about Ellesmere College, see page 276

Unlocking the benefits of boarding: your child's home away from home

King's School Rochester provides insight into the unique experience of attending a boarding school

When it comes to your child's education and personal growth, choosing the right path is a crucial decision. We understand that you want the best for your child, and that's why we invite you to explore the extraordinary world of King's School Rochester, where boarding isn't just an option; it's a transformative experience. King's offers a boutique boarding experience where no-one is a number.

A rich heritage
With a legacy spanning over 1,400 years, King's is the second oldest school in the world, nestled in the shadow of Rochester Cathedral and Rochester Castle, our school is steeped in history and tradition. Whilst a sense of place is bound to have an impact on the development of the children learning here, we prepare your child for the evolving challenges of the 21st century, emphasizing skills, experiences, and opportunities both inside and outside the classroom.

The HEART of King's
Our core values - **H**appiness, **E**ndeavour, **A**spiration, **R**oundedness and **T**eamwork (the HEART of King's) - are the guiding principles shaping the King's experience, nurturing each pupil's unique potential while fostering a profound sense of community and inner confidence.

A global community
Our boarding community mirrors the diversity of the modern world, welcoming pupils from over 20 different countries. This cultural mosaic creates an enriching environment where your child learns alongside peers from diverse backgrounds, fostering a global perspective.

Home away from home
With just 55 boarders, our community is intimate and nurturing. Our modernized Victorian boarding houses, School House for boys and St. Margaret's House for girls, offer a 'home away from home' experience, conveniently located near the School.

Flexibility for every family
We offer various boarding options to suit unique family needs, including weekday boarding for full engagement in extracurricular activities and flexi-boarding to ease the stress of commuting during exam times. Our well-structured pastoral support system ensures your child is always in capable hands, 24/7.

Exceptional dining and weekend adventures
Our chef prepares delicious two-course meals daily, offering a taste of home. Common rooms provide spaces for relaxation and socialising, mirroring the comforts of home. Weekends are brimming with exciting activities, ensuring your child has a fulfilling and enjoyable experience outside of the classroom.

A transformative journey
At King's School Rochester, we aim to foster independence while maintaining the comforting embrace of home. Our boarding experience is about creating lasting friendships, unforgettable memories, and a profound sense of belonging. Saying goodbye is often the hardest part for our pupils, who describe their time here as "the most unforgettable experience of their lives."

Choosing the right school for your child is a significant decision, and we want to ensure you have all the information you need. To learn more about King's School Rochester and how we can help shape your child's future, please visit our website at www.kings-rochester.co.uk or contact us directly at admissions@kings-rochester.co.uk.

Your child's journey begins here, with us, at King's School Rochester. Join us in creating a brighter future for your child.

For more information about King's School Rochester, see page 218

Our boarding experience is about creating lasting friendships, unforgettable memories, and a profound sense of belonging.

Cultivating environmental stewards: The Forest School experience

Heathside School Hampstead share the benefits of Forest Schools and how they help to nurture individuality and a lifelong love of learning

In today's fast-paced, technology-driven world, the traditional classroom isn't the only place where learning happens. More and more educators are recognising the value of an outdoor education, with Forest Schools leading the way. Taking children out of the conventional classroom and into the heart of nature has been shown to enrich their learning experiences.

At Heathside School Hampstead, the commitment to Forest School education is not just an extracurricular activity; it's an integral part of their educational philosophy. Here, students call North London's famous heath their playground, classroom and teacher, forging a profound connection with nature that shapes them into environmentally responsible citizens.

Headteacher, Nadia Ward, says: *"We firmly believe that taking the learning outdoors not only safeguards the essence of childhood but also encourages a more inclusive approach to play and exploration, free from the constraints of digital devices.*

"Nature becomes the canvas for their creativity, fostering a sense of equality and empowerment as they learn and grow together. This not only promotes physical activity and well-being but also nurtures social skills, teamwork, and problem-solving abilities."

In an age where screen time often supersedes outdoor adventures, Heathside stands firm in its commitment to providing a holistic education whilst not compromising on academic excellence.

Forest School emphasises hands-on exploration. In the forest, every fallen leaf, bird's nest, and stream holds a lesson waiting to be discovered. Children are encouraged to touch, feel, smell, and experience the natural world firsthand.

Nadia explains that this sensory engagement sparks curiosity and wonder, driving a deeper understanding of concepts like biology, ecology, and geology. Students also have the space and opportunity to make decisions, take risks, and explore their own interests. This autonomy builds self-confidence and encourages them to take ownership of their learning and discover their own strengths, invaluable lessons for personal growth.

Taking children out of the conventional classroom and into the heart of nature has been shown to enrich their learning experiences.

"Our approach equips students with not only knowledge but also critical thinking skills, creativity, adaptability, and a strong sense of character - all attributes they'll need to flourish in a rapidly changing world.

"At Heathside, we cherish children's formative years and give them the space and freedom to learn. Their individuality is celebrated, and this personalised approach allows students to thrive academically."

The natural world is a constant source of inspiration for every child. Forest Schools harness this creativity by encouraging children to use natural materials for their own artistic expression. Whether it's building a fairy house from sticks and leaves or painting with mud, these activities ignite a child's imagination. Creative play encourages communication, and collaboration, all while nurturing a love for art and self-expression.

Heathside takes the learning beyond the theoretical and into the real world. Children engage in authentic, practical activities like building shelters, identifying plants and animals, and cooking over an open fire. These experiences provide a tangible context for subjects like science, maths, and history, making learning more relevant and memorable. Applying what they have learnt, students are able to use these skills of ingenuity in the technology hub, working on robotics, coding and science experiments.

Children in Forest Schools learn to cooperate and collaborate with their peers in an unstructured environment. They build a sense of community, where mutual support and teamwork are essential. These social skills are transferable to any context, preparing children for success in both academic and social settings.

As educators and parents alike seek well-rounded and impactful educational experiences, Forest Schools stand as a testament to the power of nature to shape young minds and spirits for a brighter, more connected future.

Heathside stands as a shining example of how an independent education can cultivate environmental stewards and nurture individuality while upholding academic rigour to instil a lifelong love of learning.

For more information about Heathside School Hampstead, see page 144

HEATHSIDE SCHOOL
HAMPSTEAD

The importance of a character education

Ms Louise Simpson, Head of Exeter School, Devon shares their approach to creating a school of great character

For almost four centuries Exeter School has proudly provided an excellent education for its pupils.

In this time the classroom has been a challenging and exciting environment, but that has only ever been a part of what makes our education excellent. Our pupils have always had many opportunities to develop their character: on the sports field, on the moors and on the water; in the work of our chapel and community service schemes; through the CCF and the expressive and performing arts, for example.

We have been developing the character of excellent Exonians through this holistic approach for centuries.

In Ancient Greece, Aristotle said "We are what we repeatedly do; Excellence, then, is not an act, but a habit". This virtue-ethics approach is very much the philosophy that sits at the heart of our character education. Our intentional programme to develop the civic, intellectual, performance and moral virtues in our pupils gives them the traits needed to thrive in life, both at school and beyond. We want them to aspire to contribute in a positive way to the community in which they live, and to flourish in life, both at school and in adult life beyond.

We want them to aspire to contribute in a positive way to the community in which they live.

Our purpose and virtues are crucial in supporting the character development of our pupils, and making them exceptional young people, ready for whatever challenges they encounter in life. In addition, they sit at the heart of all that the school does. In being a school of character, we want our whole community to embrace this approach. This means considering others and the world around us when making decisions, ensuring that we nurture and develop our staff team, work in a sustainable way, work collaboratively with others, including our partner organisations, and ensure that we remain accountable for our choices.

Our virtues

To inspire and challenge curious minds: We are curious, independent thinkers, achieving beyond our expectations.

To act with kindness and integrity: We act with integrity, respect and kindness for others and ourselves.

To welcome and serve: We are an inclusive Exonian community, valuing diversity and equality, and giving back to others.

To endeavour and collaborate: We work together and strive for excellence in everything we do, continuing to endeavour when faced with challenge.

Academic results should be just one of the factors in the development of our pupils. The virtues we instil in them will shape the future of tomorrow. Such strong foundations have made us an exceptional school for many centuries, and we look forward to the future with excitement, just as our young people do.

For more information about Exeter School, see page 264

oneills
EXETER
SCHOOL
C
oneills
EXETER
SCHOOL

Fulfilling potential beyond the classroom

Ipswich School students reflect on the positive impact of co-curricular activities and some of the new skills they have gained

A strong co-curriculum is a key area that parents will want to consider when looking for an independent school for their child. Perhaps they already have a skill to develop further or perhaps you want them to have a broad range of opportunities. What you learn and how you develop 'soft skills' such as leadership, time management, and team work are as vital in today's society as the exam outcomes which a child achieves. We believe that a rich and varied co-curricular provision complements an excellent academic education, giving pupils the opportunity to develop many valuable transferable skills and allowing them to realise their full potential. We asked some of our pupils to explain what skills they have developed through co-curricular activities.

"Sport is an essential part of school life for many reasons. For me, being part of an elite performance based hockey programme has helped me excel beyond belief. The team ethos and overall mentality is incredible. I went from a C team goalkeeper, to an A team one in under a year! In addition to this, I am the most physically fit I have ever been, and I put much of this down to sport. Above all, the feeling of making a last minute save just cannot be beaten. I love sport and Ipswich School sport has helped me grow as a person, and as a player." - ***Adam C, Year 10***

"Nothing lets you be so creatively free like drama does. The joy in drama doesn't just come from discovering a hidden talent - far from it. The joy comes from working hard at it, and pouring yourself into it, because you know that nothing will beat the feeling of standing on stage with some of your closest friends; friends that you might have never made otherwise, and giving it everything you have. Not because you have to, but because you love it. As you take your final bow on closing night, as the hard work of so many dedicated actors, directors, and artists comes to a crescendo, you do it knowing that this has made you braver, more creative, and above all, freer." - ***Barbara S, Year 11***

"Over the past seven years we have enjoyed taking part in countless concerts and other extracurricular musical activities. Our highlights include two annual musical events: the Christmas Concert and then when the entire music department heads to Snape Maltings for the Spring Concert performance each year. Countless rehearsals and huge efforts from all go into every performance, making it possible to have concerts of such exceptional quality. Music has played a huge part in our lives at Ipswich School and we know that this will continue for others for many years to come. We personally have enjoyed our time playing in various ensembles and orchestras, whilst developing musically in the company of friends." - ***Alice C and Emily H, Year 13***

"I believe that sports are an integral part of being at Ipswich School as it helps you meet new people you may have never integrated with and helps you build relationships through your common interests of enjoying a certain sport. Additionally, sports at Ipswich School are very accessible no matter how good you are and this helps you build skills you will not learn from lessons. For example I have learnt the skills of being a leader from being the B team cricket captain for a few years and this experience helped me get into the A team in cricket last year - I think this could be linked to my increased confidence from being the captain of the B team." - ***Alex K, Year 10***

For more information about Ipswich School, see page 76

We believe that a rich and varied co-curricular provision complements an excellent academic education, giving pupils the opportunity to develop many valuable transferable skills and allowing them to realise their full potential.

VX3
VX3
VX3
GILBERT

Embracing change

Mrs Caroline Jordan, Headmistress at Headington Rye Oxford, expresses her delight about plans for the new Oxford school

For many years, our corner of Oxford has been home to two schools, both catering primarily for girls' education but carving out our own niches. We've co-existed happily, with Headington School set on a larger site, offering a wider range of activities and academic choice, while Rye St Antony's smaller class sizes offered a more intimate pastoral experience. Headington, which celebrated its 100th birthday in 2015, is separated from Rye, established in 1930, by little more than a pedestrianised lane. We have been neighbours in a very real sense, benefitting from a beautiful location just a mile from Oxford city centre, strong links with the city's two universities and a wealth of opportunities for enrichment.

That relationship is set to change and I couldn't be more excited. Over the course of the next two years, the two schools will join together to create a new senior and prep school. We are curious, confident, ambitious schools which share very similar educational and Christian values. Our mission is to take the best of both schools to create an outstanding new school for both current and future generations of children.

Headington Rye Oxford Prep School will be for girls and boys aged 3 to 11 and will be based on the current Rye site, while Headington Rye Oxford Senior School will remain a single sex school for girls aged 11 to 18 based on the Headington Senior School site. We'll continue to offer boarding for girls from age 11 and we look forward to being able to provide an even more flexible offering in future across the wealth of facilities across the two sites.

Change can be a daunting prospect but all successful institutions - schools not the least - must grow and evolve to ensure they are meeting the needs of their pupil and parent body. While staff and students at Headington, for example, work hard to embody the principles our founders laid out over 100 years ago, the reality is that the school today is almost unrecognisable from the tiny establishment set up in 1915. Rye has similarly developed and enhanced its offering over the years to reflect Oxford's changing demographics.

This is an incredibly exciting time to be a pupil at Headington Rye Oxford, both for those who are already part of our community and those who are thinking about joining us. Taking the shared experience and expertise of the staff across the two sites, Headington Rye pupils will receive a superb education, enhanced by even broader teaching, pastoral and co-curricular expertise, along with excellent facilities across 35 acres right in the heart of Oxford. There is so much scope to do more, to look at the wonderful things both schools offer and to add to already wide and varied subject and activity options.

I will lead Headington Rye School as Headmistress, ably supported by the expert teachers from both schools. We will continue to offer outstanding teaching proven to allow pupils to thrive, reaching beyond their potential. The two schools will come together in September 2024 when staff and pupils will transfer to their respective sites.

New families will join an inspirational, forward-looking school with unrivalled facilities, a wealth of teaching expertise and exceptional pastoral care. I'm really excited about being able to add more vocational options to our offering and to learning from my new colleagues about how they get the best out of their pupils. While I've been a Headmistress for many years now, there is always something new to learn. I find many of the most powerful lessons that I receive today are from the pupils in my charge. Each year I always look forward to meeting a new cohort and to see how they will challenge and inspire me as they find their feet and develop into young adults. This next year will be doubly exciting as the Rye cohort joins us, bringing their unique experience and perspectives. I cannot wait to see what they will bring to our new school.

There are of course many logistical things to be managed while we prepare for this change, which is why we have planned for a gradual merger. This will ensure that pupils get the best possible experience both during and after the transition. Our commitment to academic and pastoral excellence remains unwavering and we will, as always, place the happiness and success of our pupils at the heart of everything we do. Headington Rye Oxford will provide pupils with the best possible preparation for their future, whatever it may hold.

We are extremely lucky to have really skilled, experienced staff at both schools. We know we will be able to provide a truly fantastic experience for our current and future school community. Our new combined Prep team, from both Headington and Rye, has a wealth of experience in working with both boys and girls and we are delighted to be able to respond to the growing demand for a larger co-educational prep school in this part of Oxford.

We want everyone to feel part of this exciting journey as Headington Rye Oxford starts to take shape.

For more information about Headington Rye Oxford, see page 48

Help in funding the fees

Chris Procter, Managing Director of SFIA Wealth Management, outlines a planned approach to funding your child's school fees

Over the last year there has been greater pressure on families due to rising interest rates and an increase in the cost of living. Despite this the independent education sector remains resilient, according to the latest Independent Schools Council (ISC) survey, conducted in January 2023. The number of pupils in ISC schools stood at 554,243, a new record high.

Average school fee increases were 5.6% between the 2021/22 and 2022/23 school years, this is consistent with the higher than normal inflation that the UK economy has experienced. The average day school fees were £5,552 which is an increase of 5.8%. The average boarding school fees were £13,002 per term, an increase of 5.2%.

Fees charged by schools vary by region – for example, the average day school fees per term ranged from £4,000 in the North West to £6,676 in London.

Over £1.2bn of fee assistance was provided in the 2022/23 school year, of which 80% came from schools themselves. Over a third of pupils in ISC schools received at least one type of fee support.

£483m of means-tested fee assistance was provided, an increase of £3m on the previous year. The average means-tested bursary stood at over £11,807. Nearly half of all pupils on means-tested bursaries had more than half of their fees remitted.

The overall cost of school fees (including university fees) might seem daunting: the cost of educating one child privately could well be very similar to that of buying a house but, as with house buying, the school fees commitment for the majority of parents can be made possible by spreading it over a long period rather than funding it all from current resources.

It is vital that parents do their financial homework, plan ahead and start to save early. Grandparents who have access to capital could help out; by contributing to school fees they could also help to reduce any potential future inheritance tax liability.

Parents would be well-advised to consult a specialist financial adviser as early as possible, since a long-term plan for the payment of fees – possibly university as well – can prove very advantageous from a financial point of view and offer greater peace of mind. Funding fees is neither science, nor magic, nor is there any panacea. It is quite simply a question of planning and using whatever resources are available, such as income, capital, or tax plan planning opportunities.

The fundamental point to recognise is that you, your circumstances and your wishes or ambitions, for your children, or grandchildren are unique. They might well appear similar to those of other people but they will still be uniquely different. There will be no single solution to your problem. In fact, after a review of all your circumstances, there might not be a problem at all.

So, what are the reasons for seeking advice about education expenses?

- To reduce the overall cost
- To get some tax benefit
- To reduce your cash outflow
- To invest capital to ensure that future fees are paid
- To set aside money now for future fees
- To provide protection for school fees
- Or just to make sure that, as well as educating your children, you can still have a life

Any, some, or all of the above – or others not listed – could be on your agenda, the important thing is to develop a strategy.

At this stage, it really does not help to get hung up on which financial 'product' is the most suitable. The composition of a school fees plan will differ for each family depending on a number of factors. That is why there is no one school fees plan on offer.

The simplest strategy but in most cases, the most expensive option, is to write out a cheque for the

whole bill when it arrives and post it back to the school. Like most simple plans, that can work well, if you have the money. Even if you do have the money, is that really the best way of doing things? Do you know that to fund £1,000 of school fees as a higher rate taxpayer paying 40% income tax, you currently need to earn £1,667, this rises to £1,818 if you are an additional rate taxpayer where the rate is 45%.

How then do you start to develop your strategy? As with most things in life, if you can define your objective, then you will know what you are aiming at. Your objective in this case will be to determine how much money is needed and when.

You need to draw up a school fees schedule or what others may term a cash flow forecast. So, you need to identify:

- How many children?
- Which schools and therefore what are the fees?

(or you could use an average school fee)

- When are they due?
- Any special educational needs?
- Inflation estimate?
- Include university costs?

With this basic information, the school fees schedule/cash flow forecast can be prepared and you will have defined what it is you are trying to achieve.

Remember though, that senior school fees are typically more than prep school fees – this needs to be factored in. Also, be aware that the cost of university is not restricted to the fees alone; there are a lot of maintenance and other costs involved: accommodation, books, food, to name a few. Don't forget to build in inflation, I refer you back to the data at the beginning of this article.

You now have one element of the equation, the relatively simple element. The other side is the resources you have available to achieve the objective. This also needs to be identified, but this is a much more difficult exercise. The reason that it is more difficult, of course, is that school fees are not the only drain on your resources. You probably have a mortgage, you want to have holidays, you need to buy food and clothes, you may be concerned that you should be funding a pension.

This is a key area of expertise, since your financial commitments are unique. A specialist in the area of school fees planning can help identify these commitments, to record them and help you to distribute your resources according to your priorities.

The options open to you as parents depend completely upon your adviser's knowledge of these complex personal financial issues. (Did I forget to mention your tax position, capital gains tax allowance, other tax allowances, including those of your children and a lower or zero rate tax paying spouse or partner? These could well be used to your advantage.)

A typical school fees plan can incorporate many elements to fund short, medium and long-term fees. Each plan is designed according to individual circumstances and usually there is a special emphasis on what parents are looking to achieve, for example, to maximise overall savings and to minimise the outflow of cash.

Additionally, it is possible to protect the payment of the fees in the event of unforeseen circumstances that could lead to a significant or total loss of earnings.

Short-term fees

Short-term fees are typically the termly amounts needed within five years: these are usually funded from such things as guaranteed investments, liquid capital, loan plans (if no savings are available) or maturing insurance policies, investments etc. Alternatively, they can be funded from disposable income.

Medium-term fees

Once the short-term plan expires, the medium-term funding is invoked to fund the education costs for a further five to ten years. Monthly amounts can be invested in a low-risk, regular premium investment ranging from a building society account to a friendly society savings plan to equity ISAs. It is important to understand the pattern of the future fees and to be aware of the timing of withdrawals.

Long-term fees

Longer term funding can incorporate a higher element of risk (as long as this is acceptable to the investor), which will offer higher potential returns. Investing in UK and overseas equities could be considered. Solutions may be the same as those for medium-term fees, but will have the flexibility to utilise investments that may have an increased 'equity based' content.

Finally, it is important to remember that most investments, or financial products either mature with a single payment or provide for regular withdrawals; rarely do they provide timed termly payments.

Additionally, the overall risk profile of the portfolio should lean towards the side of caution (for obvious reasons).

There are any number of advisers in the country, but few who specialise in the area of planning to meet school and university fees. SFIA is the largest organisation specialising in school fees planning in the UK.

This article has been contributed by SFIA and edited by Chris Procter, Managing Director.

Chris can be contacted at:
SFIA, 27 Moorbridge Road,
Maidenhead,
Berkshire, SL6 8LT
Tel: 01628 566777
Email: enquiries@sfia.co.uk
Web: www.sfia.co.uk

The Independent Schools Council

The Independent Schools Council (ISC) works with its members to promote and preserve the quality, diversity and excellence of UK independent education both at home and abroad

What is the ISC?

The ISC brings together seven associations of independent schools, their heads, bursars and governors. Through our member associations we represent approximately 1,400 independent schools in the UK and overseas, which educate more than half a million children.

The ISC's work is carried out by a small team of dedicated professionals in central London. We are assisted by contributions from expert advisory groups in specialist areas. Our priorities are set by the board of directors led by our chairman, Barnaby Lenon.

ISC schools

Schools in membership of the ISC's constituent associations offer a high quality, rounded education. Whilst our schools are very academically successful, their strength also lies in the extra-curricular activities offered, helping to nurture pupils' soft skills. There are independent schools to suit every need, whether you want a day or boarding school, single-sex or co-education, a large or a small school, or schools offering specialisms, such as in the arts.

Our schools are very diverse: some are selective and highly academic, while others have very strong drama or music departments full of creative opportunities. For children with special needs there are many outstanding independent schools that offer some of the best provision in the country.

Many schools have high levels of achievement in sport, offering a wide range of facilities and excellent coaches. Independent schools excel at traditional sports like football and rugby, but also offer more unusual sports like rowing and fencing.

There is also a wealth of co-curricular opportunities available. Whether your child is into debating, sailing, or the Model United Nations, most schools offer numerous clubs and activities.

Fee assistance

Schools take affordability very seriously and are acutely aware of the sacrifices families make when choosing an independent education. Schools work hard to remain competitive whilst facing pressures on salaries, pensions and maintenance and utility costs. They are strongly committed to widening access and many schools have extended their bursary provision – this year, the amount of means-tested fee assistance has risen to a total of £494m. Over 180,000 pupils currently benefit from reduced fees, representing over a third of pupils at our schools.

School partnerships

Independent and state schools have been engaged in partnership activity for many years, with the majority of ISC schools currently involved in important cross-sector initiatives. These collaborations involve the sharing of expertise, best practice and facilities, and unlock exciting new opportunities for all involved. To learn more about these valuable partnerships, visit the Schools Together website: https://www.schoolstogether.org/

ISC Associations

There are seven member associations of the ISC, each with a distinctive ethos in their respective entrance criteria and quality assurance:

Girls' Schools Association (GSA)
The Heads' Conference (HMC)
Independent Association of Prep Schools (IAPS)
Independent Schools Association (ISA)
The Society of Heads
Association of Governing Bodies of Independent Schools (AGBIS)
Independent Schools' Bursars Association (ISBA)

Further organisations that are affiliated to the ISC: Boarding Schools' Association (BSA), Council of British International Schools (COBIS), Scottish Council of Independent Schools (SCIS) and Welsh Independent Schools Council (WISC).

The Independent Schools Council can be contacted at:
First Floor,
27 Queen Anne's Gate,
London,
SW1H 9BU
Telephone: 020 7766 7070
Website: www.isc.co.uk

Choosing a school initially

Educational institutions often belong to organisations that guarantee their standards. Here we give a brief alphabetical guide to what the initials mean

BSA

The Boarding Schools' Association

The Boarding Schools' Association (BSA) is part of the BSA Group. BSA Group supports excellence in boarding, safeguarding, inclusion and health education, serving more than 1,600 organisations and people in 40 countries worldwide.

A UK boarding school can only be a full member of the BSA if it is also a member of one of the Independent Schools Council (ISC) constituent associations, or in membership of the BSA State Boarding Forum (SBF). These two bodies require member schools to be regularly inspected by the Independent Schools' Inspectorate (ISI), Care Inspectorate (Scotland), Care Inspectorate Wales or Ofsted. Other boarding schools who are not members of these organisations can apply to be affiliate members. Similar arrangements are in place for international members. Boarding inspection of ISC-accredited independent schools has been conducted by ISI since September 2012. Ofsted retains responsibility for the inspection of boarding in state schools and non-association independent schools.

Boarding inspections must be conducted every three years. Boarding in England is judged against the National Minimum Standards for Boarding Schools which were last updated in September 2022.

Relationship with government

BSA is in regular communication with the Department for Education (DfE) on all boarding matters in England and with devolved governments for other parts of the UK. The Children Act (1989) and the Care Standards Act (2001) require boarding schools in England to conform to national legislation. The promotion of this legislation and the training required to carry it out are matters on which the DfE and BSA work together. BSA worked especially closely with the DfE and other government departments during the coronavirus pandemic, supporting the safety and continuity of education for its member schools' pupils and staff. Other governmental departments BSA work with are the Home Office, Ministry of Defence and the Foreign, Commonwealth & Development Office.

Boarding training

BSA delivers the world's largest professional development programme for boarding staff:

- Two-year courses for graduate and non-graduate boarding staff
- A Diploma course for senior experienced boarding staff
- MA in residential education
- A broad range of day seminars and webinars
- Specialist one or two-day conferences for Boarding Staff, Heads, Health & Wellbeing staff**, Marketing and Admissions staff* and State Boarding Schools staff and Safeguarding Leads**
- A course for new and aspiring boarding Heads
- Certificates in Mental Health. Safeguarding, Inclusion, School Nurses, Coaching and Mentoring
- Basic training online, for those new to boarding.

*With SACPA (Safeguarding and Child Protection Association), part of the BSA Group

**With HIEDA (Heath in Education Association) part of the BSA Group

**With BAISIS (British Association of Independent Schools with International Students), part of the BSA Group

In 2022, BSA Group launched The Institute of Boarding (TIOB), a dedicated association for supporting and recognising professional boarding school staff.

State Boarding Forum (SBF)

BSA support state boarding school members through the State Boarding Forum. There are a total of 44 state boarding schools across England, Scotland and Northern Ireland. At these schools, parents pay for boarding but not for education, so fees are substantially lower than in an independent boarding school. The latest BSA State Boarding Forum Census was published in January 2023.

Legal Services

BSA Group Legal is the trading name of BSA Group Legal Services Ltd, a law firm authorised and regulated by the Solicitors Regulation Authority of England and Wales. The BSA Group Legal team works closely with the Home Office to support members with UK immigration matters relating to independent schools. In 2023 the BSA partnered with Verisio to provide a Due Diligence service to support members.

167-169 Great Portland Street
5th Floor
London
W1W 5PF
Tel: 020 7798 1580
Email: bsa@boarding.org.uk
Website: www.boarding.org.uk

GSA

The Girls' Schools Association

The Girls' Schools Association is a membership organisation that aims to champion girls' schools, girls' education, girls, and their teachers. An expert in girls' education, GSA promotes girls' best interests and regularly commissions rigorous research to demonstrate the modern relevance, proven benefits, and enduring power of girls' schools.

Its membership is made up of Heads from a diverse range of independent and state girls' schools including many of the top performing in the UK, altogether GSA schools educate over 90,000 students. GSA schools are internationally respected and have a global reputation for excellence. Their innovative practice and academic rigour attract pupils from around the world, and abundant extra- and co-curricular activities nourish the whole student in a complete education.

The Association aims to inform and influence national and international educational debate and is a powerful and well-respected voice within the educational establishment, facilitating dialogue with policy makers on core education issues in addition to those relating to girls' schools and the education of girls. The Association has strong links with the Department for Education, OFQUAL, Awarding Bodies and Higher Education institutions.

In addition to acting as advocate, GSA provides its members and their whole school communities with expert-led professional development courses, conferences, and a unique network that provides opportunities for debate and sharing of best practice with colleagues.

Modern girls' schools come in different shapes and sizes. Some cater for 100% girls; others provide a girls-only environment with boys in the nursery and/or sixth form. Some follow a diamond model, with equal numbers of boys but separate classrooms between the ages of 11 to 16. Educational provision across the Association offers a choice of day, boarding, weekly, and flexi-boarding education. Schools range in type from large urban schools of 1000 pupils to small rural schools of around 200. Many schools have junior and pre-prep departments and can offer a complete education from age 3/4 to 18. Some also have religious affiliations. Heads of schools in the Girls' Day School Trust (GDST) are members of the GSA.

Girls' schools and girls' education achieve transformative outcomes for young women. With the most recent Department for Education data revealing that in girls' schools: girls are 2.6 times as likely to take Further Maths and more than twice as likely to take Physics and Computer Science A level compared with girls in co-ed schools; uptake in sciences is higher, Biology is 40% higher, Chemistry is 85% higher and Maths is 88% higher; Computer Science has seen the largest growth in uptake for girls, with the percentage of girls taking Computer Science doubling in girls' schools and 68% higher than in co-ed schools; girls continue to outperform students in co-ed schools in KS5; girls perform better in girls' schools than in co-ed schools in KS4, looking at all subjects as a whole, and also for Maths and English separately. The data also shows that the gap between girls in girls' school and girls in other types of schools is further widening in Further Maths, Chemistry and Computer Science, with girls' schools acting as stewards and guardians of these subjects for young women today.

The international benefits of educating girls are life changing for society; the education of girls lifts people out of poverty, grows economies, and saves lives; a child whose mother can read is 50% more likely to live beyond the age of five, and twice as likely to attend school themselves.

The GSA is one of the constituent bodies that make up the Independent Schools' Council (ISC), and its schools are required to undergo a regular cycle of inspections to ensure that these rigorous standards are maintained. Most GSA schools also belong to the Association of Governing Bodies of Independent Schools, and Heads must be in membership of the Association of School and College Leaders (ASCL) or the National Association of Headteachers (NAHT). Early Career Teachers take part in the Induction Programme overseen by ISTIP.

The Association's secretariat is based in Leicester.
Suite 105, 108 New Walk, Leicester LE1 7EA
Tel: 0116 254 1619
Email: office@gsa.uk.com
Website: www.gsa.uk.com
X @GSAUK

Chief Executive: Donna Stevens

Search for girls' schools on the dedicated www.schoolsearch.co.uk page.

HMC

HMC (The Heads' Conference) – Collective heads of world-leading independent schools

Founded in 1869 the HMC exists to enable members to discuss matters of common interest and to influence important developments in education. It looks after the professional interests of members, central to which is their wish to provide the best possible educational opportunities for their pupils.

The Heads of some 361 leading independent schools are members of The Heads' Conference, whose membership now includes Heads of boys', girls' and coeducational schools. International membership includes the Heads of around 50 schools throughout the world.

The great variety of these schools is one of the strengths of HMC, but all must exhibit high quality in the education provided.

All schools are noted for their academic excellence and achieve good results, including those with pupils from a broad ability band. Members believe that good education consists of more than academic results and schools provide pupils with a wide range of educational co-curricular activities and with strong pastoral support.

Only those schools that meet with the rigorous membership criteria are admitted and this helps ensure that HMC is synonymous with high quality in education. There is a set of membership requirements and a Code of Practice to which members must subscribe. Those who want the intimate atmosphere of a small school will find some with around 350 pupils. Others who want a wide range of facilities and specialisations will find these offered in large day or boarding schools. Many have over 1000 pupils. About 32 schools are for boys only, others are co-educational throughout or only in the sixth form. The first girls-only schools joined HMC in 2006. There are now about 49 girls-only schools.

Within HMC there are schools with continuous histories as long as any in the world and many others trace their origins to Tudor times, but HMC continues to admit to membership recently founded schools that have achieved great success. The facilities in all HMC schools will be good but some have magnificent buildings and grounds that are the result of the generosity of benefactors over many years. Some have attractive rural settings; others are sited in the centres of cities.

Pupils come from all sorts of backgrounds. Bursaries and scholarships provided by the schools give about a third of the 282,000 pupils in HMC schools help with their fees.

Entry into some schools is highly selective but others are well-suited to a wide ability range. Senior boarding schools usually admit pupils after the Common Entrance examination taken when they are 13.

Most day schools select their pupils by 11+ examination. Many HMC schools have junior schools, some with nursery and pre-prep departments. The growing number of boarders from overseas is evidence of the high reputation of the schools worldwide.

The independent sector has always been fortunate in attracting very good teachers. Higher salary scales, excellent conditions of employment, exciting educational opportunities and good pupil/teacher ratios bring rewards commensurate with the demanding expectations. Schools expect teachers to have a good education culminating in a good honours degree and a professional qualification, though some do not insist on the latter especially if relevant experience is offered. Willingness to participate in the whole life of the school is essential.

Parents expect the school to provide not only good teaching that helps their children achieve the best possible examination results, but also the dedicated pastoral care and valuable educational experiences outside the classroom in music, drama, games, outdoor pursuits and community service. Over 92% of pupils go on to higher education, many of them winning places on the most highly-subscribed university courses.

All members attend the Autumn Conference, usually held in a large conference centre in September/October. There are ten divisions covering England, Wales, Scotland and Ireland where members meet once a term on a regional basis, and a distinctive international division.

The HMC Board and Council make decisions on matters referred by membership-led committees, steering groups and working parties.

General Secretary: Dr Simon Hyde
Tel: 01858 469059

12 The Point
Rockingham Road
Market Harborough
Leicestershire LE16 7QU
Email: office@hmc.org.uk
Website: www.hmc.org.uk

IAPS

IAPS (Independent Association of Prep Schools) is a membership association representing leading heads in prep schools in the UK and overseas

With more than 660 members, IAPS schools educate almost 200,000 pupils worldwide with more than 162,000 attending schools in the UK. As the voice of independent prep school education, IAPS actively supports and promotes the interests of its members.

IAPS schools must reach a very high standard to be eligible for membership, with strict criteria on teaching a broad curriculum, maintaining excellent standards of pastoral care and keeping staff members' professional development training up-to-date. The head must be suitably qualified and schools must be accredited through a satisfactory inspection. IAPS offers its members and their staff a comprehensive and up-to-date programme of professional development courses to ensure that these high professional standards are maintained.

Member schools offer an all-round, values-led broad education which produces confident, adaptable, motivated children with a passion for learning. The targets of the National Curriculum are regarded as a basic foundation which is greatly extended by the wider programmes of study offered. Specialist teaching begins at an early age and pupils are offered a range of cultural and sporting opportunities.

IAPS organises a successful sports programme where member schools compete against each other in a variety of sports. In 2022-23, over 22,000 competitors took part in 168 events across 22 sports.

Schools offer pupils the choice of day, boarding, weekly and flexible boarding, in both singe sex and co-educational schools. Most schools are charitable trusts, some are limited companies and a few are proprietary. There are also junior schools attached to senior schools, choir schools, those with a particular religious affiliation and those that offer specialist provision, as well as some with an age range extending to age 16 or above.

Although each member school is independent and has its own ethos, they are all committed to delivering an excellent, well-rounded education to the pupils in their care, preparing them for their future.

IAPS
Bishop's House
Artemis Drive
Tachbrook Park
CV34 6UD
Tel: 01926 887833
Email: iaps@iaps.uk
Website: iaps.uk

ISA

The Independent Schools Association (ISA) brings the Headteachers of over 650 independent schools together, representing the diverse range of independent education practised across the UK and overseas.

Established in 1878, ISA is an association of headteachers of independent schools. It is one of the oldest of the associations that make up the Independent Schools Council (ISC).

ISA exists to provide professional support, fellowship and opportunity to their 650 Members who nurture and develop over 130,000 pupils within their schools. Promoting best practice and fellowship remains at the core of ISA, as it did when it began over 145 years ago.

ISA supports headteachers using their independence to meet the specific needs of their pupils. At ISA there are schools with different approaches to the curriculum, schools with different religious characters, and none, and schools with different ways of operating. This all contributes to a wide-ranging membership, not confined to any one type of school, but including all: nursery, pre-preparatory, junior and senior, all-through schools, coeducational, single-sex, boarding, day, bilingual, performing arts and specialist provision.

As well as the support and specialist professional development opportunities for ISA Members through their programme of courses and conferences, pupils in ISA schools benefit through their Head's membership with access to the extensive ISA Sport and Arts programmes. ISA Sport champions inclusion in physical activity through positive experiences for young people across a programme of 54 national (and over 150 regional) events at venues such as the Olympic Park's London Aquatics Centre.

ISA Arts helps schools inspire creativity, expression and individuality across the arts through both virtual and in-person events.

Membership is open to any Head or Proprietor, provided they meet the necessary accreditation criteria, including inspection of their school by a government-approved inspectorate.

ISA is supported by a number of committees, comprised of serving Heads and Honorary Members, who meet regularly to consider the issues that affect independent education. Some committee areas include education, monitoring developments and formulating responses to Government, also developing and promoting the principles of inclusion within the Association and supporting Members in promoting Equality, Diversity and Inclusion (EDI) in their schools.

President: Lord Lexden
Chief Executive Officer: Rudolf Eliott Lockhart

ISA House, 5-7 Great Chesterford Court, Great Chesterford, Essex CB10 1PF
Tel: 01799 523619
Email: isa@isaschools.org.uk
Website: www.isaschools.org.uk

At ISA there are schools with different approaches to the curriculum, schools with different religious characters, and none, and schools with different ways of operating.

The Society of Heads

The Society is an Association of Heads of just over 130 well-established independent schools

The Society is an Association of Heads of just over 130 well-established independent schools. It was founded in 1961 when a group of Heads decided they needed a forum in which to share ideas and experience. Since then the Society has grown substantially in size, reputation and effectiveness and represents a vibrant community of independent schools throughout England and Wales with some additional overseas members.

The Society's policy is to maintain high standards in member schools, to promote independent education, to provide an opportunity for the sharing of ideas and common concerns, to foster links with the wider sphere of higher education and to strengthen relations with the maintained sector by promoting partnerships.

Within the membership there is a wide variety of educational experience. Some schools are young, some have evolved from older foundations, some have behind them a long tradition of pioneer and specialist education; a number are at the leading edge of education in music, dance and the arts; and several are well known for their effective support for those with specific learning difficulties. The great majority are co-educational but we also have some all-boys and all-girls schools. Many have a strong boarding element; others are day only. All offer a stimulating sixth-form experience and give a sound and balanced education to pupils of widely varying abilities and interests.

The Society is one of the constituent Associations of the Independent Schools Council. Every Full Member school has been accredited through inspection by the Independent Schools Inspectorate (or Estyn in Wales and HMIE in Scotland) and is subject to regular visits to monitor standards and ensure that good practice and sound academic results are maintained. The Society is also represented on many other educational bodies.

All members are in membership of the Association of School and College Leaders (ASCL) or other union for school leaders and Full Member schools belong to AGBIS or an equivalent professional body supporting governance.

There are also categories of Alliance and Alliance Overseas Membership to which Heads are elected whose schools do not fulfil all the criteria for Full Membership but whose personal contribution to the Society is judged to be invaluable.

The Society hosts the autumn meeting, summer meeting and the annual conference for members. The Society also provides an extensive professional development programme.

The Society of Heads Office,
Office 101B, Harborough Enterprise Centre,
Compass Point Business Park,
Market Harborough,
Leicestershire LE16 9HW
Tel: 01858 433760
Email: info@thesocietyofheads.org.uk
Website: www.thesocietyofheads.org.uk

The Society has grown substantially in size, reputation and effectiveness and represents a vibrant community of independent schools throughout England and Wales with some additional overseas members.

Profiles

Channel Islands

St Michael's Preparatory School

St. Michael's Preparatory School is situated in a unique educational setting on Jersey in the Channel Islands. A forward thinking IAPS prep school preparing pupils for the rigours of secondary school education both on and off island. We place great emphasis upon the traditional values of care, consideration and courtesy.

The staff and pupils are justifiably proud of the school, and work together to create and maintain a high-achieving, well-organised and friendly environment in which every child is encouraged to do 'a little bit better' than anyone thought possible.

The curriculum is designed to give all children a broad, balanced and relevant education, which enables them to develop as enthusiastic, active and competent learners acquiring the knowledge, skills and understanding to allow them to grow up in today's world leading a full and active life. The school's ethos places emphasis on the individual and aims to encourage development in academic, physical, spiritual, moral and cultural aspects of the 'whole child'.

The teaching is multi-sensory, allowing children of all abilities and learning styles to be able to make progress in their learning. Differentiation is integral to the curriculum and children with special needs are well supported, as are the gifted and talented, who go on to achieve scholarship success.

The schemes of work are based upon the National Curriculum, the Jersey Curriculum and the requirements of the ISEB Common Entrance and Scholarship syllabuses. The curriculum is enriched and enhanced by numerous trips and visits as Jersey has an array of museums, cultural sites of interest and environmental locations.

The school prepares children for Common Entrance and Scholarships to English boarding secondary schools as well as entry to local Jersey establishments. We also offer a Shell Year (pre-GCSE) specifically to provide a bridging opportunity for Year 10 entry to our island state schools. Classes are small and there is a very low pupil to teacher ratio. All expected subjects are taught and there are flourishing and well-equipped Art, Music, Science, Design Technology and ICT departments as well as a custom built Sports Hall, Dance/Drama Studio, Gymnasium and indoor Swimming Pool, as well as new state of the art cricket facilities, including a double-aspect pavilion and soon to be completed, all-weather (Astro) hockey pitch.

As well as providing a wide range of academic subjects, the school seeks to introduce each child to a large variety of sports, performing arts, activities and challenges enabling him or her to discover, through experience, hidden talents and preferences with a view to future specialisation.

I hope St. Michael's pupils will leave us having achieved the very best they are capable of, having found out what it is that they love and are good at, having learned to challenge themselves and to value other people.

I.S.I. Inspection (Oct 2017) Key findings:

- The quality of the pupils' learning and achievements is excellent
- The quality of the pupils' personal development is excellent

"St Michael's makes ordinary children special, and special children extra-ordinary." A parent quote.

ST MICHAEL'S

(Founded 1949)

La Rue de la Houguette, Five Oaks, St Saviour, Jersey JE2 7UG UK

Tel: 01534 856904

Email: office@stmichaels.je

Website: www.stmichaels.je

Headmaster: Mr Henry Marshall

Appointed: 2023

School type: Co-educational Day Preparatory & Nursery

Age range of pupils: 3–14 years

No. of pupils enrolled as at 01/09/2023: 302

Boys: 156 ***Girls:*** 146

Fees as at 01/09/2023:

Day: £12,915–£20,304 per annum

Average class size: 19 max

Teacher/pupil ratio: 1:9

Central & West

Caldicott

Caldicott is a day and boarding country prep school for boys aged 7 - 13 in South Buckinghamshire. Situated in a beautiful 40-acre site, we are just 15 miles from Heathrow Airport and 30 minutes from London. Our expansive, growing daily bus service currently operates from Chiswick, Brook Green, Notting Hill, Marlow and the local area. We pride ourselves on our warm community where our pupils are happy and grow into confident all-rounders who have the grit and determination to succeed. Caldicott is a special place with a strong community spirit and sense of social responsibility. We encourage teamwork, intellectual curiosity and a love of learning in an atmosphere where creativity flourishes.

We have the reputation as one of the best prep schools in the UK with an excellent record in preparing boys for scholarships and Common Entrance to top UK public schools including Eton, Harrow, Radley and Wellington. Two years in a row, our leavers have attained a 'full house' of scholarships - meaning boys have excelled across art, sport, music, drama and academia. We have a strong and dynamic staffroom of dedicated and inspirational teachers and professionals - highly qualified academic teachers, expert sports coaches and musicians and drama specialists. Our recently commended pastoral care and wide range of extra-curricular activities mean boys get a full and enriching experience. Despite being successful across the major sports, our underlying philosophy is 'sports for all'; every week we have a mixture of external and House matches, giving every boy the opportunity to play in competitive fixtures week in, week out.

Boarding, compulsory in Years 7 and 8 and optional (in the form of flexi and occasional boarding) for Years 3 - 6, is caring, fun, and an integral part of the school community. Following our first year offering flexi boarding, we were proud to win BSA's 'Supporting Junior Boarders' Award. Boys live and work together in a friendly, supportive environment, build life-long friendships and develop independence before they go on to their senior schools at 13+.

We endeavour to harness the best of the school's traditions and values within a forward-looking and innovative approach all within a caring and supportive environment. Senior schools commend us for our well-mannered, considerate, confident boys who have high personal, moral and spiritual values and are striving to become their very best.

Crown Lane, Farnham Royal,
Buckinghamshire SL2 3SL UK

Tel: 01753 649301

Email: admissions@caldicott.com

Website: www.caldicott.com

Headmaster: Mr Jeremy Banks BA (Hons) QTS, MEd

Appointed: 2018

School type: Boys' Day & Boarding Preparatory

Age range of boys: 7–13 years (flexi boarding from 7)

No. of pupils enrolled as at 01/09/2023: 250

Fees as at 01/09/2023:

£7,114 – £13,265 per term

Average class size: 15

AXMINSTER®
POWER TOOL CENTRE

Downe House School

Downe House - a traditional boarding school with a modern twist. Discover a world-class education and a world of opportunities.

Downe House is one of the top all girls' boarding schools in the UK, offering a world-class traditional independent education with a modern twist. With a focus on excellence and the individual, girls are encouraged to make the most of the exceptional academic, co-curricular and enrichment opportunities on offer and to create their own paths, focus on their personal development and be authentic to themselves.

"Downe House was everything we hoped for in the next step for our daughter's education. You have evidently done a wonderful job of creating the right environment to foster achievement and happiness." (DH parent)

Supported by personal tutors, girls excel not only in their studies but in sport, creative and performing arts and music, going on to study at the top universities in the world. A Microsoft Showcase school, we equip pupils with outstanding digital skills, preparing them for a fast-developing world of work and modern life.

The school's strong global outlook prepares young women to be world-ready, offering them opportunities to study and work abroad. In Year 8, all girls spend a term at Downe House Sauveterre in France, and in years 10 and 12, girls can take part in a Global Exchange Programme, with 16 schools across five continents. The Sixth Form takes this further, offering global internships, which this year features more than 25 internships spanning five continents, alongside a Mini MBA, the Ivy House Leadership Award, and a Sixth Form Interview Training Programme which uses VR and AI technology. There is also DH LINKS, a comprehensive networking and careers initiative that connects pupils with parents and alumnae to gain professional insights and inspiration, along with our World Ready Programme, which we layer into every aspect of school life, tailored for every stage of development, to prepare them for the wider world. Girls leave Downe House with confidence - empowered to succeed.

Academically, Downe House encourages ambition and aims to ignite a love of learning through a supportive community. Although personal triumphs and individual achievements are the most celebrated within the school, the foundation of academic success is evident from its GCSE and A Level results. This year, at GCSE 80% of grades were 9–7 (58% 9–8/A**-A*) and at A Level, 84% of pupils achieved A* to B grades. Over 90% of the Class of 2023 graduates are heading off to their preferred university choice, including some of the world's top universities and institutions.

Downe House was founded as 'a school where every individual within the community matters', and we hold true to this ethos today. We work in partnership with parents to ensure that every Downe House pupil leaves school with a lifelong intellectual curiosity, the confidence, skills, and know-how to be successful and to face life's challenges, and a steadfast place in a lively school community.

Hear from our pupils, alumnae and staff about what makes Downe House special in The Downe House Podcast on all major podcast platforms.

To discover more about Downe House, visit us at one of our Open Mornings throughout the year or book an individual visit - we would love to see you.

Downe House

(Founded 1907)

Downe House, Cold Ash, Thatcham,
West Berkshire RG18 9JJ UK

Tel: +44 (0)1635 200286

Email: registrar@downehouse.net

Website: www.downehouse.net

Headmistress: Mrs Emma McKendrick BA(Liverpool)

Appointed: September 1997

School type: Girls' Day & Boarding Senior & Sixth Form

Age range of girls: 11–18 years (boarding from 11)

No. of pupils enrolled as at 01/09/2023: 580

Fees as at 01/09/2023:

Day: £11,840 per term

Full Boarding: £15,920 per term

Average class size: 15–20

Headington Rye Oxford

Headington Rye Oxford is a highly successful day and boarding school in Oxford for 800 girls aged 11–18 with a Preparatory School for 350 girls and boys aged 3–11 occupying its own site just across a pedestrianised lane. The school offers girls and boys an unrivalled opportunity to pursue academic, sporting and artistic excellence in a caring and nurturing environment.

Opening in September 2024 following a merger between Headington and Rye St Antony Schools and set in 35 acres of playing fields and gardens, the superb facilities provide the perfect backdrop for teaching and learning that extends way beyond the classroom and curriculum. Headington Rye Oxford encourages participation in all aspects of sport and culture, teamwork and leadership, challenging girls to discover and explore their own potential and achieve more than they thought possible.

Consistently in the premier league of academic schools in the UK, life at Headington Rye Oxford is about much more than exam results. Through the sheer breadth of subjects and activities at Headington Rye Oxford, the school aims to educate the complete individual, giving pupils the confidence and self-awareness to compete, contribute and succeed at school, university and in their adult lives.

Facilities

Headington Rye Oxford offers a superb range of facilities to support and enhance learning.

These include a state-of-the-art Music School complete with recording studio, 240-seat professional theatre, Dance and Fitness Centre, Swimming Pool and award-winning Library. A new Creativity and Innovation Centre opened in September 2021 and a state of the art Food and Nutrition Centre opened in April 2022, while a new boathouse for the championship-winning boat club is due to open in Autumn 2023.

Outside the classroom

More than 120 extra-curricular activities take place every week. A wide choice of subjects, sports, interests and hobbies including such diverse pastimes as Debating and Robotics, Cheerleading and CCF.

Headington Rye Oxford offers a genuinely inclusive approach to sport and encourages each girl to enjoy sport at the level that suits her. Girls can choose from more than 30 different sporting activities, from Athletics to Zumba. The school enjoys national success in a wide range of sports including Fencing, Rowing, Cross Country, Swimming and Equestrian.

Hundreds of individual music lessons take place each week while the school has a wide selection of orchestras, choirs and instrumental ensembles.

There is a busy programme of productions in our Theatre each year and pupils become involved in all aspects of theatre, from writing and producing their own plays, to lighting, costume and make up.

A huge range of dance options are on offer, from Ballet to Street Dance and Contemporary. As well as annual Dance Shows, our dance company competes in local and national competitions.

Boarding

Headington Rye Oxford has always been a boarding school and just over a quarter of the school board with us today. The five boarding houses provide the girls with a 'home from home' where, supported by a team of highly experienced staff, they learn to develop into mature and independent young people. Many boarders come from the UK and the school is also very proud of its international boarding community, made up of more than 30 nationalities from all over the world. Girls can choose between full, weekly or half-weekly boarding.

(Founded 1915)

Headington Road, Oxford, Oxfordshire OX3 7TD UK

Tel: +44 (0)1865 759100

Fax: +44 (0)1865 760268

Email: admissions@headington.org

Website: www.headington.org

Headmistress: Mrs Caroline Jordan MA(Oxon)

School type: Girls' Day & Boarding Senior & Sixth Form

Age range of girls: 11–18 years

Fees as at 01/09/2023:

Day: £6,895–£7,505 per term

Boarding: £9,238 – £15,107 per term

Prep: £3,615 – £5,530 per term

Average class size: Depends on age

Teacher/pupil ratio: 1:8

Marlborough College

Marlborough College provides an exceptional, contemporary full-boarding education set in a beautiful environment steeped in history. It is a welcoming community where ambition and scholarship are highly valued, creativity is celebrated, diversity is embraced and where each pupil is encouraged and challenged to be the best that they can be.

There is no "right" path through Marlborough College. Indeed, we celebrate and take pride in the fact that each young person's journey might be different. The children who thrive here take responsibility for their own journey, responding to the amazing opportunities and support available to them, and they want to be the best that they can be.

Founded in 1843, Marlborough College is the UK's largest co-educational full-boarding school. The College is academically ambitious, offering a progressive, challenging and enriching education both on and off the formal curriculum. Our co-curricular provision is second to none and all pupils become involved in a wide range of sporting and cultural activities. More than 80% of our pupils gain places at Russell Group Universities or Oxbridge, our sports teams regularly reach the latter stages of national competitions, our Symphony Orchestra plays in partnership with the Southbank Sinfonia and our artists exhibit in the Mount House Gallery.

Located in beautiful Wiltshire, in one of the most attractive market towns in the country, the College benefits from a 286-acre site, stunning period buildings including a Gothic Revival chapel and the neo-classical Memorial Hall, which is also a world class concert hall, as well as university-quality sporting facilities. The campus is centred around a four thousand year old Neolithic mound, reputedly the burial place of Merlin.

Marlborough College welcomes pupils from the UK and overseas. We have six girls' houses, six boys' houses and four mixed houses of 13–16 year old boys with mixed Sixth Forms of girls and boys. The pastoral care delivered through our 16 boarding houses is unrivalled, ensuring each child is known and cared for individually. The greatest strength of our school is the quality of the human relationships throughout our community. Full boarding fosters independence and interdependence. Pupils form friendships for life and develop the social and leadership skills needed to flourish in adult life.

We are a genuine community which seeks for everyone to benefit and contribute. The house and tutor systems and the great range of learned societies in the school make sure that the intellectual and emotional development of each child is nurtured, and further education and careers after school are planned carefully. We place an ethos of service to others and a love of learning at the heart of everything we do and whilst we are proud of our Anglican heritage, ours is an inclusive ethos, welcoming pupils of all faiths and none.

Connections with the College's alumni within the UK and internationally are exceptionally strong and valued. Our wholly owned subsidiary, Marlborough College Malaysia, provides an important global aspect to the Marlborough family. We are committed to access and outreach and there is a well-developed partnership with Swindon Academy and involvement with local and international schools and institutions. Our pupils are encouraged to be outward facing and to aspire to change things for the better - ultimately, we would like to be judged by the contributions made by past, present and future Marlburians to the health of wider society throughout the course of their lives.

(Founded 1843)

Bath Road, Marlborough, Wiltshire SN8 1PA UK

Tel: 01672 892200

Email: admissions@marlboroughcollege.org

Website: www.marlboroughcollege.org

Master: Mrs Louise Moelwyn-Hughes

School type:
Co-educational Boarding Senior & Sixth Form

Age range of pupils: 13–18 years

No. of pupils enrolled as at 01/09/2023: 1012

Boys: 569 ***Girls:*** 443

Fees as at 01/09/2023:

Full Boarding: £15,665 per term

Shiplake College

Shiplake College is a thriving co-educational boarding and day school for pupils aged 11–18. In September 2023 the College welcomed girls into Year 7, making up 44% of the year group, as it becomes fully co-educational, an environment already well-established in the Sixth Form. Overlooking the River Thames, two miles upstream of the famous Henley Royal Regatta stretch, students enjoy an inspirational 45-acre rural site. Flexi, weekly and full boarding is available from Year 9 (age 13).

Every pupil is placed at the heart of Shiplake life and the College's ethos is underpinned by the three Is – Inclusive, Individual and Inspirational. All pupils are valued regardless of academic prowess, artistic flair or sporting ability, with opportunities for all to join in and try new things.

Shiplake provides a friendly, supportive and structured environment to bring out the best in each and every pupil and aims to equip them with the skills they need to enter the next stage of their lives as confident, personable and talented young adults. Academically ambitious and renowned for outstanding pastoral care and personal development, the College welcomes pupils with wide-ranging skills and talents, who will make the most of the many opportunities offered to them.

Every pupil becomes well-known to their House's pastoral team, especially the Housemaster, personal tutor and matron. Each pupil's best method of learning is identified and catered for by their teachers, with high-achieving pupils continually stretched while those requiring additional support can access it in a variety of ways. There is a wide range of A Level and BTEC subjects available, with all Sixth Formers also undertaking either a EPQ or CoPE.

Interpersonal skills, confidence and talents are also discovered outside the classroom. Two afternoons are reserved for an array of clubs and activities, including a comprehensive outdoor education programme, with pupils encouraged to extend their horizons and experience new challenges and responsibilities. Sports training takes place on three afternoons a week, with the majority of fixtures on Saturday mornings.

The College recruits highly motivated teaching staff with an ability and passion to inspire future generations and we ensure pupils have the best possible learning resources and facilities at their disposal. The environment we provide encourages pupils to take inspiration from their teachers, their surroundings, and each other.

The Sixth Form Centre includes a café where Year 12 and 13 girls and boys can socialise and work independently. The Davies Centre, opened in 2020, includes storage for rowing boats and other watersports, mountain biking and outdoor education, CCF and DofE equipment, and incorporates an indoor archery/rifle range, a climbing wall, weights room and an ergo room, which transforms into a function room with a balcony overlooking the river.

Academic, Art, Music, Drama and Sport Scholarships, and means-tested bursaries, are available. The College is also offering one 100% All-Rounder scholarship to a boy or girl currently at a state-maintained primary school who would be looking to join Year 7 each September, who would not be able to attend Shiplake without substantial financial support.

Entry points are normally at Year 7 (11+), Year 9 (13+) and Year 12 (16+). Prospective families are encouraged to arrange an individual visit or attend an open morning, which take place in the Autumn Term and March each year. Please go to www.shiplake.org.uk to book your attendance, complete a registration form and explore the whole site, which includes details of admissions processes, fees, bus routes and answers to most academic, co-curricular and pastoral questions that prospective parents may have.

SHIPLAKE COLLEGE
HENLEY-ON-THAMES

(Founded 1959)

Henley-on-Thames, Oxfordshire RG9 4BW UK

Tel: +44 (0)1189 402455

Fax: +44 (0)1189 405204

Email: registrar@shiplake.org.uk

Website: www.shiplake.org.uk

Headmaster: Mr T G Howe MA, MSt, MBA

Appointed: 2019

School type:
Co-educational Day & Boarding Senior & Sixth Form

Religious Denomination: Church of England

Age range of pupils: 11–18 years

No. of pupils enrolled as at 01/09/2023: 526

Boys: 439 ***Girls:*** 87 ***Sixth Form:*** 197

No. of boarders: 158

Fees as at 01/09/2023:

Day: £22,200–£29,230 per annum

Weekly Boarding: £39,600 per annum

Full Boarding: £43,995 per annum

Flexi Boarding (2 nights per week): £34,560 per annum

Average class size: 16

Teacher/pupil ratio: 1:7

St Mary's Calne

St Mary's (founded in 1873) is an independent boarding and day school for girls aged 11–18, a happy, purposeful and flourishing community of around 360 pupils with an 80% to 20% boarding-to-day ratio. St Mary's welcomes cultural diversity and around 15% of the students come from overseas.

The school is located in the market town of Calne and amidst the Wiltshire Downs, an area of stunning natural beauty and historical significance. The school is within easy reach of the university towns of Bath, Bristol and Oxford and just over an hour by train from London. This ideal location means that the girls benefit from a huge range of co-curricular opportunities.

Focus on the individual

Small by design, St Mary's provides exceptional all-round education in a warm, nurturing environment. It is the individualised approach to every aspect of school life that makes St Mary's Calne special.

The pastoral care is outstanding. Every girl has a Tutor to support her through aspects of school life, from organisational skills and subject choices through to university application.

High Achievers

St Mary's Calne has a well-deserved reputation for academic excellence and is committed to providing an education that will challenge and inspire its pupils. In the Sunday Times Parent Power Schools' Guide 2023, St Mary's was ranked 1st independent school in Wiltshire and 3rd in the South West. St Mary's is also the first independent school in the UK to be awarded the Platinum Science Mark Award.

In 2023, the girls went on to study at a range of leading universities including Oxford, St Andrews, Durham, Edinburgh, Exeter, King's College London (KCL) and London School of Economics (LSE), Royal Holloway and Warwick. In recent years, several girls have been successful in gaining places at prestigious universities in the USA.

Outside the Classroom

Opportunities in sport, music, art and drama abound and the facilities are superb, including a £2.55 million sports complex and full-size astro, theatre, a Sixth Form Centre and a state-of-the-art new library, overlooking the orchard.

Almost 80% of girls play musical instruments and take part in a wide variety of ensembles. The girls perform at many events, both in the local community and further afield.

Drama productions in the purpose-built theatre are of the highest standard. In Year 9, pupils perform at a professional theatre and senior students perform annually at the Edinburgh Fringe Festival.

In Art, in addition to holding a triennial exhibition in London, the girls have received numerous awards, including having artwork selected for the Young Artists' Summer Show at the Royal Academy of Arts. The girls are also very active in the local community and have helped in local hospitals, residential care homes, the community library and in local schools.

Sport plays a very important part in school life and all the students are encouraged to participate, whatever their ability. Several girls represent the county in Lacrosse and Athletics and many have gone through the county development system in Netball and Hockey. Girls have represented England and Wales in Lacrosse, trained for the GB Pony Eventing Teams and competed in the English Nationals for swimming. The Tennis Academy was a National Finalist in the LTA's prestigious 2021 'School of the Year' Awards. In addition, a huge range of co-curricular sports, such as ski racing, climbing, golf and ultimate frisbee are available.

For further information, or to book onto one of our Open Days, please visit: www.stmaryscalne.org

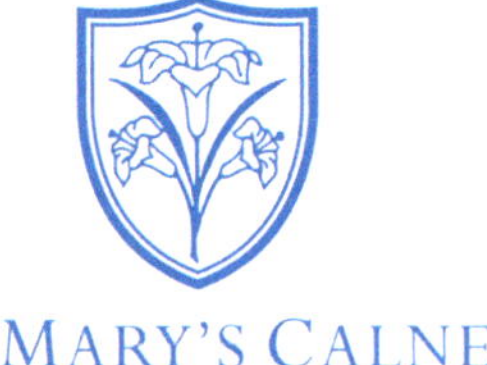

ST MARY'S CALNE

(Founded 1873)

Curzon Street, Calne, Wiltshire SN11 0DF UK

Tel: 01249 857200

Fax: 01249 857207

Email: office@stmaryscalne.org

Website: www.stmaryscalne.org

Acting Head: Mrs Diana Harrison MA (Cantab), PGCE (Bristol), CPP (Roehampton)

Appointed: January 2023

School type: Girls' Day & Boarding Senior & Sixth Form

Religious Denomination: Church of England

Age range of girls: 11–18 years (boarding from 11)

No. of pupils enrolled as at 01/09/2023: 360

Sixth Form: 119

Fees as at 01/09/2023:

Day: £34,860 per annum

Full Boarding: £46,725 per annum

Average class size: Max 17, smaller in the Sixth Form

Teacher/pupil ratio: 1:5

The Webber Independent School

Based in Milton Keynes, we are a modern, private educator for children from the age of 6 months to 16 years.

At The Webber Independent School, we build within our children a lifelong love of learning, which will equip and prepare them for their individual journey to success - whatever that might be.

Life at Webber is vibrant, inclusive and academic. Our commitment to providing first-class individualised learning experiences that drive personal growth and development within each stage of the Webber journey is unwavering, whether your child joins us at 6 months old at The Webber Nursery or when they are in Senior School ready to take on GCSE examinations.

The culture of kindness is ingrained in our family. We value inclusivity and learning from one another's experiences, backgrounds, and cultures. We understand that each child's journey may start and stop at different stages, so we want to create a warm and welcoming environment where they can achieve their full potential.

We are committed to Achieving Excellence Together, and were awarded "Excellent" in all areas of our whole-school Focused Compliance and Educational Quality ISI, Independent School Inspection.

Life at Webber ignites passions, uncovers hidden talents and prepares our students for their individual journey through life. Creating tomorrow's makers and shapers is our mission. To ensure our curriculum offering is stimulating, current, relevant, and well-rounded, we have an entire team of educators dedicated to motivating and innovating.

As well as enriching the National Curriculum, we prepare our students for the future of study and work through real world learning and entrepreneurial skills. We deliver Key Stage Learning through to GCSEs, with specialisms in STEM (Science, Technology, Engineering and Mathematics), The Arts and Modern Foreign Languages. As part of the curriculum, we offer educational trips, clubs, societies, and work experience opportunities.

Additionally, we provide opportunities for students to develop leadership skills through participation in The Army Cadet Force, The Duke of Edinburgh's Award, Prefects and The Student Council.

In modern society and the workplace, technology plays an increasingly important role, and this trend is set to continue. At The Webber Independent we blend traditional academic subjects alongside enhanced digital skills; in lessons we utilise laptops, tablets and touchscreen technology, and offer holiday clubs with a digital focus such as computer science, coding workshops and robotics. In addition to developing collaboration and agile skills, our approach to Digital Citizenship prepares students for workplaces and higher education.

Creating a strong parent, student and teacher partnership is a key priority for the Webber team, it helps us ensure your son or daughter has the best educational experience with us.

In order to help our students achieve their personal goals, we help them set SMART goals and provide continuous feedback on their progress. Continuing to ensure achievement, we will provide up to six academic reports per year, send out a weekly personal tutor email, and schedule regular parent, teacher, and student consultations.

Throughout each Form Class, two Form Tutors provide exceptional pastoral care and close academic tracking and monitoring, ensuring first-class learning experiences. It only takes a visit to fully appreciate how unique our learning environment is. To experience the school in action, meet the teachers, and speak with some of our students, we welcome you to schedule an individual visit and tour.

Soskin Drive, Stantonbury Fields, Milton Keynes, Buckinghamshire MK14 6DP UK

Tel: 01908 574740

Email: info@webberindependentschool.co.uk

Website: www.webberindependentschool.com

Principal: Mrs Hilary Marsden

School type: Co-educational Day Preparatory, Senior & Nursery

Age range of pupils: 6 months–16 years

No. of pupils enrolled as at 01/09/2023: 311

Fees as at 01/09/2023:

Day: £3,660–£5,025 per term

THE WEBBER
INDEPENDENT SCH

Thornton College

Thornton College day and boarding school for girls, located between Milton Keynes and Buckingham, is set in 25 acres of beautiful grounds. The main school building is a manor house dating back to the 14th century and it became a school in 1917, founded by the Sisters of Jesus and Mary. The school is very proud of its rich history, exceptional pastoral care for the individual and its strong emphasis on core Christian values, though it is also proud of the fact that it is a forward looking school, with exciting opportunities both in and outside the classroom, and where girls of all faiths and no faith are equally welcome and equally valued.

Thornton College is part of an international family of J&M schools in twenty nine countries around the world. This gives our students the best of opportunities for student international partnership programmes, celebrations, projects and exchanges, enabling each student to grow a unique global outlook and cultural intelligence.

Boarding is 'upstairs' in our main manor house offering a home from home experience. The boarding bedrooms and common areas are bright and spacious. We offer occasional, flexi, weekly and termly boarding for domestic and international students with a dense programme of exciting evening activities and weekend trips.

Thornton College is a one site school ensuring that there is smooth transition for students throughout pre-prep, prep, senior and sixth form and lots of leadership and role modelling opportunities.

Our academic results are comparable with high achieving competitive schools whilst having a varied ability intake and Thornton consistently ranks as one of the top non-selective schools in the UK. Girls can join us at three years old into our Pre-Reception class offering families the very best start to their daughter's education. Woodland walks, cookery, ballet, French, music and movement, library time and a host of other weekly activities excite their young minds. As a Forest School, girls at Thornton excel inside and outside the classroom with our Prep school children enjoying our outdoor classroom in our woodlands and exploring and pond dipping in our eco habitat park. Thornton College is leading the introduction of robotics into Prep school curriculum and won the Independent School of the Year Award 2020 Student Careers Programme, was a finalist in the Diversity, Equality and Inclusion 'This is Me' Awards 2022, is a Green School with Distinction 2023 as well as winning numerous Independent School Association competitions and awards over the last three years. Students in Senior and Sixth Form enjoy overseas sporting tours, World Challenges, Duke of Edinburgh (with sixth formers achieving their Gold Awards); EPQs; UCAS and careers events and debating. Our Sixth Form, which opened in 2016, offers a wide subject choice, small class sizes and individual attention with future pathway support.

Thornton College is an incredibly diverse and multi-talented community where each girl can thrive to be the best version of herself, to know her own strengths, to recognise her own challenges and to pursue with confidence the next stages of her life.

THORNTON

(Founded 1917)

College Lane, Thornton, Milton Keynes, Buckinghamshire MK17 0HJ UK

Tel: 01280 812610

Email: admissions@thorntoncollege.com

Website: www.thorntoncollege.com

Headteacher: Dr Louise Shaw

Appointed: November 2022

School type: Girls' Day & Boarding Preparatory & Senior, Nursery & Sixth Form

Age range of girls: 3–18 years (boarding from 8)

No. of pupils enrolled as at 01/09/2023: 400

No. of boarders: 60

Fees as at 01/09/2023:

Day: £15,180–£19,350 per annum

Weekly Boarding: £21,765–£27,555 per annum

Full Boarding: £27,075–£33,570 per annum

Average class size: 14

Teacher/pupil ratio: 1:20

Wycombe Abbey

Wycombe Abbey is a modern, full boarding school committed to creating tomorrow's female leaders. It has a long tradition of academic excellence, it is consistently one of the country's top performing schools.

Our learning environment is supportive, yet challenging, with a sense that pupils and their teachers are on an educational journey together. We pride ourselves on the outstanding teaching provided by our specialists who communicate a genuine love of their subject and serve to inspire the girls they teach.

We believe that education should not simply be about delivering a curriculum and examination syllabus, but that real learning stems from stimulating intellectual curiosity and nurturing a love for the subjects being taught, which will stay with our girls throughout their lives.

In all we do, boarding is the key to our continued success. The school has a culture that inspires throughout the day, seven days a week, empowering girls to achieve their best, academically and socially. Our happy and close community is a truly global one, with 29 countries represented. Each girl is known, and cherished, as an individual. Consequently, every girl's potential, whatever that might be, is explored and fulfilled.

Girls learn to be independent, to value and support others, and to develop the skills needed for future challenges in a global workplace. Given the nature of boarding life, girls are able to enjoy a wealth of co-curricular opportunities. Each and every girl carves out a unique learning path according to her interests and has the space to thrive within our magnificent grounds. Our approach to boarding is also sympathetic to the needs of today's families and pupils have the opportunity to go home regularly and parents are actively involved in the numerous school events and activities.

The school is an oasis of calm, set in 170 acres of magnificent, conservation-listed grounds and woodland. Modern, state-of-the-art facilities include the Sports Centre, with a 25-metre indoor pool, the Performing Arts Centre with a theatre and recital hall, an atrium café, dance and fitness studios, and extensive sports pitches.

Wycombe Abbey is easily accessible with excellent transport links. It is about 35 miles west of London and 30 miles east of Oxford. It is a 30-minute journey from Heathrow Airport and a 90-minute journey from Gatwick Airport by road.

To find out more about gaining a place at Wycombe Abbey, please visit our website at www.wycombeabbey.com or contact our Admissions Team on (+44) (0) 1494 897008 or by emailing admissions@wycombeabbey.com.

(Founded 1896)

Frances Dove Way, High Wycombe, Buckinghamshire HP11 1PE UK

Tel: +44 (0)1494 520381

Email: admissions@wycombeabbey.com

Website: www.wycombeabbey.com

Headmistress:
Mrs Jo Duncan MA (St Andrews), PGCE (Cantab)

Appointed: September 2019

School type: Girls' Day & Boarding Senior & Sixth Form

Religious Denomination: Church of England

Age range of girls: 11–18 years

No. of pupils enrolled as at 01/09/2023: 660

Fees as at 01/09/2023:

Day: £36,000 per annum

Full Boarding: £47,700 per annum

East

Brentwood School

Brentwood School shines out as a beacon of excellence. Our students are happy individuals who thrive on the high standards which are expected of them. They benefit from state-of-the-art facilities, set in the heart of Brentwood in Essex, and surrounded by 75 acres of green playing fields and gardens.

Academically, we sit comfortably alongside the best day and boarding schools in the country, and we enjoy an unparalleled local reputation.

We celebrate a 467-year history and take our heritage seriously. We embody our values of "virtue, learning and manners" just as those before us have been doing since 1557. We are proud of our modern inclusive community which is shaped by our Christian Foundation. Our pupils are kind, ambitious, and seek to make a positive contribution in the present and the future: our role is to help them achieve their successes - in whatever shape they may come - without any sense of entitlement.

Our pupils understand the value of perseverance and the fact that patience is a virtue. They are willing to take managed risks and celebrate their own successes and those of their peers with equal enthusiasm, whilst having the courage to fail and learn from their mistakes. We cultivate this approach by modelling the behaviours we want to help our pupils develop, and by teaching with genuine passion and intelligence in a stimulating environment.

Brentwood School pupils achieve excellent academic standards that rank among some of the best in the country. Our pupils work hard and are supported by highly professional and inspiring teachers to achieve excellent results at both GCSE level and in the Sixth Form. We offer a mixture of GCSEs and IGCSEs, A Levels, the BTEC Extended Diploma in Sport or Business, and the IB Diploma. An average of six students per year are offered places at Oxford or Cambridge and two thirds of our students progress to UK Russell Group/ Top 20 universities.

Brentwood was the first school in Essex, and one of the first in the country, to adopt the Diamond Model: single-sex classes from the age of 11–16 within an overall mixed gender environment.

Our vast and exciting co-curricular programme enjoys national prominence, and we focus on providing opportunities for all to participate, as well as the pursuit of excellence for the most able.

Our Combined Cadet Force is one of the oldest and largest in the country, we offer The Duke of Edinburgh's Award and Outdoor Learning to pupils who want to satisfy their taste for adventure, and a Voluntary Service in Action Unit which raises tens of thousands of pounds every year to help specific charitable organisations.

Our sports centre houses a 25-metre swimming pool, glass-backed squash courts, fencing salle and dance studio and pupils achieve top sporting honours both nationally and internationally.

We are proud to be a Steinway School, enabling our pupils to learn on the very best-made pianos in the world, as well as some rare instruments otherwise unavailable to them. Our musicians have played in the National Youth Orchestra, and our actors have gained places in the National Youth Theatre, RADA and other top Drama schools.

A flourishing Old Brentwoods community keeps thousands of alumni connected across the globe.

We prepare our pupils for a fast-paced and ever-changing world. They will need to solve problems we don't yet know about (in addition to those we do) and many will take on jobs that don't yet exist. Our pupils are active participants in this journey and distinguish themselves as enterprising young people who always strive to be the best version of themselves.

Brentwood School

(Founded 1557)

Middleton Hall Lane, Brentwood, Essex CM15 8EE UK

Tel: 01277 243243

Fax: 01277 243299

Email: headmaster@brentwood.essex.sch.uk

Website: www.brentwoodschool.co.uk

Headmaster: Mr Michael Bond

Appointed: September 2019

School type: Co-educational Day & Boarding Prep & Senior, Nursery & Sixth Form

Religious Denomination: Church of England

Age range of pupils: 3–18 years

No. of pupils enrolled as at 01/09/2023: 1968

Fees as at 01/09/2023:

Day: £23,472 per annum

Full Boarding: £45,996 per annum

Average class size: 20 in Prep & Senior; 8 in Sixth Form

Teacher/pupil ratio: 1:9

Framlingham College

Framlingham College is a co-educational boarding and day school for children aged 2–18, set in the beautiful surroundings of rural Suffolk. Founded in 1864 as a memorial to Prince Albert, the College was established to reflect and support the prince's interest in British educational development.

Today this legacy continues, through the College's celebration of a forward-looking and ambitious learning culture that encourages curiosity and enquiry. A school that is aspirational for every pupil, the College's vision, structure and size places emphasis on understanding, guiding and inspiring each child individually - so they can discover and develop their talents, find their own voice, confidence, self-belief and create their own life-story.

When a young person joins Framlingham College, they are welcomed because of who they are. They are valued for their experience, their history, their ambition and their belief in their future.

The school's educational approach allows teaching to go beyond textbook learning and 'learning to test'. Instead, it prepares pupils for a constantly evolving world, by providing a rigorous and challenging knowledge-rich curriculum, focussing on skills and connectivity between subjects and fostering a culture of high aspiration.

By encouraging pupils to seek out challenge, to embrace opportunity and to give them the time to reflect and learn from each experience, the school supports pupils to better understand themselves and the world around them. Pupils leave with an appreciation of the education they have experienced and an awareness of the issues facing society, inspired to give back to their community.

A focus on each child's wellbeing is paramount because a happy child will thrive. The integrated house structure at Framlingham College is an integral part of the school's pastoral care. Surrounding every pupil is the support of their House Mistress or Master, their Tutor, their teachers, the chaplain, and their peer mentors getting to know them and what makes them tick.

As a result of the House community pupils develop their deepest friendships, find their confidence and ignite sparks of admiration for the older pupils that lead to application and fulfilment in the larger community of the school.

The full, part and flexible boarding options available at the school empower pupils to grow in confidence and maturity and enables a strong sense of community. Boarding offers pupils the opportunity to further develop social and emotional skills and independent learning, whilst also enhancing each individual's understanding of their personal attributes and characteristics, their appreciation of their place as global citizens and their realisation of the importance of health and wellbeing.

The idyllic backdrop of 110 acres of bucolic Suffolk countryside - set across two sites at the Senior School and the Prep School - provides an inspiring and invigorating environment where pupils have the freedom to think and room to grow. And from here, pupils' horizons are global.

There is no typical Framlinghamian, no singular path that pupils take. Framlinghamians are academics, actors, musicians, expeditioners, sports people, innovators, scientists, ruminators, decision makers, storytellers, teammates, artists, fun lovers, nurturers and thought provokers. Often pupils are many things within one. But they are all individual with their own story to tell.

To find out more about the school, book a private tour or register for an upcoming open day please visit www.framlinghamcollege.co.uk/join/visit-us, contact the admissions team at admissions@framlinghamcollege.co.uk or ring 01728 723789.

(Founded 1864)

Framlingham, Suffolk IP13 9EY UK

Tel: +44 (0)1728 723789

Email: admissions@framlinghamcollege.co.uk

Website: www.framlinghamcollege.co.uk

Principal and Head of the Senior School: Mrs Louise North

Head of the Prep School: Mr Jonathan Egan

School type: Co-educational Day & Boarding Prep & Senior, Nursery & Sixth Form

Religious Denomination: Church of England, but all faiths are welcome

Age range of pupils: 2–18 years

No. of pupils enrolled as at 01/09/2023: 640

Fees as at 01/09/2023:

Day: £10,869–£24,795 per annum

Full Boarding: £27,428–£38,556 per annum

Haberdashers' Boys' School

Haberdashers' Boys' School is a leading independent day boys' school for students aged 4 to 18. Situated in an idyllic 100-acre co-educational campus in Hertfordshire, Habs Boys shares its wonderful location with its sibling school, Haberdashers' Girls' School. From September Habs Boys and Habs Girls will teach A Levels in co-educational classes, with students sitting a minimum of one A Level in mixed gender classes across at the other school.

At Habs Boys, our academic performance speaks for itself. At GCSE, 50% were 9 and 91% were 9 to 7. At A Level, 48% of the grades awarded were A* and 81% were A* to A.

Whilst outstanding outcomes remain a priority at Habs, great exam results are just one part of the educational journey at Habs and is not possible without the other academic and extensive co-curricular opportunities on the campus, creating relevant life skills and character development opportunities for all our students. We encourage all our students to make full use of the incredible campus, exploring their individual interests and passions, in and beyond the classroom.

As a school, our purpose is to empower our young people to make a profound and positive impact in the world. This requires personal adaptability and resilience, curiosity, genuine empathy and a sense of responsibility for the people and the world around them.

We are a diverse community with a strong global perspective. Our roots are firmly in our philanthropic founding principles and this guides our deep sense of responsibility in the world. This environment, combined with our innovative teaching approach, prepares our students for the fast-moving world.

Admissions

We offer places to bright and ambitious students who are courageous and curious in all aspects of life.

At 4+ pupils are invited to the school and will participate in a series of activities. Some will then be invited back for a second stage. Our 7+, 11+, 13+ and 16+ process involves one or multiple entrance assessments and an invitational second round interview. Our 16+ entry is also contingent on GCSE results the August before a student joins us.

Those pupils already in our Preparatory School are offered unconditional places as they move up from Year 6 to Year 7 in the Senior School.

Bursaries

At Habs, we are working to ensure every curious and ambitious child can access a Habs education. Our bursaries are means-tested and determined by a family's financial situation. The assistance provided can range from partial to full bursaries, with approximately 10% of our students currently receiving a free school place.

Scholarships

We offer a variety of different scholarships at the school from 11+. Academic, Art, Design and Technology, Drama, Music and Sport scholarships are available across our different entry levels and can offer 10–20% fee remission.

(Founded 1690)

Butterfly Lane, Elstree, Borehamwood, Hertfordshire WD6 3AF UK

Tel: 020 8266 1700

Email: office@habsboys.org.uk

Website: www.habsboys.org.uk

Headmaster: Mr Robert Sykes

Appointed: 2023

School type: Boys' Day Preparatory, Senior & Sixth Form

Age range of boys: 4–18 years

No. of pupils enrolled as at 01/09/2023: 1465

Fees as at 01/09/2023:

Sixth Form: £24,549 per annum

Senior School: £24,549 per annum

Prep: £7747 per term (including school lunches)

Pre-Prep: £6384 per term (including school lunches)

Haberdashers' Girls' School

Haberdashers' Girls' School is a leading independent day girls' school for students aged 4 to 18. Situated in an idyllic 100-acre co-educational campus in Hertfordshire, Habs Girls shares its wonderful location with its sibling school, Haberdashers' Boys' School. From September Habs Girls and Habs Boys will teach A Levels in co-educational classes, with students sitting a minimum of one A Level in mixed gender classes across at the other school.

At Habs Girls, our academic performance speaks for itself. At GCSE 45% of the grades awarded were 9 with 86% awarded 9 to 7 and A Level 43% of the school grades awarded were A* and 74% A* to A.

Whilst outstanding outcomes remain a priority at Habs, great exam results are just one part of the educational journey at Habs and is not possible without the other academic and extensive co-curricular opportunities on the campus, creating relevant life skills and character development opportunities for all our students. We encourage all our students to make full use of the incredible campus, exploring their individual interests and passions, in and beyond the classroom.

As a school, our purpose is to empower our young people to make a profound and positive impact in the world. This requires personal adaptability and resilience, curiosity, genuine empathy and a sense of responsibility for the people and the world around them.

We are a diverse community with a strong global perspective. Our roots are firmly in our philanthropic founding principles and this guides our deep sense of responsibility in the world. This environment, combined with our innovative teaching approach, prepares our students for the fast-moving world.

Admissions

We offer places to bright and ambitious students who are courageous and curious in all aspects of life.

At 4+ pupils are invited to the school and will participate in a series of activities. Some will then be invited back for a second stage. Our 7+, 11+ and 16+ process involves one or multiple entrance assessments and an invitational second round interview.

We also offer Occasional Places as spaces become available in Year 4, 5, 8, 9 and 10. The availability of these places are confirmed in February; full details can be found on our website.

Those pupils already in our Junior School are offered unconditional places as they move up from Year 6 to Year 7 in the Senior School.

Bursaries

At Habs, we are working to ensure every curious and ambitious child can access a Habs education. Our bursaries are means-tested and determined by a family's financial situation. The assistance provided can range from partial to full bursaries, with approximately 10% of our students currently receiving a free school place.

Scholarships

We offer a variety of different scholarships at the school from 11+. Academic, Art, Creative Writing, Drama, Music and Sport scholarships are available across our different entry levels and can offer 10–20% fee remission.

(Founded 1875)

Aldenham Road, Elstree, Borehamwood, Hertfordshire WD6 3BT UK

Tel: 020 8266 2300

Email: office@habsgirls.org.uk

Website: www.habsgirls.org.uk

Headmistress: Dr Hazel Bagworth-Mann

Appointed: 2023

School type: Girls' Day Preparatory, Senior & Sixth Form

Age range of girls: 4–18 years

No. of pupils enrolled as at 01/09/2023: 1170

Fees as at 01/09/2023:

Reception to Year 2: £20,310 per annum (including school lunches)

Year 3 to Year 6: £21,642 per annum (including school lunches)

Year 7 to Year 11: £23,613 per annum

Year 12 to Year 13: £23,745 per annum

Haileybury

Haileybury is a leading independent co-educational boarding and day school, situated on 500 acres of beautiful Hertfordshire countryside, just 20 miles north of London.

Haileybury's spectacular grounds are home to outstanding facilities, excellent teaching and superb pastoral care for its community of pupils.

Academic opportunity

The school offers a dedicated Lower School for Years 7 and 8 and a wide range of GCSEs and IGCSEs. In the Sixth Form, pupils can select to study for A levels or the International Baccalaureate (IB) Diploma.

Its unrivalled curriculum allows pupils to select personal pathways, such as coding and global civilisations, based on their individual passions. In the Sixth Form, electives include criminology, geopolitics and music technology.

Boarding and day

More than two-thirds of pupils are boarders and school life is centred around 12 boarding houses, Lower School benefitting from having their own house. Pupils join at 11+, 13+, 14+ or 16+ entry points. For Lower School pupils, flexiboarding is available which means families do not have to commit to boarding at this stage and pupils return home for the weekend. From Year 9 onwards, there is the additional flexibility of boarding pupils being able to return home after sporting commitments on Saturday afternoons.

Exceptional opportunities

Beyond the academic curriculum, pupils benefit from a vast array of activities, including professional sports coaching for all and regular visits from speakers and performers from the arts, sporting and academic worlds.

The co-curricular programme is packed with opportunities, from climbing and scuba diving to film making and the Model United Nations - and countless activities in between.

Haileybury also encourages pupils to immerse themselves in the Creative Arts both academically and as part of their co-curricular options. Drama, Music, Dance, LAMDA and Art are at the heart of school life. The school takes pride in hosting spectacular arts productions with multiple showcases per term and pupils are able to take part in music concerts, drama productions and public performances throughout the year.

The first school to do so in the UK, Haileybury is taking part in the global Stan-X programme, a pioneering study of genetics. Working from purpose-built labs, Haileybury pupils are contributing to efforts to find cures for diseases such as pancreatic cancer and diabetes.

Supportive environment

At Haileybury, a caring environment is crucial to a pupil's happiness and fulfilment. There is an emphasis on pastoral care with around-the-clock support from Housemasters and Housemistresses, the chaplain and tutors, as well as an onsite health centre providing a circle of care. The school is a home-from-home, with a warm and friendly feel. Every child is given the confidence to find their identity on a personal journey of discovery.

A warm welcome

Our open days and taster events take place throughout the year and families are warmly invited to come along and discover what life at Haileybury has to offer and why its pupils flourish. For further information, please contact our Admissions Department on 01992 706353 or at admissions@haileybury.com

(Founded 1862)

Haileybury, Hertford, Hertfordshire SG13 7NU UK

Tel: +44 (0)1992 706353

Email: admissions@haileybury.com

Website: www.haileybury.com

The Master: Mr Martin Collier MA BA PGCE

Appointed: September 2017

School type:
Co-educational Day & Boarding Senior & Sixth Form

Age range of pupils: 11–18 years (boarding from 11)
(entry at 11+, 13+, 14+ and 16+)

No. of pupils enrolled as at 01/09/2023: 919

Boys: 461 ***Girls:*** 458 ***Sixth Form:*** 364

No. of boarders: 539

Fees as at 01/09/2023:

Day: £7,170–£10,785 per term

Full Boarding: £9,455–£14,900 per term

Teacher/pupil ratio: 1:7

Holmwood House School

Discover Holmwood House

Holmwood House, in Colchester, provides an academically rigorous, yet broad and balanced education so that each and every girl or boy thrives and achieves their full potential. Set in 25 acres of beautiful grounds it aims to spark curiosity and ignite wonder in each child, through an inspiring learning environment and boundless opportunities for discovery and exploration.

Holmwood House firmly believes that schools are about discovery and growth which is why they focus their education on sparking curiosity and igniting wonder in and out of the classroom. Small class sizes allow their high quality teachers to create inspirational learning environments to inspire, support, and challenge each girl and boy for just that goal. Holmwood is a family school; they believe in partnership between pupils, teachers and parents to enable each individual girl and boy to thrive and achieve their potential in and out of the classroom.

The school's extensive grounds and fantastic facilities allow pupils to learn new skills and find their niche. The academic curriculum is ambitious and challenging, but with stretch and support for all individuals. Holmwood is committed to providing a broad and balanced education so that each girl or boy can discover their own academic, artistic, musical, creative and physical potential and help them to flourish.

Early Years Curriculum

Holmwood House's Early Years Curriculum in their Preschool and Reception classes provides an environment that is stimulating and exciting to young minds, enabling every child to develop as an independent learner. They provide a warm caring atmosphere where children learn to be independent, confident, sociable and develop a positive approach to learning. Every day offers dedicated time to phonics and numeracy complemented by lessons taught by specialist teachers including: French, Music, ICT, PE, Swimming, Outdoor Learning and Racket skills. The school has recently expanded their Preschool on their Lexden site and is now open to children aged 2 and over. This expanded provision complements the school's Nursery in Great Horkesley which takes children from 6 months.

Prep School and Senior School Expansion

Already well established as a successful prep school (shortlisted this year for Independent Prep School of the Year Award) the school regularly sends their children to local Grammar Schools and national boarding schools. Building on this strong foundation of the Prep School, Holmwood House has recently made the exciting announcement that it is adding a Senior School and is expanding up to the age of 16 (Year 11), so pupils can now stay on and sit their GCSEs. This exciting development will give pupils the opportunity to continue on at Holmwood House and enjoy an academically rigorous curriculum supported by a wide range of enrichment opportunities and exceptional pastoral care.

Children's learning journeys can begin at a number of stages:

- From 6 months to age 3 children can join the Nursery which is nestled in a woodland setting.
- Children age 3 and up can join Early Years, Pre-Prep and Prep School set in 25 acres of beautiful grounds.
- Age 11 pupils can join the dynamic Upper Prep and Senior elements of the school. The school recently announced that it is expanding its provision up to age 16, so pupils can now stay on and sit their GCSEs.

For more information and to book a visit please visit www.holmwood.house/admissions.

HOLMWOOD HOUSE
SCHOOL

Chitts Hill, Lexden, Colchester, Essex CO3 9ST UK

Tel: 01206 574305

Email: admissions@holmwood.house

Website: www.holmwood.house

Headmaster: Mr Edward Bond

Appointed: September 2021

School type:
Co-educational Day Preparatory, Senior & Nursery

Age range of pupils: 6 months–16 years

Fees as at 01/09/2023: Please see website

Average class size: Max 18

Ipswich School

Ipswich School is the top independent school in Suffolk. A consistently outstanding academic performance is more than matched by one of the best co-curricular programmes in the country; this is a school community with kindness at its core and this makes us a happy, busy and fun school to be at.

Each pupil is treated as an individual and that's because our teachers know their pupils really well. We have ideal class sizes and teachers have the time to understand each pupil - this means that learning can be adapted to suit individuals' needs and the result of that is pupils that enjoy lessons and thrive academically.

We have a strong and consistent academic reputation. Our students achieve excellent examination results and progress to the best universities, including Oxbridge and top Russell Group. In 2023, 39% achieved Grades 9–8 and 63% achieved Grades 9–7 in our biggest ever GCSE cohort of 143 students. A Level results were 48% A*-A and 80% A*-B again, with the school's biggest ever A Level cohort of 151 students.

We believe that a rich and varied co-curricular provision complements an excellent academic education, giving our pupils the opportunity to develop many valuable transferable skills allowing them to realise their full potential.

Our pupils are incredibly varied in their interests and achievements and we love that about them. We often see the 'Ipswich all-rounder' develop as students discover the joy in something outside of the core curriculum. Whether they are on the sports field, on stage or in the concert hall, pupils learn to take risks in a supportive environment, how to recover from setbacks, how to collaborate in a team-setting and how to become effective leaders. It's not uncommon for our rugby players to perform in the orchestra or for our musicians to discover a love of hockey. Our students want to achieve their best and progress to top universities but they also leave the school with a portfolio of wider achievements and interests.

Ipswich School has attractive boarding facilities at Westwood, a Victorian mansion set in wooded grounds about 200 metres from the school campus. We also have a Sixth Form Boarding House at Anglesea Heights, close to the centre of Ipswich and the historic Christchurch Park. As a largely day school we offer a wonderful opportunity for our small number of boarders to enjoy a close knit community with a strong sense of identity.

"As pupils move through the school, their confidence increases, nurtured by excellent welfare and pastoral support. Pupils are reflective and resilient, whether settling in as new boarders or managing the emotional aspects of forming new friendships" - ISI Inspection Report, 2022

IPSWICH SCHOOL

(Founded before 1390)

Henley Road, Ipswich, Suffolk IP1 3SG UK

Tel: 01473 408300

Email: admissions@ipswich.school

Website: www.ipswich.school

Headmaster: Mr Nicholas Weaver MA

Appointed: 2010

School type: Co-educational Day & Boarding Prep & Senior, Nursery & Sixth Form

Religious Denomination: Church of England

Age range of pupils: 0–18 years

Fees as at 01/09/2023:

Day: £19,704 per annum

Full Boarding: £40,365 per annum

Teacher/pupil ratio: 1:20

King's Ely

Nestled in the beautiful cathedral city of Ely in Cambridgeshire, King's Ely is a leading independent co-educational day and boarding school. We are located just 15 minutes from Cambridge and one hour from London, with direct rail links to both.

As one of the oldest schools in the country, King's Ely nurtures the academic and pastoral needs of around 1,100 pupils from the age of 2 through to 18. We are proud to have received an 'excellent' rating in all areas following our latest ISI Inspection, recognising the highest levels of pastoral care, academic rigour, and extra-curricular activity. Ely Cathedral serves as our school chapel and makes the perfect setting for assemblies and concerts.

The ethos of a King's Ely education enables pupils of all ages to flourish, from the children in King's Ely Acremont Pre-Prep to the young men and women in our Sixth Form. The progress that young people make throughout their King's Ely journey is astounding, and accounts for our high placement in local and national added-value rankings, including the top five in Cambridgeshire. Whether a student shines in a classroom, in a laboratory, on a stage, on a pitch or on a mountainside, we promise an abundance of opportunity for personal development, both academically and socially.

Innovative approaches to teaching and learning are the hallmark of every section of King's Ely. Through a broad and enriched curriculum, pupils develop the self-knowledge and inner resilience to enable them to face the challenges of an ever-changing world. Every year, our students secure places at their first-choice university or institution, not just in the UK, but across the globe. This year, pupils have gone on to study subjects as diverse as Mathematics and Film, to Ecology and Creative Writing.

However, our aim is for students to develop learning habits that successfully prepare them for life, not just exams. As reported in the Good Schools Guide, King's Ely "turns out well-rounded, likeable individuals who attain academically but who also realise there is more to life than just results."

Music, Drama and Theatre, Art, Fashion and Textiles, Photography and Dance are each embedded in the culture of King's Ely, with vast opportunities for pupils of all abilities and aspirations. All major Sports are offered, along with an impressive array of other activities, helping every pupil to realise their sporting potential. Rowing, athletics, golf, cricket, hockey, tennis, rugby, netball, equestrian and football - the choices are endless. Our Boat Club is located just a short walk from school, providing an uninterrupted stretch of water that runs for over 15 miles in each direction - and which Cambridge University Boat Club athletes use too.

From Mount Toubkal in Morocco to the gushing torrents of the rivers in the Alps, our unique Ely Scheme Programme also offers boundless opportunities for pupils to learn through outdoor education. We give students the chance to undertake their Duke of Edinburgh's Award at all three levels.

The range of clubs and activities on offer to pupils, both during and after school, is vast. Pre-Prep children enjoy things like Forest School and Engineering Club; Prep children enjoy clubs like Archery and Pottery, and Senior pupils enjoy clubs like Clay Pigeon Shooting and Language Leaders. There really is something for everyone.

We were delighted to be a finalist in the 2020–21 Independent Schools of the Year Awards. However, King's Ely is more than a school. We are a community, a family. We take each child on a seamless journey, travelling from one section to the next, whilst welcoming newcomers at key transition stages, giving support and adapting the offering to the needs of every child in our care. With over 35 nationalities represented at King's Ely, students enjoy their schooldays in the company of friends from a range of cultures and backgrounds.

Book your family's visit to King's Ely today!

(Founded 970 AD)

Ely, Cambridgeshire CB7 4EW UK

Tel: 01353 660707

Fax: 01353 667485

Email: admissions@kingsely.org

Website: www.kingsely.org

Principal: Mr John Attwater MA (Oxon)

Appointed: September 2019

School type: Co-educational Day & Boarding Prep & Senior, Nursery & Sixth Form

Age range of pupils: 2–18 years

No. of pupils enrolled as at 01/09/2023: 1140

Fees as at 01/09/2023:

Day: £12,477–£26,214 per annum

Full Boarding: £27,843–£38,655 per annum

Average class size: Max 20

Teacher/pupil ratio: 1:9

Mander Portman Woodward - MPW Cambridge

Cambridge is where the MPW success story began. Nearly 50 years ago, three Cambridge graduates - Messieurs Mander, Portman and Woodward came together with an ambition to create a unique secondary education experience. They focused on several elements, based on their great Alma Mater, which they considered significant to the overall learning experience. Amongst these were the following: small class sizes, a strong tutorial system and superb teaching - and all of these within an informal atmosphere, which would allow creative minds to flourish.

Move the clock forward to the present day and these elements are still very much the hallmark of an MPW education. With fewer than 10 students per class for GCSE and A level, (though in fact the college average is closer to 6 in a class), the learning experience is truly personalised. As well as simulating the small class size at Oxbridge our students experience the privilege of being treated as an individual and not a number. Small classes mean our students know their questions will be answered and that they will have genuine contact time with their tutors in every lesson. With more than 30 A level subjects on offer and no restrictions on combinations, our students can choose subjects that suit them. Whilst Maths, Business, Economics and of course the Sciences remain popular choices, less well known subjects such as Ancient History and Classical Civilisation are also available.

With a current cohort of 60% British and 40% International, MPW Cambridge offers a world-class education to all. Education, however, is much more than what happens in the classroom. Preparation for life after secondary education is important too. Students need to be especially well-informed when they begin their UCAS application. The support provided by the personal tutors to each tutee is immense. From initial, informal discussion on determining the most suitable university course, through several drafts of the personal statement, often through BMAT or other entrance tests, for some even through daunting interview prospects, the MPW Personal Tutor is there. Their mandate is to 'hold the student's hand' throughout, providing encouragement and support.

We're also proud to assist those who might not have done so well the first time around. Our weekly assessments provide diagnostics where we can see which elements require further support. They also ensure that all of our students are fully prepared for the actual exam and properly understand critical success factors such as timing and weighting.

We'll leave the final words to Ofsted, taken from our college report: *'Pupils and sixth-form students say that Mander Portman Woodward (MPW) is 'amazing' and a great place to study. They know what they want to get out of their studies and are exceptionally well motivated to learn. Staff have high expectations. Most pupils and students respond to these expectations by working hard, so they achieve very well. They are confident that the support they get from their teachers will help them to be 'the best that they can be'.'*

(Founded 1987)

3–4 Brookside, Cambridge, Cambridgeshire CB2 1JE UK

Tel: 01223 350158

Fax: 01223 366429

Email: cambridge@mpw.ac.uk

Website: www.mpw.ac.uk

Principal: Mr Tom Caston

School type:
Co-educational Day & Boarding Senior & Sixth Form

Age range of pupils: 15–19 years

Average class size: 6

Teacher/pupil ratio: 1:5

MPW

Orwell Park School

A full and exciting education in a magical setting.
Orwell Park, established in 1868, is a co-educational prep school for day pupils and boarders from 2 1/2 to 13.

The school has one of the most beautiful and expansive settings in the UK, housed in an 18th century mansion, within 110 acres of stunning grounds on the banks of the River Orwell. The adjacent pre-prep building is a new, purpose built facility that combines innovative indoor spaces with an interactive forest school setting.

This is a busy and exciting education that makes the most of superb facilities to provide an unparalleled co-curricular experience with outstanding preparation for senior schools. Facilities include six sports pitches on site, a bushcraft forest camp, an outdoor pool set within a walled garden, floodlight astros, an army designed assault course, a nine hole golf course and a working Victorian observatory that is much loved by the astronomy club. Orwell Park is linked with Mayo College in Rajasthan, India which allows Year 7 pupils to visit India and sample the education at one of India's most famous boarding schools.

Boys and girls are given every opportunity to be the best they can be, both in and outside the classroom. High expectations, small class sizes and learning strategies tailored to the individual child lead to high levels of attainment. Pupils progress to a wide range of top senior schools such as Eton, Harrow, Oundle, Uppingham, Marlborough, Radley, Winchester and Stowe.

Boarding is extremely popular with Orwell Park pupils and incorporates a comprehensive programme of evening and weekend activities. There is a strong school community and much to participate in, and this sees many local pupils also opting to flexi board. Dormitories are bright and spacious, looking out towards the River Orwell across the lawns which are often visited by the resident deer - it can seem a bit like Hogwarts! A dedicated team of boarding staff are totally committed to the happiness and wellbeing of the boys and girls in their care.

Join us at an Open Event to see for yourself what makes Orwell Park such a special and inspirational place to be.

For more information contact our Director of Admissions and External Relations, Saskia Jordan, on 01473 653224 or email admissions@orwellpark.org

ORWELL PARK SCHOOL

(Founded 1868)

Nacton, Ipswich, Suffolk IP10 0ER UK

Tel: 01473 659225

Email: admissions@orwellpark.org

Website: www.orwellpark.co.uk

Headmaster: Mr Guy Musson

Appointed: August 2023

School type: Co-educational Day & Boarding Preparatory & Nursery

Religious Denomination: Interdenominational

Age range of pupils: 2.5–13 years

No. of pupils enrolled as at 01/09/2023: 270

Fees as at 01/09/2023:

Pre-Prep Day: £3,213 – £4,570 per term

Prep Day: £6,891 – £7,638 per term

Prep Boarding: £9,406 – £13,074 per term

Average class size: 12–14

Teacher/pupil ratio: 1:12

St Cedd's School

St Cedd's School is a co-educational 3–11 Charitable Trust School offering pupils the opportunity to aspire and achieve in a caring environment that nurtures talent and supports individual endeavour. This is a school in which every child matters. We value and celebrate their many diverse talents and qualities and the grounded confidence the pupils develop results in great personal achievement.

Individual Pupil Progress

The progress of pupils, of all abilities, throughout the school is rapid. Our standardised assessment results and 11+ scores far exceed national averages and annually we celebrate an unrivalled success rate to selective grammar and independent senior schools with an impressive track record of scholarship awards. This level of achievement is significant given that the school is academically non-selective. Assessments on entry are designed to capture the strengths and areas for development of each child so that the education is tailored to the needs of the individual.

Centre of Excellence

The Independent Schools Inspectorate (ISI) placed St Cedd's School at the top level in every category of inspection in March 2022 which places the school amongst the very best 3–11 preparatory schools in the country. The accolade confirms what we witness every day: high academic achievement, outstanding records of attainment in music, an inclusive sporting ethos and successes at national tournaments, a sense of purpose and ambition that shows itself in the attitude and actions of the pupils and staff, and a very effective pastoral care system.

In December 2021, the academic excellence of the school, and our provision for the most able, was recognised by the National Association for Able Children in Education through the reaccreditation of our NACE Challenge Award.

Broad and Balanced Curriculum

With over 80 clubs and activities to choose from, extra-curricular opportunities are balanced with a firm focus on academic work. This synergy supports the development of confident, self-assured pupils ready for the challenges ahead. PE, music, art, French and science are taught by specialists with the teaching of PE, music and French starting in the Pre-School. Acknowledging the breadth of talents of pupils is an important aspect of life at St Cedd's School. To this end, our baccalaureate-style Year 6 curriculum, HOLDFAST, leads to awards in recognition of 'Holistic Opportunities to Learn and Develop, Furthering Achievement, Service and Talent'.

As a member of the Choir Schools Association our Choristers sing in the Cathedral Choir and the Junior and Senior Chamber Choirs sing at Evensong in Chelmsford Cathedral.

Nurturing the Future

For over 90 years, boys and girls at St Cedd's School have been enjoying a quality of education that is among the very best you will find. We provide the best start in our vibrant Pre-School where the children thrive in a colourful and nurturing environment that widens their horizons and instils in them a love of learning.

Breakfast Club operates from 7:30am-8:00am and a wrap-around care programme is open until 6:00pm. Fees include curriculum-linked extra-curricular activities, lunch and the majority of after-school clubs.

To attend an open day or to arrange an individual tour, please contact our Admissions Registrar on 01245 392810 or email admissions@stcedds.org.uk.

St Cedd's School

(Founded 1931)

178a New London Road, Chelmsford, Essex CM2 0AR UK

Tel: 01245 392810

Email: info@stcedds.org.uk

Website: www.stcedds.org.uk

Head: Mr Matthew Clarke

Appointed: September 2018

School type:
Co-educational Day Preparatory & Nursery

Age range of pupils: 3–11 years

No. of pupils enrolled as at 01/09/2023: 400

Boys: 200 ***Girls:*** 200

Fees as at 01/09/2023:

Day: £3,490–£4,470 per term

Average class size: 23; maximum 24

St Columba's College

St Columba's College, is a school that prides itself on an education of both the head and the heart. We are committed to excellence in all areas of our College life, from the academic rigour in the classroom through to providing our young people with a wide range of specialist programmes that will enhance and enrich their lives.

From our Prep School through to the Senior School and Sixth Form, a Columban education is instilled in our students – that success lies in the practice of Courage, Courtesy and Compassion and we see this reflected in every member of the College community. Our pastoral care is excellent and our relationships with each other reflect the core values of the College and its belief that true education is holistic.

In a rapidly changing world, we believe that St Columba's College equips our boys and girls with academic standards and values that they need for success and, in recognising the uniqueness of our students, we prepare them to be the leaders of the future.

Academic Excellence

Our students achieve the highest standards through academic challenge and rigour. Scholarship is encouraged and celebrated throughout the school at all levels. Knowledge acquisition in itself is not a singular goal, but one to be supported by developing the qualities of intellectual enquiry and acuity.

We foster a love of learning through the agency of passionate and inspirational teachers, who challenge students to step out of their comfort zones, embark on critical thinking, foster creative output, and take charge of their education. Our teachers combine the old and the new using individual Surface Pros to enhance learning as well as other innovative teaching and learning techniques. Equipping our young people with all that is needed for future work and life is a fundamental goal of our educational philosophy.

Academic achievement in public examination at GCSE and A-level is excellent. The majority of students progress to their universities of choice and embark upon study of a diverse range of disciplines. Others go on to gain prestigious apprenticeships prior to embarking on successful future careers.

Ethos & Values

St Columba's College was founded in 1939, and since 1955 it has been a member of the Brothers of the Sacred Heart global community of schools. It is unique in being the only such school in the UK. We are proud to be a Catholic school, and we welcome pupils of all faiths. Our goal is to provide a moral and religious education inspired by the charism of the Brothers.

Education in the spirit of Father Coindre's charism is a holistic education, rooted in religious values, structured through friendly discipline, nurtured by personal attention, and committed to academic excellence.

We teach our pupils the Columban values of courage, courtesy and compassion to enable them to become confident and well-rounded individuals. The ultimate aim is to leave people and places better than they find them.

St Columba's pupils are academically successful, intellectually curious, happy and empathetic.

(Founded 1939)

King Harry Lane, St Albans, Hertfordshire AL3 4AW UK

Tel: 01727 855185

Email: collegeadmin@stcolumbascollege.org

Website: www.stcolumbascollege.org

Head: Mr Karl Guest

Appointed: 1st September 2023

School type: Co-educational Day & Sixth Form

Religious Denomination: Catholic

Age range of pupils: 4–18 years

No. of pupils enrolled as at 01/09/2023: 800

Fees as at 01/09/2023:

Reception, Prep 1, 2: £12,714 per annum

Prep 3: £14,964 per annum

Prep 4, 5, 6: £16,506 per annum

Senior: £19,338 per annum

Average class size: 10–24

St Faith's

Bright Beginnings - Exciting Futures

St Faith's is a Prep School for boys and girls aged 4–13 located in a green, spacious site in the heart of Cambridge. St Faith's is part of The Leys and St Faith's Foundation. As well as enjoying use of the senior school facilities, our pupils have unique access to The Leys Preliminary Assessment via which pupils at St Faith's can gain an offer of a 13+ place at The Leys during their Lent term of Year 6.

We believe in providing a future-focused education, preparing our pupils for the needs of the modern world. Pupils need the skills of team work, an understanding of how a computer works and of the engineered world around them, and a strong grounding in Science and Maths, the Humanities and Languages, as the foundation stones for virtually every path their future lives might take.

Across our wide-ranging curriculum each child is taught, developed and nurtured, to equip them well for life. Our teachers are passionate about sharing their knowledge, exploring new ideas and instilling a life-long passion for learning. We provide a tailored education to our pupils to ensure they are supported to fulfil their potential. Top-down excellence in all lessons enables our pupils to achieve more than they thought possible. With small class sizes, exceptional teachers and excellent facilities, all subjects follow an accelerated curriculum and the vast majority of pupils work at a higher level commensurate with their age.

A school leader in the early introduction of Computing to the curriculum, we now support over 25 schools in their development of Computing. In 2015 we became the first Prep school to teach Engineering as a core curriculum subject for all children from age seven. Our curriculum explores all forms of engineering; chemical, mechanical, robotics, structural, civil, electrical and aeronautical. In 2018 The Times awarded St Faith's 'Strategic Education Initiative of the Year' for our introduction of Engineering to the curriculum. Furthermore, The Week Independent Schools Guide named us 'The Best of the Best' for STEM education in 2019.

Sport is a conduit for developing mental and physical fitness, team spirit and resilience. Twenty different individual and team sports are taught at St Faith's. Our 'Sport for All' culture ensures that all pupils, irrespective of ability, receive specialist sports teaching from the age of five. During the 2022/23 school year, team and individual national and regional titles were awarded to St Faith's in Gymnastics, Trampolining, Netball, Athletics and Hockey. There were also national and regional entries in Cricket, Fencing, Swimming, Table Tennis, Football, Rugby and Triathlon. Drama, Music and Art are subjects which not only enable pupils to develop a life-long love of the arts but also promote self-belief and confidence.

Our green and spacious 9-acre site, located in the heart of Cambridge, together with extensive playing fields a two-minute walk away, provide some of the best facilities of any prep school in the UK. The shelves in our library are stocked with over 12,000 works of fiction and non-fiction. Engineering suites provide access to tools and equipment beyond many inventors' wildest dreams. Fully-equipped Science laboratories and computer suites are used by all year groups. The Hub provides flexible large indoor spaces for interdisciplinary projects, a roof-top night sky viewing platform and a virtual reality suite allows all children to explore the universe around them in the most exciting ways.

St Faith's pupils are confident, articulate, grounded and courteous, attributes which will stand them in good stead for their futures. In 2022/2023 37 scholarships were awarded to Year 8 pupils as they moved to senior schools, with over 90% of leavers gaining a place at their first-choice school.

(Founded 1884)

Trumpington Road, Cambridge,
Cambridgeshire CB2 8AG UK

Tel: 01223 352073

Email: admissions@stfaiths.co.uk

Website: www.stfaiths.co.uk

Headmaster: Dr C Hyde-Dunn

Appointed: September 2021

School type: Co-educational Day Preparatory

Age range of pupils: 4–13 years

No. of pupils enrolled as at 01/09/2023: 576

Boys: 313 ***Girls:*** 263

Fees as at 01/09/2023:

Day: £15,735–£19,815 per annum

Average class size: 16–18

St Margaret's School, Bushey

St Margaret's School in Bushey, Hertfordshire, is an independent day and boarding school for pupils aged 2 to 18. Founded in 1749, we are one of the oldest independent schools in the UK. As well as day places for all ages, we offer a range of flexible boarding options for both UK and international pupils from the age of 11.

We are a school with a proven record of academic success in public examinations and our pupils move onto competitive courses at leading universities and institutions both here in the UK and around the world. In 2022 68% of our A-level results were A*-B grades, with 64% of all GCSE results at 9–7 grades.

Our outward looking ethos aims to encourage a genuine enthusiasm for learning and an ability to independently explore subjects beyond the classroom. Our curriculum addresses a rapidly changing world filled with complex challenges as well as exciting new possibilities.

In January 2020, we began our transition to co-education, with St Margaret's School starting the journey from being an all girls school to providing education to both girls and boys.

The pastoral care at St Margaret's is the central pillar upon which the success of the school is based and we are proud of the quality of care and opportunity given to every one of our pupils no matter what stage of their education. We offer a rich programme of extra-curricular activities and pupils are encouraged to find their talent whatever that may be.

There is no typical St Margaret's pupil; all are valued individually by our qualified and committed staff. However, they are all dedicated young people who strive to succeed in all that they do and are passionate about topics facing them today. The quality of care at St Margaret's School enables pupils to grow in an atmosphere of tolerance and understanding and leave equipped with the confidence, aptitude and skills they need for life and for work.

Our beautiful 60 acre site boasts a combination of superbly resourced historic and modern buildings and we are easily accessible from both London, the Home Counties and all the major London airports. If you have not yet visited us, please do and we will show you the love of learning, culture of achievement and relish of challenge that is the essence of St Margaret's.

17  49

ST MARGARET'S

SCHOOL

(Founded 1749)

Merry Hill Road, Bushey, Hertfordshire WD23 1DT UK

Tel: +44 (0)20 8416 4400

Email: admissions@stmargarets-school.org.uk

Website: www.stmargarets-school.org.uk

Headteacher: Lara Péchard

Appointed: January 2020

School type: Co-educational Day & Boarding Prep & Senior, Nursery & Sixth Form

Age range of pupils: 2–18 years

No. of pupils enrolled as at 01/09/2023: 740

Fees as at 01/09/2023:

Nursery (full-time): £4,480 per term

Junior: £4,704 – £5,742 per term

Senior Day: £6,873 per term

Senior Full Board: £13,080 per term

Average class size: 20

St Mary's School, Cambridge

Located close to Cambridge's academic heart, St Mary's School has been educating and empowering girls since 1898, developing engaged, compassionate young women with the aspirations, confidence, and integrity to be themselves and help shape a better world. As a World Class High Performance Learning (HPL) school, St Mary's teaches its students to understand how they learn, as well as what they learn. From the moment they start at St Mary's, girls are taught to dream big and strive to reach their full potential. The result is excellent academic outcomes and young adults who are curious, community-minded, resilient, and ready to go out and make a positive contribution to society.

A place for girls

Within Cambridgeshire, St Mary's unique all-girls offer provides a space where gender stereotypes cannot thrive. The school's first-class education status was recently exemplified when it received the highest grade of 'excellent' in its ISI (Independent Schools Inspectorate) inspection. St Mary's achieved the top grade of 'excellent' in both aspects of the Education Quality Inspection, covering the quality of pupils' academic achievements and their personal development. Inspectors also praised the quality of teaching and parents concurred, giving the school an outstanding overall satisfaction rate of 98%.

A place to be me

While academic accolades speak for themselves, studying at St Mary's is about so much more. Exam qualifications open doors, but it is a student's self-belief, persistence and drive that keeps the door open. At St Mary's, students find the inspiration, opportunity and support they need to be themselves and pursue their individual talents with confidence and joy. Whether a student's interests are in sports or STEM, St Mary's really is the place for her to be herself!

A place with no limits

At St Mary's all subjects are 'for girls'. In a nurturing, supportive environment, students are encouraged to pursue their interests with no academic path off limits. St Mary's teachers work hard to encourage a passion for Maths and Science - subjects that girls have historically been less keen to pursue, particularly in co-ed settings. The school's state-of-the-art STEM facilities, including its STEM Learning Lab located in the Junior School give pupils everything they need to experiment, explore, design, test and perfect their innovation ideas.

Students are also encouraged to excel at sport. There is access to coaching expertise for those with a passion for competitive sports and extra-curricular clubs for those who want to find an activity that supports their physical and mental wellbeing. Junior and Senior School students make good use of the school's impressive and versatile sports grounds at Long Road, which accommodates 3G, grass and artificial all-weather pitches for rugby, football, hockey, netball, tennis, athletics, and cricket nets. St Mary's Rowing Club also continues to go from strength to strength as an affiliated British Rowing Club.

A place to succeed

With 125 years' experience in girls' education, St Mary's is uniquely placed to unlock students' academic, spiritual, cultural, and personal aspirations. At St Mary's, the secret to success is student happiness. Contented girls accomplish so much more and that's reflected in the school's results, and the subjects and careers that pupils go on to pursue. Supported by first-class pastoral care, St Mary's girls grow into fulfilled young women who go on to make a difference in society and the world at large.

(Founded 1898)

Bateman Street, Cambridge,
Cambridgeshire CB2 1LY UK

Tel: +44 (0)1223 224167

Email: admissions@stmaryscambridge.co.uk

Website: www.stmaryscambridge.co.uk

Headmistress: Ms Charlotte Avery

Appointed: 2007

School type: Girls' Day & Boarding Preparatory & Senior, Nursery & Sixth Form

Age range of girls: 3–18 years (boarding from 9)

No. of pupils enrolled as at 01/09/2023: 630

Fees as at 01/09/2023:

Day: £12,663–£19,740 per annum

Full Boarding: £39,444–£41,676 per annum

Average class size:

20 in Junior School; 24 in Senior School

Teacher/pupil ratio: 1:7

The Leys School

Founded in 1875 The Leys School is Cambridge's leading co-educational boarding school for children aged 11 - 18. Unusually for a city school, it is situated within a leafy 50 acre campus, close to the banks of the River Cam, yet only a 10 minute walk from the buzz of the city centre. Our ethos is simple - to provide an excellent, all-round education for our pupils, combining the traditional values of tolerance, respect and decency with a forward-looking and collaborative approach to teaching and learning.

Our Unique Location; the Cambridge Experience

The university of Cambridge provides the kind of enrichment opportunities most schools can only dream of. Links with the University are strong and we take full advantage of this; we host world-renowned speakers in our Great Hall and attend academic lectures within university departments. Our Chapel Choir regularly joins forces with the College choirs, singing in some of the most stunning College Chapels in the world. We share our award-winning Boathouse with 3 university colleges and compete in many of their sporting fixtures. Our superb location truly does offer a world of exceptional opportunities.

Academic Life

Through the provision of a broad and balanced curriculum Leys pupils develop into articulate, confident and well-rounded individuals. Their timetables are tailored to their aptitudes, needs and interests. As pupils move up through the school they take on increased responsibility for planning their workloads, with support from a coordinated tutorial system. Class sizes are small and the school's academic results reflect the expertise, vitality and enthusiasm of its teachers.

Beyond the Classroom

Pupils at The Leys are encouraged to take part in as many wider-curricular activities as they can realistically manage. Over 100 clubs, societies and groups take place every week. 26 sports are offered from Athletics to Water Polo, alongside CCF, Duke of Edinburgh and Community Service groups. The opportunities for outdoor pursuits are endless and, combined with first class performance facilities, the school exudes an air of purposefulness and busyness.

Support and Wellbeing

The Leys is a close-knit community, based on mutual respect and shared values. Its backbone is the House system where our pupils are assured of a supportive and caring environment. Their wellbeing is at the heart of what The Leys stands for; it is a happy, inspiring and unique place.

Joining The Leys

Girls and boys join The Leys in Years 7, 9 and 12 and may either sit the school's own tests, obtain places via pre-assessment in Year 7 or apply for one of a range of scholarships, bursaries or exhibitions.

Visit The Leys

Open Mornings are held on a termly basis alongside Small Group Visits whereby up to 6 families may visit the school together. The Admissions Team is also happy to arrange Private Visits when required. To find out what makes The Leys such a special place contact The Admissions Team on 01223 508904 or email admissions@theleys.net to arrange to come and visit.

THE Leys

CAMBRIDGE

(Founded 1875)

Trumpington Road, Cambridge, Cambridgeshire CB2 7AD UK

Tel: 01223 508900

Fax: 01223 505303

Email: admissions@theleys.net

Website: www.theleys.net

Headmaster: Mr Martin Priestley

Appointed: September 2014

School type:
Co-educational Day & Boarding Senior & Sixth Form

Age range of pupils: 11–18 years

No. of pupils enrolled as at 01/09/2023: 577

Fees as at 01/09/2023:

Day: £19,965–£27,660 per annum

Full Boarding: £30,555–£41,880 per annum

Average class size: 15–20

Teacher/pupil ratio: 1:8

The Peterborough School

The Peterborough School is the city's only independent day school for boys and girls from Nursery to Sixth Form.

Situated on one beautiful, leafy campus in the heart of Peterborough, the Nursery, Prep and Senior Schools enjoy excellent transport links and shared facilities.

The combined campus means the school is a vibrant place with small classes providing boys and girls with the individual attention, opportunities, confidence and ability to exploit fully their natural potential within a happy, caring and friendly community.

The 81-place Nursery has been rated Outstanding in its last five ISI Inspections. It enjoys an excellent location in a separate building on the school site, with ample gardens and outside spaces, and is close enough to Peterborough station, with its high-speed train services to London, to make it highly attractive for working families.

In the Preparatory school (4 to 11 years), the children are encouraged to be independent and inquisitive learners and develop many important skills through the extended curriculum and numerous extra curricular clubs and activities available.

In the Senior School and Sixth Form, students' unique talents are identified and developed, whether they are in the classroom, in the creative arts or on the sports field. Closely monitored academic performance means students usually achieve levels higher than those originally expected.

The Sixth Form is going from strength to strength with consistently impressive A Level results and is an area of focus for development, with a new bespoke Sixth Form block now in place. This facility has a large, wi-fi enabled Study Room, including a student meeting space, offices and a large, well-facilitated Common Room with kitchen. This development has also created a new state-of-the art Senior Library.

Our pastoral support is extremely strong and we passionately believe that children cannot learn well unless they are happy.

Headmaster, Adrian Meadows, is proud that the long-standing traditions of the school, which was founded in 1895, remain but at the same time it is a forward-looking, progressive place where children continually surprise and delight him. *"I have seen students winning a national STEM award on the same day that the Reception Classes and Pre-schoolers enjoyed a Teddy Bear's Picnic. Being amongst children of such a wide age range is fascinating, entertaining and always interesting but overall it is incredibly rewarding and humbling to be part of such an amazing school and community."*

Visitors to the School and Nursery are very welcome. We have Open Days on Saturdays in September/October and May each year when appointments are not necessary. There is also a Sixth Form Open Evening in November. Alternatively individual visits can be booked by calling the School on 01733 343357 or by visiting the website and completing the online form: www.thepeterboroughschool.co.uk/admissions

(Founded 1895)

Thorpe Road, Peterborough, Cambridgeshire PE3 6AP UK

Tel: 01733 343357

Email: office@tpsch.co.uk

Website: www.thepeterboroughschool.co.uk

Headmaster: Mr A D Meadows BSc(Hons), NPQH

Appointed: September 2007

School type: Co-educational Day Preparatory & Senior, Nursery & Sixth Form

Age range of pupils: 6 weeks–18 years

No. of pupils enrolled as at 01/09/2023: 500

Fees as at 01/09/2023:

Day: £11,991–£19,344 per annum

Average class size: 15

The Peterborough School

East Midlands

Fairfield Prep School

Fairfield Prep School is a top-performing, independent school for boys and girls aged 3–11. It is part of the Loughborough Schools Foundation which is a charity committed to providing an education to cherish through a Nursery and four high achieving schools: The Grammar School for boys, The High School for girls and The Amherst School, a non-selective co-education school. Uniquely the schools share a beautiful campus and exceptional resources in many fields including music, STEM and sport.

Originally founded in 1929 as part of Loughborough High School, Fairfield Prep became an autonomous school within the Foundation in 1969. It is now a flourishing school of over 500 pupils and is perfectly situated to provide a first-class 21st Century Primary education.

A new chapter for each child

Fairfield Prep School is committed to the development of every pupil; the priority is to ensure that each child enjoys and benefits from their time at the school. That means a friendly and supportive community and endless exciting experiences, all backed by high academic standards.

Every pupil at Fairfield has many opportunities to thrive and to find a passion for things that matter to them. Therefore, success and achievement are both found through the inspiring and lively academic environment, as well as numerous co-curricular activities which take place outside the classroom.

Fairfield was judged 'Excellent' across all eight categories by the Independent Schools Inspectorate in both 2016 and 2021 and has been 'Highly Commended' in the Most Creative Learning Through Play category by the judges at the Muddy Stilettos Best Schools Awards 2023. Pupils move onto the next stage of their educational journey within the Foundation as happy, confident and well-rounded individuals, ready to face the wealth of challenges ahead.

Excellent ways of understanding

The pastoral care at Fairfield is excellent and all staff work hard to bring out the best in each and every child. Each child benefits from effective, sensitive and well-coordinated pastoral care that enables academic achievement with individual care and focus, alongside an excellent holistic foundation for future learning.

Excellent experiences and opportunities

From Kindergarten to Year 6, the opportunities are vast and varied. There are over 40 clubs and activities available at lunchtime and after school encompassing Sport, Music, Drama and Art. From Origami to Music Theory, these include a Running Club, Rainbows and Dance. Most importantly, each child is encouraged and given the confidence to participate and enjoy success whatever their interests.

Charity and community work are also part of the school ethos. The school Council decides upon the charity focus for each term and fundraise for a rota of local, national, overseas and animal focused causes.

Excellent spaces and facilities

In 2016, Fairfield opened a new state-of-the-art building which provides new high-tech, light and airy classrooms with access to outdoor space, a large gymnasium and performance hall, specialist Art, Science and Food Technology rooms and a purpose-built Kindergarten. There is also a Forest School in a half-acre of woodland on the campus where children can safely explore the outdoor environment and develop an appreciation of the natural world.

FAIRFIELD
Prep School

(Founded 1969)

Leicester Road, Loughborough,
Leicestershire LE11 2AE UK

Tel: 01509 215172

Email: fairfield.admissions@lsf.org

Website: www.lsf.org/fairfield

Headmaster: Mr Andrew Earnshaw

Appointed: January 2013

School type: Co-educational Day Preparatory

Age range of pupils: 3–11 years

No. of pupils enrolled as at 01/09/2023: 505

Fees as at 01/09/2023:

Kindergarten: £4,330 per term

Pre-Prep (Reception to Year 2): £4,450 per term

Upper Prep (Years 3 to 6): £4,560 per term

Loughborough Amherst School

Loughborough Amherst School is an independent Catholic day and boarding school for girls and boys aged 4 to 18. Originally, Our Lady's Convent School, the school was founded in 1850 by the Rosminian Order of the Sisters of Providence. In 2015, the school became part of the Loughborough Schools Foundation and was renamed 'Loughborough Amherst School' when it became fully co-educational in 2019. In the same year, Amherst welcomed its first boarders as part of its elite tennis programme, in partnership with Loughborough University National Tennis Academy (LUNTA).

The school is located in the centre of Loughborough on a 10 acre, self-contained campus. The original convent buildings are Gothic revival, forming a cloister quadrangle with a large chapel to the west designed by renowned architect, Charles Hansom.

At Amherst, we seek to educate the whole person, inspiring our pupils to be curious, kind to one another and to believe in themselves. High-quality teaching is complemented by an emphasis on personal development. Our pupils thrive in the context of this close-knit, happy community, and develop into compassionate, resilient and responsible young people.

At the heart of our ethos is the philosophy of our founder, Blessed Antonio Rosmini, who believed that a 'pupil must be allowed to grow and develop as an integrated human person'. This belief underpins Amherst's seamless integration of its academic curriculum, personal development programme and co-curricular offer.

Amherst's through-school, co-educational offer, from Nursery to Sixth Form, allows all pupils to progress here from infancy to young adulthood. Together with our small size, this creates a distinct, family atmosphere that makes Amherst uniquely warm and welcoming.

We are a Catholic school in the truest sense, universal and welcoming of all, regardless of faith background. We seek to nurture in every pupil a concern for the world around them, compassion for others and a deep sense of wonder.

With an excellent pupil-to-teacher ratio, we offer exceptionally high levels of individual support, giving every child the opportunity to realise their goals. As one of four schools within the Loughborough Schools Foundation, we also enjoy the significant benefits of cross-foundation collaboration and outstanding facilities, and resources in many fields including music, STEM and sport.

LOUGHBOROUGH
Amherst School

(Founded 1850)

Gray Street, Loughborough, Leicestershire LE11 2DZ UK

Tel: 01509 263901

Email: amherst.admissions@lsf.org

Website: www.lsf.org/amherst

Headmaster: Mr James Neville

Appointed: September 2023

School type:
Co-educational Day Preparatory, Senior & Sixth Form

Age range of pupils: 4–18 years

No. of pupils enrolled as at 01/09/2023: 335

Fees as at 01/09/2023:

Day Fees (Reception to Year 2): £4,040 per term

Day Fees (Years 3 to 6): £4,160 per term

Day Fees (Years 7 to 9): £5,160 per term

Day Fees (Years 10 to 11): £5,230 per term

Day Fees (Years 12 to 13): £5,270 per term

Loughborough Grammar School

Loughborough Grammar School is a top-performing, independent day and boarding school for boys aged 10–18. It is part of the Loughborough Schools Foundation which is a charity committed to providing an education to cherish through a Nursery and four high achieving schools. Uniquely the schools share a beautiful campus and exceptional resources in many fields including music, STEM and sport.

Loughborough Grammar School is one of the oldest independent schools in the country, able to trace its origins back to 1495.

A passion for life and learning

Loughborough Grammar School is a school where academic achievement is at the centre of everything. Dedicated staff and outstanding resources enable Loughborough Grammar School boys both to fulfil their potential in examinations and to embark on intellectual adventures beyond the classroom.

However, the boys encounter far more than is required for academic success. Staff at the Grammar School understand that they will only succeed if they feel happy and contented. Considerable focus is therefore placed on the development of a strong moral compass where kindness towards others and a commitment to fairness and equality are valued as key personal attributes.

So that each boy can enjoy his time at Loughborough Grammar School, there is an attentive system of pastoral care that ensures that each boy is supported by pastoral staff who fully know him, his interests and his worries, so that they can both monitor his progress and guide him towards areas in which he will feel challenged and fulfilled.

Each boy is an individual and staff want him to feel totally at ease within himself, whatever his unique interests or pursuits. The Grammar School strongly believes that pupils benefit from a well-rounded education, which is why it is so important that every boy at Loughborough Grammar School has the opportunity to discover passions that he will retain beyond his school days and into adult life.

In the early years, boys are encouraged to try as many experiences as possible, gradually finding their unique niche as they progress through the school. These activities beyond the classroom play a major part in helping boys to develop into resilient young men, who are confident yet sensitive and aware of their responsibilities to others.

The Grammar School provides a myriad of opportunities through an extensive co-curricular programme which offers sport, music and drama as well as over 100 clubs and societies. Boys are expected to take advantage of the activities and clubs that are on offer and to show pride in representing the school outside its walls.

A Loughborough Grammar School education is therefore a busy one, where each boy thrives through engaging in a broad range of activities that will complement his academic achievement, and help him to develop into a well-rounded and happy young man.

Boarding at the Grammar School

The success of the boarding community has been an enriching part of Loughborough Grammar School for much of its long history. With an active community of some 75 boarders, the boarding is like a concentration of the very best that the school offers, condensed into two wonderfully welcoming Houses within the campus.

Just like the day pupils, Boarders are supported, individually known, cared for and cared about and encouraged to make the most of all the opportunities such a high achieving school provides.

LOUGHBOROUGH
Grammar School

(Founded 1495)

Buckland House, Burton Walks, Loughborough, Leicestershire LE11 2DU UK

Tel: 01509 233233

Email: grammar.admissions@lsf.org

Website: www.lsf.org/grammar

Headteacher: Mrs Helen Foster

Appointed: September 2023

School type: Boys' Day & Boarding Senior & Sixth Form

Age range of boys: 10–18 years

No. of pupils enrolled as at 01/09/2023: 890

Fees as at 01/09/2023:

Day Fees (Years 6–9): £5,300 per term

Day Fees (Years 10–11): £5,380 per term

Day Fees (Years 12–13): £5,390 per term

Full boarding & tuition with EAL:
£13,500 – £13,590 per term

Loughborough High School

Loughborough High School is a top-performing, independent school for girls aged 11–18. It is part of the Loughborough Schools Foundation which is a charity committed to providing an education to cherish through a Nursery and four high achieving schools. Uniquely the schools share a beautiful campus and exceptional resources in many fields including music, STEM and sport.

Founded in 1850, the High School is one of the country's oldest Grammar Schools for girls. Most of the values that are upheld and the traditions that are celebrated have been established in the ensuing years, always with the goal of creating a wonderfully welcoming community within which every pupil is supported and encouraged to become all that they can be.

Achievement comes from a sense of wellbeing

Everyone is someone at Loughborough High School: whether competing on the sports field, performing with our world-class music department or volunteering to help others, the individual talents of every student are nurtured in a warm and supportive community that enjoys all the advantages of a single-sex environment within a Foundation of four closely-linked schools.

The High School takes great pride in their pupils' academic achievements but also believes that education is about so much more than excellent examination results. This is a school with a love of learning at its heart and where there are no limits placed on female aspiration: whether a pupil wants to be an astrophysicist, an actress or an anthropologist, the teachers help and encourage all the girls to achieve success. The aim is to develop adaptable, independent and socially responsible young women, who approach their learning with imagination, energy and a sense of adventure.

At the heart of everything lies the wellbeing of each pupil: diversity and difference are celebrated and the caring, committed staff support each girl in developing the self-awareness, courage and resilience needed to negotiate the challenges of modern life. As part of the Loughborough Schools Foundation, each pupil will be a lifelong member of a vibrant and happy family.

Remarkable Results

Pupils are encouraged to be enthusiastic about learning and the girls are supported by dedicated teachers who will encourage them to be curious, and question and debate in the classroom and beyond to help them develop key learning skills.

The smaller class sizes, superb teaching and well-resourced departments, and an overall environment that is ideal for learning, create the conditions where each girl can do her very best.

Remarkable Choices

The enrichment programme is extensive and constantly evolving - ranging from numerous sporting and musical pursuits to hobbies such as chess and gardening.

Activities are offered for every age range during lunchtimes and after school. This includes opportunities for the Adventure Service Challenge (Years 7 to 9) and the Duke of Edinburgh's Award Scheme (Years 9 to 13) which help girls to push boundaries and acquire new skills. Girls can also join the Combined Cadet Force where cadets not only follow the ethos of the school, but also develop core values of loyalty, integrity, courage, respect for others and selfless commitment. All High School girls are encouraged to express themselves and enjoy as wide a range of school experiences as possible.

LOUGHBOROUGH
High School

(Founded 1850)

Burton Walks, Loughborough,
Leicestershire LE11 2DU UK

Tel: 01509 212348

Email: high.admissions@lsf.org

Website: www.lsf.org/high

Head: Dr Fiona Miles

Appointed: April 2019

School type: Girls' Day Senior & Sixth Form

Age range of girls: 11–18 years

No. of pupils enrolled as at 01/09/2023: 545

Fees as at 01/09/2023:

Day Fees (Years 6 to 9): £5,300 per term

Day Fees (Years 10 to 11): £5,380 per term

Day Fees (Years 12 to 13): £5,390 per term

Greater London

Elmhurst School

Elmhurst is more than a school. It is a community who come together for the good of the pupils and work tirelessly to support them in their endeavours; something we have been doing for over 150 years. Many of our pupils continue to visit us and even rejoin the community as parents, such is the warmth and affection that the school holds. Today we focus on nurturing the brilliance in every boy through partnerships, inspiring spaces and a focus on what is best for boys.

From our youngest pupils in our Little Elms nursery, staff encourage curious, brave and determined learners to blossom. Little Elms' pupils benefit from contact with specialist teachers in Art, Music, IT, Drama and French which ensures the boys are very much a part of the school. Routines are established that continue throughout their time here and this builds a familiarity supporting pupils' transition at each stage. Parent partnerships are formed and continuity between home and school approaches, optimises learning.

As a boys' school, we understand the importance of a curriculum with literacy at its heart, driving a love of reading and learning. We also value each individual, provide a broad, challenging curriculum to enable pupils to thrive and to support each boy in his preparations for 11+ entry to local grammar and independent schools.

Sport, Drama and outdoor learning together with Art and Music ensure life at Elmhurst is always varied and performance opportunities plentiful. Boys are encouraged to take part in a range of activities through our curriculum and extensive extra-curricular clubs programme.

Responsibility too is encouraged. Our eldest pupils are asked to buddy up with our nursery pupils, writing to them to introduce themselves at the start of the year and then meeting up with them weekly for lunch and spending play times together throughout the term. These relationships are beneficial to both the older and younger pupils and become a very important part of their school life. School voice is active in Elmhurst and our school council meets regularly to feedback ideas and feelings about the community. In a similar way, our active parents association come together to share ideas with the Head and collectively ambitious school development plans are shaped.

As part of the Bellevue family of schools, we have the additional opportunity to take part in group wide initiatives and our Y6 debaters are often successful in the Prep School debating competition amongst other things. As an ISA school, we are regular participants in regional and national sports competitions, with many of our teams and pupils enjoying great success on the sporting front.

Visit us

Nestled in the heart of South Croydon with excellent transport links (adjacent to South Croydon railway station and bus stops serving no 64 and 433 routes) and a generous car park for easy pick up and drop off, we are a school proud of its local area and our pupils regularly take advantage of the excellent facilities in South Croydon as well as supporting local charities and initiatives.

We host regular open events and taster sessions throughout the year. Why not pop in and see why an Elmhurst education is the right one for your son?

For more information or to sign up to visit us, go to www.elmhurstschool.net

(Founded 1869)

44–48 South Park Hill Road, South Croydon, Surrey CR2 7DW UK

Tel: 020 8688 0661

Email: admissions@elmhurstschool.net

Website: www.elmhurstschool.net

Head of School: Mrs Sara Marriott

School type: Boys' Day Preparatory & Nursery

Age range of boys: 3–11 years

No. of pupils enrolled as at 01/09/2023: 118

Fees as at 01/09/2023:

Day: £3,900–£4,548 per term

Kew College Prep

Set in leafy South-West London, Kew College Prep provides a small, supportive and vibrant school community. The minute you walk through the door, the ethos of the school is apparent; it is a friendly and caring environment which is relaxed but purposeful. The relationship between staff and pupils is warm and open and there is a tangible buzz of creativity in the air. The children are respectful, responsible, hard-working, and fun-loving individuals who thrive given opportunities to take risks in their learning and set challenges for themselves.

The curriculum is designed to provide pupils with opportunities to create, connect and collaborate both within and beyond the classroom. Children are encouraged to ask questions and think creatively. Technology is used to enhance learning across all subject areas, and sports and arts feature prominently in school life. The school's Junior House (Years 3–6) is also the springboard for our unique 11+ programme. From Year 5 onwards, each child is provided with a tailored learning plan. The results of entrance exams to secondary schools are excellent with numerous scholarships attained.

The children display an overwhelming desire to achieve and are inspired by staff who work with boundless energy, dedication and determination. No stone is left unturned as they strive to support and nurture every child to achieve their full potential. A strong moral value system is embedded from an early age so that, by the time the pupils leave Kew College Prep, they can think independently and critically. They are inquisitive, reflective and well-rounded; true individuals who are prepared for the rigours of secondary school and for the changing world in which they live.

"Both of our boys joined the school in the Nursery and have flourished in the nurturing and caring environment the school provides. The children are all confident, articulate, well-mannered, and thoroughly nice kids who are comfortable in the company of adults. Our boys have thrived at Kew College Prep and always raced enthusiastically into school each day. The teaching and school philosophy is very much focused on helping each child to achieve their best in a happy environment. As parents, we really couldn't ask for more." The Stewart family

"We chose Kew College Prep for our four daughters for its warm atmosphere and its happy, friendly, and well-mannered pupils. We feel fortunate to have also found a school which fulfils its promise of educating our children to their highest potential. We have children with differing abilities and personalities, but Kew College Prep has provided support and education for all of them. Every child at this school is unique, but one thing that every child here has in common is that they will leave strengthened by their experience." The Ahmed Family

Registrar: registrar@kewcollegeprep.com

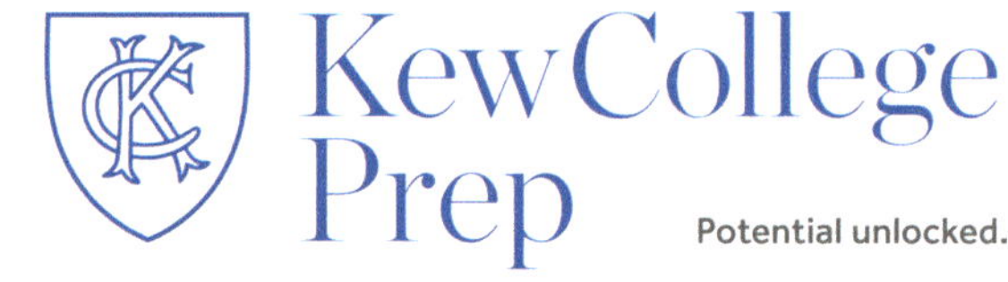

(Founded 1927)

24–26 Cumberland Road, Kew, Surrey TW9 3HQ UK

Tel: 020 8940 2039

Email: enquiries@kewcollegeprep.com

Website: www.kewcollegeprep.com

Head: Mrs Jane Bond BSc, MA(Ed), PGCE

School type:
Co-educational Day Preparatory & Nursery

Age range of pupils: 3–11 years

No. of pupils enrolled as at 01/09/2023: 284

Fees as at 01/09/2023:

Half-day Nursery: £2,730 per term

Full day Nursery: £5,105 per term

Reception - Year 6: £5,105 per term

Average class size: 20

King's House School

King's House School is a co-ed independent day prep school and nursery for children aged 3 to 13 in Richmond. Founded in 1946, the school offers each child a broad and balanced education, with a nurturing ethos and outstanding pastoral care. From September 2024 girls will be able to join the school, as KHS moves to co-education.

King's House provides a happy, supportive, and safe environment for its pupils where they can thrive and flourish. Pupils are cherished as individuals and provided with the skills and mental resilience to succeed in whatever path they choose in life. The school was recently rated 'Excellent' in all areas by ISI following their visit in June 2023.

At King's House Nursery children are taught and supported by a team of highly experienced staff, who strive to give every child the opportunity to flourish and grow. The co-ed nursery opened in January 2009 just around the corner from King's House School and benefits from light, spacious and inspiring facilities. Nestled in The Alberts, in the heart of the community, you will find an oasis of warmth, laughter and a wealth of resources to inspire little minds and create a love of learning. Children move up to school as happy, thoughtful children ready for their next journey, and all children in the nursery are offered a place in Reception.

The school aims to ensure that it keeps pace with global developments so that pupils are ready to take their place in an ever-changing world. When pupils leave the school, they are not only armed with outstanding academic results, but also with a sense of self-awareness, respectfulness, and independence. Many pupils in the Senior Department are active in the Eco-Schools Committee, and Year 8 Charity Monitors lead much of the student fundraising for both local and national charities. Academic success is a result of the happy, relaxed atmosphere at KHS, which allows pupils to simply be themselves. Pupils benefit from the school's 35-acre multi-use sports ground in Chiswick, located on the banks of the River Thames. Facilities there include two 3G pitches, an all-weather pitch used for netball and hockey, tennis courts, athletics facilities, cricket nets, and much more.

King's House is a mixed-ability inclusive school at the two main entry points, Nursery and Reception. Applications can be made anytime from birth onwards, with about half of the Reception intake coming from the Nursery. There are also small intakes at 7+, 8+ and 11+. Currently, most boys will move onto their senior schools at 13+, although all pupils are prepared for the 11+ and some will go on to local co-ed schools at the end of Year 6. The final two years allows pupils to take on leadership roles within a small year group, giving them the space to develop academically and emotionally. Pupils move on to a wide range of day, boarding, co-ed and single sex senior schools, with many achieving scholarships.

We warmly invite you to visit us and get in touch at admissions@kingshouseschool.org or 020 8940 1878.

(Founded 1946)

68 King's Road, Richmond, Surrey TW10 6ES UK

Tel: 020 8940 1878

Email: admissions@kingshouseschool.org

Website: www.kingshouseschool.org

Head: Mr Mark Turner BA, PGCE, NPQH

Appointed: 2011

School type:
Boys' Day Preparatory, Co-ed Pre-Prep & Nursery

Age range of boys: 3–13 years

Age range of girls: 3–6 years

No. of pupils enrolled as at 01/09/2023: 420

Fees as at 01/09/2023:

Day: £2,870–£6,890 per term

Laleham Lea School

Laleham Lea School was recently awarded the highest possible rating of 'Excellent' across Focused Compliance and Educational Quality Inspection including Academic Achievement following a full inspection from the Independent Schools Inspectorate. The Inspection reported that *'The quality of the pupils' academic and other achievements is excellent'* and, *'The quality of the pupils' personal development is excellent'*.

The inspectors reported that, *'Pupils make excellent progress, achieving at levels in advance of expectations for their age and ability', 'Pupils are outstanding communicators', 'Pupils develop highly effective study skills (and) are highly enthusiastic learners'*.

Along with excellent academic results and an impressive list of Senior School destinations and Scholarship Awards, Laleham Lea Catholic School is also known for and is proud of its pastoral care which was praised by the inspectors who commented that, *'The quality of the pupils' personal development is excellent', 'Pupils have high levels of self-understanding for their age and show notable resilience', 'Pupils show outstanding respect for each other and are highly inclusive'* and *'Pupils develop good relationships and demonstrate excellent social skills'*.

The Catholic life of the school was also recognised by the Inspection team who reported that, *'Pupils show excellent development of their spiritual understanding in their everyday lives'*.

At Laleham Lea we firmly believe in putting the child at the centre of everything we do. From the warm welcome as you walk through the door in the morning to the playground where all ages play, run and socialise together as one happy family. Bright, light filled classrooms and enthusiastic, experienced teachers engage young minds' thirst for knowledge, helping each developing individual to reach their full potential and ultimately move on to the school of their choice. Our pupils become happy, confident, fulfilled young people through both academic and extra-curricular activities.

Every child takes part in team sports and every child is involved in school productions and concerts. Our greatest pleasure is to watch a once shy child blossom into the confident soloist, take a leading role in school assembly or simply help a fellow pupil through a challenging moment. A high standard of teaching and learning is central to our success. Your son or daughter will be taught in well equipped classrooms and our teachers hold specialist qualifications and have experience in specific areas of the curriculum such as Science, Modern Languages, Computer Studies (ICT), Art, Music and Sports.

Together with parents, who are the first educators, we aim to lead our children towards tolerance, understanding and sensitivity to the needs of others so that they may grow up as well balanced individuals with a strong sense of personal identity and an awareness of God's love.

Our outstanding pastoral care provides for a happy, caring community for all and we invite you to come and visit Laleham Lea; we can assure you of a very warm welcome. Book your tour and secure your child's place for 2024 and beyond. 0208 660 3351. www.lalehamlea.co.uk

(Founded 1965)

29 Peaks Hill, Purley, Surrey CR8 3JJ UK

Tel: 020 8660 3351

Email: secretary@lalehamlea.co.uk

Website: www.lalehamlea.co.uk

Acting Head Teacher: Mrs Maria Reece

School type:
Co-educational Day Preparatory & Nursery

Age range of pupils: 3–11 years

No. of pupils enrolled as at 01/09/2023: 144

Fees as at 01/09/2023:

Day: from £9,960 per annum

Average class size: 18

St Catherine's School

St Catherine's is a vibrant and caring Catholic school that welcomes girls of all faiths and backgrounds. Our friendly community helps each pupil develop confidence as she explores her gifts and talents, and is inspired to meet challenges creatively. The school proudly combines excellent pastoral care with an innovative and ambitious curriculum that prepares girls for the 21st century.

Our recent excellent inspection reports from the Independent Schools Inspectorate note that *'teaching at St Catherine's is more than the sum of its classroom parts... pupils have a wrap-around experience that leads them to learn exceptionally well'* and that *'pupils flourish because of the secure, caring ethos of the school'*. We see these features in the achievements of our girls and in their readiness to learn.

In the Prep Department, we are moving toward an exclusively key stage two structure, and investing in a rich and varied curriculum and co-curricular programme for girls in Year 3–6. The emphasis on curiosity and discovery establishes firm foundations that later lead to success in the Senior School (where each pupil has a guaranteed place).

St Catherine's girls enjoy a wide range of subjects and benefit from passionate and experienced teachers who know them well, offer support and challenge at all stages, and are in regular contact with parents.

The Senior School girls certainly rise to the challenges posed by public examinations. St Catherine's is proud of its value added at GCSE and A Level, and we enjoy seeing our young women go on to university courses and careers of their choice, and to bright futures.

Those who visit St Catherine's often remark on the warm and genuine enthusiasm of our pupils. The school's Christian ethos and emphasis on values helps girls to engage with the world around them, while open discussion, time for reflection, pupil-led committees and a wide range of opportunities create a lively environment where they can feel a sense of belonging. Our emphasis on character, and on the deeper values of compassion, integrity and resilience, is also developed through a comprehensive co-curricular programme.

St Catherine's is committed to developing its facilities and over recent years we have been pleased to see girls enjoying new buildings and refurbishments, like the Science Block and Sixth Form Centre, which are designed to enhance their curriculum and social experiences. We also provide exciting trips, competitions and school events throughout the year; whether it is a trip to Iceland, regional athletics finals or a part in the latest school musical, there are plenty of opportunities for girls to develop their skills and their friendships within the school community.

Information about public examination results, co-curricular opportunities and wrap-around care can all be found on the school website: www.stcatherineschool.co.uk

ST CATHERINE'S SCHOOL
TWICKENHAM

(Founded 1914)

Cross Deep, Twickenham, Middlesex TW1 4QJ UK

Tel: 020 8891 2898

Email: info@stcatherineschool.co.uk

Website: www.stcatherineschool.co.uk

Headmistress: Mrs Johneen McPherson MA

Appointed: September 2018

School type: Girls' Day Preparatory, Senior & Sixth Form

Age range of girls: 5–18 years

No. of pupils enrolled as at 01/09/2023: 405

Fees as at 01/09/2023:

Day: £14,010–£17,910 per annum (tuition fees only)

Average class size: 15–20

Teacher/pupil ratio: 1:9

St. Catherine's School

St Helen's College

Nestled on the edge of Court Park in a quiet corner of Hillingdon, St. Helen's College is a family-run independent school for boys and girls aged 3 to 11, with a separate, thriving Kindergarten for boys and girls aged 2–3.

The school has a real family feel and has been described by inspectors as a 'haven of harmony'. Indeed, the most recent ISI quality inspection judged St. Helen's College outstanding, the quality of teaching excellent, the pupils' personal development outstanding and pupils' achievements, both academic and extra-curricular, excellent.

The report said: *'Pupils achieve high standards in academic work and a wide range of other activities. They are extremely successful in all aspects of learning…this is reflected in their success in entrance examinations both to maintained grammar and independent schools'.*

The school's values and ethos set it apart. Led by the Head, Shirley Drummond, staff create a harmonious, loving environment, nurture the individual qualities of every pupil and ensure that children develop a lifelong love of learning, find out where their talents and interests lie, and leave school with traditional values and strength of character, ready to face the challenges of adult life with confidence, resilience and joy!

The children enjoy lessons taught by highly qualified specialist teachers right from the start, allowing them to study at a high level led by teachers with a real passion for their subject. There is also an extremely wide-ranging and quite unique range of 70+ co-curricular activities available, with superb music, drama and sports provision and clubs including cookery, gardening, yoga, taekwondo, ceramics, dance and many, many more.

The school benefits from specialist modern facilities and is strongly rooted in its local community, enjoying links with local churches, Brunel University and local theatres. The safe, loving, encouraging environment at St. Helen's College fosters excellent academic achievement and well-rounded, confident pupils. Inspectors noted, *'Pupils' personal development is outstanding, well supported by excellent pastoral care. The overall feeling is of a warm, friendly community where everyone knows each other and feels safe and secure'.*

St. Helen's College operates a flexible year-round extended care provision, with Breakfast Club from 7.30 a.m. and after school care until 6 p.m. daily during term time, and Holiday Club running during school holidays to assist working parents.

Parents may register children for entry to the school at 2+ (Kindergarten) or 3+ (Nursery). This is an extremely popular school and early registration is advisable. Prospective parents may register online using the online registration form or by contacting the school using the details below.

Online and in-school open mornings are held regularly. The Head, Head of Lower School and Director of Admissions are available to answer questions and take registrations at these events.

Alternatively, prospective parents may book an individual tour one morning during term time by telephoning 01895 234371 or emailing info@sthelenscollege.com.

(Founded 1924)

Parkway, Hillingdon, Uxbridge, Middlesex UB10 9JX UK

Tel: 01895 234371

Email: info@sthelenscollege.com

Website: www.sthelenscollege.com

Head: Ms Shirley Drummond BA, PGCert, MLDP, FCCT

Appointed: 2016

School type:
Co-educational Day Preparatory & Nursery

Age range of pupils: 2–11 years

No. of pupils enrolled as at 01/09/2023: 380

Boys: 188 ***Girls:*** 192

Fees as at 01/09/2023:

Day: £10,980–£13,680 per annum

Average class size: 22

Teacher/pupil ratio: varies

Story
Time

Staines Preparatory School

We are a happy, welcoming and non-selective school that prides itself on creating a genuine family atmosphere alongside a first rate education. Our ethos of 'educating today's children for the challenges of tomorrow' is more than academics, we will be with you and your child every step of the way throughout their first stage of education.

The pupils at Staines Prep learn the value of commitment to successful learning, develop discipline and a sense of responsibility. This supportive and nurturing environment enables pupils to fulfil their potential and become more confident, independent lifelong learners across all areas of the curriculum and well–adjusted, global citizens.

As a school we adopt a 'Growth Mindset' culture. Growth Mindset is a programme which looks to empower pupils with the core belief that abilities, rather than being fixed, can be developed over time. Research shows that this powerful belief leads to an increased focus on learning, greater resilience, and superior achievement. The ISI inspectors were particularly impressed by the personal development of pupils, noting in their report that *"pupils display high levels of self-esteem due to the nurturing environment of the school"*.

Our school facilities not only include inspiring classrooms but a science lab and art, design and technology suite which many senior schools would be envious of. We have a large sports hall and theatre space which all pupils take advantage of from nursery upwards. This year we have added a state of the art home economics room.

We are very proud to have been awarded the School Games Gold award which, along with our wide range of extra-curricular activities, shows our commitment to sport and promoting a healthy lifestyle for all our pupils across all year groups. Our playgrounds are full of activities that get the pupils moving and developing a Growth Mindset outside of the classroom, from a trim trail and climbing wall for the older years through to an array of playground games for the lower school and nursery.

Our Environmental Area, The Sanctuary, allows the children to bring science to life whilst learning to safely explore the great outdoors. We use Forest School principles to teach skills that can be used in the classroom and beyond, encouraging team work, responsibility and communication as well as building self-esteem and independence. The children are not limited in what they can do but instead are taught how to access and manage the risks in nature.

We understand how hard our parents work and we aim to support them by providing wraparound care from 7.30am until 6pm. We are less than 5 minutes' walk from Staines railway station, making pick-up and drop-off that little bit easier. We also operate a bus service from the surrounding areas.

We are delighted to have been shortlisted for the Independent School Awards 4 years in a row. Our ISI 'excellent in all areas' rating following a full inspection in 2019. We are proud to have received a Primary Quality Mark accreditation for our curriculum and practice.

To come and experience the school first hand, you can arrange a private tour to fit in around your commitments or visit us at one of our popular open events which run throughout the year.

(Founded 1935)

3 Gresham Road, Staines-upon-Thames, Surrey TW18 2BT UK

Tel: 01784 450909

Email: admissions@stainesprep.co.uk

Website: www.stainesprep.co.uk

Head of School:
Ms Samantha Sawyer B.Ed (Hons), M.Ed, NPQH

Appointed: September 2014

School type:
Co-educational Day Preparatory & Nursery

Religious Denomination: Non-denominational

Age range of pupils: 3–11 years

No. of pupils enrolled as at 01/09/2023: 289

Boys: 154 ***Girls:*** 135

Fees as at 01/09/2023:

Day: £11,975–£14,610 per annum

Average class size: 15 (max 20)

SPS
SPS
SPS
SPS

The Royal Masonic School for Girls

For more than 200 years, RMS has been nurturing every pupil to develop an enduring curiosity to learn. The school continues this unwavering commitment to provide inspirational teaching, delivered by passionate and dedicated staff in a dynamic learning environment where every lesson is informative and stimulating. Emphasis is placed on developing, within their students, a commitment to and a love of learning. RMS staff appreciate that every girl is unique and they take time to get to know every individual, demonstrating total commitment to bringing out the best in every girl.

The school moved to its current Rickmansworth location in 1934 where it is situated amidst 315 acres of stunning green parkland and yet just a short walk to Rickmansworth which is served by the Metropolitan line and Chiltern Railways. With so much space, RMS offers extensive facilities such as a sports centre that also houses a fitness suite, dance studio and squash courts; an indoor heated swimming pool; an all-weather pitch; a six-hole golf course together with multiple tennis and netball courts and cricket pitches. There are separate departments for art, textiles and photography as well as a dedicated performing arts centre that includes a recital suite, a green screen and a recording studio! The younger pupils enjoy the Forest School and all pupils have access to the planetarium! To continually improve their offering, Sixth Form facilities have been extended this year with the introduction of a coffee shop, a wellbeing room, a new futures (careers) centre and a conference room.

RMS welcomes girls from Nursery to Sixth Form with boarders from age eight. The cosmopolitan boarding community provides a happy and supportive home to a mix of full, weekly and flexi boarders.

The broad and varied curriculum together with a co-curricular programme offering 100+ activities, ensures that every girl discovers her niche and thrives whilst maximising use of the extensive grounds and facilities. The prep school, known to the RMS community as Cadogan House, offers an exciting environment in which their youngest pupils thrive. The Early Years Lead works closely with the Head of the Nursery to ensure a smooth transition from Nursery to Reception. The majority of pupils continue effortlessly from the Prep School to the Senior School but with an increase in capacity in Year 7, 11+ is also a popular entry point for both boarding and day girls.

Scholarships and Bursaries are available at both 11+ and 16+ entry points for a variety of disciplines. At the 11+ entrance point, all applicants are considered as potential academic scholars and no separate application is required.

As a school that continually looks to improve and to think differently, in addition to the vast array of subjects at both GCSE and A Level currently on offer, new for September 2024 will be the introduction of an Extended Certificate in Professional Cookery by Leiths Academy.

Pupils at RMS are challenged daily and the learning style inspires pupils to dig deeper, often resulting in futures they had not imagined. As experts in girls' education, RMS understand how girls prefer to learn. The school ably guides, supports and nurtures and provides the opportunity to expand horizons. RMS pupils are encouraged to think critically, creatively and collaboratively. Above all, RMS girls are happy and balanced and will become the best version of themselves.

RMS
FOR GIRLS

(Founded 1788)

Rickmansworth Park, Rickmansworth,
Hertfordshire WD3 4HF UK

Tel: 01923 725354

Email: admissions@rmsforgirls.com

Website: www.rmsforgirls.com

Headmaster: Mr Kevin Carson M.Phil (Cambridge)

Appointed: January 2017

School type: Girls' Day & Boarding Preparatory & Senior, Nursery & Sixth Form

Religious Denomination: Non-denominational

Age range of boys: 2–3 years

Age range of girls: 2–18 years (boarding from 8)

No. of pupils enrolled as at 01/09/2023: 985

Fees as at 01/09/2023:

Day: £4,350–£7,490 per term

Full Boarding: £9,095–£13,140 per term

Whitgift School

Whitgift is one of Britain's finest independent day and boarding schools, offering a friendly, vibrant and inclusive environment for 10–18-year-old boys. Our core purpose is to educate bright and talented young men to become independent learners and thinkers, to achieve beyond what they believed they could, and to leave the school ready to give back to the society in which they will be leaders.

The school offers a variety of pathways to qualifications, including A Levels and the International Baccalaureate, and consistently ranks as a top 20 world IB school. Alongside exceptional academic standards, the co-curricular activities feature more than 100 clubs & societies, more than 40 sports and an active Outdoor Education programme that takes students worldwide. A packed Performing Arts programme performs regularly, staging first-class musicals and plays. Orchestras and choirs play at major venues, including the Royal Albert Hall, Cadogan Hall and locally the Fairfield Halls.

The school's Boarding House, which opened in 2013, is superbly-equipped and offers full, weekly and flexi-boarding to boys aged 13–18. This option allows students to make the most of their time at Whitgift without distractions or a lengthy commute. Structured homework and free time sessions, as well as organised evening and weekend activities, ensure that boarders build a strong balance between their academic studies and their co-curricular interests. For those who live further afield, there are 12 dedicated bus routes covering routes across London, Surrey, Kent and Sussex.

Whitgift takes pride in being a diverse student body and global citizenship and digital literacy are key areas of focus for the entire school community. Pastoral support is the foundation of our provision, with each pupil and his parents guaranteed a friendly face to turn to for advice and guidance. The latest ISI Report states, *"The quality of pastoral care is outstanding… a calm courteous approach pervades the school, indicated by highly civilised and positive relationships between staff and pupils."*

In 2020 Whitgift was awarded the title of Independent Boys' School of the Year and the judges said it was *"a compelling entry that radiated the school's inclusive and collaborative values in the context of an all-boys school."* In 2022, Whitgift has been shortlisted for the Community and Partnership award by Independent School Parent for our work with Primary age children throughout the academic year and during Summer School.

Open Events

We encourage you to come and visit us on one of our Open Events to get a true feel for our inspiring school community.

WHITGIFT

(Founded 1596)

Haling Park, South Croydon, Surrey CR2 6YT UK

Tel: +44 20 8633 9935

Email: admissions@whitgift.co.uk

Website: www.whitgift.co.uk

Headmaster: Mr Christopher Ramsey

Appointed: September 2017

School type: Boys' Day & Boarding Senior & Sixth Form

Religious Denomination: Accepting of all faiths

Age range of boys: 10–18 years (boarding from 13)

No. of pupils enrolled as at 01/09/2023: 1550

Fees as at 01/09/2023:

Day: £24,462 per annum

Weekly Boarding: £40,470 per annum

Full Boarding: £47,991 per annum

Average class size: 20

Teacher/pupil ratio: 1:7

London

Bassett House School

Bassett House School is a traditional prep school with an innovative soul, nestled in leafy Notting Hill. Our small size means that each child is known and nurtured by every member of staff, and each is provided with an educational journey bespoke to their strengths and needs. Committed, inspirational teachers stretch pupils who are excelling as well as providing those who require extra help, the support and tools they need to achieve their goals. Continued provision after school allows pupils the freedom to stay behind to complete homework with the help of their teachers, which has proven effective in priming a positive attitude toward learning. A plethora of clubs is on offer after this time, with wrap around care available to support busy working parents.

No two days are alike and a Bassett House pupil benefits from learning across three world-class learning spaces, complete with state of the art Performing Arts Studio, library, stage and Scandinavian inspired Montessori Early Years spaces, and all within walking distance from one another. Every child spends quality time outside every day, whether that's pursuing our sustainability curriculum in our urban garden, playing in nearby Kensington 'Rocket' Memorial Park, or partaking in sports fixtures.

With the help of expert specialist teachers, pupils are encouraged in a variety of enriching learning including entrepreneurial challenges and musical performances such as Battle of the Bands. During Art lessons, pupils learn about modern and classic artists such as Damien Hirst and Van Gogh, refining their eye for detail and manipulating a wide range of media. Pupils' artwork is proudly displayed around the school and during the annual Art Exhibition. Music classes include genres covering the popular to the gothic, fine-tuning auditory and performing skills with peripatetic lessons readily available. Pupils are encouraged to express themselves freely during end of year performances - ranging from Chitty Chitty Bang Bang to School of Rock. Teachers harness the alchemy of learning and teach a future-proof curriculum, so that pupils leave Bassett House bold and brave enough to be fearless with their dreams, in order to embark upon remarkable futures.

Residential trips are a particular highlight for Bassett children, who have recently been measuring river velocities and learning about Constable at Flatford Mill, ordering in French in a market in Normandy, and considering the Viking architecture of York (to name but a few). These experiences help to develop rounded, outward looking, tenacious pupils, which serves them well in their Senior School interviews.

Our most recent ISI report rated our outcomes as outstanding across the board, and of 16 Year 6 pupils, two thirds were awarded scholarships, with over 70 offers of a place within some of London's most superior Senior Schools.

As a member of the Dukes Education group of schools, Bassett House benefits from the sharing of best practices across the group and potential all-through schooling options. Teachers are provided with world-class Professional Development, guidance, and support from the Governing Body.

Catering for Nursery (aged 3+) to Year 6, pupils learn through our values of Courage, Compassion and Commitment. As one school leaver put it, *"At Bassett House, you learn Maths and English but more than that, you learn how to be yourself."*

Bassett House is proud to be the best small school in Notting Hill. We are small enough to be bespoke, yet big enough to thrive.

BASSETT HOUSE

SCHOOL

(Founded 1947)

60 Bassett Road, Notting Hill, London, W10 6JP UK

Tel: 020 8969 0313

Email: info@bassetths.org.uk

Website: www.bassetths.org.uk

Headmistress: Mrs Kelly Gray

School type:
Co-educational Day Preparatory & Nursery

Age range of pupils: 3–11 years

No. of pupils enrolled as at 01/09/2023: 145

Fees as at 01/09/2023:

Day: £10,818–£22,533 per annum

Average class size: 18

Teacher/pupil ratio: 1:5

City of London School

A rounded education in the Square Mile

There is no such thing as a typical CLS pupil. What characterises the education offered is a true preparation for life.

City of London School is a truly unique independent school, not least because of its unrivalled location on the banks of the Thames, between St. Paul's Cathedral and the Tate Modern. We are at the heart of the capital and our pupils benefit enormously from all that is on offer on our doorstep. Our location allows us to attract the very best outside speakers, offer top-class work shadowing placements and visit the many places of interest in this world-class city. We are a modern and forward-looking institution drawing on clever pupils from all social, economic and ethnic backgrounds and, in so doing, truly reflect the diversity of the capital in the 21st century. Pupils come from a huge number of both state primary and independent preparatory schools and, once here, receive an academic yet liberal education. Our central location allows pupils to travel to CLS from all over London, encouraging resourcefulness and self-reliance in their journey to school, and in their wider life.

Our examination results are excellent, but, more importantly, pupils leave us ready for life beyond school, with a sense of identity and an independence of thought and action which are rare among leavers from independent schools; it is significant that the vast majority of pupils go on to their first choice of university, with a large number attending Oxford and Cambridge universities, and various medical schools. Facilities are outstanding (the school moved downstream to its new buildings in 1986) and are continually updated. The state-of-the-art Winterflood Theatre and refurbished Science laboratories provide a first-rate environment in which our pupils learn and thrive. We are generously endowed with academic, music and sports scholarships and, in addition, the bursary campaign has raised significant funding for a number of full-fee places to be awarded each year to those who could not otherwise afford the fees. In this way, the school seeks to maintain the socio-economic mix which has always been its tradition and strength. Admission at 11+, 13+ and 16+ is by entrance examinations followed by interviews for those candidates who complete their examination papers to a satisfactory standard.

For dates and to book onto one of our open days please visit our website.
Tel: 020 3680 6300
Email: admissions@cityoflondonschool.org.uk

City of London School

(Founded 1442)

Queen Victoria Street, London, EC4V 3AL UK

Tel: 020 3680 6300

Email: admissions@cityoflondonschool.org.uk

Website: www.cityoflondonschool.org.uk

Head: Mr A R Bird MSc

Appointed: January 2018

School type: Boys' Day Senior & Sixth Form

Age range of boys: 10–18 years

No. of pupils enrolled as at 01/09/2023: 766

Sixth Form: 318

Fees as at 01/09/2023:

Day: £22,635 per annum

CITY OF LONDON SCHOOL
CLEANING THE RIVER TOGETHER
CITY OF LONDON SCHOOL

Durston House

Durston House is a leading London prep school for girls and boys aged 3 - 13. An education at Durston House is based upon academic rigour through excellent teaching, encouraging pupils to explore, question, take risks, and develop their creativity, communication and teamwork - all central to successful life-long learning. Durston House has a fine record of preparing pupils for Senior Schools in London and beyond. We take pride in the true and visible diversity of our community and embrace pupils and staff from all ethnic, cultural and religious backgrounds.

Durston House places an emphasis on high standards of work and targets that are commensurate with each pupil's personal development. We believe that it is hugely important to create an educational environment that encourages all pupils to be curious and enthusiastic about their opportunities to learn and grow. The manner in which this growth is guided is one of relaxed, quiet integrity of purpose, allowing pupils the freedom to develop themselves. This is the essence of our ongoing success.

In 2023 Durston House was awarded 17th on the 'Top 20 School for Academic Results' according to The Sunday Times Parent Power List, and while this is a superb accolade to have, we know the key to success is through hard work and a desire to continually improve. Placing our pupils at the centre of everything we do and making sure every opportunity is taken so that each pupil is able to flourish.

A child's education here is shaped by the development of their character, curiosity to learn, discover more, and their expanding capability. The curriculum we offer is very broad, deep and rigorous, allowing ample opportunity for pupils to question and explore.

Lessons are delivered in a range of ways, taking account of different learning styles and preferences, and the certainty that pupils should explore and experience practically, not just from a textbook. Workshops, outings, trips and outdoor adventures complement the classroom experience across all year groups. Throughout the school there is an After-School Activities Programme, offering a wide range of activities from yoga, street dance, coding, skateboarding, photography and many more! After-School Activities at Durston House aim to inspire, enthuse and develop curiosity in pupils.

We have two impressive sports fields, with over 6 acres of playing fields. Sport is strong, with both of the school's playing field sites having floodlit, all-weather facilities; fixtures against other schools are common and there has been much sporting success in recent years.

Entry into Pre-School is non-selective, children can join the Pre-School in the term after they turn 3 years old, with a September, January or April entry point. From Year 1 onwards, entry assessment procedures are in place.

(Founded 1886)

12–14 Castlebar Road, Ealing, London, W5 2DR UK

Tel: 020 8991 6530

Email: info@durstonhouse.org

Website: www.durstonhouse.org

Headmaster: Mr Giles Entwisle

Appointed: September 2020

School type: Co-educational Day Preparatory

Age range of boys: 3–13 years

No. of pupils enrolled as at 01/09/2023: 389

Fees as at 01/09/2023:

Day: £4,750–£6,180 per term

Average class size: 15

Ealing Independent College

We prepare students aged 13 to 19 from the UK and worldwide for university entry through the GCSE and A level programmes, providing expert teaching, supportive individual help and guidance.

The College offers a friendly and personalised learning environment with small class sizes, where students have a strong support system in place, both through the teachers as well as their peers.

With an average class size of ten, it gives our staff the chance to fully understand each individual student - to get to know how they best make progress - and to make a bespoke learning programme for them, geared towards ensuring that they perform to the very best of their abilities.

Ealing Independent College is a wonderful place to learn and grow, supported by passionate and dedicated staff who ensure each and every student reaches their potential and leave with grades and university destinations that they could only have dreamed of.

We encourage our students to develop confidence and resilience to succeed as they forge their own path in life. We aim to empower our students to make courageous decisions that are right for them. We encourage our students to be resourceful, analysing the options in front of them and making informed decisions about choices that impact them. We teach our students to be persistent, to push through and not to settle. We are a diverse community, where everyone has the freedom to be themselves and learn from each other.

The individual is at the core of all elements that make up our unique approach to teaching and learning. As a College we are not satisfied with just teaching the curriculum; we want to help students become the best version of themselves. We want to help them celebrate and develop their individuality and to achieve their true potential.

The learning extends beyond the classrooms, with a selection of clubs and societies available to enrich and enhance the College experience.

Physical fitness activities are some of the extra-curricular activities on offer for the students. Running club and football training take place every week, as well as a "Talk Sports Club", where students can watch and discuss sports competitions and events. Other societies include Metaphysics and Folklore society, Biomedical Society, Debating Society, Engineering Society, and a Medicine and Dentistry Interview Practice weekly session.

Finally, Ealing Independent College takes pride in giving the students opportunities to lead some of the societies themselves. The student-led clubs include Student Council and the Student Magazine Committee.

It only takes a visit to fully appreciate the unique atmosphere we provide. We encourage you to book an individual visit and tour to experience the College in action, meet relevant teachers, and speak to some of our students.

83 New Broadway, Ealing, London, W5 5AL UK

Tel: 020 8579 6668

Email: admissions@ealingindependentcollege.com

Website: www.ealingindependentcollege.com

Headteacher: Allan Cairns

School type: Co-educational Day Senior & Sixth Form

Age range of pupils: 13–19 years

No. of pupils enrolled as at 01/09/2023: 96

Average class size: 10

EALING
INDEPENDENT
COLLEGE

Eaton House Belgravia

Eaton House Belgravia is an outstanding independent school and nursery, educating boys between the ages of 2 and 11. Founded in 1897, the school has become part of the very fabric of Chelsea and Belgravia, offering a diverse and intellectually stimulating education in the heart of London. Despite its reputation for academic success, the school is notably non-selective at entry to reception. Small class sizes and an individual learning plan for each pupil ensure that each boy is stretched and supported according to their individual needs.

The school is ambitious for its pupils, committed to igniting each boy's potential beyond academic excellence, into the realms of first-rate music, drama, creative arts and sport. Mr Ross Montague, Headmaster from January 2024, intends to maintain the traditional, academic values of Eaton House Belgravia whilst bringing a fresh eye to the school. He will build on the school's philosophy of 'stretch and support'. Mr Montague says, "*we want Belgravia boys to be leaders in life; successful, public-spirited, adaptable and innovative.*"

The boys benefit from an excellent network of pastoral care, in which it is emphasised not only that the staff look after the boys, but that the boys look after each other. This, in addition to dedicated form teachers and an extensive wellbeing hub, ensures that every child can flourish emotionally as well as academically. Pupils are therefore well prepared to go on to their senior schools. These consistently include a range of top schools, such as St Paul's, Westminster, Dulwich College, King's College Wimbledon and Summer Fields.

Famous alumni that have passed through Eaton House Belgravia include Sir Laurence Olivier, Eddie Redmayne OBE, Bear Grylls OBE, Anthony Asquith and Philip Pullman CBE FRSL. The schools' most important legacy, however, continues to be the many happy children who have left Eaton House Belgravia with a passion for learning.

Entrance procedure

Nursery and Reception: Entrance to our nursery and reception is non-selective. Registration is accepted from birth and early application is advised. We welcome boys to our co-ed nursery in the September following their second birthday. The majority of our nursery pupils go on to attend reception, where they are joined by those who register for 4+ entry.

Years 1 to 6: Children registered to join Eaton House Belgravia after the initial reception entry point will be invited to visit the school for an admissions assessment before a place can be offered (subject to availability). Prospective pupils are asked to complete a formal 8+ assessment for external entry into Year 4.

EATON HOUSE BELGRAVIA

Providing an outstanding education since 1897

3–5 Eaton Gate, London, SW1W 9BA UK

Tel: 020 3917 5050

Email: admissions@eatonhouseschools.com

Website: www.eatonhouseschools.com

Interim Headmaster: Mr Brendan O'Keeffe

Headmaster from January 2024: Mr Ross Montague

School type: Boys' Day Preparatory, Co-ed Nursery

Age range of boys: 2–11 years

Age range of girls: 2–4 years

No. of pupils enrolled as at 01/09/2023: 180

Fees as at 01/09/2023:

Nursery: £3,920 for five mornings

Reception to Year 3: £7,740 per term

Year 4 to Year 6: £8,575 per term

Average class size: 16

Eaton House The Manor Boys' School

Eaton House The Manor Boys' School is an outstanding independent school and nursery, set opposite the leafy green stretches of Clapham Common. The school is formed of a Pre-Prep, which educates boys aged 4–8, and a Prep School, which educates boys aged 8–13. Despite its reputation for academic success, the school is non selective at its reception entry point. The co-educational nursery takes children between the ages of 2 and 4. A broad range of specialist subject teaching promotes intellectual curiosity and encourages each pupil to pursue his interests.

The school is committed to the individual learning of the boys, instilling in them an academic and social confidence that they carry through life. Eaton House The Manor has sent many generations of boys to Eton, Westminster, St. Paul's, King's College Wimbledon, Dulwich College and other top secondary schools. Pupils achieve scholarships every year, including four to Alleyn's School, two to St Paul's, two to Dulwich College, one to Lancing College, and one to Royal Russell in 2023. A wide range of sporting and artistic opportunities are available to the boys, with extra-curricular activities making the most of the school's high-quality facilities and access to the Common.

Pupil wellbeing is incredibly important to all at Eaton House The Manor. Staff prioritise the mental health of their pupils, as happy children achieve great results. The House system, dedicated form tutors, and an extensive wellbeing hub, contribute to a strong framework of pastoral care – ensuring that every child is championed and supported.

Eaton House The Manor Boys' School is located on the same extensive premises as Eaton House The Manor Girls' School, making it the ideal place for siblings to enjoy the benefits of a single-sex education on one site. In their 2022 report, the Independent Schools Inspectorate (ISI) found both Eaton House The Manor Boys' School and Eaton House The Manor Girls' School to be 'excellent' in all areas, which include *'the quality of pupils' academic and other achievements'*, *'diversity and inclusion'*, and *'the quality of pupils' personal development'*.

Headmistress, Mrs Sarah Segrave, says, "*A school is not a building, a curriculum or a timetable. Rather, it is a place where children grow intellectually and emotionally, guided by teachers who are determined that children succeed and are happy.*"

Entrance procedure

Nursery and Reception: Entrance to our nursery and reception is non-selective. Registration is accepted from birth and early application is advised. We welcome boys to our co-ed nursery in the September following their second birthday. The majority of our nursery pupils go on to attend reception, where they are joined by those who register for 4+ entry.

Years 1 to 8: Children registered to join Eaton House The Manor Boys' School after the initial reception entry point will be invited to visit the school for an admissions assessment before a place can be offered (subject to availability). Prospective pupils are asked to complete a formal 8+ assessment for external entry into Year 4.

EATON HOUSE THE MANOR

Boys' School

58 Clapham Common North Side, London, SW4 9RU UK

Tel: 020 3917 5050

Email: admissions@eatonhouseschools.com

Website: www.eatonhouseschools.com

Head of Prep: Mrs Sarah Segrave

Head of Pre-Prep: Mr David Wingfield

School type: Boys' Day Preparatory, Co-ed Nursery

Age range of boys: 2–13 years

Age range of girls: 2–4 years

No. of pupils enrolled as at 01/09/2023: 430

Fees as at 01/09/2023:

Nursery: £3,330 for five mornings

Reception to Year 3: £6,740 per term

Year 4 to Year 8: £8,090 per term

Average class size: 20

Eaton House The Manor Girls' School

Eaton House The Manor Girls' School is an outstanding independent school and nursery, set opposite the leafy green stretches of Clapham Common. The school offers a balanced, highly academic education to girls between the ages of 4 and 11 and is non-selective at its reception entry point. The co-educational nursery takes children between the ages of 2 and 4. A philosophy of 'sky-is-the-limit learning' allows each girl to reach her fullest potential, supported by specialist subject teaching and excellent pastoral care. Consequently, pupils leave for a range of top secondary schools, including St Paul's Girls' School, the Godolphin & Latymer School, JAGS, Alleyn's, St Mary's Ascot, Downe House and Wycombe Abbey.

Academic exploration and risk-taking are two essential ingredients in Eaton House The Manor Girls' School teaching. The girls thrive in a relaxed but highly stimulating classroom environment that promotes intellectual curiosity. Beyond an excellent core curriculum of literacy and numeracy, an equal emphasis is given to the arts and STEM subjects. Each girl is also encouraged to pursue her interests through an increasingly co-curricular attitude to learning and a sophisticated range of extracurricular activities. The school's well-rounded curriculum is reflected in the diversity of the outstanding 41 Scholarships and Awards across Academics, Sport, Drama, Music and Art in 2022 and 2023.

Pupils benefit from an exceptional wellbeing network. Form tutors provide ongoing support for each girl in their care, getting to know them on an individual level, whilst new pupils are helped to settle in by their individual 'big sisters', a role that the older girls take great pride in playing. *'The focus is on girls feeling they are 'known' and nurtured in the school. This approach is anchored by the morning ritual of the head and deputy shaking the hand of each girl as they come into school.'* (*The Good Schools Guide*, 2023).

Eaton House The Manor Girls' School is located on the same extensive 1.5 acre site as Eaton House The Manor Boys' School, making it the ideal place for siblings to enjoy the benefits of a single-sex education on one site.

In their 2022 report, the Independent Schools Inspectorate found both Eaton House The Manor Boys' School and Eaton House The Manor Girls' School to be 'excellent' in all areas, which include *'the quality of pupils' academic and other achievements'*, *'diversity and inclusion'*, and *'the quality of pupils' personal development'*.

Headmistress, Mrs Claire Fildes, says, *"I want the girls to achieve their full academic potential whilst allowing them the space to become confident and kind, ready to take the next steps on their journey as strong, impressive and independent-minded young women."*

Entrance procedure

Nursery and Reception: Entrance to our nursery and reception is non-selective. Registration is accepted from birth and early application is advised. We welcome girls to our co-ed nursery in the September following their second birthday. The majority of our nursery pupils go on to attend reception, where they are joined by those who register for 4+ entry.

Years 1 to 6: Children registered to join Eaton House The Manor Girls' School after the initial reception entry point will be invited to visit the school for an admissions assessment before a place can be offered (subject to availability). Prospective pupils are asked to complete a formal 8+ assessment for external entry into Year 4.

EATON HOUSE THE MANOR

Girls' School

58 Clapham Common North Side, London, SW4 9RU UK

Tel: 020 3917 5050

Email: admissions@eatonhouseschools.com

Website: www.eatonhouseschools.com

Headteacher: Mrs Claire Fildes

School type: Girls' Day Preparatory, Co-ed Nursery

Age range of boys: 2–4 years

Age range of girls: 2–11 years

No. of pupils enrolled as at 01/09/2023: 220

Fees as at 01/09/2023:

Nursery: £3,330 for five mornings

Reception to Year 3: £6,740 per term

Year 4 to Year 6: £7,875 per term

Average class size: 20

Cola
100

Heathside School Hampstead

Welcome to Heathside School Hampstead, a cherished haven of childhood nestled in the heart of Hampstead Village. We are a co-educational prep school spanning ages 2 to 13, driven by values of knowledge, nature, and nurture. Our unique approach blends academic excellence and the arts with the wonders of nature, forging an environment where young minds not only flourish but truly come alive.

Our commitment to nurturing both knowledge and character sets us apart. Here, teachers and students engage on first-name terms, cultivating authentic connections that spark a lifelong passion for learning. We break free from the constraints of conventional uniforms, we welcome dogs in school, and we encourage boundless play, knowing that the pursuit of knowledge knows no age limit.

As we step into a new era of growth and development, our two school buildings in the heart of Hampstead Village reflect our commitment to creating an exceptional learning environment. With newly refurbished early years facilities, state-of-the-art playgrounds, and dedicated spaces for our upper school, we are providing our pupils with the best tools to explore their potential.

Our educational philosophy embraces the wisdom of nature, fostering serenity, patience, and growth. Yet, it's also a philosophy of courage, innovation, and forward-thinking. Our outstanding 11+ and 13+ preparation programs consistently yield remarkable results, a testament to our unwavering belief in our methods. At Heathside, we champion the right for children to be children, regardless of their age.

Right on our doorstep, Hampstead Heath is an extension of our school, and adds another layer to our holistic approach. From welly boot shelves to Forest School adventures on the Heath, we instil in our students a profound connection with and respect for the natural world. This reverence extends beyond nature to encompass empathy, compassion, and respect within our school community, forging bonds that feel more like family than mere schoolmates.

But that's not all. At Heathside, we're more than just academics. We offer an extensive array of after-school clubs and enrichment activities that allow your child to explore their interests, broaden their horizons, and develop skills beyond the classroom. From chess to science, our clubs provide a platform for students to stretch themselves and discover new passions, fostering personal growth in a supportive environment.

Heathside is on a mission to empower children with the skills, knowledge, and character they need to thrive in the modern world while preserving the essence of childhood. Our nurturing yet bold environment propels students towards academic success, cultivating an enduring sense of wonder, curiosity, and achievement that will accompany them on their educational journey and into their bright futures.

In this unique educational sanctuary, we celebrate the freedom to learn, the knowledge that grows from innovation, the bond we share with nature, the nurture of empathetic hearts, and the bravery to challenge conventions. At Heathside, your child will discover not only academic excellence but also the joy of childhood preserved, ensuring they are well-prepared, confident, and eager to find their place in the world. Every day at Heathside is an opportunity for growth, wonder, and achievement.

HEATHSIDE SCHOOL
HAMPSTEAD

(Founded 1993)

84a Heath Street, Hampstead, London, NW3 1DN UK

Tel: +44 (0)20 3058 4011

Email: admissions@heathsideschoolhampstead.com

Website: www.heathsideschoolhampstead.com

Headteacher: Nadia Ward

Appointed: 2023

School type:
Co-educational Day Preparatory & Nursery

Age range of pupils: 2–13 years

No. of pupils enrolled as at 01/09/2023: 137

Fees as at 01/09/2023:

Day: £18,789–£21,273 per annum

Average class size: 15

Kensington Park School

Kensington Park School is an independent, co-educational day and boarding school for students aged 11 to 18. Founded in 2017, the school prides itself on a culture which defines excellence by the individual student, not by the cohort, and which seeks, above all, to realise and release potential. Both inside and outside the classroom, KPS students are excited, challenged, and inspired to become the best possible version of themselves.

Split across two teaching sites on either side of Kensington Gardens, the Lower School (Years 7 to 11) is situated on leafy Bark Place, while the Sixth Form overlooks the Natural History Museum on Queen's Gate. Transition through KPS is not, therefore, simply 'more of the same'. As students move through the school, they are presented with exciting new opportunities and responsibilities, and given the space to develop the independence they need to become successful life-long learners, at university and beyond. The school's boarding house, located within easy reach of both school buildings in Earl's Court, gives students in Year 9 and above the opportunity to live and study in the heart of cosmopolitan central London.

An academically purposeful school, a personalised delivery is one of the core pillars of a KPS education. Small class sizes at every level ensure teaching is tailored to students' individual needs and goals, and as students begin to select their subjects for study at GCSE and A level, the timetable is structured to allow them the flexibility to pursue their academic interests, unconstrained by set option blocks. A broad and balanced 21st century curriculum, which includes Computer Science and Mandarin introduced from Year 7, means KPS students are well-prepared for the fast-paced and ever-changing world around them.

Underpinned by an integrated personal tutor and house system, an attentive and discerning system of pastoral care not only supports students, but fosters a palpable sense of community in which all students are individually known, valued, and affirmed. Tutors play a key role in building the warm relationships between student, home, and the school, maintaining regular communication with parents and guardians on their child's personal and academic development.

An extensive sport and co-curricular programme complements the academic curriculum, enabling students to become well-rounded, balanced, and resilient individuals. The school works with a number of outstanding local facilities, such as the Porchester Centre, Will To Win, and the Old Football Pitches in Hyde Park, for activities including netball, football, swimming, rock climbing and even ice-skating. A state-of-the art theatre and creative suite offer exceptional facilities for music, drama and the arts.

A combination of academic and personal enrichment, individualised support, and outstanding pastoral care ensures KPS students achieve exceptional academic results, and every year the school's A Level graduates secure places on competitive undergraduate courses at universities including Oxford, Cambridge, and many in the Russell Group and US.

The school's selection process, which is written in-house, seeks to identify not only academic potential, but also individuals who will thrive in and contribute to the school's vibrant, diverse, and inclusive community. Academic, sport, music and art scholarships are available at 11+ and 13+, while the Kensington Scholars programme supports academically ambitious students applying to join the Sixth Form.

We welcome all prospective students and their families to join one of our Open Days, or arrange an individual visit to the school through our Admissions team.

KENSINGTON
PARK SCHOOL

KPS Lower School (Years 7 to 11):
40–44 Bark Place, Bayswater, London, W2 4AT UK

Tel: +44 (0)20 7616 4400

KPS Sixth Form:
59 Queen's Gate, South Kensington, London, SW7 5JP UK

Tel: +44 (0)20 7225 057

Email: admissions@kps.co.uk

Website: www.kps.co.uk

Headmaster: Mr Stephen Mellor

School type:
Co-educational Day & Boarding Senior & Sixth Form

Age range of pupils: 11–18 years

Fees as at 01/09/2023:

Tuition (Years 7–11 UK): £28,150 per annum

Tuition (Years 7–11 International): £30,500 per annum

Tuition (Sixth Form UK): £28,150 – £29,250 per annum

Tuition (Sixth Form International): £31,600 per annum

Lloyd Williamson School Foundation

Introduction

The Lloyd Williamson Schools Foundation has grown in both size and reputation to become the established schools they are today. The main departments are: a Nursery, a Transition School for 5–7 year olds, a Senior School for 7–11 year olds and an Secondary School for 11–16 year olds. The names Lloyd and Williamson are family names that belong to the founder. We believe they convey one of the main points of ethos at the school: that we are a family - and a strong one at that! To ensure the schools' future success, we have recently become a charitable foundation. We have an excellent reputation for strong academic standards and personalised, holistic learning for individual children. We have recently acquired another building and the Secondary School will be moving into their beautiful new building in Spring 2024. We are based in W10 in the Royal Borough of Kensington and Chelsea, with small classes to a maximum of 16 in Primary and 18 in Secondary. The schools have extended opening hours, competitive, realistic fees and Holiday Clubs.

Mission Statement and Ethos:

- Lloyd Williamson School Foundation believes that each child is an individual.
- We create the conditions for that child to reach their own unique potential.
- Teachers build positive relationships, working with each pupil to be curious, intellectual and creative. Fear of failure is banished.
- Equality and diversity permeate the fabric of our school - we are a family where everyone belongs.
- We have small class sizes with individual, tailored teaching. Children come from a wide range of backgrounds and abilities, but they are all motivated.
- We help them develop resilience, creativity and purpose. They feel safe, creative and curious, and are not stressed by education. Happy, confident students develop a rich and positive sense of who they are and can be.

Admissions

The school is open from 8:00am-5:30pm (main school hours from 8:30am-3:30 or 4:00pm).

Parents are invited to meet the Co-Principals for a personal tour of the school during school hours in order to gain a real flavour of how the school operates on a daily basis. After that, we invite the child to join us for a day. There is no formal entrance examination, but we are looking for aptitude and a positive attitude.

As a small school, everyone knows everyone from the babies up to our oldest member of staff! We cherish individuality and self-confidence and our aim is that every child will develop an organic and strong positive sense of self. We enable this through the development of positive relationships so that all our children can learn to be strong and independent.

Contact Information

www.lws.org.uk
Admissions: admin@lws.org.uk
Main School and Nursery: 020 8962 0345

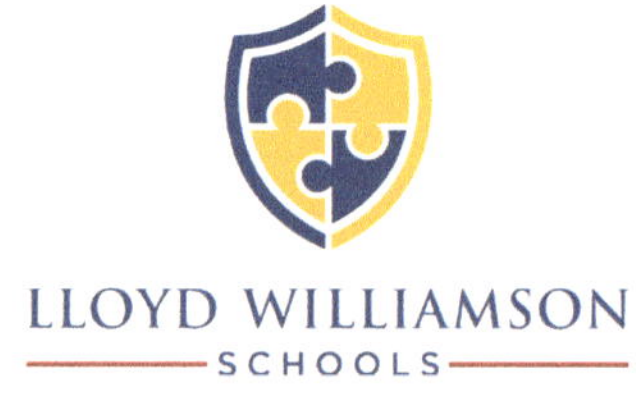

12 Telford Road, London, W10 5SH UK

Tel: 020 8962 0345

Email: admin@lws.org.uk

Website: www.lloydwilliamson.co.uk

Co-Principals: Ms Lucy Meyer & Mr Aaron Williams

Appointed: December 1999

School type:
Co-educational Day Preparatory, Senior & Nursery

Age range of pupils: 4 months–16 years

Fees as at 01/09/2023:

Day: £18,300 per annum

Nursery: £100 per day

Average class size: 12–16

Teacher/pupil ratio: 1:12

Norfolk House School

A small school with a big, beating heart.

Norfolk House School and Nursery is a leading London preparatory school for boys and girls aged 2–11. Our Nursery is located in a beautifully converted three-storey Victorian house in Princes Avenue, Muswell Hill. In Form 2, our pupils move from our Princes Avenue PrePrep site into the Junior Prep department in our school on Muswell Avenue and join our Form 3 pupils.

We are proud of the outstanding quality of education and pastoral care programmes for our children. The school takes great pride in its happy and warm environment, where each pupil is valued and supported. Pupils at Norfolk House are nurtured and guided through school life; we aim to stimulate and inspire our children, develop their interests and equip them with lifelong learning skills.

Our latest school inspection said that *"exceptionally positive attitudes to learning are evident across the school."* It went on to state that *"the quality of the pupils' academic and other achievements is excellent"* and that our *"pupils are exceptionally well prepared for the next stage of their education"* at the end of their time at Norfolk House.

We are committed to ensuring that your child thrives, enjoys school to the fullest, and realises their potential. Their experience at Norfolk House, from the small class sizes to the highly personalised learning provision, has been carefully curated to nurture and grow the unique person within.

At Norfolk House, we view academic excellence and personal growth not as competing priorities but as profoundly interdependent outcomes of quality education. A glance at our leavers' destinations demonstrates that London's leading senior schools consistently see the contribution and potential that Norfolk House pupils offer.

Though the prospect may seem distant now, we know that our pupils today will become the adult role models of tomorrow. To equip them for the fast-changing world in which they will grow up is a duty in which we take great pride. Our future-facing curriculum and time-tested values support pupils to develop into flourishing individuals, developing both self-efficacy and a life-long curiosity about the world and those with whom they share it.

Junior Prep & Senior Prep:
10 Muswell Avenue, Muswell Hill, London, N10 2EG UK

Tel: +44 (0)2088 834584

Nursery and Pre Prep:
5 Princes Avenue, Muswell Hill, London, N10 3LS UK

Tel: +44(0)2084 444399

Email: office@norfolkhouseschool.org

Website: www.norfolkhouseschool.org

Headteacher: Mr Tej Lander

Appointed: September 2022

School type:
Co-educational Day Preparatory & Nursery

Age range of pupils: 2–11 years

North Bridge House

At North Bridge House (NBH), we pride ourselves on our impressive results and academically non-selective co-education, challenging and inspiring pupils throughout every stage of their school career. With specialist expertise at the Early Years Foundation Stage all the way through to A Level, we are on a constant journey of getting to know every learner as a unique individual, helping them to find and realise their true academic and personal potential.

Celebrating results well above the national average, the Nursery and Pre-Prep Schools develop the fundamental skills upon which pupils' future successes are built. The nurturing environment combined with a broad and forward-thinking curriculum allows children to develop a genuine love of learning while benefiting from a truly individualised provision; with 7+ preparation embedded into the curriculum, pupils have the option to automatically progress to NBH Prep School or to another of the UK's highly competitive Prep schools. As well as specialist teaching in French, Italian, music and sport, progress-enhancing initiatives such as Philosophy for Children and Forest School promote children's all-important social and emotional development.

NBH Prep School excellently prepares happy, confident pupils for entry to the UK's leading senior schools - often with prestigious scholarship places. Pupils are taught entirely by subject specialists from Year 5, benefiting from an outstanding academic and co-curricular offering that encompasses everything from Philosophy, Politics and Economics to the Arts. Celebrating top results in the various 11+ and 13+ senior school entrance tests while providing highly sought-after entry to our own senior school campuses, we individually prepare pupils for the school best suited to their talents and interests - bespoke preparation for every path to success.

Preparing pupils for university and the world of work with unrivalled UCAS and careers support, our 'Excellent' (Independent Schools Inspectorate, 2023) Senior Schools in Hampstead and Islington continue to build on their highly successful track records. Students progress to top Russell Group and Oxbridge destinations, as well as renowned Arts and overseas institutions. Our expert teaching teams harness research into teen development and learning patterns to further understand and maximise pupils' potential. For example, using evidence-based research, we have implemented a later (midweek) start time for teens, which reflects current findings regarding the teenage brain and sleeping patterns, and continue to work with the Institute of Education on developing metacognition in students.

PE is essential to our school group's offering and our prime north London location sees students benefit from the best facilities for track and field, outdoor adventure, and water sports. From Bushcraft to the DofE Award, there is also a busy schedule of enrichment activities and school trips, all centred around our aim to cultivate character and promote wellbeing. This, together with the school's outstanding pastoral support, sees our students leave as articulate, confident, determined young people, proud to be themselves.

School locations:
North Bridge House Nursery School
33 Fitzjohn's Avenue, Hampstead, London NW3 5JY
North Bridge House Pre-Prep School
8 Netherhall Gardens, Hampstead, London NW3 5RR
North Bridge House Nursery & Pre-Prep West Hampstead
85–87 Fordwych Road, West Hampstead, London NW2 3TL
North Bridge House Prep School
1 Gloucester Avenue, Regent's Park, London NW1 7AB
North Bridge House Senior Hampstead
65 Rosslyn Hill, Hampstead, London NW3 5UD
North Bridge House Senior & Sixth Form Canonbury
6–9 Canonbury Place, Islington, London N1 2NQ

North Bridge House

(Founded 1939)

65 Rosslyn Hill, London, NW3 5UD UK

Tel: 020 7428 1520

Email: admissionsenquiries@northbridgehouse.com

Website: www.northbridgehouse.com

Executive Headteacher: Brendan Pavey

Heads of Nursery & Pre-Prep Schools:
Nishi Kapoor, Michelle Blaber & Eilish Sleator

Head of Prep School: Tom Le Tissier

Heads of Senior Schools:
Christopher Jones & Charlotte Tassell-Dent

School type: Co-educational Day Preparatory & Senior, Nursery & Sixth Form

Age range of pupils: 2–18 years

No. of pupils enrolled as at 01/09/2023: 1400

Fees as at 01/09/2023:

Day: £9,420–£25,302 per annum

Average class size: 15–20

Oakfield Preparatory School

Welcome to Oakfield Prep School: A World of Opportunity
Nestled in the heart of West Dulwich, Oakfield Prep is a unique day school where every child is encouraged to be the best they can be. We are dedicated to nurturing young minds, fostering individual growth, building character and preparing children for a world of endless opportunities. We're proud to be a diverse and inclusive school, welcoming boys and girls aged 2–11, reflecting the rich tapestry of London.

Location: A Hub of Learning and Diversity
Our prime location in West Dulwich provides a safe, inspiring, and culturally enriched environment for your child to grow, surrounded by modern facilities and luscious green spaces. Oakfield is a proud reflection of London's enviable diversity, celebrating the different backgrounds and experiences of our children and families and preparing our pupils to succeed in an increasingly interconnected world.

Academic Excellence: Shaping Tomorrow's Leaders
At Oakfield Prep School, we are committed to academic excellence. Our innovative curriculum teaches children how, as well as what to learn; it encourages a growth mindset, and to enquire, investigate, and solve problems collaboratively. We also provide state-of-the-art resources, including a dedicated library, iPads, individual laptops, and specialized facilities like the STEM room and Art Studio.

Our commitment to delivering exceptional education is evident in our recent 'Excellent' rating from the Independent Schools Inspectorate (ISI). Alongside our excellent record of first-choice secondary school placements, our Year 6 cohort (of 34 pupils) were offered an unparalleled 30 scholarships, and, in 2022, 97% of our early years pupils achieved a 'good level of development' in EYFSP vs the local average of 67% and the national average of 65%.

Pastoral Care and Wraparound Support: Nurturing Well-Rounded Individuals
Our approach to education places a strong emphasis on personalised care and support. Every child at Oakfield is valued and we foster a community where kindness, courtesy, and compassion are paramount. In addition to tailored academic support, we offer the most comprehensive wraparound care in the area as we believe our role includes supporting the whole family in addition to the pupils.

Preparing for the Future: A Holistic Approach
Our motto, "A World of Opportunity," encapsulates our mission to prepare pupils not only for success within our gates but also for the remarkable opportunities that await them in senior school and beyond. The Oakfield Diploma programme, completed in Year 6, equips pupils with the transferrable skills needed to excel in an ever-changing world.

We offer exceptional co-curricular experiences, from creative arts, health and wellness, forensic science and even TV production. Our sports programmes include football, athletics, cricket, rugby, hockey, netball, and gymnastics, with pupils proudly representing their school and achieving regional and national success. In music, pupils have access to a dedicated music room, one-to-one music lessons, and the opportunity to participate in school bands, orchestras, and choirs. Music technology is embedded into our lessons, providing insights into musical composition and production and we've even released a few Oakfield sessions albums and music videos for a contemporary touch.

Join us at Oakfield Prep School, where we celebrate individual strengths and interests, foster a love of learning, and prepare children for a future world of endless opportunities. We look forward to embarking on this incredible journey with you and your child.

Welcome to Oakfield Prep, where every child thrives.

(Founded 1887)

125–128 Thurlow Park Road, West Dulwich, London, SE21 8HP UK

Tel: 020 8670 4206

Email: admissions@oakfield.dulwich.sch.uk

Website: www.oakfield.dulwich.sch.uk

Head of School: Mrs Moyra Thompson

School type:
Co-educational Day Preparatory & Nursery

Age range of pupils: 2–11 years

No. of pupils enrolled as at 01/09/2023: 303

Fees as at 01/09/2023:

Years 1–6: £4,831 per term

Nursery: Tailored to each child

Average class size: 15

Orchard House School

All children can learn to thrive, regardless of learning ability. At Orchard House School, we believe tailor-made teaching opens young minds to endless possibilities, encouraging them to think creatively and form their own ideas. In addition to guiding pupils to high academic achievement, our programme of learning celebrates self-discipline and sensitivity to others, whilst developing our core values of excellence, honesty and kindness. Our pupils call it having fun. We call it being the best they can be.

Complementing our outstanding form teachers, the school is equipped with an abundance of specialist educators which has resulted in a number of awards in recent years, including; the NAACE Mark for excellence in Education Technology, and the TES Independent Schools Award for Sport. Music and Drama play a key role at Orchard House School, with pupils of all ages participating in drama and musical productions, clubs, concerts, and assemblies. Sports facilities at Rocks Lane feature football, cricket, rugby and hockey pitches, netball courts, all-weather pitches for lacrosse and a sports field for athletics and Sports Days. Our pupils benefit from nearby access to swimming facilities to ensure the breadth of sporting activities are offered.

While our school is renowned for academic excellence, pastoral care comes first. Children blossom when they feel secure, happy, and valued. No child has any doubt that teachers will lend a safe and sympathetic ear to their issues. Each child has a Pupil Pastoral Care Plan where they can note any private worries so that teachers may monitor their happiness and well-being, and our buddy system helps newcomers through their early days. The school's House system encourages teamwork and a competitive spirit, allowing children to celebrate their own success as well as the achievements of others.

Our Year 6 pupils are uniquely prepared for entrance to a senior school which is best suited to their abilities, character and interests. We prepare children for senior school life, of which the 11+ assessments are just one part. As part of their preparation, parents and pupils will attend Senior School Open Days, have individual meetings with the Form teachers and Deputy Head to discuss choices and meet with the Headteacher about all options. Our children also benefit from priority entry into Dukes Education senior schools: Hampton Court House, Eaton Square Senior and Kneller Hall.

Exciting times lie ahead for Orchard House School. A multimillion-pound redevelopment is currently underway, in partnership with neighbouring Chiswick & Bedford Park Preparatory School. With the two school nurseries now working together as one team, the main schools will be combined from September 2024 under the Orchard House School name. This new school will benefit from a full refurbishment of all three school sites as well as additional specialist teaching space in the form of a new Science, Technology and Computing Centre, additional spaces for Art, Music and Drama, a fuller timetable of enrichment and clubs, and expert subject teaching. As a thriving three form entry school, all of our children in the lower school will benefit from a full-time teaching assistant and throughout the school there will be specialist teaching staff across the curriculum, ensuring academic excellence alongside outstanding pastoral care. This investment from Dukes Education will put Orchard House School squarely on the map as one of London's premier preparatory schools.

(Founded 1993)

16 Newton Grove, Bedford Park, London, W4 1LB UK

Tel: 020 8742 8544

Email: info@orchardhs.org.uk

Website: www.orchardhs.org.uk

Headmaster: Mr Kit Thompson

Appointed: September 2021

School type:
Co-educational Day Preparatory & Nursery

Age range of pupils: 3–11 years

No. of pupils enrolled as at 01/09/2023: 301

Fees as at 01/09/2023:

Day: £10,650–£22,194 per annum

Average class size: 20

Teacher/pupil ratio: 1:7

Prospect House School

At Prospect House School, we focus on making each child feel valued and secure and on making their educational experience both challenging and fun. This allows us to develop every child to their fullest potential, as our outstanding results demonstrate. Our school was inspected by the ISI in February 2022 and we are thrilled to say that we have been judged as excellent in all areas, the highest possible achievement.

Prospect House's superb teachers provide a supportive and encouraging academic environment in which children excel. The sound of laughter is never far away, as Prospect House children discover their aptitude for sport, music, art, computing, drama or a whole host of other opportunities both within the curriculum or before or after school. Whether taking up the trombone, building a go-cart or orienteering on Putney Heath, our children relish each new challenge and emerge better able to face the next challenge that comes their way.

Music is an important part of life at Prospect House. We have over 200 individual music lessons taking place each week with a school orchestra, chamber choir and senior and junior choirs, as well as a number of ensembles. All children act in assemblies, school plays, musical productions and concerts throughout the year. Children in Years 1 to 6 enjoy drama lessons and our high-quality staging, lighting, sound and props give every production a professional feel.

Physical activity promotes wellbeing, so we offer a busy sports programme. This includes football, netball, hockey, running, cross country, athletics, cricket, dance and gymnastics. Our approach to fixtures and tournaments successfully balances participation for everyone with letting our sports stars shine.

Residential trips thrill the children with the sense of adventure, encouraging risk-taking and building self-reliance, whether on a history expedition, a bushcraft adventure, a week in the Isle of Wight engaging in a wide range of adventure activities or a week in Poole filled with sun, sea, sand and a whole lot of watersports.

We encourage our children to think for themselves, to be confident and to develop a sense of responsibility for the world in which they live. By the time they leave us aged 11, Prospect House children are ready to thrive at London's best senior schools. This is reflected in our impressive 11+ results. Every year, a notable proportion of our children win scholarships to leading senior schools.

Prospect House School is proudly non-selective. True to our belief, children are not tested and judged at the tender age of 3 or 4 years. Our stellar results repeatedly show all children can fulfil their potential, regardless of early learning ability. We encourage our high-flyers to soar, whilst children who need a little extra help are given the support they need to reach their fullest potential. At Prospect House, every child is helped to achieve a personal best.

PROSPECT HOUSE

SCHOOL

(Founded 1991)

75 Putney Hill, London, SW15 3NT UK

Tel: 020 3835 3058

Email: info@prospecths.org.uk

Website: www.prospecths.org.uk

Headmaster: Mr Michael Hodge BPED(Rhodes) QTS

Appointed: September 2017

School type:
Co-educational Day Preparatory & Nursery

Age range of pupils: 3–11 years

No. of pupils enrolled as at 01/09/2023: 300

Fees as at 01/09/2023:

Day: £10,470–£22,530 per annum

Average class size: 20

Teacher/pupil ratio: 1:7

Queen's Gate School

Queen's Gate School is an independent day school for girls between the ages of 4 and 18 years, situated in the educational and cultural heartland of South Kensington. Founded in 1891, the school has long held a reputation for its originality, such as its lack of uniform.

The school is academically aspirational, where each girl is encouraged and empowered to go beyond her academic potential. The emphasis on self-motivation and self-determination is coupled with diligent support from a highly committed staff body, which together bring outstanding academic outcomes. Pupils leave Queen's Gate to go to universities across the UK, including Russell Group institutions and Oxbridge, as well as destinations further afield such as NYU, Harvard and MIT.

The Principal, Miss Amy Wallace, joined Queen's Gate in September 2022 and continues to build on the existing strengths of the school, whilst enabling girls to enjoy new opportunities in and out of the classroom.

In the Senior School, girls follow as wide a curriculum as possible and generally take GCSEs in ten subjects that must include English, Mathematics, at least one science and a modern language. A full range of A Level subjects is offered. In the Lower Sixth girls normally take three/four subjects and in addition many complete the Extended Project Qualification (EPQ). The girls are offered excellent careers advice to assist in their UCAS and US applications.

Sport is highly valued at Queen's Gate with two compulsory sessions for all girls each week. A whole range of sports are available during the school day including netball, athletics, basketball, hockey, fencing, swimming, rowing, cross-country, biathlon and dance. Girls achieve much success, with some earning national and international status.

Co-curricular activities at Queen's Gate see girls taking part in Model United Nations conferences throughout the year, become part of clubs including the horticultural society, STEM club and Cosmetics club and experience trips around the UK and abroad to enhance their learning experience.

Music plays a large role in the school life, with concerts and recitals throughout the school year both in and out of school, and Drama productions across both the Junior and Senior schools see girls performing at venues including RADA Studios and the Chelsea Theatre.

The Junior School is situated just a few yards down the road from the Senior School at 125 and 126 Queen's Gate. The beautifully restored buildings boast spacious form rooms, three fully equipped laboratories, a state-of-the-art STEAM (Science, Technology, Engineering, Art and Mathematics) Room and an elegant Assembly Hall. Junior pupils also use Senior School facilities and benefit from specialist subject teaching from Senior School staff. Senior girls often visit the Junior School to assist with activities, thus reinforcing the continuity of education from 4–18 available at the school.

Admission is by test and interview in the Junior School. Entrance to the Senior School is by the London 11+ Consortium entrance examination. Applicants for the Sixth Form must achieve six GCSEs at Grade 7 or above with Grade 8 or 9 (or their equivalent) required in those subjects they wish to pursue at A Level.

In addition to the Open Events in the Senior and Junior Schools throughout the year, parents are always welcome to make a private visit to see the schools at work. Appointments can be made by contacting the Registrar on 0207 594 4982 or by email registrar@queensgate.org.uk.

(Founded 1891)

133 Queen's Gate, London, SW7 5LE UK

Tel: 020 7589 3587

Email: registrar@queensgate.org.uk

Website: www.queensgate.org.uk

Principal:
Miss Amy Wallace MA MPhil (Cantab), PGCE (Oxon)

Appointed: September 2022

School type: Girls' Day & Sixth Form

Age range of girls: 4–18 years

No. of pupils enrolled as at 01/09/2023: 477

Sixth Form: 90

Junior School: 112

Senior School: 365

Fees as at 01/09/2023:

Junior School: £22,860 per annum

Senior School & Sixth Form: £25,326 per annum

Average class size: 23

Teacher/pupil ratio: 1:10

St Paul's Cathedral School

Governed by the Dean and Chapter and seven lay governors, the original residential choir school, which can date its history back to the 12th century, has, since the 1980s, included non-chorister day boys and girls aged 4–13. The number of pupils is currently 260.

In its 2017 inspection, the ISI awarded the school its highest accolade of 'Excellent' in both educational attainment and pupil progress.

A broad curriculum prepares all pupils for 11+ and 13+ examinations including scholarship and Common Entrance examinations. The school has an excellent record in placing pupils in outstanding senior schools, many with scholarships. With its unique and central location, the school is able to make the most of what London can offer culturally and artistically in particular. A wide variety of sports and musical instrument tuition is offered: the school has an exceptional record in preparing pupils for ABRSM exams. Choristers receive an outstanding choral training as members of the renowned St Paul's Cathedral Choir.

The life of the school is based on the following aims and principles:

St Paul's Cathedral School is a Christian, co-educational community which holds to the values of love, justice, tolerance, respect, honesty, service and trust in its life and practice, to promote positive relationships throughout the school community and where the safety, welfare and emotional well-being of each child is of the utmost importance.

The school aims to instil a love of learning through a broad curriculum. It aims to give each pupil the opportunity to develop intellectually, socially, personally, physically, culturally and spiritually. All pupils are encouraged to work to the best of their ability and to achieve standards of excellence in all of their endeavours.

Through the corporate life of the school, and through good pastoral care, the school encourages the independence of the individual as well as mutual responsibility. It aims to make its pupils aware of the wider community, espouses the democratic process and encourages a close working relationship with parents and guardians.

Facilities: the school is situated on one site to the east of St Paul's Cathedral. It has a separate Pre-Prep department, excellent Science lab and ICT room. It has two outside play areas and a hall.

Entry is at 4+ and 7+ years. 4+ entry is held in the November preceding the September a child will enter the school and 7+ entry is held in the January preceding the September a child will enter the school. At 7+, pupils are given a short test and spend a day in school. Chorister voice trials are held throughout the year for boys between 6 and 8 years old. Occasional places in other year groups sometimes become available and, at 11+, the school now offers scholarship awards in music, the arts, sport and academics. Further information can be found on the school's website www.spcslondon.com

St Paul's Cathedral School is a registered charity (No. 312718), which exists to provide education for the choristers of St Paul's Cathedral and for children living in the local area.

ST PAUL'S CATHEDRAL SCHOOL

(Founded 12th Century or earlier)

2 New Change, London, EC4M 9AD UK

Tel: 020 7248 5156

Fax: 020 7329 6568

Email: admissions@spcs.london.sch.uk

Website: www.spcslondon.com

Head: Judith Fremont-Barnes MA (Hons), MEd

Appointed: September 2023

School type: Co-educational Pre-Prep, Day Prep & Boarding Choir School

Religious Denomination:
Church of England, admits pupils of all faiths

Age range of pupils: 4–13 years

No. of pupils enrolled as at 01/09/2023: 266

Fees as at 01/09/2023:

Day: £5,656–£6,090 per term

Full Boarding: £3,421 per term

Average class size: 15–20

Teacher/pupil ratio: 1:10

The Hampshire School, Chelsea

The Hampshire School, Chelsea, London, is an independent school for boys and girls aged 3–11. Sheltered beneath the architectural grandeur of the former Chelsea Public Library, this historic setting just off King's Road, with its expansive library, plays host to an enviable amount of space, with a desirable play area and impressive climbing structure.

As you walk through the halls of The Hampshire School, you will grasp how academically rigorous and community-focused the school is, with brilliant pupil work on display, in all subjects, where children are free to flourish at their own pace.

Last September, after being awarded an ISI Inspection of the highest honour, the Hampshire School was fortunate enough to appoint new Head, Richard Lock. Richard is ambitious about the future of the school. With a focus on providing high-quality teaching and learning, outstanding co-curricular provision and raising ambition for each child at every stage.

Richard comments: *"It is wonderful to take the reins of a particularly wonderous school. Aim high (our school motto) is a fundamental element of the broad and rigorous academic curriculum at the Hampshire School. I look forward to leading the school forward over the coming years"*

The Hampshire School Chelsea is a school with unparalleled joy, with children seizing their opportunities to be recognised for achievements, whether on the stage, on the sports field, in lessons or more. The school boasts brilliant facilities, with specialist science lessons in the extensively resourced science laboratory. The school also has a purpose-built Music and Drama room, fittingly named after the founders of the school known as 'The Anne and Susan Hampshire Music and Drama room' with their distinguished careers in the performing arts.

At The Hampshire School, we want children to flourish, that's why we offer extracurricular clubs, allowing pupils to further their talents, learn hidden skills and develop themselves in the school setting. We also provide wrap-around care to give parents extra flexibility with their child's provision.

The Hampshire School

C H E L S E A

15 Manresa Road, Chelsea, London, SW3 6NB UK

Tel: +44 (0)2073 527077

Email: info@thehampshireschoolchelsea.co.uk

Website: www.thehampshireschoolchelsea.co.uk

Headteacher: Mr Richard Lock

Appointed: September 2022

School type:
Co-educational Day Preparatory & Nursery

Age range of pupils: 3–11 years

Check-in
Departures
ship
map
EUROPE

The Merlin School

Choosing a school for your child at the age of four is an important decision providing a significant first opportunity to inspire a little learner and prepare them for the next stage of their education. At Merlin we specialise in these precious early years. The Merlin, established in 1986, is a creative and nurturing co-educational pre-prep which does not assess on entry. You will find us in the heart of Putney, in a beautiful Victorian house. We offer a warm and homely atmosphere where all staff take time to engage with our children, supporting the development of their independence and confidence. There is a vibrant buzz about the school, where the children thrive as part of a caring community. Corridors and classrooms teem with life and practical activities enhance learning and stimulate pupils' imagination.

Our school motto is 'have a go,' and we aim to evoke a thirst for learning, encouraging curiosity in the world around us. Whilst Maths and English underpin our syllabus, we pride ourselves on the depth and breadth of our curriculum. We believe in the importance of delivering a wide range of subjects and experiences, providing children with crucial and exciting opportunities and encouraging a love of learning. Our individualised approach to teaching and learning enables all children to make excellent progress. Children's learning is further enhanced by our small class sizes and high adult to child ratio, with our unique approach to teaching English and Maths creating even smaller teaching groups in these subjects. Our teachers are passionate and inspiring, and our school environment and curriculum capture the children's imagination, firing their enthusiasm, and inspiring them to want to learn. A wander around our classrooms will take you on a journey through various topics from 'Number Street' to 'The Seven Wonders of The World'.

Over half of our timetable is taught by specialist teachers including Science, Drama, Music, Computing, French and PE/Games with both our Deputy and Head being actively involved in the teaching of all year groups. Pupils relish the challenge of their first formal sports lessons, learning about teamwork and sportsmanship alongside the specific sports skills, gearing them up to find their own sporting pathway. Our children bounce into Science lessons wondering what practical activity awaits, they master the skills of thinking and creating in Computing lessons and build confidence through giving presentations and taking part in assemblies and innovative drama productions.

At the end of their school journey with us, we send our children off to their next schools with the confidence to build new relationships and the enthusiasm to learn, instilled with a positive attitude towards new challenges. Despite being a non-selective school, Merlin children make excellent progress from their individual starting points, and go on to a range of prestigious schools.

Please do book on to one of our school tours, via our website, to see for yourself - we look forward to welcoming you.

(Founded 1986)

4 Carlton Drive, Putney, London, SW15 2BZ UK

Tel: 020 8788 2769

Email: admissionenquiries@merlinschool.net

Website: www.merlinschool.net

Headteacher: Miss Violet McConville

Appointed: September 2021

Principal: Mrs Kate Prest

School type: Co-educational Day Pre-Preparatory

Age range of pupils: 4–8 years

No. of pupils enrolled as at 01/09/2023: 125

Fees as at 01/09/2023:

Day: £5,960 (Inclusive) per term

Average class size: 15

Ursuline Preparatory School

Ursuline Preparatory School is a Roman Catholic school that welcomes children of all faiths and none. Non-selective by choice, the school offers a values-driven, academic education to girls from 3–11 years of age and to boys in the Pre-School class.

Established in 1892 to promote the values of St Angela Merici OSU, Ursuline Preparatory School places equal value on the education of heart, mind and soul in the certain knowledge that only through the equal development of all three can a child truly excel. The school's mission is to develop a community that lives each day working together (Insieme) and united in harmony, valuing the contributions of all and championing the virtues of love, compassion, kindness and generosity. The children are encouraged to be grateful for the gifts they have been given and to develop these gifts to the full, in generous service to others. The school seeks to pass on the living and faith-filled tradition of Jesus Christ by having unswerving faith in every single one of our pupils and by encouraging them, in turn, to have faith and hope in others. A keen focus is to educate and create future leaders in the spirit of Serviam (I will serve), keeping justice at the centre of their lives.

The core provision of this school is three-fold:

- A strong Ursuline ethos;
- An academic provision, whether in the classroom or online, that prepares children fully for secondary school;
- A strong partnership between pupils, parents and staff.

Our children enjoy a rich diversity of experiences, both inside and outside of the classroom. Our 11+ preparation curriculum, full sporting programme, and developed range of extra-curricular activities, provides an enriching and engaging provision.

The girls at Ursuline Preparatory School follow an academic curriculum and are fully supported, securing places in their senior school of choice. As a result of the Ursuline ethos, and the academic preparation put in place, the girls here can face the 11+ process with confidence. Last year girls received offers from the following schools: ACS International; City of London, Freemans School; Claremont Fan Court; Epsom College; Emanuel; Godolphin & Latymer; Guildford High School; Kingston Grammar School; Lady Eleanor Holles; Marymount; Notre Dame; Putney High School; Surbiton High School; Sutton High School; St John's Leatherhead; Ursuline High School; and Wimbledon High School.

While we are a non-selective school our girls exceed expectations at 11+ with many scholarships offered.

An Ursuline education seeks to help the young people here grow and flourish in an environment in which every child is loved and valued. On such sure foundations, we help them become the very best that they can be. Please do come and visit; you will be made most welcome.

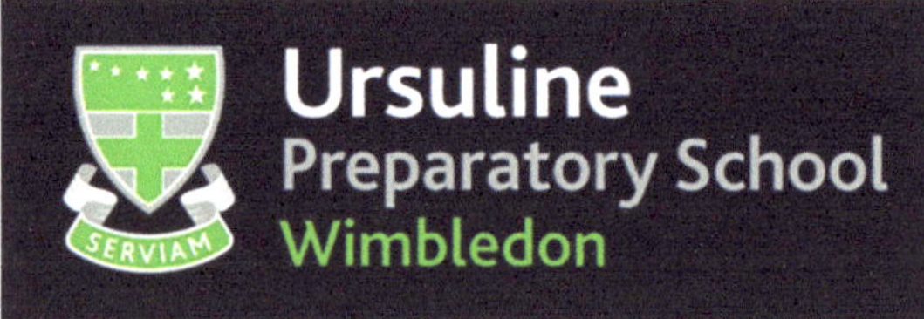

(Founded 1892)

18 The Downs, Wimbledon, London, SW20 8HR UK

Tel: 020 8947 0859

Email: headteachersoffice@ursulineprep.org

Website: www.ursulineprep.org

Head Teacher: Mrs Caroline Molina BA (Hons)

Appointed: January 2020

School type: Girls' Day Preparatory, Co-ed Nursery

Religious Denomination: Roman Catholic

Age range of boys: 3–4 years

Age range of girls: 3–11 years

No. of pupils enrolled as at 01/09/2023: 124

Fees as at 01/09/2023:

Pre-School Mornings: £2,865 per term

Pre-School - Year 6 Full Time: £4,660 per term

Average class size: 18

Teacher/pupil ratio: 1:5

Wandsworth Preparatory School

We work hard. We dream big. We achieve the extraordinary
Wandsworth Preparatory School is a co-educational independent day school for children aged 4–11. Part of the Bellevue Education group of schools, Wandsworth Prep is a school that provides an outstanding educational environment, with a broad and exciting curriculum that stimulates imagination, encourages independent learning and provides pupils with the tools to thrive.

Wandsworth Prep treats every pupil as an individual, helping each child to discover their unique talents and build their confidence in learning. Our pupils benefit from a first-class holistic education built on vital pastoral care rooted in academic excellence. Our creative curriculum brings learning to life through our engaging, thematic approach. Lessons are interactive and full of memorable experiences that inspire a love of learning, encourage curiosity, and promote independence and collaborative learning skills.

We provide classes from Reception to year 6, giving our children solid foundations for learning, with the curriculum carefully designed to ensure that each child can fulfil their individual potential. Our curriculum is challenging, diverse and engaging. We are proud of our excellent academic results, with each child reaching their goal and enabling them to attend the best schools in the area.

Last year, we welcomed our new Head, Laura Nike. Formerly Head of Prep at the Old Palace School based in Croydon, Laura brings experience, educational vision and exceptional commitment to high-quality, academically rigorous teaching and learning to the role. Laura comments: "*The strong sense of shared values within the school community allows the children here to thrive with confidence in an academic setting. Our high calibre specialist teachers enable the pupils to achieve the highest outcomes in all areas of the curriculum. Every child in our school is known and seen for who they are, and we draw alongside each child to nurture their talents, ambitions and interests.*"

The Old Library, 2 Allfarthing Lane,
London, SW18 2PQ UK

Tel: +44 (0)2088 704133

Email: office@wandsworthprep.com

Website: www.wandsworthprep.com

Headteacher: Ms Laura Nike

Appointed: September 2022

School type: Co-educational Day Preparatory

Age range of pupils: 4–11 years

North-East

Barnard Castle School

Barnard Castle School is a leading independent day and boarding school set amid stunning countryside in Northern England.

'Barney', as it is affectionately known, provides an exceptional all-round education, with a broad and balanced curriculum, first class facilities and excellent pastoral care within a happy, family environment for boys and girls aged between 4 and 18.

Through creating an inspirational, compassionate and unpretentious environment, the school develops young adults with character, where each child is nurtured and encouraged to develop their full potential.

'Barnardians' are happy, confident, resilient, intellectually curious, tolerant and driven, with an undercurrent of humility, who are ready and prepared to face, embrace and lead in an ever-changing world.

Barnard Castle School's ethos of openness means that it welcomes parents, former pupils and friends of Barney to join its community, and encourages families to visit and experience for themselves the welcoming and happy atmosphere.

Situated in an excellent rural environment, Barnard Castle School is well served by a range of transport links, with several airports and railway stations close by.

Furthermore, Barney has educated many notable former students (known as 'Old Barnardians'), counting professional athletes, television personalities as well as entrepreneurs and business leaders among its alumni.

BARNARD CASTLE SCHOOL

(Founded 1883)

Barnard Castle, Durham DL12 8UN UK

Tel: +44 (0)1833 696030

Email: admissions@barneyschool.org.uk

Website: www.barnardcastleschool.org.uk

Headmaster: Mr Tony Jackson

Appointed: March 2017

School type: Co-educational Day & Boarding Preparatory, Senior & Sixth Form

Age range of pupils: 4–18 years

No. of pupils enrolled as at 01/09/2023: 723

Fees as at 01/09/2023:

Day: £8,964–£16,995 per annum

Full Boarding: £25,740–£32,430 per annum

Average class size: 18

Teacher/pupil ratio: 1:18

North-West

Brabyns Preparatory School

Nestled on the edge of the picturesque Peak District in the small town of Marple, Brabyns Preparatory School is a co-educational independent day school and nursery for children aged two to eleven.

Unique surroundings and a warm family ethos provide a peaceful and nurturing environment for the positive development and growth of all children at the school. Children are engaged with learning and given the support, encouragement and freedom they need to develop through exploring new opportunities.

Brabyns acknowledges and appreciates each child's individual strengths and characteristics. They are instilled with confidence in our happy, caring environment whilst developing excellent life values and skills. This sits alongside their educational development to ensure every child is inspired to reach their potential. The school is committed to offering a first-class academic education within a forward-thinking and dynamic curriculum, in a way that is rewarding and engaging for children, parents and staff.

This exceptional independent school prides itself on a warm family atmosphere in which all children are valued as individuals and are encouraged and inspired to reach their full potential within a disciplined yet caring environment.

The whole school community is offered a rich and diverse experience; including a wide range of academic, sporting, language and performing arts opportunities, plus an extensive extra-curricular programme. Forest school activities help children develop a natural curiosity and love for the outdoors, equipping them with increased confidence, and physical and social skills.

Enjoyment and excellence are at the heart of an education that encompasses academic study, leadership, cultural pursuits, communication and excellent pastoral care.

Brabyns' aim is to develop confident individuals and to enable them to realise their full potential and contribute fully to the world in which they grow. Every child's individual talent is nurtured and their achievements are celebrated. Brabyns values its close partnership with parents; through working collaboratively the school identifies each child's strength to assist in the pursuit of excellence.

Each and every child has a part to play in Brabyns' life and every child is respected. By the time children leave us at the end of Year 6 they have built firm foundations not only for secondary school but for life ahead, and they move on with life-long memories.

34–36 Arkwright Road, Marple, Stockport, Cheshire SK6 7DB UK

Tel: 0161 427 2395

Email: admin@brabynsprepschool.co.uk

Website: www.brabynsprepschool.co.uk

Headteacher: Mrs Cath Carrasco

School type:
Co-educational Day Preparatory & Nursery

Age range of pupils: 2–11 years

Fees as at 01/09/2023:

Day: £2,354–£3,264 per term

f
f
r

Forest Park Preparatory School

Forest Park Preparatory School provides an excellent educational start for your child. It is a unique school underpinned by core values that support the development of every child.

Rated 'Excellent' in all areas within our most recent Inspection Report (2019), this is a school where children are inspired and challenged from their very first day with us. Challenged to think independently and creatively, to enjoy and participate fully in their learning, and to achieve their full potential.

There is a real sense of belonging and family at Forest Park. From their first days in Pre Prep, children encourage one another to live the school motto, 'I can and I will'. In our warm and supportive environment, children learn to value themselves and each other, to take risks and responsibility, to learn from their mistakes and build on their successes year by year.

With a broad and exciting curriculum, and supported and encouraged by excellent specialist teachers, our children steadily build knowledge and understanding, key skills and a robust work ethic year on year. When the time comes, they are able to take senior school entrance exams for the local state and independent grammar schools comfortably in their stride, without the pressures of intensive preparation.

We are dedicated to ensuring our children succeed with their 11+ examinations, without undue pressure.

As a result, our pupils gain places in the region's top grammar schools, with 100% recently passing for a school of their choice last year. Most importantly, every child is ready for the next step, confident, optimistic, and ready and willing to make the most of all the opportunities life presents.

Parents choose Forest Park Preparatory School because they want their children to be happy and to develop in a dynamic and challenging, yet caring environment.

FOREST PARK
PREPARATORY SCHOOL

Lauriston House, 27 Oakfield, Sale,
Greater Manchester M33 6NB UK

Tel: 0161 973 4835

Email: office@forestparkprep.co.uk

Website: www.forestparkprep.co.uk

Headteacher: Mr Nick Tucker

School type:
Co-educational Day Preparatory & Nursery

Age range of pupils: 3–11 years

Forest Preparatory School & Nursery

Situated in the attractive suburb of Timperley, Forest Preparatory School is an outstanding co-educational, independent day school for children aged two to eleven.

At Forest, staff provide a happy, stimulating and well-disciplined environment, and encourage each child to strive for excellence, and reach their full potential in all areas of school life.

Excellent pastoral care is built on knowledge of every child as an individual, and with an 'open door' policy strong links are formed with parents, allowing for excellent communication between home and school. In our most recent Early Years Inspection Report, inspectors noted that "nurturing and supportive staff have successfully created a homely and welcoming environment that contributes positively to children's achievements." This is something we feel very passionate about at Forest. In addition, our Wraparound Care enables children to be safely looked after in school from 7:30am until 5:55pm each day.

Our vision is embedded in putting pupil success at the heart of every decision. We believe in developing pupils' self-esteem so that they have the confidence to use their individual talents, skills and knowledge effectively and leave Forest equipped to be lifelong learners.

We value the partnership which exists between school, parents and community and the part it plays in realising this vision.

Though the school is not selective at infant level, Forest has great expectations, resulting in high aspirations from the children, and great achievements occurring both in and out of the classroom.

Parents at Forest Preparatory School are very fortunate with the extensive choice of highly respected secondary schools available in the area and we aim to help them choose the right school for their child.

Our curriculum goes beyond the demands of the National Curriculum; it is personally structured and, in the later years, there is a clear focus placed on the requirements of the Independent and State Grammar Schools entrance examinations at 11+. The curriculum remains broad and balanced with a continued emphasis on creativity, questioning, and independent thinking. A priority for Forest is to help guide and prepare our children for their future schools.

The Early Years Department comprises of the Nursery (2–3 year olds), Kindergarten (3–4 year olds) and Reception. Our Early Years department provides a stimulating, caring and vibrant environment where children aged 2–5 years of age learn important social skills and thrive on the planned learning opportunities, particularly in early reading, writing, mathematics, technology and creativity.

Children feel happy, secure and valued. They gain a wealth of learning experiences including Computing, PE, French and Music tuition from specialist teachers. There is also the opportunity for children to attend a range of after-school activities including Yoga, Spanish, Science, Art, Dance and Kiddy Cook.

Nursery children may start with their academic year group from the September after their second birthday and they may attend for any combination of mornings, afternoons or full days. Reception is a natural progression from Kindergarten, combining a warm, welcoming atmosphere with a bright, spacious and stimulating environment, which provides a wide variety of learning areas. The children are well-motivated learners, who continue to work within the seven areas of learning from the Foundation Stage curriculum, with an increased focus on the teaching of reading, writing and numeracy.

We believe that Forest is a great place to be and we would love to help your children learn. We hold a number of events for prospective parents throughout the year and our next Open Morning is Saturday 2nd March 2024 10am - 12pm.

FOREST PREPARATORY SCHOOL

(Founded 1924)

Moss Lane, Timperley, Altrincham,
Greater Manchester WA15 6LJ UK

Tel: 0161 980 4075

Email: enquiries@forestschool.co.uk

Website: www.forestschool.co.uk

Headmaster: Mr Graeme Booth

School type:
Co-educational Day Preparatory & Nursery

Age range of pupils: 2–11 years

Lime House School

"Fun,Fab, Fair", Lime House School is a great place to learn to be your best self.

Lime House School - www.limehouseschool.co.uk - just south of Carlisle on the edge of the Lake District National Park, is an independent, co-educational boarding and day school which welcomes pupils, aged seven to 18, from all over the world.

Lime House School offers a rigorous academic and intellectual education which will challenge and engage your child. Supportive and nurturing in approach, the school empowers pupils to establish secure foundations for independent learning from which to launch their futures in tertiary education, and the careers of their choice.

The school has a wide and varied curriculum at both Primary and Secondary levels, with a dynamic range of subjects offered to Sixth Form. Pupils of all abilities are welcome, those with Special Education Needs are supported by a dedicated team of professionals.

Headteacher, Mr Andy Guest, says: *"It is a privilege to lead a school of such vibrancy. The academic programme is rich and fulfilling, with pupils benefiting from tailored programmes, delivered by subject specialists, who enthuse our learners with their passion. The super-curricular opportunities inform the academic life of the school with a range of cultural, performance, and sporting activities.*

"Pupils are guided in their growth as future global citizens and custodians, by their personal development tutors, and are encouraged to explore their dreams and define their path. Lime House School is a joyous and enriching place for all who are involved in our community."

The school's ethos is that learning should be integrated and fun, extending beyond the classroom and informing all we do.

The activities programme includes: sporting; music; art; photography; debating; environmental and strategic thinking. Pupils engage wholeheartedly with their beautiful surroundings with Forest School enhancing wellbeing and resilience. Weekends are structured, with pupils exploring diverse educational, cultural and fun filled experiences.

Lime House is a school of outstanding potential, its vibrancy and tolerance reflected in each of its pupils. Why not arrange a visit to see what we can offer your child?

(Founded 1899)

Holm Hill, Dalston, Carlisle, Cumbria CA5 7BX UK

Tel: 01228 710225

Email: office@limehouseschool.co.uk

Website: www.limehouseschool.co.uk

Headteacher: Mr Andy Guest

Appointed: September 2022

School type: Co-educational Day & Boarding Preparatory, Senior & Sixth Form

Age range of pupils: 7–18 years

No. of pupils enrolled as at 01/09/2023: 168

Fees as at 01/09/2023: £35,550 per annum

Average class size: 12

Teacher/pupil ratio: 1:8

South-East

Bethany School

Set on a 60 acre rural campus in the beautiful Kent countryside, Bethany School is a flourishing co-educational day, full and weekly boarding school that provides a welcoming and caring environment for pupils between the ages of 11 and 18. The school was delighted to have achieved the highest accolades possible after their ISI inspection in April 2023, receiving 'excellent' in all areas.

Bethany enjoys an excellent reputation as a particularly friendly and happy community. It is a strong, thriving school with an enviable building programme, including recent and regular upgrading of boarding school facilities; a fantastic six lane 25 metre indoor swimming pool, state-of-the-art fitness suite, a sixth form centre with excellent facilities and an expansive outdoor high ropes course.

Location

Situated in Kent, known as the 'Garden of England', Bethany has an idyllic location with easy accessibility. London is less than an hour by train, Gatwick Airport one hour by taxi and Heathrow an hour and a half. The Eurostar terminal at Ashford International is just 30 minutes away.

The very best academic education

As a mainstream school, Bethany prides itself on nurturing academic excellence while catering for pupils with a broad range of abilities. The school offers a wide variety of subjects in modern classrooms with specialist facilities, including a Science Centre with modern laboratories.

The entire campus is served by a wireless network and all pupils have their own laptop. Much of the curriculum is delivered through ICT and pupils gain important digital skills. Almost all of our sixth formers progress on to university courses, leaving Bethany with a mature, self-confident sense of purpose.

CReSTeD registered since 1994, Bethany's Learning Support department enjoys an international reputation for its success in giving specialist help to dyslexic pupils within the mainstream curriculum. In addition, for those pupils who require it, we offer support for English as an Additional Language.

Boarding life and overseas pupils

Our boarding community brings great diversity to Bethany. We are a small school and yet we have boarders coming from over 20 different countries, enriching our education with a variety of experiences and backgrounds.

We aim to inspire individual excellence in every pupil and this approach underlies everything we do at Bethany. Its success is evidenced by the excellent transition from school to university made by our pupils each year. Sixth form boarders benefit from single bedrooms with en suite bathrooms, all with easy access to kitchens and laundry rooms. This experience, combined with our Body for Life programme, is designed to be a stepping stone to life at university, all within the supportive environment of the school.

Outside the classroom

At Bethany, we believe that pursuits outside the classroom are very important in developing pupils' personalities. Everyone takes part in sport at least three times a week, and chooses from a huge array of extra-curricular activities including horse riding, chef school, golf, fishing, clay pigeon shooting, archery, orchestra and country pursuits. The Duke of Edinburgh's Award is hugely popular and very successful at Bethany.

The Headmaster firmly believes that school should be enjoyed rather than endured and it is the positive and nurturing atmosphere and the level of focus given to each individual pupil, that helps makes Bethany 'refreshingly different'.

Bethany
since 1866

(Founded 1866)

Curtisden Green, Goudhurst, Cranbrook,
Kent TN17 1LB UK

Tel: 01580 211273

Email: registrar@bethanyschool.org.uk

Website: www.bethanyschool.org.uk

Headmaster: Mr Francie Healy BSc, HDipEd, NPQH

Appointed: 2010

School type:
Co-educational Day & Boarding Senior & Sixth Form

Age range of pupils: 11–18 years

No. of pupils enrolled as at 01/09/2023: 366

Boys: 247 ***Girls:*** 119 ***Sixth Form:*** 79

No. of boarders: 69

Fees as at 01/09/2023:

Day: £20,415–£22,545 per annum

Weekly Boarding: £31,680–£34,980 per annum

Full Boarding: £34,155–£38,445 per annum

Average class size: 15–17

Teacher/pupil ratio: 1:8

Brighton College Prep School

The Nursery at Brighton College sees its young learners start their educational journey at just three years old, taught by qualified teachers. They attend five mornings a week and many enjoy staying for a flexible afternoon offering themed learning time in French, yoga, beach school, art and movement, which can be followed by the in-house after-school care group which runs until 5.45pm. The Nursery day is a highly flexible offering which suits the school's many types of parent. The curriculum has been developed to place an emphasis upon play-based learning and on supporting the individual interests and abilities of the children. Its innovative approach incorporates a programme of fine motor skill development and an emphasis on role-play in teaching, alongside an embedded use of technology including classroom CTouch screens, remote controlled devices and simple coding software and tablets.

Each year the Nursery pupils move on to Reception classes, fully prepared for their first year of school. They take with them a strong foundation and which ensures that they are keen learners who are ready to flourish. Alongside French and Mandarin teaching, the curriculum in Reception includes specialist art, PE, games and music lessons. Pupils from Reception upwards also benefit from weekly lessons in computing, teaching vital IT literacy and e-safety, and library lessons aimed at inspiring all pupils to read and learn about a range of literacy genres from the earliest age. At six years, children are given the opportunity to take up individual instrumental lessons taught by music specialists and become confident performers in weekly assemblies and annual concerts. Swimming lessons start when the children are five, adding to their action packed week of learning.

As the children progress into Year 4, their world of learning expands to incorporate curriculum drama, home economics, design and technology and Latin, alongside the traditional maths, English, science and humanities subjects. The co-curricular provision is also extended, incorporating LAMDA courses, choirs, music ensembles and orchestras. Over 50 clubs and activities are offered to the children during lunchtimes and after school, ranging from sewing or chess to debating or hockey. A programme of residential trips also begins in Year 5 which assists pupils to gain vital team-building and independence skills learnt in experiences outside of the classroom.

As the main feeder school into Year 9 at Brighton College, pupils here look forward to moving across from Year 8. They are well prepared for the next chapter in their education, having enjoyed a full programme of transition during their final term, 'Chapter IX', which, in liaison with the College, ensures that they are fully prepared. Many are successful in taking with them scholarship awards in both academic and co-curricular subjects.

Walpole Lodge, Walpole Road,
Brighton, East Sussex BN2 0EU UK

Tel: 01273 704343

Email: prepadmissions@brightoncollege.net

Website: www.brightoncollege.org.uk

Headmaster: Mr Ant Falkus

Appointed: August 2022

School type:
Co-educational Day Preparatory & Nursery

Age range of pupils: 3–13 years

No. of pupils enrolled as at 01/09/2023: 510

Fees as at 01/09/2023:

Day: £4,400–£7,430 per term

Burgess Hill Girls

"The community at Burgess Hill Girls is very special. The way we bond with our teachers is not something you come across every day. I feel very lucky to be a part of this school."

Laura, Year 10, Burgess Hill Girls

A transformative education

Burgess Hill Girls is an Excellent rated independent school in Sussex for girls aged 2 to 18 years of age.

Whatever the stage at which your daughter joins Burgess Hill Girls you can be confident of two things: that she will be known for who she is as an individual and she will be provided with an outstanding, transformative education of the whole person.

I am, I can, I should, I will

Our school motto, 'I am, I can, I should, I will', conveys and underpins our whole approach, identifying and realising the potential of your daughter as she proceeds, giving her the very best possible opportunities to become a successful women of the future.

As parents, success will be having a happy and healthy daughter who loves going to school, loves to learn, loves participating, and is able to make friends for life. For the girls, success may be doing well in lessons and tests, being part of a team, playing a musical instrument and having fun with friends.

At Burgess Hill Girls we pride ourselves on unlocking the academic talent that is found within our girls and strongly believe each individual will thrive in our high-achieving environment. Whilst Burgess Hill Girls aims to provide the very best opportunities for everyone to excel, we believe that success is more than obtaining the highest marks and grades. We recognise just as much all those fantastic qualities that are not materialistic or target driven. Success at our school is when we produce bright, confident and independent young women who have and will continue to achieve great things.

Perfectly located

Burgess Hill Girls stands in 14 acres of beautiful grounds within a conservation area close to Burgess Hill's town centre in the centre of Sussex. All aspects of the school are located on this one campus; Nursery, Pre-Prep & Prep, Senior, Sixth Form and Boarding Houses. The school is only a five minute walk from the railway station (on the London to Brighton line) and close to excellent road networks (10 miles from Brighton and only 20 miles from London Gatwick Airport); the school is easily accessible for local and international students. A flexible, daily minibus service is provided for girls across Sussex and beyond.

Visit Burgess Hill Girls

We would be very pleased to meet you, put a name to a face and show you round our school. Please get in touch to arrange a visit.

BURGESS HILL

— GIRLS —

Tomorrow's Women

(Founded 1906)

Keymer Road, Burgess Hill, West Sussex RH15 0EG UK

Tel: 01444 241050

Email: admissions@burgesshillgirls.com

Website: burgesshillgirls.com

Head of School: Lars Fox

Appointed: 2022

School type: Girls' Day & Boarding, Co-ed Nursery

Religious Denomination: Interdenominational

Age range of boys: 2.5–4 years

Age range of girls: 2.5–18 years

No. of pupils enrolled as at 01/09/2023: 503

Boys: 19 ***Girls:*** 484 ***Sixth Form:*** 59

No. of boarders: 50

Fees as at 01/09/2023:

Day: £10,500–£23,940 per annum

Full Boarding: £36,960–£42,540 per annum

Average class size: Max 20

Teacher/pupil ratio: 1:11

3
4

Churcher's College

Churcher's College

Churcher's College is an independent day school for girls and boys aged 3 to 18 which delivers an inspiring education with opportunities for pupils to flourish and grow both inside and outside the classroom. We enjoy recognition as one of the most accomplished independent, co-educational day schools in the country.

Limitless Potential

We offer pupils the widest range of experiences and opportunities to excel. Our aim is to develop the full academic, creative and sporting talents of the girls and boys, within the context of social awareness, fully preparing them to make informed decisions on issues they will face in today's dynamic and challenging world. We nurture the children to be fittingly prepared for their futures, ready to succeed in life.

Pastoral Care is at the heart of all that we do

Our welcoming, nurturing and secure environment ensures that every pupil feels valued and supported, thus enabling them to succeed academically, and in the many and varied extra-curricular activities that are on offer.

Our pastoral system is one based upon excellent interactions, both formal and informal, between pupils and staff. Our pupils have a wide range of adults in the school community to whom they can talk, and who will have concern and compassion for them.

Another key feature of our pastoral provision is a strong partnership between school and home. Open dialogue with parents is actively encouraged, and contributes significantly to maintaining the happiness and wellbeing of our pupils.

Perhaps most importantly, Churcher's pupils also share problems with each other, and are incredibly supportive, tolerant and understanding of their peers; we see this as one of the defining characteristics of our school.

A countryside location

Just one hour from London, the school is located on two beautiful countryside campus sites in Hampshire, on the borders of Surrey and West Sussex. Our Junior School and Nursery is nestled in leafy Liphook, just ten minutes from the Senior School and Sixth Form in Petersfield, both boast generous on-site playing fields and unrivalled facilities in green and open countryside locations.

Our community

Churcher's is proud to be an inclusive school where parents, children, staff and friends all contribute to the rich and broad education provided.

"The quality of the pupils' personal development... academic and other activities is excellent" ISI Inspection 2022

"Big enough to give a broad offering but small enough to know and care." Churcher's Parent

"I know I have made life-long friends and have built the strongest platform to start my next chapter, which I am so thankful for." Sixth Form Student

Visit us to discover more

The best way to discover Churcher's College is to join us at an Open Event to explore for yourself, please check the website for all details. We really look forward to meeting you soon.

ChurchersCollege.com

01730 263 033

(Founded 1722)

Petersfield, Hampshire GU31 4AS UK

Tel: 01730 263033

Email: admissions@churcherscollege.com

Website: www.ChurchersCollege.com

Headmaster: Mr Simon Williams , MA, BSc

Appointed: September 2004

School type: Co-educational Independent Day

Age range of pupils: 3–18 years

No. of pupils enrolled as at 01/09/2023:

Senior School: 1000

Junior School: 235

Fees as at 01/09/2023:

Day: £12,525–£18,735 per annum

Average class size: 22

Teacher/pupil ratio: 1:12

Claremont School

Thriving at Claremont means welcoming you as you are, empowering you to find your own unique path to your best, and supporting you in reaching it, then bettering it.

Claremont Senior School and Sixth Form

Founded in 2011, Claremont Senior School is situated in the heart of historic Bodiam, famous for its picturesque 14th Century castle. With 'student voice' at its heart, the school has an unrelenting focus on attitude and activism as the central pillars of its holistic educational philosophy and offers a dynamic learning environment where young people consistently say they can be themselves. Never before has there been so many career paths, university courses and avenues for teenagers to explore, as the forces of technological change transform our world. By presenting students with challenge, opportunity and experimentation the school seeks to give them the confidence to fulfil their individual potential and face their futures with self-assurance, optimism and a boundless drive to be the best version of themselves. Relaxed, but ambitious and rigorous in approach, Claremont is a local school with an international perspective. It is a special place to work and a unique place to learn.

An extensive extra curricular, enrichment and service programme recognises that, for many young people, the greatest learning experiences can come from outside the classroom. The Co Curricular programme is inspired by the eight core skills valued by universities, apprenticeship courses and ultimately future careers, with the aim of giving students opportunities to explore new talents as well as become masters of the things they love.

Student outcomes are outstanding with over 90% of Sixth Form students able to access their first choice of university, of which a third are Russell Group institutions.

Claremont has been judged 'Outstanding' by Ofsted in its last 3 consecutive inspections and in October 2021, was named Independent School of the Year for the Performing Arts.

'Being able to prepare young people for Maths degrees at Harvard as effectively as for Fashion courses in London is something all our staff are deeply proud of.' Ed Dickie, Head of Senior School

Claremont Prep School

Founded in 1925, Claremont Prep is a magical place to learn and grow. It's a joyful environment where children feel happy, secure and valued, where they further skills and knowledge and start to learn to adapt to the ever changing demands of the modern world. The school is based in rural St Leonards just 5 miles from the seaside and surrounded by over 100 acres of wonderful grounds to include extensive sports and playing fields and a locally renowned cross county track, alongside some truly magnificent woodlands. The main house is steeped in history, with curious winding corridors and beautiful spaces to learn in. There is even an icehouse hidden in the forest.

In lessons, the approach to learning is all about 'getting better', that it is good to aim high and there are no limits to furthering skills and knowledge in and outside the classroom. Many teachers are secondary school trained so are very knowledgeable about senior school life and how best to prepare children for GCSEs and all the challenges and opportunities that come with this next crucial stage in their education. All this, whilst nurturing an environment of friendship and kindness where children can most definitely still be children.

Green Flag and BBC Young Reporter School status

The Prep School holds the much coveted Green Flag and BBC Reporter school status. The children write and publish an award winning student magazine, called The Arrow. The school is one of the first (if not the first) schools to have its own Eco Store.

Bodiam, Nr Robertsbridge, East Sussex TN32 5UJ UK

Tel: 01580 830396

Email: admissions@claremontschool.co.uk

Website: www.claremontschool.co.uk

Principal: Severine Collins

School type: Co-educational Day & Boarding Prep & Senior, Nursery & Sixth Form

Age range of pupils:

1–18 years (boarding from 10)

Cranleigh School

Cranleigh is Surrey's leading co-educational independent school offering both day and boarding education for children aged 7–18, enabling siblings to be educated together.

Set on adjacent hills, the Preparatory School and the Senior School enjoy a spectacular 280-acre rural setting on the Surrey/West Sussex border, by the Surrey Hills, an Area of Outstanding Natural Beauty; yet they are conveniently situated close to the mainline city of Guildford, roughly equidistant between Gatwick and Heathrow, and only an hour's drive from London, where Cranleigh pupils regularly visit professional exhibitions and performances.

Both the Prep and the Senior Schools are proud of their excellent academic track records, culminating in outstanding performances at Common Entrance, GCSE and A-level. 99% of pupils go on to Higher Education, and Cranleigh also has a consistently strong Oxbridge contingent.

Such academic excellence does not come at the expense of co-curricular success at Cranleigh and the schools currently boast national and county level representatives in a wide range of sports, including cricket, riding, hockey, rugby and swimming.

Pupil participation in sport, music and drama is actively encouraged at all levels; most Saturdays see every pupil playing sport for the school. More than 10 dramatic productions each academic year provide acting opportunities for all and the hugely popular Technical Theatre encourages the development of backstage skills.

Around 40 per cent of pupils play at least one musical instrument. Many take the opportunity to perform in more than 30 concerts a year, with over 10 musical groups, including symphony orchestra, wind band, chapel choir, big band, strings, trios, quartets and several other choirs.

The schools offer outstanding facilities alongside new academic blocks. Sports facilities enjoyed by both the Prep and the Senior School include a double-sized indoor sports centre, four artificial playing surfaces, full equestrian centre, two expansive hard court areas for netball and tennis, a generous array of rugby and cricket pitches, a three-par, nine-hole golf course and an indoor pool. Equally outstanding sports staff includes former England players, an England national coach and an Olympic Gold Medallist (Hockey).

The schools also boast professional-standard theatre facilities, rehearsal rooms, beautiful art studio spaces and a modern design centre fully equipped with 3D printers. The students have the opportunity to showcase their work in professional exhibitions several times a year.

Most importantly, Cranleigh prides itself on providing a happy, nurturing environment, founded upon an extremely supportive pastoral system (every pupil has their own tutor) and a high staff to pupil ratio, underscored by an invariably passionate house spirit. In such an environment, pupils can flourish into the well-rounded, self-motivated and confident individuals Cranleighans are famed for becoming, well prepared for life after school and invariably blessed with a circle of lifelong friends.

Pupils enter Cranleigh following a process of holistic review, at the main entry points of 13 and 16, and in other years where places are available. We also offer an 11+ entry point, to include two years at our Prep School followed by entry into the Senior School. Regular Welcome Mornings are held and a wide range of academic and non-academic Scholarships are available.

CRANLEIGH

EX CULTU ROBUR

(Founded 1865)

Horseshoe Lane, Cranleigh, Surrey GU6 8QQ UK

Tel: +44 (0) 1483 273666

Fax: +44 (0) 1483 267398

Email: admissions@cranleigh.org

Website: www.cranleigh.org

Headmaster: Mr Martin Reader MA, MPhil, MBA

Appointed: September 2014

School type:
Co-educational Day & Boarding & Sixth Form

Age range of pupils: 7–18 years (including Prep School)

No. of pupils enrolled as at 01/09/2023: 695

Boys: 407 ***Girls:*** 288 ***Sixth Form:*** 281

No. of boarders: 514

Fees as at 01/09/2023:

Day: £37,905 per annum

Full Boarding: £46,035 per annum

Average class size: 20 (9 in Sixth Form)

Teacher/pupil ratio: 1:6

Ditcham Park School

Ditcham Park School is a co-educational Independent School for children aged rising 3 to 16.

Situated near Petersfield, in the heart of the South Downs National Park, with spectacular views of the rolling Hampshire hills and south across the Solent as far as the Isle of Wight, we provide the perfect environment for your child to flourish.

We offer an outstanding education, which equips our children with excellent academic qualifications, skills and self-confidence. We believe that children learn best and develop self-esteem when they are encouraged in a caring and supportive environment. Our school's size and stunning location creates a genuinely friendly, nurturing environment where 'every child is known and valued'.

Relatively small class sizes, excellent teaching, strong pastoral care and opportunities for personal development through sport, the arts and outdoor activities, set on our beautiful 16-acre site, are unique to the education children receive here. Furthermore our innovative STEAM programme offers all year groups an exciting experiential style of learning that combines the disciplines of Science, Technology, Engineering, the Arts and Maths. Children have the chance to try out the latest technologies and hands-on activities that have authentic real-world applications to build the flexible and creative problem-solving skills that will be most valued by employers of the future. The annual STEAM Festival attracts top technology and engineering giants such as McLaren, Google and the Royal Navy to our school to give careers advice and inspiring hands-on demonstrations.

Our extensive parkland and state-of-the-art learning environments lend themselves perfectly to a large variety of extra-curricular activities for all pupils. These include bushcraft, mountain biking, tennis, Lego, Greenpower Challenge and modern dance. Our children are conscious of the environment around them, and we have a vibrant cross-school Eco Committee that has recently won Ditcham the prestigious Green Flag status.

We are proud of our school's academic progress and achievements. Children in Juniors regularly exceed expected levels of literacy and numeracy and our curriculum provides rich opportunities for learning across all subject areas. Regular learning experiences beyond the classroom mean that our Juniors have the chance to see the application of their subjects taught by inspirational specialist teachers such as science, modern foreign languages and music.

Within our Senior school, we offer a dedicated three-year GCSE programme that really is the jewel in our academic crown. We currently offer 19 different subjects from Computer Science, Sport, Latin, Business studies, Music, Art and Drama, alongside all three sciences and Design Technology. Year on year, our GCSE results far exceed the national average, allowing our pupils to move on into A-levels at a range of competitive independent and state sixth form colleges. University destinations for Ditcham Park students include the top Russell Group universities such as Oxford, Cambridge, Southampton and Newcastle to name a few.

Our children leave the school happy, confident and enthusiastic - always willing to come back and inspire the next generation with their learning journey.

(Founded 1976)

Ditcham Park, Petersfield, Hampshire GU31 5RN UK

Tel: 01730 825659

Email: admissions@ditchampark.com

Website: www.ditchampark.com

Headmaster: Mr Graham Spawforth MA, MEd

Appointed: April 2017

School type:
Co-educational Day Preparatory, Senior & Nursery

Age range of pupils: 2.5–16 years

No. of pupils enrolled as at 01/09/2023: 430

Boys: 240 ***Girls:*** 190

Fees as at 01/09/2023:

Day: £3,327–£5,633 per term

Average class size: 18

Dolphin School

Dolphin School is unique. It is a school where our core values of Freedom, Discovery, Challenge, Confidence and Kindness are lived out each and every day. Whether it is through our extensive and varied trips programme, our subject specialist teaching from nursery upwards, our lack of uniform, or the first name terms between students and teachers, Dolphin is a school that is different, and proudly so.

Children are encouraged to be curious, volunteer their own insights and ask questions. Debate and discourse are actively encouraged as stimuli for learning. Whenever visitors encounter our students in their learning environments, they comment on the genuine enthusiasm shown by our boys and girls, as they vie for the opportunity to tell our guests what they are studying and what they have been doing.

At the very heart of our educational philosophy is our belief that children learn best when they are happy and comfortable in their learning environment, whether in the classroom, outside, or away on a trip. Our children flourish in small classes, in an atmosphere filled with warmth and enthusiasm, where individuality is celebrated and relationships between teacher and child are cherished. We are not constrained to the classroom or bound by tradition, and strive to maintain a learning environment where our children love coming into school and have the opportunity to learn at their own pace and in their own way.

For the last few years, we have been developing our Dolphin Project Qualification (DPQ): an extended, cross-curricular undertaking that affords children real-life learning experiences, fosters a plethora of 'soft' skills and celebrates multiple pathways to success.

Now running across Years 3–8, these projects take a variety of forms tailored to the specific year group (from a travel vlog based on a residential trip to Boulogne in Year 5, to a TED talk devised around the 'zeitgeist' in Year 8). Each one has a literacy, numeracy and IT strand - to reflect the central importance of these competencies - but beyond that, students are encouraged to consider the relevance of as many of their subject areas as possible. Designed to reflect the requirements of later life more faithfully than traditional forms of assessment, we emphasise the importance of students' oracy, as well as the production of a portfolio of evidence to demonstrate their independence, initiative and collaboration.

We would be delighted to welcome you to visit our school and meet our Headmaster, Adam Hurst. Please contact Kate Spooner at admissions@dolphinschool.com or call us on 0118 934 1277 to book your personal tour.

Waltham Road, Hurst, Reading, Berkshire RG10 0FR UK

Tel: 0118 934 1277

Email: enquiries@dolphinschool.com

Website: www.dolphinschool.com

Headmaster: Mr Adam Hurst

School type:
Co-educational Day Preparatory & Nursery

Age range of pupils: 3–13 years

No. of pupils enrolled as at 01/09/2023: 223

Fees as at 01/09/2023:

Nursery (full time) to Reception: £3,965 – £4,185 per term

Years 1 to 2: £4,610 per term

Years 3 to 4: £5,520 per term

Years 5 to 6: £5,675 per term

Years 7 to 8: £5,730 per term

GRYFFINDOR

Durlston School

Welcoming our first Year 9 pupils

The start of term is always an exciting time but this year is extra special - not only are we welcoming new children to Kindergarten, Pre-Prep, Middle Prep and Upper Prep but we are also welcoming our first ever Year 9 Senior pupils. Celebrating 120 years since the school was first founded, Durlston is marking the next stage as we extend to 16 and GCSE.

Durlston has a long-standing reputation for all-round educational excellence - combining academic, creative and sporting opportunities with the pastoral support to help our children grow in ability and confidence and to ultimately achieve their very best. We are thrilled that we can now offer children the opportunity to continue their education at Durlston through to Year 11 and to GCSE examinations.

We welcome children at any point. Our Pre-Prep children enjoy a vibrant and nurturing environment where they can experience their journey of discovery at their own pace. The children have a myriad of opportunities and develop the confidence to embrace challenge in the classroom and in music, sport, drama and dance as well. Outdoor challenges in the Forest School develop resilience and perseverance, and experiences like dancing the Charleston at a 1920s afternoon tea dance, really bring learning to life.

Children in Middle Prep explore new and exciting opportunities and as they grow in independence children continue to make amazing progress inside and outside the classroom. They are encouraged to find what they love, participating in the range of experiences such as: starting a band; learning to sail; growing vegetables in the Middle School Garden; representing the school in a team, and the list goes on.

The adventure continues in the Upper Prep and Senior years. The children at Durlston are challenged and supported by specialist, inspirational teachers in wonderful purpose built facilities. We encourage the children to take advantage of all the opportunities on offer from competing in a STEM competition to taking the lead in a charity music concert.

Our purpose is to provide an exceptional education in an environment where each child is properly known by all members of staff. Our small class sizes and 'family feel' ensure that we truly know our children and it is the quality of the relationship between our staff and children that makes Durlston such a very special place to learn and grow.

"If you are looking for an exceptional school, then look to Durlston."

We invite you and your family to find out more.

(Founded 1903)

Becton Lane, Barton-on-Sea, New Milton, Hampshire BH25 7AQ UK

Tel: 01425 610010

Email: registrar@durlstonschool.co.uk

Website: www.durlstonschool.co.uk

Headmaster: Mr Richard May

Appointed: 2015

School type: Co-educational Day & Nursery

Age range of pupils: 2–16 years

No. of pupils enrolled as at 01/09/2023: 260

Fees as at 01/09/2023: Please see website

Average class size: 15

Eagle House School

Eagle House is a coeducational, boarding and day Prep, Pre-Prep and Nursery located in Berkshire and only 50 minutes from London, benefitting from a close relationship with Wellington College. The school's superb grounds and excellent facilities are the background to an experience where success, confidence and happiness are paramount. The school is proud of its academic record, preparing children for a host of top independent schools and boasting a diverse and robust curriculum.

In September 2023, Ed Venables took over as Head.

Younger pupils follow the International Primary Curriculum and our older children have embarked on a new 'Curriculum 200', specially created for Years 5 to 8 that links subjects through topics and themes. Great teaching, new technology and a focus on the basics mean that children make good progress and love to be in the classroom. Independent learning is a focus for all children and our Extended Project programme helps drive inquisitive minds.

We unashamedly offer lots as part of our Golden Eagle activities experience. Children benefit from a huge range of opportunities in sport, music, drama, art, outward bound and community programmes. Busy children are happy and fulfilled children and we like to think that all pupils are Learning for Life.

Learning for Life means that children benefit from the best all-round education. They can feel confident in the classroom, on the games field, on stage, in the concert hall and in the community. Everyone is given the chance to stretch themselves in every area. Challenge is an important part of growing up and at Eagle House we learn that success and failure are both positive experiences.

Bright learning environments, outdoor learning areas and wonderful sporting facilities are important, but it is the community that shapes a young person. Through the excellent pastoral care and tutor system, coupled with a buddy structure, ensuring children have an older pupil to support them, Eagle House seeks to develop wellbeing from the youngest to the oldest.

Recognising how to be a positive influence within a community is also part of the Eagle House journey. Our wonderful Learning for Life programme teaches children about themselves and the wider community. Through community service we aim to make all our pupils responsible and independent as well as able to show empathy and understanding towards others. Time for reflection in chapel and assemblies also improves the way we look at the world and mindfulness sessions help us all take stock.

Boarding is a popular option and allows children to experience a varied evening programme of activities as well as being part of a vibrant and caring community. Boarding encourages independence but it is also great fun and whether full, weekly or flexi, boarders have the most wonderful time.

We often say that Eagle House children have the time of their lives and we firmly believe this. Learning for Life at Eagle House opens the doors to all sorts of opportunities and this results in children who are highly motivated and enthusiastic in all they do.

Eagle House buzzes with achievement and laughter - not a bad way to grow up!

Eagle House is a registered charity (No 309093) for the furtherance of education.

(Founded 1820)

Sandhurst, Berkshire GU47 8PH UK

Tel: 01344 772134

Email: info@eaglehouseschool.com

Website: www.eaglehouseschool.com

Head: Mr E Venables

Appointed: September 2023

School type:
Co-educational Day & Boarding Preparatory & Nursery

Age range of pupils: 3–13 years

No. of pupils enrolled as at 01/09/2023: 354

No. of boarders: 50

Fees as at 01/09/2023:

Day: £14,145–£22,125 per annum

Full Boarding: £29,730 per annum

Average class size: 17

Teacher/pupil ratio: 1:10

Farlington School

About Farlington School

Located in Horsham, West Sussex, Farlington School is a co-educational independent day and boarding school and nursery for ages 6 months to 18 years. Set within 33 acres of parkland on the borders of Sussex and Surrey, Farlington offers a perfect rural backdrop with plenty of space to grow. Formerly an all-girls' school, Farlington began welcoming boys in 2018 and has been fully co-educational since September 2021.

At Farlington, we strive to help our students develop confidence and self-belief, both inside and outside the classroom. Our core values constantly seek to develop Individuality, Opportunity and Community. **Individuality** is about recognising and celebrating each student's voice. Our constant aim is to enable **opportunities** for our pupils to learn across our full and extensive curriculum. As a true 'through school' and nursery, we provide a caring and cohesive **community**, in which each child is recognised as a valued and valuable member.

Pastoral care, wellbeing and fun are at the heart of a Farlington education, and we passionately believe that happiness enables success. Here, friendships are forged for life, and our emphasis is on promoting respect for others, celebrating teamwork, and developing collective responsibility.

Extra-Curricular Provision

Farlington offers an extensive extra-curricular provision, incorporating sporting, creative and enrichment options. Our twice daily activities programme allows every pupil to be involved in an enrichment activity - outdoors or indoors; practical, intellectual or unusual. We offer a range of extra-curricular art, music, dance and drama clubs, and provide a varied and inclusive extra-curricular sports programme.

Academic Success

Farlington students consistently achieve outstanding results at GCSE and A-Level. In 2023, our A-Level results were exceptional: 74% of grades awarded to Farlington students were A*-B and 84% of grades were A*-C. Our 'value added' was especially impressive, with 83% of students achieving one grade above expected in at least one A-Level, and 21% of all grades awarded being two grades above expected. Furthermore, 83% of our Year 13 students secured a place at their first choice of university, beating the national average. Our GCSE results in 2023 were equally impressive: 35% of grades awarded to Farlington students were 9–8; 54% of grades were 9–7; and 95% of grades were 9–4. The number of grade 9s achieved by Farlington students has almost tripled since pre-pandemic examinations in 2019.

Alumni & Awards

Notable Farlington alumni include Olivier Award-winning actor and puppeteer Romina Hytten, and Issy Hayes, now a successful triathlete and part of the England Next Generation talent squad. Over recent years, Farlington art students have triumphed in prestigious art competitions, including the ISA National Art Competition and the RBA's Rising Stars and Star Students Competitions. Farlington was shortlisted for the Outstanding Response to Covid-19 Award at the Independent Schools of the Year Awards 2021.

Recent Developments

Following the arrival of Headmaster James Passam in 2021, exciting developments at Farlington have included a stylish new Sixth Form Refectory, and the introduction of design & technology, together with a brand new D&T Workshop and Graphic Design Lab. Farlington has also improved its dance offering, with a new fully equipped Dance Studio and the subject now available to students both as part of the curriculum and in the form of extra-curricular examination and non-examination classes. In September 2023, Farlington opened its own nursery provision, Little Farlington, which caters for babies and children from 6 months to 4 years.

(Founded 1896)

Strood Park, Horsham, West Sussex RH12 3PN UK

Tel: 01403 282573

Email: admissions@farlingtonschool.com

Website: www.farlingtonschool.com

Headmaster: Mr James Passam

Appointed: September 2021

School type: Co-educational Day & Boarding Prep & Senior, Nursery & Sixth Form

Age range of pupils: 6 months–18 years

No. of pupils enrolled as at 01/09/2023: 413

Fees as at 01/09/2023:

Day: £2,200–£6,690 per term

Weekly Boarding: £11,300 per term

Full Boarding: £12,150 per term

Flexi Boarding: from £65 per night

Nursery: from £75 per day

Average class size: Prep: 16; Senior: 14; Sixth Form: 8

Gordon's School

Built by public subscription over a century ago at the insistence of Queen Victoria, Gordon's School is the national monument to General Charles Gordon of Khartoum, is listed as one of Britain's outstanding schools by Her Majesty's Chief Inspector and Tes Boarding School of the Year for 2022.

A non-selective, co-educational residential and day boarding school, while Gordon's School embraces modern ideas, General Gordon's legacy of traditional values remains. The school's ethos is that high performance without good character is not true success.

To this end, it's not just in the classrooms where students excel. Successes are achieved in drama and the arts; debating and public speaking; dance and sport. The school also boasts an enviable record in attaining Duke of Edinburgh awards.

While the individual is celebrated, the whole school unites for parades. Since its inception, students have marched and there has always been a Pipes and Drums band. Dressed in their Blues uniform, the students parade around eight times a year and the school is the only one permitted to march along Whitehall - an annual tradition in remembrance of General Gordon.

Set in over 50 acres of beautiful Surrey countryside within easy access of major airports and roads, the school is home to some 980 students and offers Day and Residential (weekly and termly) Boarding.

At the start of September 2020, Gordon's School entered one of the most exciting chapters in its 135 year history. A new sports hub and additional all-weather pitch was added to the already extensive facilities on the Surrey site and the school announced its partnership with Harlequins. As a result of the partnership, promising rugby players can now follow a pathway to a career in the game while receiving a first class education.

Each student is assigned to one of the ten Houses - four residential boarding and six day boarding. Recently opened has been a dedicated Year 7 bespoke Residential Boarding House for our youngest students. Inter-House competitions are fiercely contested.

Spiritual guidance and support is given through chapel services and informal worship. And Houseparents provide a 'home from home', lending special atmosphere to each Boarding House and ensuring that free time off for students is fun, with numerous activities.

There are three main admission points - at 11 years old; 13 years old and for Sixth Form.

Scholarships are offered for those coming into the Sixth Form. The scholarships enable those awarded to benefit from a programme to enhance their development and give them wider opportunities to progress in their field. Bursaries are also available.

The real judgement of Gordon's is the students. All who visit are struck by the friendliness, discipline and vibrancy throughout the school and by the family atmosphere, exemplified by the special rapport between staff and students. This is borne from a community that strives to live with integrity, to be courteous, enthusiastic and diligent, even in adversity.

Gordon's School is unique. Please book a visit and find out why.

(Founded 1885)

West End, Woking, Surrey GU24 9PT UK

Tel: 01276 858084

Fax: 01276 855335

Email: registrar@gordons.school

Website: www.gordons.school

Head Teacher: Andrew Moss MEd

Appointed: September 2010

School type: State Boarding & Day School

Age range of pupils: 11–18 years

No. of pupils enrolled as at 01/09/2023: 979

Boys: 523 ***Girls:*** 456 ***Sixth Form:*** 353

Fees as at 01/09/2023:

Day Boarding: £9,807 per annum

Weekly Boarding: £20,664 per annum

Full Boarding: £22,050 per annum

Average class size: 20

Teacher/pupil ratio: 1:12

Kent College, Canterbury

Kent College is an outstanding day and boarding school that celebrates both its 130 years of history and tradition, and its forward-looking, innovative approach to education. It has a reputation as a friendly school, and is most definitely a place where teachers really get to know the pupils, with the time and space to give individual attention, both academically and pastorally. Music, drama and sport all play central roles in the life of the school, and many pupils also enjoy the opportunities provided by the school's Farm and Riding Centre.

Part of the Methodist Schools group, Kent College is deeply rooted in the Methodist tradition that welcomes all pupils of every faith and none. 'Do all the good you can' is a guiding principle, and one that allows pupils to develop into confident young adults, aware of their responsibilities and their place in the world.

Location

The school's location, on the outskirts of the historic city of Canterbury, provides a safe, healthy and beautiful environment for pupils to grow up. The school sits in 80 acres (32 hectares) of land with extensive sports fields, as well as the Farm and Riding Centre. Yet the centre of Canterbury, with its wide selection of shops, restaurants, theatres, cinemas and world-heritage site, within which sits Canterbury Cathedral, is only a 5-minute journey by car. A high-speed train service links Canterbury to London, and the school is within 100 minutes of Gatwick, Heathrow, Stansted and City of London airports.

Boarding

Kent College has a long history of welcoming boarding pupils from abroad, as well as from British families resident in the UK or working overseas. Boarders make up around one third of pupils, and there are over 42 countries represented in the boarding community. The five friendly and comfortable Senior boarding houses truly become a 'home away from home'. The school also offers weekly and occasional boarding.

Academic Success

The bespoke approach to the curriculum differentiates the college's approach and ensures highly personalised teaching resulting in excellent results. The school regularly ranks in the top 10 small cohort schools for the International Baccalaureate with an average score of 37 for the last 7 years. 75% of students achieve A* - B at A Level and 98% of students regularly go to their first university of choice.

Beyond the classroom

The performing arts are a particular strength at Kent College, with an impressive line-up of vocal and instrumental ensembles, and many opportunities to perform for all ages and abilities. The Great Hall is an impressive 600-seat auditorium that allows students to gather for worship and to showcase their musical, theatrical and performance talents within a world-class theatre. In sport, the aim is to provide something for every pupil, from recreational sport and promoting fitness to top-level coaching for our elite players. Kent College teams make formidable competitors in any sport. Hockey and cricket are a particular strength with regular representation by our pupils in county, regional and national squads. The school's scholarship programme offers talented individuals individual support in art, design, drama, music and sport. There is also a wide-ranging list of activities and clubs on offer for all pupils, including a full Duke of Edinburgh programme, horse riding and Farm Club at the School Farm.

KENT COLLEGE
CANTERBURY

(Founded 1885)

Whitstable Road, Canterbury, Kent CT2 9DT UK

Tel: +44 (0)1227 763 231

Email: admissions@kentcollege.co.uk

Website: www.kentcollege.com

Head of Kent College: Mr Mark Turnbull

School type: Co-educational Day & Boarding Prep & Senior, Nursery & Sixth Form

Religious Denomination: Methodist

Age range of pupils:
3 months–18 years (boarding from 7 years)

Garden Cottage Nursery: 3 months–3 years

No. of pupils enrolled as at 01/09/2023: 800

Fees as at 01/09/2023:

Day: £3,964–£7,487 per term

Full Boarding: £10,072–£13,860 per term

Average class size: 15, max 18

King Edward VI School

King Edward VI School, Southampton, has been at the heart of the city for over 460 years and is one of the UK's leading independent 11–18 co-educational day schools.

King Edward's undoubtedly has high academic standards and expectations. Under the guidance of an expert teaching staff, our pupils perform at the highest levels in public examinations, and both GCSE and A level outcomes are consistently exceptional.

With a reputation for academic excellence, the school boasts a thriving Sixth Form that produces consistently excellent A Level examination results ensuring students continue on to a range of competitive institutions, most to one of the UK's top 25 universities and, on average, approximately 10% of students proceed to Oxford or Cambridge.

King Edward VI School places every child at the heart of all they do. The pastoral duty as a school encompasses all aspects of life and this responsibility of the children is reflected in their story. King Edward's aspires for children to be kind, caring young people committed to helping others as well as developing their own unique personality strengths and character. Last year saw the rebuild of a new Wellbeing Centre in the heart of the school. Wellbeing in the King Edward's curriculum, peer support schemes, wellbeing surveys and the KES cyber ambassadors being awarded Pathfinder of the Year 2023, by Hampshire's Deputy Police and Crime Commissioner are amongst some of the measures KES have introduced to transform how wellbeing is talked about. The school were shortlisted as a finalist in the category of outstanding pastoral care in the 2023 Muddy Stilettos Best Schools Awards. This shortlist reflects genuine and sustained progress over the past few years.

King Edward's aims to foster a sense of personal worth in every pupil through a wide range of co-curricular activities, particularly with an active engagement in community work, so that every individual emerges as a fully responsible member of society.

Annually, students take part in excursions to worldwide destinations. Recent cocurricular trips have included a cultural exchange with a school in North Carolina, and a trekking expedition in Tanzania. Language students participate in the exchange programmes on offer to Germany, France and Spain. Closer to home the school also organises an annual summer camp to Swanage for local young carers, run by our Sixth Formers.

Sport and the arts are an integral part of school life. Students are given the opportunity to represent the school across the major team games as well as individual sports. Overseas tours, regular fixtures and tournaments offer a competitive sporting environment and King Edward's boasts 33 acres of sports ground, a fully equipped brand-new, purpose-built gym and multiple all-weather pitches. The Creative Arts Faculty offers an array of facilities from recital rooms, a recording studio and music technology suite to a custom-built dance studio. The state-of-the-art Dobson Theatre provides a superb venue for our talented dramatists and musicians.

Students are actively encouraged to become involved in fund-raising and community work and take part in some of the 150 clubs and societies that are available outside of lesson time.

Seventeen bus routes extend throughout south Hampshire, allowing students from the New Forest, Salisbury, Winchester and east of Southampton easy, direct access to the school.

King Edward VI School is pleased to announce a momentous milestone in its partnership with its Preparatory, Stroud School. After 10 years of a highly successful partnership, Stroud School have revealed that from September 2024, their new name will be King Edward VI Preparatory. The decision to change the name of the prep institution reflects the deepening relationship between Stroud and KES.

(Founded 1553)

Wilton Road, Southampton, Hampshire SO15 5UQ UK

Tel: 023 8070 4561

Fax: 023 8070 5937

Email: registrar@kes.hants.sch.uk

Website: kes.school

Head Master: Mr N T Parker

Appointed: August 2019

School type: Co-educational Day Senior & Sixth Form

Age range of pupils: 11–18 years

No. of pupils enrolled as at 01/09/2023: 988

Fees as at 01/09/2023:

Day: £19,995 per annum

Average class size: 22

Teacher/pupil ratio: 1:10

King Edward's Witley

Pupils thrive at King Edward's. We encourage them to be the best versions of themselves because individual achievement and personal growth count for more than league tables. Our unique heritage and place among British co-educational independent schools means that we can provide the best preparation for adult life to a wider range of young people than almost any other institution.

King Edward's offers your son or daughter a school that can feel as warm and welcoming as home. A springboard to a lifelong love of learning which can nurture confidence, foster collaboration and prepare them for life in a multicultural world. Most of all it can help them discover who they are. This is a school shaped by generosity of spirit, not by background.

Academic focus

A King Edward's education is a rounded education. All academic staff are subject specialists, GCSE/IGCSE in Year 11 followed by a choice of A-level courses in the Sixth Form. Young people discover skills, talents and enthusiasms they never knew they had and are encouraged to set their sights high and be ambitious in their learning. Our rich co-curricular programme broadens their horizons.

Pastoral

All our pupils benefit from small class sizes and our House system with its supportive pastoral networks at the heart of school life. Each House is committed to strong connections uniting and blending boarders and day pupils into a single team. Diversity has been a strength since our foundation in 1553 and while most of our 440 pupils are local, we attract international pupils from more than 30 countries. They help teach us what it means to be part of the wider human family.

Boarding

King Edward's is a thriving community with four senior boys and two senior girls Houses for day, weekly and flexi boarders. Lower School pupils in Years 7 and 8 reside in Queen Mary House, an impressive family-oriented building steeped in history. Each House has a pastoral team consisting of a House parent and assistant House parent, Matron and an academic tutor. Additionally, there is a 24-hour Medical Centre and an on-site chaplain.

Mindful of our responsibility to prepare our pupils for the next stage in their educational journey, in September 2022 we opened an impressive Upper Sixth Form House that represents a stepping-stone to the independence and the full university experience. The House provides a unique opportunity, allowing pupils to study independently while honing important life skills, in a vibrant, communal environment consistent with student campus accommodation.

Hobbies and activities

On our leafy, 100-acre site amid the Surrey Hills we have space for all the sport, drama, music, hobbies, and intellectual pursuits a young mind can take. King Edward's is a wonderfully safe place for youthful adventure and curiosity.

The school creates a foundation for life both now and for the future. Our timeless education reaches far beyond the exciting and challenging academic curriculum and the broad range of opportunities in all areas of school life - sporting, artistic, social and cultural.

Pupils leave as independent free-thinkers - agile, motivated, and self-disciplined. The creative, entrepreneurial thinking they develop here gives the next generation of inventors, designers and problem-solvers the ability to grasp life with both hands.

Petworth Road, Godalming, Surrey GU8 5SG UK

Tel: 01428 686700

Email: admissions@kesw.org

Website: www.kesw.org

Head: Mrs Joanna Wright

School type:
Co-educational Day & Boarding Senior & Sixth Form

Religious Denomination: Christian

Age range of pupils: 11–18 years

No. of pupils enrolled as at 01/09/2023: 484

Fees as at 01/09/2023:

Day: £20,025–£23,985 per annum

Weekly Boarding: £35,985–£36,990 per annum

Full Boarding: £38,205–£38,955 per annum

Average class size: 12–20

King's School Rochester

King's School Rochester is a remarkable school with a rich and diverse heritage, where pupils have been educated for over 1,400 years under the watchful gaze of Rochester Cathedral and Rochester Castle. Founded in 604AD, King's is the second oldest school in the world and the world's oldest Cathedral Choir School.

While a sense of place is bound to have an impact on the development of the children learning here, it is the skills, experiences and opportunities provided to them, both inside and outside the classroom, that will enable them to thrive in an uncertain and fast-changing world.

At King's, we believe in preparing children for the 21st century through educating the whole child. Our priority though, is ensuring that happy children perform to their best and the school is an exceptionally happy and friendly place where moral values, self-discipline, emotional intelligence and a Christion spirit underpin our family community.

Our academic results ore excellent at all levels but we believe that building a love of learning and developing independent thinking skills are just as important as achieving the best grades. We keep our class sizes small so that teachers know their pupils as individuals and can help each of them shine. We ore a school where all are cared for and where links between home and school ore a real strength.

We offer and encourage pupils to take part in a huge range of co-curricular opportunities to ignite and nurture their interests, providing experiences which will develop confidence in them for life. Sport, Music, Drama, Outdoor Pursuits, CCF and a range of clubs and societies are integral to the school's commitment to provide a broad education al experience.

Music is a huge strength and we are privileged to use Rochester Cathedral as our chapel. We hold seasonal concerts throughout the year in the Nave and the Cathedral. Choristers are educated in our Preparatory School. Music Scholars go on to leading international conservatoires.

Under the refurbished Vines Church is our Drama studio, equipped with digital sound and lighting. We are a proud Royal Shakespeare Company Associate School and our pupils have staged productions across Kent. King's has a strong reputation for exceptional drama performances and productions of "Titanic the Musical" and "Fiddler on the Roof" have been comparable to the standard of productions in the West End.

Our coaches and many of our pupils play at county, national and international level. The King's School Rochester Sports Centre provides pupils with extensive facilities to train, in addition to playing fields, a heated indoor swimming pool and boat house situated on the bank of the River Medway, while the Paddock is regarded as one of the finest cricket fields in the county.

The boarding community at King's reflects the personal approach of the school. Boarding starts from age 11 and we have 55 beds across our two boarding houses, St Margaret's House for girls and School House for boys. The small boarding community ensures o real boutique and family-feel to both boarding houses which are comprised of both British and international pupils.

We offer co-education from 3 to 18 and our structure of Pre-Prep, Prep and Senior Schools enables us to offer a tailor-made experience for each age group while giving access to the excellent facilities of the whole school.

King's School Rochester is in every sense a school for life.

(Founded 604 AD)

Satis House, Boley Hill, Rochester, Kent ME1 1TE UK

Tel: 01634 888555

Email: admissions@kings-rochester.co.uk

Website: www.kings-rochester.co.uk

Principal: Mr B Charles

Appointed: 2019

School type: Co-educational Day & Boarding Prep & Senior, Nursery & Sixth Form

Age range of pupils: 3–18 years

No. of pupils enrolled as at 01/09/2023: 680

Sixth Form: 105

No. of boarders: 55

Fees as at 01/09/2023:

Day: £2,895–£7,765 per term

Full Boarding: £8,870–£12,860 per term

Average class size: 18

Teacher/pupil ratio: 1:9 (Years 1–8) & 1:7 (Years 9–13)

Maltman's Green School

Our Approach

At Maltman's Green we believe in the pursuit of excellence with a sense of fun. Girls are inspired to do their best inside and outside of the classroom through an ambitious and dynamic curriculum, extensive extra-curricular opportunities, a nurturing environment and dedicated staff. We prepare girls for the modern world through a relevant, adaptable and innovative approach that is supported by a foundation of traditional values. Our girls are given every opportunity to succeed across multiple disciplines, fostering confidence and self-belief, and empowering them for whatever future awaits.

We believe that the emotional, social and physical wellbeing of our girls is paramount. By providing a personalised learning experience in an encouraging and nurturing environment, we ensure our girls feel happy, confident and valued - a perfect foundation from which children can flourish.

Games and The Arts

Our sports provision is an outstanding feature of the school, with dedicated facilities and daily lessons. All girls enjoy friendly tournaments between houses and within year groups where those with the talent and inclination can progress to squad level to compete locally, regionally or nationally, usually with exceptional results.

Music is a very important part of life at Maltman's Green. Specialist teaching, exceptional facilities and lots of choice give our girls plenty of opportunity to explore and showcase their musical talents. Many of our girls participate in various choirs and we have a wide choice of musical instrument lessons available as well as a variety of instrumental ensemble groups to join. Drama too has a big part to play in school life where regular performances and workshops give girls a strong sense of confidence and creative expression. Our dedicated performance space with high-quality staging, lighting, costumes and props give our shows a professional feel.

Achievements

Our girls are encouraged to be independent thinkers, to challenge themselves and to always try their best. Maltman's Green provides a firm foundation, preparing girls to face senior school and beyond with confidence, determination and a lifelong love of learning. This is reflected in our impressive Bucks Secondary Transfer Test (11+) results, 81% qualification rate for 2021/22, and twenty scholarships awarded to Independent Senior Schools. This, combined with our girls' impressive achievements across sport, music and drama, affirm our position as one of the foremost prep schools in the country.

Outstanding Characteristics

Our rigorous approach and excellent teaching were highlighted by the Independent Schools Inspectorate (ISI) at their most recent inspection in February 2022, when Maltman's Green was awarded "excellent" in all areas - an outstanding achievement. *"The quality of the pupils' academic and other achievements is excellent. Pupils of all ages and abilities make excellent progress over time because of the systematic use of the assessment framework in planning for individual needs. Pupils' linguistic and other mathematical skills are outstanding, and pupils apply these with great confidence to other areas of learning. Pupils demonstrate excellent attitudes to learning when the curriculum creates opportunities for them to develop independence in their learning. Pupils readily think for themselves and acquire higher-order thinking skills which they instinctively apply to all areas of learning."*

(Founded 1918)

Maltmans Lane, Gerrards Cross, Buckinghamshire SL9 8RR UK

Tel: 01753 883022

Email: registrar@maltmansgreen.com

Website: www.maltmansgreen.com

Headmistress: Mrs Jill Walker BSc (Hons), MA Ed, PGCE

Appointed: 2020

School type: Girls' Day Preparatory & Nursery

Age range of girls: 2–11 years

No. of pupils enrolled as at 01/09/2023: 330

Fees as at 01/09/2023:

Day: £2,850 Nursery (5 mornings & 1 afternoon)–£6,500 Year 6 (per term)

Meet my bear!

Manor House School, Bookham

Founded in 1920 and having celebrated its Centenary Year in 2020–2021, Manor House School can be found nestled amidst seventeen acres of gardens, woodland and sports fields in the village of Bookham, Surrey.

Manor House School is a selective independent Day School for girls aged 4–16 with a Co-Educational Nursery and Lower Prep. It provides a smaller, nurturing learning environment producing consistently great academic results in a happy, friendly, and caring school environment.

Our staff are passionate about laying strong foundations for the children in Nursery and Lower Prep. As a member of the GSA (Girls' School Association) our aim is to support and develop happy individuals who love coming to school and believe in their abilities to learn and succeed.

Manor House School is one of the three schools in the Effingham Schools Trust partnership, which forms a dynamic triumvirate. Effingham Schools Trust diamond model offers benefits to the co-ed classroom for very young pupils, the benefits of single sex education in later, Prep and Secondary years, before returning to a co-educational Sixth Form. Families joining the Trust will have provision for boys and/or girls from 2–18 years across the three schools.

There is an extensive co-curricular enrichment programme with over 50 extra-curricular clubs and activities operating across the school each term. Pupils are encouraged to seek out new experiences and try something new. Manor House School achieves excellent Key Stage 2 and GCSE results. For more information on their latest results, please visit www.manorhouseschool.org/academic-results/gcseresults.

Seven School values form the foundations of school life and the school motto 'To Love is to Live' was chosen in 1921 by the Bishop of Plymouth, Dr Masterman, who was a close friend of one of the school's original founders.

Manor House School pupils enjoy high levels of success in all areas of Sport boasting some future world class athletes. There is a popular Senior Scholarships programme from Year 7 (application in Year 6) offering Major and Minor Academic Scholarships and Art, Sport, Drama and Music awards.

Facilities include an award-winning Nursery, Forest School which transforms into a seated theatre space for professional productions, outdoor swimming pool, a Tennis Academy, Tennis and Netball courts, Football and Hockey pitches and purpose-built Science blocks. Pupils enjoy many opportunities in the creative and expressive arts, with additional music, singing and drama lessons a popular choice.

The school day operates from 7:45am to 6pm to accommodate working and/or busy parents. Fees include a daily hot lunch and there is a minibus service in the morning and afternoons and a late bus to Effingham train station which is serviced by good rail connections, The school bus routes service Ashtead, Dorking, Claygate, Cobham, Epsom, Esher, Fetcham, Guildford, Hinchley Wood, Kingswood, Kinston, Walton-on-Thames, West Byfleet, Weybridge, Wimbledon and surrounding areas.

For more information visit www.manorhouseschool.org. There are three main Open Morning events per year in October, March and May. For more information contact admissions@manorhouseschool.org.

(Founded 1920)

Manor House Lane, Little Bookham, Leatherhead, Surrey KT23 4EN UK

Tel: 01372 457077

Email: admin@manorhouseschool.org

Website: www.manorhouseschool.org

Headteacher: Ms Tracey Fantham BA (Hons) MA NPQH

School type:
Girls' Day, Co-ed Pre-Preparatory & Nursery

Age range of boys: 2–6 years

Age range of girls: 2–16 years

No. of pupils enrolled as at 01/09/2023: 280

Fees as at 01/09/2023:

Day: £10,980–£20,634 per annum

Average class size: 15–20

Northbourne Park School

Northbourne Park School is an independent day and boarding school for children from 2 to 13. Set in over 100 acres of beautiful park and woodland in rural Kent, the school is within easy reach from central London, Eurostar and Gatwick Airport. Northbourne Park School provides children with a first-class education focusing on the individual needs of every child, inspiring them to succeed across a wide range of learning experiences. Our setting offers each child a safe environment with freedom and space and countless opportunities to grow in confidence and succeed.

Academic

Northbourne Park School is an environment where each and every child can flourish. Pupils gain confidence in their learning and through inspirational teaching from dedicated staff and an engaging and stimulating curriculum, their results are phenomenal. We focus on individual needs and consistently achieve academic excellence, with many of our pupils gaining scholarships to top Senior Schools. The school's Language Programme helps every child develop foreign languages in an integrated learning environment. The result is a clear advantage when they move on to Senior Schools.

Sport

We are passionate about sport and through an excellent sports programme the pupils develop key skills and learn the importance of teamwork and leadership. We coach traditional sports as well as more diverse activities such as archery. The school has excellent facilities including a brand new all-weather sports pitch.

Creative Arts

We nurture a love for all the Arts. Many pupils learn one or more instruments in our purpose-built Music suite. They have the opportunity to take part in the choir, band, orchestra, string and brass groups performing regularly within the school and in the local area. Other opportunities include LAMDA lessons, regular drama productions and Public Speaking that ensure the pupils are articulate and confident in their performances. Artistic talents are encouraged through a range of media including sculpture, costume design, 3D printing and pottery.

Community

Pupils are provided with a first-class level of pastoral care in a safe and nurturing environment with a real family atmosphere. Our welcoming boarding community provides a home-from-home environment and a continuous boarding service at weekends throughout the term. Boarders enjoy regular excursions and activities, and the accompanied services to London and Paris provide opportunities for weekends at home. Northbourne Park School holds a Child Student Sponsor Licence for non-European pupils requiring visas under the UK Visa and Immigration Service scheme.

Extra Curricular

We provide the pupils with a fun and extensive programme of afternoon clubs that help develop their interests and skills. Love of the outdoors and respect for the environment begins in the Pre-Prep and develops through into the Prep School with fun physical adventures. Whether they are playing in the woods, camping out overnight or following our Outdoor Education Programme, children love Northbourne Park life.

The children are at the heart of everything we do and it is important to us that they learn with confidence and enjoy each and every day at school. All prospective pupils are welcome and we offer a wide range of scholarships.

Every day is an Open Day at Northbourne Park School, come and visit us!

(Founded 1936)

Betteshanger, Deal, Kent CT14 0NW UK

Tel: 01304 611215

Email: admissions@northbournepark.com

Website: www.northbournepark.com

Headmaster: Mr Mark Hammond BA (Hons), PGCE, MA

Appointed: September 2023

School type:
Co-educational Day & Boarding Preparatory & Nursery

Age range of pupils: 2–13 years (boarding from 7)

No. of pupils enrolled as at 01/09/2023: 176

Boys: 97 ***Girls:*** 79

No. of boarders: 43

Fees as at 01/09/2023:

Day: £11,025–£18,663 per annum

Weekly Boarding: £23,490 per annum

Full Boarding: £27,198 per annum

Average class size: 15

Ryde School with Upper Chine

A Breath of Fresh Air Every Day

Based on the Isle of Wight just off the south coast of England (one of the warmest locations in the UK), we are a Round Square and IB World School, an island school with a global outlook. The importance of community sits at the heart of our school and we expect pupils to be true to our values of ambition, responsibility, courage and respect. Our pupils work hard and we challenge them to make the most of their talents and the opportunities in front of them.

The school is located in the Victorian town of Ryde with its high-speed connections to mainland rail and air services. Cowes, the home of international sailing, is 30 minutes away.

Boarding is in two beautifully appointed boarding houses in the school grounds in Ryde. Our Junior Boarding house, Millfield, for boys and girls in Years 6 to 10 and our Senior Boarding house, Centenary, for Year 11 and Sixth Form.

We pride ourselves on aiming high for our pupils and offering many diverse activities alongside our academic teaching to build resilient, confident pupils ready to embrace the wider world. Main sports, such as netball, cricket, rugby and hockey are played against schools on and off island with football, athletics, croquet and riding also on offer. Sailing is built into the curriculum with beginner to elite sailors thriving at Ryde. The school has an excellent record of academic achievement throughout all age groups and was the first independent school in the UK to offer the IB Career-related Programme alongside the IB Diploma Programme and our A Level Plus Programme, through which pupils study for A Levels but also take advantage of the IB courses on offer and add them as enrichment options. We also offer a one year GCSE and Pre-Sixth Form course providing excellent preparation for entry into the Sixth Form.

Pupils leave to go on to study at Oxbridge, medical schools, other Russell Group Universities and Art, Music and Drama colleges. Pupils succeed academically and are well-mannered, characterful, happy and independent; a result of Ryde School's dynamic yet welcoming environment.

Boarding pupils live in two boarding houses within the 17 acres of school grounds: Millfield, a sensitively renovated Victorian villa for the younger boarders or the new purpose-built Centenary House, with stunning sea views, designed to prepare older students for university and adult life. Both houses have multiple common rooms, study areas and single and twin bedrooms, mostly en-suite. Weekends are spent learning to paddle board, go-karting or simply enjoying long walks on the beaches with a boarding house dog. Barbecues and football are regular pursuits as well as cooking and now bee keeping with our Ryde bee hives and cooking in our new cookery school.

Day pupils range from local Island families to those travelling to the school daily from Portsmouth and the surrounding areas on the mainland via the 10 minute hovercraft service. Boarding options include full, weekly and flexi with a diverse boarding community including around 13 different nationalities. Ryde is only 90 minutes from Heathrow and parents embrace the weekly and flexi boarding option to enable them to live on the island or nearby and commute more widely to work, on the mainland and further afield. Breakfast and supper clubs and school buses across the island augment that flexibility for our pupils.

Our Open Mornings are a great time to view the school as is our annual Summer School during four weeks of July and August. We also offer individual tours throughout the year and will work with you to find a suitable time if you are visiting the Island for a short period.

RYDE SCHOOL
WITH UPPER CHINE

(Founded 1921)

Queen's Road, Ryde, Isle of Wight PO33 3BE UK

Tel: 01983 562229

Email: admissions@rydeschool.net

Website: www.rydeschool.org.uk

Headmaster: Mr Will Turner

Appointed: August 2022

School type: Co-educational Day & Boarding Prep & Senior, Nursery & Sixth Form

Age range of pupils: 2–18 years (boarding from 10)

No. of pupils enrolled as at 01/09/2023: 795

Fees as at 01/09/2023:

Day: £3,128–£5,542 per term

Weekly Boarding: £10,766–£10,950 per term

Full Boarding: £12,099–£12,283 per term

Average class size: 15–22

Teacher/pupil ratio: 1:12

Seaford College

Seaford College is a coeducational independent day and boarding school for pupils aged 5 to 18, situated amid 400 acres of picturesque parkland in West Sussex. The College, with its excellent amenities and outstanding panoramic views, offers an inspirational environment that nurtures academic excellence, sporting success and creative talent.

The college uses its resources to provide and enhance educational, cultural, spiritual and social opportunities so that students leave school as confident, articulate and well-rounded individuals.

Pupils in the Preparatory School at Seaford College share the superb facilities with the Senior School and enjoy a seamless education from 6 to 18. The Prep School prides itself on its friendly atmosphere.

Boarding is offered to students from the age of 10 and many pupils elect to board in order to take full advantage of the social, sporting and extracurricular activities on offer. The College offers full boarding, weekly and flexible boarding in order to meet the needs of pupils and their parents.

A new boys' boarding house, has individual and twin bedrooms opened in 2011. Girls board in the historic Mansion house. Recent developments include a new music suite, which consists of individual teaching and practice rooms, a computer and keyboard room, a sound-proofed band practice room and outdoor concert arena.

A state-of-the-art maths and science block offers the latest technologies and facilities, while the College has long been recognised as a centre of excellence for art and design. A large exhibition gallery is incorporated into the purpose-built arts faculty.

Seaford College offers outstanding sports facilities, including an all-weather water-based Astroturf hockey pitch, golf course and driving range. Students regularly play at county level. A state-of-the-art sports centre was opened in 2017.

Overseas students are expected to study English as a foreign language and study for the International Language Testing System, which is a requirement for UK university entrance.

Seaford opened an impressive Sixth Form centre in September 2019. They have their own social areas, study areas and cafe. Seaford sees its Sixth Form very much as a transitional stage. They have their own social centre, which has facilities for individual study, a lounge area and several classrooms where subjects such as Economics, Business Studies and Media Studies are taught.

Sixth Form boarders have study bedrooms, as well as their own common room. Students are divided into small tutor groups, but most commonly meet on a 1-to-1 basis with their tutors to discuss aspects of their work and progress.

Many of Seaford's Sixth Formers go on to university or higher education – all are equipped with self-confidence, as well as a passion for life and a willingness to succeed.

Entry to the College is by test and Trial Day and, although intake is non-selective, expectations are high. If your child is talented and enthusiastic, the College offers a range of scholarships at 11+, 13+ and Sixth Form, including Academic Studies, Music, Art and Sport.

The college has its own dedicated learning support unit, catering for pupils with dyslexia, dyscalculia and dyspraxia.

Whatever their chosen path, Seaford College seeks to prepare young people for adult life so that they have the personal skills and confidence to make it a success. The school allows its pupils to achieve their potential and beyond, inspiring personal ambition and success so that personal ambitions are achieved inside and outside the classroom.

(Founded 1884)

Lavington Park, Petworth, West Sussex GU28 0NB UK

Tel: 01798 867392

Fax: 01798 867606

Email: headmasterpa@seaford.org

Website: www.seaford.org

Headmaster: J P Green MA BA

School type: Co-educational Day & Boarding Preparatory, Senior & Sixth Form

Age range of pupils: 5–18 years

No. of pupils enrolled as at 01/09/2023: 943

Boys: 560 ***Girls:*** 383 ***Sixth Form:*** 264

No. of boarders: 214

Fees as at 01/09/2023:

Day: £12,720–£26,355 per annum

Weekly Boarding: £26,475–£35,685

Full Boarding: £40,740 per annum

Average class size: 15–20

Teacher/pupil ratio: 1:9

Sherborne House School

Sherborne House School is a small co-ed day school just outside of Chandlers Ford. Sitting in four acres of woodland, in the quiet village of Hiltingbury, it caters for 272 pupils between the ages of 6 months and 11 years, with average class sizes of just twelve.

The school was inspected by the Independent Schools Inspectorate in July 2021, which rated it 'excellent in all areas'. Being part of Bellevue Education, a world-class group of exceptional schools, Sherborne House remains dedicated to providing the best possible education to their children.

In addition, personal development at the school was ranked Excellent in the last ISI report and is something the school is particularly proud of. *"We tell the children all the time to make the most of every opportunity they're given. That really does prepare them for the future in which they can embrace and explore everything that comes their way."*

The nursery provision from 6 months to 4 years is award winning. Fully renovated in 2020, the nursery takes children aged between 6 months to 3 years. Close, nurturing attention is paid to the small classes and weekly specialist French, music and P.E. lessons for those aged two upwards.

Through the purposeful and busy atmosphere within the school gates, it is evident that each child at Sherborne House is encouraged to explore. The children learn by pursuing their own interests, cultivating their curiosity, developing tenacity and providing the confidence to own their own voice.

The school's language of learning encourages children to reflect on the mental processes and the skills they use and apply in their self-driven learning journey. Rather than simply praising success (or a final outcome), they celebrate effort, persistence and positive attitudes to the frequent challenges in the process of learning. By empowering their children to develop their 'learning to learn' skills, the school aims to improve outcomes for all.

Sherborne House boasts a curriculum which is irresistible; allowing children to embrace challenges with resilience and to enjoy the effort and mistakes that come with learning. Indeed, children at Sherborne House are evidently intrigued by the how and why of mistakes made; acting on constructive feedback and offering praise for a job well done. This visibly consistent approach was articulated most profoundly to us by children during our visit. When talking about their learning, the children spoke proudly about the focus their teachers have on relevance, on their interests and on fun; 'Our teachers listen to us and we lead our learning with their support.'

This is mirrored in the school's aim; to engender confidence in exploration entwined with awe about learning - to sew a golden thread which interweaves throughout a child's life enabling their enquiring mind, to go on to write their own extraordinary story.

39 Lakewood Road, Chandlers Ford, Eastleigh, Hampshire SO53 1EU UK

Tel: 02380 252440

Email: info@sherbornehouse.co.uk

Website: www.sherbornehouse.co.uk

Head of School: Mrs Cordelia Cripps

Appointed: September 2023

School type:
Co-educational Day Preparatory & Nursery

Age range of pupils: 6 months–11 years

Sherfield School

Sherfield School is a leading co-educational independent day and boarding school for children from 3 months to 18 years. It offers an outstanding, all-round academic, active and creative environment where children of all ages have the opportunity to thrive and flourish as they experience the excitement and enjoyment of learning.

Set in 76 acres of idyllic parkland in Hampshire, the 12th Century manor house is at the heart of Sherfield school and boasts a wealth of history linked to the local community. Sherfield School lies nestled in beautiful countryside between Reading and Basingstoke. With good public transport links and its own minibus service, Sherfield is set in a safe, semi-rural setting, yet within close proximity to London.

Pupils at Sherfield benefit from rich and diverse learning experiences, both within and outside the classroom. There are a range of high quality facilities including indoor sports hall, drama studio, two synthetic all-weather surfaces, fitness suite, recording studio and extensive woodland. The state of the art boarding house offers full, weekly and flexi boarding options, in a vibrant and engaging environment offered to domestic and international pupils.

The co-curricular provision is extensive, with provision from 7.30am to 6pm for day pupils and evening and weekend activities for boarders. Sherfield runs an extraordinary enrichment programme which promotes the life-skills needed for everyday life, develop "soft-skills" that employers and universities look for, while also giving pupils the opportunity to find out more about their interests and passions. Outdoor learning is embedded in the ethos of the school, providing opportunities for pupils to learn in different contexts and develop a blend of academic and non-academic experiences.

At Sherfield, we strongly believe in a holistic approach to learning, and one that results in continued development, unleashing the true potential of passionate and creative problem solvers that make up this vibrant school. Children are ready to continue their journey long after leaving Sherfield and contribute to an ever changing global society.

An education at Sherfield is unique, as every pupil receives personalised support and guidance, identifying their individual talents and nurturing their potential. The Sherfield experience enables young people to thrive and flourish as they experience the excitement and enjoyment of learning. Pupils at Sherfield are ambitious, enterprising, inventive, thoughtful, inquisitive and supportive of each other. As a close knit community, they develop the confidence and desire to be the best they can possibly be as they take control of their futures. In an ever changing and evolving society, Sherfield pupils are adept at developing the necessary skills, qualities and experiences to meet the challenges of the future.

At Sherfield great academic results are just a by-product of something even bigger, a brilliant, well-rounded education that identifies and celebrates every child's strengths, and teaches them how to become the best version of themselves. As our Latin motto 'Ad Vitam Paramus' suggests, Sherfield prepares children for life.

South Drive, Sherfield-on-Loddon, Hook, Hampshire RG27 0HU UK

Tel: 01256 884800

Email: admissions@sherfieldschool.co.uk

Website: www.sherfieldschool.co.uk

Headmaster: TBC

School type: Co-educational Day & Boarding Prep & Senior, Nursery & Sixth Form

Age range of pupils: 3 months–18 years (boarding from 9)

No. of pupils enrolled as at 01/09/2023: 609

Fees as at 01/09/2023: Please see website

Sir William Perkins's School

Making your mark on the world begins on day one at Sir William Perkins's School.

We are an independent day school for girls aged 11 to 18 where every student is supported to achieve great things, and where curiosity, ambition and generosity thrive. We are home to approximately 600 students who join us from independent and maintained schools, and who flourish within a diverse, vibrant, and happy community.

At SWPS, students are at our heart. We expect the best from them, and in return they can expect the best from us. We provide teaching of the highest quality, where every individual is stretched and challenged and given tailored support and attention. SWPS is a warm and friendly school: the staff know our students, their talents, hopes and aspirations, and we work with them to develop innate confidence, leadership skills and an ability to collaborate with others.

Set in 13 acres of attractive green-belt grounds in Surrey, Sir William Perkins's School is a beautiful environment in which every student can flourish. With first-rate facilities equipped to the highest standard, students have space in which to study, relax, exercise and express themselves.

Academic success is consistently high at SWPS. Our students' most recent GCSE and A Level results stem from a winning formula; they are testament to students' determination and resilience, coupled with our excellent teaching resources. We are delighted that the 2023 GCSE results were 39% grade 9 and 80% grades 9–7. For A Level, 84% were grades A* - B and 51% were grades A* - A. Students consistently achieve outstanding results in STEM subjects - Chemistry, Biology, Maths, Further Maths, Physics and Computer Science. However, the culture is such that education is about far more than achieving top grades. Students are encouraged to become involved in many of the 150 co-curricular activities on offer, with clubs as diverse as Sewing and Dissection. Almost all our students take part in the Duke of Edinburgh Award Scheme, with the number taking the Gold Award among the highest in Surrey.

We pride ourselves on our commitment to pastoral care, with a fully staffed wellbeing room and even a visiting therapy dog. Music, Art and Drama permeate through the school with concerts, productions and exhibitions throughout the year. Sport is high on the agenda and students play competitive fixtures in netball, hockey, tennis, cricket and athletics. Other activities are available such as football, trampolining and dance. We are an elite rowing school - currently ranked in the top 5 girls' schools in the country and this year have achieved notable successes at, among others, the National Schools Regatta and the Henley Royal Regatta where SWPS was one of only two girls' school programmes to have qualified both a quad and an eight, meaning that thirteen of our students experienced the magic of Henley, with the global livestream, the thrill of the atmosphere, and the top-level international competition.

The school's Sixth Form Centre offers education to the highest standard, as well as welcoming spaces for students to study or relax. Sir William Perkins's School's UCAS preparation programme starts mid-way through Year 12 and continues to the end of Year 13. This focused approach also includes a Higher Education Fair featuring 50 of the most prestigious learning establishments, and a UCAS conference day with specialist speakers providing advice on a wide range of subjects.

SWPS students are prepared for all aspects of life beyond school, most recently 90% of our Sixth Form students secured their first choice university place, and 75% of our students went onto Russell Group universities.

(Founded 1725)

Guildford Road, Chertsey, Surrey KT16 9BN UK

Tel: 01932 574900

Fax: 01932 574901

Email: reg@swps.org.uk

Website: www.swps.org.uk

Head: Ms D Picton

Appointed: September 2023

School type: Girls' Day Senior & Sixth Form

Age range of girls: 11–18 years

No. of pupils enrolled as at 01/09/2023: 600

Fees as at 01/09/2023:

Day: £6,808 per term

Average class size: Senior School: 24, Sixth Form: 10

Teacher/pupil ratio: 1:8

Skippers Hill Manor Preparatory School

"Skippers is a magical school. A place where every child can be the child they want to be. The school caters brilliantly for all three of my very different children who are happy and thriving. It's a gem of a place with a fab reputation, I wouldn't hesitate recommending Skippers." Current parent 2023

The children at Skippers Hill are at the heart of the school and ensuring their happiness and wellbeing is key. The high academic achievement, broad range of talents and impressive social confidence that the children show year after year is embedded in the school's core ethos. Their smiles speak for themselves!

An excellent team of specialist staff provide exciting opportunities for the children to achieve to the best of their abilities in all areas. Whether they thrive on academic challenge, feel a burning desire to perform, are bursting with creative spirit or can't wait to hit the sports field, the children are encouraged to make the most of every opportunity.

The strong academic results speak for themselves, with children consistently performing above national and local averages at every stage of their education. For a mixed ability school, Skippers has an excellent reputation for gaining significant numbers of scholarships for entry to top senior schools at 13+ across a range of disciplines. The school has strong, long-standing relationships with the senior schools in the area and Skippers children are highly sought-after for their sound academic grounding, strong sense of community spirit and overall zest for life.

Skippers is privileged to enjoy a stunning rural setting in 22 acres of beautiful Sussex countryside that truly enables the all-round development of the children in their care. Children are provided with the space to flourish in every sense and the bespoke programme of outdoor learning is interwoven throughout the curriculum for all ages.

Skippers is a warm and welcoming community; a visit to the school would be strongly advised in order to experience the energy for yourself and to gain a deeper understanding of what a special place Skippers is.

"I was completely blown away by how happy everyone was! The atmosphere was calm and extremely happy and I loved the relationship that has so clearly been built up between all the adults and the children." Prospective parent 2023

After a recent visit the headmaster of Tonbridge, James Priory commented:

"I was really impressed by their gentle confidence, the enthusiasm they showed for academic subjects and co-curricular pursuits, and the extent to which they knew and encouraged each other in their interests."

Five Ashes, Mayfield, East Sussex TN20 6HR UK

Tel: 01825 830234

Email: info@skippershill.com

Website: www.skippershill.com

Headmaster: Mr Phillip Makhouli

School type:
Co-educational Day Preparatory & Nursery

Age range of pupils: 2–13 years

Fees as at 01/09/2023:

Day: £3,402–£5,391 per term

St George's Ascot

St George's is a thriving independent boarding and day school for girls aged 11–18 offering an ambitious, connected and future-facing education tailored for girls to realise their potential both at school and in fulfilling adult lives ahead. Awarded 'excellent' in its November 2022 ISI inspection, the report speaks of pupils demonstrating 'healthy self-knowledge, well developed study skills, first-class social skills and an awareness of the world around them.'

The St George's ethos, and education, focuses on developing Confident, Capable and Connected young women who are thoroughly prepared for the world beyond school. Learning in an all-girls environment fosters confidence as girls are emboldened to innovate, lead and express informed views free from gender stereotypes. They are, as a recent Head Girl explained, at 'the centre of their own story' throughout their time at the school. They are exposed to a wide range of opportunities both inside and outside of the classroom, developing excellence in academic, sporting, musical, dramatic and creative pursuits. Throughout their time at St George's pupils are encouraged to connect across the diverse school community but also with the world around them and so they develop a strong sense of what they want to bring to and how they will challenge the society they will ultimately join.

Pupils enjoy facilities that 'might easily belong to a school three times the size' (2023 Good Schools Guide review), with four art studios, a state of the art 6-lane swimming pool, a 300-seat theatre, a Cookery & Food Technology room, and brand new music recording studio. Yet the school is small enough to develop markedly strong relationships across the community. Each pupil is known and supported by a close network of boarding, teaching and pastoral staff who help shape and develop each individual. Examination results are excellent with regular Oxbridge success, a high percentage attending Russell Group universities in both the sciences and humanities and a strong number of girls choosing post-18 options in the Arts in courses ranging from visual effects, fine art, textiles and fashion to photography. A recent value-added figure for the school at GCSE placed St George's 7th out of 344 schools. In 2023, the school maintained the excellent A Level standards achieved in 2022, with 43% of grades awarded at A*-A, 72% of grades at A*-B and nearly a third of the Upper Sixth leavers achieving all A* and A grades.

The school is a finalist in the Independent Girls School of the Year category for the upcoming Independent Schools of the Year 2023 Awards. During 2022, St George's was also shortlisted for a number of industry awards and chosen as a finalist in the prestigious Tes Awards' category for Innovative Learning. After a demanding application process, the school was also recently awarded Google for Education Reference School status as a mark of the tremendous work that has been done to integrate technology in the classroom and innovate teaching methodology in collaboration with Google Education. The History Department was also proud to have been awarded the Historical Association's Gold Quality Mark with assessors noting the department's 'strong desire to become a centre of excellence for the transformation of history education.'

Pupils benefit from a sizeable and diverse co-curricular programme with over 70 clubs on offer through the 'working week' for the girls to enjoy. With sports clubs in abundance, a Gardening Club, the SGA 'Googley' Google Diploma Club, Amnesty International, a Cultural Diversity Club and Model United Nations on the list, there is plenty to spark the girls' interest.

ST GEORGE'S
ASCOT

Wells Lane, Ascot, Berkshire SL5 7DZ UK

Tel: 01344 629900

Email: admissions@stgeorges-ascot.org.uk

Website: www.stgeorges-ascot.org.uk

Head: Mrs Liz Hewer MA (Hons) (Cantab) PGCE

Appointed: 2016

School type: Girls' Day & Boarding Senior & Sixth Form

Age range of girls: 11–18 years (boarding from 11)

No. of pupils enrolled as at 01/09/2023: 270

Fees as at 01/09/2023: Please see website

Average class size: 17

St Lawrence College

Founded in 1879, St Lawrence College is a thriving independent day and boarding school, providing a first class education for boys and girls from 3 to 18 years. Currently, we have approximately 535 pupils - 127 in the Junior School and 408 in the Senior School, of which 169 are boarders (boarding from 7 years of age).

Located in the Kent coastal town of Ramsgate, and within easy walking distance of the sea, the school is set in 45 acres of safe and spacious grounds, housing both beautiful historic architecture and outstanding contemporary facilities.

In the Classroom

Academic standards are high across the school, which offers an extensive choice of GCSEs and A-levels, with an excellent success rate of pupils going on to their first choice of university. We ensure pupils attain their personal best academically, whilst preparing them for life in a rapidly changing global society. Modern facilities combined with traditional values, based on our Christian roots, draw out the talents of each pupil, whilst our policy for keeping class sizes small ensures that our teachers can look after the individual needs of each pupil.

Outside the Classroom

Sporting facilities are exceptional, and expert coaching is provided at all levels in a variety of disciplines, including rugby, netball, hockey and cricket. The magnificent sports centre houses a fitness suite, squash courts, climbing wall, dance studio and a large sports hall for activities such as badminton and basketball.

Music and drama flourish, enhanced by the school's 500-seat theatre, and there are many opportunities for pupils to perform. All pupils benefit from an extensive activities programme which in the Senior School includes the CCF (Combined Cadet Force) and a thriving Duke of Edinburgh's Award Scheme, as well as chess, archery, golf, fencing, football, sailing, horse riding, swimming, table tennis, musical theatre and many more activities.

Boarding at St Lawrence

Strong pastoral care, high quality teaching and a great emphasis on extra-curricular activity make this a very special community in which to live and learn. Boarding is central to the school's life and is one of our great strengths. A wide range of evening and weekend activities are provided for boarders, along with additional events and fun day trips. We offer full time and weekly boarding options, and we aim to provide a 'home-from-home' for our boarding pupils, both in terms of comfort and atmosphere. In recent years, a substantial programme of investment has created exceptional boarding facilities, with all rooms en-suite.

Location

The self-contained campus is situated within easy walking distance of the historic seaside town of Ramsgate. It has excellent transport links to the continent, being near to both Dover and the Channel Tunnel. London is only 75 minutes away by high-speed rail link to St Pancras International. Gatwick and Heathrow are under two hours away.

ST LAWRENCE
COLLEGE

(Founded 1879)

College Road, Ramsgate, Kent CT11 7AE UK

Tel: 01843 572931

Email: admissions@slcuk.com

Website: www.slcuk.com

Head of College: Mr Barney Durrant

School type: Co-educational Day & Boarding Prep & Senior, Nursery & Sixth Form

Age range of pupils: 3–18 years

No. of pupils enrolled as at 01/09/2023: 535

No. of boarders: 169

Fees as at 01/09/2023:

Day: £8,814–£20,877 per annum

Full Boarding: £29,454–£40,899 per annum

Teacher/pupil ratio: 1:8

TAYLOR HALL

St Swithun's School

Compassion, integrity, and a quiet sense of self-confidence
St Swithun's School is a renowned independent boarding and day school for girls set in 45 acres overlooking the Hampshire Downs on the outskirts of Winchester, yet only 55 minutes by train from central London. It offers excellent teaching, sporting and recreational facilities.

Boarding at St Swithun's is designed with the modern family in mind. The range of boarding options allows parents to balance the demands of a busy lifestyle, reassured that their daughter has access to a huge breadth of opportunities, first class academic and pastoral support, further education expertise and the secure, homely atmosphere of a contemporary British boarding house.

The school has a long-standing reputation for academic rigour and success. Girls are prepared for public examinations and higher education in a stimulating environment in which they develop intellectual curiosity, independence of mind and the ability to take responsibility for their own learning. They achieve almost one grade higher at GCSE than their already significant baseline ability would suggest, and approximately half a grade higher at A level. St Swithun's offers a comprehensive careers and higher education support service throughout the school years. Its Oxbridge preparation is part of a whole-school academic enrichment programme providing additional challenge and stimulation.

St Swithun's describes itself as an 'appropriately academic' school, celebrating intellectual curiosity and the life of the mind, but not to the exclusion of all else. They expect their pupils to develop individual passions and through them to acquire a range of skills and characteristics. These characteristics will include a willingness to take risks, to question and to debate, and to persevere in the face of difficulty. In the words of Samuel Beckett: *"Ever tried. Ever failed. No matter. Try again. Fail again. Fail better."*

Whilst achieving academic excellence, girls also have the opportunity to do 'something else'. There is an extensive co-curricular programme of over 100 weekly and 50 weekend activities to choose from. As well as academic classrooms and science laboratories, there is a magnificent performing arts centre with a 600-seat auditorium, a music school, an art and technology block, a sports hall and a full-size indoor swimming pool. There is an impressive library and ICT facility. The grounds are spacious and encompass sports fields, tennis courts and gardens.

With kindness and tolerance at the heart of its community, St Swithun's provides award winning pastoral care as well as a civilized and caring environment in which all girls are valued for their individual gifts. By the time a girl leaves she will be courageous, compassionate, committed and self-confident with a love of learning, a moral compass and a sense of humour.

Open days provide an excellent introduction to the school and include a student-led tour, an opportunity to meet the staff and a presentation from the head giving an overview of the unique atmosphere and opportunities at St Swithun's. To book a place on an open day, or to arrange an individual visit at a more convenient time, please contact Kate Cairns on 01962 835703 or email registrar@stswithuns.com. Keep up to date with latest news by visiting www.stswithuns.com, or on instagram and facebook @stswithunsgirls.

St Swithun's
WINCHESTER

(Founded 1884)

Alresford Road, Winchester, Hampshire SO21 1HA UK

Tel: 01962 835700

Fax: 01962 835779

Email: office@stswithuns.com

Website: www.stswithuns.com

Head of School: Jane Gandee MA(Cantab)

Appointed: 2010

School type: Girls' Day & Boarding Senior & Sixth Form

Age range of girls: 11–18 years

No. of pupils enrolled as at 01/09/2023: 517

Sixth Form: 142

No. of boarders: 214

Fees as at 01/09/2023:

Day: £25,356 per annum

Full Boarding: £42,651 per annum

Stroud, King Edward VI Preparatory School

Stroud School is an exciting, independent preparatory school where boys and girls aged 3 to 11 thrive in its unique family environment. With an ISI Excellent rating, it is the preparatory school for King Edward VI School, Southampton.

Highwood House is an impressive Victorian building standing in 22 acres of beautiful rural countryside. With only six former heads since its foundation in 1926, Stroud has always been a school that values the family ethos. It is a school with a strong academic record, fantastic sports facilities and links to strong academic secondary schools. Stroud's curriculum achieves the highest academic standard without compromising the key skills its children need to be successful in the workplace and generally in life.

The school ethos and curriculum is centred around the Stroud Spirit values, which provide pupils with a strong sense of community; this character curriculum not only fosters creativity and curiosity, but it equips its children with empathy, celebrates individuality and encourages its children to live up to the school motto, in aeternum intrepidus - Forever Undaunted - every day.

Specialist teaching begins in Nursery with specialist sport, music, languages and computing, and this develops along with the children, until they receive a curriculum that is entirely specialist taught from the beginning of Year 6. With small classes, dedicated teachers and an exciting extra-curricular clubs and activities programme, children are exposed to many activities which will hopefully ignite their passions. Additionally, there's an outdoor pool, huge sports hall, riding paddock, dance studio, music practice rooms, a science lab, dedicated ICT suites for both KS1 and KS2/3 plus a brand new Masterchef-style food tech kitchen and a newly-expanded Wellbeing centre.

Stroud has always been a school that believes in children thriving when they are happy and have plenty of access to the great outdoors. In a world where education is increasingly digitised, Stroud wants its children to flourish outside, whether that's during Forest School sessions in the woods, conducting science experiments down by the ponds or caring for the school farm animals. Its farm is home to chickens (fed by the little ones), beehives and pygmy goats, which live alongside three ponies. There are large ponds used for pond dipping and ecology studies, and a newly-built bird hide nestled into their woodland to allow children to get closer to nature. Veg boxes sit just outside the classrooms and the school has held an Eco School Green Flag for more than 10 years, recognising our commitment to sustainability.

Sport assumes an inclusive approach at Stroud and the school regularly uses the pitches at its Wellington Sports Ground, its Outward Bound Centre in the Dartmoor National Park, and facilities at its senior school King Edward VI. Traditional sports are part of school life: boys play rugby, football, hockey and cricket, while girls take on netball, hockey and cricket.

Stroud was, in fact, one of the first schools to offer cricket to all boys and girls from Year 3 upwards, suggesting a willingness to embrace new ideas. Certainly, alternative sports play a big part in the curriculum, such as handball, ultimate Frisbee and lacrosse, alongside athletics and swimming in the Summer Term.

Several new initiatives over the last two years have been demonstrative of how well Stroud is moving forward. And further planned developments allow for new facilities that will keep pace with a 21st Century educational need. What has not changed at Stroud, however, is the opportunities that it provides for its pupils.

STROUD SCHOOL
King Edward VI Preparatory

(Founded 1926)

Highwood House, Highwood Lane, Romsey, Hampshire SO51 9ZH UK

Tel: 01794 513231

Email: registrar@stroud-kes.org.uk

Website: stroud.kes.school

Headmistress: Mrs Rebecca Smith

School type:
Co-educational Day Preparatory & Nursery

Age range of pupils: 3–11 years

Fees as at 01/09/2023:

Day: £4,060–£6,525 per term

Average class size: 16–18

The Abbey School

One of the country's foremost independent girls' schools from 3–18 The Abbey is a place where academic excellence becomes a natural process of growth and curiosity at every stage of the journey, from the age of 3 to 18. We are a school that celebrates success in all its forms, and every girl is encouraged to explore her own unique strengths and discover her passions through a vast choice of opportunities - both inside and outside the classroom.

For many years The Abbey Junior School has been developing a leading system of inquiry-based study where students are in charge of their own learning. We help them to cover topics with active, questing intelligence, led by questions, finding their own answers. Our teachers support, encourage and guide so that students have the confidence to make discoveries of their own.

From September 2021, we embraced the internationally recognised and renowned Primary Years Programme (PYP) as an IB Candidate School, combining it with our own Abbey Ideas and Passion (Abbey IP). Together they support our theme of Human Intelligence.

The programme is academically challenging, robust, supporting curriculum milestones and going far beyond them. It is innovative and outward-looking, prioritising creativity and connections. It is full of joy, reward and illumination. Simply put: it is the most exciting, innovative and rigorous curriculum available anywhere in the country.

Throughout the Senior School, we seek to provide a 'real-world' education that goes outside the classroom to offer a myriad of opportunities for students to explore, identify and cultivate their passions. Far from being a blank canvas, every individual arrives with a rich palette of her own unique colours - and we encourage them to embrace them in all their glory. Our exceptional co-curricular provision sets us apart: whatever your daughter's enthusiasm, there will be an activity just right for her and lots of new things to try.

Sixth Form provides a pathway to suit each student through our A Level and IB curriculum offerings. Our internationally-minded ethos means that we collaborate across divides and strive to provide an education that prepares students to step out into an uncertain world with confidence, empathy, and at ease with those from all cultures. Our pioneering methods put the 'why' back at the heart of learning and our holistic approach places equal emphasis on academic achievement, intellectual agility and emotional wellbeing.

The academic results attained speak for themselves. The A Level cohorts regularly achieve upwards of 70% A*-A grades - enabling them to move on to study at the university that is right for them. The school is also one of the top performing IB schools academically - not only in the UK, but globally. In 2023, our students achieved an average of 38 points, compared to the global average of 30, placing The Abbey as one of the leading IB Schools in the World.

Above all, The Abbey is passionate about creating a learning experience that is joyful and meaningful. Our self-regulating culture helps us all to look after each other, and our inspiring teachers are dedicated to fostering a special relationship with each and every individual.

(Founded 1887)

Kendrick Road, Reading, Berkshire RG1 5DZ UK

Tel: 0118 987 2256

Email: admissions@theabbey.co.uk

Website: www.theabbey.co.uk

Head: Mr Will le Fleming

Appointed: September 2020

School type:
Girls' Day Preparatory & Senior, Nursery & Sixth Form

Age range of girls: 3–18 years

No. of pupils enrolled as at 01/09/2023: 987

Fees as at 01/09/2023:

Day: £13,500–£21,750 per annum

The Oratory Prep School

The Oratory Prep School is a leading independent day and boarding Catholic school for children aged 2 - 13, set within 65 acres of South Oxfordshire countryside.

Pupils benefit from an excellent education enriched by outstanding facilities including extensive woodland, ponds and adventure playgrounds; a learner pool and a 25 metre heated indoor swimming pool; a full size 3G pitch; and a raked 300-seater auditorium with state-of-the-art sound and lighting systems.

Our impressive scholarship record and consistently high grades provides testament to the hard work of the whole school family and, whilst our vision is to provide outstanding learning opportunities for all, we are conscious of the importance to strike the right educational balance, so that our children are prepared for their future endeavours, whilst very much enjoying the journey that they are embarking on. This is crucial in our every-changing global climate.

At The Oratory Prep School, we are proud of the work of all our children and are passionate about ensuring their emotional and social wellbeing. Our commitment to excellent pastoral support, with an emphasis on Catholic values, is central to all aspects of school life.

Beyond the classroom, we provide a wealth of opportunities enabling pupils to thrive in a variety of fields, whether in orchestra, choir, on the stage or on the rugby field. Our action-packed Activity Programmes offer activities ranging from fencing to cookery alongside our diverse Newman Programme including modules in debating, interview and presentation skills and orienteering. Outstanding Performing Arts opportunities are also available, through LAMDA from Year 1, instrument and vocal tuition, and musical and drama productions.

Little Oaks Nursery is where the journey begins. We welcome children from two years of age where we instil a spirit of exploring and discovery and an appetite for trying out new things.

We nurture aspiration from the earliest age through an excited and varied curriculum that challenges and extends our children academically and is rich in music, art, sport and outdoor learning.

In Junior Prep (Reception to Year 4) and Senior Prep (Year 5 to 8), our pupils achieve academic success through a well-rounded, hands on education that brings out the best in each child.

We balance academic rigour with fostering a continuous love for learning, making it fresh and fun and engendering a raft of skills and attitudes - such as being inquisitive, creative and adventurous.

Alongside this, we offer a wealth of extra-curricular trips and activities to enrich learning and provide a breadth of experience that enables each child to discover talents and passions that prepare them for senior school and for life beyond.

Boarding is an integral part of school life. We provide full, weekly and flexi-boarding to children from the time that they enter Year 3 upwards with many taking advantage of our weekly flexi-boarding programmes. Boarders enjoy a full and varied calendar of activities throughout the year - from our Newman Programme and sports matches to various outings and cultural trips.

Here at The Oratory Prep School, our focus is to work with you and your child to ensure that his or her learning journey continues - not only in a way that challenges them intellectually, but in a manner that inspires their curiosity and enables them to dream.

Great Oaks, Goring Heath, Reading,
Berkshire RG8 7SF UK

Tel: 0118 984 4511

Email: office@oratoryprep.co.uk

Website: www.oratoryprep.co.uk

Headteacher: Mr Andrew De Silva

Appointed: September 2022

School type: Co-educational Day & Boarding Preparatory & Nursery

Age range of pupils: 2–13 years (boarding from 7)

No. of pupils enrolled as at 01/09/2023: 300

Fees as at 01/09/2023:

Day: £3,855–£6,635 per term

Full Boarding: £8,535–£9,910 per term

Average class size: 16–18

The Royal School, Haslemere

The Royal is a vibrant, independent day and boarding school for girls and boys aged 9 to 18. Located on a safe and idyllic 26-acre site in the historic, charming market town of Haslemere, Surrey, yet only 50 minutes by train from central London.

As an organisation we embrace modern ideas but are steeped in tradition and history. We are honoured to have HRH The Princess Royal as our President and hold our close connection to the Royal Family and our history with great affection.

Our school motto

'Per Aspera Ad Astra' is as valuable to our community today as it was in 1840, when our school was founded. Our modern interpretation of our motto - 'Through challenge to the Stars' - inspires our pupils to free their minds and to look forward to their future with a sense of purpose and hope. Our pupils are considerate of others, ambitious for themselves and their friends, confident and strong in character; they embrace challenge for what it is and set high value on hard work and being kind.

Future Ready: An educational philosophy

We believe that everything we do, every single day, prepares our pupils for the future and that education is not about forcing pupils to fit a predetermined mould. Our Future Ready philosophy goes beyond traditional academic knowledge and focuses on fostering and developing emotional intelligence, practical skills, and critical thinking abilities. We aim to empower our pupils to become adaptable, resilient, and caring individuals who can thrive in an unpredictable future.

Academic excellence remains a cornerstone of Future Ready education and our pupils gain excellent academic profiles which become their passport to accessing the life-defining opportunities they so richly deserve. Our approach to academic learning is ever-evolving, and we embrace the challenges that new technologies bring. We focus on cultivating a deep understanding of subjects, fostering curiosity, and promoting a love for learning.

We believe that the world is human-led and tech-powered and are proud that, in an increasingly interconnected world, our Future Ready pupils have a sense of global citizenship. They learn to appreciate diverse cultures, understand global challenges, and collaborate with peers from different backgrounds. It is this holistic approach to education that nurtures life-long learners, compassionate global citizens, and adaptable problem-solvers who are ready to make a positive impact on society.

Home-from-Home Boarding from age 10+

Our happy, home-from-home boarding environment allows for a sense of community and belonging, where each child is known and nurtured. The rapport between staff and pupils is excellent. Many of our boarders establish life-long friendships across the globe.

High Achievers Programme

The Royal Scholarship Programme is a fantastic opportunity for those who excel academically or possess exceptional talent in Art, Music, Performing Arts and Sports to develop their skills and passions whilst making a powerful contribution to our vibrant and forward-looking school.

Discover our unique approach to education

Choosing a school is rather like buying a house: you have to see it, touch it, and hear it to imagine yourself living in it. We encourage families to visit us, meet the staff and, more importantly, our pupils, so that you can imagine for yourself your own son or daughter being part of our unique community.

(Founded 1840)

Farnham Lane, Haslemere, Surrey GU27 1HQ UK

Tel: 01428 605805

Email: admissions@royal.surrey.sch.uk

Website: www.royal-school.org

Executive Headmaster: Mr Matthew Close BA, MSc

Appointed: September 2023

President: HRH The Princess Royal

School type: Co-educational Day & Boarding Preparatory, Senior & Sixth Form

Religious Denomination: Church of England

Age range of pupils: 9–18 years (boarding from 10+)

No. of pupils enrolled as at 01/09/2023: 180

No. of boarders: 40

Fees as at 01/09/2023:

Day: £4,662–£6,863 per term

Weekly Boarding: £10,097 per term

Full Boarding: £11,483 per term

Average class size: 15–20

Teacher/pupil ratio: 1:15

JINYJIA
The Royal School
PRACTICALLY · INTELLECTUALLY · EMOTIONALLY ·
FUTURE READY

Upton House School

Upton House is a progressive and highly regarded Nursery, Pre-Prep and Prep school educating boys and girls from aged 2–11 years. Located in the heart of Windsor, Upton boasts excellent academic standards, high calibre staff and a warm and nurturing environment where children blossom and are prepared with confidence for the very best senior schools. Individual talent is developed, and a progressive curriculum offers a balanced co-education ensuring children are equipped with vital life skills for the future.

"Our children progress to their next schools as confident, successful and independent individuals. We were delighted to be awarded 'Excellent' in all areas in our Independent Schools Inspection Report." Rhian Thornton, Headmistress

Although non-selective, 30% of pupils in the past 3 years have achieved one or more scholarships to their chosen senior school. Details of scholarships and next schools can be found on the website.

Little Upton Pre-Nursery and Nursery is a very special environment where children begin their Upton journey from as young as age 2. Little Upton is open a flexible 48 weeks a year should parents require and benefits from being in a beautiful whole school setting. Staff are highly qualified, experienced practitioners and engage the children in stimulating, challenging and exciting activities that enable them to develop their love of learning within the Early Years Foundation Stage. Specialist subjects include French from 2 years old and Mandarin from 3 years old as well as regular PE and music lessons.

Facilities in the Pre-Prep and Prep departments at Upton House include an arts block which houses music rooms, an art and DT studio and a music studio which enables all the children to create and record as part of music technology lessons. A wide range of individual music instrument and singing lessons are also available. A vibrant and creative technology curriculum is rich with cross-curricular digital innovations, whilst our pioneering live-streamed events run by our Broadcasting Club share our events and activities to our global family online. More specialist subject teachers from Form 3 results in wonderful achievements and results for every child. All classrooms are furnished with interactive white boards and iPads are used daily by pupils to support learning throughout the school. Facilities also include a broadcasting studio, drama and dance studio, gymnasium and two libraries. Diverse sporting activities include netball, rugby, football, hockey, cricket and athletics as well as judo, fencing and ballet. Sporting fixtures are a key weekly part of Upton life and we hold home matches at the beautiful York Club in Windsor Great Park. We have a dedicated swim team, squad training twice each week and have achieved great success in the IAPS swimming championship finals for the last two years. We have received the NACE Challenge Award - external validation of school-wide high-quality provision/challenge for all.

Children at Upton House enjoy breakfast club from 7.45am, healthy meals prepared on site and a wide range of after school extra-curricular activities until 6pm. Holiday clubs are run on site outside of term time.

To book for an open morning, or to arrange a personal tour of the school, please register online or contact Mrs Deborah Bates: registrar@uptonhouse.org.uk.

We look forward to welcoming you!

(Founded 1936)

115 St Leonard's Road, Windsor, Berkshire SL4 3DF UK

Tel: 01753 862610

Email: registrar@uptonhouse.org.uk

Website: www.uptonhouse.org.uk

Head: Mrs Rhian Thornton BA (Hons) NPQH LLE PGCE

Appointed: September 2016

School type: Co-educational Prep, Pre-Prep & Nursery

Age range of pupils: 2–11 years

No. of pupils enrolled as at 01/09/2023: 290

Boys: 100 ***Girls:*** 190

Fees as at 01/09/2023:

Day: £2,982–£5,980 per term

Average class size: 16

STORIES
BOYS

Vinehall

Overview

Vinehall is a school where every child thrives, and children come first. We are a proud member of the Repton Family of Schools. At Vinehall, we believe that in providing a wide range of opportunities we can allow our children to achieve success, instilling in them a strong sense of purpose and self confidence. Our staff and parents work together to create a warm and thriving community, where kindness and tolerance towards others are leading values. The school's ethos is encapsulated in our motto, 'to do our best for the benefit of others'.

Idyllic Setting

Located in 50 acres of picturesque East Sussex countryside, Vinehall provides a unique learning experience that allows our children to thrive in an expansive and nurturing family environment, giving every child the opportunity to succeed both academically and personally, while allowing them to remain children for as long as possible. Our wonderful site means our pupils have a freedom rarely found these days, providing opportunities to explore and play outside, including climbing trees and building dens. The school offers a range of outstanding facilities, including an all-weather pitch, indoor swimming pool, nine-hole golf course, 250-seater theatre, full-size sports hall and an impressive library and classroom building.

Outstanding Education

Vinehall upholds high standard of academic achievement as well as offering a range of co-curricular opportunities. We are a vibrant and busy school with high expectations all round. Vinehall is a warm, caring, family school, and promoting positive mental and physical wellbeing is at the heart of what we do. Our size means that the teachers know all of the children well, and that every child is treated as an individual, supported and challenged during their time with us. Our broad and stimulating curriculum provides children with relevant and engaging learning experiences, enabling all pupils to fulfil their potential. Our aim is to foster a love of learning by encouraging children to ask questions and think for themselves.

We encourage our children to develop a sense of purpose and self-confidence, while also fostering a strong sense of community where tolerance and kindness towards others are leading values. These values are embedded throughout our curriculum, and we encourage our children to develop creativity, critical thinking skills, and an awareness of ethical issues. This helps our children to become modern global citizens who are well-equipped to succeed in the twenty-first century world.

Full, weekly and flexible boarding

Located within the heart of the main school, our boarding house is very much an extended family. It is valued as a home away from home for our boarders; creating a relaxed and comfortable environment separate from academic life at the school. We offer full, weekly or flexible boarding open to all. For full boarders there are regular exeat weekend breaks every two or three weeks. Most boarders describe the weekends at Vinehall as the highlight of their week, with a wide range of trips and activities on offer. Weekly boarding is available for those wishing to spend weekends with their families. Flexible boarding is on offer to provide a helping hand to day pupils.

Vinehall

A REPTON SCHOOL

(Founded 1938)

Robertsbridge, East Sussex TN32 5JL UK

Tel: 01580 880413

Email: admissions@vinehallschool.com

Website: www.vinehallschool.com

Headmaster: Joff Powis

Appointed: September 2017

School type: Co-educational Day & Boarding Preparatory & Nursery

Age range of pupils: 2–13 years

No. of pupils enrolled as at 01/09/2023: 201

Fees as at 01/09/2023:

Day: £11,100–£21,675 per annum

Weekly Boarding: £26,925 per annum

Full Boarding: £29,925 per annum

Average class size: 15

Teacher/pupil ratio: 1:6

Vinehall
A REPTON SCHOOL

Wellington College

Wellington College is a vibrant and inspiring coeducational boarding and day school set in 400 acres of parkland, 40 minutes from Heathrow. The College, whose educational philosophy is based on values of kindness, courage, respect, integrity and responsibility, is celebrated not only for its academic achievements but also for its sporting, artistic and dramatic successes. Stellar examination results, outstanding provision across all co-curricular areas, and a raft of national accolades contribute to the College's national and international reputation. Wellingtonians study GCSEs, followed by the IB Diploma or A Levels and, whichever route they take, results are superb: in 2023, 37% of grades at GCSE were 9s (the most common grade for Wellingtonians) and 86% 9–7. The combined total of IB and A Level grades in 2023 were impressive: 31% achieved A*/7; 74% A* A/7 6. Remarkably of the 234 pupils in the Upper Sixth, 50% secured either Higher Level 7s and 6s at IB or A* and A at A Level, with 19 students achieving straight HL 7s or A*s. On average 20 of the cohort gain Oxbridge places every year while entry to Russell Group universities is almost a given. In 2023, 24 students went to US universities, many to Ivy League institutions.

In 2022/23 there were over 20 different sports on offer at Wellington, involving 200 teams in around 1,500 fixtures, and it was yet another bumper year with over 30 Wellingtonians involved in National level sport, and 12 teams or individuals taking part in National Finals. Wellington remains committed to adding to its reputation as one of the UK's strongest and most diverse schools on the sporting front, offering both challenge and support at all sporting levels and to all pupils.

Performing Arts are equally strong. Music, Dance and Drama are stunning, with 60% of pupils taking instrumental or LAMDA lessons with some 1,000 lessons taking place each week and over 50 visiting teachers. 2022/23 was an outstanding year for the Arts at Wellington. Not only have we continued to provide a whole range of activities for our students but have been externally recognised by the award of Artsmark Platinum and been nominated for a TES Excellence in Creative Arts Award for our Festival of Musical Theatre, the finale of our wonderful Arts Festival. The Speech Day show, in a 4,000-seater Big Top, provides a fitting finale, with musicians, singers, actors and dancers able to reprise many of the highlights of the year.

Leadership, service to others and developing an international outlook are central to the College's core values: co-curricular activities include CCF, DofE, and a pioneering Global Social Leaders scheme, in which pupils create and run innovative social action projects, tackling local and global issues.

Clubs and societies range from Green Power Racing to the Field Gun team, from WTV (Wellington's own television company) and its pupil-run radio station DukeBox, to a full range of more traditional pastimes such as Photography, Creative Writing, Debating and MUN.

Wellington builds strong external partnerships to broaden impact in education and continues to have mutually beneficial partnerships with a wide variety of schools, including Special Schools, Secondary and Primary schools. The Wellington family of schools includes Eagle House prep school and eight schools in China, India and Thailand, with new schools in development. This network supports opportunities for cultural dialogue and understanding and broadens access to world-class education through bursaries and regional education initiatives.

Further information including details about Visitors Days can be found on the website and the Admissions Office can be contacted on +44 (0)1344 444013.

WELLINGTON
COLLEGE

(Founded 1853)

Duke's Ride, Crowthorne, Berkshire RG45 7PU UK

Tel: +44 (0)1344 444000

Email: admissions@wellingtoncollege.org.uk

Website: www.wellingtoncollege.org.uk

Master: Mr James Dahl

Appointed: September 2019

Director of IB: Mr Richard Atherton

School type:
Co-educational Day & Boarding Senior & Sixth Form

Religious Denomination: Church of England

Age range of pupils: 13–18 years

No. of pupils enrolled as at 01/09/2023: 1104

Boys: 585 ***Girls:*** 519 ***Sixth Form:*** 489

No. of boarders: 868

Fees as at 01/09/2023:

Day: £35,760 per annum

Full Boarding: £48,930 per annum

Average class size:
Lower + Middle = 20
Upper School = 12

Teacher/pupil ratio: 1:7

Weston Green School

Inspiring individuals and nurturing potential for a successful future

A warm welcome to Weston Green School!

As you step through the doors of our wonderful school we hope that you will soon feel part of this special place where children thrive within wonderful surroundings. From age 2–11, our children grow to become independent and confident young people, achieve exceptionally well academically and most of all enjoy their experiences through the immense joy and wonder of learning.

We were recently awarded 'Excellent' in all areas by the Independent Schools Inspectorate (ISI) for the academic achievement and personal development of our pupils, reinforcing our objectives to celebrate childhood and give pupils a breadth of enrichment opportunities to achieve individual success.

Weston Green takes pride in its well-regarded reputation for being a warm and welcoming school where children secure high academic achievement and successfully go on to attain their choices of future schools.

From Nursery and Early Years though to when they leave us at Year 6, every individual is nurtured so that they will not only develop and achieve academically, but also personally, socially and emotionally. Our academic excellence is founded on a focus on the development of the whole person, that each child is provided with the opportunities to enable them to flourish and our partnership with you is key in delivering this successfully.

Our pupils are happy and confident and as a result are successful learners. We guide them through every step to ensure they are well prepared personally, socially and academically for their next phase of education. We call this our Future Schools Programme. Feeding into a broad range of schools, we work closely with families to identify and support the preparation and application for the school that is the right fit for your child.

Our dedicated and specialist teachers have a wealth of experience, expertise and curriculum knowledge, having aspirations for each child to become inquisitive and creative learners, undaunted by their mistakes and eager to face increasingly complex challenges. You will see a school day which places a high priority on the core areas of reading, writing, mathematics and science, yet engages a child in learning these in a highly imaginative and innovative curriculum. In this way children develop crucial skills for learning which then benefits the broad, diverse and rich thematic curriculum we offer.

If you're looking for a school place (for boys and girls aged 2 - 11 years), please come along for a personal tour - contact info@westongreenschool.org.uk to book your place. We look forward to welcoming you soon.

Weston Green School

Weston Green Road, Thames Ditton, Surrey KT7 0JN UK

Tel: 020 8398 2778

Email: info@westongreenschool.org.uk

Website: www.westongreenschool.org.uk

Head Teacher: Mrs Sarah Evans BA Hons, NPQH

School type:
Co-educational Day Preparatory & Nursery

Age range of pupils: 2–11 years

No. of pupils enrolled as at 01/09/2023: 179

Fees as at 01/09/2023:

Please see website

Woldingham School

A leading day and boarding school for girls aged 11–18 set in 700 acres of the most beautiful Surrey countryside, Woldingham is an inspiring place for students to become confident, compassionate and courageous young women. It's a place where students learn to 'write your own story' through excellent teaching, boundless opportunities and first-rate pastoral care.

Despite Woldingham's rural and peaceful location the school is remarkably easy to get to. With Woldingham station adjoining the school grounds, London is just 30 minutes away by train and the school is only 30 minutes from Gatwick and 45 minutes from Heathrow airports.

Main House, the stunning 19th century mansion at the centre of the school, sits alongside purpose-built science labs, humanities and language hubs, and studios for art, drama and music. With a professional standard auditorium seating 630, it's no surprise that award-winning actors Emma Corrin and Carey Mulligan both attended Woldingham.

Students achieve outstanding GCSE and A Level results to secure places at leading UK and international universities, opening doors to exciting careers. Students choose from a wide range of academic enrichment opportunities, including a vibrant talks programme from leading academics, annual philosothon, and dynamic scholarship programmes to stretch and challenge scholars.

Woldingham has an exceptional programme of sport, clubs, performing arts and outreach into the local community, enabling students to develop an excellent range of skills, expertise and interests. In 2022, Woldingham opened an Outdoor Education & Adventure Centre - a perfect addition to the school's wonderful 700 acres.

Woldingham has excellent indoor and outdoor sports facilities onsite. Hockey and netball teams compete locally and regionally with first-class training from specialist coaches. The tennis dome means tennis can be played year round, as well as on outside courts in the summer. There is an indoor swimming pool, squash courts, fitness suites, dance studio and newly-refurbished sports hall with cricket nets.

The beauty and peace of Woldingham in the Surrey Hills makes it the perfect place to board. Boarders live with their own year group in comfortable and well-equipped boarding houses, and there is a great sense of community. Enthusiastic and experienced housemistresses understand how to help new girls settle in quickly and make the most of school life. Flexi-boarding is a great option and weekly boarding, where students spend their weekends at home, is increasingly popular.

One of the UK's oldest girls' schools, Woldingham is proud to be a pioneer of women's education and its staff are experts in teaching in an all-girls environment. Woldingham's supportive and stimulating single-sex environment enables students to become authors of their own life story, growing into independent women who make a positive contribution to the world.

Woldingham is a Sacred Heart Catholic school, warmly welcoming students of all faiths and none.

(Founded 1842)

Marden Park, Woldingham, Surrey CR3 7YA UK

Tel: 01883 349431

Email: registrar@woldinghamschool.co.uk

Website: www.woldinghamschool.co.uk

Head of School: Mrs Julia Harrington

School type: Girls' Day & Boarding Senior & Sixth Form

Age range of girls: 11–18 years (boarding from 11)

No. of pupils enrolled as at 01/09/2023: 580

Fees as at 01/09/2023:

Day: £24,090–£27,390 per annum

Weekly Boarding: £37,410–£40,830 per annum

Full Boarding: £42,585–£46,350 per annum

South-West

Exeter School

Welcome to Exeter School: a school of great character.
At Exeter School, we believe that education is not just about academic excellence but also about nurturing the character and potential of each individual. Exeter School has a rich history spanning nearly four hundred years, during which we have been committed to providing a holistic and well-rounded educational experience to our pupils.

We are now a day school for approximately 1,030 pupils aged 3–18 years, having welcomed Exeter Pre-Prep into the family. Our early years are based in The Avenue, Exminster, with Years 3+ based at our 25 acre campus in the heart of Exeter city itself, on Victoria Park Road.

With a dedicated team of passionate educators, we strive to create a supportive and inclusive environment that fosters the growth and development of our pupils. Our emphasis on character education is what sets us apart. We believe in instilling strong values, integrity, and resilience in our pupils, preparing them to become responsible global citizens who make a positive impact on the world.

Academic excellence forms the cornerstone of our educational philosophy. Our rigorous curriculum, combined with innovative teaching methods, encourages critical thinking, creativity, and problem-solving skills. We empower our pupils to explore their passions and unlock their full potential, helping them excel academically and beyond.

Beyond the classroom, our extensive co-curricular activities provide opportunities for pupils to develop leadership skills, teamwork, and a healthy competitive spirit. Whether it's through participating in our renowned music and drama programmes, engaging in community service, or excelling on the sports field, our pupils learn valuable life lessons that shape their character.

Exeter School is proud of its strong sense of community. Our dedicated parents, alumni, and staff work collaboratively to create a nurturing and inspiring environment. We believe in open communication and actively involve our Exeter School community in the educational journey of our pupils.

We are committed to staying at the forefront of educational innovation and provide state-of-the-art facilities and resources for our pupils. Our passionate and experienced staff continually seek new ways to enhance the learning experience and ensure our pupils receive a world-class education.

Come and visit us
We invite you to learn more about our community either by booking a personal tour of either of our campuses or by registering for any of our open mornings or taster days hosted throughout the year. Let us show you how you could embark on an educational journey that will shape your future.

For more information, please contact our friendly admissions team on: 01392 307080 or admissions@exeterschool.org.uk.

(Founded 1633)

Victoria Park Road, Exeter, Devon EX2 4NS UK

Tel: 01392 307080

Email: admissions@exeterschool.org.uk

Website: www.exeterschool.org.uk

Head: Ms Louise Simpson

Appointed: 2020

School type:
Co-educational Day Preparatory, Senior & Sixth Form

Age range of pupils: 3–18 years

No. of pupils enrolled as at 01/09/2023: 1031

Boys: 640 ***Girls:*** 391

Fees as at 01/09/2023:

Day: £2,900–£5,570 per term

Teacher/pupil ratio: 1:9 (Pre-Prep) & 1:20 (age and subject selection dependent)

King's College

King's College is an independent co-educational boarding and day school for boys and girls from the aged 13 to 18. Situated in the picturesque county town of Somerset and only three hours from London by train, the school seeks to develop well-rounded, balanced individuals with a love of learning and academic curiosity. Boarding and pastoral care are core to life at King's, and there is a strong sense of community with so many pupils and staff living on-site in centrally located boarding houses.

The school holds the position of being one of the top academic secondary institutions in the county, regularly leading the tables in both GCSE and A-level results. As well as academic excellence, the breadth of sport and other co-curricular activities are unparalleled for a school of King's size.

As well as being an exceptionally happy school, they are busy and purposeful. Pupils leave well qualified, but more importantly, they leave as well-rounded, intellectually curious and balanced individuals who have been nurtured and encouraged to grow, develop and explore.

Much of what sets King's apart from other schools stems is their strong boarding ethos. The houses are centrally placed (two are in the main school building) and boarding is central. Boarders come from far and wide; many boarders are local with a few live closer to school than some of their day pupil friends, others come from the south west of England or further afield in the UK, and some from overseas. This makes for a varied and vibrant community within the houses. Wherever pupils come from, they soon develop a strong sense of loyalty to their house, which makes for exciting and hotly contested inter-house competition in sport and many other activities.

King's believes that boarding is a rich and life-affirming experience for pupils and is confident that they leave the school well prepared for the demands and challenges of university life. Their friendships are extraordinarily long-lived, and they are independent, resilient, resourceful, cheerful, tolerant, pro-active, kind, capable young men and women who go on to make their mark on the world.

Pupils are challenged by enthusiastic and dedicated specialist teachers both inside and outside the classroom. Careful planning has devised a programme of visits, lectures, tutoring and prep to support learning. House-based tutors each support seven or eight boys or girls throughout their time at the school. Pupils are also prepared with care for examinations (GCSE and A-levels) and university, and are encouraged to develop independent thought and inquiring minds.

Sport is pivotal at King's, and the school aims to engage and develop all pupils so they have fun. First class facilities include two floodlit Astros, a tennis/netball dome, 25m swimming pool, strength and conditioning suite, a climbing wall and an equestrian centre. For those with elite aspirations, excellent technical coaching is backed up by mentoring and support maintaining a healthy life balance. The school has a Cricket Performance Centre and is an accredited England hockey performance centre. King's also has a vast array of co-curricular activities unparalleled for a school of its size, from drama, music, outdoor pursuits and CCF, to dance, cookery and debating. Outdoor activities are well catered for under the umbrella of the CCF (Royal Navy, Royal Marines and Army sections), and alongside that are the Duke of Edinburgh Bronze and Gold award schemes. Kayaking and water polo are popular, as is climbing - we have our own indoor wall and climbing club.

(Founded 1880)

South Road, Taunton, Somerset TA1 3LA UK

Tel: 01823 328204

Email: admissions@kings-taunton.co.uk

Website: www.kings-taunton.co.uk

Headmaster: Mr Michael Sloan

School type:
Co-educational Day & Boarding Senior & Sixth Form

Age range of pupils: 13–18 years

No. of pupils enrolled as at 01/09/2023: 490

Fees as at 01/09/2023:

Day: £27,480 per annum

Average class size: 20 max

Teacher/pupil ratio: 1:9

Kingsley School

Welcome to Kingsley School

There are many reasons students could fall in love with Kingsley School, an independent co-educational boarding and day school located in Bideford on the banks of the River Torridge in North Devon.

One reason could be location - Kingsley is set in 25 acres of playfields and woodland, surrounded by stunning countryside, and just five minutes from popular surfing beaches. And another reason could be the school's strong academic tradition - at Kingsley every sixth form student typically goes on to university, including top-tier higher education institutes like Oxford and Cambridge.

But ultimately our students rate the opportunity to find their place, the exceptional support they receive and the welcome as the prime reasons they just can't see themselves going anywhere else but Kingsley.

Kingsley School is an inclusive day and boarding school where every child is important and is treated with dignity and respect. As a relatively small school of around 400 boys and girls, Kingsley's atmosphere is like that of a large family where everybody knows each other well.

The school's philosophy encourages personal qualities such as courage, generosity, honesty, imagination, tolerance and kindness. In addition, we develop the students' wider interests and skills in sport, music, art, and drama. Kingsley also has a national reputation for its Learning Development Centre which provides additional support for students with moderate learning needs. Overall, a Kingsley education develops the individual character and talents of each and every student both inside and outside the classroom.

Becoming part of the family: The boarding houses at Kingsley help form part of the family atmosphere at the school. Students live in three comfortable and well-equipped houses in the school's grounds; one for boys, one for girls and a mixed Sixth Form house. Each house has 30–40 students who are supervised by two teachers and their families who live in the houses as well.

Kingsley School Earth Centre: Kingsley is located within the UNESCO North Devon biosphere and the school's Earth Centre is a unique and very exciting ongoing project for all pupils at school. In response to the challenges of our time, the Earth Centre puts the natural world and environmental sustainability at the core of education here at Kingsley. Kingsley is very proud to be named ISA Sustainability and Environmental Education School of the Year, and a finalist for the Green Award in the Independent School of the Year Awards.

Sport and Clubs: Sport includes traditional sports plus surfing, judo, handball and gymnastics squads competing at a National level. As part of the National Theatre Connections programme, the school drama cast performed at the Theatre Royal, Plymouth and the National Theatre, London. Popular extra-curricular clubs include the Duke of Edinburgh's Award Scheme, Ten Tors, orchestra, computing, art, film making, choir and surfing.

Transport: we run an accompanied coach service to and from Heathrow Airport and Bristol Airport at the beginning and end of each term. Weekly boarding options with transport to London and the South East.

Do follow us on social media

Facebook: Kingsley Devon
Instagram: Kingsley School
Twitter: @KingsleyDevon
YouTube: @KingsleyDevon
www.kingsleydevon.com

(Founded 1884)

Northdown Road, Bideford, Devon EX39 3LY UK

Tel: 01237 426200

Fax: 01237 425981

Email: admissions@kingsleyschoolbideford.co.uk

Website: www.kingsleydevon.com

Headteacher: Mr Robert Pavis

Appointed: February 2022

Head of the Prep School: Mr Andrew Trythall

School type: Co-educational Day & Boarding Prep & Senior, Nursery & Sixth Form

Age range of pupils: 0–18 years (boarding from 9)

No. of pupils enrolled as at 01/09/2023: 395

No. of boarders: 100

Fees as at 01/09/2023:

Day: £5,220 per term

Weekly Boarding: £8,370 per term

Full Boarding (UK & Non-Visa): £11,545 per term

Full Boarding (International): £12,650 per term

Average class size: 14

Teacher/pupil ratio: 1:9

West Midlands

Denstone College

The ambition to explore every possible version of yourself at Denstone College

Denstone College and The Prep at Denstone College are an independent day and boarding school set in rural Staffordshire. The school has a rich history of 150 years and has just under 800 pupils.

The school shapes its ethos and vision around 'Denstonacity' which is described as 'the abition to explore every possible version of yourself'. Head of Denstone, Lotte Tulloch asks for pupils who jump up and down and make a difference in the world.

Denstone is filled with pupils from 4 years of age up to 18, all taking part is academia as well as a large array of sporting, musical or performance related activities with performance pathways into Leicester Tigers, Loughborough Lightning and England Cricket.

As well as education and co-curricular activities, Denstone is very much focused on the health and wellbeing of the pupils, with a newly branded Health and Wellbeing Centre on site with a dedicated team helping pupils deal with the world around them.

Junior-school pupils have a broader timetable, encompassing art, D&T, drama, music, PHSE and computing alongside the core subjects, giving them a 'solid academic foundation' together with their sporting and extracurricular pursuits.

The build-up to GCSE sees a real emphasis on the core subjects, and there's a requirement to take at least three additional subjects, totalling eight to 10 for most. Everyone starts off with triple science but with the option to adjust to a combined science programme (culminating in two science GCSEs rather than three separate subject exams) after the basics have been covered. Most pupils opt for a foreign language (French and Spanish are on offer here), and the majority of subjects are taught across five or six ability groups per subject, with plenty of individual attention for each pupil in these relatively small cohorts.

Sixth-formers set out with four A-levels but most eventually drop down to three. An EPQ is offered as a side option for the upper sixth. Traditional subjects are all on the table (plus the likes of D&T, computer science and psychology), but a BTEC in sport and a CTEC in ICT is also up for grabs. Science, computer science and ICT is a notably popular combo - most likely a result of a significant parental workforce in local tech giants such as Rolls-Royce, AstraZeneca, JCB and Merlin.

Pupils end up at a suitably rounded variety of destinations, from local degree apprenticeships to US rugby scholarships. Close to 50 per cent of pupils win places at Russell Group universities each year, and one of this year's cohort has an Oxbridge offer on the table. As the product of a US degree herself, Ms Tulloch is keen to encourage pupils who are enthused by the idea of a North American or European destination but equally buoyed by the fact that 19 students opted for the apprenticeship route last year.

DENSTONE
COLLEGE

Uttoxeter, Staffordshire ST14 5HN UK

Tel: 01889 590484

Email: admissions@denstonecollege.net

Website: www.denstonecollege.org

Head of School: Miss Lotte Tulloch

School type: Co-educational Day & Boarding Preparatory, Senior & Sixth Form

Age range of pupils: 4–18 years (boarding from 7)

No. of pupils enrolled as at 01/09/2023: 777

Boys: 458 ***Girls:*** 319

Fees as at 01/09/2023:

Day: £15,048 + per annum

Full Boarding: £30,936 + per annum

SB

Edenhurst Preparatory School

Edenhurst Preparatory School is an independent, coeducational day school located in Newcastle under Lyme, Staffordshire for pupils aged three months to eleven years.

Our aim is to inspire and support pupils in their learning, and to build a solid foundation for future success. Our dedicated staff and small class sizes help us to achieve this by creating a positive learning environment, with a healthy mix of play, discovery and responsibility. When the time comes for our pupils to leave Edenhurst, we take pride in their confidence and individuality, their passion for learning, and their ability to embrace all challenges they may encounter in later life.

We are very mindful of the importance of developing a partnership between school and home, maintaining regular contact between teaching staff and parents in order to best serve the needs of each child.

We have a vision to equip children with the necessary skills and attributes to thrive in a rapidly changing world which gives our children the 'Edenhurst Edge' - that little bit extra that sets them above their peers.

Our core values are clearly understood and shared by every member of the Edenhurst school community and we:

- nurture - developing children's individual talents and gifts by providing an appropriate level of challenges.
- inspire - using the latest technology to provide a broad and balanced curriculum delivered by Specialist teachers.
- achieve - fostering a love of learning and equipping children with the necessary skills to succeed, achieving excellent results in all areas of school life.

The Edenhurst Nursery caters for children from the age of three months to four years old, offering the highest quality care in a safe, engaging and nurturing environment. Our qualified, friendly staff are dedicated to providing each child with all of the support and encouragement they need to learn and grow.

In Edenhurst Pre-Prep we work closely with each and every child, in order to support them in developing the skills and interests cultivated in the Early Years Foundation Stage. As well as English and Mathematics, pupils in Pre-Prep study Science, Geography, History and Religious Studies. In addition, children benefit from specialist teaching in Music, Art, ICT, French and P.E., which includes swimming. Upon entering the Prep Forms, a specialist subject based approach is adopted. Each subject is led by a teacher who is a specialist in their own field, allowing the children to benefit from their expertise and an enthusiasm derived from a genuine interest in each subject.

Pupils in the Prep Forms continue to build on their skills in English and Mathematics, as well as other core subjects, and preparation for entrance examinations at 11+ is an ongoing process at Edenhurst. Small class sizes of 20 or below are maintained to allow for the most advantageous pupil to adult ratio.

Children benefit from a careful and sensitive familiarisation with the demands of examinations, and parents are also invited to join the Headteacher for a discussion about future schooling. Edenhurst has an excellent record in preparing children for transfer to senior school at age 11, and each year a number of children gain scholarships to a range of schools.

Westlands Avenue, Newcastle-under-Lyme, Staffordshire ST5 2PU UK

Tel: 01782 619348

Email: office@edenhurst.co.uk

Website: www.edenhurst.co.uk

Headteacher: Mrs Emma Mousley

School type:
Co-educational Day Preparatory & Nursery

Age range of pupils: 3 months–11 years

Fees as at 01/09/2023:

Day: £3,200–£4,120 per term

Ellesmere College

Since its founding in 1884, Ellesmere College has become renowned for its individual focus on student's academic and personal success. An incredibly friendly co-ed boarding, weekly and day school, 600 students from ages 7 to 18, and from all across the globe, are encouraged to explore, engage and evolve to the best of their potential through the College's innovative, dynamic and world class academic and co-curricular opportunities.

At every entry point to the College students are offered a broad choice of academic subjects as well as a vast range of co-curricular activities (DofE, CCF, ESB, EPQ, ILM, Survive and Thrive with the John Muir Award, expeditions, career conventions, affiliations, etc) that develop essential life skills - leadership, initiative, confidence, teambuilding, and above all a belief in themselves that they can achieve if they try their best - the ethos at the heart of the school - to be 'Life:Ready'.

Academic

Ellesmere College has recently been reaccredited as a High Performance Leaning (HPL) World Class School - one of only 39 in the world. At Key Stages 2 & 3 we offer a wide curriculum preparing them for their choice of i/GCSEs as they move up to Middle School at age 13. Our award winning Support for Learning department supports those students with diverse academic needs including dyslexia, dyspraxia and dyscalculia.

In Sixth Form, students choose A Levels, BTEC or International Baccalaureate (IB), and our students regularly gain entrance to their first-choice university including Oxford, Cambridge and Russell Group institutions. We are ranked in the top 20 British schools offering the IB.

Pastoral Care

All students at the College - whether day pupils or boarders - are assigned to a House, under which they compete in termly House Competitions. Our student accommodation provides a high-quality, comfortable and secure environment for our students from Year 8, with residential staff on site to tend to the pupils' personal and pastoral needs 24 hours a day.

Drama, Music and the Arts

The College was the first independent school to be awarded Artsmark Platinum by the Arts Council of Great Britain for its commitment and delivery of the arts from the traditional to more modern media. Singing is an area of real excellence with four award winning choirs and a wide range of ensembles with opportunities to perform. Participation at every level is encouraged and supported by ESB, LAMDA, ballet & dance classes, and individual tuition.

Sports

We are immensely proud of our sporting tradition at Ellesmere College and physical education is an integral part of the curriculum - playing for ones' house or school, or at national, international and Olympic level. We are an accredited WAoS (World Academy of Sport) Athlete Friendly Education Centre (AFEC), allowing students to balance their studies with demanding training and competition schedules. There are seven distinct Sports Academies – rugby, cricket, tennis, swimming, shooting, football and golf - as well as a High Performance Hockey Programme and many other sports.

We believe very strongly that the foundations for a successful adult life are built at a young age - and at Ellesmere College we empower and enrich our students to become confident, strong and exceptional young adults - truly 'Life Ready'.

(Founded 1884)

Ellesmere, Shropshire SY12 9AB UK

Tel: 01691 622321

Fax: 01691 623286

Email: registrar@ellesmere.com

Website: www.ellesmere.com

Head of School: Mr Brendan Wignall MA, FRSA, MCMI

School type: Co-educational Day & Boarding Preparatory, Senior & Sixth Form

Age range of pupils: 7–18 years (boarding from 12)

No. of pupils enrolled as at 01/09/2023: 600

Fees as at 01/09/2023:

Day: £4,565–£7,450 per term

Weekly Boarding: £9,170–£9,670 per term

Full Boarding: £10,855–£13,545 per term

Teacher/pupil ratio: 1:8

Mander Portman Woodward - MPW Birmingham

MPW Birmingham was founded in 1980 with the goal of ensuring that students experience an education based on the Oxford and Cambridge tutorial system. This means that lessons are more relaxed and informal than a typical school, but are also academically stimulating and demanding. With fewer than ten students in any class, lessons are intensive but rewarding with plenty of opportunity for individual attention and personalised teaching.

MPW Birmingham guides students in their learning by encouraging them to focus on our model of success: aspiration, attitude, attendance, application and achievement. We help students obtain results that all too often they never thought were possible. With almost 30 subjects to choose from at A level and many at GCSE, MPW Birmingham provides a breadth of study opportunity that is unique for a small college. MPW helps students demystify the examination process and develop both the technical skills and academic knowledge needed to perform well under timed conditions. We offer all of our students the opportunity to sit weekly assessments enabling students to perfect examination technique.

We run a university support programme that values every student in equal measure regardless of aspiration; we treat all students as though they are elite. We prepare students for a range of courses including medicine, dentistry and Oxbridge and ensure that they are well equipped to cope with the demands of university life.

Students benefit from outstanding pastoral care with each student being allocated a Personal Tutor. This builds upon our core values of diligence, respect, tolerance and care. We expect our students to work hard but we also expect to provide more support to our students than they would receive at other schools. Our culture is one based on high expectations but one that is both nurturing and unpretentious. We run a non-compulsory enrichment programme in which many students participate, developing both sporting and cultural interests. There is no glass ceiling in MPW Birmingham and we strive to enable all students to reach their potential and use their talents without inhibition.

Our mission is to be one of the leading colleges of its type within the country, enabling students to develop confidence, maturity, knowledge and skills, turning academic aspirations into reality. MPW helps build the character of students enabling them to develop good self-discipline regarding work, intellectual curiosity and a sense of duty regarding community. Our best ambassadors are our students and we are rightly proud of what they achieve with us and what they go on to achieve afterwards. We change lives for the better and help bring about progress and success. Irrespective of where a student is starting from, MPW helps young people achieve special things.

(Founded 1980)

16–18 Greenfield Crescent, Edgbaston, Birmingham, West Midlands B15 3AU UK

Tel: 0121 454 9637

Fax: 0121 454 6433

Email: birmingham@mpw.ac.uk

Website: www.mpw.ac.uk

Principal: Mr Mark Shingleton

School type: Co-educational Day Senior & Sixth Form

Age range of pupils: 14–19 years

Average class size: 8

M|P|W
Mander Portman Woodward
18

Stafford Grammar School

The first building you come to when coming up our drive is a Pugin designed manor house that many of our pupils fondly call the Harry Potter building with its wonderful wooden staircase winding its way around our main foyer after walking across the moat bridge. It is the beginning of what we hope is a magical experience for every pupil and visitor to the school!

At Stafford Grammar School our focus is on ensuring our pupils come away every day with a smile on their faces. We pride ourselves on our excellent academic results but we take just as much pride from helping our pupils discover hitherto unknown talents and instilling in them an insatiable curiosity to explore and challenge themselves. Fulfilling potential is our driving ambition and there are opportunities for every pupil to pursue a plethora of subjects and activities in their journey of personal discovery, whether that is in the forest school for our Prep pupils or in the Labs or theatre or on the sports fields for our budding scientists, thespians and athletes.

The performing arts ensure the school is high on endorphins and the annual school musical showcases exceptional talent with a number of our pupils having subsequently pursued careers on the stage and in the media. With 18 different music groups meeting for rehearsals every week and nearly 40 concerts every year, the opportunities for our musicians to perform at the highest level and in some of the country's best performance venues, gives them experiences they will cherish for the rest of their lives.

Classes are small, typically 13–20 pupils in a class up until their A Levels where the class size will generally drop below 10 in a class. This ensures individualised support for pupils of all levels. Our academic results at GCSE and A Level are excellent and the majority of our pupils achieve their first choice of University, including Oxbridge and Russell Group institutions, with good numbers going to study Medicine.

Our House system ensures that every pupil is provided with excellent pastoral support from their Form Tutor and Housemaster/mistress and every pupil is able to participate in the abundant range of competitions so that they genuinely enjoy the sense of shared achievement and collaboration.

Despite being a smaller school of roughly 440 pupils, we have enjoyed some wonderful successes in sport with several pupils achieving county, regional and national honours. Beyond the typical sports we have a very successful ski team and several pupils representing the school in horse riding. We believe wholeheartedly in the notion of 'a healthy body, healthy mind' and participation in sport for all our pupils is significant to the success they enjoy elsewhere in their life at school.

Pupils' mental health is something we take very seriously and we are due to open our new Well-being Centre imminently where the pupils will know they can go for support when it is needed or where they can escape from the hustle and bustle if in need of a quiet space.

We have 7 core values – Excellence, Respect, Compassion, Responsibility, Integrity, Creativity and perhaps most importantly, Courage. Winston Churchill said *'Courage is rightly esteemed the first of human qualities, because, as has been said, it is the quality which guarantees all others.'* The world is full of challenges to overcome but for those with courage, they are already half way to meeting them head on and emerging victorious and that is what we want for our pupils.

(Founded – 1982)

Burton Manor, Burton Manor Road, Stafford ST18 9AT

Tel: 01785 249752

Email: admissions@staffordgrammar.co.uk

Website: www.staffordgrammar.co.uk

Headmaster: Mr W P N Pietrek

School type: Co-educational Day Preparatory & Senior, Nursery & Sixth Form

Age range of pupils: 4–18 years

No. of pupils enrolled as at 01/09/2023: (provisionally – 421)

Fees as at 01/09/2023: £2,100 - £4,960 per term

Average class size: GCSE: 15, A Level: 8

The Royal School, Wolverhampton

The building works continue! After opening as a Free school/ State Boarding School in 2016, and following the ambitious and successful growth programme in pupil numbers over the past five years, The Royal School's exciting building programme is now well under way to develop first class teaching facilities for pupils from five to 19. Phase one of the school's development plan saw a new Sixth Form Centre and refurbished classrooms. Phase two starts in the summer with renovation and more classrooms coming on line.

At the centre of all that we do is our inclusive community where students study, play and live together harmoniously. The Royal is a small, cohesive community with a friendly atmosphere for both day pupils and boarders alike. Our strong academic tradition is based upon individual attention and encouragement, as well as excellent pastoral care founded on respect, tolerance and understanding of others. Students achieve their full academic potential, whilst a wide range of extended-day activities is available to develop character and leadership. We prepare pupils for Oxbridge and other top universities while also catering to pupils of all abilities. The school regularly achieves high standards in both A-Level and GCSE results, particularly in STEM subjects of mathematics and the sciences. The Royal combines traditional values with a modern outlook and a 'real-world' attitude. At The Royal, education is about developing the whole individual.

Developing the 'whole person' in sport, drama, music and adventurous activity, young people at The Royal are also better placed to make the best of their opportunities to become well-rounded individuals with confidence and empathy for those around them.

The Royal School

Wolverhampton

Penn Road, Wolverhampton,
West Midlands WV3 0EG UK

Tel: +44 (0)1902 341230

Email: info@theroyal.school

Website: theroyalschool.co.uk

Principal: Mr Mark Heywood

School type: State Boarding & Day School

Age range of pupils: 4–19 years (boarding from 11)

No. of pupils enrolled as at 01/09/2023: 1476

Fees as at 01/09/2023:

Full Boarding: £16,254 per annum

Average class size: 25

Yorkshire & Humberside

Pocklington School

Pocklington is an inclusive, family focussed and academic school that offers incredible experiences inside and outside the classroom. We believe in encouraging pupils to seize opportunities from the broad range of activities we offer. Along with our approach to teaching and learning, these help to form our young Pocklingtonians' character and grow the qualities that support our values. Our sense of community, care for each other and pride in the school is tangible. This is no more evident than in our outstanding boarding provision. At the heart of this ethos lie our Values and Virtues. They guide us at Pocklington and mean our pupils leave with a deep sense of social responsibility and the ability to shape their own future.

Pocklington School lies 12 miles east of York on the edge of a vibrant, friendly market town, on a 50-acre campus with good public transport links and its own bus service. The school, founded in 1514, blends strong traditions with innovation and flexibility, encouraging pupils to have the courage to take chances with their learning and achieve the best that they can.

Numerous co-curricular activities for day and boarding pupils take place every day until 5pm, and each pupil is encouraged to pursue their own interests to help develop the depth of character and self-awareness to tackle life's challenges on their own terms. Facilities include a 300-seat theatre, an indoor sports hall, strength and conditioning room and swimming pool, plus 21-acres of grass sports pitches and two full-sized synthetic pitches.

Full, weekly and part-time boarding options are available, in outstanding boarding houses that create a home from home for all our boarders.

Right through from Prep School, where the Curiosity Project curriculum enables children to expand their critical thinking skills through structured and creative enquiry, to the Sixth Form where independent thought is prized, our pupils are encouraged to be resilient, resourceful learners. To support the school's strategic goal of further improving academic performance, increasing pupils' independence and meeting the needs of modern family life, pupils engage in a 5-day academic week, Monday to Friday. Saturdays are reserved for sports fixtures, and boarders enjoy a full weekend programme of activities and trips.

We employ the best educational tools and new technology to ensure youngsters are enthused and inspired by the world of knowledge available to them. Our Art and Design Technology Centre has every facility to encourage the pursuit of traditional arts and crafts, as well as providing cutting-edge equipment for digital and computer design, and manufacturing technology. An individual approach, supported by flexible learning platforms allows each pupil to progress at their own pace, boosting their confidence and self-esteem so they often exceed their expectations.

Our Sixth Form has spacious communal areas, a study centre, and a comprehensive library. Students are encouraged to work both collaboratively and independently as they begin to make the transition to university study and/or workplace success.

Recent former pupils who retain links with the school include Davis Cup winner Kyle Edmund, England rugby star Rob Webber and world-renowned concert pianist Alexandra Dariescu.

We aim to instil the Pocklington Values and Virtues into all our pupils, to engage with our families and support them in raising the Pocklingtonians of tomorrow and to be open to innovation, conscious of tradition and so secure our Foundation's future.

(Founded 1514)

West Green, Pocklington, York,
North Yorkshire YO42 2NJ UK

Tel: 01759 321200

Fax: 01759 306366

Email: admissions@pocklingtonschool.com

Website: www.pocklingtonschool.com

Headmaster: Mr Toby Seth MA (Cantab)

Appointed: January 2019

School type: Co-educational Day & Boarding Prep & Senior, Nursery & Sixth Form

Religious Denomination:
Christian ethos welcoming all faiths and none

Age range of pupils: 2–18 years

No. of pupils enrolled as at 01/09/2023: 725

Boys: 363 ***Girls:*** 362 ***Sixth Form:*** 160

No. of boarders: 76

Fees as at 01/09/2023:

Day: £18,798 per annum

Weekly Boarding: £31,875 per annum

Full Boarding: £34,656 per annum
(See website for full range of boarding options)

Sorting Algorithms

Queen Ethelburga's Collegiate

Students and staff at Queen Ethelburga's College and Faculty are celebrating another successful year, following the publishing of the 2023 A level and BTEC examination results. In 2023, across the two senior schools the combined percentage of A*/A grades at A Level is 79%, with the percentage of BTEC Distinction* and Distinction grades in QE Faculty reaching 76%.

QE is an Excellent rated Collegiate (ISI 2019), known locally, nationally, and internationally as a group of four schools that promotes the highest standards in all that it does. The Collegiate welcomes girls and boys from 3 months and supports them through four schools - Chapter House (3 months to Year 5), King's Magna (Year 6 to 9), The College and The Faculty (both Year 10 to 13).

QE also places great emphasis on our students growing into resilient, caring, compassionate and confident adults, who develop independence and initiative, and who can take responsibility for their own learning and futures. We provide opportunities for students to take part in a range of wider enrichment and extra-curricular activities to help them to gain skills in leadership, teamwork and collaboration, and decision making.

Students at QE have access to an impressive 150 sports and activities each week, including popular sports such as hockey, football, netball, cricket, swimming, basketball, rounders, tennis, dance, gymnastics, trampolining, athletics, badminton, and volleyball. Our team of sports staff cater for all abilities and encourage each student to make the most of all the fantastic opportunities on offer during their time here. We have a well-honed mix of physical education teachers and specialist sports coaches, many of whom are ex-professional sportspeople themselves. This means there really is no limit to the level our students can train to. Health and fitness is so central to school life for students that many continue with sport and exercise, either recreationally or as a route of study, that it continues to be a key part of their lives long after they have left us for the next step in their education or career.

What enables us to deliver all of this sporting activity so successfully of course is the outstanding range of high quality facilities on campus. We're pretty unique in that we have a dedicated Sports Village to which all students have access to inside and outside of formal school hours. The Village is home to a 25-metre swimming pool, triple court sports hall, 100 station fitness suite and free weights centre. Outside we have a four-lane synthetic cushioned running track and over 30 acres of both grass and artificial 3G pitches. We also have a number of specialist studios used for; martial arts, wrestling, dance, gymnastics, table tennis, cycling, archery, fencing and boxing.

Care is the most important element within the QE community; every member of the Collegiate, staff and student, is responsible for the pastoral care and happiness of the site. QE offers support and guidance to all students and parents to ensure that we are all working to support individual students needs and equipping them with the right skills, not only to be successful in education, but to excel in their chosen career and life in general. Our dedicated THRIVE@QE programme offers all students a huge range of activities to support their positive mental health and wellbeing.

QE's Hill Standard is 'To be the best that I can with the gifts that I have' providing every child with a springboard to their individual successes, whichever pathway they choose.

(Founded 1912)

Thorpe Underwood Hall, Ouseburn, York, North Yorkshire YO26 9SS UK

Tel: 01423 33 33 30

Email: admissions@qe.org

Website: www.qe.org

Principal: Dan Machin

School type: Co-educational Day & Boarding Prep & Senior, Nursery & Sixth Form

Religious Denomination: Multi-Denominational

Age range of pupils: 3–19 years (boarding from 7)

No. of pupils enrolled as at 01/09/2023: 1400

Average class size: 18

Teacher/pupil ratio: 1:10

Rishworth School

Adventure awaits at Rishworth School. After all, this is a school whose past teachers included the real James Bond himself. Patrick Dalzel-Job was *"an unusual officer who possesses no fear of danger,"* the kind who would evacuate all civilians from a large town called Narvik just before it was destroyed by German bombers - courage and charisma that would inspire a decades-long blockbuster series.

At Rishworth School, Dalzel-Job taught Chemistry and ran the Combined Cadets Force (CCF). His legacy prevails. At any given day, life at the school is action-packed - the kind that would lead to an excellent education both in and out of the classroom.

Each week, there are over 90 enrichment and extension activities available to students. From skiing and rock climbing to astronomy and mystery solving, these let students live the school's motto *"Res Non Verba"* (Deeds Not Words).

Such spirit and adventure are found from the Nursery through to Sixth Form. They start young exploring the great outdoors during forest school. By the time they reach the end of their schooling journey, students are bold and courageous in their academic achievements. Many set off to top universities such as Cambridge to study law, or even taking exciting routes such as commercial pilot training.

Founded in 1724, Rishworth School has been around for almost 300 years. It offers a curriculum designed to cater to every child's needs. Small classes - 15 on average at the Senior School and eight on average in the Sixth Form - allow teachers to understand each child's character and talents. It's an approach that's led to outstanding exam results. Based on the 2023 summer A Level examinations, students of Rishworth School achieved a 100% pass rate, and 80% of students scored A* to C.

Located in the countryside within Ryburn Valley, the 140-acre campus overlooks moors, fields, hills and the reservoir - the perfect backdrop for the spirit of community and the sense of belonging every students feels here.

It is a home away from home with a blend of people, practices, provisions, and place where students can thrive. Boarders feel happy, cared for, healthy and secure. *"Rishworth School taught independence and gave me confidence. Boarding at Rishworth solidified these attributes,"* says former student Andy McPhail.

Still, academic excellence is only one aspect of success Rishworth School students achieve. Self-discovery, finding new passions, trying new things and learning new skills outside of the classroom are some achievements a student will experience during their years here.

Understanding the role that learning outside the classroom plays in students' development, Rishworth introduced enrichment programmes that range from music and sports to photography and film.

Fancy learning to Kayak or learning how to code? Rishworth School has both a kayaking club and a coding programme for students. On top of that, F1 remote control, cooking club, orchestra and community projects are some of the other options available.

RISHWORTH
SCHOOL

(Founded 1724)

Oldham Road, Sowerby Bridge, Halifax,
West Yorkshire HX6 4QA UK

Tel: 01422 822217

Email: admissions@rishworth-school.co.uk

Website: www.rishworth-school.co.uk

Head: Dr Anthony Wilkins

Appointed: November 2020

School type: Co-educational Day & Boarding Prep & Senior, Nursery & Sixth Form

Age range of pupils: 3–18 years (boarding from 11)

Fees as at 01/09/2023: Please see website

Average class size: 15–20 (8–12 in Sixth Form)

The Froebelian School

The Froebelian School, Horsforth is one of Leeds' leading independent preparatory schools.

A Froebelian School education starts at three years of age as pupils enter our Lower Kindergarten and continues to Form IV (Year 6). School life is varied, exciting, and fast-paced. There is never a dull moment as we embody our ethos of 'Giving a Flying Start to the Citizens of Tomorrow'.

Since The Froebelian School's foundation in 1913, influenced by German educationalist, Friedrich Froebel, it has become one of the North's leading educational success stories. Our academic results are outstanding, but the school offers much more than an excellent academic education: we firmly believe in laying solid foundations for a lifelong love of learning, to gain knowledge and skills and develop personal attributes, relevant to each and every child's future.

The sense of community at Froebelian is second to none and we value our place in our local community, too. The breadth of opportunity on offer means that there is something for everyone to discover and in which to thrive. Our pupils are confident and our talented and passionate staff guide and support each individual on their personal journeys of discovery.

Children are at the heart of everything we do and we are passionate that they enjoy a positive experience, in a warm, friendly, caring, structured and secure environment where they are known as individuals and supported at each step of their journey through the school.

"We chose Froebelian because it feels like a family. The nurturing environment that Froebelian provides brings out the best in our children." - A Parent

We are clear that a pupil's education should be a broad and varied experience and our pupils are encouraged to step outside their comfort zone and take risks in a safe and supportive environment, discovering new talents and interests which provide much happiness at school and, critically, develop their self-confidence, problem solving abilities and interpersonal skills.

Sport, Drama and Music all play important roles in school life. Games receives a more generous time allocation than in many schools and our pupils represent the school in fixtures in a wide range of sports. There are a multitude of opportunities to be involved in musical ensembles, groups and performances. House Drama competitions give large numbers of pupils the opportunity to tread the boards, and our end of year productions are of exceptional quality, playing to large audiences at Yeadon Town Hall.

We have a very active Outdoor Education Curriculum which provides residential experiences across the UK and all pupils in Year 6 undertake our very own version of the Duke of Edinburgh's Award Scheme - The FIVe (sic) Steps Challenge - through which they acquire self-reliance, resilience and teamwork whilst learning the importance of service to the community.

We have made significant investment in our early years provision creating bespoke-designed classrooms and continuous access to an exceptional outdoor space including our hidden, secret forest and treehouse. With 51 weeks a year provision for all children, funding available for our youngest children, and plans for further investment and development in STEM we aim to balance both academic and co-curricular spheres of school life.

The latest Independent Schools Inspectorate report judged The Froebelian School as 'excellent' for the quality of the pupils' achievements and the quality of pupils' personal development - this is the highest judgement available. *"The pupils' attitudes to learning are exceptional."* - ISI Inspectorate

Our children adore their school and are justly proud of all they do. They love learning and there is a true sense of fun. We would love you to experience the warmth of our Froebelian Family for yourselves - please do come and meet them! Visit www.froebelian.com to find out more.

(Founded 1913)

Clarence Road, Horsforth, Leeds,
West Yorkshire LS18 4LB UK

Tel: 0113 2583047

Email: office@froebelian.co.uk

Website: www.froebelian.com

Head Teacher: Mrs Anna Coulson

Appointed: 2023

School type:
Co-educational Day Preparatory & Nursery

Age range of pupils: 3–11 years

No. of pupils enrolled as at 01/09/2023: 150

Fees as at 01/09/2023:

Day: £6,255–£9,300 (compulsory school lunches £804 per annum)

Teacher/pupil ratio: 1:10

Scotland

Loretto School

Our changing world is full of challenges and opportunities for young people. Finding a school that can provide an all-round education to fully prepare them for what lies ahead is vital. Loretto is that school.

Founded in 1827, Loretto is Scotland's first boarding school. Today an independent, private, boarding and day school, it welcomes girls and boys, from 3 to 18 years.

Set in a safe, leafy 85-acre campus just six miles from Edinburgh, Loretto enjoys all the advantages of this rural setting while being globally connected - the school is just nine kilometres/six miles from Scotland's capital city, its international airport, rail, and road networks.

Welcoming just over 500 pupils, the first thing you notice when you enter Loretto's campus is the warmth and energy of both pupils and staff. Relationships are marked by kindness, care and respect; a truly special environment for providing the confidence and know-how to thrive in life beyond Loretto. More than nine pupils out of ten achieve places at their chosen onwards destination, many attending top universities such as, Oxford, Cambridge, St Andrews, Newcastle, and Durham, as well as American universities.

Loretto, with its superb location on Scotland's Golf Coast, also has a strong tradition of top-level golf. The school's surrounding area of East Lothian offers a choice of magnificent links courses, and in 2002 this tradition blossomed into The Golf Academy. The Academy is now regarded as one of Europe's leading golf academies where pupils can develop their sporting talent in tandem with an exceptional education.

Directed by a team of top-class PGA Professional coaches, Loretto offers golfers access to state-of-the-art practice centres, and an abundance of local, accessible golf courses. With innovative practice facilities, including a nine-hole artificial putting green, several driving bays, bunker and chipping areas, and a putting studio with video analysis and Trackman.

From day one, Loretto's founder was dedicated to blending academic excellence with a wealth of experiences beyond the classroom. The enormous range of co-curricular activities offered ensures that each pupil can grow and develop wherever their interests and talents may lie. The school's achievements in music, art, drama and its strong reputation in sporting endeavours - both in major team sports and other sports, are testament to that.

Ultimately, to really understand the warm and welcoming atmosphere that makes Loretto different, you have to experience the school in person. So please come along for a visit - you will soon see why our pupils are so proud to be called Lorettonians.

Loretto

(Founded 1827)

Linkfield Road, Musselburgh, East Lothian EH21 7RE UK

Tel: +44 (0)131 653 4455

Email: admissions@loretto.com

Website: www.loretto.com

Head of School: Dr. Graham R. W. Hawley

Appointed: 2014

School type: Co-educational Day & Boarding Prep & Senior, Nursery & Sixth Form

Age range of pupils: 3–18 years

No. of pupils enrolled as at 01/09/2023: 500

Fees as at 01/09/2023:

Day: £3,212–£9,182 per term

Full Boarding: £8,782–£13,485 per term

Flexi Boarding: £7,479 – £11,191 per term

Average class size: Junior 14; Senior 17; Exam Years 15

Teacher/pupil ratio: 1:7

BEST IN BLOOM
BEST IN BLOOM

Overseas

Ecole Jeannine Manuel - Lille

École Jeannine Manuel Lille is a non-profit coeducational school founded in 1992 and welcomes students from nursery to 12th grade. As the sister campus of École Jeannine Manuel Paris, the school has the same educational project and mission: promoting international understanding through bilingual education. An associated UNESCO school, École Jeannine Manuel Lille is the only non-denominational independent school in Nord-Pas-de-Calais, with over 900 pupils representing 40 nationalities and every major cultural tradition. The school's academic excellence matches it diversity: École Jeannine Manuel Lille is regularly ranked among the best French high schools (ranked first for four consecutive years). The school is accredited by the French Ministry of Education, the International Baccalaureate Organization (IBO), the Council of International Schools (CIS), and the New England Association of Schools and Colleges (NEASC).

Ecole Jeannine Manuel Lille's campus extends over 8.5 acres. It includes a boarding house, a dining hall, and state-of-the-art sports facilities including a 1600 m2 gym with its own climbing wall, a 300m racing track, and two outdoor playing fields. The boarding house currently welcomes 120 pupils from 6th to 12th grade.

Each year, École Jeannine Manuel Lille welcomes non-French speaking students. These students integrate the school through the adaptation program, which provides intensive instruction in French, support in English as needed, help in understanding and adjusting to French culture, and differentiated coursework and assessment during their adaptation period. The lower and middle school follow the French national curriculum with several exceptions: English is taught every day and, in middle school, experimental sciences, history and geography are taught in English. The curriculum is enriched at all levels, not only with a more advanced English language and literature curriculum, but also, for example, with Chinese language instruction (compulsory in grades 3–4–5), an integrated science program in lower school, and independent research projects in middle school.

In upper school, tenth graders follow the French national curriculum, albeit taught 50% in French and 50% in English. In 11th grade, pupils choose between the French track (*Baccalauréat Français International*, BFI) and the International Baccalaureate Diploma Programme (IBDP). Approximately 25% of our pupils opt for the IBDP.

Admission

Although admission is competitive, the school makes every effort to reserve space for international applicants, including children of families who expect to remain in France for a limited period of time and wish to combine a cultural immersion in French education with the ability to re-enter their own school systems and excel.

(Founded 1992)

418 bis rue Albert Bailly, Marcq-en-Baroeul, 59700 France

Tel: +33 3 20 65 90 50

Email: admissions-lille@ejm.net

Website: www.ecolejeanninemanuel.org

Head of School: Constance Devaux

School type: Co-educational Day & Boarding

Age range of pupils: 3–18 years

No. of pupils enrolled as at 01/09/2023: 980

Fees as at 01/09/2023:

Day: €6,632 per annum

Full Boarding: €25,875 per annum

IB Classes: €23,945 per annum

Average class size: 25 (15 in IBDP)

Ecole Jeannine Manuel - Paris

École Jeannine Manuel is a non-profit pre-K-12 coeducational school founded in 1954 with the mission to promote international understanding through bilingual (French/English) education. An associated UNESCO school, École Jeannine Manuel welcomes pupils representing 80 nationalities and every major cultural tradition. The school's academic excellence matches its diversity: École Jeannine Manuel is regularly ranked among the best French high schools (state and independent) for its overall academic performance (ranked first for ten consecutive years). The school is accredited by the French Ministry of Education, the International Baccalaureate Organization (IBO), the Council of International Schools (CIS) and the New England Association of Schools and Colleges (NEASC).

Each year, the school welcomes more than 100 new non-French speaking pupils. These students integrate the school through our adaptation program, which provides intensive instruction in French, support in English as needed, help in understanding and adjusting to French culture, and differentiated coursework and assessment during their adaptation period.

The lower and middle school follow the French national curriculum with several exceptions: English is taught every day and, in middle school, experimental sciences, history and geography are taught in English. The curriculum is enriched at all levels, not only with a more advanced English language and literature curriculum, but also, for example, with Chinese language instruction (compulsory in grades 3–4–5), an integrated science program in lower school, and independent research projects in middle school.

In upper school, tenth graders follow the French national curriculum, albeit taught 50% in French and 50% in English. In 11th grade, pupils choose between the French track (*Baccalauréat Français International*, BFI) and the International Baccalaureate Diploma Programme (IBDP). Approximately 25% of our pupils opt for the IBDP.

Over the past three years, around 13% of our graduating students attended US colleges or universities, 41% chose to study in the UK, and 29% entered the French higher education system. Around 7% of graduating students go on to study in countries all over the world such as the Netherlands, Switzerland, Belgium, Germany, Spain, Italy, and Australia.

Admission

Admission is competitive and applications typically exceed available spaces by a ratio of 7:1. The school nonetheless makes every effort to reserve space for international applicants, including children of families who expect to remain in France for a limited period of time and wish to combine a cultural immersion in French education with the ability to seamlessly re-enter the school system in their home country.

(Founded 1954)

70 rue du Théâtre, Paris, 75015 France

Tel: +33 1 44 37 00 80

Email: admissions@ejm.net

Website: www.ecolejeanninemanuel.org

Principal: Jérôme Giovendo

School type: Co-educational Day

Age range of pupils: 4–18 years

No. of pupils enrolled as at 01/09/2023: 2400

Fees as at 01/09/2023:

Day: €7,935–€8,749 per annum

IB Classes: €28,065 per annum

Average class size: 25

EARTH
A
LOL!
GAP
GAP

Geographical directory of schools

KEY TO SYMBOLS

- Boys' school
- Girls' school
- International school
- Tutorial or sixth form college
- A levels
- Boarding accommodation
- Bursaries
- International Baccalaureate
- Learning support
- Entrance at 16+
- Vocational qualifications
- Independent Association of Preparatory Schools
- The Headmasters' & Headmistresses' Conference
- Independent Schools Association
- Girls' School Association
- Boarding Schools' Association
- Society of Heads

Unless otherwise indicated, all schools are coeducational day schools. Single-sex and boarding schools will be indicated by the relevant icon.

Channel Islands

KEY TO SYMBOLS

- Boys' school
- Girls' school
- International school
- Tutorial or sixth form college
- A levels
- Boarding accommodation
- Bursaries
- International Baccalaureate
- Learning support
- Entrance at 16+
- Vocational qualifications
- Independent Association of Preparatory Schools
- The Headmasters' & Headmistresses' Conference
- Independent Schools Association
- Girls' School Association
- Boarding Schools' Association
- Society of Heads

Unless otherwise indicated, all schools are coeducational day schools. Single-sex and boarding schools will be indicated by the relevant icon.

Guernsey

Elizabeth College
The Grange, St Peter Port,
Guernsey GY1 2PY
Tel: 01481 726544
Principal: Ms Jenny Palmer
Age range: 21/2–18 years
Ⓐ £ 16

Elizabeth College Junior School
Beechwood, Queen's Road, St
Peter Port, Guernsey GY1 1PU
Tel: 01481 722123
Headteacher: Mr Richard Fyfe
Age range: 21/2–11 years

The Ladies' College
Les Gravées, St Peter Port,
Guernsey GY1 1RW
Tel: 01481 721602
Principal: Ms Ashley Clancy
Age range: G21/2–18 years
Ⓐ 16

Jersey

Beaulieu Convent School
Wellington Road, St Helier,
Jersey JE2 4RJ
Tel: 01534 731280
Executive Headmaster: Mr Chris Beirne
Age range: B16–19 years G3–19 years
Ⓐ £ 16

De La Salle College
Wellington Road, St Saviour,
Jersey JE2 7TH
Tel: 01534 754100
Head of College: Mr Jason Turner
Age range: B3–18 years
Ⓐ 16

FCJ Primary School
Deloraine Road, St Saviour,
Jersey JE2 7XB
Tel: 01534 723063
Headteacher: Ms Donna Lenzi
Age range: 4–11 years

Helvetia House School
14 Elizabeth Place, St
Helier, Jersey JE2 3PN
Tel: 01534 724928
Headmistress: Mrs Lindsey
Woodward BA, DipEd
Age range: G4–11 years

Jersey College For Girls
Le Mont Millais, St Saviour,
Jersey JE2 7YB
Tel: 01534 516200
Principal: Mr Carl Howarth
Age range: G11–18 years

St George's Preparatory School
La Hague Manor, Rue de la
Hague, St Peter, Jersey JE3 7DB
Tel: 01534 481593
Headmaster: Mr Cormac Timothy
Age range: 2–11 years
£

ST MICHAEL'S PREPARATORY SCHOOL
For further details see p. 40
La Rue de la Houguette, Five
Oaks, St Saviour, Jersey JE2 7UG
Tel: 01534 856904
Email: office@stmichaels.je
Website: www.stmichaels.je
Headmaster: Mr Henry Marshall
Age range: 3–14 years
No. of pupils: 302
Fees: Day £12,915–£20,304
£

St. Christopher's School
1901 Building, Rue De La Chapelle,
St. Clement, Jersey JE2 6LN
Tel: +44 (0)1534 724758
Age range: 3–11 years

Victoria College
Mont Millais, St Helier, Jersey JE1 4HT
Tel: 01534 638200
Head Teacher: Dr Gareth Hughes
Age range: B11–18 years
Ⓐ 16

Victoria College Preparatory School
Pleasant Street, St Helier, Jersey JE2 4RR
Tel: 01534 723468
Head Teacher: Mr Dan Pateman
Age range: B7–11 years

Central & West

KEY TO SYMBOLS

- *Boys' school*
- *Girls' school*
- *International school*
- *Tutorial or sixth form college*
- *A levels*
- *Boarding accommodation*
- *Bursaries*
- *International Baccalaureate*
- *Learning support*
- *Entrance at 16+*
- *Vocational qualifications*
- *Independent Association of Preparatory Schools*
- *The Headmasters' & Headmistresses' Conference*
- *Independent Schools Association*
- *Girls' School Association*
- *Boarding Schools' Association*
- *Society of Heads*

Unless otherwise indicated, all schools are coeducational day schools. Single-sex and boarding schools will be indicated by the relevant icon.

Buckinghamshire

Akeley Wood School
Akeley Wood House, Buckingham, Buckinghamshire MK18 5AE
Tel: 01280 814110
Headmaster: Mr Simon Antwis
Age range: 12 months–18 years
No. of pupils: 700 VIth100
Fees: Day £10,665–£15,900

Ashfold School
Dorton House, Dorton, Aylesbury, Buckinghamshire HP18 9NG
Tel: 01844 238237
Headmaster: Mr Colin MacIntosh
Age range: 3–13 years

Baytul Ilm Secondary School
12a Clarke Road, Bletchley, Milton Keynes, Buckinghamshire MK1 1LG
Tel: 01908 804163
Age range: B11–16 years

Broughton Manor Preparatory School
Newport Road, Broughton, Milton Keynes, Buckinghamshire MK10 9AA
Tel: 01908 665234
Heads: Mr J Smith & Mrs R Smith
Age range: 2 months–11 years

CALDICOTT
For further details see p. 44
Crown Lane, Farnham Royal, Buckinghamshire SL2 3SL
Tel: 01753 649301
Email: admissions@caldicott.com
Website: www.caldicott.com
Headmaster: Mr Jeremy Banks BA (Hons) QTS, MEd
Age range: B7–13 years (flexi boarding from 7)
No. of pupils: 250

Chesham Preparatory School
Two Dells Lane, Chesham, Buckinghamshire HP5 3QF
Tel: 01494 782619
Headmaster: Mr Jonathan Beale
Age range: 3–13 years

Child First Aylesbury Pre-School
35 Rickfords Hill, Aylesbury, Buckinghamshire HP20 2RT
Tel: 01296 433224
Age range: 3–5 years

Crown House Preparatory School
Bassetsbury Manor, Bassetsbury Lane, High Wycombe, Buckinghamshire HP11 1QX
Tel: 01494 529927
Headteacher: Mrs Sarah Hobby
Age range: 3–11 years

Dair House School
Bishops Blake, Beaconsfield Road, Farnham Royal, Buckinghamshire SL2 3BY
Tel: 01753 643964
Head of School: Mrs Janine Bull
Age range: 3–11 years
No. of pupils: 125
Fees: Day £1,020–£4,850

Gateway School
1 High Street, Great Missenden, Buckinghamshire HP16 9AA
Tel: 01494 862407
Head of School: Mrs Cath Bufton-Green
Age range: 2–11 years

Godstowe Preparatory School
Shrubbery Road, High Wycombe, Buckinghamshire HP13 6PR
Tel: 01494 529273
Headmistress: Ms Kate Bailey
Age range: B3–7 years G3–13 years (boarding from 7)

Griffin House Preparatory School
Little Kimble, Aylesbury, Buckinghamshire HP17 0XP
Tel: 01844 346154
Headmaster: Mr Tim Walford
Age range: 3–11 years

Heatherton School
10 Copperkins Lane, Amersham, Buckinghamshire HP6 5QB
Tel: 01494 726433
Headteacher: Mrs Nicola Nicoll
Age range: B3–4 years G3–11 years
No. of pupils: 160
Fees: Day £3,525–£5,300

High March
23 Ledborough Lane, Beaconsfield, Buckinghamshire HP9 2PZ
Tel: 01494 675186
Head of School: Mrs Kate Gater
Age range: B3–4 years G3–11 years
No. of pupils: 282
Fees: Day £6,255–£17,325

Milton Keynes Preparatory School
Tattenhoe Lane, Milton Keynes, Buckinghamshire MK3 7EG
Tel: 01908 642111
Head of School: Mr Simon Driver
Age range: 2 months–11 years

Pipers Corner School
Pipers Lane, Great Kingshill, High Wycombe, Buckinghamshire HP15 6LP
Tel: 01494 718 255
Headmistress: Mrs H J Ness-Gifford BA(Hons), PGCE
Age range: G4–18 years

Stowe School
Buckingham, Buckinghamshire MK18 5EH
Tel: 01280 818000
Headmaster: Dr Anthony Wallersteiner
Age range: 13–18 years

Swanbourne House School
Swanbourne, Milton Keynes, Buckinghamshire MK17 0HZ
Tel: 01296 720264
Head of School: Mrs Jane Thorpe
Age range: 4–13 years

The Beacon School
15 Amersham Road, Chesham Bois, Amersham, Buckinghamshire HP6 5PF
Tel: 01494 433654
Headmaster: Mr William Phelps
Age range: B3–13 years

The Chalfonts Independent Grammar School
19 London Road, High Wycombe, Buckinghamshire HP11 1BJ
Tel: +44 (0)1494 875502
Principal: Mr David Shandley
Age range: 11–18 years

The Grove Independent School
Redland Drive, Loughton, Milton Keynes, Buckinghamshire MK5 8HD
Tel: 01908 690590
Principal: Mrs Deborah Berkin
Age range: 3 months–13 years

The Royal Grammar School
Amersham Road, High Wycombe, Buckinghamshire HP13 6QT
Tel: 01494 524955
Headmaster: Mr Philip Wayne
Age range: B11–18 years

THE WEBBER INDEPENDENT SCHOOL
For further details see p. 56
Soskin Drive, Stantonbury Fields, Milton Keynes, Buckinghamshire MK14 6DP
Tel: 01908 574740
Email: info@webberindependentschool.co.uk
Website: www.webberindependentschool.com
Principal: Mrs Hilary Marsden
Age range: 6 months–16 years
No. of pupils: 311
Fees: Day £3,660–£5,025

THORNTON COLLEGE
For further details see p. 58
College Lane, Thornton, Milton Keynes, Buckinghamshire MK17 0HJ
Tel: 01280 812610
Email: admissions@thorntoncollege.com
Website: www.thorntoncollege.com
Headteacher: Dr Louise Shaw
Age range: G3–18 years (boarding from 8)
No. of pupils: 400
Fees: Day £15,180–£19,350 WB £21,765–£27,555 FB £27,075–£33,570

Walton Pre-Preparatory School & Nursery
The Old Rectory, Walton Drive, Milton Keynes, Buckinghamshire MK7 6BB
Tel: 01908 678403
Head of School: Mrs Chantelle McLaughlan
Age range: 2 months–5 years

WYCOMBE ABBEY
For further details see p. 60
Frances Dove Way, High Wycombe, Buckinghamshire HP11 1PE
Tel: +44 (0)1494 520381
Email: admissions@wycombeabbey.com
Website: www.wycombeabbey.com
Headmistress: Mrs Jo Duncan MA (St Andrews), PGCE (Cantab)
Age range: G11–18 years
No. of pupils: 660
Fees: Day £36,000 FB £47,700

Gloucestershire

Al-Ashraf Primary School
Al-Ashraf Cultural Centre, Stratton Road, Gloucester, Gloucestershire GL1 4HB
Tel: 01452 503533
Head Teacher: Mr Abdullah Patel
Age range: 2–11 years

Al-Ashraf Secondary School for Girls
Sinope Street, off Widden Street, Gloucester, Gloucestershire GL1 4AW
Tel: 01452 300465
Head Teacher: Abdullah Patel
Age range: G11–16 years

Beaudesert Park School
Minchinhampton, Stroud, Gloucestershire GL6 9AF
Tel: 01453 832072
Headmaster: Mr C D Searson
Age range: 3–13 years (boarding from 8)

Berkhampstead School
Pittville Circus Road, Cheltenham, Gloucestershire GL52 2QA
Tel: 01242 523263
Headmaster: Richard Cross
Age range: 3 months–11 years
No. of pupils: 260
Fees: Day £3,015–£4,330

Bredon School
Pull Court, Bushley, Tewkesbury, Gloucestershire GL20 6AH
Tel: 01684 293156
Headmaster: Mr Nick Oldham
Age range: 7–18 years

Cheltenham College
Bath Road, Cheltenham, Gloucestershire GL53 7LD
Tel: 01242 265600
Head of School: Mrs Nicola Huggett
Age range: 13–18 years

Cheltenham College Preparatory School
Thirlestaine Road, Cheltenham, Gloucestershire GL53 7AB
Tel: 01242 522697
Head of School: Mr Tom O'Sullivan
Age range: 3–13 years

Cheltenham Ladies' College
Bayshill Road, Cheltenham, Gloucestershire GL50 3EP
Tel: +44 (0)1242 520691
Principal: Eve Jardine-Young MA
Age range: G11–18 years (boarding from 11)
No. of pupils: 862
Fees: Day £9,900–£11,300 FB £15,050–£16,900

Dean Close Airthrie
27–29 Christ Church Road, Cheltenham, Gloucestershire GL50 2NY
Tel: 01242 512837
Headmaster: Mr Jason Dobbie
Age range: 4–11 years
No. of pupils: 80

Dean Close Pre-Preparatory & Preparatory School
Lansdown Road, Cheltenham, Gloucestershire GL51 6QS
Tel: +44 (0)1242 512217
Headmaster Preparatory School: Mr Paddy Moss
Age range: 2–13 years (boarding from 7)

Dean Close School
Shelburne Road, Cheltenham, Gloucestershire GL51 6HE
Tel: +44 (0)1242 258000
Headmaster: Mr Bradley Salisbury MEd, PGCE
Age range: 13–18 years (boarding from 13)
No. of pupils: 490
Fees: Day £8,470–£8,980 FB £12,625–£13,150

Dean Close St John's
Castleford Hill, Tutshill, Gloucestershire NP16 7LE
Tel: 01291 622045
Head: Mr Nick Thrower
Age range: 3–13 years (boarding from 7)

Edward Jenner School
The Elms, 44 London Road, Gloucester, Gloucestershire GL1 3NZ
Tel: 01452 380808
Head Teachers: Ms. Manda & Mr. Phil Brookes
Age range: 5–16 years

Hatherop Castle School
Hatherop, Cirencester, Gloucestershire GL7 3NB
Tel: 01285 750206
Headmaster: Mr Nigel Reed M.Ed, B.Sc (Hons), PGCE
Age range: 2–13 years

Hopelands Preparatory School
38/40 Regent Street, Stonehouse, Gloucestershire GL10 2AD
Tel: 01453 822164
Heads: Mrs Sonja Jones & Mrs Maria Boix
Age range: 3–11 years

Immanuel Christian School
Rodford Tabernacle, Westerleigh Road, Westerleigh, Gloucestershire BS37 8QG
Tel: 01454 311710
Head Teacher: Ms Joanna Gulliford
Age range: 4–16 years

Kitebrook Preparatory School
Kitebrook House, Moreton-in-Marsh, Gloucestershire GL56 0RP
Tel: 01608 674350
Headmistress: Mrs Susan McLean
Age range: 3–13 years

OneSchool Global UK Bristol Campus
Station Road, Wanswell, Berkeley, Gloucestershire GL13 9RS
Tel: 01453 511282
Age range: 7–18 years

OneSchool Global UK Gloucester Campus
Eastbrook Road, Gloucester, Gloucestershire GL4 3DB
Tel: 01452 417722
Age range: 7–18 years

Rendcomb College
Rendcomb, Cirencester, Gloucestershire GL7 7HA
Tel: 01285 831213
Head of School: Mr Rob Jones
Age range: 3–18 years

St Edward's Preparatory School
London Road, Charlton Kings, Cheltenham, Gloucestershire GL52 6NR
Tel: +44 (0)1242 388550
Head of Prep School: Mr Paul Fathers BA (Hons) PGCE
Age range: 1–11 years

St Edward's Senior School & Sixth Form
Cirencester Road, Charlton Kings, Cheltenham, Gloucestershire GL53 8EY
Tel: +44 (0)1242 388555
Principal: Mr Matthew Burke BA (Hons), PGCE, Ad dip Ed, NPQH
Age range: 11–18 years

The Acorn School
Church Street, Nailsworth, Stroud, Gloucestershire GL6 0BP
Tel: 01453 836508
Headmaster: Mr Graeme E B Whiting
Age range: 6–18 years

The King's School
Gloucester, Gloucestershire GL1 2BG
Tel: 01452 337337
Headmaster: Mr David Morton
Age range: 3–18 years

The Richard Pate School
Southern Road, Leckhampton, Cheltenham, Gloucestershire GL53 9RP
Tel: 01242 522086
Headmaster: Mr Robert MacDonald
Age range: 3–11 years

Westonbirt Prep School
Westonbirt, Tetbury, Gloucestershire GL8 8QG
Tel: 01666 881400
Headmaster: Mr Sean Price
Age range: 2–11 years

Westonbirt School
Westonbirt, Tetbury, Gloucestershire GL8 8QG
Tel: 01666 880333
Headmistress: Mrs Natasha Dangerfield
Age range: 11–18 years

Wotton House International School
Wotton House, Horton Road, Gloucester, Gloucestershire GL1 3PR
Tel: +44 (0)1452 764248
Principal: Dr Daniel Sturdy
Age range: 7–16 years

Wycliffe College
Bristol Road, Stonehouse, Gloucestershire GL10 2AF
Tel: 01453 822432
Senior School Head: Mr Nick Gregory BA, MEd
Age range: 3–19 years (boarding from 7)
No. of pupils: 696
Fees: Day £9,675–£20,985 FB £20,625–£38,115

Oxfordshire

Abingdon Preparatory School
Josca's House, Kingston Road, Frilford, Oxfordshire OX13 5NX
Tel: +44 (0)1865 391570
Headmaster: Mr Craig Williams
Age range: B4–13 years

Abingdon School
Park Road, Abingdon, Oxfordshire OX14 1DE
Tel: +44 (0)1235 849029
Headmaster: Mr Michael Windsor
Age range: B11–18 years

Bloxham School
Bloxham, Banbury, Oxfordshire OX15 4PE
Tel: 01295 720222
Headmaster: Mr Paul Sanderson
Age range: 11–18 years

Burford School
Cheltenham Road, Burford, Oxfordshire OX18 4PL
Tel: 01993 823303
Headteacher: Mr M Albrighton
Age range: 11–18 years

Carfax College
39–42 Hythe Bridge Street, Oxford, Oxfordshire OX1 2EP
Tel: +44 (0)1865 200676
Principal: Carl Morris
Age range: 11–21 years
No. of pupils: 24

Carrdus School
Overthorpe Hall, Banbury, Oxfordshire OX17 2BS
Tel: 01295 263733
Head: Mr Edward Way
Age range: 3–11 years

Chandlings
Bagley Wood, Kennington, Oxford, Oxfordshire OX1 5ND
Tel: 01865 730771
Head: Christine Cook
Age range: 2–11 years

Cherwell College Oxford
St George's Mansion, George Street, Oxford, Oxfordshire OX1 2AR
Tel: 01865 953362
Principal: Mr Stephen Clarke
Age range: 12–18 years

Christ Church Cathedral School
3 Brewer Street, Oxford, Oxfordshire OX1 1QW
Tel: 01865 242561
Headmaster: Mr Richard Murray
Age range: B2–13 years (boarding from 7) G2–4 years

Cokethorpe School
Witney, Oxfordshire OX29 7PU
Tel: 01993 703921
Headmaster: Mr D Ettinger BA, MA, PGCE
Age range: 4–18 years

Cothill House
Cothill, Oxfordshire OX13 6JL
Tel: 01865 390800
Headmaster: Mr D M Bailey
Age range: B8–13 years

Cranford House School
Moulsford, Wallingford, Oxfordshire OX10 9HT
Tel: 01491 651218
Headmaster: Dr James Raymond
Age range: 3–18 years
No. of pupils: 525
Fees: Day £3,650–£6,175

d'Overbroeck's
333 Banbury Road, Oxford, Oxfordshire OX2 7PL
Tel: 01865 688 600
Principal: Mr Jonathan Cuff
Age range: 11–18 years

Dragon School
Bardwell Road, Oxford, Oxfordshire OX2 6SS
Tel: 01865 315405
Head: Emma Goldsmith
Age range: 4–13 years
No. of pupils: 798
Fees: Day £7,473 FB £10,931

EF Academy Oxford
Pullens Lane, Headington, Oxfordshire OX3 0DT
Tel: +41 (0) 43 430 41 00
Head of School: Mr. Mark Fletcher-Single
Age range: 16–19 years
Fees: Day £29,500 FB £44,500

Emmanuel Christian School
Sandford Road, Littlemore, Oxford, Oxfordshire OX4 4PU
Tel: 01865 395236
Principal: Mrs Elizabeth Nesbitt
Age range: 3–11 years

Greene's College Oxford
45 Pembroke Street, Oxford, Oxfordshire OX1 1BP
Tel: 01865 664400
Principal: Mrs. Carmen Dare
Age range: 16–18 years
No. of pupils: VIth60

Headington Preparatory School
26 London Road, Oxford, Oxfordshire OX3 7PB
Tel: +44 (0)1865 759400
Head: Mrs Jane Crouch BA (Hons), MA
Age range: G3–11 years

HEADINGTON RYE OXFORD
For further details see p. 48
Headington Road, Oxford, Oxfordshire OX3 7TD
Tel: +44 (0)1865 759100
Email: admissions@headington.org
Website: www.headington.org
Headmistress: Mrs Caroline Jordan MA(Oxon)
Age range: G11–18 years
Fees: Day £6,895–£7,505

Kingham Hill School
Kingham, Chipping Norton, Oxfordshire OX7 6TH
Tel: 01608 658999
Head of School: Mr Pete Last
Age range: 11–18 years
No. of pupils: 370
Fees: Day £20,565–£23,325 WB £29,025–£35,880 FB £29,985–£39,525

Kings Oxford
Temple Road, Oxford, Oxfordshire OX4 2UJ
Tel: +44 (0)1865 711829
Principal: Mr John Gale
Age range: 14–25 years

Magdalen College School
Cowley Place, Oxford, Oxfordshire OX4 1DZ
Tel: 01865 242191
Master: Miss Helen Pike
Age range: B7–18 years G16–18 years

Moulsford Preparatory School
Moulsford-on-Thames, Oxfordshire OX10 9HR
Tel: 01491 651438
Headmaster: Mr B Beardmore-Gray
Age range: B3–13 years G3–7 years
No. of pupils: 382
Fees: FB £8,235

New College School
2 Savile Road, Oxford, Oxfordshire OX1 3UA
Tel: 01865 285 560
Head of School: Dr Matthew Jenkinson
Age range: B4–13 years
No. of pupils: 156
Fees: Day £11,100–£17,700

Our Lady's Abingdon School
Radley Road, Abingdon-on-Thames, Oxfordshire OX14 3PS
Tel: 01235 524658
Principal: Mr Stephen Oliver
Age range: 7–18 years
No. of pupils: 374 VIth61
Fees: Day £11,280–£16,815

Oxford High School GDST
Belbroughton Road, Oxford, Oxfordshire OX2 6XA
Tel: 01865 559888
Headmistress: Ms Marina Gardiner Legge
Age range: G4–18 years

Oxford International College
1 London Place, Oxford, Oxfordshire OX4 1BD
Tel: +44 (0)1865 203988
Principal: Ms Kim Terrar
Age range: 14–19 years

Oxford Montessori School
Forest Farm School, Elsfield, Oxford, Oxfordshire OX3 9UW
Tel: 01865 352062
Age range: 2–16 years

Oxford Sixth Form College
12 King Edward Street, Oxford, Oxfordshire OX1 4HT
Tel: +44 (0)1865 793233
Principal: Mr Mark Love
Age range: 15–19 years

Radley College
Radley, Abingdon, Oxfordshire OX14 2HR
Tel: 01235 543000
The Warden: Mr J S Moule
Age range: B13–18 years

Rupert House School
90–92 Bell Street, Henley-on-Thames, Oxfordshire RG9 2BN
Tel: 01491 574263
Head: Mr Nick Armitage
Age range: 3–11 years

Rye St Antony
Pullen's Lane, Oxford, Oxfordshire OX3 0BY
Tel: 01865 762802
Head of School: Ms Joanne Croft
Age range: B3–11 years G3–18 years (boarding from 9)

SHIPLAKE COLLEGE
For further details see p. 52
Henley-on-Thames, Oxfordshire RG9 4BW
Tel: +44 (0)1189 402455
Email: registrar@shiplake.org.uk
Website: www.shiplake.org.uk
Headmaster: Mr T G Howe MA, MSt, MBA
Age range: 11–18 years
No. of pupils: 526 VIth197
Fees: Day £22,200–£29,230 WB £39,600 FB £43,995

Sibford School
Sibford Ferris, Banbury, Oxfordshire OX15 5QL
Tel: 01295 781200
Head: Mr Toby Spence
Age range: 3–18 years

St Clare's, Oxford
139 Banbury Road, Oxford, Oxfordshire OX2 7AL
Tel: +44 (0)1865 552031
Head of School: Mr Duncan Reith
Age range: 15–19 years
No. of pupils: 280
Fees: Day £21,196 FB £44,118

St Edward's, Oxford
Woodstock Road, Oxford, Oxfordshire OX2 7NN
Tel: +44 (0)1865 319200
Warden: Alastair Chirnside
Age range: 13–18 years
No. of pupils: 800
Fees: Day £11,550 FB £14,433

St Helen and St Katharine
Faringdon Road, Abingdon, Oxfordshire OX14 1BE
Tel: 01235 520173
Headmistress: Mrs Rebecca Dougall BA MA
Age range: G9–18 years

St Hugh's School
Carswell Manor, Faringdon, Oxfordshire SN7 8PT
Tel: 01367 870700
Headmaster: Mr James Thompson
Age range: 3–13 years
Fees: Day £12,285–£21,195 WB £23,655–£25,350

St John's Priory School
St John's Road, Banbury, Oxfordshire OX16 5HX
Tel: 01295 259607
Headmistress: Mrs Tracey Wilson
Age range: 3–11 years

St Mary's Preparatory School
13 St Andrew's Road, Henley-on-Thames, Oxfordshire RG9 1HS
Tel: 01491 573118
Headmaster: Mr Rob Harmer (BA)Hons
Age range: 2–11 years
No. of pupils: 129
Fees: Day £4,010

Summer Fields
Mayfield Road, Oxford, Oxfordshire OX2 7EN
Tel: 01865 454433
Headmaster: Mr David Faber MA(Oxon)
Age range: B4–13 years (boarding from 8)

The King's School, Witney
New Yatt Road, Witney, Oxfordshire OX29 6TA
Tel: 01993 778463
Principal: Mr Matthew Cripps
Age range: 3–16 years

The Manor Preparatory School
Faringdon Road, Abingdon, Oxfordshire OX13 6LN
Tel: 01235 858458
Headmaster: Mr Alastair Thomas
Age range: 2–11 years
No. of pupils: 372

The Unicorn School
20 Marcham Road, Abingdon, Oxfordshire OX14 1AA
Tel: 01235 530222
Headteacher: Mr. Andrew Day BEd (Hons)University of Wales (Cardiff)
Age range: 7–16 years

Tudor Hall School
Wykham Park, Banbury, Oxfordshire OX16 9UR
Tel: 01295 263434
Headmistress: Ms Julie Lodrick
Age range: G11–18 years (boarding from 11)

Windrush Valley School
The Green, London Lane, Ascott-under-Wychwood, Oxfordshire OX7 6AN
Tel: 01993 831793
Headteacher: Mrs Amanda Douglas
Age range: 3–11 years
No. of pupils: 120
Fees: Day £7,005–£7,341

Wychwood School
74 Banbury Road, Oxford, Oxfordshire OX2 6JR
Tel: +44 (0)18655 57976
Headmistress: Mrs A K Johnson BSc (Dunelm)
Age range: G11–18 years (boarding from 11)
16

West Berkshire

Brockhurst & Marlston House Schools
Hermitage, Newbury, West Berkshire RG18 9UL
Tel: 01635 200293
Headmaster: Mr David Fleming MA (Oxon), MSc
Age range: 2–13 years (boarding from 7)

Cheam School
Headley, Newbury, West Berkshire RG19 8LD
Tel: +44 (0)1635 268242
Headmaster: Mr William Phelps
Age range: 2–13 years (boarding from 8)

DOWNE HOUSE SCHOOL
For further details see p. 46
Downe House, Cold Ash, Thatcham, West Berkshire RG18 9JJ
Tel: +44 (0)1635 200286
Email: registrar@downehouse.net
Website: www.downehouse.net
Headmistress: Mrs Emma McKendrick BA(Liverpool)
Age range: G11–18 years (boarding from 11)
No. of pupils: 580
Fees: Day £11,840 FB £15,920
A £ 16

Horris Hill
Newtown, Newbury, West Berkshire RG20 9DJ
Tel: 01635 40594
Headmaster: Mr Rob Stewart
Age range: B2–13 years (boarding from 8)

St Gabriel's
Sandleford Priory, Newbury, West Berkshire RG20 9BD
Tel: 01635 555680
Principal: Mr Ricki Smith
Age range: 6 months–18 years
A 16

St. Michael's School
Harts Lane, Burghclere, Newbury, West Berkshire RG20 9JW
Tel: 01635 278137
Headmaster: Rev. Fr. John Brucciani
Age range: B4–18 years (boarding from 11) G4–11 years

Wiltshire

Avondale Preparatory School
27–29 High Street, Bulford, Salisbury, Wiltshire SP4 9DR
Tel: 01980 632387
Head of School: Mr Stuart Watson
Age range: 2–11 years

Bishopstrow College
Barrow House, Bishopstrow Road, Bishopstrow, Warminster, Wiltshire BA12 9HU
Tel: +44 (0)1985 219210
Principal: Mario Di Clemente
Age range: 7–17 years

Chafyn Grove School
33 Bourne Avenue, Salisbury, Wiltshire SP1 1LR
Tel: 01722 333423
Headmaster: Mr Simon Head
Age range: 3–13 years (boarding from 7)
£

Cricklade Manor Prep
The Manor House, Calcutt Street, Cricklade, Wiltshire SN6 6BB
Tel: 01793 750275
Headmaster: Mr Guy Barrett
Age range: 2–11 years

Dauntsey's
High Street, West Lavington, Devizes, Wiltshire SN10 4HE
Tel: 01380 814500
Head Master: Mr Mark Lascelles
Age range: 11–18 years (boarding from 11)
A £ 16

Emmaus School
School Lane, Staverton, Trowbridge, Wiltshire BA14 6NZ
Tel: 01225 782684
Headteacher: Ms Miriam Wiltshire
Age range: 5–16 years

Godolphin Preparatory School
Laverstock Road, Salisbury, Wiltshire SP1 2RB
Tel: +44 (0)1722 430545
Head: Ms Julia Miller
Age range: G3–11 years (boarding from 7)
£

Godolphin School
Milford Hill, Salisbury, Wiltshire SP1 2RA
Tel: +44 (0)722 430545
Head: Ms Emma Hattersley
Age range: G11–18 years (boarding from 11)
A £ 16

Heywood Prep
The Priory, Priory Street, Corsham, Wiltshire SN13 0AP
Tel: 01249 713379
Headmistress: Ms Rebecca Mitchell
Age range: 2–11 years
No. of pupils: 200
Fees: Day £9,525–£10,755

Leehurst Swan School
19 Campbell Road, Salisbury, Wiltshire SP1 3BQ
Tel: 01722 333094
Headteacher: Mrs Mandy Bateman
Age range: 4–16 years
£

Maranatha Christian School
Queenlaines Farm, Sevenhampton, Swindon, Wiltshire SN6 7SQ
Tel: 01793 762075
Headteacher: Mr Tom Price
Age range: 3–18 years

MARLBOROUGH COLLEGE
For further details see p. 50
Bath Road, Marlborough,
Wiltshire SN8 1PA
Tel: 01672 892200
Email: admissions@marlboroughcollege.org
Website: www.marlboroughcollege.org
Master: Mrs Louise Moelwyn-Hughes
Age range: 13–18 years
No. of pupils: 1012
Fees: FB £15,665

OneSchool Global UK Salisbury Campus
The Hollows, Wilton, Salisbury,
Wiltshire SP2 0JE
Tel: 01722 741910
Age range: 7–18 years

Pinewood School
Bourton, Shrivenham, Swindon,
Wiltshire SN6 8HZ
Tel: 01793 782205
Headmaster: Mr Neal Bailey
Age range: 3–13 years
(boarding from 9)

Salisbury Cathedral School
The Old Palace, 1 The Close,
Salisbury, Wiltshire SP1 2EQ
Tel: 01722 555300
Head Master: Mr Clive Marriott BEd MA
Age range: 3–13 years
(boarding from 7)

Sandroyd School
Rushmore, Tollard Royal,
Salisbury, Wiltshire SP5 5QD
Tel: 01725 516264
Headmaster: Mr Alastair Speers
Age range: 2–13 years (boarding from 7, mandatory in years 7 & 8)

St Francis School
Marlborough Road, Pewsey,
Wiltshire SN9 5NT
Tel: 01672 563228
Headmaster: Mr David Lee
Age range: 0–13 years

St Margaret's Preparatory School
Curzon Street, Calne, Wiltshire SN11 0DF
Tel: 01249 857220
Headmaster: Mr Luke Bromwich
Age range: 2–11 years

ST MARY'S CALNE
For further details see p. 54
Curzon Street, Calne,
Wiltshire SN11 0DF
Tel: 01249 857200
Email: office@stmaryscalne.org
Website: www.stmaryscalne.org
Acting Head: Mrs Diana Harrison MA (Cantab), PGCE (Bristol), CPP (Roehampton)
Age range: G11–18 years
(boarding from 11)
No. of pupils: 360 VIth119
Fees: Day £34,860 FB £46,725

Stonar School
Cottles Park, Atworth, Melksham,
Wiltshire SN12 8NT
Tel: 01225 701740
Head of School: Mr Matthew Way
Age range: 2–18 years
(boarding from 10)

The Wellington Academy
Tidworth, Wiltshire SP11 9RR
Tel: 01264 405060
Headteacher: Mr S Paddock
Age range: 11–18 years

Warminster School
Church Street, Warminster,
Wiltshire BA12 8PJ
Tel: +44 (0)1985 210100
Headmaster: Mr Matt Williams BA MA
Age range: 2–18 years
(boarding from 7)
No. of pupils: 551
Fees: Day £5,970 FB £12,241

East

KEY TO SYMBOLS

- *Boys' school*
- *Girls' school*
- *International school*
- *Tutorial or sixth form college*
- *A levels*
- *Boarding accommodation*
- *Bursaries*
- *International Baccalaureate*
- *Learning support*
- *Entrance at 16+*
- *Vocational qualifications*
- *Independent Association of Preparatory Schools*
- *The Headmasters' & Headmistresses' Conference*
- *Independent Schools Association*
- *Girls' School Association*
- *Boarding Schools' Association*
- *Society of Heads*

Unless otherwise indicated, all schools are coeducational day schools. Single-sex and boarding schools will be indicated by the relevant icon.

Bedfordshire

Al Hikmah Boys School
145 High Street, Luton,
Bedfordshire LU4 9LE
Tel: 01582 594885
Acting Headteacher: Adil Rahman
Age range: B11–16 years

Al Hikmah Girls School
82–86 Dunstable Road, Luton,
Bedfordshire LU1 1EH
Tel: 01582 728196
Acting Headteacher: Adil Rahman
Age range: G9–19 years

Bedford Girls' School
Cardington Road, Bedford,
Bedfordshire MK42 0BX
Tel: 01234 361900
Headmistress: Ms Gemma Gibson
Age range: G7–18 years

Bedford Greenacre Independent School
58–60 Shakespeare Road,
Bedford, Bedfordshire MK40 2DL
Tel: 01234 352031
Principal: Mr Ian Daniel
Age range: 3–18 years

Bedford Modern School
Manton Lane, Bedford,
Bedfordshire MK41 7NT
Tel: 01234 332500
Headmaster: Mr Alex Tate
Age range: 7–18 years
No. of pupils: 1289
Fees: Day £10,528–£14,443

Bedford Preparatory School
De Parys Avenue, Bedford,
Bedfordshire MK40 2TU
Tel: 01234 362274
Headmaster: Mr Ian Silk
Age range: B7–13 years

Bedford School
De Parys Avenue, Bedford,
Bedfordshire MK40 2TU
Tel: 01234 362200
Head Master: Mr James Hodgson BA
Age range: B7–18 years

E-Spired Centre of Excellence
The Raleigh Centre, Ampthill Road,
Bedford, Bedfordshire MK42 9HE
Tel: 01234 363400
Principal & CEO: Mr Mark Hudson
Age range: 14–18 years

Jamiatul Uloom Al Islamia
364–370 Leagrave Road,
Luton, Bedfordshire LU3 1RF
Tel: 01582 595535
Headteacher: Mohd A Ali
Age range: B11–16 years

King's House School
33–43 High Street, Leagrave,
Luton, Bedfordshire LU4 9JY
Tel: 01582 491430
Head of School: Ms Jade Pawaar
Age range: 2–11 years

Mehria Primary School
23 Westbourne Road, Luton,
Bedfordshire LU4 8JD
Tel: 01582 484617
Headteacher: Mr Zia Qazi
Age range: 4–11 years

Oakwood Primary School
117 Tennyson Road, Luton,
Bedfordshire LU1 3RR
Tel: 01582 518800
Headteacher: Mrs F Salihi
Age range: 3–11 years

OneSchool Global UK Biggleswade Campus
The Oaks, Potton Road, Biggleswade,
Bedfordshire SG18 0EP
Tel: 01767 602800
Age range: 7–18 years

OneSchool Global UK Dunstable Campus
Ridgeway Avenue, Dunstable,
Bedfordshire LU5 4QL
Tel: 01582 665676
Age range: 7–18 years

Orchard School & Nursery
Higham Gobion Road, Barton le Clay,
Bedford, Bedfordshire MK45 4RB
Tel: 01582 882054
Headmistress: Mrs Anne Burton
Age range: 0–9 years

Pilgrims Pre-Preparatory School
Brickhill Drive, Bedford,
Bedfordshire MK41 7QZ
Tel: 01234 369555
Head: Mrs J Webster BEd(Hons), EYPS
Age range: 3 months–7 years

Polam School
45 Lansdowne Road, Bedford,
Bedfordshire MK40 2BU
Tel: 01234 261864
Head: Darren O'Neil
Age range: 1–7 years
No. of pupils: 110
Fees: Day £10,080

St George's School
28 Priory Road, Dunstable,
Bedfordshire LU5 4HR
Tel: 01582 661471
Head of School: Mr Stuart Compton
Age range: 3–11 years

Cambridgeshire

Abbey College Cambridge
Homerton Gardens, Purbeck Road,
Cambridge, Cambridgeshire CB2 8EB
Tel: 01223 578280
Principal: Dr Elena Hesse
Age range: 13–21 years

Cambridge Seminars College
87–89 Cherry Hinton Road,
Cambridge, Cambridgeshire CB1 7BS
Tel: +44 (0)1223 300 123
Principal: Mr Phil Scherb
Age range: 16–20 years

Cambridge Steiner School
Hinton Road, Fulbourn, Cambridge,
Cambridgeshire CB21 5DZ
Tel: 01223 882727
Education Manager: Ms Sarah Fox
Age range: 2½–16 years

Cardiff Sixth Form College, Cambridge
89 Regent Street, Cambridge,
Cambridgeshire CB2 1AW
Tel: +44 (0)1223 903080
Principal: Mr Gareth Collier
Age range: 15–18 years

CATS Cambridge
Elizabeth House, 1 High Street,
Chesterton, Cambridge,
Cambridgeshire CB4 1NQ
Tel: +44 (0)1223 314431
Principal: Mr Dominic Tomalin
Age range: 14–19+ years

Heritage School
17–19 Brookside, Cambridge,
Cambridgeshire CB2 1JE
Tel: 01223 350615
Headmaster: Mr Jason Fletcher
Age range: 4–16 years

Iqra Academy
Enterprise Way, North
Bretton, Peterborough,
Cambridgeshire PE3 8YQ
Tel: 01733 331433
Principal: Dr Michael Wright
Age range: G11–19 years

Kimbolton School
Kimbolton, Huntingdon,
Cambridgeshire PE28 0EA
Tel: 01480 860505
Headmaster: Mr Jonathan Belbin
Age range: 4–18 years

King's College School
West Road, Cambridge,
Cambridgeshire CB3 9DN
Tel: 01223 365814
Head: Mrs Yvette Day
BMus, MMus, GDL
Age range: 4–13 years

KING'S ELY
For further details see p. 78
Ely, Cambridgeshire CB7 4EW
Tel: 01353 660707
Email: admissions@kingsely.org
Website: www.kingsely.org
Principal: Mr John
Attwater MA (Oxon)
Age range: 2–18 years
No. of pupils: 1140
Fees: Day £12,477–£26,214
FB £27,843–£38,655

Landmark International School
The Old Rectory, 9 Church
Lane, Fulbourn, Cambridge,
Cambridgeshire CB21 5EP
Tel: 01223 755100
Headteacher: Gareth Turnbull-Jones
Age range: 4–16 years
No. of pupils: 100

Magdalene House Preparatory School
Chapel Road, Wisbech, Cambridgeshire PE13 1RH
Tel: 01945 583631
Senior Deputy Head, Prep School: Mrs Keryn Neaves
Age range: 3–11 years

MANDER PORTMAN WOODWARD - MPW CAMBRIDGE
For further details see p. 80
3-4 Brookside, Cambridge, Cambridgeshire CB2 1JE
Tel: 01223 350158
Email: cambridge@mpw.ac.uk
Website: www.mpw.ac.uk
Principal: Mr Tom Caston
Age range: 15–19 years

Oaks International School
Cherry Hinton Road, Cambridge, Cambridgeshire CB1 8DW
Tel: +44 (0) 1223 416938
Headteacher: Ms Amanda Gibbard
Age range: 2–11 years

Sancton Wood School
2 St Paul's Road, Cambridge, Cambridgeshire CB1 2EZ
Tel: +44 (0)1223 471703
Head of School: Mr Richard Settle
Age range: 1–16 years

St Andrew's College Cambridge
13 Station Road, Cambridge, Cambridgeshire CB1 2JB
Tel: +44 (0)1223 903048
Principal: Wayne Marshall
Age range: 14–19 years

ST FAITH'S
For further details see p. 88
Trumpington Road, Cambridge, Cambridgeshire CB2 8AG
Tel: 01223 352073
Email: admissions@stfaiths.co.uk
Website: www.stfaiths.co.uk
Headmaster: Dr C Hyde-Dunn
Age range: 4–13 years
No. of pupils: 576
Fees: Day £15,735–£19,815

St John's College School
73 Grange Road, Cambridge, Cambridgeshire CB3 9AB
Tel: 01223 353652
Headmaster: Mr N. Chippington MA(Cantab), FRCO
Age range: 4–13 years
No. of pupils: 463

ST MARY'S SCHOOL, CAMBRIDGE
For further details see p. 92
Bateman Street, Cambridge, Cambridgeshire CB2 1LY
Tel: +44 (0)1223 224167
Email: admissions@stmaryscambridge.co.uk
Website: www.stmaryscambridge.co.uk
Headmistress: Ms Charlotte Avery
Age range: G3–18 years (boarding from 9)
No. of pupils: 630
Fees: Day £12,663–£19,740 FB £39,444–£41,676

Stephen Perse Junior School, Fitzwilliam Building
Shaftesbury Road, Cambridge, Cambridgeshire CB2 8AA
Tel: 01223 454700 (Ext:2000)
Age range: 5–11 years

Stephen Perse Nurseries & Early Years
Cambridge Road, Madingley, Cambridge, Cambridgeshire CB23 8AH
Tel: 01223 454700 (Ext:5000)
Age range: 1–5 years

Stephen Perse Senior School
Union Road, Cambridge, Cambridgeshire CB2 1HF
Tel: 01223 454700 (Ext:1000)
Age range: 11–16 years

THE LEYS SCHOOL
For further details see p. 94
Trumpington Road, Cambridge, Cambridgeshire CB2 7AD
Tel: 01223 508900
Email: admissions@theleys.net
Website: www.theleys.net
Headmaster: Mr Martin Priestley
Age range: 11–18 years
No. of pupils: 577
Fees: Day £19,965–£27,660 FB £30,555–£41,880

The Perse Pelican Pre-Prep & Nursery
92 Glebe Road, Cambridge, Cambridgeshire CB1 7TD
Tel: 01223 403940
Head: Ms Francesca Heftman
Age range: 3–7 years

The Perse Prep School
Trumpington Road, Cambridge, Cambridgeshire CB2 8EX
Tel: 01223 403920
Head: Mr James Piper
Age range: 7–11 years

The Perse Upper School
Hills Road, Cambridge, Cambridgeshire CB2 8QF
Tel: 01223 403800
Head: Mr Ed Elliott
Age range: 11–18 years

THE PETERBOROUGH SCHOOL
For further details see p. 96
Thorpe Road, Peterborough, Cambridgeshire PE3 6AP
Tel: 01733 343357
Email: office@tpsch.co.uk
Website: www.thepeterboroughschool.co.uk
Headmaster: Mr A D Meadows BSc(Hons), NPQH
Age range: 6 weeks–18 years
No. of pupils: 500
Fees: Day £11,991–£19,344

Whitehall School
117 High Street, Somersham, Cambridgeshire PE28 3EH
Tel: 01487 840966
Head of School: Chris Holmes
Age range: 6 months–11 years

Wisbech Grammar School
Chapel Road, Wisbech, Cambridgeshire PE13 1RH
Tel: 01945 583631
Head of School: Mr Barnaby Rimmer
Age range: 11–18 years

Essex

Alleyn Court School
Wakering Road, Southend-on-Sea, Essex SS3 0PW
Tel: 01702 582553
Headmaster: Mr Rupert W.J. Snow B.Ed, NPQH
Age range: 2½–11 years

Brentwood Preparatory School
Shenfield Road, Brentwood, Essex CM15 8BD
Tel: +44 (0)1277 243300
Headmaster: Mr Jason Whiskerd
Age range: 3–11 years
No. of pupils: 584

BRENTWOOD SCHOOL
For further details see p. 64
Middleton Hall Lane, Brentwood, Essex CM15 8EE
Tel: 01277 243243
Email: headmaster@brentwood.essex.sch.uk
Website: http://www.brentwoodschool.co.uk
Headmaster: Mr Michael Bond
Age range: 3–18 years
No. of pupils: 1968
Fees: Day £23,472 FB £45,996

Colchester High School
Wellesley Road, Colchester, Essex CO3 3HD
Tel: 01206 573389
Headteacher: Ms Karen Gracie-Langrick
Age range: 2½–16 years
No. of pupils: 320
Fees: Day £9,465–£13,620

Colchester Royal Grammar School
6 Lexden Road, Colchester, Essex CO3 3ND
Tel: 01206 509100
Headmaster: Mr John Russell
Age range: B11–18 years G16–18 years

Coopersale Hall School
Flux's Lane, off Stewards Green Road, Epping, Essex CM16 7PE
Tel: 01992 577133
Headmistress: Ms Moreen Barnard
Age range: 2½–11 years

Elm Green Preparatory School
Parsonage Lane, Little Baddow, Chelmsford, Essex CM3 4SU
Tel: 01245 225230
Principal: Ms Ann Milner
Age range: 4–11 years

Felsted Preparatory School
Felsted, Great Dunmow, Essex CM6 3JL
Tel: 01371 822610
Headmaster: Mr Simon James
Age range: 4–13 years

Felsted School
Felsted, Great Dunmow, Essex CM6 3LL
Tel: +44 (0)1371 822600
Headmaster: Mr Chris Townsend
Age range: 4–18 years
A £ IB 16

Gosfield School
Cut Hedge Park, Halstead Road, Gosfield, Halstead, Essex CO9 1PF
Tel: 01787 474040
Head of School: Mr Rod Jackson
Age range: 2–18 years
Fees: Day £7,680–£17,250

Heathcote School
Eves Corner, Danbury, Chelmsford, Essex CM3 4QB
Tel: 01245 223131
Head of School: Mrs Samantha Scott
Age range: 2–11 years
No. of pupils: 105
Fees: Day £9,450
£

HOLMWOOD HOUSE SCHOOL
For further details see p. 74
Chitts Hill, Lexden, Colchester, Essex CO3 9ST
Tel: 01206 574305
Email: admissions@holmwood.house
Website: www.holmwood.house
Headmaster: Mr Edward Bond
Age range: 6 months–16 years

Littlegarth School
Horkesley Park, Nayland, Colchester, Essex CO6 4JR
Tel: 01206 262332
Head of School: Ms Kathy Uttley
Age range: 2½–11 years

Maldon Court Preparatory School
Silver Street, Maldon, Essex CM9 4QE
Tel: 01621 853529
Headteacher: Elaine Mason
Age range: 1–11 years

New Hall School
The Avenue, Boreham, Chelmsford, Essex CM3 3HS
Tel: 01245 467588
Principal: Mrs Katherine Jeffrey MA, BA, PGCE, MA(Ed Mg), NPQH
Age range: 1–18 years (boarding from 7)
No. of pupils: 1329
£ 16

Octavia House School, Great Baddow
High Street, Great Baddow, Essex CM2 7HH
Tel: 020 3651 4396 (option 4)
Assistant Principal: Ms Aboukhshem
Age range: 5–11 years

OneSchool Global UK Colchester Campus
Sudbury Road, Stoke By Nayland, Colchester, Essex CO6 4RW
Tel: 01206 264230
Age range: 7–18 years

Oxford House School
2–4 Lexden Road, Colchester, Essex CO3 3NE
Tel: 01206 576686
Head Teacher: Mrs Sarah Leyshon
Age range: 2½–11 years

Saint Nicholas School
Hillingdon House, Hobbs Cross Road, Harlow, Essex CM17 0NJ
Tel: 01279 429910
Headmaster: Mr Terence Ayres
Age range: 2½–16 years
£

Saint Pierre School
16 Leigh Road, Leigh-on-Sea, Southend-on-Sea, Essex SS9 1LE
Tel: 01702 474164
Headmaster: Mr Peter Spencer-Lane
Age range: 2½–11 years

ST CEDD'S SCHOOL
For further details see p. 84
178a New London Road, Chelmsford, Essex CM2 0AR
Tel: 01245 392810
Email: info@stcedds.org.uk
Website: http://www.stcedds.org.uk
Head: Mr Matthew Clarke
Age range: 3–11 years
No. of pupils: 400
Fees: Day £3,490–£4,470

St John's School
Stock Road, Billericay, Essex CM12 0AR
Tel: 01277 623070
Headteacher: Mr A. Angeli BA (Hons)
Age range: 2–16 years

St Margaret's Preparatory School
Hall Drive, Gosfield, Halstead, Essex CO9 1SE
Tel: 01787 472134
Headteacher: Mrs Carolyn Moss
Age range: 2–11 years
Fees: Day £3,240–£4,055
£

St Mary's School
91 Lexden Road, Colchester, Essex CO3 3RB
Tel: 01206 572544
Principal: Mrs Nicola Griffiths
Age range: B3–4 years G3–16 years
£

St Michael's Church Of England Preparatory School
198 Hadleigh Road, Leigh-on-Sea, Southend-on-Sea, Essex SS9 2LP
Tel: 01702 478719
Headmaster: Mr James Mobbs
Age range: 3–11 years

St Philomena's Catholic School
Hadleigh Road, Frinton-on-Sea, Essex CO13 9HQ
Tel: 01255 674492
Head of School: Mrs P Mathews ACIS, BA Hons, PGCE, MA, NPQH
Age range: 4–11 years

St. Anne's Preparatory School
154 New London Road, Chelmsford, Essex CM2 0AW
Tel: 01245 353488
Head of School: Valerie Eveleigh
Age range: 3–11 years

Stephen Perse Junior School, Dame Bradbury's School
Ashdon Road, Saffron Walden, Essex CB10 2AL
Tel: 01223 454700 (Ext: 4000)
Age range: 1–11 years

Thorpe Hall School
Wakering Road, Southend-on-Sea, Essex SS1 3RD
Tel: 01702 582340
Headmaster: Mr Stephen Duckitt
Age range: 2–16 years

TLG Tendring
Frinton Free Church, Connaught Avenue, Frinton-on-Sea, Essex CO13 9PW
Tel: 01255 679585
Head of Centre: Mr Ben Pratt
Age range: 11–16 years

Ursuline Preparatory School
Old Great Ropers, Great Ropers Lane, Warley, Brentwood, Essex CM13 3HR
Tel: 01277 227152
Headmistress: Mrs Pauline Wilson MSc
Age range: 3–11 years

Widford Lodge Preparatory School
Widford Road, Chelmsford, Essex CM2 9AN
Tel: 01245 352581
Headteacher: Miss Michelle Cole A.C.I.B. – P.G.C.E.
Age range: 2½–11 years

Woodlands School, Great Warley
Warley Street, Great Warley, Brentwood, Essex CM13 3LA
Tel: 01277 233288
Head: Mr David Bell
Age range: 2–11 years

Woodlands School, Hutton Manor
428 Rayleigh Road, Hutton, Brentwood, Essex CM13 1SD
Tel: 01277 245585
Head: Ms Paula Hobbs
Age range: 3–11 years

Hertfordshire

Abbot's Hill School
Bunkers Lane, Hemel Hempstead, Hertfordshire HP3 8RP
Tel: 01442 240333
Headmistress: Mrs K Gorman BA, MEd (Cantab)
Age range: G4–16 years
No. of pupils: 482

Aldenham School
Elstree, Hertfordshire WD6 3AJ
Tel: 01923 858122
Headmaster: Mr James Fowler
Age range: 3–18 years
16

Aldwickbury School
Wheathampstead Road, Harpenden, Hertfordshire AL5 1AD
Tel: 01582 713022
Headmaster: Mr Paul Symes
Age range: B4–13 years

Beechwood Park School
Beechwood Park, Pickford Lane, Markyate, Nr St Albans, Hertfordshire AL3 8AW
Tel: 01582 840333
Head of School (until July 2023): Mrs Maureen Cussans
Age range: 3 months–13 years
No. of pupils: 529
Fees: Day £13,170

Berkhamsted School
Overton House, 131 High Street, Berkhamsted, Hertfordshire HP4 2DJ
Tel: 01442 358001
Principal: Mr Richard Backhouse MA(Cantab)
Age range: 3–18 years
No. of pupils: 1961 VIth443
Fees: Day £11,025–£25,275 WB £34,650 FB £41,310
A £ 16

Bishop's Stortford College
School House, Maze Green Road, Bishop's Stortford, Hertfordshire CM23 2PQ
Tel: +44 (0)1279 838575
College Head: Ms Kathy Crewe-Read
Age range: 13–18 years
16

Bishop's Stortford College Prep School
School House, Maze Green Road, Bishop's Stortford, Hertfordshire CM23 2PQ
Tel: +44 (0)1279 838583
Head of the Prep School: Mr Bill Toleman
Age range: 4–13 years

Charlotte House Preparatory School
88 The Drive, Rickmansworth, Hertfordshire WD3 4DU
Tel: 01923 772101
Head: Miss P Woodcock
Age range: G3–11 years

Duncombe School
4 Warren Park Road, Bengeo, Hertford, Hertfordshire SG14 3JA
Tel: 01992 414100
Headmaster: Mr Jeremy Phelan M.A. (Ed)
Age range: 2–11 years
No. of pupils: 301
Fees: Day £10,380–£14,565

Edge Grove School
Aldenham Village, Watford, Hertfordshire WD25 8NL
Tel: 01923 855724
Head of School: Mr Ed Balfour
Age range: 3–13 years
No. of pupils: 500

Egerton Rothesay School
Durrants Lane, Berkhamsted, Hertfordshire HP4 3UJ
Tel: 01442 865275
Headteacher: Mr Colin Parker BSc(Hons), Dip.Ed (Oxon), PGCE, C.Math MIMA
Age range: 6–19 years

Gurukula - The Hare Krishna Primary School
Hartspring Cottage, Elton Way, Watford, Hertfordshire WD25 8HB
Tel: 01923 851 005
Head of School: Ms Gunacuda Dasi (Gwyneth Milan)
Age range: 4–12 years

HABERDASHERS' BOYS' SCHOOL
For further details see p. 68
Butterfly Lane, Elstree, Borehamwood, Hertfordshire WD6 3AF
Tel: 020 8266 1700
Email: office@habsboys.org.uk
Website: www.habsboys.org.uk
Headmaster: Mr Robert Sykes
Age range: B4–18 years
No. of pupils: 1465
16

HABERDASHERS' GIRLS' SCHOOL
For further details see p. 70
Aldenham Road, Elstree, Borehamwood, Hertfordshire WD6 3BT
Tel: 020 8266 2300
Email: office@habsgirls.org.uk
Website: www.habsgirls.org.uk
Headmistress: Dr Hazel Bagworth-Mann
Age range: G4–18 years
No. of pupils: 1170
16

HAILEYBURY
For further details see p. 72
Haileybury, Hertford, Hertfordshire SG13 7NU
Tel: +44 (0)1992 706353
Email: admissions@haileybury.com
Website: www.haileybury.com
The Master: Mr Martin Collier MA BA PGCE
Age range: 11–18 years (boarding from 11)
No. of pupils: 919 VIth364
Fees: Day £7,170–£10,785 FB £9,455–£14,900
A £ IB 16

Heath Mount School
Woodhall Park, Watton-at-Stone, Hertford, Hertfordshire SG14 3NG
Tel: 01920 830230
Headmaster: Mr Chris Gillam BEd(Hons)
Age range: 3–13 years
No. of pupils: 492 B270 G222
Fees: Day £12,435–£19,185

Howe Green House School
Great Hallingbury, Bishop's Stortford, Hertfordshire CM22 7UF
Tel: 01279 657706
Headmistress: Ms Deborah Mills BA (Hons) Q.T.S
Age range: 2–11 years
No. of pupils: 177
Fees: Day £433–£4,313

Immanuel College
87/91 Elstree Road, Bushey, Hertfordshire WD23 4EB
Tel: 020 8950 0604
Head: Mr Mike Buchanan
Age range: 4–18 years
16

Kingshott
Stevenage Road, St Ippolyts, Hitchin, Hertfordshire SG4 7JX
Tel: 01462 432009
Headmaster: Mr David Weston
Age range: 3–13 years
No. of pupils: 400
Fees: Day £6,555–£14,115

Little Acorns Montessori School
Building 19 & 21, The Lincolnsfield Centre, Bushey Hall Drive, Bushey, Hertfordshire WD23 2ES
Tel: 01923 230705
Age range: 3 months–5 years

Lochinver House School
Heath Road, Little Heath, Potters Bar, Hertfordshire EN6 1LW
Tel: 01707 653064
Headmaster: Mr Ben Walker BA(Hons)
Age range: B4–13 years
No. of pupils: 345
Fees: Day £12,060–£15,840

Lockers Park
Lockers Park Lane, Hemel Hempstead, Hertfordshire HP1 1TL
Tel: 01442 251712
Headmaster: Mr Gavin Taylor
Age range: B4–13 years
No. of pupils: 171
Fees: Day £11,505–£18,225 WB £26,325

Longwood School
Bushey Hall Drive, Bushey, Hertfordshire WD23 2QG
Tel: 01923 253715
Headteacher: Ms Claire May
Age range: 3 months–11 years

Manor Lodge School
Rectory Lane, Ridge Hill, Shenley, Hertfordshire WD7 9BG
Tel: 01707 642424
Head Teacher: Mrs A Lobo BEd(Hons)
Age range: 3–11 years
No. of pupils: 456
Fees: Day £3,820–£4,500

Merchant Taylors' Prep
Moor Farm, Sandy Lodge Road, Rickmansworth, Hertfordshire WD3 1LW
Tel: 01923 825648
Head of School: Dr Karen McNerney
Age range: B3–13 years

Queenswood
Shepherd's Way, Brookmans Park, Hatfield, Hertfordshire AL9 6NS
Tel: 01707 602500
Principal: Mrs Jo Cameron
Age range: G11–18 years (boarding from 11)
No. of pupils: 418
Fees: Day £7,115–£8,440 WB £7,325–£10,615 FB £8,395–£11,810

Radlett Preparatory School
Kendal Hall, Watling Street, Radlett, Hertfordshire WD7 7LY
Tel: 01923 856812
Principal: Mr M Pipe BA Hons, QTS
Age range: 4–11 years

Sherrardswood School
Lockleys, Welwyn, Hertfordshire AL6 0BJ
Tel: 01438 714282
Headmistress: Mrs Anna Wright
Age range: 2–18 years

St Albans High School for Girls
Townsend Avenue, St Albans, Hertfordshire AL1 3SJ
Tel: 01727 853800
Head: Ms Amber Waite
Age range: G4–18 years

St Albans Independent College
69 London Road, St Albans, Hertfordshire AL1 1LN
Tel: 01727 842348
Principals: Mr. A N Jemal & Mr Elvis Cotena
Age range: 14–19 years

St Albans School
Abbey Gateway, St Albans, Hertfordshire AL3 4HB
Tel: 01727 855521
Headmaster: Mr JWJ Gillespie MA(Cantab), FRSA
Age range: B11–18 years G16–18 years

St Christopher School
Barrington Road, Letchworth Garden City, Hertfordshire SG6 3JZ
Tel: 01462 650 850
Head of School: Ms Emma-Kate Henry
Age range: 3–18 years

ST COLUMBA'S COLLEGE
For further details see p. 86
King Harry Lane, St Albans, Hertfordshire AL3 4AW
Tel: 01727 855185
Email: collegeadmin@stcolumbascollege.org
Website: www.stcolumbascollege.org
Head: Mr Karl Guest
Age range: 4–18 years
No. of pupils: 800 VIth150

St Edmund's College & Prep School
Old Hall Green, Nr Ware, Hertfordshire SG11 1DS
Tel: 01920 824247
Headmaster: Mr Matthew Mostyn BA (Hons) MA (Ed)
Age range: 3–18 years (boarding from 11)

St Francis' College
Broadway, Letchworth Garden City, Hertfordshire SG6 3PJ
Tel: 01462 670511
Headmistress: Mrs B Goulding
Age range: B3–11 years G3–18 years (boarding from 10)

St George's School
Sun Lane, Harpenden, Hertfordshire AL5 4TD
Tel: 01582 765477
Headmistress: Miss Helen Barton
Age range: 11–18 years

St Hilda's School
28 Douglas Road, Harpenden, Hertfordshire AL5 2ES
Tel: 01582 712307
Headmaster: Mr Dan Sayers
Age range: B21/2–4 years G21/2–11 years
No. of pupils: 150
Fees: Day £3,285–£4,260

St Hilda's School, Bushey
High Street, Bushey, Hertfordshire WD23 3DA
Tel: 020 8950 1751
Headmistress: Miss Sarah-Jane Styles MA
Age range: B2–4 years G2–11 years

St Joseph's In The Park
St Mary's Lane, Hertingfordbury, Hertford, Hertfordshire SG14 2LX
Tel: 01992 513810
Head of School: Mr Douglas Brown
Age range: 2–11 years

ST MARGARET'S SCHOOL, BUSHEY
For further details see p. 90
Merry Hill Road, Bushey, Hertfordshire WD23 1DT
Tel: +44 (0)20 8416 4400
Email: admissions@stmargarets-school.org.uk
Website: www.stmargarets-school.org.uk
Headteacher: Lara Péchard
Age range: 2–18 years
No. of pupils: 740

St. John's Prep School
The Ridgeway, Potters Bar, Hertfordshire EN6 5QT
Tel: +44 (0)1707 657294
Head Teacher: Mrs C Tardios
Age range: 3–11 years

Stanborough Primary School
Appletree Walk, Watford, Hertfordshire WD25 0DQ
Tel: 01923 673291
Head of School: Mrs T Madden
Age range: 3–11 years

Stanborough Secondary School
Stanborough Park, Garston, Watford, Hertfordshire WD25 9JT
Tel: 01923 673268
Interim Head: Mr K. James
Age range: 11–18 years

Stormont
The Causeway, Potters Bar, Hertfordshire EN6 5HA
Tel: 01707 654037
Head Teacher: Miss Louise Martin
Age range: G4–11 years

The Christian School (Takeley)
Dunmow Road, Brewers End, Takeley, Bishop's Stortford, Hertfordshire CM22 6QH
Tel: 01279 871182
Headmaster: Mr M E Humphries
Age range: 3–16 years

The King's School
Elmfield, Ambrose Lane, Harpenden, Hertfordshire AL5 4DU
Tel: 01582 767566
Headteacher: Mr Andy Reeves
Age range: 2–16 years

The Purcell School, London
Aldenham Road, Bushey, Hertfordshire WD23 2TS
Tel: 01923 331100
Principal: Mr Paul Bambrough
Age range: 10–18 years

Tring Park School for the Performing Arts
Mansion Drive, Tring, Hertfordshire HP23 5LX
Tel: 01442 824255
Principal: Mr Stefan Anderson MA, ARCM, ARCT
Age range: 8–19 years
No. of pupils: 370 VIth171
Fees: Day £15,405–£24,885 FB £26,190–£37,605

Westbrook Hay Prep School
London Road, Hemel Hempstead, Hertfordshire HP1 2RF
Tel: 01442 256143
Headmaster: Mark Brain
Age range: 3–13 years
No. of pupils: 340
Fees: Day £10,905–£15,690

York House School
Sarratt Road, Croxley Green, Rickmansworth, Hertfordshire WD3 4LW
Tel: 01923 772395
Headmaster: Mr Jon Gray BA(Ed)
Age range: 3–13 years
No. of pupils: 395
Fees: Day £3,876–£5,164

Norfolk

All Saints School
School Road, Lessingham, Norwich, Norfolk NR12 0DJ
Tel: 01692 582083
Head of School: Samantha Dangerfield
Age range: 7–16 years

Beeston Hall School
Beeston Regis, West Runton, Cromer, Norfolk NR27 9NQ
Tel: 01263 837324
Headmaster: Mr Fred de Falbe BA(Hons) PGCE
Age range: 4–13 years

Downham Preparatory School & Montessori Nursery
The Old Rectory, Stow Bardolph, Kings Lynn, Norfolk PE34 3HT
Tel: 01366 388066
Principal: Mrs E J Laffeaty-Sharpe
Age range: 3 months–13 years

Glebe House School & Nursery
Cromer Road, Hunstanton, Norfolk PE36 6HW
Tel: 01485 532809
Headmaster: Mr Adrian Stewart
Age range: 0–13 years (boarding from 7)

Gresham's Nursery and Pre-Prep School
Market Place, Holt, Norfolk NR25 6BB
Tel: 01263 714575
Head: Ms Sarah Hollingsworth
Age range: 2–7 years

Gresham's Prep School
Holt, Norfolk NR25 6EY
Tel: 01263 714600
Head: Mrs Cathy Braithwaite
Age range: 7–13 years

Gresham's Senior School
Cromer Road, Holt, Norfolk NR25 6EA
Tel: 01263 714500
Headmaster: Mr Douglas Robb MA, MEd
Age range: 13–18 years
No. of pupils: 540
Fees: Day £27,450 FB £39,345

Langley Pre-Prep & Prep School
Taverham, Norwich, Norfolk NR8 6HU
Tel: 01603 868206
Head of Prep: Mr Mike A Crossley NPQH, BEd(Hons)
Age range: 6 months–13 years

Langley Senior School & Sixth Form
Langley Park, Loddon, Norwich, Norfolk NR14 6BJ
Tel: 01508 520210
Headmaster: Mr Jon Perriss
Age range: 10–18 years

Norwich High School for Girls GDST
95 Newmarket Road, Norwich, Norfolk NR2 2HU
Tel: 01603 453265
Head: Ms Alison Sefton
Age range: G3–18 years

Norwich School
71a The Close, Norwich, Norfolk NR1 4DD
Tel: 01603 728430
Head: Mr Steffan D A Griffiths
Age range: 4–18 years

Norwich Steiner School
Hospital Lane, Norwich, Norfolk NR1 2HW
Tel: 01603 611175
Age range: 3–19 years

Notre Dame Preparatory School
147 Dereham Road, Norwich, Norfolk NR2 3TA
Tel: 01603 625593
Headmaster: Mr Rob Thornton MA
Age range: 2–11 years

OneSchool Global UK Swaffham Campus
Turbine Way, Swaffham, Norfolk PE37 7XD
Tel: 01760 336939
Age range: 7–18 years

Riddlesworth Hall Preparatory School
Hall Lane, Diss, Norfolk IP22 2TA
Tel: 01953 681246
Head: Mrs V White
Age range: 2–13 years

Thetford Grammar School
Bridge Street, Thetford, Norfolk IP24 3AF
Tel: 01842 752840
Head: Mr Michael Brewer
Age range: 3–19 years

Town Close School
14 Ipswich Road, Norwich, Norfolk NR2 2LR
Tel: 01603 620180
Headteacher: Mr Chris Wilson
Age range: 3–13 years
No. of pupils: 450
Fees: Day £3,081–£4,673

Wymondham College
Golf Links Road, Wymondham, Norfolk NR18 9SZ
Tel: 01953 609000
Principal: Mrs Zoe Fisher
Age range: 11–18 years

Wymondham College Prep School
Golf Links Road, Wymondham, Norfolk NR18 9SZ
Tel: 01953 609000 (option 3)
Headteacher: Mr Simon Underhill
Age range: 4–11 years
No. of pupils: 150
Fees: FB £12,165

Suffolk

Barnardiston Hall Preparatory School
Hall Road, Barnardiston, Nr Haverhill, Suffolk CB9 7TG
Tel: 01440 786316
Headmaster: Lt Col K A Boulter MA(Cantab)
Age range: 6 months–13 years

Brookes UK
Flempton Road, Risby, Bury St Edmunds, Suffolk IP28 6QJ
Tel: 01284 760531
Principal: Ms Natalie Taylor
Age range: 2–16 years

Culford School
Bury St Edmunds, Suffolk IP28 6TX
Tel: +44 (0)1284 728615
Headmaster: Mr J F Johnson-Munday MA, MBA
Age range: 1–18 years

Fairstead House School
Fairstead House, Fordham Road, Newmarket, Suffolk CB8 7AA
Tel: 01638 662318
Head of School: Mr Michael Radford
Age range: 3 months–11 years
No. of pupils: 95
Fees: Day £10,704–£11,934

Finborough School
The Hall, Great Finborough, Stowmarket, Suffolk IP14 3EF
Tel: +44 (0)1449 773600
Headmaster: Mr Steven T. Clark
Age range: 2–18 years
No. of pupils: 663
Fees: Day £10,800–£16,650 WB £20,250–£27,150 FB £25,260–£33,840

FRAMLINGHAM COLLEGE
For further details see p. 66
Framlingham, Suffolk IP13 9EY
Tel: +44 (0)1728 723789
Email: admissions@framlinghamcollege.co.uk
Website: www.framlinghamcollege.co.uk
Principal and Head of the Senior School: Mrs Louise North
Age range: 2–18 years
No. of pupils: 640
Fees: Day £10,869–£24,795 FB £27,428–£38,556

Ipswich High School
Woolverstone, Ipswich, Suffolk IP9 1AZ
Tel: 01473 780201
Head of School: Mr Dan Browning
Age range: 3–18 years
No. of pupils: 500
Fees: Day £11,355–£17,955 WB £29,925 FB £40,110

IPSWICH SCHOOL
For further details see p. 76
Henley Road, Ipswich, Suffolk IP1 3SG
Tel: 01473 408300
Email: admissions@ipswich.school
Website: www.ipswich.school
Headmaster: Mr Nicholas Weaver MA
Age range: 0–18 years
Fees: Day £19,704 FB £40,365

Old Buckenham Hall School
Old Buckenham Hall, Brettenham Park, Ipswich, Suffolk IP7 7PH
Tel: 01449 740252
Headmaster: Mr David Griffiths
Age range: 3–13 years
No. of pupils: 221
Fees: Day £7,295 FB £9,505

ORWELL PARK SCHOOL
For further details see p. 82
Nacton, Ipswich, Suffolk IP10 0ER
Tel: 01473 659225
Email: admissions@orwellpark.org
Website: www.orwellpark.co.uk
Headmaster: Mr Guy Musson
Age range: 2½–13 years
No. of pupils: 270

Saint Felix School
Halesworth Road, Southwold, Suffolk IP18 6SD
Tel: +44 (0)15027 22175
Headmaster: Mr. James Harrison
Age range: 2–18 years (boarding from 7)

South Lee Preparatory School
Nowton Road, Bury St Edmunds, Suffolk IP33 2BT
Tel: 01284 754654
Acting Head: Mrs Sarah Catchpole
Age range: 4 months–13 years

St Joseph's College
Belstead Road, Ipswich, Suffolk IP2 9DR
Tel: +44 (0)1473 690281
Principal: Mrs Danielle Clarke
Age range: 2–18 years

Stoke College
Ashen Lane, Stoke by Clare, Sudbury, Suffolk CO10 8JE
Tel: +44 (0)1787 278141
Principal: Dr. Gareth P. Lloyd
Age range: 11–18 years

Summerhill School
Westward Ho, Leiston, Suffolk IP16 4HY
Tel: 01728 830540
Principal: Mrs Zoe Readhead
Age range: 5–18 years

The Meadows Montessori School
32 Larchcroft Road, Ipswich, Suffolk IP1 6AR
Tel: 01473 233782
Headteacher: Ms Samantha Sims
Age range: 3–16 years

The Old School Henstead
Toad Row, Henstead, Beccles, Suffolk NR34 7LG
Tel: 01502 741150
Head: Mr W J McKinney
Age range: 2½–11 years

The Royal Hospital School
Holbrook, Ipswich, Suffolk IP9 2RX
Tel: 01473 326136
Headmaster: Mr Simon Lockyer BSc MEd
Age range: 11–18 years
No. of pupils: 730
Fees: Day £18,207–£20,253 WB £27,825–£34,542 FB £29,211–£37,614

Woodbridge School
Burkitt Road, Woodbridge, Suffolk IP12 4JH
Tel: +44 (0)1394 615000
Head of School: Miss Shona Norman
Age range: 4–18 years
Fees: Day £11,148–£18,885 WB £26,844–£29,178 FB £34,998

East Midlands

KEY TO SYMBOLS

- Boys' school
- Girls' school
- International school
- Tutorial or sixth form college
- A levels
- Boarding accommodation
- Bursaries
- International Baccalaureate
- Learning support
- Entrance at 16+
- Vocational qualifications
- Independent Association of Preparatory Schools
- The Headmasters' & Headmistresses' Conference
- Independent Schools Association
- Girls' School Association
- Boarding Schools' Association
- Society of Heads

Unless otherwise indicated, all schools are coeducational day schools. Single-sex and boarding schools will be indicated by the relevant icon.

Derbyshire

Barlborough Hall School
Park Street, Barlborough, Chesterfield, Derbyshire S43 4ES
Tel: 01246 810511
Headteacher: Mrs Karen Keeton
Age range: 3–11 years

Dame Catherine Harpur's School
Rose Lane, Ticknall, Derby, Derbyshire DE73 7JW
Tel: 01332 862792
Headteacher: Lorna Harvey
Age range: 3–11 years

Derby Grammar School
Rykneld Hall, Rykneld Road, Littleover, Derby, Derbyshire DE23 4BX
Tel: 01332 523027
Head: Mr Paul Logan
Age range: 4–18 years

Derby High School
Hillsway, Littleover, Derby, Derbyshire DE23 3DT
Tel: 01332 514267
Headteacher: Mrs Amy Chapman
Age range: 3–18 years

Emmanuel School
Juniper Lodge, 43 Kedleston Road, Derby, Derbyshire DE22 1FP
Tel: 01332 340505
Headteacher: Mr Ben Snowdon
Age range: 3–11 years

Mount St Mary's College
College Road, Spinkhill, Near Sheffield, Derbyshire S21 3YL
Tel: 01246 433388
Headmaster: Dr Dan Wright
Age range: 11–18 years
No. of pupils: 350
Fees: Day £12,870–£14,790 WB £20,220–£25,980 FB £24,780–£32,445
A 16·

Normanton House School
Normanton House, Village Street, Derby, Derbyshire DE23 8DF
Tel: 01332 769333
Head of School: Ms A Ahmed
Age range: 5–16 years

Old Vicarage School
11 Church Lane, Darley Abbey, Derby, Derbyshire DE22 1EW
Tel: 01332 557130
Head of School: Mrs Kerry Wise
Age range: 3–13 years

Repton Prep
Milton, Derby, Derbyshire DE65 6EJ
Tel: 01283 707100
Head of School: Mrs Vicky Harding
Age range: 3–13 years

Repton School
The Hall, Repton, Derbyshire DE65 6FH
Tel: 01283 559200
Head of School: M J Semmence MA, MBA
Age range: 13–18 years
A 16·

S. Anselm's School
Stanedge Road, Bakewell, Derbyshire DE45 1DP
Tel: 01629 812734
Headmaster: Mr Frank Thompson
Age range: 2–13 years

St Peter & St Paul School
Brambling House, Hady Hill, Chesterfield, Derbyshire S41 0EF
Tel: 01246 278522
Headteacher: Mrs Jill Phinn
Age range: 3 months–11 years

St Wystan's School
High Street, Repton, Derbyshire DE65 6GE
Tel: 01283 703258
Head Teacher: Ms Kara Lebihan
Age range: 21/2–11 years

Watchorn Christian School
Watchorn Church, Derby Road, Alfreton, Derbyshire DE55 7AQ
Tel: 07387 721877
Age range: 3–11 years

Leicestershire

Al-Aqsa Schools Trust
The Wayne Way, Leicester, Leicestershire LE5 4PP
Tel: 01162 760953
Headteacher: Arafat Q Hingora
Age range: 4–16 years

Brooke House College
12 Leicester Road, Market Harborough, Leicestershire LE16 7AU
Tel: 01858 462452
Principal: Mr Ian Smith
Age range: 11–19 years

Brooke House School
Croft Road, Cosby, Leicester, Leicestershire LE9 1SE
Tel: 0116 286 7770
Principal: Mrs Joy Parker
Age range: 3–18 years

Darul Uloom Leicester
119 Loughborough Road, Leicester, Leicestershire LE4 5LN
Tel: 0116 2668922
Principal: Moulana Ishaq Boodi
Age range: B11–23 years (boarding from 11)

Emmanuel Christian School, Leicester
Didsbury Street, Braunstone, Leicester, Leicestershire LE3 1QP
Tel: 0116 222 0792
Age range: 4–16 years

FAIRFIELD PREP SCHOOL
For further details see p. 100
Leicester Road, Loughborough, Leicestershire LE11 2AE
Tel: 01509 215172
Email: fairfield.admissions@lsf.org
Website: www.lsf.org/fairfield
Headmaster: Mr Andrew Earnshaw
Age range: 3–11 years
No. of pupils: 505

Jameah Boys Academy
33 Wood Hill, Leicester, Leicestershire LE5 3SQ
Tel: 01162 927746
Age range: B5–16 years

Jameah Girls Academy
49 Rolleston Street, Leicester, Leicestershire LE5 3SD
Tel: 0116 262 7745
Age range: G5–16 years

Leicester Grammar Junior School
London Road, Great Glen, Leicester, Leicestershire LE8 9FL
Tel: 0116 259 1950
Head of School: Mrs S Ashworth Jones
Age range: 3–11 years
No. of pupils: 391
Fees: Day £11,493–£12,212

Leicester Grammar School
London Road, Great Glen, Leicester, Leicestershire LE8 9FL
Tel: 0116 259 1900
Headmaster: Mr John Watson
Age range: 10–18 years
No. of pupils: 856
Fees: Day £14,130
A 16·

Leicester High School for Girls
454 London Road, Leicester, Leicestershire LE2 2PP
Tel: 0116 2705338
Headmaster: Mr Alan Whelpdale
Age range: G3–18 years
16·

Leicester Islamic Academy
320 London Road, Leicester, Leicestershire LE2 2PJ
Tel: 01162 705343
Headteacher: Mrs T. Jakhura
Age range: 3–11 years

Leicester Preparatory School
2 Albert Road, Leicester,
Leicestershire LE2 2AA
Tel: 01162 707414
Headmistress: Ms Claudette Salmon
Age range: 2–11 years

LGS Stoneygate
London Road, Great Glen,
Leicester, Leicestershire LE8 9DJ
Tel: 01162 592282
Headmaster: Mr J F Dobson
Age range: 4–16 years

LOUGHBOROUGH AMHERST SCHOOL
For further details see p. 102
Gray Street, Loughborough,
Leicestershire LE11 2DZ
Tel: 01509 263901
Email: amherst.admissions@lsf.org
Website: www.lsf.org/amherst
Headmaster: Mr James Neville
Age range: 4–18 years
No. of pupils: 335

LOUGHBOROUGH GRAMMAR SCHOOL
For further details see p. 104
Buckland House, Burton
Walks, Loughborough,
Leicestershire LE11 2DU
Tel: 01509 233233
Email: grammar.admissions@lsf.org
Website: www.lsf.org/grammar
Headteacher: Mrs Helen Foster
Age range: B10–18 years
No. of pupils: 890

LOUGHBOROUGH HIGH SCHOOL
For further details see p. 106
Burton Walks, Loughborough,
Leicestershire LE11 2DU
Tel: 01509 212348
Email: high.admissions@lsf.org
Website: www.lsf.org/high
Head: Dr Fiona Miles
Age range: G11–18 years
No. of pupils: 545

Ratcliffe College
Fosse Way, Ratcliffe on the Wreake,
Leicester, Leicestershire LE7 4SG
Tel: +44 (0)1509 817000
Headmaster: Mr Jon Reddin
BSc, MSc, NPQH
Age range: 3–18 years
(boarding from 11)

St Crispin's School
6 St Mary's Road, Stoneygate,
Leicester, Leicestershire LE2 1XA
Tel: 01162 707648
Headmaster: Mr Andrew Atkin
Age range: 2–16 years

The Dixie Grammar School
Market Place, Market Bosworth,
Leicestershire CV13 0LE
Tel: 01455 292244
Headmaster: Mr Richard Lynn MA
Age range: 3–18 years

Lincolnshire

Ayscoughfee Hall School
Welland Hall, London Road,
Spalding, Lincolnshire PE11 2TE
Tel: 01775 724733
Headteacher: Ms Theresa Wright
Age range: 3–11 years

Burton Hathow Preparatory School
Odder Farm, Saxilby Road, Burton,
Lincoln, Lincolnshire LN1 2BB
Tel: 01522 274616
Head Teacher: Ms Penny Ford
Age range: 2–11 years

Copthill School
Barnack Road, Uffington,
Stamford, Lincolnshire PE9 3AD
Tel: 01780 757506
Headmaster: Mr J A Teesdale
BA(Hons), PGCE
Age range: 2–11 years

Dudley House School
1 Dudley Road, Grantham,
Lincolnshire NG31 9AA
Tel: 01476 400184
Headteacher: Ms Jenny Johnson
Age range: 3–11 years

Grantham Preparatory International School
Gorse Lane, Grantham,
Lincolnshire NG31 7UF
Tel: +44 (0)1476 593293
Headmistress: Mrs K A Korcz
Age range: 3–11 years

Greenwich House Independent School
106 High Holme Road, Louth,
Lincolnshire LN11 0HE
Tel: 01507 609252
Headmistress: Mrs J Brindle
Age range: 9 months–11 years

Handel House Preparatory School
The Northolme, Gainsborough,
Lincolnshire DN21 2JB
Tel: 01427 612426
Headteacher: Mr Mark Raisborough
Age range: 3–11 years

Kirkstone House School
Main Street, Baston, Peterborough,
Lincolnshire PE6 9PA
Tel: 01778 560350
Headteacher: Mr Stuart Judge
Age range: 5–18 years

Lincoln Minster School
The Prior Building, Upper Lindum
Street, Lincoln, Lincolnshire LN2 5RW
Tel: 01522 551300
Headmistress: Mrs Maria Young
Age range: 4–18 years
No. of pupils: 500

St George's Preparatory School & Little Dragons Nursery
126 London Road, Boston,
Lincolnshire PE21 7HB
Tel: 01205 317600
Directors: Mark & Sarah Whelan
Age range: 3–11 years

St Hugh's School
Cromwell Avenue, Woodhall
Spa, Lincolnshire LN10 6TQ
Tel: 01526 352169
Headmaster: Mr Jeremy Wyld
Age range: 2–13 years

Stamford High School
St. Martin's Street, Stamford,
Lincolnshire PE9 2LL
Tel: 01780 484200
Head of School: Mrs Vicky Buckman
Age range: G11–18 years
(boarding from 11)

Stamford Junior School
Kettering Road, Stamford,
Lincolnshire PE9 2LR
Tel: 01780 484400
Headteacher: Mr Matthew O'Reilly
Age range: 2–11 years
(boarding from 7)

Stamford School
Southfields House, Stamford,
Lincolnshire PE9 2BQ
Tel: 01780 750300
Headmaster: Mr Nick Gallop
Age range: B11–18 years
(boarding from 11)

Viking School
140 Church Road North, Skegness,
Lincolnshire PE25 2QJ
Tel: 01754 765749
Principal: Ms Laura Middlebrook
Age range: 3–11 years

Witham Hall Preparatory School
Witham-on-the-Hill, Stamford,
Lincolnshire PE10 0JJ
Tel: +44(0)1778 590222
Headmaster: Mr William Austen
Age range: 4–13 years

Northamptonshire

Beachborough School
Westbury, Nr. Brackley,
Northamptonshire NN13 5LB
Tel: 01280 700071
Headteacher: Mrs Simone Mitchell
Age range: 2–13 years
No. of pupils: 400
Fees: Day £12,885–£20,235

Bosworth Independent School
The Newton Building, Avenue Campus,
St Georges Avenue, Northampton,
Northamptonshire NN2 6JB
Tel: +44 (0)1604 239995
Headteacher: Mr Jason Lewis
Age range: 11–19 years
A

Laxton Junior School
East Road, Oundle,
Northamptonshire PE8 4BX
Tel: 01832 277275
Head: Mr Sam Robertson
Age range: 4–11 years

Maidwell Hall
Maidwell, Northampton,
Northamptonshire NN6 9JG
Tel: 01604 686234
Headmaster: Mr R A
Lankester MA, PGCE
Age range: 4–13 years
Fees: FB £27,966
£

Northampton High School GDST
Newport Pagnell Road,
Hardingstone, Northampton,
Northamptonshire NN4 6UU
Tel: 01604 765765
Head: Dr May Lee
Age range: G2–18 years
No. of pupils: 600
Fees: Day £3,576–£5,254
A £ 16·

OneSchool Global UK Northampton Campus
Billing Road East, Northampton,
Northamptonshire NN3 3LF
Tel: 01604 633819
Age range: 7–18 years

Oundle School
The Great Hall, New Street, Oundle,
Northamptonshire PE8 4GH
Tel: +44 (0)1832 277122
Head of School: Mrs Sarah Kerr-Dineen
Age range: 11–18 years
16·

Overstone Park School
Overstone Park,
Overstone, Northampton,
Northamptonshire NN6 0DT
Tel: 01604 643787
Principal: Mrs M F Brown
BA(Hons), PGCE
Age range: 2–18 years

Pitsford School
Pitsford Hall, Pitsford, Northampton,
Northamptonshire NN6 9AX
Tel: 01604 880306
Headteacher: Dr Craig Walker
Age range: 3–18 years
Fees: Day £8,751–£15,183
A £ 16·

Quinton House School
Upton Hall, Upton, Northampton,
Northamptonshire NN5 4UX
Tel: 01604 752050
Headteacher: Mr Tim Hoyle
Age range: 2–18 years
No. of pupils: 390
Fees: Day £8,040–£11,985
A £ 16·

Spratton Hall
Smith Street, Spratton,
Northamptonshire NN6 8HP
Tel: 01604 847292
Head Master: Mr Simon Clarke
Age range: 4–13 years
No. of pupils: 400
Fees: Day £11,985–£18,600
£

St Peter's School
52 Headlands, Kettering,
Northamptonshire NN15 6DJ
Tel: 01536 512066
Headteacher: Mr Mark Thomas
Age range: 3–11 years

Wellingborough School
London Road, Wellingborough,
Northamptonshire NN8 2BX
Tel: 01933 222427
Headmaster: Mr A N Holman
Age range: 3–18 years
16·

Winchester House School
High Street, Brackley,
Northamptonshire NN13 7AZ
Tel: 01280 702483
Head: Ms Antonia Lee
Age range: 3–13 years
(boarding from 7)

Nottinghamshire

Colston Bassett Preparatory School
School Lane, Colston
bassett, Nottingham,
Nottinghamshire NG12 3FD
Tel: 01949 81118
Headteacher: Mrs C Newcombe
Age range: 4–11 years

Coteswood House Pre-school & Day Nursery
19 Thackeray's Lane, Woodthorpe,
Nottingham, Nottinghamshire NG5 4HT
Tel: 01159 676551
Age range: 2–5 years

Fig Tree Primary School
30 Bentinck Road, Nottingham,
Nottinghamshire NG7 4AF
Tel: 01159 788152
Headteacher: Mrs Nabeela Hussain
Age range: 5–11 years

Highfields School
London Road, Newark,
Nottinghamshire NG24 3AL
Tel: 01636 704103
Headteacher: Mrs Sarah H Lyons
Age range: 2–11 years

Hollygirt School
Elm Avenue, Nottingham,
Nottinghamshire NG3 4GF
Tel: 0115 958 0596
Head of School: Dr. Helen Barsham
Age range: 3–16 years

Jamia Al-Hudaa Residential College
Forest House, Berkeley Avenue,
Mapperley Park, Nottingham,
Nottinghamshire NG3 5TT
Tel: 01159 690800
Principal: Raza ul-Haq Siakhvy
Age range: 11–19 years

Nottingham Girls' High School GDST
9 Arboretum Street, Nottingham,
Nottinghamshire NG1 4JB
Tel: 01159 417663
Head: Julie Keller
Age range: G3–18 years
No. of pupils: 690
16·

Nottingham High School
Waverley Mount, Nottingham,
Nottinghamshire NG7 4ED
Tel: 01159 786056
Headmaster: Mr Kevin Fear BA
Age range: 4–18 years
16·

OneSchool Global UK Nottingham Campus
Wellington Street, Long
Eaton, Nottingham,
Nottinghamshire NG10 4HR
Tel: 0115 973 3568
Age range: 7–18 years

Plumtree School
Church Hill, Plumtree, Nottingham,
Nottinghamshire NG12 5ND
Tel: 0115 937 5859
Head Teacher: Phil Simpson
Age range: 3–11 years

Salterford House School
Salterford Lane, Calverton, Nottingham, Nottinghamshire NG14 6NZ
Tel: 01159 652127
Head: Ms Kimberley Venables
Age range: 3–11 years

Saville House School
11 Church Street, Mansfield Woodhouse, Mansfield, Nottinghamshire NG19 8AH
Tel: 01623 904418
Headteacher: Ms Claire King
Age range: 3–11 years

St Joseph's School
33 Derby Road, Nottingham, Nottinghamshire NG1 5AW
Tel: 01159 418356
Head Teacher: Mr Ashley Crawshaw
Age range: 1–11 years

The Iona School
310 Sneinton Dale, Nottingham, Nottinghamshire NG3 7DN
Tel: 01159 415295
Chair of College: Mr Rob Strafford
Age range: 3–11 years

The Orchard School
South Leverton, Retford, Nottinghamshire DN22 0DJ
Tel: 01427 880395
Head Teacher: Mrs Sandra Fox BA, PGCE
Age range: 5–16 years

Trent College and The Elms
Derby Road, Long Eaton, Nottingham, Nottinghamshire NG10 4AD
Tel: 0115 8494949
Head: Mr Bill Penty
Age range: 0–18 years
No. of pupils: 1121
Fees: Day £14,994–£18,789
A £ 16

Wellow House School
Wellow, Newark, Nottinghamshire NG22 0EA
Tel: 01623 861054
Headmistress: Ms Kirsty Lamb
Age range: 3–13 years

Worksop College
Cuthbert's Avenue, Worksop, Nottinghamshire S80 3AP
Tel: 01909 537100
Headmaster: Dr John Price
Age range: 11–18 years
16

Worksop College, Ranby House
Retford, Nottinghamshire DN22 8HX
Tel: 01777 703138
Headmaster: Mr David Thorpe
Age range: 3–11 years

Rutland

Brooke Priory School
Station Approach, Oakham, Rutland LE15 6QW
Tel: 01572 724778
Headmaster: Mr Duncan Flint
Age range: 2–11 years

Oakham School
Chapel Close, Oakham, Rutland LE15 6DT
Tel: 01572 758758
Headmaster: Mr Henry Price MA (Oxon)
Age range: 10–18 years
No. of pupils: 1022 VIth376
Fees: Day £19,740–£24,420 WB £23,730–£38,370 FB £30,300–£40,650
A £ IB 16

Uppingham School
Uppingham, Rutland LE15 9QE
Tel: +44 (0)1572 822216
Headmaster: Dr Richard Maloney
Age range: 13–18 years
16

Greater London

KEY TO SYMBOLS

- *Boys' school*
- *Girls' school*
- *International school*
- *Tutorial or sixth form college*
- *A levels*
- *Boarding accommodation*
- *Bursaries*
- *International Baccalaureate*
- *Learning support*
- *Entrance at 16+*
- *Vocational qualifications*
- *Independent Association of Preparatory Schools*
- *The Headmasters' & Headmistresses' Conference*
- *Independent Schools Association*
- *Girls' School Association*
- *Boarding Schools' Association*
- *Society of Heads*

Unless otherwise indicated, all schools are coeducational day schools. Single-sex and boarding schools will be indicated by the relevant icon.

Essex

Apex Primary School
60–62 Argyle Road, Ilford, Essex IG1 3BG
Tel: 020 8554 1208
Head Teacher: Ms Meherun Hamid
Age range: 3–11 years

Avon House Preparatory School
490 High Road, Woodford Green, Essex IG8 0PN
Tel: 020 8504 1749
Headteacher: Mrs Amanda Campbell
Age range: 3–11 years
No. of pupils: 268
Fees: Day £3,530–£3,950

Bancroft's School
High Road, Woodford Green, Essex IG8 0RF
Tel: 020 8505 4821
Head: Mr Simon Marshall MA, PGCE (Cantab), MA, MPhil (Oxon)
Age range: 7–18 years
A £ 16·

Beehive Preparatory School
233 Beehive Lane, Redbridge, Ilford, Essex IG4 5ED
Tel: 020 8550 3224
Head Teacher: Mr Jamie Gurr
Age range: 2½–11 years

Braeside School
130 High Road, Buckhurst Hill, Essex IG9 5SD
Tel: 020 8504 1133
Headmistress: Ms Chloe Moon
Age range: 2½–16 years

Chigwell School
High Road, Chigwell, Essex IG7 6QF
Tel: 020 8501 5700
Head Teacher: Mr Damian King
Age range: 4–18 years
No. of pupils: 1057
A £ 16·

Daiglen School
68 Palmerston Road, Buckhurst Hill, Essex IG9 5LG
Tel: 020 8504 7108
Headteacher: Mrs P Dear
Age range: 3–11 years

Eastcourt Independent School
1–5 Eastwood Road, Goodmayes, Ilford, Essex IG3 8UW
Tel: 020 8590 5472
Headmistress: Mrs Christine Redgrave BSc(Hons), DipEd, MEd
Age range: 3–11 years
No. of pupils: 220
Fees: Day £2,600

Gidea Park Preparatory School & Nursery
2 Balgores Lane, Gidea Park, Romford, Essex RM2 5JR
Tel: 01708 740381
Head of School: Mr Callum Douglas
Age range: 2–11 years
No. of pupils: 100
Fees: Day £10,775

Guru Gobind Singh Khalsa College
Roding Lane, Chigwell, Essex IG7 6BQ
Tel: 020 8559 9160
Principal: Mr Amarjit Singh Toor BSc(Hons), BSc, BT
Age range: 3–19 years

Immanuel School
Havering Grange, Havering Road, Romford, Essex RM1 4HR
Tel: 01708 764449
Principal: Ms Sarah Williams
Age range: 3–16 years

Loyola Preparatory School
103 Palmerston Road, Buckhurst Hill, Essex IG9 5NH
Tel: 020 8504 7372
Headmistress: Mrs K R Anthony
Age range: B3–11 years
No. of pupils: 200
Fees: Day £11,610
£

Oakfields Preparatory School
Harwood Hall, Harwood Hall Lane, Upminster, Essex RM14 2YG
Tel: 01708 220117
Headmistress: Katrina Carroll
Age range: 2½–11 years
No. of pupils: 202
Fees: Day £10,296–£11,121

Oaklands School
6–8 Albion Hill, Loughton, Essex IG10 4RA
Tel: 020 8508 3517
Headmistress: Ms Sue Belej
Age range: 2½–11 years

Park School for Girls
20–22 Park Avenue, Ilford, Essex IG1 4RS
Tel: 020 8554 2466
Head Teacher: Mrs Catherine Redfern
Age range: G4–16 years
16·

St Aubyn's School
Bunces Lane, Woodford Green, Essex IG8 9DU
Tel: 020 8504 1577
Headmaster: Mr Leonard Blom BEd(Hons) BA NPQH
Age range: 3–13 years

St Mary's Hare Park School & Nursery
South Drive, Gidea Park, Romford, Essex RM2 6HH
Tel: 01708 761220
Headteacher: Mr Ludovic Bernard
Age range: 2½–11 years

The Ursuline Preparatory School Ilford
2–4 Coventry Road, Ilford, Essex IG1 4QR
Tel: 020 8518 4050
Acting Headteacher: Mrs Lorraine Pereira
Age range: 3–11 years

Woodford Green Preparatory School
Glengall Road, Woodford Green, Essex IG8 0BZ
Tel: 020 8504 5045
Head: Miss Lisa McDonald
Age range: 3–11 years
No. of pupils: 385
Fees: Day £3,945
£

Hertfordshire

Lyonsdown School
3 Richmond Road, New Barnet, Barnet, Hertfordshire EN5 1SA
Tel: 020 8449 0225
Head: Mrs Rittu Hall
Age range: G3–11 years
No. of pupils: 180
Fees: Day £11,199–£12,237

Mount House School
Camlet Way, Hadley Wood, Barnet, Hertfordshire EN4 0NJ
Tel: 020 8449 6889
Head: Mrs Sarah Richardson
Age range: 11–18 years
IB 16·

Susi Earnshaw Theatre School
The Bull Theatre, 68 High Street, Barnet, Hertfordshire EN5 5SJ
Tel: 020 8441 5010
Headteacher: Ms Julia Hammond
Age range: 9–16 years
£

THE ROYAL MASONIC SCHOOL FOR GIRLS
For further details see p. 124
Rickmansworth Park, Rickmansworth, Hertfordshire WD3 4HF
Tel: 01923 725354
Email: admissions@rmsforgirls.com
Website: www.rmsforgirls.com
Headmaster: Mr Kevin Carson M.Phil (Cambridge)
Age range: B2–3 years G2–18 years (boarding from 8)
No. of pupils: 985
Fees: Day £4,350–£7,490 FB £9,095–£13,140
£ 16·

Kent

Ashgrove School
116 Widmore Road,
Bromley, Kent BR1 3BE
Tel: 020 8460 4143
Head of School: Dr Patricia Ash
Age range: 3–11 years

Babington House School
Grange Drive, Chislehurst, Kent BR7 5ES
Tel: 020 8467 5537
Headmaster: Mr Tim Lello
MA, FRSA, NPQH
Age range: 3–18 years
No. of pupils: 466
A £

Benedict House Preparatory School
1–5 Victoria Road, Sidcup,
Kent DA15 7HD
Tel: 020 8300 7206
Headteacher: Mr Craig Wardle
Age range: 3–11 years

Bickley Park School
14 & 24 Page Heath Lane,
Bickley, Bromley, Kent BR1 2DS
Tel: 020 8467 2195
Head of School: Ms Tammy Howard
Age range: B21/2–13 years
G21/2–4 years

Bishop Challoner School
228 Bromley Road, Shortlands,
Bromley, Kent BR2 0BS
Tel: 020 8460 3546
Headteacher: Mr Mark
Wallace BA (Hons), MBA
Age range: 3–18 years
A £ 16

Breaside Preparatory School
41–43 Orchard Road,
Bromley, Kent BR1 2PR
Tel: 020 8460 0916
Executive Principal: Mrs Karen A
Nicholson B.Ed, NPQH, Dip EYs
Age range: 21/2–11 years
No. of pupils: 376
Fees: Day £11,580–£13,494

Bromley High School GDST
Blackbrook Lane, Bickley,
Bromley, Kent BR1 2TW
Tel: 020 8781 7000/1
Head: Mrs A M Drew
BA(Hons), MBA (Dunelm)
Age range: G4–18 years
A £ 16

Darul Uloom London
Foxbury Avenue, Perry Street,
Chislehurst, Kent BR7 6SD
Tel: 020 8295 0637
Principal: Mufti Muhammed
Kamil Sheikh
Age range: B11–19 years

Farringtons School
Perry Street, Chislehurst, Kent BR7 6LR
Tel: 020 8467 0256
Head: Mr David Jackson
Age range: 3–18 years
No. of pupils: 700 VIth100
Fees: Day £18,720 WB £31,770 FB £39,870
A £ 16

Kings London
25 Beckenham Road,
Beckenham, Kent BR3 4PR
Tel: +44 (0)2086 505891
Director of Studies: Mr Danny Carroll
Age range: 14–25 years
A

Merton Court Preparatory School
38 Knoll Road, Sidcup, Kent DA14 4QU
Tel: 020 8300 2112
Headmaster: Mr Dominic
Price BEd, MBA
Age range: 3–11 years
No. of pupils: 308
Fees: Day £3,250–£4,925
£

St Christopher's The Hall School
49 Bromley Road, Beckenham,
Kent BR3 5PA
Tel: 020 8650 2200
Headteacher: Mr Tom Carter
Age range: 3–11 years

St David's Prep
Justin Hall, Beckenham Road,
West Wickham, Kent BR4 0QS
Tel: 020 8777 5852
Head Teacher: Ms Julia Foulger
Age range: 3–11 years

West Lodge School
36 Station Road, Sidcup, Kent DA15 7DU
Tel: 020 8300 2489
Head Teacher: Mr Robert Francis
Age range: 3–11 years

Middlesex

ACS Hillingdon International School
108 Vine Lane, Hillingdon,
Uxbridge, Middlesex UB10 0BE
Tel: +44 (0) 1895 259771
Head of School: Mr Martin Hall
Age range: 4–18 years
IB 16

Alpha Preparatory School
21 Hindes Road, Harrow,
Middlesex HA1 1SH
Tel: 020 8427 1471
Headmaster: Mr Pádraic Fahy
Age range: 3–11 years

Ashton House School
50–52 Eversley Crescent,
Isleworth, Middlesex TW7 4LW
Tel: 020 8560 3902
Headteacher: Mrs Angela Stewart
Age range: 3–11 years

Buckingham Preparatory School
458 Rayners Lane, Pinner,
Harrow, Middlesex HA5 5DT
Tel: 020 8866 2737
Head of School: Mrs Sarah Hollis
Age range: B3–11 years

Buxlow Preparatory School
5/6 Castleton Gardens, Wembley,
Middlesex HA9 7QJ
Tel: 020 8904 3615
Headteacher: Mr D May
Age range: 2–11 years

Edgware Jewish Girls - Beis Chinuch
296 Hale Lane, Edgware,
Middlesex HA8 8NP
Tel: 020 8905 4376
Headteacher: Mr M Cohen
Age range: G3–11 years

Halliford School
Russell Road, Shepperton,
Middlesex TW17 9HX
Tel: 01932 223593
Headmaster: Mr James Davies BMus
(Hons) LGSM FASC ACertCM PGCE
Age range: B11–18 years G16–18 years
No. of pupils: 450
Fees: Day £19,200
A £ 16

Hampton Prep and Pre-Prep School
Gloucester Road, Hampton,
Middlesex TW12 2UQ
Tel: 020 8979 1844
Headmaster: Mr Tim Smith
Age range: B3–11 years G3–7 years

Hampton School
Hanworth Road, Hampton,
Middlesex TW12 3HD
Tel: 020 8979 5526
Headmaster: Mr Kevin
Knibbs MA (Oxon)
Age range: B11–18 years
16

Harrow School
5 High Street, Harrow on the
Hill, Middlesex HA1 3HP
Tel: 020 8872 8000
Head Master: Mr Alastair Land
Age range: B13–18 years
16

Holland House School
1 Broadhurst Avenue, Edgware,
Middlesex HA8 8TP
Tel: 020 8958 6979
Headteacher: Mrs Emily Brown
Age range: 4–11 years
No. of pupils: 147

Jack & Jill Family of Schools
20 First Cross Road, Twickenham,
Middlesex TW2 5QA
Tel: 03333 444630
Age range: B2–4 years G2–11 years

Greater London: ENGLAND

John Lyon School
Middle Road, Harrow on the Hill, Middlesex HA2 0HN
Tel: 020 8515 9443
Head: Miss Katherine Haynes BA, MEd, NPQH
Age range: 11–18 years
No. of pupils: 600
Ⓐ Ⓛ 16·

Kew House School
Kew House, 6 Capital Interchange Way, London, Middlesex TW8 0EX
Tel: 0208 742 2038
Headmaster: Mr Will Williams
Age range: 11–18 years
No. of pupils: 595
Fees: Day £8,073
Ⓐ 16·

Lady Eleanor Holles
Hanworth Road, Hampton, Middlesex TW12 3HF
Tel: 020 8979 1601
Head of School: Mrs Heather Hanbury
Age range: G7–18 years
No. of pupils: 970
Fees: Day £21,738
Ⓐ £ 16·

Lady Nafisa School
Inglenook, Sipson Road, Sipson, West Drayton, Middlesex UB7 0JG
Tel: 02087 070001
Headteacher: Ms Fouzia Butt
Age range: G11–16 years

Menorah Foundation School
Abbots Road, Edgware, Middlesex HA8 0QS
Tel: 020 8906 9992
Headteacher: Karen Kent
Age range: B11–21 years

Merchant Taylors' School
Sandy Lodge, Northwood, Middlesex HA6 2HT
Tel: 01923 820644
Head Master: Mr S J Everson MA (Cantab)
Age range: B11–18 years
16·

Newland House School
Waldegrave Park, Twickenham, Middlesex TW1 4TQ
Tel: 020 8865 1234
Head of School: Mr Chris Skelton
Age range: 3–13 years
No. of pupils: 448
£

North London Collegiate School
Canons, Canons Drive, Edgware, Middlesex HA8 7RJ
Tel: +44 (0)20 8952 0912
Headmistress: Ms Vicky Bingham
Age range: G4–18 years
No. of pupils: 1080
Fees: Day £6,283–£7,436
Ⓐ £ IB 16·

Northwood College for Girls GDST
Maxwell Road, Northwood, Middlesex HA6 2YE
Tel: 01923 825446
Head of School: Mrs Rebecca Brown
Age range: G3–18 years
No. of pupils: 844
Ⓐ £ 16·

Oak Heights
2–3 Red Lion Court, Alexandra Road, Hounslow, Middlesex TW3 1JS
Tel: 020 8577 1827
Head: Mr S Dhillon
Age range: 11–16 years

Orley Farm School
South Hill Avenue, Harrow, Middlesex HA1 3NU
Tel: 020 8869 7600
Headmaster: Mr Tim Calvey
Age range: 4–13 years

Quainton Hall School & Nursery
91 Hindes Road, Harrow, Middlesex HA1 1RX
Tel: 020 8515 9500
Headmaster: S Ford BEd (Hons), UWE Bristol
Age range: 3–11 years
Fees: Day £11,850–£13,050

Radnor House
Pope's Villa, Cross Deep, Twickenham, Middlesex TW1 4QG
Tel: +44 (0)20 8891 6264
Head: Mr Darryl Wideman MA Oxon, PGCE
Age range: 9–18 years
16·

Reddiford School
36–38 Cecil Park, Pinner, Middlesex HA5 5HH
Tel: 020 8866 0660
Headteacher: Mrs J Batt CertEd, NPQH
Age range: 3–11 years

Regent College London
Regent House, 167 Imperial Drive, Harrow, Middlesex HA2 7HD
Tel: +44 (0)20 3870 6666
Co-Principals: Dr Selva Pankaj & Mrs Tharshiny Pankaj
Age range: 14–24 years
16· 16·

Roxeth Mead School
Buckholt House, 25 Middle Road, Harrow, Middlesex HA2 0HW
Tel: 020 8422 2092
Co-Headteachers: Mrs Suzanne Goodwin & Mrs Sarah Mackintosh
Age range: 0–7 years

St Catherine's Prep
Cross Deep, Twickenham, Middlesex TW1 4QJ
Tel: 020 8891 2898
Headmistress: Mrs Johneen McPherson MA
Age range: G5–11 years
No. of pupils: 95
Fees: Day £13,395–£14,085

ST CATHERINE'S SCHOOL
For further details see p. 118
Cross Deep, Twickenham, Middlesex TW1 4QJ
Tel: 020 8891 2898
Email: info@stcatherineschool.co.uk
Website: www.stcatherineschool.co.uk
Headmistress: Mrs Johneen McPherson MA
Age range: G5–18 years
No. of pupils: 405
Fees: Day £14,010–£17,910
Ⓐ £ 16·

St Christopher's School
71 Wembley Park Drive, Wembley, Middlesex HA9 8HE
Tel: 020 8902 5069
Head of School: Mr Jonathan Coke
Age range: 2–11 years

ST HELEN'S COLLEGE
For further details see p. 120
Parkway, Hillingdon, Uxbridge, Middlesex UB10 9JX
Tel: 01895 234371
Email: info@sthelenscollege.com
Website: www.sthelenscollege.com
Head: Ms Shirley Drummond BA, PGCert, MLDP, FCCT
Age range: 2–11 years
No. of pupils: 380
Fees: Day £10,980–£13,680

St Helen's School
Eastbury Road, Northwood, Middlesex HA6 3AS
Tel: +44 (0)1923 843210
Headmistress: Mrs Alice Lucas
Age range: G3–18 years
No. of pupils: 1150
16·

St John's School
Potter Street Hill, Northwood, Middlesex HA6 3QY
Tel: 020 8866 0067
Headmaster: Mr Sean Robinson
Age range: B3–13 years

St Martin's School
40 Moor Park Road, Northwood, Middlesex HA6 2DJ
Tel: 01923 825740
Headmaster: Mr S Dunn BEd (Hons)
Age range: B3–13 years

St. John's Senior School
North Lodge, The Ridgeway, Enfield, Middlesex EN2 8BE
Tel: +44 (0)20 8366 0035
Head Teacher: Mr A Tardios
Age range: 11–18 years

Tashbar of Edgware
Mowbray Road, Edgware, Middlesex HA8 8JL
Age range: B3–11 years

The Hall Pre-Preparatory School & Nursery
The Grange Country House, Rickmansworth Road, Northwood, Middlesex HA6 2RB
Tel: 01923 822807
Headmistress: Mrs S M Goodwin
Age range: 0–7 years

The Mall School
185 Hampton Road, Twickenham, Middlesex TW2 5NQ
Tel: 0208 977 2523
Headmaster: Mr D C Price BSc, MA
Age range: B4–11 years

The St Michael Steiner School
Park Road, Hanworth Park, London, Middlesex TW13 6PN
Tel: 0208 893 1299
Age range: 3–18 years

Twickenham Preparatory School
Beveree, 43 High Street, Hampton, Middlesex TW12 2SA
Tel: 020 8979 6216
Headmaster: Mr Oliver Barrett
Age range: B4–13 years G4–11 years

Surrey

Al-Khair School
109–117 Cherry Orchard Road, Croydon, Surrey CR0 6BE
Tel: 020 8662 8664
Headteacher: Mrs Aisha Chaudhry
Age range: 2–16 years

Broomfield House School
Broomfield Road, Kew Gardens, Richmond, Surrey TW9 3HS
Tel: 020 8940 3884
Head of School: Ms Susie Byers
Age range: 3–11 years

Cambridge Tutors College
Water Tower Hill, Croydon, Surrey CR0 5SX
Tel: 020 8688 5284/7363
Principal: Dr Chris Drew
Age range: 14–23 years
16· A 16·

Canbury School
Kingston Hill, Kingston upon Thames, Surrey KT2 7LN
Tel: 020 8549 8622
Headmistress: Ms Carolyn Yates
Age range: 11–18 years

Collingwood School
3 Springfield Road, Wallington, Surrey SM6 0BD
Tel: 020 8647 4607
Headmaster: Mr Leigh Hardie
Age range: 3–11 years

Croydon High School GDST
Old Farleigh Road, Selsdon, South Croydon, Surrey CR2 8YB
Tel: 02082 607543
Head: Ms Annabel Davies
Age range: G3–18 years
A £ 16·

Cumnor House School for Boys
168 Pampisford Road, South Croydon, Surrey CR2 6DA
Tel: 020 8645 2614
Head of School: Miss Emma Edwards
Age range: B4–13 years
No. of pupils: 423
Fees: Day £3,880–£4,655

Cumnor House School for Girls
1 Woodcote Lane, Purley, Surrey CR8 3HB
Tel: 020 8668 0050
Head of School: Mrs Amanda McShane
Age range: G4–11 years

Date Valley School Trust
Mitcham Court, Cricket Green, Mitcham, Surrey CR4 4LB
Tel: +44 (0)20 8648 4647
Headteacher: Neena Lone
Age range: 3–11 years

Educare Small School
12 Cowleaze Road, Kingston upon Thames, Surrey KT2 6DZ
Tel: 020 8547 0144
Head Teacher: Mrs E Steinthal
Age range: 3–11 years

ELMHURST SCHOOL
For further details see p. 110
44–48 South Park Hill Road, South Croydon, Surrey CR2 7DW
Tel: 020 8688 0661
Email: admissions@elmhurstschool.net
Website: www.elmhurstschool.net
Head of School: Mrs Sara Marriott
Age range: B3–11 years
No. of pupils: 118
Fees: Day £3,900–£4,548

Falcons Prep Richmond
41 Kew Foot Road, Richmond, Surrey TW9 2SS
Tel: 020 8948 9490
Headmistress: Ms Olivia Buchanan
Age range: B3–13 years

Hampton Court House
Hampton Court Road, Richmond upon Thames, London, Surrey KT8 9BS
Tel: 020 8614 0865
Headteacher: Katherine Vintiner
Age range: 2–18 years
No. of pupils: 300
Fees: Day £15,075–£22,044
A

Holy Cross Preparatory School
George Road, Kingston upon Thames, Surrey KT2 7NU
Tel: 020 8942 0729
Headteacher: Mrs S Hair BEd(Hons)
Age range: G3–11 years
£

Homefield Preparatory School
Western Road, Sutton, Surrey SM1 2TE
Tel: 02086 420965
Headmaster: Mr John Towers
Age range: B4–13 years

KEW COLLEGE PREP
For further details see p. 112
24–26 Cumberland Road, Kew, Surrey TW9 3HQ
Tel: 020 8940 2039
Email: enquiries@kewcollegeprep.com
Website: www.kewcollegeprep.com
Head: Mrs Jane Bond BSc, MA(Ed), PGCE
Age range: 3–11 years
No. of pupils: 284
£

Kew Green Preparatory School
Layton House, Ferry Lane, Kew Green, Richmond, Surrey TW9 3AF
Tel: 020 8948 5999
Headteacher: Mrs Sasha Davies
Age range: 2–11 years
No. of pupils: 275
Fees: Day £6,632

KING'S HOUSE SCHOOL
For further details see p. 114
68 King's Road, Richmond, Surrey TW10 6ES
Tel: 020 8940 1878
Email: admissions@kingshouseschool.org
Website: www.kingshouseschool.org
Head: Mr Mark Turner BA, PGCE, NPQH
Age range: B3–13 years G3–6 years
No. of pupils: 420
Fees: Day £2,870–£6,890

Kingston Grammar School
London Road, Kingston upon Thames, Surrey KT2 6PY
Tel: 02085 465875
Head Master: Mr Stephen Lehec
Age range: 11–18 years
A £ 16·

LALEHAM LEA SCHOOL
For further details see p. 116
29 Peaks Hill, Purley, Surrey CR8 3JJ
Tel: 020 8660 3351
Email: secretary@lalehamlea.co.uk
Website: www.lalehamlea.co.uk
Acting Head Teacher: Mrs Maria Reece
Age range: 3–11 years
No. of pupils: 144
£

Marymount International School London
George Road, Kingston upon Thames, Surrey KT2 7PE
Tel: +44 (0)20 8949 0571
Headmistress: Mrs Margaret Giblin
Age range: G11–18 years
No. of pupils: 248
Fees: Day £28,830 WB £46,740 FB £48,810
£ IB 16·

Oakwood School
Coombe Road, Lloyd Park, Croydon, Surrey CR0 5RD
Tel: 02086 688080
Headmistress: Ms Debbie Morrison
Age range: 3–11 years

Old Palace of John Whitgift School
Old Palace Road, Croydon, Surrey CR0 1AX
Tel: 02086 882027
Head of School: Mrs Jane Burton
Age range: G3–18 years
No. of pupils: 650
Fees: Day £3,300–£5,536
£ 16·

Old Vicarage School
46–48 Richmond Hill, Richmond, Surrey TW10 6QX
Tel: 020 8940 0922
Headmistress: Mrs G D Linthwaite
Age range: G3–11 years
No. of pupils: 200
Fees: Day £5,200

Park Hill School
8 Queens Road, Kingston upon Thames, Surrey KT2 7SH
Tel: 020 8546 5496
Headmaster: Mr Alistair Bond
Age range: 2–11 years

Rokeby School
George Road, Kingston upon Thames, Surrey KT2 7PB
Tel: 020 8942 2247
Head: Mr J R Peck
Age range: B4–13 years

Royal Russell Junior School
Coombe Lane, Croydon, Surrey CR9 5BX
Tel: +44 (0)20 8657 4433
Junior School Headmaster: Mr John Evans
Age range: 3–11 years

Royal Russell School
Coombe Lane, Croydon, Surrey CR9 5BX
Tel: +44 (0)20 8657 4433
Headmaster: Mr Christopher Hutchinson
Age range: 11–18 years
A £ 16·

Seaton House School
67 Banstead Road South, Sutton, Surrey SM2 5LH
Tel: 020 8642 2332
Headteacher: Mr Carl Bates
Age range: B3–5 years G3–11 years

Shrewsbury House School
107 Ditton Road, Surbiton, Surrey KT6 6RL
Tel: 020 8399 3066
Executive Head: Ms Joanna Hubbard MA BA(Hons) PGCE PGDipSEN
Age range: B7–13 years

St David's School
Woodcote Valley Road, Purley, Surrey CR8 3AL
Tel: 020 8660 0723
Headmistress: Cressida Mardell
Age range: 3–11 years

St James Senior Boys' School
Church Road, Ashford, Surrey TW15 3DZ
Tel: 01784 266930
Headmaster: Mr David Brazier
Age range: B11–18 years
A £ 16·

STAINES PREPARATORY SCHOOL
For further details see p. 122
3 Gresham Road, Staines-upon-Thames, Surrey TW18 2BT
Tel: 01784 450909
Email: admissions@stainesprep.co.uk
Website: www.stainesprep.co.uk
Head of School: Ms Samantha Sawyer B.Ed (Hons), M.Ed, NPQH
Age range: 3–11 years
No. of pupils: 289
Fees: Day £11,975–£14,610
£

Surbiton High School
13–15 Surbiton Crescent, Kingston upon Thames, Surrey KT1 2JT
Tel: 02085 465245
Principal: Mrs Rebecca Glover
Age range: B4–11 years G4–18 years
A £ 16·

Sutton High School GDST
55 Cheam Road, Sutton, Surrey SM1 2AX
Tel: 020 8642 0594
Head of School: Ms Beth Dawson
Age range: G3–18 years
A £ 16·

The Royal Ballet School (White Lodge)
White Lodge, Richmond Park, Richmond, Surrey TW10 5HR
Tel: 020 8392 8440
Head of School: Mr David Gajadharsingh
Age range: 11–19 years (boarding from 11)

The Study School
57 Thetford Road, New Malden, Surrey KT3 5DP
Tel: 020 8942 0754
Headmaster: Mr Alistair Bond
Age range: 2–11 years

Trinity School
Shirley Park, Croydon, Surrey CR9 7AT
Tel: 020 8656 9541
Head: Mr Alasdair Kennedy
Age range: B10–18 years G16–18 years
A £ 16·

Unicorn School
238 Kew Road, Richmond, Surrey TW9 3JX
Tel: 020 8948 3926
Headteacher: Mrs Polly Fraley
Age range: 3–11 years

Westbury House
80 Westbury Road, New Malden, Surrey KT3 5AS
Tel: 020 8942 5885
Headteacher: Miss Clare King
Age range: 2–11 years

WHITGIFT SCHOOL
For further details see p. 126
Haling Park, South Croydon, Surrey CR2 6YT
Tel: +44 20 8633 9935
Email: admissions@whitgift.co.uk
Website: www.whitgift.co.uk
Headmaster: Mr Christopher Ramsey
Age range: B10–18 years (boarding from 13)
No. of pupils: 1550
Fees: Day £24,462 WB £40,470 FB £47,991
A £ IB 16·

London

KEY TO SYMBOLS

- *Boys' school*
- *Girls' school*
- *International school*
- *Tutorial or sixth form college*
- *A levels*
- *Boarding accommodation*
- *Bursaries*
- *International Baccalaureate*
- *Learning support*
- *Entrance at 16+*
- *Vocational qualifications*
- *Independent Association of Preparatory Schools*
- *The Headmasters' & Headmistresses' Conference*
- *Independent Schools Association*
- *Girls' School Association*
- *Boarding Schools' Association*
- *Society of Heads*

Unless otherwise indicated, all schools are coeducational day schools. Single-sex and boarding schools will be indicated by the relevant icon.

London

Central London

Charterhouse Square School
40 Charterhouse Square,
London EC1M 6EA
Tel: 020 7600 3805
Headteacher: Mrs Caroline Lloyd BEd (Hons)
Age range: 3–11 years

City Junior School
4 Gray's Inn Place, London WC1R 5EY
Tel: 020 3814 3506
Head: Ms Rachel Thompson
Age range: 7–11 years

CITY OF LONDON SCHOOL
For further details see p. 132
Queen Victoria Street,
London EC4V 3AL
Tel: 020 3680 6300
Email: admissions@cityoflondonschool.org.uk
Website: www.cityoflondonschool.org.uk
Head: Mr A R Bird MSc
Age range: B10–18 years
No. of pupils: 766 VIth318
Fees: Day £22,635

City of London School for Girls
St Giles' Terrace, Barbican,
London EC2Y 8BB
Tel: 020 7847 5500
Headmistress: Ms Jenny Brown
Age range: G11–18 years

Dallington School
8 Dallington Street, Islington,
London EC1V 0BW
Tel: 020 7251 2284
Head of School: Mr James Griffiths
Age range: 3–11 years
No. of pupils: 81
Fees: Day £12,450–£15,660

École Jeannine Manuel - London
Bloomsbury, London WC1B 3DN
Tel: 020 3829 5970
Head of School: Pauline Prévot
Age range: 3–18 years
No. of pupils: 620
Fees: Day £22,740

Guildhouse School
43–45 Bloomsbury Square,
London WC1A 2RA
Tel: +44 (0)1223 341300
Acting Headmaster: Mr Craig Wilson
Age range: 15–24 years

Italia Conti Academy of Theatre Arts
Italia Conti House, 23 Goswell Road, London EC1M 7AJ
Tel: 020 7608 0047
Director: Chris White
Age range: 10–21 years

ST PAUL'S CATHEDRAL SCHOOL
For further details see p. 162
2 New Change, London EC4M 9AD
Tel: 020 7248 5156
Email: admissions@spcs.london.sch.uk
Website: http://www.spcslondon.com
Head: Judith Fremont-Barnes MA (Hons), MEd
Age range: 4–13 years
No. of pupils: 266
Fees: Day £5,656–£6,090 FB £3,421

The Lyceum School
65 Worship Street, London EC2A 2DU
Tel: +44 (0)20 7247 1588
Headmaster: Mr Mike Stanley
Age range: 4–11 years

The Royal Ballet School (Covent Garden)
46 Floral Street, Covent Garden,
London WC2E 9DA
Tel: 020 7836 8899
Head of School: Mr David Gajadharsingh
Age range: 11–19 years
(boarding from 11)

East London

Al-Falah Primary School
48 Kenninghall Road,
Hackney, London E5 8BY
Tel: 020 8985 1059
Headteacher: Mr M A Hussain
Age range: 5–11 years

Al-Mizan School
46 Whitechapel Road, London E1 1JX
Tel: 020 7650 3070
Headteacher: Mr Mohammed Badr
Age range: B7–11 years

Azhar Academy Girls School
235a Romford Road, Forest
Gate, London E7 9HL
Tel: 020 8534 5959
Executive Head Teacher: Rookshana Adam
Age range: G11–16 years

Azhar Academy Primary School
470 High Road, Leytonstone,
London E11 3HN
Tel: 020 3327 1150
Headteacher: Ms Saima Ahmed
Age range: 3–11 years

Beis Trana Girls' School
186 Upper Clapton Road,
London E5 9DH
Tel: 020 8815 8000
Age range: G3–16 years

Buttercup Primary School
181 Cannon Street Road,
London E1 2LX
Tel: 020 3759 7408
Headteacher: Ms Rena Begum
Age range: 3–11 years

Chingford House Nursery
22 Marlborough Road, Waltham
Forest, London E4 9AL
Tel: 02085 272902
Age range: 6 months–5 years

Darul Hadis Latifiah
1 Cornwall Avenue, Bethnal
Green, London E2 0HW
Tel: 020 8980 2673
Principal: Mr Maulana Muhammad Hasan Chowdhury
Age range: B11–18 years

Faraday Prep School
Old Gate House, 7 Trinity Buoy
Wharf, London E14 0JW
Tel: 020 8965 7374
Head Teacher: Lucas Motion
Age range: 4–11 years
No. of pupils: 100
Fees: Day £4,320

Forest School
College Place, Snaresbrook,
London E17 3PY
Tel: 020 8520 1744
Warden: Mr Marcus Cliff Hodges
Age range: 4–18 years

Gatehouse School
Sewardstone Road, Victoria
Park, London E2 9JG
Tel: 020 8980 2978
Headteacher: Mrs Sevda Korbay
Age range: 3–11 years

Grangewood Independent School
Chester Road, Forest
Gate, London E7 8QT
Tel: 020 8472 3552
Headteacher: Mrs Beverley Roberts
Age range: 2–11 years

Hafs Academy
26 Maryland Road, Stratford,
London E15 1JW
Tel: 020 8555 4260
Head of School: Mr Kazi Hussain
Age range: B7–16 years

Jamiatul Ummah School
56 Bigland Street, London E1 2ND
Tel: 020 7790 7878
Principal: Mr Nojarul Islam
Age range: B11–16 years

Jasper City School
90A Lawson Close, London E16 3LU
Tel: 07957 163043
Head Teacher: Ms Michelle Kintu
Age range: 3–16 years

Lantern of Knowledge Secondary School
30–36 Lindley Road, Leyton,
London E10 6QT
Tel: 020 8539 5183
Head of School: Mr Shakil Ahmed
Age range: B11–16 years

Learningsure College
90a Lawson Close, Custom
House, London E16 3LU
Tel: 020 7511 3444
Head of School: Mr John Ajiferuke
Age range: 11–16 years

London East Academy
46 Whitechapel Road, London E1 1JX
Tel: 020 7650 3070
Headteacher: Askor Ali
Age range: B11–16 years

London Islamic School
18–22 Damien Street, London E1 2HX
Tel: 020 7265 9667
Principal: Hafiz Mawlana Shamsul Haque
Age range: B11–16 years

Lubavitch House School (Junior Boys)
135 Clapton Common, London E5 9AE
Tel: 020 8800 1044
Head: Mr R Leach
Age range: B5–11 years
No. of pupils: 101

Madani Girls School
Myrdle Street, London E1 1HL
Tel: 020 7377 1992
Principal: Muhammad S. Rahman
Age range: G11–18 years

Mazahirul Uloom London
241 Mile End Road, Stepney Green, London E1 4AA
Tel: 020 7702 8533
Principal: Moulana Imdadur Rahman Al-Madani
Age range: 11–16 years

Noor ul Islam Primary School
135 Dawlish Road, Leyton, London E10 6QW
Tel: 020 8558 0786
Interim Head Teacher: Aslam Hansa
Age range: 4–11 years

Normanhurst School
68–74 Station Road, Chingford, London E4 7BA
Tel: 020 8529 4307
Headmistress: Mrs Jacqueline Job
Age range: 21/2–16 years

Ohr Emes
148 Upper Clapton Road, London E5 9JZ
Tel: 020 8800 8932
Age range: B3–7 years

Pillar Box Montessori Nursery & Pre-Prep School
107 Bow Road, London E3 2AN
Tel: 020 8980 0700
Director: Lorraine Redknapp
Age range: 0–5 years
Fees: Day £12,000

Quwwat-ul-Islam Girls' School
16 Chaucer Road, Forest Gate, London E7 9NB
Tel: 020 8548 4736
Headteacher: Ms Shazia Member
Age range: G4–16 years

River House Montessori School
Great Eastern Enterprise, 3 Millharbour, London E14 9XP
Tel: 020 7538 9886
Principal: Ms Sarah Greenwood
Age range: 3–16 years

Snaresbrook Preparatory School
75 Woodford Road, South Woodford, London E18 2EA
Tel: 020 8989 2394
Headteacher: Mr Ralph Dalton
Age range: 31/2–11 years

Talmud Torah Machzikei Hadass School
1 Belz Terrace, Clapton, London E5 9SN
Tel: 020 8800 6599
Age range: B3–16 years

UK Community College (UKCC)
566 Romford Road, London E12 5AF
Tel: 07979 547727
Age range: 7–18 years

Walthamstow Montessori School
Penrhyn Hall, Penrhyn Avenue, Walthamstow, London E17 5DA
Tel: 020 8523 2968
Principal: Ms Lorna Mahoney
Age range: 2–6 years

Winston House Preparatory School
140 High Road, London E18 2QS
Tel: 020 8505 6565
Head Teacher: Mrs Marian Kemp
Age range: 3–11 years

North London

Annemount School
18 Holne Chase, Hampstead Garden Suburb, London N2 0QN
Tel: 020 8455 2132
Principal: Mrs G Maidment BA(Hons), MontDip
Age range: 2–7 years

Avenue Pre-Prep & Nursery School
2 Highgate Avenue, Highgate, London N6 5RX
Tel: 020 8348 6815
Head of School: Ms Sarah Tapp
Age range: 2–7 years

Beis Chinuch Lebonos Girls School
Woodberry Down Centre, Woodberry Down, London N4 2SH
Tel: 020 88097 737
Head of School: Mrs Leah Klein
Age range: G2–16 years

Beis Malka Girls School
93 Alkham Road, London N16 6XD
Tel: 020 8806 2070
Head of School: Mrs G Wind
Age range: G2–16 years

Beis Rochel D'Satmar Girls School
51–57 Amhurst Park, London N16 5DL
Tel: 020 8800 9060
Head of School: Mrs Elka Katz
Age range: G2–18 years

Bnois Jerusalem School
79–81 Amhurst Park, London N16 5DL
Tel: 020 8211 7136
Head of School: Mrs M Landau
Age range: G2–16 years

Bobov Primary School
87–90 Egerton Road, London N16 6UE
Tel: 020 8809 1025
Head of School: Mr Yossi Elzas
Age range: B2–13 years

Channing School
The Bank, Highgate, London N6 5HF
Tel: 020 8340 2328
Headmistress: Mrs Lindsey Hughes
Age range: G4–18 years
£ 16·

Dania Scandinavian School
Curran House, 3 Highbury Crescent, London N5 1RN
Tel: 07933 619674
Headteacher: Ms Katie Howard
Age range: 2–11 years

Dwight School London
6 Friern Barnet Lane, London N11 3LX
Tel: 020 8920 0600
Head: Chris Beddows
Age range: 2–18 years
£ IB 16·

Finchley & Acton Yochien School
6 Hendon Avenue, Finchley, London N3 1UE
Tel: 020 8343 2191
Head of School: Ms Junko Tanabe
Age range: 2–6 years

Grange Park Preparatory School
13 The Chine, Grange Park, Winchmore Hill, London N21 2EA
Tel: 020 8360 1469
Headteacher: Ms Flavia Rizzo
Age range: 3–11 years

Greek Secondary School of London
22 Trinity Road, London N22 8LB
Tel: +44 (0)20 8881 9320
Headteacher: Ms Sandra Doropoulou
Age range: 12–18 years

Highgate
North Road, Highgate, London N6 4AY
Tel: 020 8340 1524
Head Master: Mr Adam Pettitt MA
Age range: 4–18 years
No. of pupils: 1935
A £ 16·

Highgate Junior School
Cholmeley House, 3 Bishopswood Road, London N6 4PL
Tel: 020 8340 9193
Principal: Ms Philippa Studd
Age range: 7–11 years
£

Highgate Pre-Preparatory School
7 Bishopswood Road, London N6 4PH
Tel: 020 8340 9196
Principal: Ms Sally Hancock
Age range: 4–7 years

Hyland House School
Holcombe Road, Tottenham, London N17 9AB
Tel: 0208 520 4186
Headteacher: Mr Errol Gayle
Age range: 2–11 years

Keble Prep
Wades Hill, Winchmore Hill, London N21 1BG
Tel: 020 8360 3359
Headmaster: Mr Perran Gill BA (Hons)
Age range: 3–13 years

Kerem School
Norrice Lea, Hampstead Garden Suburb, London N2 0RE
Tel: 020 8455 0909
Head Teacher: Ms Naomi Simon
Age range: 3–11 years

Lubavitch House School (Senior Girls)
107–115 Stamford Hill, Hackney, London N16 5RP
Tel: 020 8800 0022
Headmaster: Rabbi Shmuel Lew FRSA
Age range: G11–18 years
No. of pupils: 102
Fees: Day £3,900

NORFOLK HOUSE SCHOOL
For further details see p. 150
10 Muswell Avenue, Muswell Hill, London N10 2EG
Tel: +44 (0)2088 834584
Email: office@norfolkhouseschool.org
Website: www.norfolkhouseschool.org
Headteacher: Mr Tej Lander
Age range: 2–11 years

NORTH BRIDGE HOUSE SENIOR CANONBURY
For further details see p. 152
6–9 Canonbury Place, Islington, London N1 2NQ
Tel: 020 7428 1520
Head of School: Mr Brendan Pavey
Age range: 11–18 years
No. of pupils: 220
Fees: Day £19,230–£21,735

North London Grammar School
110 Colindeep Lane, Hendon, London NW9 6HB
Tel: 0208 205 0052
Headteacher: Mr Fatih Adak
Age range: 7–18 years

North London Rudolf Steiner School
1–3 The Campsbourne, London N8 7PN
Tel: 020 8341 3770
Age range: 0–6 years

Palmers Green High School
104 Hoppers Road, London N21 3LJ
Tel: 020 8886 1135
Head: Ms Sarah Proudlove
Age range: G3–17 years

Pardes House Grammar School
Hendon Lane, Finchley, London N3 1SA
Tel: 020 8349 4222
Head of School: Rabbi Yitzchok Lev
Age range: B10–16 years

Phoenix Academy
85 Bounces Road, Edmonton, London N9 8LD
Tel: 020 8887 6888
Head Teacher: Mr Paul Kelly
Age range: 5–18 years

Rosemary Works Independent School
1 Branch Place, London N1 5PH
Tel: 02077 393950
Headteacher: Ms Amanda Parker NPQH, MPhil
Age range: 3–11 years

Salcombe Preparatory School
Green Road, London N14 4AD
Tel: 020 8441 5356
Headmistress: Miss Nicola Sands
Age range: 3–11 years

Shakhsiyah School, London
1st Floor, 277 St Ann's Road, London N15 5RG
Tel: 020 8802 8651
Executive Headteacher: Mr Ziaur Rahman
Age range: 3–14 years

St Paul's Steiner School
1 St Paul's Road, Islington, London N1 2QH
Tel: 020 7226 4454
Head Teacher: Ms Anna Retsler
Age range: 3–14 years

Sunrise Nursery, Stoke Newington
1 Cazenove Road, Stoke Newington, Hackney, London N16 6PA
Tel: 020 8806 6279
Principal: Didi Ananda Manika
Age range: 15 months–5 years

Sunrise Primary School
55 Coniston Road, Tottenham, London N17 0EX
Tel: 020 8806 6279 (Office); 020 8885 3354 (School)
Head: Mrs Mary-Anne Lovage MontDipEd, BA
Age range: 2–11 years
No. of pupils: 30
Fees: Day £5,550

Talmud Torah Chaim Meirim School
26 Lampard Grove, London N16 6XB
Tel: 020 8806 0898
Age range: B5–13 years

Talmud Torah Yetev Lev School
111–115 Cazenove Road, London N16 6AX
Tel: 020 8806 3834
Age range: B3–11 years

Tawhid Boys School
21 Cazenove Road, Stamford Hill, London N16 6PA
Tel: 020 8806 2999
Headteacher: Mr Usman Mapara
Age range: B11–16 years

Tayyibah Girls School
88 Filey Avenue, Hackney, London N16 6JJ
Tel: 020 8880 0085
Head Teacher: Mrs Sumeya Patel
Age range: G4–18 years

The Children's House Nursery School
77 Elmore Street, London N1 3AQ
Tel: 020 7354 2113
Age range: 21/2–4 years

The Children's House Upper School
King Henry's Walk, London N1 4PB
Tel: 020 7249 6273
Headteacher: Ms Ellie Grunewald
Age range: 4–7 years

The Gower School Nursery
18 North Road, Islington, London N7 9EY
Tel: 020 7700 2445
Principal: Miss Emma Gowers
Age range: 3 months–5 years

The Gower School Primary
10 Cynthia Street, Barnsbury, London N1 9JF
Tel: 020 7278 2020
Principal: Miss Emma Gowers
Age range: 4–11 years

TTTYY School
14 Heathland Road, London N16 5NH
Tel: 020 8802 1348
Head of School: Rabbi Y.Y. Friesel
Age range: B2–13 years

Vita et Pax School
6a Priory Close, Green Road, Southgate, London N14 4AT
Tel: 020 8449 8336
Headteacher: Ms Allana Gay
Age range: 3–11 years

Yesodey Hatorah Senior Girls' School
Egerton Road, London N16 6UB
Tel: 020 8826 5500
Acting Head Teacher: Mrs C Neuberger
Age range: 3–16 years
No. of pupils: 920

North-West London

Al-Sadiq & Al-Zahra Schools
134 Salusbury Road, London NW6 6PF
Tel: 020 7372 7706
Heads: Mr Seyed Alireza Khoei & Mrs Zamina Rizvi
Age range: 3–16 years

Arnold House School
1 Loudoun Road, St John's Wood, London NW8 0LH
Tel: 020 7266 4840
Headmaster: Mr Giles F Tollit
Age range: B3–13 years

Barnet Hill Academy
10A Montagu Road, Hendon, London NW4 3ES
Tel: 020 3411 2660
Principal: Mr Alim Shaikh MA, PGCE, MPhil, NPQH
Age range: 3–11 years

Beis Soroh Schneirer
Arbiter House, Wilberforce Road, London NW9 6AX
Tel: 020 8201 7771
Head of School: Mrs Sonia Mossberg
Age range: G2–11 years

Belmont, Mill Hill Preparatory School
The Ridgeway, London NW7 4ED
Tel: 020 8906 7270
Headmaster: Mr Leon Roberts MA
Age range: 7–13 years
No. of pupils: 550
Fees: Day £19,560

Beth Jacob Grammar School for Girls
Stratford Road, Hendon, London NW4 2AT
Tel: 020 8203 4322
Age range: G11–17 years

Brampton College
Lodge House, Lodge Road, Hendon, London NW4 4DQ
Tel: 020 8203 5025
Principal: Mr Bernard Canetti
Age range: 15–19 years
16 A

Broadhurst School
19 Greencroft Gardens, London NW6 3LP
Tel: 020 7328 4280
Headmistress: Mrs Zoe Sylvester
Age range: 2–5 years

Brondesbury College
8 Brondesbury Park, London NW6 7BT
Tel: 020 8830 4522
Headteacher: Mr Amzad Ali
Age range: B11–16 years

Collège Français Bilingue de Londres (CFBL)
87 Holmes Road, Kentish Town, London NW5 3AX
Tel: 020 7993 7400
Head of School: Mr David Gassian
Age range: 3–15 years
No. of pupils: 700

Devonshire House Preparatory School
2 Arkwright Road, Hampstead, London NW3 6AE
Tel: 020 7435 1916
Headmistress: Mrs S. Piper BA(Hons)
Age range: B2½–13 years G2½–11 years
No. of pupils: 543
Fees: Day £9,870–£20,475
£

Francis Holland School, Regent's Park, NW1
Clarence Gate, Ivor Place, Regent's Park, London NW1 6XR
Tel: 020 7723 0176
Head of School: Mrs Katharine Woodcock
Age range: G11–18 years
No. of pupils: 556 VIth120
Fees: Day £22,890
A £ 16

Goodwyn School
Hammers Lane, Mill Hill, London NW7 4DB
Tel: 020 8959 3756
Principal: Mr Struan Robertson
Age range: 3–11 years

Grimsdell, Mill Hill Pre-Preparatory School
Winterstoke House, Wills Grove, Mill Hill, London NW7 1QR
Tel: 020 8959 6884
Head: Mrs Kate Simon BA, PGCE
Age range: 3–7 years
No. of pupils: 188
Fees: Day £15,095

Hampstead Fine Arts College
Centre Studios, 41–43 England's Lane, London NW3 4YD
Tel: +44 (0)207 586 0312
Principal: Ms Candida Cave
Age range: 13–19 years
16

Hampstead Hill School
St Stephen's Hall, Pond Street, Hampstead, London NW3 2PP
Tel: 020 7435 6262
Headteacher: Mr Ross Montague
Age range: 2–7+ years

HEATHSIDE SCHOOL HAMPSTEAD
For further details see p. 144
84a Heath Street, Hampstead, London NW3 1DN
Tel: +44 (0)20 3058 4011
Email: admissions@heathsideschoolhampstead.com
Website: www.heathsideschoolhampstead.com
Headteacher: Nadia Ward
Age range: 2–13 years
No. of pupils: 137
Fees: Day £18,789–£21,273

Hendon Prep School
20 Tenterden Grove, Hendon, London NW4 1TD
Tel: 020 8203 7727
Headteacher: Mrs Tushi Gorasia
Age range: 3–11 years
No. of pupils: 170
£

Hereward House School
14 Strathray Gardens, Hampstead, London NW3 4NY
Tel: 020 7794 4820
Headmaster: Mr Pascal Evans
Age range: B4–13 years
No. of pupils: 173
Fees: Day £19,350–£19,890

IRIS School
100 Carlton Vale, London NW6 5HE
Tel: 020 7372 8051
Headteacher: Mr Seyed Abbas Hosseini
Age range: 6–16 years

Islamia Girls School
129 Salusbury Road, London NW6 6PE
Tel: 020 7372 3472
Headteacher: Mr Amzad Ali
Age range: G11–16 years

Lyndhurst House Prep School
24 Lyndhurst Gardens, Hampstead, London NW3 5NW
Tel: 020 7435 4936
Head of School: Mr Andrew Reid MA (Oxon)
Age range: B4–13 years
No. of pupils: 125
Fees: Day £18,360–£20,790

Maple Walk Prep School
62A Crownhill Road, London NW10 4EB
Tel: 020 8963 3890
Head Teacher: Claire Murdoch
Age range: 4–11 years
No. of pupils: 170
Fees: Day £4,194
£

Maria Montessori Institute
26 Lyndhurst Gardens, Hampstead, London NW3 5NW
Tel: 020 7435 3646
Director of Training & School: Mrs Lynne Lawrence BA, Mont Int Dip(AMI)
Age range: 2–12 years
No. of pupils: 50
Fees: Day £5,580–£13,560
16

Maria Montessori School - Hampstead
26 Lyndhurst Gardens, Hampstead, London NW3 5NW
Tel: 020 7435 3646
Age range: 2½–12 years

Mill Hill School
The Ridgeway, Mill Hill Village, London NW7 1QS
Tel: 020 8959 1176
Head: Mrs Jane Sanchez BSc (Hons) PGCE
Age range: 13–18 years (boarding from 13)
No. of pupils: 876 VIth312
Fees: Day £21,987 WB £31,140 FB £36,900
A £ 16

Naima Jewish Preparatory School
21 Andover Place, London NW6 5ED
Tel: 020 7328 2802
Headmaster: Mr Bill Pratt
Age range: 2–11 years

Nancy Reuben Primary School
48 Finchley Lane, Hendon, London NW4 1DJ
Tel: 020 8202 5646
Head Teacher: Mr Anthony Wolfson
Age range: 2–11 years

NORTH BRIDGE HOUSE NURSERY AND PRE-PREP HAMPSTEAD
For further details see p. 152
8 Netherhall Gardens, London NW3 5RR
Tel: 020 7428 1520
Head of School: Mrs Christine McLelland
Age range: 2–7 years
No. of pupils: 190

NORTH BRIDGE HOUSE NURSERY AND PRE-PREP WEST HAMPSTEAD
For further details see p. 152
85–87 Fordwych Rd, London NW2 3TL
Tel: 020 7428 1520
Head of School: Mrs Christine McLelland
Age range: 2–7 years

NORTH BRIDGE HOUSE PREP SCHOOL REGENT'S PARK
For further details see p. 152
1 Gloucester Avenue, London NW1 7AB
Tel: 020 7428 1520
Head of School: Mr Tom Le Tissier
Age range: 7–13 years
No. of pupils: 385
Fees: Day £20,193–£21,855
£

NORTH BRIDGE HOUSE SENIOR HAMPSTEAD
For further details see p. 152
65 Rosslyn Hill, London NW3 5UD
Tel: 020 7428 1520
Email: joinus@northbridgehouse.com
Website: www.northbridgehouse.com
Executive Headteacher: Brendan Pavey
Age range: 2–18 years
No. of pupils: 1400
Fees: Day £9,420–£25,302

Rainbow Montessori School
13 Woodchurch Road, Hampstead, London NW6 3PL
Tel: 020 7328 8986
Head Mistress: Maggy Miller MontDip
Age range: 2–5 years

Saint Christina's School
25 St Edmund's Terrace, St John's Wood, London NW8 7PY
Tel: 020 7722 8784
Headteacher: Mr Alastair Gloag
Age range: 3–11 years

Sarum Hall School
15 Eton Avenue, London NW3 3EL
Tel: 020 7794 2261
Headmistress: Miss Karen Coles BEd (Hons), Exon
Age range: G3–11 years
No. of pupils: 185

South Hampstead High School GDST
3 Maresfield Gardens, London NW3 5SS
Tel: 020 7435 2899
Headmistress: Mrs Victoria Bingham MA (Oxon)
Age range: G4–18 years

Southbank International School - Hampstead
16 Netherhall Gardens, London NW3 5TH
Tel: 020 3890 1969
Head of School: Stuart Bain
Age range: 2–11 years
IB

St Christopher's School
32 Belsize Lane, Hampstead, London NW3 5AE
Tel: 020 7435 1521
Head: Ms Sandrine Paillasse
Age range: G4–11 years

St John's Wood Pre-Preparatory School
St Johns Hall, Lords Roundabout, London NW8 7NE
Tel: 020 7722 7149
Principal: Adrian Ellis
Age range: 3–7 years

St Margaret's School
18 Kidderpore Gardens, Hampstead, London NW3 7SR
Tel: 020 7435 2439
Principal: Mr Mark Webster BSc, PGCE
Age range: G4–16 years

St Martin's School
22 Goodwyn Avenue, Mill Hill, London NW7 3RG
Tel: 020 8959 1965
Headteacher: Mrs Samantha Mbah
Age range: 3–11 years

St Mary's School Hampstead
47 Fitzjohn's Avenue, Hampstead, London NW3 6PG
Tel: 020 7435 1868
Headteacher: Miss Charlotte Owen
Age range: G2 years 9 months–11 years
No. of pupils: 300
Fees: Day £9,330–£17,250

St Nicholas School
22 Salmon Street, London NW9 8PN
Tel: 020 8205 7153
Headmaster: Mr Matt Donaldson BA (Hons), PGCE, PGDip (Surv)
Age range: 3 months–11 years

St. Anthony's School for Boys
90 Fitzjohn's Avenue, Hampstead, London NW3 6NP
Tel: 020 7431 1066
Head of School: Mr Richard Berlie MA (Cantab)
Age range: B21/2–13 years G21/2–4 years
No. of pupils: 280

St. Anthony's School for Girls
Ivy House, 94–96 North End Road, London NW11 7SX
Tel: 020 3869 3070
Head of School: Mr Donal Brennan
Age range: G21/2–11 years
No. of pupils: 85
Fees: Day £18,000

The Academy School
3 Pilgrims Place, Rosslyn Hill, Hampstead, London NW3 1NG
Tel: 020 7435 6621
Headteacher: Mr Garth Evans BA (Lond)
Age range: 6–13 years

The American School in London
One Waverley Place, London NW8 0NP
Tel: +44 (0)20 7449 1200
Head of School: Ms Coreen R. Hester
Age range: 4–18 years

The Cavendish School
31 Inverness Street, Camden Town, London NW1 7HB
Tel: 020 7485 1958
Head of School: Mrs Taryn Lombard
Age range: G3–11 years

The Hall School
23 Crossfield Road, Hampstead, London NW3 4NU
Tel: 020 7722 1700
Headmaster: Mr Chris Godwin
Age range: B4–13 years

The King Alfred School
North End Road, London NW11 7HY
Tel: 020 8457 5200
Head: Robert Lobatto MA (Oxon)
Age range: 4–18 years
No. of pupils: 670

The Mount, Mill Hill International
Milespit Hill, London NW7 2RX
Tel: +44 (0)20 3826 33
Head of School: Ms Sarah Bellotti
Age range: 13–17 years
No. of pupils: 80
Fees: Day £27,000 WB £37,500 FB £44,250

The Mulberry House School
7 Minster Road, West Hampstead, London NW2 3SD
Tel: 020 8452 7340
Headteacher: Ms Victoria Playford BA Hons, QTS
Age range: 2–7+ years

The Village Prep School
2 Parkhill Road, Belsize Park, London NW3 2YN
Tel: 020 7485 4673
Head of School: Ms Morven MacDonald
Age range: G21/2–11 years

Torah Vodaas
Brent Park Road, West Hendon Broadway, London NW9 7AJ
Tel: 020 3670 4670
Head of School: Rabbi Y Feldman
Age range: B2–11 years

Trevor-Roberts School
55–57 Eton Avenue, London NW3 3ET
Tel: 020 7586 1444
Co-Heads: Simon & Amanda Trevor-Roberts
Age range: 5–13 years

University College School Hampstead (UCS) Junior
11 Holly Hill, Hampstead, London NW3 6QN
Tel: 020 7435 3068
Headmaster: Mr Lewis Hayward
Age range: B7–11 years

University College School Hampstead (UCS) Pre-Prep
36 College Crescent, Hampstead, London NW3 5LF
Tel: 020 7722 4433
Headmistress: Ms Zoe Dunn
Age range: B4–7 years

University College School Hampstead (UCS) Senior
Frognal, Hampstead, London NW3 6XH
Tel: 020 7435 2215
Headmaster: Mr Mark J Beard
Age range: B11–18 years G16–18 years

Wentworth College
6–10 Brentmead Place, London NW11 9LH
Tel: 020 8458 8524
Principal: Mr Manuel Guimaraes
Age range: 14–19 years

South-East London

Alleyn's School
Townley Road, Dulwich, London SE22 8SU
Tel: 020 8557 1500
Head of School: Ms Jane Lunnon
Age range: 4–18 years

Arco Academy
Camberwell Leisure Centre, Artichoke Place, London SE5 8TS
Tel: 020 3189 1193
Principal: Ms Lisa Miller
Age range: 11–16 years

Blackheath High School GDST
Vanbrugh Park, Blackheath, London SE3 7AG
Tel: 020 8853 2929
Acting Head: Ms Natalie Argile
Age range: G3–18 years

Blackheath Prep
4 St Germans Place, Blackheath, London SE3 0NJ
Tel: 020 8858 0692
Head: Mr Alex Matthews
Age range: 3–11 years
No. of pupils: 385

Colfe's Junior School
Upwood Road, London SE12 8AA
Tel: 020 8463 8266
Head of School: Mrs M-C Gilfedder-Bonnar
Age range: 3–11 years

Colfe's School
Horn Park Lane, London SE12 8AW
Tel: 020 8852 2283
Head of School: Mr R Russell
Age range: 3–18 years

DLD College London
199 Westminster Bridge Road, London SE1 7FX
Tel: +44 (0)20 7935 8411
Principal: Mr Irfan H Latif
Age range: 13–19 years

Dulwich College
Dulwich Common, London SE21 7LD
Tel: 020 8693 3601
Master: Dr J A F Spence
Age range: B6 months–18 years G6 months–7 years
Fees: Day £24,693 WB £48,324 FB £51,546

Dulwich College Kindergarten & Infants School
Eller Bank, 87 College Road, London SE21 7HH
Tel: 020 8693 1538
Head: Mrs Miranda Norris
Age range: 3 months–7 years
No. of pupils: 251

Dulwich Prep London
42 Alleyn Park, Dulwich, London SE21 7AA
Tel: 020 8766 5500
Head Master: Miss Louise Davidson
Age range: B3–13 years (boarding from 8) G3–5 years

Eltham College
Grove Park Road, Mottingham, London SE9 4QF
Tel: 0208 857 1455
Headmaster: Mr Guy R Sanderson
Age range: 7–18 years

Greenwich Steiner School
90 Mycenae Road, London SE3 7SE
Tel: 020 8858 4404
Executive Principal: Mr Allan Osborne
Age range: 3–18 years

Heath House Preparatory School
37 Wemyss Road, Blackheath, London SE3 0TG
Tel: 020 8297 1900
Head Teacher: Mrs Sophia Laslett CertEd PGDE
Age range: 3–11 years

Herne Hill School
The Old Vicarage, 127 Herne Hill, London SE24 9LY
Tel: 020 7274 6336
Headteacher: Mrs Ngaire Telford
Age range: 2–7 years

James Allen's Girls' School
144 East Dulwich Grove, Dulwich, London SE22 8TE
Tel: 020 8693 1181
Head of School: Mrs Alex Hutchinson
Age range: G4–18 years

Kings Kids Christian School
100 Woodpecker Road, Newcross, London SE14 6EU
Tel: 020 8259 3659
Headteacher: Mrs M Okenwa
Age range: 3–11 years

London Christian School
40 Tabard Street, London SE1 4JU
Tel: 02031 306430
Head Teacher: Miss Nicola Collett-White
Age range: 3–11 years

Marathon Science School
1–9 Evelyn Street, Surrey Quays, London SE8 5RQ
Tel: 020 7231 3232
Headteacher: Mr Mehmet Yilmaz
Age range: B11–18 years

OAKFIELD PREPARATORY SCHOOL
For further details see p. 154
125–128 Thurlow Park Road, West Dulwich, London SE21 8HP
Tel: 020 8670 4206
Email: admissions@oakfield.dulwich.sch.uk
Website: www.oakfield.dulwich.sch.uk
Head of School: Mrs Moyra Thompson
Age range: 2–11 years
No. of pupils: 303

Octavia House School, Kennington
214b Kennington Road, London SE11 6AU
Tel: 020 3651 4396 (option 3)
Assistant Principal: Ms Knight
Age range: 14–16 years

Octavia House School, Vauxhall
Vauxhall Street, London SE11 5LG
Tel: 020 3651 4396 (option 1)
Assistant Principal: Ms Ross
Age range: 5–11 years

Octavia House School, Walworth
Larcom Street, London SE17 1RT
Tel: 020 3651 4396 (option 2)
Assistant Principal: Mr Dickens
Age range: 11–14 years

Riverston School
63/69 Eltham Road, Lee, London SE12 8UF
Tel: 020 8318 4327
Headmaster: Mr David A T Ward MA
Age range: 9 months–19 years

Rose House Montessori School
Vancouver Road, Forest Hill, London SE23 2AG
Tel: 020 8699 9260
Principal: Mrs Dawn Nasser
Age range: 2–11 years

Rosemead Preparatory School & Nursery, Dulwich
70 Thurlow Park Road, Dulwich, London SE21 8HZ
Tel: 020 8670 5865
Headmaster: Mr Phil Soutar
Age range: 21/2–11 years

St Dunstan's College
Stanstead Road, London SE6 4TY
Tel: 020 8516 7200
Head of School: Mr Nick Hewlett
Age range: 3–18 years

St Olave's Preparatory School
106–110 Southwood Road, New Eltham, London SE9 3QS
Tel: 020 8294 8930
Headteacher: Miss Claire Holloway BEd, QTS
Age range: 3–11 years

Sydenham High School GDST
15 & 19 Westwood Hill, London SE26 6BL
Tel: 020 8557 7004
Head of School: Ms Antonia Geldeard
Age range: G4–18 years

The Cedars School
147 Central Hill, Upper Norwood, London SE19 1RS
Tel: 020 8185 7770
Headmaster: Mr Robert Teague
Age range: B11–18 years

The Laurels School
1 Our Lady's Close, Upper Norwood, London SE19 3FA
Tel: 020 8674 7229
Headmistress: Mrs Linda Sanders BA Hons (Bristol), MA (Madrid)
Age range: G11–18 years

The New School London
St. Mary's Lodge, 149 Central Hill, London SE19 1RT
Tel: 020 4513 0505
Co-Headteachers: Dhama Sangarabalan & Callie Sharma
Age range: 4–16 years

The Pointer School
19 Stratheden Road, Blackheath, London SE3 7TH
Tel: 020 8293 1331
Head of School: Ms Charlotte Crookes MA (Cantab), MA, PGCE
Age range: 3–11 years

The Villa School & Nursery
54 Lyndhurst Grove, Peckham, London SE15 5AH
Tel: 020 7703 6216
Head Teacher: Ms Louise Maughan
Age range: 2–7 years

South-West London

Al-Risalah Secondary School
145 Upper Tooting Road, London SW17 7TJ
Tel: 020 8767 6057
Executive Principal: Suhayl Lee
Age range: 11–16 years

Beechwood Nursery School
55 Leigham Court Road, Streatham, London SW16 2NJ
Tel: 020 8677 8778
Age range: 0–5 years

Bertrum House Nursery
290 Balham High Road, London SW17 7AL
Tel: 020 8767 4051
Age range: 2–5 years

Broomwood Prep, Boys
26 Bolingbroke Grove, London SW11 6EL
Tel: 020 8682 8888
Head (and Group Principal): Mr Kevin Doble
Age range: B7–13 years
No. of pupils: 200
Fees: Day £7,535

Broomwood Prep, Girls
68–74 Nightingale Lane, London SW12 8NR
Tel: 020 8682 8810
Head: Mrs Louisa McCafferty
Age range: G7–13 years
No. of pupils: 200
Fees: Day £7,535

Broomwood Pre-Prep and Little Broomwood
192 Ramsden Road, London SW12 8RQ
Tel: 020 8682 8840
Head: Mrs Caron Mackay
Age range: 3–7 years
No. of pupils: 300

Cameron Vale School
4 The Vale, Chelsea, London SW3 6AH
Tel: 020 7352 4040
Headteacher: Ms Alison Melrose
Age range: 2–11 years
£

Centre Academy London
92 St John's Hill, Battersea, London SW11 1SH
Tel: 020 7738 2344
Head of School: Mrs. Kas Lee-Douglas
Age range: 9–19 years
16·

Collingham College
23 Collingham Gardens, London SW5 0HL
Tel: 020 7244 7414
Principal: Ms Sally Powell
Age range: 13–19 years
16· A

Dolphin School
106 Northcote Road, London SW11 6QW
Tel: 020 7924 3472
Head Teacher: Mr S Gosden
Age range: 2–11 years
No. of pupils: 162
Fees: Day £13,395–£14,670
£

Donhead Preparatory School
33 Edge Hill, Wimbledon, London SW19 4NP
Tel: 020 8946 7000
Headteacher: Mr P J J Barr
Age range: B4–11 years

EATON HOUSE BELGRAVIA
For further details see p. 138
3–5 Eaton Gate, London SW1W 9BA
Tel: 020 3917 5050
Email: admissions@eatonhouseschools.com
Website: www.eatonhouseschools.com
Interim Headmaster: Mr Brendan O'Keeffe
Age range: B2–11 years G2–4 years
No. of pupils: 180

EATON HOUSE THE MANOR BOYS' SCHOOL
For further details see p. 140
58 Clapham Common North Side, London SW4 9RU
Tel: 020 3917 5050
Email: admissions@eatonhouseschools.com
Website: www.eatonhouseschools.com
Head of Prep: Mrs Sarah Segrave
Age range: B2–13 years G2–4 years
No. of pupils: 430

EATON HOUSE THE MANOR GIRLS' SCHOOL
For further details see p. 142
58 Clapham Common North Side, London SW4 9RU
Tel: 020 3917 5050
Email: admissions@eatonhouseschools.com
Website: www.eatonhouseschools.com
Headteacher: Mrs Claire Fildes
Age range: B2–4 years G2–11 years
No. of pupils: 220

Eaton Square Prep School
55–57 Eccleston Square, London SW1V 1PP
Tel: 0207 225 3131
Head of School: Ms Trish Watt
Age range: 4–11 years

École Primaire Marie D'Orliac
60 Clancarty Road, London SW6 3AA
Tel: +44 (0)20 7736 5863
Director: Mr Blaise Fenart
Age range: 4–11 years

Emanuel School
Battersea Rise, London SW11 1HS
Tel: 020 8870 4171
Headmaster: Mr Robert Milne
Age range: 10–18 years
A £ 16·

Eveline Day School
Swan House, 207 Balham High Road, London SW17 7BQ
Tel: 020 8673 3188
Head Teacher: Ms Eveline Drut
Age range: 2–11 years

Evergreen Primary School
9 Swan Mews, Fulham, London SW6 4QT
Tel: 07429 112217
Headteacher: Ms Rena Begum
Age range: 3–11 years

Falcons School for Girls
11 Woodborough Road, Putney, London SW15 6PY
Tel: 020 8992 5189
Headmistress: Ms Sara Williams-Ryan
Age range: G4–11 years

Falkner House
19 Brechin Place, South Kensington, London SW7 4QB
Tel: 02073 734501
Headteachers: Mrs Flavia Rogers & Mrs Eleanor Dixon
Age range: 2–11 years

Finton House School
171 Trinity Road, London SW17 7HL
Tel: 020 8682 0921
Head of School: Mr Ben Freeman
Age range: 4–11 years

Francis Holland School, Sloane Square, SW1
39 Graham Terrace, London SW1W 8JF
Tel: 020 7730 2971
Head: Mr Rob Cawley (MA, BA, PGCE, FRSA)
Age range: G4–18 years
A £ 16·

Garden House School
Turks Row, Chelsea, London SW3 4TW
Tel: 020 7730 1652/6652
Principals: Mr Christian Warland & Mrs Sophie Strafford
Age range: 3–11 years

Glendower Preparatory School
86/87 Queen's Gate, London SW7 5JX
Tel: 020 7370 1927
Headmistress: Mrs Nina Kingsmill Moore
Age range: G3–11 years

Hall School Wimbledon
17, The Downs, Wimbledon, London SW20 8HF
Tel: 020 8879 9200
Headmaster: Mr. A Hammond
Age range: 5–18 years
No. of pupils: 160
Fees: Day £4,570–£6,140

Harrodian
Lonsdale Road, London SW13 9QN
Tel: 020 8748 6117
Headmaster: Mr James R Hooke
Age range: 4–18 years
A £ 16·

Hill House
17 Hans Place, Chelsea, London SW1X 0EP
Tel: 020 7584 1331
Headmaster: Mr Richard Townend
Age range: 4–13 years

Hornsby House School
Hearnville Road, Balham, London SW12 8RS
Tel: 020 8673 7573
Headmaster: Mr Edward Rees
Age range: 4–11 years

Hurlingham School
122 Putney Bridge Road, Putney, London SW15 2NQ
Tel: 020 8103 0823
Headmaster: Mr Simon Gould
Age range: 4–11 years

Ibstock Place School
Clarence Lane, Roehampton, London SW15 5PY
Tel: 020 8876 9991
Head of School: Mr Christopher J Wolsey
Age range: 4–18 years

KENSINGTON PARK SCHOOL
For further details see p. 146
40–44 Bark Place, Bayswater, London W2 4AT
Tel: +44 (0)20 7616 4400
Email: admissions@kps.co.uk
Website: www.kps.co.uk
Headmaster: Mr Stephen Mellor
Age range: 11–18 years

Kensington Prep School
596 Fulham Road, London SW6 5PA
Tel: 0207 731 9300
Head of School: Mrs Caroline Hulme-McKibbin
Age range: G4–11 years
Fees: Day £6,954

King's College School
Southside, Wimbledon Common, London SW19 4TT
Tel: 020 8255 5300
Head: Dr Anne Cotton
Age range: B7–18 years G16–18 years
No. of pupils: 1478

Knightsbridge School
67 Pont Street, Knightsbridge, London SW1X 0BD
Tel: +44 (0)20 7590 9000
Head: Miss Shona Colaço
Age range: 3–16 years
No. of pupils: 400
Fees: Day £7,452

L'Ecole de Battersea
Trott Street, Battersea, London SW11 3DS
Tel: 020 7371 8350
Principal: Mrs F Brisset
Age range: 3–11 years
No. of pupils: 250
Fees: Day £5,075

L'Ecole des Petits
2 Hazlebury Road, Fulham, London SW6 2NB
Tel: 020 7371 8350
Principal: Mrs F Brisset
Age range: 3–6 years
No. of pupils: 120
Fees: Day £4,935

London Park School, Clapham
7–11 Nightingale Lane, Clapham South, London SW4 9AH
Tel: 020 8161 0301
Head: Mr Paul Vanni
Age range: 11–16 (plus 16–18 in standalone Sixth Form)
No. of pupils: 250
Fees: Day £7,535

Lycée Français Charles de Gaulle de Londres
35 Cromwell Road, London SW7 2DG
Tel: 020 7584 6322
Head of School: TBC
Age range: 3–18 years
No. of pupils: 3450
Fees: Day £7,631–£15,965

Mander Portman Woodward - MPW London
90–92 Queen's Gate, London SW7 5AB
Tel: 020 7835 1355
Principal: Mr Steve Boyes BA, MSc, PGCE
Age range: 14–19 years
No. of pupils: 600
Fees: Day £10,765

More House School
22–24 Pont Street, Knightsbridge, London SW1X 0AA
Tel: 020 7235 2855
Head: Ms Faith Hagerty
Age range: G11–18 years
No. of pupils: 145
Fees: Day £7,750

Newton Prep
149 Battersea Park Road, London SW8 4BX
Tel: 020 7720 4091
Headmistress: Mrs Alison Fleming BA, MA Ed, PGCE
Age range: 3–13 years
No. of pupils: 646
Fees: Day £10,575–£22,395

Oliver House Preparatory School
7 Nightingale Lane, London SW4 9AH
Tel: 020 8772 1911
Headteacher: Mr Rob Farrell
Age range: 3–11 years
No. of pupils: 144
Fees: Day £6,600–£15,090

Parkgate House School
80 Clapham Common North Side, London SW4 9SD
Tel: +44 (0)20 7350 2461
Principal: Miss Catherine Shanley
Age range: 21/2–11 years

Parsons Green Prep School
1 Fulham Park Road, Fulham, London SW6 4LJ
Tel: 020 7371 9009
Head: Dr Pamela Edmonds
Age range: 4–11 years

Prince's Gardens Preparatory School
10–13 Prince's Gardens, London SW7 1ND
Tel: 0207 591 4622
Headmistress: Mrs Alison Melrose
Age range: 3–11 years

PROSPECT HOUSE SCHOOL
For further details see p. 158
75 Putney Hill, London SW15 3NT
Tel: 020 3835 3058
Email: info@prospecths.org.uk
Website: www.prospecths.org.uk
Headmaster: Mr Michael Hodge BPED(Rhodes) QTS
Age range: 3–11 years
No. of pupils: 300
Fees: Day £10,470–£22,530

Putney High School GDST
35 Putney Hill, London SW15 6BH
Tel: 020 8788 4886
Headmistress: Mrs Suzie Longstaff BA, MA, PGCE
Age range: G4–18 years

QUEEN'S GATE SCHOOL
For further details see p. 160
133 Queen's Gate, London SW7 5LE
Tel: 020 7589 3587
Email: registrar@queensgate.org.uk
Website: www.queensgate.org.uk
Principal: Miss Amy Wallace MA MPhil (Cantab), PGCE (Oxon)
Age range: G4–18 years
No. of pupils: 477 VIth90

Redcliffe Gardens School
47 Redcliffe Gardens, Chelsea, London SW10 9JH
Tel: 020 7352 9247
Head: Mrs Sarah Glencross
Age range: 21/2–11 years

Sinclair House Preparatory School
59 Fulham High Street, Fulham, London SW6 3JJ
Tel: 0207 736 9182
Principal: Mrs Carlotta T M O'Sullivan
Age range: 2–11 years
No. of pupils: 120
Fees: Day £5,280–£17,025

St Mary's Summerstown Montessori
46 Wimbledon Road, Tooting, London SW17 0UQ
Tel: 020 8947 7359
Head: Liz Maitland NNEB, RSH, MontDip
Age range: 18 months–5 years
No. of pupils: 30
Fees: Day £1,300

St Paul's School
Lonsdale Road, Barnes, London SW13 9JT
Tel: 020 8748 9162
High Master: Ms Sally-Anne Huang
Age range: B7–18 years

St Philip's School
6 Wetherby Place, London SW7 4NE
Tel: 020 7373 3944
Head Master: Mr A Thomas
Age range: B7–13 years

Streatham & Clapham High School GDST
42 Abbotswood Road, London SW16 1AW
Tel: 020 8677 8400
Executive Head: Mrs Isabel Tobias MA (Cantab), PGCE
Age range: G3–18 years

Sussex House School
68 Cadogan Square, London SW1X 0EA
Tel: 020 7584 1741
Headmaster: Mr N P Kaye MA(Cantab), ACP, FRSA, FRGS
Age range: B8–13 years

Swedish School in London
82 Lonsdale Road, Barnes, London SW13 9JS
Tel: 020 8741 1751
Head of School: Ms. Jenny Abrahamsson
Age range: 3–18 years

Thames Christian School
12 Grant Road, London SW11 2FR
Tel: 020 7228 3933
Head of School: Mr Stephen Holsgrove PhD
Age range: 11–16 years

THE HAMPSHIRE SCHOOL, CHELSEA
For further details see p. 164
15 Manresa Road, Chelsea, London SW3 6NB
Tel: +44 (0)2073 527077
Email: info@thehampshireschoolchelsea.co.uk
Website: www.thehampshireschoolchelsea.co.uk
Headteacher: Mr Richard Lock
Age range: 3–11 years

THE MERLIN SCHOOL
For further details see p. 166
4 Carlton Drive, Putney, London SW15 2BZ
Tel: 020 8788 2769
Email: admissionenquiries@merlinschool.net
Website: www.merlinschool.net
Headteacher: Miss Violet McConville
Age range: 4–8 years
No. of pupils: 125
Fees: Day £5,960

The Montessori Pavilion - The Kindergarten School
Vine Road, Barnes, London SW13 0NE
Tel: 07554 277 746
Headmistress: Ms Georgina Dashwood
Age range: 3–8 years
No. of pupils: 50

The Norwegian School in London
28 Arterberry Road, Wimbledon, London SW20 8AH
Tel: 020 8947 6617
Headteacher: Ms Lise Meling Karlsen
Age range: 6–16 years

The Roche School
11 Frogmore, London SW18 1HW
Tel: 020 8877 0823
Headmistress: Mrs Vania Adams BA(Hons), PGCE, MA
Age range: 2–11 years
No. of pupils: 270
Fees: Day £16,470–£17,190

The Rowans School
19 Drax Avenue, Wimbledon, London SW20 0EG
Tel: 020 8946 8220
Head of School: Miss Elizabeth Spratt BMus PGCE Primary QTS
Age range: 3–7 years

The Study Preparatory School
Wilberforce House, Camp Road, Wimbledon Common, London SW19 4UN
Tel: 020 8947 6969
Interim Head: Ms Helen Lowe
Age range: G4–11 years

The White House Preparatory School & Woodentops Kindergarten
24 Thornton Road, Clapham, London SW12 0LF
Tel: 020 8674 9514
Headmaster: Mr. Tony Lewis
Age range: 3–11 years

Thomas's Academy
New King's Road, London SW6 4LY
Tel: 020 7736 2318
Head of School: Ms Suzanne Kelly
Age range: 4–11 years

Thomas's Battersea
28–40 Battersea High Street, London SW11 3JB
Tel: 020 7978 0900
Head of School: Mr Ben Thomas
Age range: 4–13 years

Thomas's Clapham
Broomwood Road, London SW11 6JZ
Tel: 020 7326 9300
Head of School: Mr Nathan Boller
Age range: 4–13 years

Thomas's Fulham
Hugon Road, London SW6 3ES
Tel: 020 7751 8200
Head of School: Ms Annette Dobson
Age range: 4–11 years

Thomas's Outdoors
Stroud Crescent, London SW15 3EQ
Tel: 020 7751 8200
Head of School: Mr Paul Wild
Age range: 4–18 years

Thomas's Putney Vale
Stroud Crescent, London SW15 3EH
Tel: 020 3653 1640
Heads of School: Therese Andrews & Emma Oliver
Age range: 13–16 years

Tower House School
188 Sheen Lane, East Sheen, London SW14 8LF
Tel: 020 8876 3323
Head: Mr Gregory Evans
Age range: B4–13 years

URSULINE PREPARATORY SCHOOL
For further details see p. 168
18 The Downs, Wimbledon, London SW20 8HR
Tel: 020 8947 0859
Email: headteachersoffice@ursulineprep.org
Website: www.ursulineprep.org
Head Teacher: Mrs Caroline Molina BA (Hons)
Age range: B3–4 years G3–11 years
No. of pupils: 124

WANDSWORTH PREPARATORY SCHOOL
For further details see p. 170
The Old Library, 2 Allfarthing Lane, London SW18 2PQ
Tel: +44 (0)2088 704133
Email: office@wandsworthprep.com
Website: www.wandsworthprep.com
Headteacher: Ms Laura Nike
Age range: 4–11 years

Westminster Abbey Choir School
Dean's Yard, Westminster, London SW1P 3NY
Tel: 020 7654 4918
Acting Headmaster: Mr Mark Mitchell
Age range: B8–13 years

Westminster Cathedral Choir School
Ambrosden Avenue, London SW1P 1QH
Tel: 020 7798 9081
Headmaster: Mr Neil McLaughlan
Age range: B4–13 years

Westminster School
17A Dean's Yard, Westminster, London SW1P 3PB
Tel: 020 7963 1000
Head Master: Dr Gary Savage
Age range: B13–18 years G16–18 years

Westminster Tutors
86 Old Brompton Road, South Kensington, London SW7 3LQ
Tel: 020 7584 1288
Principal: Sean Doherty
Age range: 14+ years
No. of pupils: VIth40
Fees: Day £4,000–£25,000

Westminster Under School
27 Vincent Square, London SW1P 2NN
Tel: 020 7821 5788
Master: Mrs C J Jefferson
Age range: B7–13 years

Wetherby Kensington
4 Wetherby Gardens, London SW5 0JN
Tel: 020 3910 9760
Executive Head: Mr Mark Snell
Age range: B4–8 years

Willington Independent Preparatory School
Worcester Road, Wimbledon, London SW19 7QQ
Tel: 020 8944 7020
Headmaster: Mr Keith Brown
Age range: 3–11 years
£

Wimbledon Common Preparatory School
113 Ridgway, Wimbledon, London SW19 4TA
Tel: 020 8946 1001
Head Teacher: Mr Andrew Forbes
Age range: B4–7 years

Wimbledon High School GDST
Mansel Road, Wimbledon, London SW19 4AB
Tel: 020 8971 0900
Head of School: Ms Fionnuala Kennedy
Age range: G4–18 years
A £ 16

West London

Abercorn School
38 Portland Place, London W1B 1LS
Tel: 020 7100 4335
Headmaster: Mr Christopher Hammond
Age range: 2–13 years

Albemarle Independent College
18 Dunraven Street, Mayfair, London W1K 7FE
Tel: 02074 097273
Co-Principals: Beverley Mellon & James Eytle
Age range: 14–19 years
16 A 16

ArtsEd Day School & Sixth Form
14 Bath Road, Chiswick, London W4 1LY
Tel: 020 8987 6666
Headteacher: Mr Matthew Bulmer
Age range: 11–18 years

Ashbourne College
17 Old Court Place, Kensington, London W8 4PL
Tel: 020 7937 3858
Principal: Mr Michael Kirby MSc, BApSc, MInstD
Age range: 13–21 years
16 A £

Avenue House School
70 The Avenue, Ealing, London W13 8LS
Tel: 020 8998 9981
Headteacher: Mr Conall Chivers
Age range: 4–11 years

AZBUKA Russian-English Bilingual School
Studland Hall, Studland Street, Hammersmith, London W6 0JS
Tel: 020 8392 2286
Head Teacher: Ms Maria Gavrilova
Age range: 2–11 years

Bales College
2 Kilburn Lane, London W10 4AA
Tel: 020 8960 5899
Principal: Mr William Moore
Age range: 11–18 years
16 A £

BASSETT HOUSE SCHOOL
For further details see p. 130
60 Bassett Road, Notting Hill, London W10 6JP
Tel: 020 8969 0313
Email: info@bassetths.org.uk
Website: www.bassetths.org.uk
Headmistress: Mrs Kelly Gray
Age range: 3–11 years
No. of pupils: 145
Fees: Day £10,818–£22,533

Bute House Preparatory School for Girls
Bute House, Luxemburg Gardens, London W6 7EA
Tel: 020 7603 7381
Head of School: Ms Sian Bradshaw
Age range: G4–11 years
£

Chepstow House School
108a Lancaster Road, Notting Hill, London W11 1QS
Tel: 020 7243 0243
Headteacher: Ms Angela Barr
Age range: 21/2–11 years

Chiswick & Bedford Park Prep School
Priory House, Priory Avenue, London W4 1TX
Tel: 020 8994 1804
Head of School: Ms Henrietta Adams
Age range: B3–7+ years G3–11 years

Clifton Lodge School
8 Mattock Lane, Ealing, London W5 5BG
Tel: 020 8579 3662
Head of School: Mr Michael Belsito
Age range: 3–11 years
No. of pupils: 130
Fees: Day £13,650–£16,305
£

Connaught House School
47 Connaught Square, Westminster, London W2 2HL
Tel: 020 7262 8830
Principal: Ms Victoria Hampton
Age range: 4–11 years
£

David Game College
31 Jewry Street, London EC3N 2ET
Tel: 02072 216665
Principal: D T P Game MA, MPhil
Age range: 13–22 years
16 A 16

DURSTON HOUSE
For further details see p. 134
12–14 Castlebar Road, Ealing, London W5 2DR
Tel: 020 8991 6530
Email: info@durstonhouse.org
Website: www.durstonhouse.org
Headmaster: Mr Giles Entwisle
Age range: B3–13 years
No. of pupils: 389
Fees: Day £4,750–£6,180
£

EALING INDEPENDENT COLLEGE
For further details see p. 136
83 New Broadway, Ealing, London W5 5AL
Tel: 020 8579 6668
Email: admissions@ealingindependentcollege.com
Website: www.ealingindependentcollege.com
Headteacher: Allan Cairns
Age range: 13–19 years
No. of pupils: 96
16 A 16

Eaton Square Senior School
106 Piccadilly, Mayfair, London W1J 7NL
Tel: +44 (0)20 7491 7393
Headteacher: Dr Adrian Rainbow
Age range: 11–18 years

Ecole Française de Londres Jacques Prévert
59 Brook Green, Hammersmith, London W6 7BE
Tel: 020 7602 6871
Director: Ms Sylvie Wanin
Age range: 4–11 years

Falcons Pre-Preparatory Chiswick
2 Burnaby Gardens, Chiswick, London W4 3DT
Tel: 020 8747 8393
Head: Ms Liz McLaughlin
Age range: B2–7 years G2–4 years

Fulham School
1–3 Chesilton Road, London SW6 5AA
Tel: 020 8154 6751
Executive Head of Fulham: Bex Tear
Age range: 3–18 years
No. of pupils: 650
Fees: Day £20,310–£23,775
A

Godolphin and Latymer School
Iffley Road, Hammersmith, London W6 0PG
Tel: +44 (0)20 8741 1936
Head Mistress: Dr Frances Ramsey
Age range: G11–18 years
No. of pupils: 800
Fees: Day £25,185
A £ IB 16

Great Beginnings Montessori Nursery
39 Brendon Street, London W1H 5JE
Tel: 020 7258 1066
Head: Mrs Wendy Innes
Age range: 2–6 years

Greek Primary School of London
3 Pierrepoint Road, Acton, London W3 9JR
Tel: 020 8896 2118
Primary School Head Teacher: Ms Katerina Papagianni
Age range: 4–11 years

Halcyon London International School
33 Seymour Place, London W1H 5AU
Tel: +44 (0)20 7258 1169
Director: Mr Barry Mansfield
Age range: 11–18 years

Harvington School
20 Castlebar Road, Ealing, London W5 2DS
Tel: 020 8997 1583
Headteacher: Mr Giles Entwisle
Age range: B3–7 years G3–11 years

Hawkesdown House School Kensington
27 Edge Street, Kensington, London W8 7PN
Tel: 020 7727 9090
Headmistress: Mrs S Gillam BEd (Cantab)
Age range: 2–8 years
No. of pupils: 100
Fees: Day £4,725–£21,120

Heathfield House School
Heathfield Gardens, Chiswick, London W4 4JU
Tel: 020 8994 3385
Headteacher: Ms Caroline Goodsman
Age range: 4–11 years

Holland Park Pre Prep School and Day Nursery
5, Holland Road, Kensington, London W14 8HJ
Tel: 020 7602 9066/020 7602 9266
Head Mistress: Mrs Kitty Mason
Age range: 3 months–8 years
No. of pupils: 39
Fees: Day £9,180–£18,120

ICS London
7B Wyndham Place, London W1H 1PN
Tel: +44 (0)20 729 88800
Head of School: Alec Jiggins
Age range: 3–19 years
No. of pupils: 160
Fees: Day £20,970–£30,930

Instituto Español Vicente Cañada Blanch
317 Portobello Road, London W10 5SZ
Tel: +44 (0) 20 8969 2664
Head of School: Mr Antonio Simón Saiz
Age range: 3–18 years

International School of London (ISL)
139 Gunnersbury Avenue, London W3 8LG
Tel: +44 (0)20 8992 5823
Principal: Mr Richard Parker
Age range: 3–18 years
No. of pupils: 420
Fees: Day £20,850–£28,850

Kensington Wade School
Fulham Palace Road, London W6 9ER
Tel: 020 3096 2888
Head: Mr Huw May
Age range: 3–11 years
No. of pupils: 108
Fees: Day £6,830

King Fahad Academy
Bromyard Avenue, Acton, London W3 7HD
Tel: 020 8743 0131
Director General: Dr Tahani Aljafari
Age range: 3–18 years

La Petite Ecole Française
73 Saint Charles Square, London W10 6EJ
Tel: +44 (0)20 8960 1278
Age range: 3–11 years

Latymer Prep School
36 Upper Mall, Hammersmith, London W6 9TA
Tel: 020 7993 0061
Principal: Ms Andrea Rutterford
Age range: 7–11 years

Latymer Upper School
King Street, Hammersmith, London W6 9LR
Tel: 020 8629 2024
Head: Mr David Goodhew
Age range: 11–18 years

Le Herisson
River Court Methodist Church, Rover Court Road, Hammersmith, London W6 9JT
Tel: 020 8563 7664
Director: Maria Frost
Age range: 2–6 years
Fees: Day £8,730–£8,970

L'Ecole Bilingue
St David's Welsh Church, St Mary's Terrace, London W2 1SJ
Tel: 020 7224 8427
Headteacher: Ms Veronique Ferreira
Age range: 3–11 years

Leiths School of Food & Wine
16–20 Wendell Road, Shepherd's Bush, London W12 9RT
Tel: 020 8749 6400
Age range: 17+ years

LLOYD WILLIAMSON SCHOOL FOUNDATION
For further details see p. 148
12 Telford Road, London W10 5SH
Tel: 020 8962 0345
Email: admin@lws.org.uk
Website: www.lloydwilliamson.co.uk
Co-Principals: Ms Lucy Meyer & Mr Aaron Williams
Age range: 4 months–16 years
Fees: Day £18,300

London Welsh School Ysgol Gymraeg Llundain
Hanwell Community Centre, Westcott Crescent, London W7 1PD
Tel: 020 8575 0237
Headteacher: Ms Tracey O'Brien
Age range: 3–11 years

Maida Vale School
18 Saltram Crescent, London W9 3HR
Tel: 020 4511 6000
Headmaster: Mr Magnus Bashaarat
Age range: 11–18 years
No. of pupils: 160
Fees: Day £8,073

Maria Montessori School - Bayswater
St Matthew's Church, St Petersburgh Place, Bayswater, London W2 4LA
Tel: 020 7435 3646
Age range: 21/2–12 years

Norland Place School
162–166 Holland Park Avenue, London W11 4UH
Tel: 020 7603 9103
Headmaster: Mr Patrick Mattar MA
Age range: 4–11 years

Notting Hill & Ealing High School GDST
2 Cleveland Road, West Ealing, London W13 8AX
Tel: (020) 8799 8400
Headmaster: Mr Matthew Shoults
Age range: G4–18 years

Notting Hill Preparatory School
95 Lancaster Road, London W11 1QQ
Tel: 020 7221 0727
Head of School: Mrs Sarah Knollys
Age range: 4–13 years
No. of pupils: 444
Fees: Day £7,689

ORCHARD HOUSE SCHOOL
For further details see p. 156
16 Newton Grove, Bedford Park, London W4 1LB
Tel: 020 8742 8544
Email: info@orchardhs.org.uk
Website: www.orchardhs.org.uk
Headmaster: Mr Kit Thompson
Age range: 3–11 years
No. of pupils: 301
Fees: Day £10,650–£22,194

Pembridge Hall School
18 Pembridge Square, London W2 4EH
Tel: 020 7229 0121
Head: Mrs Sophie Banks
Age range: G4–11 years

Portland Place School
56–58 Portland Place, London W1B 1NJ
Tel: 020 7307 8700
Headmaster: Mr David Bradbury
Age range: 10–16 years

Queen's College
43–49 Harley Street, London W1G 8BT
Tel: 020 7291 7000
Principal: Mr Richard Tillet
Age range: G11–18 years

Queen's College Preparatory School
61 Portland Place, London W1B 1QP
Tel: 020 7291 0660
Headmistress: Mrs Laura Hall
Age range: G4–11 years

Ravenscourt Park Preparatory School
16 Ravenscourt Avenue, London W6 0SL
Tel: 020 8846 9153
Headmaster: Mr Carl Howes MA (Cantab), PGCE (Exeter)
Age range: 4–11 years
No. of pupils: 418
Fees: Day £6,632

Ray Cochrane Beauty School
118 Baker Street, London W1U 6TT
Tel: 02033 896888
Heads of Education: Xubin Yuan & Eleonora Androva
Age range: 16+ years

Southbank International School - Kensington
36–38 Kensington Park Road, London W11 3BU
Tel: 020 3890 1969
Head of School: David MacMorran
Age range: 2–18 years
IB

Southbank International School - Westminster
63–65 Portland Place, London W1B 1QR
Tel: 020 3890 1969
Head of School: Angela Liu
Age range: 11–18 years
IB

St Augustine's Priory
Hillcrest Road, Ealing, London W5 2JL
Tel: 020 8997 2022
Headteacher: Mrs Sarah Raffray M.A., N.P.Q.H
Age range: B3–4 years G3–18 years
A

St Benedict's School
54 Eaton Rise, Ealing, London W5 2ES
Tel: 020 8862 2000
Headmaster: Mr A Johnson BA
Age range: 3–18 years
No. of pupils: 1083 VIth185
Fees: Day £14,940–£19,575
A £

St James Preparatory School
Earsby Street, London W14 8SH
Tel: 02073 481794
Headmistress: Mrs Hilary Wyatt
Age range: 3–11 years
£

St James Senior Girls' School
Earsby Street, London W14 8SH
Tel: 02073 481777
Headmistress: Mrs Sarah Labram BA
Age range: G11–18 years
A £

St Paul's Girls' School
Brook Green, Hammersmith, London W6 7BS
Tel: 020 7603 2288
High Mistress: Mrs Sarah Fletcher
Age range: G11–18 years
A £

Sylvia Young Theatre School
1 Nutford Place, London W1H 5YZ
Tel: 020 7258 2330
Principal: Sylvia Young OBE
Age range: 10–16 years
£

Tabernacle School
32 St Anns Villas, Holland Park, London W11 4RS
Tel: 020 7602 6232
Principal: Mrs P Wilson
Age range: 3–16 years

The Japanese School in London
87 Creffield Road, Acton, London W3 9PU
Tel: 020 8993 7145
Age range: 6–16 years

Thomas's Kensington
17–19 Cottesmore Gardens, London W8 5PR
Tel: 020 7361 6500
Head of School: Ms Kelly Miller
Age range: 4–11 years

TLG West London
Tasso Baptist Church, 138 Greyhound Road, London W6 8NS
Tel: 07494486851
Head of Centre: Ms Tina Amadi
Age range: 11–16 years

Wetherby Preparatory School
Bryanston Square, London W1H 2EA
Tel: 020 7535 3520
Headmaster: Mr Mark White MA (Hons), PGCE
Age range: B8–13 years

Wetherby Pre-Preparatory School
11 Pembridge Square, London W2 4ED
Tel: 020 7727 9581
Headmaster: Mr Mark Snell
Age range: B21/2–8 years

Wetherby Senior School
100 Marylebone Lane, London W1U 2QU
Tel: 020 7535 3530
Headmaster: Mr Joe Silvester
Age range: B11–18 years

Young Dancers Academy
25 Bulwer Street, London W12 8AR
Tel: 020 8743 3856
Head: Mrs K Williams
Age range: 11–16 years
Fees: Day £12,237–£12,690

North-East

KEY TO SYMBOLS

- Boys' school
- Girls' school
- International school
- Tutorial or sixth form college
- A levels
- Boarding accommodation
- Bursaries
- International Baccalaureate
- Learning support
- Entrance at 16+
- Vocational qualifications
- Independent Association of Preparatory Schools
- The Headmasters' & Headmistresses' Conference
- Independent Schools Association
- Girls' School Association
- Boarding Schools' Association
- Society of Heads

Unless otherwise indicated, all schools are coeducational day schools. Single-sex and boarding schools will be indicated by the relevant icon.

Durham

BARNARD CASTLE SCHOOL
For further details see p. 174
Barnard Castle, Durham DL12 8UN
Tel: +44 (0)1833 696030
Email: admissions@barneyschool.org.uk
Website: www.barnardcastleschool.org.uk
Headmaster: Mr Tony Jackson
Age range: 4–18 years
No. of pupils: 723
Fees: Day £8,964–£16,995
FB £25,740–£32,430

Delta Independent School
Parliament Street, Consett, Durham DH8 5DH
Tel: 01207 502680
Principal: Ms Helen Daglish
Age range: 13–16 years

Durham High School for Girls
Farewell Hall, South Road, Durham DH1 3TB
Tel: 0191 384 3226
Headmistress: Mrs Simone Niblock
Age range: G3–18 years
No. of pupils: 347

Durham School
Quarryheads Lane, Durham DH1 4SZ
Tel: +44 (0)191 731 9270
Headmaster: Mr Kieran McLaughlin
Age range: 11–18 years

The Chorister School (Bow)
South Road, Durham DH1 3LS
Tel: 0191 731 9270
Head of School: Ms Sally Harrod
Age range: 3–7 years

The Chorister School (Cathedral)
The College, Durham DH1 3EL
Tel: +44 (0)191 731 9270
Head of School: Ms Sally Harrod
Age range: 7–11 years

The Independent Grammar School: Durham
Claypath, Durham DH1 1RH
Tel: 07984 619739
Principal: Mr Chris Gray
Age range: 4–13 years

Northumberland

Longridge Towers School
Longridge Towers, Berwick-upon-Tweed, Northumberland TD15 2XQ
Tel: 01289 307584
Headmaster: Mr Jonathan Lee
Age range: 3–19 years
No. of pupils: 350

Mowden Hall School
Newton, Stocksfield, Northumberland NE43 7TP
Tel: 01661 842147
Head: Ms Kate Martin
Age range: 3–13 years
No. of pupils: 200

Stockton-on-Tees

Red House School
36 The Green, Norton, Stockton-on-Tees TS20 1DX
Tel: 01642 553370
Head: Dr Rebecca Ashcroft
Age range: 3–16 years

Teesside High School
The Avenue, Eaglescliffe, Stockton-on-Tees TS16 9AT
Tel: 01642 782095
Head of School: Mrs K Mackenzie
Age range: 3–18 years

Yarm School
The Friarage, Yarm, Stockton-on-Tees TS15 9EJ
Tel: 01642 786023
Head of School: Dr Huw Williams
Age range: 3–18 years

Tyne & Wear

Argyle House School
19–20 Thornhill Park, Sunderland, Tyne & Wear SR2 7LA
Tel: 01915 100726
Headteacher: Mr. Chris Johnson
Age range: 3–16 years

Dame Allan's Boys' School
Fowberry Crescent, Fenham, Newcastle upon Tyne, Tyne & Wear NE4 9YJ
Tel: 01912 750608
Head of School: Mr D Ridley
Age range: B11–16 years

Dame Allan's Girls' School
Fowberry Crescent, Fenham, Newcastle upon Tyne, Tyne & Wear NE4 9YJ
Tel: 01912 750608
Head of School: Mrs E Fiddaman
Age range: G11–16 years

Dame Allan's Junior School & Nursery
Hunters Road, Spital Tongues, Newcastle upon Tyne, Tyne & Wear NE2 4NG
Tel: 01912 750608
Headteacher: Mr Geoff Laidler
Age range: 3–11 years

Dame Allan's Sixth Form
Fowberry Crescent, Fenham, Newcastle upon Tyne, Tyne & Wear NE4 9YJ
Tel: 01912 750608
Head of School: Mr P Terry
Age range: 16–18 years

Gateshead Jewish Boarding School
10 Rydal Street, Gateshead, Tyne & Wear NE8 1HG
Tel: 01914 771431
Age range: B10–16 years

Gateshead Jewish Primary School
18–22 Gladstone Terrace, Gateshead, Tyne & Wear NE8 4EA
Tel: 01914 772154
Age range: B5–11 years

Newcastle High School for Girls GDST
Tankerville Terrace, Jesmond, Newcastle upon Tyne, Tyne & Wear NE2 3BA
Tel: 01912 016511
Head: Mr Michael Tippett
Age range: G3–18 years

Newcastle Preparatory School
6 Eslington Road, Jesmond, Newcastle upon Tyne, Tyne & Wear NE2 4RH
Tel: 01912 811769
Head of School: Miss Gemma Strong
Age range: 3–11 years
No. of pupils: 286
Fees: Day £4,313

Newcastle School for Boys
30 West Avenue, Gosforth, Newcastle upon Tyne, Tyne & Wear NE3 4ES
Tel: 01912 559300
Headmaster: Mr David Tickner
Age range: B3–18 years

OneSchool Global UK York (Springwell) Campus
60 Peareth Hall Road, Springwell, Gateshead, Tyne & Wear NE9 7NT
Tel: 01904 663300
Age range: 7–18 years

Royal Grammar School
Eskdale Terrace, Newcastle upon Tyne, Tyne & Wear NE2 4DX
Tel: 01912 815711
Headmaster: Mr Geoffrey Stanford
Age range: 7–18 years

Westfield School
Oakfield Road, Gosforth, Newcastle upon Tyne, Tyne & Wear NE3 4HS
Tel: 01912 553980
Headmaster: Mr Neil Walker
Age range: G3–18 years

North-West

KEY TO SYMBOLS

- *Boys' school*
- *Girls' school*
- *International school*
- *Tutorial or sixth form college*
- *A levels*
- *Boarding accommodation*
- *Bursaries*
- *International Baccalaureate*
- *Learning support*
- *Entrance at 16+*
- *Vocational qualifications*
- *Independent Association of Preparatory Schools*
- *The Headmasters' & Headmistresses' Conference*
- *Independent Schools Association*
- *Girls' School Association*
- *Boarding Schools' Association*
- *Society of Heads*

Unless otherwise indicated, all schools are coeducational day schools. Single-sex and boarding schools will be indicated by the relevant icon.

Cheshire

Abbey Gate College
Saighton Grange, Saighton, Chester, Cheshire CH3 6EN
Tel: 01244 617352
Head: Mr Craig Jenkinson
Age range: 4–18 years

Alderley Edge School for Girls
Wilmslow Road, Alderley Edge, Cheshire SK9 7QE
Tel: 01625 583028
Head of School: Ms Nicola Smillie
Age range: G2–18 years

Beech Hall School
Beech Hall Drive, Tytherington, Macclesfield, Cheshire SK10 2EG
Tel: 01625 422192
Headmaster: Mr James Allen
Age range: 6 months–16 years

Bowdon Preparatory School for Girls
Ashley Road, Bowdon, Altrincham, Cheshire WA14 2LT
Tel: 0161 928 0678
Headmistress: Mrs Helen Gee
Age range: G3–11 years

BRABYNS PREPARATORY SCHOOL
For further details see p. 178
34–36 Arkwright Road, Marple, Stockport, Cheshire SK6 7DB
Tel: 0161 427 2395
Email: admin@brabynsprepschool.co.uk
Website: www.brabynsprepschool.co.uk
Headteacher: Mrs Cath Carrasco
Age range: 2–11 years
Fees: Day £2,354–£3,264

Cornerstone Academy
c/o Marlfields Primary Academy, Waggs Road, Congleton, Cheshire CW12 4BT
Tel: 01270 304094
Headteacher: Mr Damien Sweeney
Age range: 5–11 years

Cransley School
Belmont Hall, Belmont Road, Great Budworth, Northwich, Cheshire CW9 6HN
Tel: 01606 891747
Head of School: Mr Richard Pollock LL.B, PGCE, PG Dip (RNCM)
Age range: 4–16 years

Green Meadow Independent School
Robson Way, Lowton, Warrington, Cheshire WA3 2RD
Tel: 01942 671138
Head of School: Mrs S Green
Age range: 3–14 years

Greenbank Preparatory School
64 Heathbank Road, Cheadle Hulme, Stockport, Cheshire SK8 6HU
Tel: 0161 485 3724
Head of School: Mr Malcolm Johnson
Age range: 6 months–11 years
No. of pupils: 283
Fees: Day £9,480

Hale Preparatory School
Broomfield Lane, Hale, Cheshire WA15 9AS
Tel: 0161 928 2386
Headmaster: Mr J F Connor
Age range: 4–11 years

Lady Barn House School
Schools Hill, Cheadle, Cheshire SK8 1JE
Tel: 0161 428 2912
Head of School: Ms Louise Higson
Age range: 3–11 years
No. of pupils: 479

OneSchool Global UK Northwich Campus
Hartford Manor, Greenbank Lane, Northwich, Cheshire CW8 1HW
Tel: 01606 210320
Age range: 7–18 years

Pownall Hall School
Carrwood Road, Pownall Park, Wilmslow, Cheshire SK9 5DW
Tel: 01625 523141
Headmaster: Mr David Goulbourn
Age range: 6 months–11 years

Terra Nova School
Jodrell Bank, Holmes Chapel, Crewe, Cheshire CW4 8BT
Tel: 01477 571251
Headmaster: Mr Paul Campbell
Age range: 2½–13 years (boarding from 8)

The Firs School
45 Newton Lane, Upton, Chester, Cheshire CH2 2HJ
Tel: 01244 322443
Head Teacher: Miss Rosemary Evans
Age range: 2–11 years

The Grange School
Bradburns Lane, Hartford, Northwich, Cheshire CW8 1LU
Tel: 01606 533431
Senior Head: Dr Lorraine Earps
Age range: 4–18 years

The Hammond School
Mannings Lane, Chester, Cheshire CH2 4ES
Tel: 01244 305350
Principal: Ms Jennifer Roscoe
Age range: 11–19+ years

The King's School in Macclesfield
Alderley Road, Prestbury, Cheshire SK10 4SP
Tel: 01625 260000
Headmaster: Mr Jason Slack
Age range: 3–18 years

The King's School, Chester
Wrexham Road, Chester, Cheshire CH4 7QL
Tel: 01244 689500
Headmaster: Mr George Hartley
Age range: 4–18 years

The Queen's School
City Walls Road, Chester, Cheshire CH1 2NN
Tel: 01244 312078
Headmistress: Mrs Sue Wallace-Woodroffe
Age range: G4–18 years
No. of pupils: 450

The Ryleys School
Ryleys Lane, Alderley Edge, Cheshire SK9 7UY
Tel: 01625 583241
Headteacher: Mrs Julia Langford
Age range: 1–11 years

Wilmslow Preparatory School
Grove Avenue, Wilmslow, Cheshire SK9 5EG
Tel: 01625 524246
Headteacher: Mr Bradley Lavagna-Slater
Age range: 3–11 years

Yorston Lodge Prep School
18 St John's Road, Knutsford, Cheshire WA16 0DP
Tel: 01565 746 841
Headmistress: Mrs Janet Dallimore
Age range: 3–11 years

Cumbria

Austin Friars School
Etterby Scaur, Carlisle, Cumbria CA3 9PB
Tel: 01228 528042
Headmaster: Mr Matt Harris
Age range: 3–18 years

Casterton, Sedbergh Preparatory School
Casterton, Kirkby Lonsdale, Cumbria LA6 2SG
Tel: 01524 279200
Headmaster: Mr Will Newman BA(Ed) Hons MA
Age range: 3–13 years

Dallam School
Main Street, Milnthorpe, Cumbria LA7 7DD
Tel: 015395 65165
Headteacher: Mr S Henneberry
Age range: 11–19 years

Hunter Hall School
Frenchfield, Penrith, Cumbria CA11 8UA
Tel: 01768 891291
Head Teacher: Mrs Donna Vinsome
Age range: 3–11 years

Keswick School
Vicarage Hill, Keswick, Cumbria CA12 5QB
Tel: 017687 72605
Headteacher: Mr Simon Jackson
Age range: 11–18 years

LIME HOUSE SCHOOL
For further details see p. 184
Holm Hill, Dalston, Carlisle, Cumbria CA5 7BX
Tel: 01228 710225
Email: office@limehouseschool.co.uk
Website: www.limehouseschool.co.uk
Headteacher: Mr Andy Guest
Age range: 7–18 years
No. of pupils: 168
(A) (£) (16)

Sedbergh School
Station Road, Sedbergh, Cumbria LA10 5HG
Tel: 015396 20535
Headmaster: Mr Dan Harrison
Age range: 3–19 years
(A) (£) (16)

St Bees School
Wood Lane, St Bees, Cumbria CA27 0DS
Tel: 01946 828000
Headmaster: Mr Robin Silk
Age range: 11–18 years

Windermere School
Patterdale Road, Windermere, Cumbria LA23 1NW
Tel: 015394 46164
Headmaster: Mr Tom Hill
Age range: 3–18 years (boarding from 7)
No. of pupils: 350
Fees: Day £20,190 WB £34,400 FB £35,985
(£) (IB) (16)

Greater Manchester

Abbey College Manchester
5–7 Cheapside, Off King Street, Manchester, Greater Manchester M2 4WG
Tel: 0161 817 2700
Principal: Mr Chris Randell
Age range: 15–21 years
(16) (A) (£) (16)

Abbotsford Preparatory School
211 Flixton Road, Urmston, Manchester, Greater Manchester M41 5PR
Tel: 0161 748 3261
Head of School: Mrs Catherine Howard B.Ed(Hons)
Age range: 4 months–11 years

Altrincham Preparatory School
Marlborough Road, Bowdon, Altrincham, Greater Manchester WA14 2RR
Tel: 0161 928 3366
Headmaster: Mr N J Vernon
Age range: B2–11 years

Beech House School
184 Manchester Road, Rochdale, Greater Manchester OL11 4JQ
Tel: 01706 646309
Principal: Mr Kevin Sartain
Age range: 2–16 years

Beis Ruchel Girls School
87 Devonshire Street, Salford, Greater Manchester M7 4AE
Tel: 01617 951830
Age range: G2–16 years

Bnos Yisroel School
Leicester Road, Salford, Greater Manchester M7 4DA
Tel: 01617 923896
Headmaster: Rabbi R Spitzer
Age range: G3–16 years

Bolton School
Chorley New Road, Bolton, Greater Manchester BL1 4PA
Tel: 01204 840201
Head of Foundation: Philip Britton
Age range: 0–18 years
Fees: Day £10,380–£12,972
(A) (£) (16)

Branwood Preparatory School
Stafford Road, Monton, Eccles, Manchester, Greater Manchester M30 9HN
Tel: 0161 789 1054
Headmaster: Mr Andrew Whittell
Age range: 3–11 years

Bridgewater School
Drywood Hall, Worsley Road, Worsley, Manchester, Greater Manchester M28 2WQ
Tel: 0161 794 1463
Head Teacher: Mrs JAT Nairn CertEd(Distinction)
Age range: 3–18 years
No. of pupils: 475
(A) (£) (16)

Bury Grammar Schools
Tenterden Street, Bury, Greater Manchester BL9 0HN
Tel: 0161 696 8600
Headmistress: Mrs J Anderson
Age range: 3–18 years

Cheadle Hulme School
Claremont Road, Cheadle Hulme, Cheadle, Greater Manchester SK8 6EF
Tel: 0161 488 3330
Head: Mr Neil Smith
Age range: 3–18 years
(16)

Chetham's School of Music
Long Millgate, Manchester, Greater Manchester M3 1SB
Tel: 0161 834 9644
Joint Principals: Nicola Smith & Tom Redmond
Age range: 8–18 years
No. of pupils: 300
(A) (16)

Clarendon Cottage School
Ivy Bank House, Half Edge Lane, Eccles, Manchester, Greater Manchester M30 9BJ
Tel: 0161 950 7868
Head of School: Miss E Bagnall
Age range: 3–11 years

Clevelands Preparatory School
425 Chorley New Road, Bolton, Greater Manchester BL1 5DH
Tel: 01204 843898
Head of School: Mr Keith Cahillane
Age range: 2–11 years

Covenant Christian School
The Hawthorns, 48 Heaton Moor Road, Stockport, Greater Manchester SK4 4NX
Tel: 0161 432 3782
Head: Dr Roger Slack
Age range: 5–16 years

Darul Hadis Latifiah Northwest
Plum Street, Oldham, Greater Manchester OL8 1TJ
Tel: 01616 274422
Head of School: Mr Salman Ahmed Chowdhury
Age range: B11–16 years

Darul Uloom Al Arabiya Al Islamiya (Darul Uloom Bury)
Holcombe Hall, Holcombe, Bury, Greater Manchester BL8 4NG
Tel: 01706 826106
Head: Mr Mohammed Mulla
Age range: B11–23 years

Darul Uloom Al Jamiatul Islamiyah (Darul Uloom Bolton)
Mount St Joseph's Convent, Willows Lane, Bolton, Greater Manchester BL3 4HF
Tel: 01204 62622
Head of School: Irfan Ibrahim
Age range: B11–25 years

Farrowdale House Preparatory School
Farrow Street, Shaw, Oldham, Greater Manchester OL2 7AD
Tel: 01706 844533
Headteacher: Miss Z. N. Campbell BA (Hons) PGCE
Age range: 3–11 years

FOREST PARK PREPARATORY SCHOOL
For further details see p. 180
Lauriston House, 27 Oakfield, Sale, Greater Manchester M33 6NB
Tel: 0161 973 4835
Email: office@forestparkprep.co.uk
Website: www.forestparkprep.co.uk
Headteacher: Mr Nick Tucker
Age range: 3–11 years

FOREST PREPARATORY SCHOOL & NURSERY
For further details see p. 182
Moss Lane, Timperley, Altrincham, Greater Manchester WA15 6LJ
Tel: 0161 980 4075
Email: enquiries@forestschool.co.uk
Website: www.forestschool.co.uk
Headmaster: Mr Graeme Booth
Age range: 2–11 years

Greater Manchester Independent School
Unit 3, Peel Street, Failsworth, Manchester, Greater Manchester M35 0UF
Tel: 0161 222 8168
Executive Head: Ms Louise Hodson
Age range: 11–18 years

Hulme Hall Grammar School
Beech Avenue, Stockport, Greater Manchester SK3 8HA
Tel: 0161 485 3524
Headmaster: Mr Dean Grierson
Age range: 2–16 years
No. of pupils: 200
Fees: Day £2,840–£3,300

Kassim Darwish Grammar School for Boys
Hartley Hall, Alexandra Road South, Manchester, Greater Manchester M16 8NH
Tel: 0161 8607676
Executive Headteacher: Mrs M Mohamed
Age range: B11–16 years

King of Kings School
142 Dantzic Street, Manchester, Greater Manchester M4 4DN
Tel: 0161 834 4214
Headteacher: Mrs Brenda Lewis
Age range: 3–18 years

Lord's School
Green Lane, Bolton, Greater Manchester BL3 2EF
Tel: 01204 523731
Headteacher: Mrs Anne Ainsworth
Age range: 7–18 years

Loreto Preparatory School
Dunham Road, Altrincham, Greater Manchester WA14 4GZ
Tel: 0161 928 8310
Headteacher: Mrs Anne Roberts
Age range: G3–11 years

Madrasatul Imam Muhammad Zakariya
Keswick Street, Bolton, Greater Manchester BL1 8LX
Tel: 01204 384434
Headteacher: Mrs Amena Sader
Age range: G11–19 years

Manchester High School for Girls
Grangethorpe Road, Manchester, Greater Manchester M14 6HS
Tel: 0161 224 0447
Head Mistress: Mrs Helen F Jeys
Age range: G4–18 years
No. of pupils: 1000

Manchester Islamic Grammar School for Girls
55 High Lane, Chorlton, Manchester, Greater Manchester M21 9FA
Tel: 0161 881 2127
Headmistress: Mrs Mona Mohamed
Age range: G11–16 years

Manchester Junior Girls School
64 Upper Park Road, Salford, Greater Manchester M7 4JA
Tel: 0161 740 0566
Head of School: Mrs Hannah Ehrentreu
Age range: G3–13 years

Manchester Muslim Preparatory School
551 Wilmslow Road, Withington, Manchester, Greater Manchester M20 4BA
Tel: 0161 445 5452
Headteacher: Ms D Ghafori-Kanno
Age range: 3–11 years

Mechinoh School
13 Upper Park Road, Salford, Greater Manchester M7 4HY
Tel: 0161 7959275
Head of School: Rabbi N Baddiel
Age range: B11–16 years

Moor Allerton Preparatory School
131 Barlow Moor Road, West Didsbury, Manchester, Greater Manchester M20 2PW
Tel: 0161 445 4521
Headmistress: Ms Kathryn Unsworth
Age range: 6 months–11 years

Oholei Yosef Yitzchok (OYY) Lubavitch Boys School
4 Upper Park Road, Salford, Greater Manchester M7 4HL
Tel: 01617 400923
Head of School: Mendel Cohen
Age range: 5–16 years

Oholei Yosef Yitzchok (OYY) Lubavitch Girls School
460 Bury New Road, Park Lane, Salford, Greater Manchester M7 4LH
Tel: 01617 050483
Head of School: Mrs Avigail Di Veroli
Age range: G2–17 years

Oldham Hulme Grammar School
Chamber Road, Oldham, Greater Manchester OL8 4BX
Tel: 0161 624 4497
Principal: Mr CJD Mairs
Age range: 3–18 years

Prestwich Preparatory School
St Margaret's Building, 400 Bury Old Road, Prestwich, Manchester, Greater Manchester M25 1PZ
Tel: 0161 773 1223
Headmistress: Miss P Shiels
Age range: 2–11 years

Rochdale Islamic Academy Boys School (RIAB)
36 Taylor Street, Rochdale, Greater Manchester OL12 0HX
Tel: 01706 347344
Head of School: Mr Arshad Ashraf
Age range: B11–16 years

Rochdale Islamic Academy Girls School (RIAG)
Greenbank Road, Rochdale, Greater Manchester OL12 0HZ
Tel: 01706 710184
Head of School: Mr Arshad Ashraf
Age range: G11–16 years

St Ambrose Preparatory School
Hale Barns, Altrincham, Greater Manchester WA15 0HF
Tel: 0161 903 9193
Headmaster: F J Driscoll
Age range: 3–11 years

St. Bede's College
Alexandra Park, Manchester, Greater Manchester M16 8HX
Tel: 0161 226 3323
Headteacher: Mrs Sandra Pike
Age range: 3–18 years

Stella Maris School
St. John's Road, Heaton Mersey, Stockport, Greater Manchester SK4 3BR
Tel: 0161 432 0532
Headteacher: Mrs N Johnson
Age range: 3–11 years

Stockport Grammar School
Buxton Road, Stockport, Greater Manchester SK2 7AF
Tel: 0161 456 9000
Headmaster: Dr Paul Owen
Age range: 3–18 years

Tashbar of Manchester
20 Upper Park Road, Salford, Greater Manchester M7 4HL
Tel: 01617 208254
Head of School: Rabbi David Hammond
Age range: B3–12 years

The Chadderton Preparatory Grammar School
Broadway, Chadderton, Oldham, Greater Manchester OL9 0AD
Tel: 0161 620 6570
Headteacher: Mrs Caroline Greenwood
Age range: 2–11 years

The Manchester Grammar School
Old Hall Lane, Fallowfield, Manchester, Greater Manchester M13 0XT
Tel: 0161 224 7201
High Master: Dr Martin Boulton
Age range: B7–18 years

TLG Bolton
Concorde House, 2 Frederick Street, Farnworth, Bolton, Greater Manchester BL4 9AL
Tel: 01204 201355
Head of Centre: Mr Gareth Crossley
Age range: 11–16 years

TLG Manchester
Carisbrook Street, Harpurhey, Manchester, Greater Manchester M9 5UX
Tel: 07903050587
Head of Centre: Ms Judith Skelton
Age range: 11–16 years

Trinity Christian School
Birbeck Street, Off High Street, Stalybridge, Greater Manchester SK15 1SH
Tel: 0161 303 0674
Head: Mr Michael Stewart
Age range: 3–16 years

Withington Girls' School
100 Wellington Road, Fallowfield, Manchester, Greater Manchester M14 6BL
Tel: 0161 224 1077
Headmistress: Mrs S J Haslam BA
Age range: G7–18 years

Isle of Man

King William's College
Castletown, Isle of Man IM9 1TP
Tel: +44 (0)1624 820110
Principal: Mr Damian Henderson
Age range: 11–18 years
No. of pupils: 340
Fees: Day £20,345–£26,995
FB £34,940–£41,590

The Buchan School
Westhill, Arbory Road, Castletown, Isle of Man IM9 1RD
Tel: +44 (0)1624 820110
Head of School: Mrs Janet Billingsley Evans
Age range: 2–11 years

Lancashire

Abrar Academy
34–36 Garstang Road, Preston, Lancashire PR1 1NA
Tel: 01772 82 87 32
Head of School: Mr A Chowdhury
Age range: B11–21 years

AKS Lytham
Clifton Drive South, Lytham St Annes, Lancashire FY8 1DT
Tel: 01253 784100
Headmaster: Mr David Harrow
Age range: 0–18 years

Al Islah Girls High School
108 Audley Range, Blackburn, Lancashire BB1 1TF
Tel: 01254 261573
Headteacher: Apa Nikhat
Age range: G11–16 years

Ashbridge Independent School
Lindle Lane, Hutton, Preston, Lancashire PR4 4AQ
Tel: 01772 619900
Headteacher: Ms Karen Mehta
Age range: 0–11 years

Highfield Priory School
58 Fulwood Row, Fulwood, Preston, Lancashire PR2 5RW
Tel: 01772 709624
Headteacher: Jeremy M Duke
Age range: 2–11 years
No. of pupils: 210
Fees: Day £8,370

Islamiyah Girls High School
Willow Street, Blackburn, Lancashire BB1 5NQ
Tel: 01254 661259
Interim Head Teacher: Salma Patel
Age range: G11–16 years

Jamea Al Kauthar
Ashton Road, Lancaster, Lancashire LA1 5AJ
Tel: +44 (0)1524 389898
Age range: G11–18 years (boarding from 11)

Jamiatul Ilm Wal Huda
15 Moss Street, Blackburn, Lancashire BB1 5JT
Tel: 01254 673105
Principal: Mr Abdus-Samad Ahmed
Age range: B11–25 years

Kirkham Grammar School
Ribby Road, Kirkham, Preston, Lancashire PR4 2BH
Tel: 01772 684264
Headmaster: Mr Daniel Berry
Age range: 3–18 years
No. of pupils: 930 VIth180

Lancaster Royal Grammar School
East Road, Lancaster, Lancashire LA1 3EF
Tel: 01524 580600
Head of School: Dr C J Pyle
Age range: B11–18 years

Lancaster Steiner School
Lune Road, Lancaster, Lancashire LA1 5QU
Tel: 01524 381876
Principal: Patricia Williams
Age range: 0–11 years

Markazul Uloom
Park Lee Road, Blackburn, Lancashire BB2 3NY
Tel: 01254 581569
Head of School: Mr Sajid Bargit
Age range: B11–16 years

Moorland School
Ribblesdale Avenue, Clitheroe, Lancashire BB7 2JA
Tel: 01200 423833
Headteacher: Mrs. Deborah Frost
Age range: 3 months–18 years (boarding from 7)

Oakhill School & Nursery
Wiswell Lane, Whalley, Clitheroe, Lancashire BB7 9AF
Tel: 01254 823546
Principal: Ms Jane Buttery BA (Hons) NPQH
Age range: 0–16 years

OneSchool Global UK Lancaster Campus
Melling Road, Hornby, Lancashire LA2 8LH
Tel: 01524 222159
Age range: 7–18 years

Rossall School
Broadway, Fleetwood, Lancashire FY7 8JW
Tel: +44 (0)1253 774201
Head: Mr Jeremy Quartermain
Age range: 0–18 years
No. of pupils: 843 VIth220
Fees: Day £9,435–£15,150 WB £16,050–£26,085 FB £23,865–£38,685

Scarisbrick Hall School
Southport Road, Scarisbrisk, Ormskirk, Lancashire L40 9RQ
Tel: 01704 841151
Headmaster: Mr J Shaw
Age range: 0–18 years

St Joseph's Park Hill School
Padiham Road, Burnley, Lancashire BB12 6TG
Tel: 01282 455622
Headteacher: Mrs Maria Whitehead
Age range: 3–11 years

St Pius X Catholic Preparatory School
Oak House, 200 Garstang Road, Fulwood, Preston, Lancashire PR2 8RD
Tel: 01772 719937
Headmaster: Mr Patrick Gush
Age range: 2–11 years

St. Annes College Grammar School
293 Clifton Drive South, Lytham St Annes, Lancashire FY8 1HN
Tel: +44 (0)1253 725815
Head of School: S R Welsby
Age range: 2–18 years

Stonyhurst College
Stonyhurst, Clitheroe, Lancashire BB7 9PZ
Tel: 01254 827073
Headmaster: Mr John Browne BA LLB MBA
Age range: 3–18 years
No. of pupils: 799
Fees: Day £22,920 WB £33,075
FB £37,860–£41,265

The Alternative School
Suite 4a, Ribble Court, 1 Mead Way, Padiham, Lancashire BB12 7NG
Tel: 01282 851800
Head of School: Ms Kirsty Swierkowski
Age range: 5–18 years

Westholme School
Wilmar Lodge, Meins Road, Blackburn, Lancashire BB2 6QU
Tel: 01254 506070
Principal: Dr Richard Robson
Age range: 4–18 years

Merseyside

Auckland College
65–67 Parkfield Road, Aigburth, Liverpool, Merseyside L17 4LE
Tel: 01517 270083
Headteacher: Miss Stephanie Boyd
Age range: 3–16 years

Avalon School
Caldy Road, West Kirby, Wirral, Merseyside CH48 2HE
Tel: 01516 256993
Headteacher: Ms Joanna Callaway
Age range: 2–11 years

Birkenhead School
58 Beresford Road, Oxton, Wirral, Merseyside CH43 2JD
Tel: 01516 524014
Headmaster: Mr Paul Vicars
Age range: 3 months–18 years
16·

Carleton House Preparatory School
145 Menlove Avenue, Liverpool, Merseyside L18 3EE
Tel: 01517 220756
Headteacher: Mrs Sandy Coleman
Age range: 3–11 years

Christian Fellowship School
Overbury Street, Edge Hill, Liverpool, Merseyside L7 3HL
Tel: 01517 091642
Head Teacher: Mrs R Boulton (BA Tons, PGCE)
Age range: 0–16 years

Liverpool College
Queens Drive, Liverpool, Merseyside L18 8BG
Tel: 01517 244000
Principal: Mr H van Mourik Broekman
Age range: 4–19 years

Prenton Preparatory School
12 Mount Pleasant, Oxton, Wirral, Merseyside CH43 5SY
Tel: 01516 523182
Headteacher: Mr M Jones BSC Hons, PGCE
Age range: 2–11 years

St. Mary's College
Everest Road, Crosby, Liverpool, Merseyside L23 5TW
Tel: 01519 243926
Principal: Mr Michael Kennedy Bsc, MA
Age range: 0–18 years
16·

Stanfield Preparatory School
Liverpool Road, Crosby, Liverpool, Merseyside L23 0QP
Tel: 01519 499400
Headmistress: Miss E Lynan
Age range: 4–11 years

The Belvedere Preparatory School
23 Belvidere Road, Princes Park, Aigburth, Liverpool, Merseyside L8 3TF
Tel: 01514 711137
Headmistress: Miss Clare Burnham
Age range: 3–11 years

The Merchant Taylors' Boys' School
Liverpool Road, Crosby, Liverpool, Merseyside L23 0QP
Tel: 01519 499400
Headmaster: Mr David Wickes
Age range: B11–18 years
16·

The Merchant Taylors' Girls' School
Liverpool Road, Crosby, Liverpool, Merseyside L23 0QP
Tel: 01519 499400
Headmistress: Mrs Claire Tao
Age range: G11–18 years
16·

Tower College
Mill Lane, Rainhill, Prescot, Merseyside L35 6NE
Tel: 01514 264333
Head of School: Ms Andrea Bingley
Age range: 3 months–16 years

South-East

KEY TO SYMBOLS

- *Boys' school*
- *Girls' school*
- *International school*
- *Tutorial or sixth form college*
- *A levels*
- *Boarding accommodation*
- *Bursaries*
- *International Baccalaureate*
- *Learning support*
- *Entrance at 16+*
- *Vocational qualifications*
- *Independent Association of Preparatory Schools*
- *The Headmasters' & Headmistresses' Conference*
- *Independent Schools Association*
- *Girls' School Association*
- *Boarding Schools' Association*
- *Society of Heads*

Unless otherwise indicated, all schools are coeducational day schools. Single-sex and boarding schools will be indicated by the relevant icon.

Berkshire

Alder Bridge Steiner-Waldorf School
Bridge House, Mill Lane, Padworth, Reading, Berkshire RG7 4JU
Tel: 0118 971 4471
Head of School: Lucia Dimarco
Age range: 3–14 years

Al-Madani Girls School
339–341 Bath Road, Slough, Berkshire SL1 5PR
Tel: 01628 298841
Head of School: Tazmul Islam Rahman
Age range: G11–16 years

Al-Madani Independent Grammar School
1 Whittle Parkway, Slough, Berkshire SL1 6FE
Tel: 01753 202203
Age range: B11–16 years

Bradfield College
Bradfield, Berkshire RG7 6AU
Tel: 0118 964 4516
Headmaster: Dr Christopher Stevens
Age range: 13–18 years
No. of pupils: 820
Fees: Day £33,732 FB £42,165

Caversham Preparatory School
16 Peppard Road, Caversham, Reading, Berkshire RG4 8JZ
Tel: 01189 478 684
Head of School: Mrs Naomi Williams
Age range: 3–11 years

Claires Court Junior Boys
Ridgeway, The Thicket, Maidenhead, Berkshire SL6 3QE
Tel: 01628 327400
Head of Juniors: Ms Leanne Kirby
Age range: B4–11 years

Claires Court Nursery, Girls and Sixth Form
1 College Avenue, Maidenhead, Berkshire SL6 6AW
Tel: 01628 327500
Head of Juniors: Ms Leanne Kirby
Age range: B16–18 years G2–18 years

Claires Court Senior Boys
Ray Mill Road East, Maidenhead, Berkshire SL6 8TE
Tel: 01628 327600
Head of Senior Boys: Mr James Wilding
Age range: B11–16 years

Crosfields School
Shinfield Road, Reading, Berkshire RG2 9BL
Tel: 0118 987 1810
Headmaster: Mr Craig Watson
Age range: 3–16 years

Darul Madinah Slough
50 Darvills Lane, Slough, Berkshire SL1 2PH
Tel: 01753 553841
Age range: 2–6 years

Deenway Montessori School & Unicity College
3–5 Sidmouth Street, Reading, Berkshire RG1 4QX
Tel: 0118 9574737
Headmaster: Mr Munawar Karim LL.B (Hons), M.A, Mont. Dip.
Age range: 3–18+ years

DOLPHIN SCHOOL
For further details see p. 202
Waltham Road, Hurst, Reading, Berkshire RG10 0FR
Tel: 0118 934 1277
Email: enquiries@dolphinschool.com
Website: www.dolphinschool.com
Headmaster: Mr Adam Hurst
Age range: 3–13 years
No. of pupils: 223

EAGLE HOUSE SCHOOL
For further details see p. 206
Sandhurst, Berkshire GU47 8PH
Tel: 01344 772134
Email: info@eaglehouseschool.com
Website: www.eaglehouseschool.com
Head: Mr E Venables
Age range: 3–13 years
No. of pupils: 354
Fees: Day £14,145–£22,125 FB £29,730

Elstree School
Woolhampton Hill, Woolhampton, Reading, Berkshire RG7 5TD
Tel: 01189 713302
Headmaster: Mr Sid Inglis B.A. (Hons), P.G.C.E.
Age range: 3–13 years
No. of pupils: 270

Eton College
Windsor, Berkshire SL4 6DW
Tel: +44 (0)1753 370 611
Head Master: Mr Simon Henderson MA
Age range: B13–18 years
No. of pupils: 1342
Fees: FB £44,094

Eton End School
35 Eton Road, Datchet, Slough, Berkshire SL3 9AX
Tel: 01753 541075
Head of School: Mrs Rachael Cox
Age range: 3–11 years
No. of pupils: 210
Fees: Day £11,106–£14,193

Heathfield School
London Road, Ascot, Berkshire SL5 8BQ
Tel: 01344 898343
Head of School: Ms Sarah Wilson
Age range: G11–18 years (boarding from 11)
Fees: Day £8,589–£8,772 WB £13,174–£13,481 FB £13,868–£14,190

Hemdean House School
Hemdean Road, Caversham, Reading, Berkshire RG4 7SD
Tel: 0118 947 2590
Head Teacher: Mrs Helen Chalmers
Age range: 4–11 years
Fees: Day £3,250–£3,540

Herries Preparatory School
Dean Lane, Cookham Dean, Berkshire SL6 9BD
Tel: 01628 483350
Headteacher: Mr Robert Grosse
Age range: 3–11 years

Highfield Preparatory School
2 West Road, Maidenhead, Berkshire SL6 1PD
Tel: 01628 624918
Headteacher: Mrs Joanna Leach
Age range: B2–7 years G2–11 years

Holme Grange School
Heathlands Road, Wokingham, Berkshire RG40 3AL
Tel: 0118 978 1566
Headteacher: Mrs Claire Robinson BA (Open) PGCE NPQH
Age range: 3–16 years
No. of pupils: 660
Fees: Day £10,665–£16,140

Holyport College
Ascot Road, Holyport, Berkshire SL6 3LE
Tel: 01628 640150
Headmaster: Mr Ben McCarey
Age range: 11–19 years

Lambrook School
Winkfield Row, Nr Ascot, Berkshire RG42 6LU
Tel: 01344 882717
Headmaster: Mr Jonathan Perry
Age range: 3–13 years
No. of pupils: 600

Langley Hall Arts Academy
Symphony House, 4 Waterside Court, Langley, Berkshire SL3 6EZ
Tel: 01753 900470
Principal: Mr Claudio Di Meo
Age range: 12–18 years

Leighton Park School
Shinfield Road, Reading, Berkshire RG2 7ED
Tel: 0118 987 9600
Head: Mr Matthew L S Judd BA, PGCE
Age range: 11–18 years
No. of pupils: 550

Long Close School
Upton Court Road, Upton, Slough, Berkshire SL3 7LU
Tel: 01753 520095
Headteacher: Miss K Nijjar BA (Hons), Med, MA
Age range: 2–16 years
No. of pupils: 329

Luckley House School
Luckley Road, Wokingham, Berkshire RG40 3EU
Tel: 0118 978 4175
Head: Mrs Areti Bizior
Age range: 11–18 years

Ludgrove
Wokingham, Berkshire RG40 3AB
Tel: 0118 978 9881
Head of School: Mr Simon Barber
Age range: B8–13 years

LVS Ascot
London Road, Ascot, Berkshire SL5 8DR
Tel: 01344 882770
Principal: Mrs Christine Cunniffe BA (Hons), MMus, MBA
Age range: 4–18 years
No. of pupils: 833
Fees: Day £11,640–£20,985 FB £29,760–£36,660

Meadowbrook Montessori School
Malt Hill, Warfield, Berkshire RG42 6JQ
Tel: 01344 890869
Director of Education: Ms Serena Gunn
Age range: 4–11 years

Newbold School
Popeswood Road, Binfield, Bracknell, Berkshire RG42 4AH
Tel: 01344 421088
Headteacher: Mrs Jaki Crissey MA, BA, PGCE Primary
Age range: 3–11 years

OneSchool Global UK Reading Campus (Primary)
401 Old Whitley Wood Lane, Reading, Berkshire RG2 8QA
Tel: 0118 931 2938
Age range: 7–11 years

OneSchool Global UK Reading Campus (Senior)
The Quad, 14 Arkwright Road, Reading, Berkshire RG2 0LU
Tel: 03000 700421
Age range: 11–18 years

Our Lady's Preparatory School
19 The Avenue, Crowthorne, Wokingham, Berkshire RG45 6PB
Tel: 01344 773394
Headmaster: Mr Michael Stone
Age range: 4–11 years
No. of pupils: 130
Fees: Day £8,748

Padworth College
Sopers Lane, Reading, Berkshire RG7 4NR
Tel: 0118 983 2644
Principal: Lorraine Atkins
Age range: 14–19 years
A £ 16·

Pangbourne College
Pangbourne, Reading, Berkshire RG8 8LA
Tel: 0118 984 2101
Headmaster: Thomas J C Garnier
Age range: 11–18 years
No. of pupils: 458
Fees: Day £6,300–£8,540 WB £8,210–£11,510 FB £9,050–£12,680
A £ 16·

Papplewick School
Windsor Road, Ascot, Berkshire SL5 7LH
Tel: 01344 621488
Headmaster: Mr Tom Bunbury
Age range: B6–13 years

Queen Anne's School
6 Henley Road, Caversham, Reading, Berkshire RG4 6DX
Tel: 0118 918 7300
Head: Ms Elaine Purves
Age range: G11–18 years (boarding from 11)
No. of pupils: G450
Fees: Day £8,370 FB £13,590
A £ 16·

Reading Blue Coat School
Holme Park, Sonning Lane, Sonning, Reading, Berkshire RG4 6SU
Tel: 0118 944 1005
Headmaster: Mr Peter Thomas
Age range: B11–18 years G16–18 years
A £ 16·

Reading School
Erleigh Road, Reading, Berkshire RG1 5LW
Tel: 0118 9015600
Headmaster: Mr A.M. Robson
Age range: B11–18 years

Reddam House Berkshire
Bearwood Road, Sindlesham, Wokingham, Berkshire RG41 5BG
Tel: +44 (0)118 974 8300
Principal: Mr Rick Cross
Age range: 3 months–18 years
No. of pupils: 675
Fees: Day £12,006–£19,248 WB £29,241–£33,696 FB £30,855–£35,310
A £ 16·

Shakhsiyah School, Slough
Cippenham Lodge, Cippenham Lane, Slough, Berkshire SL1 5AN
Tel: 01753 518000
Acting-Head Teacher: Ms Sajeada Ahmed
Age range: 3–11 years

St Andrew's School
Buckhold, Pangbourne, Reading, Berkshire RG8 8QA
Tel: 0118 974 4276
Head Master: Ed Graham
Age range: 3–13 years (boarding from 7)
Fees: Day £3,890–£6,525

St Bernard's Preparatory School
Hawtrey Close, Slough, Berkshire SL1 1TB
Tel: 01753 521821
Headteacher: Mrs A Verma
Age range: 2½–11 years

St Edward's Prep
64 Tilehurst Road, Reading, Berkshire RG30 2JH
Tel: 0118 957 4342
Headteacher: Mr Jonathan Parsons
Age range: 3–11 years

ST GEORGE'S ASCOT
For further details see p. 238
Wells Lane, Ascot, Berkshire SL5 7DZ
Tel: 01344 629900
Email: admissions@stgeorges-ascot.org.uk
Website: www.stgeorges-ascot.org.uk
Head: Mrs Liz Hewer MA (Hons) (Cantab) PGCE
Age range: G11–18 years (boarding from 11)
No. of pupils: 270
A £ 16·

St George's School Windsor Castle
Windsor Castle, Windsor, Berkshire SL4 1QF
Tel: 01753 865553
Head Master: Mr W Goldsmith BA (Hons), FRSA, FCCT
Age range: 3–13 years (boarding from 8)
IB

St John's Beaumont Preparatory School
Priest Hill, Old Windsor, Berkshire SL4 2JN
Tel: 01784 494 053
Headmaster: Mr P Barr
Age range: B3–13 years G3–7 years
No. of pupils: 220
Fees: Day £3,788–£7,502 FB £3,807
£

St Joseph's College
Upper Redlands Road, Reading, Berkshire RG1 5JT
Tel: 0118 966 1000
Head of School: Mrs Laura Stotesbury
Age range: 3–18 years
A £ 16·

St Mary's School Ascot
St Mary's Road, Ascot, Berkshire SL5 9JF
Tel: 01344 296614
Headmistress: Mrs Danuta Staunton
Age range: G11–18 years (boarding from 11)
A £ 16·

St Piran's School
Gringer Hill, Maidenhead, Berkshire SL6 7LZ
Tel: 01628 594300
Headmaster: Mr Sebastian Sales
Age range: 2–11 years

Sunningdale School
Dry Arch Road, Sunningdale, Berkshire SL5 9PY
Tel: 01344 620159
Headmaster: Tom Dawson MA, PGCE
Age range: B7–13 years

THE ABBEY SCHOOL
For further details see p. 246
Kendrick Road, Reading, Berkshire RG1 5DZ
Tel: 0118 987 2256
Email: admissions@theabbey.co.uk
Website: www.theabbey.co.uk
Head: Mr Will le Fleming
Age range: G3–18 years
No. of pupils: 987
Fees: Day £13,500–£21,750
A £ IB 16·

The King's House School, Windsor
King's House, 77A Frances Road, Windsor, Berkshire SL4 3AQ
Tel: 01753 834850
Headteacher: Mrs Lyndsey Harding
Age range: 3–11 years

The Marist Preparatory School
King's Road, Sunninghill, Ascot, Berkshire SL5 7PS
Tel: 01344 624291
Vice Principal Prep Phase: Mrs Jane Gow
Age range: G2–11 years

The Marist School
King's Road, Sunninghill, Ascot, Berkshire SL5 7PS
Tel: 01344 624291
Principal: Ms Jo Smith
Age range: G2–18 years

THE ORATORY PREP SCHOOL
For further details see p. 248
Great Oaks, Goring Heath, Reading, Berkshire RG8 7SF
Tel: 0118 984 4511
Email: office@oratoryprep.co.uk
Website: www.oratoryprep.co.uk
Headteacher: Mr Andrew De Silva
Age range: 2–13 years (boarding from 7)
No. of pupils: 300
Fees: Day £3,855–£6,635 FB £8,535–£9,910

The Oratory School
Woodcote, Reading, Berkshire RG8 0PJ
Tel: 01491 683500
Head Master: Mr Joe Smith BA(Hons), MEd, PGCE
Age range: 11–18 years

The Vine Christian School
Three Mile Cross Church, Basingstoke Road, Three Mile Cross, Reading, Berkshire RG7 1HF
Tel: 0118 988 6464
Head of School: Mrs René Esterhuizen
Age range: 3–18 years

TLG Reading
Empress Road Centre, Empress Road Calcot, Reading, Berkshire RG31 4XR
Tel: 01189 432978
Head of Centre: Ms Rachel Owen
Age range: 11–16 years

Trinity Christian School
11 Glebe Road, Reading, Berkshire RG2 7AG
Tel: 0118 336 0477
Head of School: Ms Pearl Linkens
Age range: 4–11 years

UPTON HOUSE SCHOOL
For further details see p. 252
115 St Leonard's Road, Windsor, Berkshire SL4 3DF
Tel: 01753 862610
Email: registrar@uptonhouse.org.uk
Website: www.uptonhouse.org.uk
Head: Mrs Rhian Thornton BA (Hons) NPQH LLE PGCE
Age range: 2–11 years
No. of pupils: 290
Fees: Day £2,982–£5,980

Waverley Preparatory School & Day Nursery
Waverley Way, Finchampstead, Wokingham, Berkshire RG40 4YD
Tel: 0118 973 1121
Principal: Mr Guy Shore
Age range: 3 months–11 years

WELLINGTON COLLEGE
For further details see p. 256
Duke's Ride, Crowthorne, Berkshire RG45 7PU
Tel: +44 (0)1344 444000
Email: admissions@wellingtoncollege.org.uk
Website: www.wellingtoncollege.org.uk
Master: Mr James Dahl
Age range: 13–18 years
No. of pupils: 1104 VIth489
Fees: Day £35,760 FB £48,930

Buckinghamshire

Davenies
Station Road, Beaconsfield, Buckinghamshire HP9 1AA
Tel: 01494 685400
Headmaster: Mr Carl Rycroft BEd (Hons)
Age range: B4–13 years
No. of pupils: 334
Fees: Day £12,825–£19,350

Gayhurst School
Bull Lane, Gerrards Cross, Buckinghamshire SL9 8RJ
Tel: 01753 969538
Headmaster: Gareth R A Davies
Age range: 3–11 years

International School of Creative Arts (ISCA)
Framewood Road, Wexham, Buckinghamshire SL2 4QS
Tel: +44 (0)1753 208820
Head of School: Mr Robert Hunter
Age range: 15–19 years
No. of pupils: 85

MALTMAN'S GREEN SCHOOL
For further details see p. 220
Maltmans Lane, Gerrards Cross, Buckinghamshire SL9 8RR
Tel: 01753 883022
Email: registrar@maltmansgreen.com
Website: www.maltmansgreen.com
Headmistress: Mrs Jill Walker BSc (Hons), MA Ed, PGCE
Age range: G2–11 years
No. of pupils: 330
Fees: Day £2,850–£6,500

St Mary's School
94 Packhorse Road, Gerrards Cross, Buckinghamshire SL9 8JQ
Tel: 01753 883370
Head of School: Mrs Patricia Adams
Age range: G3–18 years

Teikyo School UK
Framewood Road, Wexham, Buckinghamshire SL2 4QS
Tel: 01753 663711
Age range: 15–18 years

Thorpe House School
Oval Way, Gerrards Cross, Buckinghamshire SL9 8QA
Tel: 01753 882474
Headmaster: Mr Nicholas Pietrek
Age range: B4–16 years

East Sussex

Annan The Froebel School
Lewes Road, Easons Green, Uckfield, East Sussex TN22 5RE
Tel: 01825 841410
Principal: Ms Debby Hunter
Age range: 2–11 years

Bartholomews Tutorial College
22–23 Prince Albert Street, Brighton, East Sussex BN1 1HF
Tel: 01273 205965/205141
Age range: 14+ years
No. of pupils: 40
Fees: Day £22,000

Battle Abbey School
High Street, Battle, East Sussex TN33 0AD
Tel: 01424 772385
Headmaster: Mr David Clark BA, M Phil (Cantab)
Age range: 3 months–18 years (boarding from 11)

Bede's Prep School
Duke's Drive, Eastbourne, East Sussex BN20 7XL
Tel: 01323 356939
Head: Mrs Leigh-Anne Morris
Age range: 3 months–13 years (boarding from 9)
No. of pupils: 336
Fees: Day £3,660–£6,390 FB £2,990

Bede's Senior School
Upper Dicker, Hailsham, East Sussex BN27 3QH
Tel: 01323 356609
Head: Mr Peter Goodyer
Age range: 13–18 years (boarding from 13)
No. of pupils: 832
Fees: Day £8,300 WB £12,240 FB £12,990

Brighton & Hove Montessori School
67 Stanford Avenue, Brighton, East Sussex BN1 6FB
Tel: 01273 702485
Headteacher: Mrs Daisy Cockburn AMI, MontDip
Age range: 2–12 years

Brighton College
Eastern Road, Brighton, East Sussex BN2 0AL
Tel: 01273 704200
Head Master: Richard Cairns
Age range: 3–18 years

BRIGHTON COLLEGE PREP SCHOOL
For further details see p. 190
Walpole Lodge, Walpole Road, Brighton, East Sussex BN2 0EU
Tel: 01273 704343
Email: prepadmissions@brightoncollege.net
Website: www.brightoncollege.org.uk
Headmaster: Mr Ant Falkus
Age range: 3–13 years
No. of pupils: 510
Fees: Day £4,400–£7,430

Brighton Girls GDST
Montpelier Road, Brighton, East Sussex BN1 3AT
Tel: 01273 280280
Head: Ms Rosie McColl
Age range: G4–18 years

Brighton International School
5 Old Steine, Brighton, East Sussex BN1 1EJ
Tel: 07796 997780
Head of School: Ms Juliet Cassells
Age range: 15–17 years

Buckswood School
Broomham Hall, Rye Road, Guestling, Hastings, East Sussex TN35 4LT
Tel: 01424 813 813
Co-Principals: Michael Shaw & Kevin Samson
Age range: 10–19 years

CLAREMONT SCHOOL
For further details see p. 196
Bodiam, Nr Robertsbridge, East Sussex TN32 5UJ
Tel: 01580 830396
Email: admissions@claremontschool.co.uk
Website: www.claremontschool.co.uk
Age range: 1–18 years (boarding from 10)

Darvell School
Darvell, Brightling Road, Robertsbridge, East Sussex TN32 5DR
Tel: 01580 883300
Age range: 6–14 years

Didac School
16 Trinity Trees, Eastbourne, East Sussex BN21 3LE
Tel: +44 1323 417276
Age range: 16–18 years

Eastbourne College
Old Wish Road, Eastbourne, East Sussex BN21 4JX
Tel: 01323 452323 (Admissions)
Headmaster: Mr Tom Lawson MA (Oxon)
Age range: 13–18 years

Greenfields Independent Day & Boarding School
Priory Road, Forest Row, East Sussex RH18 5JD
Tel: +44 (0)1342 822189
Executive Head: Mr. Jeff Smith
Age range: 2–18 years (boarding from 10)

Kings Brighton
27–33 Ditchling Road, Brighton, East Sussex BN1 4SB
Tel: +44 (0)1273 443403
Principal: Mr Nigel Addison
Age range: 14–25 years

Lancing Prep Hove
The Droveway, Hove, East Sussex BN3 6LU
Tel: 01273 503452
Headmistress: Mrs Kirsty Keep BEd
Age range: 3–13 years

Lewes Old Grammar School
140 High Street, Lewes, East Sussex BN7 1XS
Tel: 01273 472634
Headmaster: Mr Robert Blewitt
Age range: 3–18 years

Mayfield School
The Old Palace, Mayfield, East Sussex TN20 6PH
Tel: 01435 874642
Head: Ms Antonia Beary MA, MPhil (Cantab), PGCE
Age range: G11–18 years (boarding from 11)
No. of pupils: 425

Michael Hall School
Kidbrooke Park, Priory Road, Forest Row, East Sussex RH18 5JA
Tel: 01342 822275
Head of School: Emmeline Hawker
Age range: 0–19 years

Roedean School
Roedean Way, Brighton, East Sussex BN2 5RQ
Tel: 01273 667500
Head of School: Niamh Green
Age range: G11–18 years (boarding from 11)
No. of pupils: 700
Fees: Day £6,290–£8,220 WB £11,120–£12,400 FB £12,180–£14,745

Sacred Heart School
Mayfield Lane, Durgates, Wadhurst, East Sussex TN5 6DQ
Tel: 01892 783414
Headteacher: Ms Johanna Collyer
Age range: 2–11 years

SKIPPERS HILL MANOR PREPARATORY SCHOOL
For further details see p. 236
Five Ashes, Mayfield, East Sussex TN20 6HR
Tel: 01825 830234
Email: info@skippershill.com
Website: www.skippershill.com
Headmaster: Mr Phillip Makhouli
Age range: 2–13 years
Fees: Day £3,402–£5,391

St Andrew's Prep
Meads Street, Eastbourne, East Sussex BN20 7RP
Tel: 01323 733203
Headmaster: Tom Gregory BA(Hons), PGCE
Age range: 9 months–13 years
No. of pupils: 374

St Christopher's School
33 New Church Road, Hove, East Sussex BN3 4AD
Tel: 01273 735404
Head of School: Ms Elizabeth Lyle
Age range: 4–13 years

The Brighton Waldorf School
Roedean Road, Brighton, East Sussex BN2 5RA
Tel: 01273 386300
School Director: Mr Damian Mooncie
Age range: 0–16 years

The Drive Prep School
101 The Drive, Hove, East Sussex BN3 6GE
Tel: 01273 738444
Head Teacher: Mrs S Parkinson CertEd, CertPerfArts
Age range: 7–16 years

The Montessori Place
45 Cromwell Road, Hove, East Sussex BN3 3ER
Tel: 01273 773 764
Head of School: Mr Rob Gueterbock
Age range: 15 months–18 years

VINEHALL
For further details see p. 254
Robertsbridge, East Sussex TN32 5JL
Tel: 01580 880413
Email: admissions@vinehallschool.com
Website: www.vinehallschool.com
Headmaster: Joff Powis
Age range: 2–13 years
No. of pupils: 201
Fees: Day £11,100–£21,675 WB £26,925 FB £29,925

Windlesham School
190 Dyke Road, Brighton, East Sussex BN1 5AA
Tel: 01273 553645
Headmaster: Mr John Ingrassia
Age range: 3–11 years

Hampshire

Alton School
Anstey Lane, Alton,
Hampshire GU34 2NG
Tel: 01420 82070
Headmaster: Mr Karl Guest
Age range: 0–18 years
No. of pupils: 400

Ballard School
Fernhill Lane, New Milton,
Hampshire BH25 5SU
Tel: 01425 626900
Headmaster: Mr Andrew McCleave
Age range: 2–16 years
No. of pupils: 472
Fees: Day £3,105–£5,715

Bedales Prep, Dunhurst & Pre-Prep, Dunannie
Alton Road, Steep, Petersfield,
Hampshire GU32 2DR
Tel: 01730 300200 / 01730 300400
Head of Bedales Prep, Dunhurst: Mr Colin Baty
Age range: 3–13 years

Bedales School
Church Road, Steep, Petersfield,
Hampshire GU32 2DG
Tel: 01730 300100
Head of School: Mr Will Goldsmith
Age range: 13–18 years

Boundary Oak School
Roche Court, Wickham Road,
Fareham, Hampshire PO17 5BL
Tel: 01329 280955
Executive Headmaster: Mr James Polansky MA (Cantab) PGCE
Age range: 2–16 years
No. of pupils: 348
Fees: Day £9,195–£14,886 WB £16,155–£21,078 FB £18,144–£23,067

Brockwood Park School
Brockwood Park, Bramdean,
Alresford, Hampshire SO24 0LQ
Tel: +44 (0)1962 771744
Principal: Mr Antonio Autor
Age range: 14–19 years

Charlton House Independent School
55–57 Midanbury Lane, Southampton,
Hampshire SO18 4DJ
Tel: 023 8067 1739
Head Teacher: Mr Matthew Robinson
Age range: 9 months–11 years

CHURCHER'S COLLEGE
For further details see p. 194
Petersfield, Hampshire GU31 4AS
Tel: 01730 263033
Email: admissions@churcherscollege.com
Website: www.ChurchersCollege.com
Headmaster: Mr Simon Williams , MA, BSc
Age range: 3–18 years
Fees: Day £12,525–£18,735

Daneshill School
Stratfield Turgis, Basingstoke,
Hampshire RG27 0AR
Tel: 01256 882707
Head of School: Jim Massey
Age range: 2–13 years
No. of pupils: 303
Fees: Day £11,550–£15,615

DITCHAM PARK SCHOOL
For further details see p. 200
Ditcham Park, Petersfield,
Hampshire GU31 5RN
Tel: 01730 825659
Email: admissions@ditchampark.com
Website: www.ditchampark.com
Headmaster: Mr Graham Spawforth MA, MEd
Age range: 21/2–16 years
No. of pupils: 430
Fees: Day £3,327–£5,633

DURLSTON SCHOOL
For further details see p. 204
Becton Lane, Barton-on-Sea, New Milton, Hampshire BH25 7AQ
Tel: 01425 610010
Email: registrar@durlstonschool.co.uk
Website: www.durlstonschool.co.uk
Headmaster: Mr Richard May
Age range: 2–16 years
No. of pupils: 260

Embley
Embley Park, Romsey,
Hampshire SO51 6ZE
Tel: 01794 512206
Headteacher: Mr Cliff Canning
Age range: 2–18 years
No. of pupils: 600
Fees: Day £9,165–£17,004 WB £29,310 FB £9,598–£33,636

Farleigh School
Red Rice, Andover,
Hampshire SP11 7PW
Tel: 01264 710766
Headmaster: Fr Simon Everson
Age range: 3–13 years
No. of pupils: 460

Farnborough Hill
Farnborough Road, Farnborough,
Hampshire GU14 8AT
Tel: 01252 545197
Head: Mrs A Neil BA, MEd, PGCE
Age range: G11–18 years

Fitrah SIPS
55 Northumberland Road,
Southampton, Hampshire SO14 0EJ
Tel: 02380 570 849
Age range: 4–16 years

Forres Sandle Manor
Fordingbridge, Hampshire SP6 1NS
Tel: 01425 653181
Head of School: Mr Mark Howe
Age range: 2–16 years
No. of pupils: 180

Glenhurst School
16 Beechworth Road, Havant,
Hampshire PO9 1AX
Tel: 023 9248 4054
Age range: 3 months–5 years

Grantham Farm Montessori School & The Children's House
Grantham Farm, Baughurst,
Tadley, Hampshire RG26 5JS
Tel: 0118 981 5821
Head Teacher: Ms Emma Wetherley
Age range: 2–7 years

Highfield and Brookham School
Highfield Lane, Liphook,
Hampshire GU30 7LQ
Tel: 01428 728000
Headteacher: Mrs Suzannah Cryer BA (QTS)
Age range: 2–13 years
No. of pupils: 468

Hurst Lodge School
Yateley Hall, Firgrove Road,
Yateley, Hampshire GU46 6HJ
Tel: 01252 227002
Principal: Ms Victoria Smit
Age range: 4–19 years

Inwoods Small School
Brockwood Park, Bramdean,
Alresford, Hampshire SO24 0LQ
Tel: +44 (0)1962 771065
Age range: 5–11 years

KING EDWARD VI SCHOOL
For further details see p. 214
Wilton Road, Southampton,
Hampshire SO15 5UQ
Tel: 023 8070 4561
Email: registrar@kes.hants.sch.uk
Website: kes.school
Head Master: Mr N T Parker
Age range: 11–18 years
No. of pupils: 988
Fees: Day £19,995

Kingscourt School
182 Five Heads Road, Catherington,
Hampshire PO8 9NJ
Tel: 023 9259 3251
Head of School: Amanda Bembridge
Age range: 3–11 years
No. of pupils: 158
Fees: Day £2,856

Lord Wandsworth College
Long Sutton, Hook,
Hampshire RG29 1TA
Tel: 01256 862201
Head of School: Mr Adam Williams
Age range: 11–18 years
No. of pupils: 700
Fees: Day £8,400–£9,880 WB £11,930–£13,390 FB £12,350–£14,000

Mayville High School
35–37 St Simon's Road, Southsea,
Portsmouth, Hampshire PO5 2PE
Tel: 023 9273 4847
Headteacher: Mrs Rebecca Parkyn
Age range: 2–16 years

Meoncross School
Burnt House Lane, Stubbington, Fareham, Hampshire PO14 2EF
Tel: 01329 662182
Headmaster: Mr Mark Cripps
Age range: 21/2–16 years
No. of pupils: 405
Fees: Day £8,736–£12,576

Moyles Court School
Moyles Court, Ringwood, Hampshire BH24 3NF
Tel: 01425 472856
Headmaster: Mr Richard Milner-Smith
Age range: 2–16 years

Peter Symonds College
Owens Road, Winchester, Hampshire SO22 6RX
Tel: 01962 857500
Age range: 16–19 years

Portsmouth High School GDST
Kent Road, Southsea, Portsmouth, Hampshire PO5 3EQ
Tel: 023 9282 6714
Headmistress: Mrs Jane Prescott BSc NPQH
Age range: G3–18 years
No. of pupils: 500
Fees: Day £2,574–£4,800

Prince's Mead School
Worthy Park House, Kings Worthy, Winchester, Hampshire SO21 1AN
Tel: 01962 888000
Headmaster: Mr Peter Thacker
Age range: 3–11 years

Ringwood Waldorf School
Folly Farm Lane, Ashley, Ringwood, Hampshire BH24 2NN
Tel: 01425 472664
Age range: 3–18 years

Rookwood School
Weyhill Road, Andover, Hampshire SP10 3AL
Tel: 01264 325900
Headmaster: Mr A Kirk-Burgess BSc, PGCE, MSc (Oxon)
Age range: 2–18 years (boarding from 7)

Salesian College
119 Reading Road, Farnborough, Hampshire GU14 6PA
Tel: 01252 893000
Headmaster: Mr Gerard Owens
Age range: B11–18 years G16–18 years

SHERBORNE HOUSE SCHOOL
For further details see p. 230
39 Lakewood Road, Chandlers Ford, Eastleigh, Hampshire SO53 1EU
Tel: 02380 252440
Email: info@sherbornehouse.co.uk
Website: www.sherbornehouse.co.uk
Head of School: Mrs Cordelia Cripps
Age range: 6 months–11 years

SHERFIELD SCHOOL
For further details see p. 232
South Drive, Sherfield-on-Loddon, Hook, Hampshire RG27 0HU
Tel: 01256 884800
Email: admissions@sherfieldschool.co.uk
Website: www.sherfieldschool.co.uk
Headmaster: TBC
Age range: 3 months–18 years (boarding from 9)
No. of pupils: 609

St Neot's School
St Neot's Road, Eversley, Hampshire RG27 0PN
Tel: 0118 9739650
Headmaster: Mr Jonathan Slot
Age range: 2–13 years

St Nicholas' School
Redfields House, Redfields Lane, Church Crookham, Fleet, Hampshire GU52 0RF
Tel: 01252 850121
Headmistress: Dr O Wright PhD, MA, BA Hons, PGCE
Age range: B3–7 years G3–16 years

St Swithun's Prep
Alresford Road, Winchester, Hampshire SO21 1HA
Tel: 01962 835750
Head of School (retiring summer 2023): Mr Jonathan Brough
Age range: B3–4 years G3–11 years
No. of pupils: 209

ST SWITHUN'S SCHOOL
For further details see p. 242
Alresford Road, Winchester, Hampshire SO21 1HA
Tel: 01962 835700
Email: office@stswithuns.com
Website: www.stswithuns.com
Head of School: Jane Gandee MA(Cantab)
Age range: G11–18 years
No. of pupils: 517 VIth142
Fees: Day £25,356 FB £42,651

Stockton House School
Stockton Avenue, Fleet, Hampshire GU51 4NS
Tel: 01252 616323
Early Years Manager: Mrs Jenny Bounds BA EYPS
Age range: 2–5 years

STROUD, KING EDWARD VI PREPARATORY SCHOOL
For further details see p. 244
Highwood House, Highwood Lane, Romsey, Hampshire SO51 9ZH
Tel: 01794 513231
Email: registrar@stroud-kes.org.uk
Website: stroud.kes.school
Headmistress: Mrs Rebecca Smith
Age range: 3–11 years
Fees: Day £4,060–£6,525

The Gregg Prep School
17–19 Winn Road, Southampton, Hampshire SO17 1EJ
Tel: 023 8055 7352
Headteacher: Mr M Pascoe
Age range: 4–11 years

The Gregg School
Townhill Park House, Cutbush Lane, Southampton, Hampshire SO18 3RR
Tel: 023 8047 2133
Headteacher: Mrs S Sellers
Age range: 11–16 years

The King's School
Lakesmere House, Allington Lane, Fair Oak, Eastleigh, Southampton, Hampshire SO50 7DB
Tel: 023 8060 0986
Headteacher: Mrs Heather Bowden
Age range: 4–16 years

The New Forest Small School
1 Southampton Road, Lyndhurst, Hampshire SO43 7BU
Tel: 02380 284415
Headteacher: Mr Alex James
Age range: 3–16 years

The Pilgrims' School
3 The Close, Winchester, Hampshire SO23 9LT
Tel: 01962 854189
Interim Head of School: Mr Alistair Duncan
Age range: B4–13 years

The Portsmouth Grammar School
High Street, Portsmouth, Hampshire PO1 2LN
Tel: +44 (0)23 9236 0036
Age range: 21/2–18 years
IB

Thorngrove School
The Mount, Highclere, Newbury, Hampshire RG20 9PS
Tel: 01635 253172
Headmaster: Mr Adam King
Age range: 21/2–13 years

Twyford School
Twyford, Winchester, Hampshire SO21 1NW
Tel: 01962 712269
Headmaster: Mr Andrew Harvey
Age range: 2–13 years

Walhampton
Walhampton, Lymington, Hampshire SO41 5ZG
Tel: 01590 613300
Head: Mr Jonny Timms
Age range: 2–13 years (boarding from 7)

West Hill Park School
St Margaret's Lane, Titchfield, Hampshire PO14 4BS
Tel: 01329 842356
Headmaster: Mr Chris Ward
Age range: 3–13 years

Winchester College
College Street, Winchester, Hampshire SO23 9NA
Tel: 01962 621100
Headmaster: Dr. T R Hands
Age range: B13–18 years (boarding from 13)

Yateley Manor School
51 Reading Road, Yateley, Hampshire GU46 7UQ
Tel: 01252 405500
Headmaster: Mr Robert Upton
Age range: 3–13 years

Isle of Wight

Priory School of Our Lady of Walsingham
Beatrice Avenue, Whippingham, Isle of Wight PO32 6LP
Tel: 01983 861222
Principal: Mr David EJJ Lloyd
Age range: 4–18 years
No. of pupils: 176
Fees: Day £6,690–£10,500

RYDE SCHOOL WITH UPPER CHINE
For further details see p. 226
Queen's Road, Ryde, Isle of Wight PO33 3BE
Tel: 01983 562229
Email: admissions@rydeschool.net
Website: www.rydeschool.org.uk
Headmaster: Mr Will Turner
Age range: 2–18 years (boarding from 10)
No. of pupils: 795
Fees: Day £3,128–£5,542 WB £10,766–£10,950 FB £12,099–£12,283

Kent

Ashford School
East Hill, Ashford, Kent TN24 8PB
Tel: +44 (0)1233 625171
Head: Mr Michael Hall
Age range: 3 months–18 years (boarding from 11)
No. of pupils: 1034 VIth140
Fees: Day £9,030–£19,026 WB £27,846 FB £38,778

Beech Grove School
Forest Drive, Nonington, Dover, Kent CT15 4FB
Tel: 01304 843 707
Headteacher: Timothy Maas
Age range: 6–18 years

Beechwood School
12 Pembury Road, Tunbridge Wells, Kent TN2 3QD
Tel: 01892 532747
Headmaster: Mr Justin Foster-Gandey
Age range: 3–18 years

Benenden School
Cranbrook, Kent TN17 4AA
Tel: 01580 240592
Headmistress: Ms Samantha Price
Age range: G11–18 years (boarding from 11)

BETHANY SCHOOL
For further details see p. 188
Curtisden Green, Goudhurst, Cranbrook, Kent TN17 1LB
Tel: 01580 211273
Email: registrar@bethanyschool.org.uk
Website: www.bethanyschool.org.uk
Headmaster: Mr Francie Healy BSc, HDipEd, NPQH
Age range: 11–18 years
No. of pupils: 366 VIth79
Fees: Day £20,415–£22,545 WB £31,680–£34,980 FB £34,155–£38,445

Bronte School
7 Pelham Road, Gravesend, Kent DA11 0HU
Tel: 01474 533805
Headmistress: Ms Emma Wood
Age range: 4–11 years

Bryony School
Marshall Road, Rainham, Gillingham, Kent ME8 0AJ
Tel: 01634 231511
Head of School: Mrs N Gee
Age range: 2–11 years

Chartfield School
45 Minster Road, Westgate on Sea, Kent CT8 8DA
Tel: 01843 831716
Head & Proprietor: Miss L P Shipley
Age range: 3–11 years

Cobham Hall School
Brewers Road, Cobham, Kent DA12 3BL
Tel: 01474 823371
Headteacher: Mrs Wendy Barrett
Age range: B16–18 years G11–18 years (boarding from 11)
No. of pupils: 150
Fees: Day £7,100–£8,250 FB £11,500–£13,250

Cranbrook School, Kent
Waterloo Road, Cranbrook, Kent TN17 3JD
Tel: 01580 711800
Head of School: Mr W Chuter
Age range: 11–18 years

Dover College
Effingham Crescent, Dover, Kent CT17 9RH
Tel: 01304 205969
Head of School: Mr Simon Fisher
Age range: 3–18 years

Dulwich Prep Cranbrook
Coursehorn, Cranbrook, Kent TN17 3NP
Tel: 01580 712179
Headmaster: Mr Paul David BEd(Hons)
Age range: 2–16 years

Earlscliffe
29 Shorncliffe Road, Folkestone, Kent CT20 2NB
Tel: 01303 253951
Headteacher: Mr Joss Williams
Age range: 15–19 years
No. of pupils: 130
Fees: Day £9,100 WB £11,745 FB £13,650

Fosse Bank School
Mountains, Noble Tree Road, Hildenborough, Tonbridge, Kent TN11 8ND
Tel: 01732 834212
Acting Head: Mrs Shiralee Davies
Age range: 2–11 years

Gad's Hill School
Gravesend Road, Higham, Rochester, Kent ME3 7PA
Tel: 01474 822366
Headmaster: Mr Paul Savage
Age range: 3–16 years

Haddon Dene School
57 Gladstone Road, Broadstairs, Kent CT10 2HY
Tel: 01843 861176
Headmistress: Mrs Joanne Parpworth
Age range: 3–11 years

Hilden Grange School
62 Dry Hill Park Road, Tonbridge, Kent TN10 3BX
Tel: 01732 352706
Headmaster: Mr Malcolm Gough
Age range: 3–13 years

Hilden Oaks Preparatory School & Nursery
38 Dry Hill Park Road, Tonbridge, Kent TN10 3BU
Tel: 01732 353941
Head of School: Mrs. K Joiner
Age range: 3 months–11 years

Holmewood House School
Barrow Lane, Langton Green, Tunbridge Wells, Kent TN3 0EB
Tel: 01892 860000
Head of School: Mrs Ruth O'Sullivan
Age range: 3–13 years
No. of pupils: 450

Kent College Pembury
Old Church Road, Pembury, Tunbridge Wells, Kent TN2 4AX
Tel: +44 (0)1892 822006
Head of School: Miss Katrina Handford
Age range: B3–11 years G3–18 years (boarding from 8)
No. of pupils: 500
Fees: Day £22,575 WB £28,200 FB £35,700

KENT COLLEGE, CANTERBURY
For further details see p. 212
Whitstable Road, Canterbury, Kent CT2 9DT
Tel: +44 (0)1227 763 231
Email: admissions@kentcollege.co.uk
Website: www.kentcollege.com
Head of Kent College: Mr Mark Turnbull
Age range: 3 months–18 years (boarding from 7 years)
No. of pupils: 800
Fees: Day £3,964–£7,487 FB £10,072–£13,860

KING'S SCHOOL ROCHESTER
For further details see p. 218
Satis House, Boley Hill, Rochester, Kent ME1 1TE
Tel: 01634 888555
Email: admissions@kings-rochester.co.uk
Website: www.kings-rochester.co.uk
Principal: Mr B Charles
Age range: 3–18 years
No. of pupils: 680 VIth105
Fees: Day £2,895–£7,765 FB £8,870–£12,860

Lorenden Preparatory School
Painter's Forstal, Faversham, Kent ME13 0EN
Tel: 01795 590030
Head of School: Mr Richard McIntosh
Age range: 3–11 years
No. of pupils: 122

Marlborough House School
High Street, Hawkhurst, Kent TN18 4PY
Tel: 01580 753555
Head: Mr Eddy Newton
Age range: 2½–13 years
No. of pupils: 250
Fees: Day £9,165–£18,690

NORTHBOURNE PARK SCHOOL
For further details see p. 224
Betteshanger, Deal, Kent CT14 0NW
Tel: 01304 611215
Email: admissions@northbournepark.com
Website: www.northbournepark.com
Headmaster: Mr Mark Hammond BA (Hons), PGCE, MA
Age range: 2–13 years (boarding from 7)
No. of pupils: 176
Fees: Day £11,025–£18,663 WB £23,490 FB £27,198

OneSchool Global UK Maidstone Campus
Heath Road, Maidstone, Kent ME17 4HT
Tel: 03000 700 507
Age range: 7–18 years

Radnor House, Sevenoaks
Combe Bank Drive, Sevenoaks, Kent TN14 6AE
Tel: 01959 563720
Head of School: Mr Fraser Halliwell
Age range: 2–18 years

Rochester Independent College
254 St Margaret's Banks, Rochester, Kent ME1 1HY
Tel: +44 (0)163 482 8115
Head of School: Mr Alistair Brownlow
Age range: 11–18 years

Rose Hill School
Coniston Avenue, Tunbridge Wells, Kent TN4 9SY
Tel: 01892 525591
Head: Ms Emma Neville
Age range: 3–13 years

Russell House School
Station Road, Otford, Sevenoaks, Kent TN14 5QU
Tel: 01959 522352
Headmaster: Mr Craig McCarthy
Age range: 2–11 years

Sackville School
Tonbridge Road, Hildenborough, Tonbridge, Kent TN11 9HN
Tel: 01732 838888
Headteacher: Ms Leoni Ellis
Age range: 11–18 years

Saint Ronan's School
Water Lane, Hawkhurst, Kent TN18 5DJ
Tel: 01580 752271
Headmaster: Mr William Trelawny-Vernon BSc(Hons)
Age range: 3–13 years

Sevenoaks Preparatory School
Godden Green, Sevenoaks, Kent TN15 0JU
Tel: 01732 762336
Headmaster: Mr Luke Harrison
Age range: 2–13 years

Sevenoaks School
High Street, Sevenoaks, Kent TN13 1HU
Tel: +44 (0)1732 455133
Head of School: Mr Jesse R Elzinga AB MSt FCCT
Age range: 11–18 years
No. of pupils: 1189
Fees: Day £26,721–£30,348 FB £42,921–£46,566

Solefield School
Solefields Road, Sevenoaks, Kent TN13 1PH
Tel: 01732 452142
Headmistress: Ms Helen McClure
Age range: B4–13 years

Somerhill
Tonbridge, Kent TN11 0NJ
Tel: 01732 352124
Principal: Mr Duncan Sinclair
Age range: 2–13 years

Spring Grove School
Harville Road, Wye, Kent TN25 5EZ
Tel: 01233 812337
Head of School: Mrs Therésa Jaggard
Age range: 2–11 years
No. of pupils: 229
Fees: Day £9,780–£13,775

St Andrew's School
24–28 Watts Avenue, Rochester, Medway, Kent ME1 1SA
Tel: 01634 843479
Principal: Mrs E Steinmann-Gilbert
Age range: 2½–11 years

St Edmund's School
St Thomas Hill, Canterbury, Kent CT2 8HU
Tel: 01227 475601
Head: Mr Edward O'Connor MA (Cantab), MPhil (Oxon), MEd (Cantab)
Age range: 2–18 years (boarding from 11)
No. of pupils: 602

St Faith's Prep
5 The Street, Ash, Canterbury, Kent CT3 2HH
Tel: 01304 813409
Headmaster: Mr Lawrence Groves
Age range: 2–11 years

ST LAWRENCE COLLEGE
For further details see p. 240
College Road, Ramsgate, Kent CT11 7AE
Tel: 01843 572931
Email: admissions@slcuk.com
Website: www.slcuk.com
Head of College: Mr Barney Durrant
Age range: 3–18 years
No. of pupils: 535
Fees: Day £8,814–£20,877 FB £29,454–£40,899

St Michael's Preparatory School
Otford Court, Row Dow, Otford, Sevenoaks, Kent TN14 5RY
Tel: 01959 522137
Head: Mr Nik Pears
Age range: 2–13 years

Steephill School
Off Castle Hill, Fawkham, Longfield, Kent DA3 7BG
Tel: 01474 702107
Head: Mr John Abbott
Age range: 3–11 years

Sutton Valence Preparatory School
Church Road, Chart Sutton, Maidstone, Kent ME17 3RF
Tel: 01622 842117
Head: Miss C Corkran
Age range: 2–11 years

Sutton Valence School
North Street, Sutton Valence, Kent ME17 3HL
Tel: 01622 845200
Headmaster: Mr James A Thomas MA (Cantab) MA (London) NPQH
Age range: 11–18 years (boarding from 11)
No. of pupils: 557

The Duke of York's Royal Military School
Guston, Dover, Kent CT15 5EQ
Tel: 01304 245023
Principal: Mr Alex Foreman
Age range: 11–18 years

The Granville School
2 Bradbourne Park Road, Sevenoaks, Kent TN13 3LJ
Tel: 01732 453039
Headmistress: Mrs Louise Lawrance B. Prim. Ed. (Hons)
Age range: B3–4 years G3–11 years

The Junior King's School, Canterbury
Milner Court, Sturry, Canterbury, Kent CT2 0AY
Tel: 01227 714000
Head of School: Ms Emma Károlyi
Age range: 3–13 years

The King's School, Canterbury
Lattergate Office, 25 The Precincts, Canterbury, Kent CT1 2ES
Tel: 01227 595501
Head of School: Ms Jude Lowson
Age range: 13–18 years

The Mead School
16 Frant Road, Tunbridge Wells, Kent TN2 5SN
Tel: 01892 525837
Headmistress: Ms Catherine Openshaw
Age range: 3–11 years

The New Beacon School
Brittains Lane, Sevenoaks, Kent TN13 2PB
Tel: 01732 452131
Head of School: Mrs Sarah Brownsdon
Age range: B3–13 years
No. of pupils: 350

The Worthgate School
68 New Dover Road, Canterbury, Kent CT1 3LQ
Tel: +44 (0)1227 866540
Acting Principal: Dr Nicola Robinson
Age range: 13–21 years
No. of pupils: 450
Fees: Day £17,370–£27,990 FB £13,230–£19,140

Tonbridge School
High Street, Tonbridge, Kent TN9 1JP
Tel: 01732 304297
Headmaster: Mr James Priory MA (Oxon)
Age range: B13–18 years
No. of pupils: 795
Fees: Day £35,067 FB £46,740

Walthamstow Hall School
Holly Bush Lane, Sevenoaks, Kent TN13 3UL
Tel: 01732 451334
Headmistress: Miss Stephanie Ferro
Age range: G3–18 years

Wellesley House
114 Ramsgate Road, Broadstairs, Kent CT10 2DG
Tel: 01843 862991
Headmaster: Mr G D Franklin
Age range: 2–13 years

Portsmouth

Madani Academy
Merefield House, Nutfield Place, , Portsmouth PO1 4JZ
Tel: 02392 830764
Headteacher: Mr Luthfur Rahman
Age range: 4–16 years

Surrey

Aberdour School
Brighton Road, Burgh Heath, Tadworth, Surrey KT20 6AJ
Tel: +44 (0)1737 354119
Headmaster: Mr S. D. Collins
Age range: 2–11 years
No. of pupils: 335
Fees: Day £4,920–£17,070

ACS Cobham International School
Heywood, Portsmouth Road, Cobham, Surrey KT11 1BL
Tel: +44 (0) 1932 867251
Head of School: Mr Barnaby Sandow
Age range: 2–18 years

ACS Egham International School
London Road, Egham, Surrey TW20 0HS
Tel: +44 (0) 1784 430800
Head of School: Mr Jeremy Lewis
Age range: 4–18 years

Aldro School
Lombard Street, Shackleford, Godalming, Surrey GU8 6AS
Tel: 01483 810266
Headmaster: Mr Chris Carlier
Age range: 7–13 years

Amesbury School
Hazel Grove, Hindhead, Surrey GU26 6BL
Tel: 01428 604322
Head of School: Mr Jonathan Whybrow
Age range: 2–13 years

Banstead Preparatory School
Sutton Lane, Banstead, Surrey SM7 3RA
Tel: 01737 363601
Head of School: Mr Jon Chesworth
Age range: 2–11 years

Barfield School
Guildford Road, Runfold, Farnham, Surrey GU10 1PB
Tel: 01252 782271
Headmaster: Mr Andy Boyle
Age range: 2–11 years

Barrow Hills School
Roke Lane, Witley, Godalming, Surrey GU8 5NY
Tel: +44 (0)1428 683639
Headmaster: Mr John Towers
Age range: 2–13 years
No. of pupils: 221
Fees: Day £11,985–£19,500

Belmont School
Pasturewood Road, Holmbury St Mary, Dorking, Surrey RH5 6LQ
Tel: 01306 730852
Age range: 3–16 years
No. of pupils: 190

Bishopsgate School
Bishopsgate Road, Englefield Green, Egham, Surrey TW20 0YJ
Tel: 01784 432109
Headmaster: Mr R Williams
Age range: 3–13 years
No. of pupils: 370

Box Hill School
London Road, Mickleham, Dorking, Surrey RH5 6EA
Tel: 01372 373382
Headmaster: Cory Lowde
Age range: 11–18 years
No. of pupils: 410
Fees: Day £21,585 WB £31,635

Caterham School
Harestone Valley Road, Caterham, Surrey CR3 6YA
Tel: 01883 343028
Headmaster: Mr C. W. Jones MA(Cantab)
Age range: 3–18 years

Charterhouse
Godalming, Surrey GU7 2DX
Tel: +44 (0)1483 291501
Head: Dr Alex Peterken
Age range: B13–18 years (boarding from 13) G16–18 years
No. of pupils: 940
Fees: Day £12,180 FB £14,740

Chinthurst School
52 Tadworth Street, Tadworth, Surrey KT20 5QZ
Tel: 01737 812011
Head: Miss Catherine Trundle
Age range: 3–11 years

City of London Freemen's School
Ashtead Park, Ashtead, Surrey KT21 1ET
Tel: +44 (0)1372 822400
Headmaster: Mr Roland J. Martin
Age range: 7–18 years

Claremont Fan Court School
Claremont Drive, Esher, Surrey KT10 9LY
Tel: 01372 473794
Head: Mr William Brierly
Age range: 21/2–18 years
No. of pupils: 1100

Coworth Flexlands School
Chertsey Road, Chobham, Surrey GU24 8TE
Tel: 01276 855707
Head of School: Miss Nicola Cowell
Age range: 21/2–11 years
No. of pupils: 120

CRANLEIGH SCHOOL
For further details see p. 198
Horseshoe Lane, Cranleigh, Surrey GU6 8QQ
Tel: +44 (0) 1483 273666
Email: admissions@cranleigh.org
Website: www.cranleigh.org
Headmaster: Mr Martin Reader MA, MPhil, MBA
Age range: 7–18 years (including Prep School)
No. of pupils: 695 VIth281
Fees: Day £37,905 FB £46,035

Cranmore School
Epsom Road, West Horsley, Surrey KT24 6AT
Tel: 01483 280340
Headmaster: Mr Barry Everitt
Age range: 2–18 years

Danes Hill School
Leatherhead Road, Oxshott, Surrey KT22 0JG
Tel: 01372 842509
Head of School: Mrs Maxine Shaw
Age range: 3–13 years
No. of pupils: 706
Fees: Day £4,952–£6,984

Danesfield Manor School
Rydens Avenue, Walton-on-Thames, Surrey KT12 3JB
Tel: 01932 220930
Head Teacher: Mrs Jo Smith
Age range: 2–11 years

Downsend School
1 Leatherhead Road, Leatherhead, Surrey KT22 8TJ
Tel: 01372 372197
Headmaster: Mr Ian Thorpe
Age range: 2–16 years
No. of pupils: 792
Fees: Day £11,970–£17,985

Duke of Kent School
Peaslake Road, Ewhurst, Surrey GU6 7NS
Tel: 01483 277313
Head: Mrs Sue Knox BA(Hons) MBA MEd
Age range: 3–16 years
No. of pupils: 316
Fees: Day £2,740–£6,540

Dunottar School
High Trees Road, Reigate, Surrey RH2 7EL
Tel: 01737 761945
Headmaster: Mr Mark Tottman
Age range: 11–18 years

Edgeborough
84 Frensham Road, Frensham, Farnham, Surrey GU10 3AH
Tel: 01252 792495
Headmaster: Mr Daniel Cox
Age range: 2–13 years (boarding from 7)
No. of pupils: 370

Epsom College
College Road, Epsom, Surrey KT17 4JQ
Tel: 01372 821000
Acting Headmaster: Mr Paul Williams
Age range: 11–18 years (boarding from 13)

Essendene Lodge School
Essendene Road, Caterham, Surrey CR3 5PB
Tel: 01883 348349
Headteacher: Mrs K Ali
Age range: 2–11 years

Ewell Castle School
Church Street, Ewell, Epsom, Surrey KT17 2AW
Tel: 020 8393 1413
Principal: Mr Silas Edmonds
Age range: 3–18 years
No. of pupils: 670
Fees: Day £5,382–£18,141

Feltonfleet School
Byfleet Road, Cobham, Surrey KT11 1DR
Tel: 01932 862264
Headmistress: Mrs Shelley Lance
Age range: 3–13 years (boarding from 7)
No. of pupils: 492

Frensham Heights
Rowledge, Farnham, Surrey GU10 4EA
Tel: 01252 792561
Head: Mr Andrew Fisher
Age range: 3–18 years (boarding from 11)

Glenesk School
Ockham Road North, East Horsley, Surrey KT24 6NS
Tel: 01483 282329
Headmistress: Mrs Sarah Bradley
Age range: 2–7 years
No. of pupils: 120
Fees: Day £12,762–£14,424

GORDON'S SCHOOL
For further details see p. 210
West End, Woking, Surrey GU24 9PT
Tel: 01276 858084
Email: registrar@gordons.school
Website: www.gordons.school
Head Teacher: Andrew Moss MEd
Age range: 11–18 years
No. of pupils: 979 VIth353
Fees: WB £20,664 FB £22,050

Greenfield School
Old Woking Road, Woking, Surrey GU22 8HY
Tel: 01483 772525
Headmistress: Mrs. Tania Botting MEd
Age range: 6 months–11 years
No. of pupils: 347

Guildford High School
London Road, Guildford, Surrey GU1 1SJ
Tel: 01483 561440
Headmistress: Mrs F J Boulton BSc, MA
Age range: G4–18 years

Hall Grove School
London Road, Bagshot, Surrey GU19 5HZ
Tel: 01276 473059
Principal: Mr Alastair Graham
Age range: 3–13 years (boarding from 8)

Halstead St Andrew's School (Lower)
Woodham Rise, Woking, Surrey GU21 4EE
Tel: 01483 772682
Head of School: Mr Dominic Fitzgerald
Age range: 2–8 years
Fees: Day £1,425–£4,580

Halstead St Andrew's School (Upper)
Church Hill House, Wilson Way, Horsell, Woking, Surrey GU21 4QW
Tel: 01483 760943
Head of School: Mr Dominic Fitzgerald
Age range: 8–13 years (16 from Sept 2026)
Fees: Day £5,420–£6,135

Hazelwood School
Wolf's Hill, Limpsfield, Oxted, Surrey RH8 0QU
Tel: 01883 712194
Head: Mrs Lindie Louw
Age range: 9 months–13 years
No. of pupils: 572
Fees: Day £3,800–£6,055

Hoe Bridge School
Hoe Place, Old Woking Road, Woking, Surrey GU22 8JE
Tel: 01483 760018
Headmaster: Mr C Webster MA BSc (Hons) PGCE
Age range: 2–16 years

Hurtwood House
Holmbury St. Mary, Dorking, Surrey RH5 6NU
Tel: 01483 279000
Principal: Mr Cosmo Jackson
Age range: 16–18 years
No. of pupils: 360
Fees: Day £29,748 FB £44,622

KING EDWARD'S WITLEY
For further details see p. 216
Petworth Road, Godalming, Surrey GU8 5SG
Tel: 01428 686700
Email: admissions@kesw.org
Website: www.kesw.org
Head: Mrs Joanna Wright
Age range: 11–18 years
No. of pupils: 484
Fees: Day £20,025–£23,985 WB £35,985–£36,990 FB £38,205–£38,955

Kingswood House School
56 West Hill, Epsom, Surrey KT19 8LG
Tel: 01372 723590
Headmaster: Mr Duncan Murphy BA (Hons), MEd, FRSA
Age range: 4–16 years
No. of pupils: 250

Lingfield College
St Piers Lane, Lingfield, Surrey RH7 6PN
Tel: 01342 832407
Headmaster: Mr Richard Bool
Age range: 0–18 years
No. of pupils: 940
Fees: Day £3,500–£6,810

Little Downsend Ashtead
Ashtead Lodge, 22 Oakfield Road, Ashtead, Surrey KT21 2RE
Tel: 01372 385439
Head of School: Ms Vanessa Conlan
Age range: 2–6 years

Little Downsend Epsom
Epsom Lodge, 6 Norman Avenue, Epsom, Surrey KT17 3AB
Tel: 01372 385438
Head of School: Ms Vanessa Conlan
Age range: 2–6 years

Little Downsend Leatherhead
13 Epsom Road, Leatherhead, Surrey KT22 8ST
Tel: 01372 385437
Head of School: Ms Vanessa Conlan
Age range: 2–6 years

Longacre School
Hullbrook Lane, Shamley Green, Guildford, Surrey GU5 0NQ
Tel: 01483 893225
Head of School: Mr Matthew Bryan MA(Cantab.), MA(Oxon.), MSc, FRSA
Age range: 2–11 years

Lyndhurst School
36 The Avenue, Camberley, Surrey GU15 3NE
Tel: 01276 22895
Head: Mr Andrew Rudkin
Age range: 3–11 years

MANOR HOUSE SCHOOL, BOOKHAM
For further details see p. 222
Manor House Lane, Little Bookham, Leatherhead, Surrey KT23 4EN
Tel: 01372 457077
Email: admin@manorhouseschool.org
Website: www.manorhouseschool.org
Headteacher: Ms Tracey Fantham BA (Hons) MA NPQH
Age range: B2–6 years G2–16 years
No. of pupils: 280
Fees: Day £10,980–£20,634

Micklefield School
10 Somers Road, Reigate, Surrey RH2 9DU
Tel: 01737 224212
Head: Mr R Ardé
Age range: 3–11 years
No. of pupils: 210
Fees: Day £10,965–£13,935

Milbourne Lodge School
Arbrook Lane, Esher, Surrey KT10 9EG
Tel: 01372 462737
Head: Mrs Judy Waite
Age range: 4–13 years
No. of pupils: 278
Fees: Day £14,475–£18,195

Notre Dame School
Cobham, Surrey KT11 1HA
Tel: 01932 869990
Head of Seniors: Mrs Anna King MEd, MA (Cantab), PGCE
Age range: B2–7 years G2–18 years

Oakhyrst Grange School
160 Stanstead Road, Caterham, Surrey CR3 6AF
Tel: 01883 343344
Headmaster: Mr Alex Gear
Age range: 4–11 years

OneSchool Global UK Hindhead Campus
Tilford Road, Hindhead, Surrey GU26 6SJ
Tel: 01428 601800
Age range: 7–18 years

OneSchool Global UK Kenley Campus
Victor Beamish Avenue, Kenley, Surrey CR3 5FX
Tel: 01883 338634
Age range: 7–18 years

Parkside School
The Manor, Stoke d'Abernon, Cobham, Surrey KT11 3PX
Tel: 01932 862749
Headteacher: Ms Nicole Janssen
Age range: B2–13 years G2–4 years
No. of pupils: 270

Prior's Field
Priorsfield Road, Godalming, Surrey GU7 2RH
Tel: 01483 810551
Head of School: Mrs Tracey Kirnig
Age range: G11–18 years (boarding from 11)

Reed's School
Sandy Lane, Cobham, Surrey KT11 2ES
Tel: 01932 869001
Headmaster: Mr Mark Hoskins
Age range: B11–18 years (boarding from 11) G16–18 years

Reigate Grammar School
Reigate Road, Reigate, Surrey RH2 0QS
Tel: 01737 222231
Headmaster: Mr Shaun Fenton MA (Oxon) MEd (Oxon)
Age range: 11–18 years

Reigate St Mary's Prep & Choir School
Chart Lane, Reigate, Surrey RH2 7RN
Tel: 01737 244880
Headmaster: Mr Marcus Culverwell MA
Age range: 2–11 years

RGS Guildford
High Street, Guildford, Surrey GU1 3BB
Tel: 01483 880600
Headmaster: Dr J M Cox BSc, PhD
Age range: B11–18 years

RGS Guildford Prep
Maori Road, Guildford, Surrey GU1 2EL
Tel: 01483 880650
Head of School: Mr Toby Freeman-Day
Age range: B3–11 years

Ripley Court School
Rose Lane, Ripley, Surrey GU23 6NE
Tel: 01483 225217
Headmistress: Ms Aislinn Clarke
Age range: 3–11 years

Rowan Preparatory School
6 Fitzalan Road, Claygate, Esher, Surrey KT10 0LX
Tel: 01372 462627
Headmistress: Mrs Susan Clarke BEd, NPQH
Age range: G2–11 years

Royal Alexandra and Albert School
Gatton Park, Reigate, Surrey RH2 0TD
Tel: 01737 649 000
Headteacher: Mr M.P. Thomas
Age range: 7–18 years

Aberdeen

Albyn School
17–23 Queen's Road,
Aberdeen AB15 4PB
Tel: 01224 322408
Headmaster: Mr Stefan Horsman
Age range: 2–18 years

International School of Aberdeen
Pitfodels House, North Deeside Road,
Pitfodels, Cults, Aberdeen AB15 9PN
Tel: 01224 730300
Head of School: Mr Nick Little
Age range: 3–18 years

Robert Gordon's College
Schoolhill, Aberdeen AB10 1FE
Tel: 01224 646346
Head of College: Mr
Robin Macpherson
Age range: 3–18 years

St Margaret's School for Girls
17 Albyn Place, Aberdeen AB10 1RU
Tel: +44 (0)1224 584466
Headmistress: Miss Anna Tomlinson
Age range: B3–5 years G3–18 years

Aberdeenshire

OneSchool Global UK Caledonia (North) Campus
Millden, Balmedie,
Aberdeenshire AB23 8YY
Tel: 01259 303030
Age range: 7–18 years

Angus

Lathallan School
Brotherton Castle, Johnshaven,
Montrose, Angus DD10 0HN
Tel: 01561 362220
Headmaster: Mr Richard Toley
Age range: 6 months–18 years

Argyll & Bute

Lomond School
10 Stafford Street, Helensburgh,
Argyll & Bute G84 9JX
Tel: +44 (0)1436 672476
Principal: Mrs Johanna Urquhart
Age range: 3–18 years
No. of pupils: 360

Borders

St. Mary's School
Abbey Park, Melrose, Borders TD6 9LN
Tel: 01896 822517
Headmaster: Mr Liam Harvey
Age range: 2–13 years

Clackmannanshire

Dollar Academy
Dollar, Clackmannanshire FK14 7DU
Tel: 01259 742511
Rector: Mr Ian Munro
Age range: 4–18 years
(boarding from 10)
No. of pupils: 1340
Fees: Day £10,899–£14,571 WB
£28,197–£31,869 FB £30,051–£33,723

OneSchool Global UK Caledonia (South) Campus
The Pavillions, Stirling Road, Alloa,
Clackmannanshire FK10 1TA
Tel: 01259 303030
Age range: 7–18 years

Dundee

High School of Dundee
Euclid Crescent, Dundee DD1 1HU
Tel: 01382 202921
Rector: Mrs Lise Hudson
Age range: 3–18 years
No. of pupils: 1000
Fees: Day £9,618–£13,650

East Lothian

Belhaven Hill School
Belhaven Road, Dunbar,
East Lothian EH42 1NN
Tel: 01368 862785
Headmaster: Mr. Olly Langton
Age range: 5–13 years

Loretto Junior School
North Esk Lodge, 1 North High Street,
Musselburgh, East Lothian EH21 6JA
Tel: 0131 653 4570
Headmaster: Mr Andrew Dickenson
Age range: 3–12 years

LORETTO SCHOOL
For further details see p. 296
Linkfield Road, Musselburgh,
East Lothian EH21 7RE
Tel: +44 (0)131 653 4455
Email: admissions@loretto.com
Website: www.loretto.com
Head of School:
Dr. Graham R. W. Hawley
Age range: 3–18 years
No. of pupils: 500
Fees: Day £3,212–£9,182
FB £8,782–£13,485

The Compass School
West Road, Haddington,
East Lothian EH41 3RD
Tel: 01620 822642
Headmaster: Mr Mark Becher
MA(Hons), PGCE
Age range: 3–12 years

Edinburgh

Basil Paterson School & College
65/66 Queen Street, Edinburgh EH2 4NA
Tel: 01312 253802
Age range: 14–16+ years

Cargilfield School
45 Gamekeeper's Road,
Edinburgh EH4 6HU
Tel: 0131 336 2207
Headmaster: Mr. Robert Taylor
Age range: 3–13 years

Clifton Hall School
Newbridge, Edinburgh EH28 8LQ
Tel: 0131 333 1359
Headmaster: Mr R Grant
Age range: 3–18 years

Edinburgh Montessori Arts School
18N Liberton Brae, Edinburgh EH16 6AE
Tel: 0131 600 0123
Principal: Ms Emma Rattigan
Age range: 1–18 years

Edinburgh Steiner School
60–64 Spylaw Road,
Edinburgh EH10 5BR
Tel: 0131 337 3410
Age range: 2–18 years
No. of pupils: 380

ESMS Junior School
11 Queensferry Terrace,
Edinburgh EH4 3EQ
Tel: +44 (0)131 311 1111
Head of School: Mr Mike Kane
Age range: 3–11 years

Fettes College
Carrington Road, Edinburgh EH4 1QX
Tel: +44 (0)131 332 2281
Head of School: Mrs Helen Harrison
Age range: 13–18 years

West Sussex

Ardingly College
College Road, Ardingly, Haywards Heath, West Sussex RH17 6SQ
Tel: +44 (0)1444 893320
Headmaster: Mr Ben Figgis
Age range: 13–18 years

Ardingly College Preparatory School
College Road, Haywards Heath, West Sussex RH17 6SQ
Tel: +44 (0)1444 893320
Head of Prep School: Mr Harry Hastings
Age range: 21/2–13 years

Brambletye
Brambletye, East Grinstead, West Sussex RH19 3PD
Tel: 01342 321004
Headmaster: Mr Will Brooks
Age range: 2–13 years

BURGESS HILL GIRLS
For further details see p. 192
Keymer Road, Burgess Hill, West Sussex RH15 0EG
Tel: 01444 241050
Email: admissions@burgesshillgirls.com
Website: http://burgesshillgirls.com
Head of School: Lars Fox
Age range: B21/2–4 years G21/2–18 years
No. of pupils: 503 VIth59
Fees: Day £10,500–£23,940 FB £36,960–£42,540

Christ's Hospital
Horsham, West Sussex RH13 0LJ
Tel: 01403 211293
Head Teacher: Mr Simon Reid
Age range: 11–18 years

Conifers School
Egmont Road, Easebourne, Midhurst, West Sussex GU29 9BG
Tel: 01730 813243
Head of School: Miss Emma Fownes
Age range: 2–13 years

Copthorne Prep School
Effingham Lane, Copthorne, West Sussex RH10 3HR
Tel: 01342 712311
Headmaster: Mr Nathan Close
Age range: 2–13 years

Cottesmore School
Buchan Hill, Pease Pottage, West Sussex RH11 9AU
Tel: 01293 520648
Head of School: Mr Tom Rogerson
Age range: 4–13 years

Cumnor House Sussex
London Road, Danehill, Haywards Heath, West Sussex RH17 7HT
Tel: 01825 790347
Headmaster: Mr Fergus Llewellyn
Age range: 2–13 years (boarding from 11)

Dorset House School
The Manor, Church Lane, Bury, Pulborough, West Sussex RH20 1PB
Tel: 01798 831456
Headmaster: Mr Matt Thomas Med BA Ed (Hons) (Exeter) FRGS
Age range: 4–13 years (boarding from 9)
No. of pupils: 140
Fees: Day £9,315–£18,945 WB £1,258–£4,488

FARLINGTON SCHOOL
For further details see p. 208
Strood Park, Horsham, West Sussex RH12 3PN
Tel: 01403 282573
Email: admissions@farlingtonschool.com
Website: www.farlingtonschool.com
Headmaster: Mr James Passam
Age range: 6 months–18 years
No. of pupils: 413
Fees: Day £2,200–£6,690 WB £11,300 FB £12,150

Great Ballard School
Eartham House, Eartham, Nr Chichester, West Sussex PO18 0LR
Tel: 01243 814236
Head of School: Mr Matt King
Age range: 21/2–16 years
No. of pupils: 136
Fees: Day £8,580–£16,200

Great Walstead School
East Mascalls Lane, Lindfield, Haywards Heath, West Sussex RH16 2QL
Tel: 01444 483528
Headmaster: Mr Chris Calvey
Age range: 21/2–13 years
No. of pupils: 345
Fees: Day £3,098–£5,938

Handcross Park School
London Road, Handcross, Haywards Heath, West Sussex RH17 6HF
Tel: 01444 400526
Headmaster: Mr Richard Brown
Age range: 2–13 years (boarding from 8)

Hurst College
College Lane, Hurstpierpoint, West Sussex BN6 9JS
Tel: 01273 833636
Headmaster: Mr. Dominic Mott
Age range: 4–18 years (boarding from 13)
No. of pupils: 1295

Lancing College
Lancing, West Sussex BN15 0RW
Tel: 01273 452213
Head Master: Mr Dominic T Oliver MPhil
Age range: 13–18 years

Lancing Prep Worthing
Broadwater Road, Worthing, West Sussex BN14 8HU
Tel: 01903 201123
Head: Mrs Heather Beeby
Age range: 2–13 years

Oakwood Preparatory School
Chichester, West Sussex PO18 9AN
Tel: 01243 575209
Headteacher: Mrs Clare Bradbury
Age range: 21/2–11 years
No. of pupils: 310
Fees: Day £3,450–£5,520

Our Lady of Sion School
Gratwicke Road, Worthing, West Sussex BN11 4BL
Tel: 01903 204063
Headmaster: Mr Steven Jeffery
Age range: 3–18 years

Pennthorpe School
Church Street, Horsham, West Sussex RH12 3HJ
Tel: 01403 822391
Hea: Ms Lydia Waller
Age range: 2–13 years

Rikkyo School in England
Guildford Road, Rudgwick, Horsham, West Sussex RH12 3BE
Tel: +44 (0)1403 822107
Principal: Mr Tohru Okano
Age range: 10–18 years

SEAFORD COLLEGE
For further details see p. 228
Lavington Park, Petworth, West Sussex GU28 0NB
Tel: 01798 867392
Email: headmasterpa@seaford.org
Website: www.seaford.org
Headmaster: J P Green MA BA
Age range: 5–18 years
No. of pupils: 943 VIth264
Fees: Day £12,720–£26,355 WB £26,475–£35,685 FB £40,740

Shoreham College
St Julian's Lane, Shoreham-by-Sea, West Sussex BN43 6YW
Tel: 01273 592681
Principal: Mrs Sarah Bakhtiari
Age range: 3–16 years

Slindon College
Slindon House, Top Road, Slindon, Arundel, West Sussex BN18 0RH
Tel: 01243 814320
Headteacher: Mrs Sotiria Vlahodimou
Age range: B8–18 years (boarding from 11)

Sompting Abbotts Preparatory School
Church Lane, Sompting, West Sussex BN15 0AZ
Tel: 01903 235960
Headmaster: Mr Stuart Douch
Age range: 2–13 years

Steyning Grammar School
Shooting Field, Steyning,
West Sussex BN44 3RX
Tel: 01903 814555
Headteacher: Mr Adam Whitehead
Age range: 11–18 years

The Prebendal School
52–55 West Street, Chichester,
West Sussex PO19 1RT
Tel: 01243 772220
Head: Ms Alison Napier
Age range: 3–13 years
(boarding from 7)

Westbourne House School
Coach Road, Chichester,
West Sussex PO20 2BH
Tel: 01243 782739
Headmaster: Mr Martin Barker
Age range: 2½–13 years
(boarding from 7)

Windlesham House School
London Road, Washington,
Pulborough, West Sussex RH20 4AY
Tel: 01903 874700
Headmaster: Mr Ben Evans
Age range: 4–13 years
(boarding from 7)
£

Worth School
Paddockhurst Road, Turners Hill,
Crawley, West Sussex RH10 4SD
Tel: +44 (0)1342 710200
Head Master: Mr Stuart McPherson
Age range: 11–18 years
(boarding from 13)
A £ IB 16·

South-East: ENGLAND

South-West

KEY TO SYMBOLS

- *Boys' school*
- *Girls' school*
- *International school*
- *Tutorial or sixth form college*
- *A levels*
- *Boarding accommodation*
- *Bursaries*
- *International Baccalaureate*
- *Learning support*
- *Entrance at 16+*
- *Vocational qualifications*
- *Independent Association of Preparatory Schools*
- *The Headmasters' & Headmistresses' Conference*
- *Independent Schools Association*
- *Girls' School Association*
- *Boarding Schools' Association*
- *Society of Heads*

Unless otherwise indicated, all schools are coeducational day schools. Single-sex and boarding schools will be indicated by the relevant icon.

Bath & North-East Somerset

Bath Academy
27 Queen Square, Bath, Bath & North-East Somerset BA1 2HX
Tel: 01225 334577
Principal: Mr Tim Naylor
Age range: 14–19+ years

Beechen Cliff School
Kipling Avenue, Bath, Bath & North-East Somerset BA2 4RE
Tel: 01225 480466
Headteacher: Mr Tim Markall
Age range: B11–18 years G16–18 years

Downside School
Stratton-on-the-Fosse, Radstock, Bath, Bath & North-East Somerset BA3 4RJ
Tel: 01761 235100
Head Master: Mr Andrew Hobbs
Age range: 11–18 years
No. of pupils: 360
Fees: Day £18,705–£22,200 FB £28,245–£37,905

King Edward's Junior School
North Road, Bath, Bath & North-East Somerset BA2 6JA
Tel: 01225 464218
Head of School: Mr Greg Taylor
Age range: 7–11 years

King Edward's Pre-Prep & Nursery School
Weston Lane, Bath, Bath & North-East Somerset BA1 4AQ
Tel: 01225 421681
Head of School: Ms Jayne Gilbert
Age range: 3–7 years

King Edward's Senior & Sixth Form School
North Road, Bath, Bath & North-East Somerset BA2 6HU
Tel: 01225 464313
Head of School: Mr Martin J Boden
Age range: 11–18 years

Kingswood School
Lansdown Road, Bath, Bath & North-East Somerset BA1 5RG
Tel: 01225 734200
Headmaster: Mr Andrew Gordon-Brown
Age range: 9 months–18 years

Monkton Prep School
Church Road, Combe Down, Bath, Bath & North-East Somerset BA2 7ET
Tel: 01225 831200
Head: Mrs Catherine Winchcombe
Age range: 2–13 years (boarding from 7)
No. of pupils: 275

Monkton Senior School
Monkton Combe, Bath, Bath & North-East Somerset BA2 7HG
Tel: 01225 721133
Principal: Mr Chris Wheeler
Age range: 13–18 years (boarding from 13)
No. of pupils: 395 VIth173
Fees: Day £25,500–£26,790 WB £37,770–£38,790 FB £41,625–£42,735

Prior Park College
Ralph Allen Drive, Bath, Bath & North-East Somerset BA2 5AH
Tel: +44 (0)1225 835353
Headmaster: Mr Ben Horan
Age range: 11–18 years

Royal High School Bath, GDST
Lansdown Road, Bath, Bath & North-East Somerset BA1 5SZ
Tel: +44 (0)1225 313877
Head: Mrs Kate Reynolds
Age range: G3–18 years (boarding from 11)
No. of pupils: 580
Fees: Day £5,294–£5,526 FB £11,965–£12,577

The Paragon School
Lyncombe House, Lyncombe Vale, Bath, Bath & North-East Somerset BA2 4LT
Tel: 01225 310837
Head of School: Ms Rosie Allen
Age range: 3–11 years

Bristol

Badminton School
Westbury Road, Westbury-on-Trym, Bristol BS9 3BA
Tel: 0117 905 5200
Headmistress: Mrs Rebecca Tear BSc, MA, PGCE
Age range: G3–18 years (boarding from 9)

Bristol Grammar School
University Road, Bristol BS8 1SR
Tel: 0117 973 6006
Headmaster: Mr Jaideep Barot
Age range: 4–18 years

Bristol International College
Torwood House, 8 Durdham Park, Redland, Bristol BS6 6XA
Tel: +44 (0)117 374 4888
CEO & Principal: Mr John Milne
Age range: 14–18 years

Bristol Steiner School
Redland Hill House, Redland, Bristol BS6 6UX
Tel: 0117 933 9990
Acting Head Teacher: Lorraine Swords
Age range: 3–11 years
No. of pupils: 128
Fees: Day £7,977

Cleve House School
254 Wells Road, Knowle, Bristol BS4 2PN
Tel: 0117 9777218
Head of School: Ms Clare Fraser
Age range: 2–11 years

Clifton College
32 College Road, Clifton, Bristol BS8 3JH
Tel: 0117 315 7000
Head of College: Dr Tim Greene MA DPhil
Age range: 13–18 years (boarding from 13)

Clifton College Preparatory School
The Avenue, Clifton, Bristol BS8 3HE
Tel: +44 (0)117 315 7502
Head of Preparatory School: Mr Jim Walton
Age range: 2–13 years (boarding from 8)

Clifton High School
College Road, Clifton, Bristol BS8 3JD
Tel: 0117 973 0201
Head of School: Mr Matthew Bennett
Age range: 3–18 years
No. of pupils: 734
Fees: Day £3,110–£5,285

Collegiate School, Bristol
Stapleton, Bristol BS16 1BJ
Tel: 0117 965 5207
Headmaster: Mr Jeremy McCullough
Age range: 3–18 years
No. of pupils: 816
Fees: Day £8,055–£14,625

Ecole Française de Bristol
Stanton Road, Southmead, Bristol BS10 5SJ
Tel: +44 (0)117 9692410
Age range: 3–16 years

Fairfield School
Fairfield Way, Backwell, Bristol BS48 3PD
Tel: 01275 462743
Headmistress: Mrs Lesley Barton
Age range: 2–11 years

Gracefield Preparatory School
266 Overndale Road, Fishponds, Bristol BS16 2RG
Tel: 0117 956 7977
Headteacher: Mr J Gunter
Age range: 4–11 years

LPW School
Princess Street, Bedminster, Bristol BS3 4AG
Tel: 0117 907 4500
Headteacher: Mr Dan Carter
Age range: 14–16 years

Queen Elizabeth's Hospital
Berkeley Place, Clifton, Bristol BS8 1JX
Tel: 0117 930 3040
Head: Mr Rupert Heathcote
Age range: B7–18 years G16–18 years

Redmaids' High Junior School
Grange Court Road, Westbury-on-Trym, Bristol BS9 4DP
Tel: 0117 962 9451
Headteacher: Mrs Lisa Brown BSc (Hons)
Age range: G7–11 years

Redmaids' High School Senior & Sixth Form
Westbury Road, Westbury-on-Trym, Bristol BS9 3AW
Tel: 0117 962 2641
Head: Mr Paul Dwyer
Age range: G11–18 years

The Downs Preparatory School
Wraxall, Bristol BS48 1PF
Tel: 01275 852008
Head: Ms Debbie Isaachsen
Age range: 4–13 years

Tockington Manor School
Washingpool Hill Road, Tockington, Bristol BS32 4NY
Tel: 01454 613229
Headmaster: Mr Stephen Symonds
Age range: 2–13 years

Torwood House School
8 Durdham Park, Redland, Bristol BS6 6XA
Tel: 01179 736620
Head Teacher: Mrs Dionne Seagrove B.Ed, M.Ed
Age range: 0–11 years

Cornwall

Polwhele House School
Truro, Cornwall TR4 9AE
Tel: 01872 273011
Head of School: Mrs Hilary Mann
Age range: 3–13 years

St Joseph's School
15 St Stephen's Hill, Launceston, Cornwall PL15 8HN
Tel: 01566 772580
Head Teacher: Mr Oliver Scott
Age range: 4–16 years

St. Piran's School
14 Trelissick Road, Hayle, Cornwall TR27 4HY
Tel: 01736 752612
Headteacher: Mrs Lucy Draycott
Age range: 4–16 years

Truro High School for Girls
Falmouth Road, Truro, Cornwall TR1 2HU
Tel: 01872 272830
Headmistress: Mrs Sarah Matthews
Age range: G4–18 years (boarding from 9)

Truro School
Trennick Lane, Truro, Cornwall TR1 1TH
Tel: 01872 272763
Head of School: Mr Andy Johnson
Age range: 3–18 years

Devon

Abbey School
Hampton Court, St Marychurch, Torquay, Devon TQ1 4PR
Tel: 01803 327868
Principal: Mrs Sylvia Greinig
Age range: 0–11 years

Blundell's Preparatory School
Milestones House, Blundell's Road, Tiverton, Devon EX16 4NA
Tel: 01884 252393
Head Master: Mr Andrew Southgate BA Ed (Hons)
Age range: 3–11 years

Blundell's School
Tiverton, Devon EX16 4DN
Tel: 01884 252543
Head: Mr Bart Wielenga BComm, Natal & Johannesburg, BEd
Age range: 11–18 years

Chances School
Red Rock, Sandy Lane, Dawlish, Devon EX7 0AF
Tel: 01626 864412
Headteacher: Mr Gary Hayes
Age range: 11–16 years

Exeter Cathedral School
The Chantry, Palace Gate, Exeter, Devon EX1 1HX
Tel: 01392 255298
Headmaster: James Featherstone
Age range: 3–13 years (boarding from 8)
No. of pupils: 271
Fees: Day £2,992–£4,900 FB £2,886

EXETER SCHOOL
For further details see p. 264
Victoria Park Road, Exeter, Devon EX2 4NS
Tel: 01392 307080
Email: admissions@exeterschool.org.uk
Website: www.exeterschool.org.uk
Head: Ms Louise Simpson
Age range: 3–18 years
No. of pupils: 1031
Fees: Day £2,900–£5,570

Fletewood School
88 North Road East, Plymouth, Devon PL4 6AN
Tel: 01752 663782
Headteacher: Mrs R Gray
Age range: 3–11 years

King's School
Hartley Road, Mannamead, Plymouth, Devon PL3 5LW
Tel: 01752 771789
Head of School: Mrs Clare Page
Age range: 8 months–11 years

KINGSLEY SCHOOL
For further details see p. 268
Northdown Road, Bideford, Devon EX39 3LY
Tel: 01237 426200
Email: admissions@kingsleyschoolbideford.co.uk
Website: www.kingsleydevon.com
Headteacher: Mr Robert Pavis
Age range: 0–18 years (boarding from 9)
No. of pupils: 395
Fees: Day £5,220 WB £8,370

Mount Kelly
Parkwood Road, Tavistock, Devon PL19 0HZ
Tel: +44 (0)1822 813100
Head of School: Mr. Guy Ayling
Age range: 3–18 years

OneSchool Global UK Plymouth Campus
Foulston Avenue, Plymouth, Devon PL5 1HL
Tel: 01752 363290
Age range: 7–18 years

Park School
Park Road, Dartington Hall, Totnes, Devon TQ9 6EQ
Tel: 01803 864588
Headteacher: Arnet Donkin
Age range: 3–12 years

Plymouth College
Ford Park, Plymouth, Devon PL4 6RN
Tel: 01752 505100
Headteacher: Mrs Jo Hayward
Age range: 3–18 years
No. of pupils: 569

Sands School
48 East Street, Ashburton, Devon TQ13 7AX
Tel: 01364 653666
Age range: 11–17 years

Shebbear College
Shebbear, Beaworthy, Devon EX21 5HJ
Tel: 01409 282000
Head: Ms Caroline Kirby
Age range: 4–18 years

South Devon Steiner School
Hood Manor, Buckfastleigh Road, Dartington, Totnes, Devon TQ9 6AB
Tel: 01803 897377
Education Manager: Jeff van Zyl
Age range: 3–19 years

St Christopher's Prep School & Nursery
Mount Barton, Staverton, Devon TQ9 6PF
Tel: 01803 762202
Headmistress: Mrs Alexandra Cottell
Age range: 3–11 years

St John's School
Broadway, Sidmouth, Devon EX10 8RG
Tel: 01395 513984
Head of School: Mr Bryan Kane
Age range: 2–18 years
(boarding from 8)

St Peter's Preparatory School
Harefield, Lympstone,
Exmouth, Devon EX8 5AU
Tel: 01395 272148
Head: Mrs Charlotte Johnston
Age range: 3–13 years

St Wilfrid's School
25–29 St David's Hill, Exeter,
Devon EX4 4DA
Tel: 01392 276171
Headteacher: Mr Ross Bovingdon
Age range: 3–16 years

Stover School
Stover, Newton Abbot,
Devon TQ12 6QG
Tel: +44 (0)1626 354505
Headmaster: Mr R W D Notman
Age range: 3–18 years

The Maynard School
Denmark Road, Exeter, Devon EX1 1SJ
Tel: 01392 273417
Headmistress: Mrs Liz Gregory
Age range: G4–18 years

TLG Torbay
Upton Vale Baptist Church, St.
Marychurch Road, Castle Circus,
Torquay, Devon TQ1 3HY
Tel: 07706 334965
Head of Centre: Ms Sharon Chapman
Age range: 11–16 years

Totnes Progressive School
Windmill House, 21 Ashburton
Road, Totnes, Devon TQ9 5JT
Tel: 01803 864484
Head Teacher: Ms Laura Manley
Age range: 11–16 years

Trinity School
Buckeridge Road, Teignmouth,
Devon TQ14 8LY
Tel: 01626 774138
Headmaster: Mr Lawrence Coen
Age range: 3–18 years
(boarding from 9)

West Buckland School
Barnstaple, Devon EX32 0SX
Tel: 01598 760000
Headmaster: Mr Phillip Stapleton
Age range: 3–18 years

Dorset

Bournemouth Christian School
29- 35 Wimborne Road,
Bournemouth, Dorset BH2 6NA
Tel: 01202 402021
Acting Head Teacher: Miss
Vicky Nutburn
Age range: 7–18 years

Bournemouth Collegiate School (BCS Prep)
40 St. Osmund's Road, Lower
Parkstone, Poole, Dorset BH14 9JY
Tel: 01202 714110
Head of Prep: Mrs Karen Wyborn
Age range: 2–11 years

Bournemouth Collegiate School (BCS Senior)
College Road, Southbourne,
Bournemouth, Dorset BH5 2DY
Tel: 01202 436550
Principal: Mrs Maria Coulter
Age range: 11–18 years

Bryanston Prep
Durweston, Blandford, Dorset DT11 0PY
Tel: 01258 452065
Head of School: Mr Will Lockett
Age range: 3–13 years

Bryanston School
Blandford Forum, Dorset DT11 0PX
Tel: 01258 484633
Head: Richard Jones
Age range: 3–18 years
No. of pupils: 806
Fees: Day £11,850 FB £14,450

Canford School
Canford Magna, Wimborne,
Dorset BH21 3AD
Tel: 01202 841254
Headmaster: Mr B A M Vessey MA, MBA
Age range: 13–18 years

Castle Court School
Knoll Lane, Corfe Mullen,
Wimborne, Dorset BH21 3RF
Tel: 01202 694438
Headmaster: Mr Luke Gollings
Age range: 2–13 years

Clayesmore School
Blandford Road, Iwerne
Minster, Dorset DT11 8LL
Tel: 01747 813111
Head of School: Mrs Jo Thomson
Age range: 3–18 years

Dumpton School
Deans Grove House, Deans Grove,
Wimborne, Dorset BH21 7AF
Tel: 01202 883818
Headmaster: Mr Christian Saenger
Age range: 2–13 years

Hanford School
Child Okeford, Blandford
Forum, Dorset DT11 8HN
Tel: 01258 860219
Headmaster: Mr Rory Johnston
Age range: G7–13 years
(boarding from 7)

Leweston Prep School
Sherborne, Dorset DT9 6EN
Tel: 01963 210790
Head of School: Ms Alanda Phillips
Age range: 0–11 years

Leweston Senior School
Sherborne, Dorset DT9 6EN
Tel: 01963 210691
Head of School: Mr John
Paget-Tomlinson
Age range: 11–18 years

Milton Abbey School
Blandford Forum, Dorset DT11 0BZ
Tel: 01258 880484
Head: Judith Fremont-Barnes
Age range: 13–18 years

Park School
43 Queens Park South Drive,
Bournemouth, Dorset BH8 9BJ
Tel: 01202 396640
Headteacher: Mrs Melanie Dowler
Age range: 3 months–11 years

Port Regis
Motcombe Park, Shaftesbury,
Dorset SP7 9QA
Tel: 01747 857800
Headmaster: Mr Titus Mills
Age range: 2–13 years
(boarding from 7)

Shaftesbury School
Salisbury Road, Shaftesbury,
Dorset SP7 8ER
Tel: 01747 854498
Headteacher: Ms Donna London-Hill
Age range: 11–18 years

Sherborne Girls
Bradford Road, Sherborne,
Dorset DT9 3QN
Tel: 01935 812245
Headmistress: Dr Ruth Sullivan
BSc, PGCE, MSc, PhD
Age range: G11–18 years
(boarding from 11)

Sherborne International
Newell Grange, Newell,
Sherborne, Dorset DT9 4EZ
Tel: +44 (0)1935 814743
Principal: Mr Tim Waters MA
(Oxon), MSc (Oxon)
Age range: 8–17 years

Sherborne Preparatory School
Acreman Street, Sherborne,
Dorset DT9 3NY
Tel: 01935 812097
Head: Ms Natalie Bone
Age range: 3–13 years
(boarding from 7)

Sherborne School
Abbey Road, Sherborne, Dorset DT9 3LF
Tel: +44 (0)1935 812249
Headmaster: Dr Dominic Luckett BA, DPhil, FRSA,FHA
Age range: B13–18 years

St Martin's School
15 Stokewood Road, Bournemouth, Dorset BH3 7NA
Tel: 01202 292011
Headteacher: Ms Laura Richards
Age range: 4–11 years

Sunninghill Preparatory School
South Court, South Walks Road, Dorchester, Dorset DT1 1EB
Tel: 01305 262306
Headmaster: Mr David Newberry
Age range: 3–13 years

Talbot Heath
Rothesay Road, Talbot Woods, Bournemouth, Dorset BH4 9NJ
Tel: 01202 761881
Senior School Head: Mrs A Holloway MA (Oxon) PGCE
Age range: G3–18 years (boarding from 11)

Talbot House Preparatory School
8 Firs Glen Road, Talbot Park, Bournemouth, Dorset BH9 2LR
Tel: 01202 510348
Headteacher: Mrs Emma Haworth
Age range: 3–11 years

Yarrells School & Nursery
Yarrells House, Upton, Poole, Dorset BH16 5EU
Tel: 01202 622229
Head: Mrs Sally Moulton
Age range: 2–11 years
No. of pupils: 257

Somerset

All Hallows Preparatory School
Cranmore Hall, Shepton Mallet, Somerset BA4 4SF
Tel: 01749 881600
Headmaster: Dr Trevor Richards
Age range: 3–13 years

Brymore Academy
Brymore Way, Cannington, Bridgwater, Somerset TA5 2NB
Tel: 01278 652369
Headteacher: Mr Mark Thomas
Age range: B11–18 years

Chard School
Fore Street, Chard, Somerset TA20 1QA
Tel: 01460 63234
Headteacher: Ms Katie Hill
Age range: 4–11 years

Hazlegrove Prep School
Hazlegrove House, Sparkford, Somerset BA22 7JA
Tel: +44 (0)1963 442606
Headmaster: Mr Ed Benbow BA MEd PGCE
Age range: 2–13 years
No. of pupils: 386
Fees: Day £3,199–£6,486 FB £7,524–£9,600

King's Bruton
The Plox, Bruton, Somerset BA10 0ED
Tel: 01749 814200
Headmaster: Mr I S Wilmshurst MA
Age range: 13–18 years
No. of pupils: 360
Fees: Day £24,723 FB £35,568

KING'S COLLEGE
For further details see p. 266
South Road, Taunton, Somerset TA1 3LA
Tel: 01823 328204
Email: admissions@kings-taunton.co.uk
Website: www.kings-taunton.co.uk
Headmaster: Mr Michael Sloan
Age range: 13–18 years
No. of pupils: 490
Fees: Day £27,480

King's College Prep School
Kingston Road, Taunton, Somerset TA2 8AA
Tel: 01823 285920
Head: Mr Justin Chippendale
Age range: 2–13 years
No. of pupils: 300
Fees: Day £8,850–£18,750

Millfield Preparatory School
Edgarley Hall, Glastonbury, Somerset BA6 8LD
Tel: 01458 832446
Headmaster: Dan Thornburn
Age range: 2–13 years
No. of pupils: 472

Millfield School
Butleigh Road, Street, Somerset BA16 0YD
Tel: 01458 442291
Headmaster: Mr Gavin Horgan
Age range: 13–18 years
No. of pupils: 1301
Fees: Day £27,165 FB £41,355

Perrott Hill
North Perrott, Crewkerne, Somerset TA18 7SL
Tel: 01460 72051
Headmaster: Mr Alex McCullough
Age range: 3–13 years

Queen's College
Trull Road, Taunton, Somerset TA1 4QS
Tel: +44 (0)1823 272559
Head of College: Mr Julian Noad
Age range: 3 months–18 years

Richard Huish College
South Road, Taunton, Somerset TA1 3DZ
Tel: 01823 320800
Principal: Ms Emma Fielding
Age range: 16–19 years

Sexey's School
Cole Road, Bruton, Somerset BA10 0DF
Tel: 01749 813393
Headteacher: Mrs Helen Cullen
Age range: 11–18 years

Sidcot School
Oakridge Lane, Winscombe, Somerset BS25 1PD
Tel: 01934 843102
Headmaster: Iain Kilpatrick BA MEd FRSA
Age range: 3–18 years (boarding from 11)
No. of pupils: 603
Fees: Day £2,900–£6,510 FB £9,830–£12,030

Springmead Preparatory School & Nursery
13 Castle Corner, Beckington, Frome, Somerset BA11 6TA
Tel: 01373 831555
Headteacher: Ms Sally Cox
Age range: 3–11 years

Taunton School
Staplegrove Road, Taunton, Somerset TA2 6AD
Tel: +44 (0)1823 703703
Headmaster, Taunton School: Mr. James Johnson
Age range: 0–18 years
No. of pupils: 1182

Wellington School
South Street, Wellington, Somerset TA21 8NT
Tel: 01823 668800
Headmaster: Mr Eugene du Toit
Age range: 3–18 years

Wells Cathedral School
The Liberty, Wells, Somerset BA5 2ST
Tel: +44 (0)1749 834200
Head Master: Mr Alastair Tighe
Age range: 2–18 years

West Midlands

KEY TO SYMBOLS

- Boys' school
- Girls' school
- International school
- Tutorial or sixth form college
- A levels
- Boarding accommodation
- Bursaries
- International Baccalaureate
- Learning support
- Entrance at 16+
- Vocational qualifications
- Independent Association of Preparatory Schools
- The Headmasters' & Headmistresses' Conference
- Independent Schools Association
- Girls' School Association
- Boarding Schools' Association
- Society of Heads

Unless otherwise indicated, all schools are coeducational day schools. Single-sex and boarding schools will be indicated by the relevant icon.

Herefordshire

Hereford Cathedral School
The Old Deanery, The Cathedral Close, Hereford, Herefordshire HR1 2NG
Tel: 01432 363 500
Headmaster: Dr Michael Gray Gray
Age range: 3–18 years

Lucton School
Lucton, Herefordshire HR6 9PN
Tel: 01568 782000
Headmaster: Mr David Bicker-Caarten
Age range: 6 months–18 years (boarding from 7)
No. of pupils: 300
Fees: Day £7,500–£14,250 WB £24,345–£28,695 FB £35,130

Shropshire

Adcote School for Girls
Little Ness, Shrewsbury, Shropshire SY4 2JY
Tel: 01939 260202
Headmistress: Mrs Diane Browne
Age range: G7–18 years (boarding from 7)
Fees: Day £9,141–£14,838 FB £19,618–£38,100

Bedstone College
Bedstone, Bucknell, Shropshire SY7 0BG
Tel: 01547 530303
Headmaster: Mr Toby Mullins
Age range: 4–18 years

Birchfield School
Albrighton, Wolverhampton, Shropshire WV7 3AF
Tel: 01902 372534
Headmistress: Sarah Morris
Age range: 4–16 years
No. of pupils: 142
Fees: Day £7,500–£11,000

Castle House School
Chetwynd End, Newport, Shropshire TF10 7JE
Tel: 01952 567600
Headteacher: Mr Ian Sterling
Age range: 2–11 years

Concord College
Acton Burnell Hall, Acton Burnell, Shrewsbury, Shropshire SY5 7PF
Tel: +44 (0)1694 731631
Principal: Dr Michael R Truss
Age range: 13–18 years
No. of pupils: 600
Fees: Day £16,200 FB £48,900

ELLESMERE COLLEGE
For further details see p. 276
Ellesmere, Shropshire SY12 9AB
Tel: 01691 622321
Email: registrar@ellesmere.com
Website: www.ellesmere.com
Head of School: Mr Brendan Wignall MA, FRSA, MCMI
Age range: 7–18 years (boarding from 12)
No. of pupils: 600
Fees: Day £4,565–£7,450 WB £9,170–£9,670 FB £10,855–£13,545

Haberdashers' Adams
High Street, Newport, Shropshire TF10 7BD
Tel: 01952 953810
Headmaster: Mr Gary Hickey
Age range: B11–18 years G16–18 years
No. of pupils: 1050
Fees: FB £4,619–£5,045

Moor Park
Richards Castle, Ludlow, Shropshire SY8 4DZ
Tel: 01584 876 061
Head: Mr Brendan Brady
Age range: 0–13 years
No. of pupils: 209
Fees: Day £2,385–£6,610 FB £8,185–£9,805

Moreton Hall
Weston Rhyn, Oswestry, Shropshire SY11 3EW
Tel: +44 (0)1691 773671
Principal: Mr George Budd
Age range: 11–18 years

Moreton Hall Prep
Weston Rhyn, Oswestry, Shropshire SY11 3EW
Tel: 01691 776028
Head: Mrs Deborah Speakman
Age range: 6 months–11 years
No. of pupils: 140
Fees: Day £11,190–£15,900 FB £25,800

Oswestry School
Upper Brook Street, Oswestry, Shropshire SY11 2TL
Tel: +44 (0)1691 655711
Headmaster: Mr Peter Middleton
Age range: 4–18 years

Packwood Haugh School
Ruyton XI Towns, Shrewsbury, Shropshire SY4 1HX
Tel: 01939 260217
Headmaster: Mr Robert Fox
Age range: 4–13 years

Prestfelde Preparatory School
London Road, Shrewsbury, Shropshire SY2 6NZ
Tel: 01743 245400
Head of School: Mrs F Orchard
Age range: 3–13 years

Shrewsbury High School GDST
32 Town Walls, Shrewsbury, Shropshire SY1 1TN
Tel: 01743 494000
Headteacher: Ms Jo Sharrock
Age range: G4–18 years

Shrewsbury School
The Schools, Shrewsbury, Shropshire SY3 7BA
Tel: 01743 280552
Headmaster: Mr. Leo Winkley
Age range: 13–18 years
No. of pupils: 845
Fees: Day £27,930 FB £42,210

St Winefride's RC Independent School
Belmont, Shrewsbury, Shropshire SY1 1TE
Tel: 01743 369883
Headteacher: Mrs E Devey
Age range: 3–11 years

The Old Hall School
Stanley Road, Wellington, Shropshire TF1 3LB
Tel: 01952 223117
Head of School: Ms Anna Karacan
Age range: 4–11 years
No. of pupils: 232
Fees: Day £9,270–£14,580

Thomas Adams School
Lowe Hill, Wem, Shropshire SY4 5UB
Tel: 01939 237000
Headteacher: Mr Mark Cooper
Age range: 11–18 years

Wrekin College
Wellington, Shropshire TF1 3BH
Tel: +44 (0)1952 265600
Headmaster: Mr Tim Firth
Age range: 11–18 years

Staffordshire

Abbotsholme School
Rocester, Uttoxeter, Staffordshire ST14 5BS
Tel: 01889 590217
Head of School: Mr Simon Ruscoe-Price
Age range: 2–18 years
No. of pupils: 285
Fees: Day £8,985–£22,485 WB £18,525–£27,450 FB £24,585–£33,750

Chase Grammar School
Convent Close, Cannock, Staffordshire WS11 0UR
Tel: +44 (0)1543 501800
Principal: Mr Michael Hartland
Age range: 2–19 years

DENSTONE COLLEGE
For further details see p. 272
Uttoxeter, Staffordshire ST14 5HN
Tel: 01889 590484
Email: admissions@denstonecollege.net
Website: www.denstonecollege.org
Head of School: Miss Lotte Tulloch
Age range: 4–18 years (boarding from 7)
No. of pupils: 777
Fees: Day £15,048 FB £30,936

EDENHURST PREPARATORY SCHOOL
For further details see p. 274
Westlands Avenue, Newcastle-under-Lyme, Staffordshire ST5 2PU
Tel: 01782 619348
Email: office@edenhurst.co.uk
Website: www.edenhurst.co.uk
Headteacher: Mrs Emma Mousley
Age range: 3 months–11 years
Fees: Day £3,200–£4,120

Lichfield Cathedral School
The Palace, The Close, Lichfield, Staffordshire WS13 7LH
Tel: 01543 306170
Head: Mrs Susan E Hannam BA (Hons) MA PGCE
Age range: 2½–18 years

Maple Hayes Hall School
Abnalls Lane, Lichfield, Staffordshire WS13 8BL
Tel: 01543 264387
Principal: Dr N E Brown MSc, BA, MINS, MSCMe, AFBPsS, CPsychol, FRSA, CSci
Age range: 7–17 years

Newcastle under Lyme School
Mount Pleasant, Newcastle-under-Lyme, Staffordshire ST5 1DB
Tel: 01782 631197
Headmaster: Mr Michael Getty BA, NPQH
Age range: 3–18 years
No. of pupils: 879 VIth152
Fees: Day £3,152–£4,330

St Joseph's Preparatory School
Rookery Lane, Trent Vale, Stoke-on-Trent, Staffordshire ST4 5RF
Tel: 01782 417533
Headteacher: Mr D Hood BA (Joint Hons), PGCE
Age range: 3–11 years

St. Dominic's Grammar School
32 Bargate Street, Brewood, Staffordshire ST19 9BA
Tel: 01902 850248
Headmaster: Mr Peter McNabb BSc Hons, PGCE
Age range: 4–18 years

St. Dominic's Priory School Stone
37 Station Road, Stone, Staffordshire ST15 8ER
Tel: +44 (0)1785 814181
Headteacher: Mrs Rebecca Harrison
Age range: 3–16 years

STAFFORD GRAMMAR SCHOOL
For further details see p. 280
Burton Manor, Burton Manor Road, Stafford, Staffordshire ST18 9AT
Tel: 01785 249752
Email: admissions@staffordgrammar.co.uk
Website: www.staffordgrammar.co.uk
Headmaster: Mr W P N Pietrek
Age range: 4–18 years
No. of pupils: 421
Fees: Day £2,100–£4,960

Yarlet School
Yarlet, Stafford, Staffordshire ST18 9SU
Tel: 01785 286568
Headmaster: Mr I Raybould BEd(Hons)
Age range: 2–13 years

Warwickshire

Arnold Lodge School
15–17 Kenilworth Road, Leamington Spa, Warwickshire CV32 5TW
Tel: 01926 778050
Headmaster: Mr David Preston
Age range: 4–18 years

Bilton Grange Preparatory School
Dunchurch, Rugby, Warwickshire CV22 6QU
Tel: 01788 810217
Headmaster: Mr Gareth Jones
Age range: 3–13 years (boarding from 8)

Crackley Hall School
St Joseph's Park, Kenilworth, Warwickshire CV8 2FT
Tel: 01926 514444
Headmaster: Mr Rob Duigan
Age range: 4–11 years

King's High School
Banbury Road, Warwick, Warwickshire CV34 6YE
Tel: 01926 494485
Head Master: Dr Stephen Burley
Age range: G11–18 years

OneSchool Global UK Atherstone Campus
Long Street, Atherstone, Warwickshire CV9 1AE
Tel: 01827 721751
Age range: 7–18 years

Princethorpe College
Leamington Road, Princethorpe, Rugby, Warwickshire CV23 9PX
Tel: 01926 634200
Headmaster: Mr Ed Hester
Age range: 11–18 years

Rugby School
Lawrence Sheriff Street, Rugby, Warwickshire CV22 5EH
Tel: +44 (0)1788 556216
Head Master: Mr Gareth Parker-Jones
Age range: 13–18 years (boarding from 13)

Stratford Preparatory School
Church House, Old Town, Stratford-upon-Avon, Warwickshire CV37 6BG
Tel: 01789 297993
Head of School: Ms Tracey Woodcock
Age range: 2–11 years

The Crescent School
Bawnmore Road, Bilton, Rugby, Warwickshire CV22 7QH
Tel: 01788 521595
Headmaster: Mr J.P. Thackway B.A.Hons, P.G.C.E.
Age range: 4–11 years

The Croft Preparatory School
Alveston Hill, Loxley Road, Stratford-upon-Avon, Warwickshire CV37 7RL
Tel: 01789 293795
Headmaster: Mr Marcus Cook
Age range: 3–11 years

The Kingsley School
Beauchamp Hall, Beauchamp Avenue, Leamington Spa, Warwickshire CV32 5RD
Tel: 01926 895358
Headteacher: Mr James Mercer-Kelly
Age range: B3–11 years G3–18 years

Twycross House Pre-Preparatory School (The Hollies)
The Green, Twycross (Near Atherstone), Warwickshire CV9 3PQ
Tel: 01827 880725
Age range: 4–8 years

Twycross House School
The Green, Twycross (Near Atherstone), Warwickshire CV9 3PQ
Tel: 01827 880651
Headmaster: Mr S D Assinder
Age range: 8–18 years

Warwick Preparatory School
Banbury Road, Warwick, Warwickshire CV34 6PL
Tel: 01926 491545
Headmistress: Ms Hellen Dodsworth
Age range: B3–7 years G3–11 years

Warwick School
Myton Road, Warwick, Warwickshire CV34 6PP
Tel: 01926 776400
Head Master: Mr James Barker
Age range: B7–18 years

West Midlands

Abu Bakr Girls School
Shelly Campus, Scarborough Road, Walsall, West Midlands WS2 9TY
Tel: 01922 612361
Acting Head Teacher: Moulana M Luqman
Age range: G4–16 years

Al Ameen Primary School
Stanfield House, 447 Warwick Way, Tyseley, Birmingham, West Midlands B11 2JR
Tel: 0121 706 3322
Head Teacher: Maulana Mohammed Aminur Rahman
Age range: 3–11 years

Al-Burhan Grammar School
Spring Road Centre, 258 Spring Road, Tyseley, Birmingham, West Midlands B11 3DW
Tel: 01214 405454
Headteacher: Dr Mohammad Nasrullah BSc MSc PhD
Age range: G11–16 years

Al-Furqan Primary School
Reddings Lane, Tyseley, Birmingham, West Midlands B11 3EY
Tel: 01217 772222
Executive Head Teacher: Ms Susan Barratt
Age range: 4–11 years

Bablake School
Coundon Road, Coventry, West Midlands CV1 4AU
Tel: 02476 271200
Headmaster: Mr Andrew Wright
Age range: 3–18 years

Birchfield Independent Girls' School
30 Beacon Hill, Aston, Birmingham, West Midlands B6 6JU
Tel: 01213 277707
Head Teacher: Ms Rehana Mogra
Age range: G11–17 years

Darul Uloom Islamic High School (Darul Uloom Birmingham)
521–527 Coventry Road, Small Heath, Birmingham, West Midlands B10 0LL
Tel: 0121 688 6507
Head of School: Ustaadh Azharul Islam
Age range: B11–16 years

Edgbaston High School for Girls
Westbourne Road, Edgbaston, Birmingham, West Midlands B15 3TS
Tel: 01214 545831
Headmistress: Mrs Clare Macro
Age range: G21/2–18 years
No. of pupils: 880
Fees: Day £3,106–£4,695

Elmfield Rudolf Steiner School
14 Love Lane, Stourbridge, West Midlands DY8 2EA
Tel: 01384 394633
Age range: 3–17 years

Elmhurst Ballet School
249 Bristol Road, Edgbaston, Birmingham, West Midlands B5 7UH
Tel: +44 (0)1214 726655
Principal: Ms Jessica Ward
Age range: 11–19 years (boarding from 11)

Emmanuel School (Walsall)
36 Wolverhampton Road, Walsall, West Midlands WS2 8PR
Tel: 01922 635810
Head Teacher: Mr Jonathan Swain BA PGCE
Age range: 3–16 years

Eversfield Preparatory School
Warwick Road, Solihull, West Midlands B91 1AT
Tel: 0121 705 0354
Headmaster: Mr Robert A Yates MA, BA, PGCE, LPSH
Age range: 3–11 years
No. of pupils: 335
Fees: Day £8,410–£12,300

Green Heath School
43–51 Whitmore Road, Small Heath, Birmingham, West Midlands B10 0NR
Tel: 0121 213 1171
Head of School: Mr Z Khan
Age range: 11–19 years

Green Oak Academy
11–15 Woodstock Road, Moseley, Birmingham, West Midlands B13 9BB
Tel: 01214 496690
Head Teacher: Dr Razia Ghani
Age range: G11–16 years

Greenfields Primary School
472 Coventry Road, Small Heath, Birmingham, West Midlands B10 0UG
Tel: 01217 724567
Headteacher: Mr Matthew Williams
Age range: 5–11 years

Hallfield School
48 Church Road, Edgbaston, Birmingham, West Midlands B15 3SJ
Tel: 0121 454 1496
Head Master: Mr Keith Morrow
Age range: 3 months–13 years

Hamd House School
The Custard House, 29–43 Blake Lane, Birmingham, West Midlands B9 5QT
Tel: +44 (0)1217 713030
Age range: 5–16 years

Highclare School
10 Sutton Road, Erdington, Birmingham, West Midlands B23 6QL
Tel: 01213 737400
Headmaster: Dr Richard Luker
Age range: 2–18 years

Hydesville Tower School
25 Broadway North, Walsall, West Midlands WS1 2QG
Tel: 01922 624374
Headteacher: Mrs Raj Samra
Age range: 3–16 years
No. of pupils: 289
Fees: Day £9,738–£13,758

Jamia Islamia Birmingham School & College
Fallows Road, Sparkbrook, Birmingham, West Midlands B11 1PL
Tel: 01217 726400
Headteacher: Monzoor Hussain NPQH PGCE Bsc
Age range: 11–18 years

King Edward VI High School for Girls
Edgbaston Park Road, Birmingham, West Midlands B15 2UB
Tel: 01214 721834
Principal: Mrs Kirsty von Malaisé
Age range: G11–18 years

King Edward's School
Edgbaston Park Road, Birmingham, West Midlands B15 2UA
Tel: 01214 721672
Chief Master: Dr Katy Ricks
Age range: B11–18 years
No. of pupils: 876
Fees: Day £5,175

King Henry VIII Preparatory School
Warwick Road, Coventry, West Midlands CV3 6AQ
Tel: 02476 271160
Headmaster: Mr J. Holtby
Age range: 3–11 years

King Henry VIII School
Warwick Road, Coventry, West Midlands CV3 6AQ
Tel: 02476 271111
Headmaster: Mr Philip Dearden BA (Hons), MA Ed
Age range: 11–18 years

Kingswood School
St James Place, Shirley, Solihull, West Midlands B90 2BA
Tel: 01217 447883
Headmaster: Mr Rob Luckham BSc(Hons), PGCE
Age range: 2–16 years

Lambs Christian School
113 Soho Hill, Hockley, Birmingham, West Midlands B19 1AY
Tel: 01215 543790
Headteacher: Mrs Patricia Ekhuenelo
Age range: 3–11 years

Lote Tree Primary
643 Foleshill Road, Coventry, West Midlands CV6 5JQ
Tel: 02476 261803
Headteacher: Ms Mariam Ashique
Age range: 2–11 years

MANDER PORTMAN WOODWARD - MPW BIRMINGHAM
For further details see p. 278
16–18 Greenfield Crescent, Edgbaston, Birmingham, West Midlands B15 3AU
Tel: 0121 454 9637
Email: birmingham@mpw.ac.uk
Website: www.mpw.ac.uk
Principal: Mr Mark Shingleton
Age range: 14–19 years

Mayfield Preparatory School
Sutton Road, Walsall, West Midlands WS1 2PD
Tel: 01922 624107
Headmaster: Mr Matthew Draper
Age range: 2–11 years

Newbridge Preparatory School
51 Newbridge Crescent, Tettenhall, Wolverhampton, West Midlands WV6 0LH
Tel: 01902 751088
Headmistress: Mrs Sarah Fisher
Age range: B2–7 years G2–11 years

Norfolk House School
4 Norfolk Road, Edgbaston, Birmingham, West Midlands B15 3PS
Tel: 01214 547021
Susannah: Ms Susannah Palmer
Age range: 3–11 years

Old Swinford Hospital
Heath Lane, Stourbridge, West Midlands DY8 1QX
Tel: 01384 817300
Headmaster: Mr Paul Kilbride
Age range: 11–18 years

Pattison School
86–90 Binley Road, Coventry, West Midlands CV3 1FQ
Tel: 024 7645 5031
Head of School: Mr Graeme Delaney
Age range: 2–18 years

Priory School
39 Sir Harry's Road, Edgbaston, Birmingham, West Midlands B15 2UR
Tel: 0121 440 4103
Headmaster: Mr J Cramb
Age range: 6 months–18 years

Rosslyn School
1597 Stratford Road, Hall Green, Birmingham, West Midlands B28 9JB
Tel: 01217 442743
Head of School: Mrs Irina Jones
Age range: 11 months–11 years

Ruckleigh School
17 Lode Lane, Solihull, West Midlands B91 2AB
Tel: 01217 052773
Headmaster: Mr Dominic Smith
Age range: 3–11 years

Solihull School
Warwick Road, Solihull, West Midlands B91 3DJ
Tel: 01217 050958
Head of Senior School: Mr Sean A Morgan
Age range: 3–18 years

St George's School, Edgbaston
31 Calthorpe Road, Edgbaston, Birmingham, West Midlands B15 1RX
Tel: 01216 250398
Head of School: Mr Gary Neal BEd (Hons)
Age range: 3–18 years

Tettenhall College
Wood Road, Tettenhall, Wolverhampton, West Midlands WV6 8QX
Tel: 01902 751119
Headteacher: Mr Christopher McAllister
Age range: 2–18 years (boarding from 10)
No. of pupils: 440

The Blue Coat School
Somerset Road, Edgbaston, Birmingham, West Midlands B17 0HR
Tel: 01214 106800
Headmaster: Mr N G Neeson
Age range: 3–11 years

THE ROYAL SCHOOL, WOLVERHAMPTON
For further details see p. 282
Penn Road, Wolverhampton, West Midlands WV3 0EG
Tel: +44 (0)1902 341230
Email: info@theroyal.school
Website: theroyalschool.co.uk
Principal: Mr Mark Heywood
Age range: 4–19 years (boarding from 11)
No. of pupils: 1476
Fees: FB £16,254

The Shrubbery School
Walmley Ash Road, Walmley, Sutton Coldfield, West Midlands B76 1HY
Tel: 01213 511582
Head Teacher: Mrs Amanda Lees
Age range: 3–11 years

TLG North Birmingham
240–244 Lozells Road, Lozells, Birmingham, West Midlands B19 1NP
Tel: 07943 183021
Head of Centre: Mr James Lawlor
Age range: 11–16 years

West House School
24 St James's Road, Edgbaston, Birmingham, West Midlands B15 2NX
Tel: 0121 440 4097
Headmaster: Mr Alistair M J Lyttle BA(Hons), PGCE, NPQH
Age range: B6 months–11 years G6 months–4 years
No. of pupils: 350
Fees: Day £2,200–£4,226

Wolverhampton Grammar School
Compton Road, Wolverhampton, West Midlands WV3 9RB
Tel: 01902 421326
Head: Mr Alex Frazer
Age range: 4–18 years

Worcestershire

Bowbrook House School
Main Street, Peopleton, Pershore, Worcestershire WR10 2EE
Tel: 01905 841242
Headmaster: Mr C D Allen BSc(Hons)
Age range: 31/2–16 years

Bromsgrove Preparatory School
Old Station Road, Bromsgrove, Worcestershire B60 2BU
Tel: 01527 579679
Headmaster: Mr Mike Marie
Age range: 7–13 years (boarding from 7)

Bromsgrove Pre-preparatory & Nursery School
Avoncroft House, Hanbury Road, Bromsgrove, Worcestershire B60 4JS
Tel: 01527 579679 (Ext:204)
Headmaster: Mr Mike Marie
Age range: 2–7 years

Bromsgrove School
Worcester Road, Bromsgrove, Worcestershire B61 7DU
Tel: +44 (0)1527 579679
Headmaster: Michael Punt
Age range: 7–18 years (boarding from 7)
No. of pupils: 1650
Fees: Day £18,840 WB £27,945 FB £42,165

Heathfield Knoll School
Wolverley, Kidderminster, Worcestershire DY10 3QE
Tel: 01562 850204
Head of School: Mr. L. G. Collins B.Sc.(Hons), M.A.,P.G.C.E.
Age range: 3 months–18 years
No. of pupils: 243
Fees: Day £9,045–£14,283

King's Hawford
Lock Lane, Claines, Worcester, Worcestershire WR3 7SD
Tel: 01905 451292
Acting Head: Ms Caroline Knight
Age range: 2–11 years
No. of pupils: 270
Fees: Day £2,661–£4,789

King's St Alban's
Mill Street, Worcester, Worcestershire WR1 2NJ
Tel: 01905 354906
Head of School: Mr Richard Chapman
Age range: 2–11 years
No. of pupils: 182
Fees: Day £2,538–£4,593

King's Worcester
5 College Green, Worcester, Worcestershire WR1 2LL
Tel: 01905 721700
Headmaster: Mr Gareth Doodes
Age range: 11–18 years
A £ 16·

Madinatul Uloom Al Islamiya School
Heath Lane, Summerfield, Kidderminster, Worcestershire DY10 4BS
Tel: 01562 66894
Age range: B11–28 years
A 16·

Malvern College
College Road, Malvern, Worcestershire WR14 3DF
Tel: +44 (0)1684 581515
Headmaster: Keith Metcalfe MA (Cantab)
Age range: 13–18 years
No. of pupils: 660
A £ IB 16·

Malvern St James Girls' School
15 Avenue Road, Great Malvern, Worcestershire WR14 3BA
Tel: 01684 892288
Headteacher: Mrs Olivera Raraty BA PGCE
Age range: G3–18 years (boarding from 7)
A £ 16·

RGS Dodderhill
Dodderhill Road, Droitwich Spa, Worcestershire WR9 0BE
Tel: 01905 778290
Headmistress: Mrs Sarah Atkinson
Age range: B2–11 years G2–16 years
£

RGS Springfield
Springfield, Britannia Square, Worcester, Worcestershire WR1 3DL
Tel: 01905 24999
Headmistress: Mrs Laura Brown
Age range: 2–11 years
£

RGS The Grange
Grange Lane, Claines, Worcester, Worcestershire WR3 7RR
Tel: 01905 451205
Headmaster: Mr Gareth Hughes
Age range: 2–11 years
£

RGS Worcester
Upper Tything, Worcester, Worcestershire WR1 1HP
Tel: 01905 613391
Headmaster: Mr John Pitt
Age range: 11–18 years
A £ 16·

The Abbey College
253 Wells Road, Malvern Wells, Malvern, Worcestershire WR14 4JF
Tel: 01684 892300
Principal: Mr Daniel Booker
Age range: 13–19 years
16·

The Downs Malvern
Brockhill Road, Malvern, Worcestershire WR13 6EY
Tel: 01684 544100
Headmaster: Mr Andy Nuttall
Age range: 3–13 years (boarding from 7)
£

The Elms
Colwall, Malvern, Worcestershire WR13 6EF
Tel: 01684 540344
Interim Co-Headmasters: Mr Jonathan Bungard & Mr David Pearce
Age range: 3–13 years
£

The River School
Oakfield House, Rose Bank, Worcester, Worcestershire WR3 7ST
Tel: 01905 457047
Headteacher: Mr Adrian Parsonage
Age range: 2–16 years

Winterfold House School
Chaddesley Corbett, Kidderminster, Worcestershire DY10 4PW
Tel: 01562 777234
Headmistress: Mrs Denise Toms BA (Hons) QTS, NPQH
Age range: 3 months–13 years

Yorkshire & Humberside

KEY TO SYMBOLS

- *Boys' school*
- *Girls' school*
- *International school*
- *Tutorial or sixth form college*
- *A levels*
- *Boarding accommodation*
- *Bursaries*
- *International Baccalaureate*
- *Learning support*
- *Entrance at 16+*
- *Vocational qualifications*
- *Independent Association of Preparatory Schools*
- *The Headmasters' & Headmistresses' Conference*
- *Independent Schools Association*
- *Girls' School Association*
- *Boarding Schools' Association*
- *Society of Heads*

Unless otherwise indicated, all schools are coeducational day schools. Single-sex and boarding schools will be indicated by the relevant icon.

East Riding of Yorkshire

Froebel House School
5 Marlborough Avenue, Kingston upon Hull, East Riding of Yorkshire HU5 3JP
Tel: 01482 342272
Head Teacher: Mr A Roberts M.Ed BA Hons PGCE
Age range: 4–11 years

Hessle Mount School
Jenny Brough Lane, Hessle, East Riding of Yorkshire HU13 0JZ
Tel: 01482 643371
Principal: Miss Sarah Cutting
Age range: 3–8 years

Hymers College
Hymers Avenue, Kingston upon Hull, East Riding of Yorkshire HU3 1LW
Tel: 01482 343555
Headmaster: Mr Justin Stanley
Age range: 8–18 years

Tranby
Tranby Croft, Anlaby, Kingston upon Hull, East Riding of Yorkshire HU10 7EH
Tel: 01482 657016
Headmistress: Mrs Alex Wilson BA (Surrey) PGCE (Cantab) MA (London)
Age range: 3–18 years
No. of pupils: 576

North Yorkshire

Ampleforth College
York, North Yorkshire YO62 4ER
Tel: 01439 766000
Head: Mr Peter Roberts
Age range: 11–18 years

Ashville College
Green Lane, Harrogate, North Yorkshire HG2 9JP
Tel: +44 (0)1423 566358
Head: Mrs Rhiannon Wilkinson
Age range: 2–18 years

Aysgarth School
Newton le Willows, Bedale, North Yorkshire DL8 1TF
Tel: 01677 450240
Head of School: Mr Rob Morse
Age range: B3–13 years (boarding from 8) G3–8 years

Belmont Grosvenor School
Swarcliffe Hall, Birstwith, Harrogate, North Yorkshire HG3 2JG
Tel: 01423 771029
Headmaster: Mr Nathan Sadler
Age range: 3 months–11 years

Bootham Junior School
Rawcliffe Lane, York, North Yorkshire YO30 6NP
Tel: 01904 655021
Head: Mrs Helen Todd
Age range: 3–11 years
Fees: Day £2,475–£3,700

Bootham School
York, North Yorkshire YO30 7BU
Tel: 01904 623261
Head: Mr Chris Jeffery BA, FRSA
Age range: 11–18 years

Brackenfield School
128 Duchy Road, Harrogate, North Yorkshire HG1 2HE
Tel: 01423 508558
Headteacher: Mr Joe Masterson
Age range: 2–11 years

Chapter House Preparatory School
Thorpe Underwood Hall, Ouseburn, York, North Yorkshire YO26 9SS
Tel: 01423 33 33 30
Head Teacher: Mrs Karen Kilkenny BSc
Age range: 3 months–10 years

Cundall Manor School
Cundall, North Yorkshire YO61 2RW
Tel: 01423 360200
Headmaster: Mr Christopher James-Roll
Age range: 2–16 years (boarding from 7)
Fees: Day £10,785–£17,805 WB £22,395–£23,115

Fyling Hall School
Robin Hood's Bay, Whitby, North Yorkshire YO22 4QD
Tel: 01947 880353
Headmaster: Mr. Steven Allen
Age range: 4–18 years

Giggleswick Junior School
Settle, North Yorkshire BD24 0DG
Tel: 01729 893100
Headmaster: Mr Sam Hart
Age range: 2–11 years
No. of pupils: 98
Fees: Day £9,195–£14,505 WB £23,175 FB £24,000

Giggleswick School
Settle, North Yorkshire BD24 0DE
Tel: 01729 893000
Headmaster: Mr Sam Hart
Age range: 11–18 years (boarding from 8)

Harrogate Ladies' College
Clarence Drive, Harrogate, North Yorkshire HG1 2QG
Tel: 01423 504543
Principal: Mrs Sylvia Brett
Age range: G11–18 years (boarding from 11)

Highfield Prep School
Clarence Drive, Harrogate, North Yorkshire HG1 2QG
Tel: 01423 537060
Head: Mr James Savile
Age range: 2–11 years

POCKLINGTON SCHOOL
For further details see p. 286
West Green, Pocklington, York, North Yorkshire YO42 2NJ
Tel: 01759 321200
Email: admissions@pocklingtonschool.com
Website: www.pocklingtonschool.com
Headmaster: Mr Toby Seth MA (Cantab)
Age range: 2–18 years
No. of pupils: 725 VIth160
Fees: Day £18,798 WB £31,875 FB £34,656

QUEEN ETHELBURGA'S COLLEGIATE
For further details see p. 288
Thorpe Underwood Hall, Ouseburn, York, North Yorkshire YO26 9SS
Tel: 01423 33 33 30
Email: admissions@qe.org
Website: www.qe.org
Principal: Dan Machin
Age range: 3–19 years (boarding from 7)
No. of pupils: 1400

Queen Margaret's School
Escrick Park, York, North Yorkshire YO19 6EU
Tel: 01904 727600
Head: Ms Sue Baillie
Age range: G11–18 years (boarding from 11)

Queen Mary's School
Baldersby Park, Topcliffe, Thirsk, North Yorkshire YO7 3BZ
Tel: 01845 575000
Head: Carole Cameron
Age range: B4–7 years G4–16 years (boarding from 7)

Ripon Grammar School
16 Clotherholme Road, Ripon, North Yorkshire HG4 2DG
Tel: 01765 602 647
Headmaster: Mr Jonathan M Webb
Age range: 11–18 years

Scarborough College
Filey Road, Scarborough, North Yorkshire YO11 3BA
Tel: +44 (0)1723 360620
Headmaster: Mr Guy Emmett
Age range: 3–18 years (boarding from 11)
No. of pupils: 528
Fees: Day £8,250–£16,680 FB £20,502–£34,536

St Peter's 13–18
Clifton, York, North Yorkshire YO30 6AB
Tel: 01904 527300
Head Master: Mr Jeremy Walker
Age range: 13–18 years

St Peter's 2–8
Clifton, York, North Yorkshire YO30 6AB
Tel: 01904 527361
Head of School: Mr Phil Hardy
Age range: 2–8 years

St Peter's 8–13
Queen Anne's Road, York, North Yorkshire YO30 7AA
Tel: 01904 527416
Head of School: Mr Andy Falconer
Age range: 8–13 years

Terrington Hall
Terrington, York, North Yorkshire YO60 6PR
Tel: 01653 648227
Headmaster: Mr. Simon Kibler
Age range: 3–13 years

The Mount School York
Dalton Terrace, York, North Yorkshire YO24 4DD
Tel: 01904 667500
Principal: Mr David Griffiths
Age range: G3–18 years (boarding from 11)
16·

The Read School
Drax, Selby, North Yorkshire YO8 8NL
Tel: 01757 618248
Head: Ms Ruth Ainley
Age range: 4–18 years (boarding from 8)
16·

Wharfedale Montessori School
Bolton Abbey, Skipton, North Yorkshire BD23 6AN
Tel: 01756 710452
Age range: 6 months–11 years

York Steiner School
Danesmead, Fulford Cross, York, North Yorkshire YO10 4PB
Tel: 01904 654983
Headteacher: Ms Annabel Gibb
Age range: 0–14 years

North-East Lincolnshire

OneSchool Global UK Ridgeway Campus
Ridge Way, Scunthorpe, North-East Lincolnshire DN17 1BS
Tel: 03300 552611
Age range: 7–18 years

St Martin's Preparatory School
63 Bargate, Grimsby, North-East Lincolnshire DN34 5AA
Tel: 01472 878907
Headmaster: Mr Joel Jackson
Age range: 2–11 years

St. James School
22 Bargate, Grimsby, North-East Lincolnshire DN34 4SY
Tel: 01472 503260
Headmistress: Ms Trudy Harris
Age range: 11–18 years
16·

The Children's House
Station Road, Stallingborough, North-East Lincolnshire DN41 8AJ
Tel: 01472 886000
Headteacher: Ms Theresa Ellerby
Age range: 4–11 years

South Yorkshire

Al-Mahad-Al-Islam School
1 Industry Road, Sheffield, South Yorkshire S9 5FP
Tel: 01142 431224
Headteacher: Mrs Juwairiah Khan
Age range: G11–17 years

Bethany School
Finlay Street, Sheffield, South Yorkshire S3 7PS
Tel: 0114 272 6994
Head of School: Mr David Charles B.Eng. (Hons) (Sheffield) PGCE
Age range: 4–16 years

Birkdale School
4 Oakholme Road, Sheffield, South Yorkshire S10 3DH
Tel: 01142 668408
Head of School: Mr Peter Harris
Age range: 4–18 years
16·

Hill House School
6th Avenue, Auckley, Doncaster, South Yorkshire DN9 3GG
Tel: +44 (0)1302 776300
Headmaster: Mr David Holland
Age range: 3–18 years

Mylnhurst Preparatory School & Nursery
Button Hill, Woodholm Road, Ecclesall, Sheffield, South Yorkshire S11 9HJ
Tel: 0114 2361411
Headmaster: Mr Michael Hibbert
Age range: 3–11 years

Sheffield Girls' GDST
10 Rutland Park, Sheffield, South Yorkshire S10 2PE
Tel: 01142 660324
Head: Mrs Nina Gunson
Age range: G4–18 years
16·

Sycamore Hall Preparatory School
1 Hall Flat Lane, Balby, Doncaster, South Yorkshire DN4 8PT
Tel: 01302 856800
Headmistress: Miss Jane Spencer
Age range: 3–11 years

Westbourne School
60 Westbourne Road, Sheffield, South Yorkshire S10 2QT
Tel: 01142 660374
Headmaster: Mr Chris Hattam
Age range: 3–16 years

West Yorkshire

Ackworth School
Pontefract Road, Ackworth, Pontefract, West Yorkshire WF7 7LT
Tel: 01977 233 600
Headteacher: Mr. Anton Maree BA Rhodes (HDE)
Age range: 2½–18 years (boarding from 10)
No. of pupils: 494
Fees: Day £3,195–£5,256 FB £8,984–£12,988
A £ 16·

Al Mu'min Primary School
Clifton Street, Bradford, West Yorkshire BD8 7DA
Tel: 01274 488593
Headteacher: Mr M M Azam
Age range: 3–18 years

Al-Furqaan Preparatory School
Drill Hall House, Bath Street, Dewsbury, West Yorkshire WF13 2JR
Tel: 01924 453661
Head of School: Ms Shaheda Ughratdar
Age range: 2–11 years

Bradford Christian School
Livingstone Road, Bolton Woods, Bradford, West Yorkshire BD2 1BT
Tel: 01274 532649
Head Teacher: Ms Jane Prothero
Age range: 4–16 years

Bradford Grammar School
Keighley Road, Bradford, West Yorkshire BD9 4JP
Tel: 01274 542492
Headmaster: Dr Simon Hinchliffe
Age range: 6–18 years
A £ 16·

Brontë House School
Apperley Bridge, Bradford, West Yorkshire BD10 0NR
Tel: 0113 250 2811
Head: Mrs Sarah Chatterton
Age range: 2–11 years
No. of pupils: 302
Fees: Day £10,200–£13,323

Crystal Gardens Primary School
38–40 Greaves Street, Bradford, West Yorkshire BD5 7PE
Tel: 01274 573004
Headteacher: Ms Rashta Bibi
Age range: 4–11 years

Dale House Independent School & Nursery
Ruby Street, Carlinghow, Batley, West Yorkshire WF17 8HL
Tel: 01924 422215
Headmistress: Mrs S M G Fletcher BA, CertEd
Age range: 2–11 years

Darul Uloom Dawatul Imaan (Darul Uloom Bradford)
Harry Street, Off Wakefield Road, Bradford, West Yorkshire BD4 9PH
Tel: 01274 402233
Headteacher: Moulana Abdurrahman Kayat Sahib
Age range: B11–25 years

Eternal Light Secondary School
Christopher Street, Off Little Horton Lane, Bradford, West Yorkshire BD5 9DH
Tel: 01274 501597
Headteacher: Mr Yusuf Collector
Age range: B11–23 years

Fulneck School
Fulneck, Pudsey, Leeds, West Yorkshire LS28 8DS
Tel: +44 (0)113 257 0235
Principal: Ms Francine Smith
Age range: 3–18 years (boarding from 11)

Gateways School
Leeds Road, Harewood, Leeds, West Yorkshire LS17 9LE
Tel: 0113 2886345
Head: Dr Tracy Johnson
Age range: B2–15 years G2–18 years
No. of pupils: 430
Fees: Day £9,270–£14,865

Ghyll Royd School and Pre-School
Greystone Manor, Ilkley Road, Burley in Wharfedale, West Yorkshire LS29 7HW
Tel: 01943 865575
Headteacher: Mr David Martin BA MA PGCE
Age range: 2–11 years
No. of pupils: 100
Fees: Day £3,200

Hipperholme Grammar School
Bramley Lane, Hipperholme, Halifax, West Yorkshire HX3 8JE
Tel: 01422 202256
Headteacher: Mr Nicholas James
Age range: 3–16 years
Fees: Day £10,410–£13,002

Huddersfield Grammar School
Royds Mount, Luck Lane, Marsh, Huddersfield, West Yorkshire HD1 4QX
Tel: 01484 424549
Headmistress: Mrs Donna Holmes
Age range: 3–16 years
No. of pupils: 546
Fees: Day £9,009–£11,103

Institute of Islamic Education
South Street, Savile Town, Dewsbury, West Yorkshire WF12 9NG
Tel: 01924 455762
Executive Headteacher: Mr Yusuf Seedat
Age range: B11–25 years

Islamic Tarbiyah Preparatory School
Ambler Street, Bradford, West Yorkshire BD8 8AW
Tel: 01274 490462
Headteacher: Mr S A Nawaz
Age range: 3–11 years

Jaamiatul Imaam Muhammad Zakaria School
Thornton View Road, Clayton, Bradford, West Yorkshire BD14 6JX
Tel: 01274 882007
Head of School: Ms Zebunnisa Hajee
Age range: G11–23 years

Lady Lane Park School
College Road, Bingley, West Yorkshire BD16 4AP
Tel: 01274 551168
Headmaster: Mr Nigel Saunders
Age range: 2–11 years

Leeds Menorah School
399 Street Lane, Leeds, West Yorkshire LS17 6HQ
Tel: 0113 2697709
Head Teacher: Mrs Ethel Refson
Age range: 3–11 years

Madni Academy
40–42 Scarborough Street, Savile Town, Dewsbury, West Yorkshire WF12 9AY
Tel: 01924 500335
Headteacher: Mrs Shakera A Mirza
Age range: G2–16 years

Moorfield School
Wharfedale Lodge, 11 Ben Rhydding Road, Ilkley, West Yorkshire LS29 8RL
Tel: 01943 607285
Headmistress: Mrs Tina Herbert
Age range: 2–11 years
No. of pupils: 110
Fees: Day £10,395

Moorlands School
Foxhill Drive, Weetwood Lane, Leeds, West Yorkshire LS16 5PF
Tel: 0113 2785286
Head of School: Ms Jacqueline Atkinson
Age range: 2–11 years

New Horizon Community School
Newton Hill House, Newton Hill Road, Leeds, West Yorkshire LS7 4JE
Tel: 0113 262 4001
Headteacher: Mr Mohammed Sheikh
Age range: G11–16 years

OneSchool Global UK York Campus
Bishopthorpe Road, York, West Yorkshire YO23 2QA
Tel: 01904 663300
Age range: 7–18 years

Paradise Primary School
1 Bretton Street, Dewsbury, West Yorkshire WF12 9BB
Tel: 01924 439803
Head of School: Mrs A Patel
Age range: 2–11 years

Queen Elizabeth Grammar School (Junior Section)
158 Northgate, Wakefield, West Yorkshire WF1 3QY
Tel: 01924 373821
Director of Junior Section: Mr Richard Thompson BA (Hons), PGCE
Age range: B7–11 years

Queen Elizabeth Grammar School (Senior Section)
154 Northgate, Wakefield, West Yorkshire WF1 3QX
Tel: 01924 373943
Head: Dr Richard Brookes MChem
Age range: B11–18 years

Queenswood School
Queen Street, Morley, Leeds, West Yorkshire LS27 9EB
Tel: 01132 534033
Headteacher: Mrs Julie Tanner MMus, BA, FTCL, ARCO
Age range: 4–11 years

Richmond House School
168–170 Otley Road, Leeds, West Yorkshire LS16 5LG
Tel: 0113 2752670
Headteacher: Mrs Sharon Young BA (Hons), PGCE, MEd
Age range: 3–11 years

RISHWORTH SCHOOL
For further details see p. 290
Oldham Road, Sowerby Bridge, Halifax, West Yorkshire HX6 4QA
Tel: 01422 822217
Email: admissions@rishworth-school.co.uk
Website: www.rishworth-school.co.uk
Head: Dr Anthony Wilkins
Age range: 3–18 years (boarding from 11)

Silcoates School
Wrenthorpe, Wakefield, West Yorkshire WF2 0PD
Tel: 01924 291614
Headmaster: Mr Chris Wainman MA
Age range: 3–18 years

The Branch Christian School
Dewsbury Revival Centre, West Park Street, Dewsbury, West Yorkshire WF13 4LA
Tel: +44 (0)1924 452511
Head Teacher: Mrs Jill Holt
Age range: 3–18 years

THE FROEBELIAN SCHOOL
For further details see p. 292
Clarence Road, Horsforth,
Leeds, West Yorkshire LS18 4LB
Tel: 0113 2583047
Email: office@froebelian.co.uk
Website: www.froebelian.com
Head Teacher: Mrs Anna Coulson
Age range: 3–11 years
No. of pupils: 150
Fees: Day £6,255–£9,300

The Gleddings School
Birdcage Lane, Savile Park,
Halifax, West Yorkshire HX3 0JB
Tel: 01422 354605
Head Teacher: Ms Jill Wilson
Age range: 3–11 years

The Grammar School at Leeds
Alwoodley Gates, Harrogate Road,
Leeds, West Yorkshire LS17 8GS
Tel: 0113 2291552
Principal: Mrs Sue Woodroofe
Age range: 3–18 years
16·

The Mount School
3 Binham Road, Edgerton,
Huddersfield, West Yorkshire HD2 2AP
Tel: 01484 426432
Head Teacher: Mr Euan Burton-Smith
Age range: 3–11 years

TLG Wakefield
All Saints Church, High Street,
Normanton, Wakefield,
West Yorkshire WF6 1NT
Tel: 01924 895375
Head of Centre: Mr Gavin Budby
Age range: 11–16 years

Wakefield Girls' High School (Junior Section)
2 St. John's Square, Wakefield,
West Yorkshire WF1 2QX
Tel: 01924 374577
Director of Junior Section: Mr S Rowley BSc (Hons), PGCE, MSc
Age range: G7–11 years

Wakefield Girls' High School (Senior Section)
Wentworth Street, Wakefield,
West Yorkshire WF1 2QS
Tel: 01924 372490
Head: Ms Heidi-Jayne Boyes BSc (Hons), PGCE
Age range: G11–18 years

Wakefield Grammar Pre-Preparatory School
Margaret Street, Wakefield,
West Yorkshire WF1 2DG
Tel: 01924 231618
Head: Mrs Emma Gill
Age range: 3–7 years

Wakefield Independent School
The Nostell Centre, Doncaster Road, Nostell, Wakefield,
West Yorkshire WF4 1QG
Tel: 01924 865757
Headmistress: Mrs K E Caryl
Age range: 3–16 years

Westville House School
Carter's Lane, Middleton, Ilkley,
West Yorkshire LS29 0DQ
Tel: 01943 608053
Headteacher: Mrs Nikki Hammond BA(Hons) PGCE
Age range: 2–11 years

Woodhouse Grove School
Apperley Bridge, Bradford,
West Yorkshire BD10 0NR
Tel: 0113 250 2477
Headmaster: Mr James Lockwood
Age range: 11–18 years
No. of pupils: 768 VIth203
Fees: Day £15,240–£15,444
FB £32,085–£32,256
A £ 16·

Northern Ireland

KEY TO SYMBOLS

- *Boys' school*
- *Girls' school*
- *International school*
- *Tutorial or sixth form college*
- *A levels*
- *Boarding accommodation*
- *Bursaries*
- *International Baccalaureate*
- *Learning support*
- *Entrance at 16+*
- *Vocational qualifications*
- *Independent Association of Preparatory Schools*
- *The Headmasters' & Headmistresses' Conference*
- *Independent Schools Association*
- *Girls' School Association*
- *Boarding Schools' Association*
- *Society of Heads*

Unless otherwise indicated, all schools are coeducational day schools. Single-sex and boarding schools will be indicated by the relevant icon.

County Antrim

Ballymoney Independent Christian School
55 Market Street, Ballymoney, County Antrim BT53 6ED
Tel: 028 2766 3402
Principal: Mrs J Boyd
Age range: 3–11 years

Belfast Royal Academy
5–17 Cliftonville Road, Belfast, County Antrim BT14 6JL
Tel: 028 9074 0423
Principal: Mrs Hilary Woods
Age range: 11–18 years

Bloomfield Collegiate School
Astoria Gardens, Upper Newtownards Road, Belfast, County Antrim BT5 6HW
Tel: 028 90 471214
Principal: Mr G Greer
Age range: G11–18 years

Campbell College
Belmont Road, Belfast, County Antrim BT4 2ND
Tel: 028 9076 3076
Headmaster: Mr Robert Robinson
Age range: B11–18 years

Campbell College Junior School
Belmont Road, Belfast, County Antrim BT4 2ND
Tel: 028 9076 3076
Head of Junior School: Miss Andrea Brown
Age range: B3–11 years G3–4 years

Dominican College
38 Fortwilliam Park, Belfast, County Antrim BT15 4AQ
Tel: 028 90 370298
Principal: Ms Lynda Catney
Age range: G11–18 years

Hunterhouse College
Upper Lisburn Road, Finaghy, Belfast, County Antrim BT10 0LE
Tel: 028 9061 2293
Principal: Mr Andrew Gibson MA, DipEd, PQH
Age range: G11–18 years

Inchmarlo
Cranmore Park, Belfast, County Antrim BT9 6JR
Tel: 028 9038 1454
Headteacher: Mrs A Morwood
Age range: B4–11 years

Methodist College
1 Malone Road, Belfast, County Antrim BT9 6BY
Tel: 028 9020 5205
Principal: Mr Scott Naismith
Age range: 4–18 years

Newtownabbey Independent Christian school
307–309 Ballyclare Road, Glengormley, Newtownabbey, County Antrim BT36 4TQ
Tel: 028 9084 4937
Principal: Mrs L McClung
Age range: 4–18 years

Royal Belfast Academical Institution
College Square East, Belfast, County Antrim BT1 6DL
Tel: 028 9024 0461
Principal: Ms Janet Williamson
Age range: B11–18 years

St Mary's Christian Brothers' Grammar School
147a Glen Road, Belfast, County Antrim BT11 8NR
Tel: 028 9029 4000
Head of School: Mrs Siobhan Kelly
Age range: B11–19 years

Victoria College Belfast
2A Cranmore Park, Belfast, County Antrim BT9 6JA
Tel: 028 9066 1506
Principal: Mrs Karen Quinn
Age range: G3–19 years

County Armagh

Portadown Independent Christian School
Levaghery Gardens, Portadown, County Armagh BT63 5EQ
Tel: 028 3833 6733
Principal: Miss Diane Haffey
Age range: 3–16 years

The Royal School, Armagh
College Hill, Armagh, County Armagh BT61 9DH
Tel: 02837 522807
Headmaster: Mr Graham G W Montgomery
Age range: 4–18 years (boarding from 8)

County Down

Bangor Grammar School
84 Gransha Road, Bangor, County Down BT19 7QU
Tel: 028 91 473734
Headteacher: Mrs E P Huddleson
Age range: B11–18 years

Bangor Independent Christian School
277A Clandeboye Road, Bangor, County Down BT19 1AA
Tel: 028 9145 0240
Headteacher: Miss Anna Priestley
Age range: 3–16 years

Harmony Christian School
17–19 Main Street, Ballynahinch, County Down BT24 8DH
Tel: 028 9756 3487
Principal: Mrs Leanne Woods
Age range: 4–18 years

Holywood Steiner School
34 Croft Road, Holywood, County Down BT18 0PR
Tel: 028 9042 8029
Headteacher: Mr Peter Chambers
Age range: 3–17 years

Mourne Independent Christian School
5 Carrigenagh Road, Kilkeel, County Down BT34 4NE
Tel: 028 417 62712
Principal: Mrs H Campbell
Age range: 4–16 years

OneSchool Global UK Newry Campus
22 Rampart Road, Newry, County Down BT34 2QU
Tel: 02830 260777
Age range: 7–18 years

Rockport School
15 Rockport Road, Craigavad, Holywood, County Down BT18 0DD
Tel: 028 9042 8372
Headmaster: Mr George Vance
Age range: 3–18 years

County Londonderry

Coleraine Grammar School
23–33 Castlerock Road, Coleraine, County Londonderry BT51 3LA
Tel: 028 7034 4331
Headmaster: Dr David Carruthers
Age range: 11–18 years

OneSchool Global UK Knockloughrim Campus
23 Rocktown Road, Knockloughrim, County Londonderry BT45 8QE
Tel: 02879 645191
Age range: 7–18 years

County Tyrone

Clogher Valley Independent Christian School
150 Ballagh Road, Fivemiletown, County Tyrone BT75 0QP
Tel: 028 89521851
Principal: Mrs R Carscadden
Age range: 4–16 years

Kilskeery Independent Christian School
19 Old Junction Road, Kilskeery, Omagh, County Tyrone BT78 3RN
Tel: 028 89 561 560
Principal: Mrs Pamela Foster
Age range: 4–18 years

The Royal School, Dungannon
2 Ranfurly Road, Dungannon, County Tyrone BT71 6EG
Tel: 02887 722710
Headmaster: Dr David Burnett
Age range: 11–18 years (boarding from 11)

Scotland

KEY TO SYMBOLS

- *Boys' school*
- *Girls' school*
- *International school*
- *Tutorial or sixth form college*
- *A levels*
- *Boarding accommodation*
- *Bursaries*
- *International Baccalaureate*
- *Learning support*
- *Entrance at 16+*
- *Vocational qualifications*
- *Independent Association of Preparatory Schools*
- *The Headmasters' & Headmistresses' Conference*
- *Independent Schools Association*
- *Girls' School Association*
- *Boarding Schools' Association*
- *Society of Heads*

Unless otherwise indicated, all schools are coeducational day schools. Single-sex and boarding schools will be indicated by the relevant icon.

Aberdeen

Albyn School
17–23 Queen's Road,
Aberdeen AB15 4PB
Tel: 01224 322408
Headmaster: Mr Stefan Horsman
Age range: 2–18 years

International School of Aberdeen
Pitfodels House, North Deeside Road,
Pitfodels, Cults, Aberdeen AB15 9PN
Tel: 01224 730300
Head of School: Mr Nick Little
Age range: 3–18 years

Robert Gordon's College
Schoolhill, Aberdeen AB10 1FE
Tel: 01224 646346
Head of College: Mr
Robin Macpherson
Age range: 3–18 years

St Margaret's School for Girls
17 Albyn Place, Aberdeen AB10 1RU
Tel: +44 (0)1224 584466
Headmistress: Miss Anna Tomlinson
Age range: B3–5 years G3–18 years

Aberdeenshire

OneSchool Global UK Caledonia (North) Campus
Millden, Balmedie,
Aberdeenshire AB23 8YY
Tel: 01259 303030
Age range: 7–18 years

Angus

Lathallan School
Brotherton Castle, Johnshaven,
Montrose, Angus DD10 0HN
Tel: 01561 362220
Headmaster: Mr Richard Toley
Age range: 6 months–18 years

Argyll & Bute

Lomond School
10 Stafford Street, Helensburgh,
Argyll & Bute G84 9JX
Tel: +44 (0)1436 672476
Principal: Mrs Johanna Urquhart
Age range: 3–18 years
No. of pupils: 360

Borders

St. Mary's School
Abbey Park, Melrose, Borders TD6 9LN
Tel: 01896 822517
Headmaster: Mr Liam Harvey
Age range: 2–13 years

Clackmannanshire

Dollar Academy
Dollar, Clackmannanshire FK14 7DU
Tel: 01259 742511
Rector: Mr Ian Munro
Age range: 4–18 years
(boarding from 10)
No. of pupils: 1340
Fees: Day £10,899–£14,571 WB
£28,197–£31,869 FB £30,051–£33,723

OneSchool Global UK Caledonia (South) Campus
The Pavillions, Stirling Road, Alloa,
Clackmannanshire FK10 1TA
Tel: 01259 303030
Age range: 7–18 years

Dundee

High School of Dundee
Euclid Crescent, Dundee DD1 1HU
Tel: 01382 202921
Rector: Mrs Lise Hudson
Age range: 3–18 years
No. of pupils: 1000
Fees: Day £9,618–£13,650

East Lothian

Belhaven Hill School
Belhaven Road, Dunbar,
East Lothian EH42 1NN
Tel: 01368 862785
Headmaster: Mr. Olly Langton
Age range: 5–13 years

Loretto Junior School
North Esk Lodge, 1 North High Street,
Musselburgh, East Lothian EH21 6JA
Tel: 0131 653 4570
Headmaster: Mr Andrew Dickenson
Age range: 3–12 years

LORETTO SCHOOL
For further details see p. 296
Linkfield Road, Musselburgh,
East Lothian EH21 7RE
Tel: +44 (0)131 653 4455
Email: admissions@loretto.com
Website: www.loretto.com
Head of School: Dr.
Graham R. W. Hawley
Age range: 3–18 years
No. of pupils: 500
Fees: Day £3,212–£9,182
FB £8,782–£13,485

The Compass School
West Road, Haddington,
East Lothian EH41 3RD
Tel: 01620 822642
Headmaster: Mr Mark Becher
MA(Hons), PGCE
Age range: 3–12 years

Edinburgh

Basil Paterson School & College
65/66 Queen Street, Edinburgh EH2 4NA
Tel: 01312 253802
Age range: 14–16+ years

Cargilfield School
45 Gamekeeper's Road,
Edinburgh EH4 6HU
Tel: 0131 336 2207
Headmaster: Mr. Robert Taylor
Age range: 3–13 years

Clifton Hall School
Newbridge, Edinburgh EH28 8LQ
Tel: 0131 333 1359
Headmaster: Mr R Grant
Age range: 3–18 years

Edinburgh Montessori Arts School
18N Liberton Brae, Edinburgh EH16 6AE
Tel: 0131 600 0123
Principal: Ms Emma Rattigan
Age range: 1–18 years

Edinburgh Steiner School
60–64 Spylaw Road,
Edinburgh EH10 5BR
Tel: 0131 337 3410
Age range: 2–18 years
No. of pupils: 380

ESMS Junior School
11 Queensferry Terrace,
Edinburgh EH4 3EQ
Tel: +44 (0)131 311 1111
Head of School: Mr Mike Kane
Age range: 3–11 years

Fettes College
Carrington Road, Edinburgh EH4 1QX
Tel: +44 (0)131 332 2281
Head of School: Mrs Helen Harrison
Age range: 13–18 years

Fettes College Preparatory School
East Fettes Avenue, Edinburgh EH4 1DL
Tel: +44 (0)131 332 2976
Headmaster: Mr A A Edwards
Age range: 7–13 years

George Heriot's School
Lauriston Place, Edinburgh EH3 9EQ
Tel: 0131 229 7263
Principal: Mr Gareth Warren
Age range: 3–18 years

George Watson's College
69–71 Colinton Road,
Edinburgh EH10 5EG
Tel: 0131 446 6000
Principal: Mr Melvyn Roffe
Age range: 3–18 years

Mannafields Christian School
Unit B12, St Margaret's House, 151
London Road, Edinburgh EH7 6AE
Tel: 131516 3221
Age range: 5–14 years

Merchiston Castle School
294 Colinton Road, Edinburgh EH13 0PU
Tel: 0131 312 2200
Headmaster: Mr Jonathan Anderson
Age range: B7–18 years
(boarding from 7)
No. of pupils: 400
Fees: Day £15,930–£27,090
FB £22,950–£37,320

Regius School
69a Whitehill Street, Newcraighall,
Edinburgh EH21 8QZ
Tel: 0131 669 2913
Head of School: Mr James Steward
Age range: 5–14 years

St George's School for Girls
Garscube Terrace, Edinburgh EH12 6BG
Tel: 0131 311 8000
Head: Mrs Alex Hems
Age range: B3–5 years G3–18
years (boarding from 10)

St Mary's Music School
Coates Hall, 25 Grosvenor
Crescent, Edinburgh EH12 5EL
Tel: 0131 538 7766
Headteacher: Dr Kenneth Taylor
BSc Hons, PhD, PGCE, PG Dip
Age range: 9–19 years

Stewart's Melville College
Queensferry Road, Edinburgh EH4 3EZ
Tel: +44 (0)131 311 1000
Head of School: Mr Anthony Simpson
Age range: B12–18 years

The Edinburgh Academy
42 Henderson Row, Edinburgh EH3 5BL
Tel: 0131 556 4603
Rector: Barry Welsh
Age range: 2–18 years

The Mary Erskine School
Ravelston, Edinburgh EH4 3NT
Tel: +44 (0)131 347 5700
Head of School: Ms Kirsty Nicholson
Age range: G12–18 years
(boarding from 12)

Fife

St Leonards School
South Street, St Andrews, Fife KY16 9QJ
Tel: 01334 472126
Head: Mr Simon Brian
Age range: 5–18 years
(boarding from 10)
No. of pupils: 593

Glasgow

Belmont House School
Sandringham Avenue, Newton
Mearns, Glasgow G77 5DU
Tel: 0141 639 2922
Principal: Mr Melvyn D Shanks
BSc, DipEd, MInstP, CPhys, SQH
Age range: 3–18 years

Fernhill School
Fernbrae Avenue, Burnside,
Rutherglen, Glasgow G73 4SG
Tel: 01416 342674
Head Teacher: Mr Mark Donnelly
Age range: 3–18 years
No. of pupils: 230
Fees: Day £8,900–£13,500

Hutchesons' Grammar School
21 Beaton Road, Glasgow G41 4NW
Tel: 0141 423 2933
Rector: Mr Colin Gambles
BSc (Hons) PGCE
Age range: 3–18 years

Kelvinside Academy
33 Kirklee Road, Glasgow G12 0SW
Tel: 0141 357 3376
Rector: Mr Daniel J Wyatt BA (Ed) Hons
Age range: 3–18 years

Olivewood Primary School
81 Lister Street, Glasgow G4 0BZ
Age range: 5–11 years

St Aloysius' College
45 Hill Street, Glasgow G3 6RJ
Tel: 0141 332 3190
Head Master: Mr Matthew Bartlett
MA (Cantab), PGCE, NLE, NPQH
Age range: 3–18 years

The Glasgow Academy, Kelvinbridge
Colebrooke Street, Kelvinbridge,
Glasgow G12 8HE
Tel: 0141 334 8558
Rector: Mr Matthew K
Pearce BA (Dunelm)
Age range: 3–18 years

The Glasgow Academy, Milngavie
Mugdock Road, Milngavie,
Glasgow G62 8NP
Tel: 0141 956 3758
Rector: Mr Matthew K
Pearce BA (Dunelm)
Age range: 3–8 years

The Glasgow Academy, Newlands
54 Newlands Road, Newlands,
Glasgow G43 2JG
Tel: 0141 632 0736
Rector: Mr Matthew K
Pearce BA (Dunelm)
Age range: 3–8 years

The High School of Glasgow
637 Crow Road, Glasgow G13 1PL
Tel: 0141 954 9628
Rector: Mr John O'Neill
Age range: 3–18 years

Moray

Drumduan School
Clovenside Road, Forres,
Moray IV36 2RD
Tel: + 44 (0)1309 676300
Principal Teacher: Krzysztof
Zajaczkowski
Age range: 3–18 years

Gordonstoun
Elgin, Moray IV30 5RF
Tel: 01343 837837
Principal: Ms Lisa Kerr BA
Age range: 41/2–18 years

Perth & Kinross

Ardvreck School
Crieff, Perth & Kinross PH7 4EX
Tel: 01764 653112
Headmistress: Mrs Ali Kinge
Age range: 3–13 years
(boarding from 7)

Craigclowan School & Nursery
Edinburgh Road, Perth,
Perth & Kinross PH2 8PS
Tel: 01738 626310
Head of School: Liz Henderson
Age range: 3–13 years
No. of pupils: 219
Fees: Day £5,330

Glenalmond College, Perth
Glenalmond, Perth, Perth
& Kinross PH1 3RY
Tel: 01738 842000
Warden: Mr Mark Mortimer
Age range: 12–18 years

Kilgraston School
Bridge of Earn, Perth, Perth & Kinross PH2 9BQ
Tel: 01738 812257
Head of School: Mrs Tanya Davie
Age range: B4–12 years G4–18 years (boarding from 8)
No. of pupils: 235
Fees: Day £13,410–£22,785 FB £29,730–£42,045

Morrison's Academy
Ferntower Road, Crieff, Perth & Kinross PH7 3AN
Tel: 01764 653885
Rector: Mr A J McGarva
Age range: 2–18 years

Strathallan School
Forgandenny, Perth, Perth & Kinross PH2 9EG
Tel: 01738 812546
Headmaster: Mr Mark Lauder MA Hons
Age range: 7–18 years
No. of pupils: 545
Fees: Day £16,092–£25,452 FB £26,649–£38,199

Perthshire

Queen Victoria School
Dunblane, Perthshire FK15 0JY
Tel: 01786 822288
Head: Donald Shaw BSc(Hons) PGCE
Age range: 11–18 years

Renfrewshire

Al-Qalam Primary & High School
Ben Nevis Road, Paisley, Renfrewshire PA2 7LA
Tel: 014123 72236
Executive Head: Mr Shoeb Sarguroh
Age range: 5–14 years

Cedars School of Excellence
31 Ardgowan Square, Greenock, Renfrewshire PA16 8NJ
Tel: 01475 723905
Interim Head: Ms Jennifer Offord
Age range: 5–18 years

St Columba's School
Duchal Road, Kilmacolm, Renfrewshire PA13 4AU
Tel: 01505 872238
Rector: Ms Victoria J. Reilly
Age range: 3–18 years

South Ayrshire

Wellington School
Carleton Turrets, 1 Craigweil Road, Ayr, South Ayrshire KA7 2XH
Tel: 01292 269321
Head: Mr S Johnson MA (Cantab) PGCE
Age range: 3–18 years

South Lanarkshire

Hamilton College
Bothwell Road, Hamilton, South Lanarkshire ML3 0AY
Tel: 01698 282700
Headteacher: Mr Richard Charman
Age range: 2–18 years
No. of pupils: 400
Fees: Day £8,985–£12,588

Stirling

Fairview International School, Bridge of Allan
52 Kenilworth Road, Bridge of Allan, Stirling FK9 4RY
Tel: +44 (0)1786 231952
Headteacher: Mr David Hicks
Age range: 5–18 years
No. of pupils: 64

Wales

KEY TO SYMBOLS

- *Boys' school*
- *Girls' school*
- *International school*
- *Tutorial or sixth form college*
- *A levels*
- *Boarding accommodation*
- *Bursaries*
- *International Baccalaureate*
- *Learning support*
- *Entrance at 16+*
- *Vocational qualifications*
- *Independent Association of Preparatory Schools*
- *The Headmasters' & Headmistresses' Conference*
- *Independent Schools Association*
- *Girls' School Association*
- *Boarding Schools' Association*
- *Society of Heads*

Unless otherwise indicated, all schools are coeducational day schools. Single-sex and boarding schools will be indicated by the relevant icon.

Cardiff

Cardiff Sixth Form College
1–3 Trinity Court, 21–27 Newport Road, , Cardiff CF24 0AA
Tel: +44 (0)29 2049 3121
Principal: Mr Gareth Collier
Age range: 15–18 years

Carmarthenshire

Llandovery College
Queensway, Llandovery, Carmarthenshire SA20 0EE
Tel: +44(0)1550 723000
Warden: Mr Dominic Findlay
Age range: 4–18 years

St. Michael's School
Bryn, Llanelli, Carmarthenshire SA14 9TU
Tel: 01554 820325
Headmaster: Mr Benson Ferrari
Age range: 3–18 years

Clwyd

Rydal Penrhos Preparatory School
Pwllycrochan Avenue, Colwyn Bay, Clwyd LL29 7BT
Tel: +44 (0)1492 530 381
Head of School: Mrs Lucy Davies
Age range: 2–11 years

Rydal Penrhos Senior School
Pwllycrochan Avenue, Colwyn Bay, Clwyd LL29 7BT
Tel: +44 (0)1492 530155
Head of School: Mr Phil Sutton
Age range: 11–18 years

St David's College
Gloddaeth Hall, Llandudno, Clwyd LL30 1RD
Tel: 01492 875974
Headmaster: Mr Andrew Russell
Age range: 9–19 years (boarding from 9)

Denbighshire

Fairholme Preparatory School
The Mount, Mount Road, St. Asaph, Denbighshire LL17 0DH
Tel: 01745 583 505
Principal: Mrs E Perkins MA(Oxon)
Age range: 3–11 years

Myddelton College
Peakes Lane, Denbigh, Denbighshire LL16 3EN
Tel: +44 174 547 2201
Head Teacher: Mr Andrew Allman
Age range: 4–18 years

Ruthin School
Mold Road, Ruthin, Denbighshire LL15 1EE
Tel: 01824 702543
Interim Head: Ms Sue Frencham
Age range: 11–18 years

Glamorgan

Cardiff Academy
Harlech Court, Bute Terrace, Cardiff, Glamorgan CF10 2FE
Tel: 02920 318 318
Principal: Mrs Caroline Williams
Age range: 16–19 years

Cardiff Montessori School
Golden Gate, 73 Ty Glas Avenue, Llanishen, Cardiff, Glamorgan CF14 5DX
Tel: 02920 567311
Head of School: Ms Esma Izzidien
Age range: 2–12 years

Cardiff Muslim Primary School
Merthyr Street, Cathays, Cardiff, Glamorgan CF24 4JL
Tel: 029 2034 2040
Headteacher: Sakhawat Ali
Age range: 4–11 years

Cardiff Steiner School
Hawthorn Road West, Llandaff North, Cardiff, Glamorgan CF14 2FL
Tel: 029 2056 7986
Age range: 3–18 years

Ely Presbyterian Church School
4–6 Archer Road, Cardiff, Glamorgan CF5 4FR
Tel: 02920 596410
Headteachers: Mrs Julia Haines & Stephanie Williams
Age range: 3–16 years

Ffynone House School
36 St James's Crescent, Swansea, Glamorgan SA1 6DR
Tel: 01792 464967
Headteacher: Mr Michael Boulding
Age range: 11–18 years

Howell's School, Llandaff GDST
Cardiff Road, Llandaff, Cardiff, Glamorgan CF5 2YD
Tel: 029 2056 2019
Principal: Mrs Sally Davis BSc
Age range: B16–18 years G3–18 years

Kings Monkton School
6 West Grove, Cardiff, Glamorgan CF24 3XL
Tel: 02920 482854
Principal: Mr Paul Norton
Age range: 3–18 years

Oakleigh House School
38 Penlan Crescent, Uplands, Swansea, Glamorgan SA2 0RL
Tel: 01792 298537
Headmistress: Mrs Catrin Sherwood
Age range: 21/2–11 years

OneSchool Global UK Swansea Campus
Sway Road, Morriston, Swansea, Glamorgan SA6 6JA
Tel: 01792 581221
Age range: 7–18 years

St Clare's School
Newton, Porthcawl, Glamorgan CF36 5NR
Tel: 01656 782509
Head of School: Helen Hier
Age range: 21/2–18 years
No. of pupils: 250
Fees: Day £6,753–£11,799

St John's College, Cardiff
College Green, Old St Mellons, Cardiff, Glamorgan CF3 5YX
Tel: 029 2077 8936
Headteacher: Mr Shaun Moody BA (Hons) PGCE
Age range: 3–18 years

The Cathedral School, Llandaff
Cardiff Road, Llandaff, Cardiff, Glamorgan CF5 2YH
Tel: 029 2056 3179
Head: Ms Clare Sherwood
Age range: 3–18 years

Ummul Mumineen Academy
142 Penarth Road, Grangetown, Cardiff, Glamorgan CF11 6NJ
Tel: 02920 220 383
Age range: 8–16 years

Westbourne School
Hickman Road, Penarth, Glamorgan CF64 2AJ
Tel: 029 2070 5705
Headteacher: Dr GW Griffiths BSc, PhD, ARCS, PGCE
Age range: 2–18 years
No. of pupils: 382
Fees: Day £9,192–£16,152
FB £38,950–£40,620

Gwynedd

Bangor Independent School
The Old Canonry, 39 Ffordd Gwynedd, Bangor, Gwynedd LL57 1DT
Tel: 01248 354635
Headteacher: Mr Paul Gash
Age range: 3–11 years

St Gerard's School
Ffriddoedd Road, Bangor, Gwynedd LL57 2EL
Tel: 01248 351656
Head Teacher: Mr Campbell Harrison
Age range: 4–18 years
No. of pupils: 138
Fees: Day £8,250–£12,480

Treffos School
Llansadwrn, Nr. Menai Bridge, Isle of Anglesey, Gwynedd LL59 5SD
Tel: 01248 712322
Headmaster: Dr S. Humphreys
Age range: 3–11 years

Monmouthshire

Llangattock School Monmouth
Llangattock-Vibon-Avel, Monmouth, Monmouthshire NP25 5NG
Tel: 01600 772 213
Principal: Ms Rosemary Whaley
Age range: 2–19 years

Monmouth Prep School
Hadnock Road, Monmouth, Monmouthshire NP25 3NG
Tel: 01600 715930
Age range: 3–11 years (boarding from 7)

Monmouth School for Boys
Almshouse Street, Monmouth, Monmouthshire NP25 3XP
Tel: 01600 713143
Age range: B11–18 years (boarding from 11)

Monmouth School for Girls
Hereford Road, Monmouth, Monmouthshire NP25 5XT
Tel: 01600 711100
Age range: G11–18 years (boarding from 11)

Rougemont School
Llantarnam Hall, Malpas Road, Newport, Monmouthshire NP20 6QB
Tel: 01633 820800
Headmaster: Mr Robert Carnevale
Age range: 3–18 years

Pembrokeshire

Castle School Pembrokeshire
Glenover House, Scarrowscant Lane, Haverfordwest, Pembrokeshire SA61 1ES
Tel: 01437 558010
Director: Ms Harriet Harrison
Age range: 3–18 years

Nant-y-Cwm Steiner School
Llanycefn, Clunderwen, Pembrokeshire SA66 7QJ
Tel: +44 (0)1437 563640
Age range: 3–14 years

Redhill High School
Clynderwen House, Clynderwen, Pembrokeshire SA66 7PN
Tel: 01437 211003
Headmaster: Mr Alun Millington
Age range: 11–18 years

Redhill Preparatory School
The Garth, St David's Road, Haverfordwest, Pembrokeshire SA61 2UR
Tel: 01437 762472
Head Teacher: Mr Adrian Thomas
Age range: 0–11 years

Powys

Christ College
Brecon, Powys LD3 8AF
Tel: 01874 615440
Head: Mr Gareth Pearson
Age range: 7–18 years
No. of pupils: 370
Fees: Day £9,582–£19,584
FB £19,431–£34,419

OneSchool Global UK Newtown Campus
Sarn, Newtown, Powys SY16 4EJ
Tel: 01686 670152
Age range: 7–18 years

Vale of Glamorgan

UWC Atlantic
St Donat's Castle, St Donat's, Llantwit Major, Vale of Glamorgan CF61 1WF
Tel: +44 (0)1446 799000
Principal: Naheed Bardai
Age range: 16–19 years
No. of pupils: 350

Examinations and qualifications

Common Entrance

What is Common Entrance?

The Common Entrance examinations are used in UK independent schools (and some independent schools overseas) for transfer from junior to senior schools at the ages of 11+ and 13+. They were first introduced in 1904 and are internationally recognised as being a rigorous form of assessment following a thorough course of study. The examinations are produced by the Independent Schools Examinations Board and backed by HMC (Headmasters' and Headmistresses' Conference), GSA (Girls' Schools Association), and IAPS (Independent Association of Prep Schools) which together represent the leading independent schools in the UK, and many overseas.

Common Entrance is not a public examination as, for example, GCSE, and candidates may normally be entered only in one of the following circumstances:

a) they have been offered a place at a senior school subject to their passing the examination, or

b) they are entered as a 'trial run', in which case the papers are marked by the junior school concerned

Candidates normally take the examination in their own junior or preparatory schools, either in the UK or overseas.

How does Common Entrance fit into the progression to GCSEs?

Rapid changes in education nationally and internationally have resulted in regular reviews of the syllabuses for all the Common Entrance examinations. Reviews of the National Curriculum, in particular, have brought about a number of changes, with the Board wishing to ensure that it continues to set high standards. It is also a guiding principle that Common Entrance should be part of the natural progression from 11-16, and not a diversion from it.

Common Entrance at 11+

At 11+, the examination consists of papers in English, mathematics and science. It is designed so that it can be taken by candidates either from independent preparatory schools or by candidates from schools in the maintained sector or overseas who have had no special preparation. The examination is normally taken in January for entrance to senior schools in the following September.

Common Entrance at 13+

At 13+, most candidates come from independent preparatory schools. The compulsory subjects are English, mathematics and science. Papers in French, geography, German, Classical Greek, history, Latin, religious studies and Spanish are also available and candidates usually offer as many subjects as they can. In most subjects, papers are available at more than one level to cater for candidates of different abilities. There are three examination sessions each year, with the majority of candidates sitting in the summer prior to entry to their senior schools in September.

Marking and grading

The papers are set centrally but the answers are marked by the senior school for which a candidate is entered. Mark schemes are provided by the Board but senior schools are free to set their own grade boundaries. Results are available within two weeks of the examinations taking place.

Pre-Testing and the ISEB Common Pre-Tests

A number of senior independent schools 'pre-test' pupils for entry, prior to them taking their main entrance examinations at a later date. Usually, these pre-tests take place when a pupil is in Year 6 or Year 7 of his or her junior school and will then be going on to sit Common Entrance in Year 8. The tests are designed to assess a pupil's academic potential and suitability for a particular senior school so that the child, the parents and the school know well in advance whether he/she is going to be offered a place at the school, subject to a satisfactory performance in the entrance examinations. The tests enable senior schools to manage their lists and help to ensure that pupils are not entered for examinations in which they are unlikely to be successful. In short, it reduces uncertainty for all concerned.

Pre-tests may be written specifically for the senior school for which the candidate is entered but a growing number of schools are choosing to use the Common Pre-Tests provided by the Independent Schools Examinations Board. These online tests are usually taken in the candidate's own junior school and one of their main advantages is that a pupil need sit the tests only once, with the results then made available to any senior school which wishes to use them. The multiple-choice tests cover verbal reasoning, non-verbal reasoning, English and mathematics, with the results standardised according to the pupil's age when they are taken. Further information is available on the ISEB website at www.iseb.co.uk.

Parents are advised to check the entrance requirements for senior schools to see if their child will be required to sit a pre-test.

Further information

Details of the Common Entrance examinations and how to register candidates are available on the ISEB website www.iseb.co.uk. Copies of past papers and a wide range of textbooks and other resources can be purchased from Galore Park Publishing Ltd at www.galorepark.co.uk. Support materials are also available from Hodder Education and other publishers; see the Resources section of the ISEB website for details.

Independent Schools Examinations Board
Endeavour House, Crow Arch Lane,
Ringwood, Hampshire BH24 1HP

Telephone: 01425 470555
Email: enquiries@iseb.co.uk
Web: www.iseb.co.uk

7+ Entrance Exams

What is the 7+?

The 7+ is the descriptive name given to the entrance exams set by an increasing number of independent schools for pupils wishing to gain admission into their Year 3.

7+ entrance exams may be simply for admission into a selective preparatory school, which will then prepare the child for Common Entrance exams to gain a place at senior school. Alternatively, the 7+ can be a route into a school with both prep and senior departments, therefore often effectively bypassing the 11+ or 13+ Common Entrance exams.

The Independent Schools Examinations Board provides Common Entrance examinations and assessments for pupils seeking entry to independent senior schools at 11+ and 13+, but there is as yet no equivalent for the 7+. The testing is largely undertaken by the individual schools, although some schools might commission the test from external agencies. Many schools in the incredibly competitive London area offer entrance exams at 7+ and some share specimen papers on their website to clarify what 7+ children will face.

Who sits the 7+?

The 7+ is sat by Year 2 children, who may be moving from a state primary school or a stand-alone pre-prep school to an independent prep school (although many prep schools now have their own pre-prep department, with a cohort of children poised to pass into Year 3 there).

Registration for 7+ entrance exams usually closes in the November of Year 2, with the exams then sat in January or February, for entry that September.

How is the 7+ assessed?

Written exam content will be primarily English and maths based, whilst spelling, dictation, mental arithmetic and more creative skills may be assessed verbally on a one-to-one basis. Group exercises are also sometimes used to look at a child's initiative and their ability to work with others.

Schools will not only be looking for academic potential, but also good citizens and a mixture of personalities to produce a well-rounded year group. For this reason, children are often asked to attend an interview. Some schools interview all candidates, whilst others may call back a limited number with good test results. They will be looking for a child's ability to look an adult in the eye and think on their feet, but also simply to show some spark and personality.

After the assessments, children will be told if they have been successful in gaining a firm place, or a place on a waiting list.

Further Information

As the 7+ is not centrally regulated, it is best for parents to seek accurate admissions and testing information direct from the schools in which they are interested. In addition to a school's facilities and ethos, choosing a school for admission at 7+ will probably also involve whether the school has a senior department and if not, the prep school's record in gaining its students places at target senior schools.

Experienced educational consultants may be able to help parents decide which independent prep school is best suited for their child, based on their personality, senior school ambitions and academic potential. Many parents enlist the help of tutors to prepare children for the 7+, if only to reduce the fear of the unknown in these very young children. This is achieved by teaching them the required curriculum, what to expect on their test and interview days, and giving them the opportunity to practice tackling the type of assessments they will face.

The Pre-Senior Baccalaureate

What is the Pre-Senior Baccalaureate?

The Pre-Senior Baccalaureate (PSB) is part of the Learning Skills Trust (LST) which operates 2 frameworks of study. The PSB is designed for Years 2 – 8 and the Skills Development Framework (SDF) for Years 9 – 11. The frameworks focus on the active development and assessment of 6 core skills: Communication, Collaboration, Leadership, Independence, Reviewing and Improving and Thinking and Learning. Member schools promote the core skills across all areas of school life, and provide guidance for pupils in progressing these skills, which are seen as essential for developing capable and balanced adults, able to make the most of the opportunities of a fast-changing world. A strong but appropriate knowledge base compliments this, with the use of focused tutoring, pastoral care and Well Being programmes.

Schools do not work to a prescribed curriculum and the emphasis is upon promoting an independent approach which works for each individual school. There are subject INSET days for LST school staff annually, supported by specialist colleagues, to ensure that work done in LST schools compliments the demands of education at higher levels.

The development of skills is recognised as essential by the Independent Schools Inspectorate (ISI), and recent ISI reports on PSB schools highlight the excellent contribution the PSB has in schools achieving excellence.

Assessment

The PSB has a 10-point scale for all subjects studied with a compulsory spine covering: English, Maths, Science, Modern Languages, The Humanities, Art, Design Technology, Music, Sport and PE with each pupil additionally completing a cross curricular project - The Pre-Senior Project Qualification. Optional subjects are agreed with schools, but these must be supported by a scheme of work clearly identifying appropriate core skills which are assessed on a narrative scale. The 10-point scale cross references both ISEB and National Curriculum assessment levels. Pupils moving on to senior school do so via individual senior school pre-testing arrangements, the award of the PSB certificate, core ISEB papers or a combination of the above.

The SDF is a commitment to enable students across 3 years to experience authentic interdisciplinary experiences through extended project work. Schools have freedom to work within the framework and adapt it to their specific setting and existing programmes can be adapted to the SDF. The assessment of core skills is across all aspects of school life and not focused on academic subjects, which have their own particular demands. Time is given for students to reflect on the development of core skills, progression academically and contributions more widely to school life. A particular emphasis is given to the successful transition to independent study and away from closed learning tasks assessed on knowledge retention rather than student reflection.

Membership categories

All schools join as Partner Members and progress to full membership following an audit.

Affiliated membership is for schools that have developed their own skills-based approach, in line with LST principles; staff can participate in training opportunities and the Heads of Affiliated Schools join committee meetings as guests.

Membership of the above categories is dependent upon strong ISI reports, the development of a skills-based curriculum, with skills clearly identified in schemes of work, and excellent teaching.

Foundation membership is for organisations that actively support the LST by providing funding which enables the charity to invest in research, IT, etc. They also provide staff for meetings and conferences and offer a valuable perspective on the operation of the charity.

Further details

The LST is an entirely independent charity overseen by a Board of Trustees who have expertise in both primary and secondary education. Details of the LST can be found on the website – psbacc.org – together with contact details for the Operations Manager who can provide further details on request. .

General Certificate of Secondary Education (GCSE)

What are the GCSE qualifications?

GCSE qualifications were first introduced in 1986 and are the principal means of assessment at Key Stage 4 across a range of academic subject areas. They command respect and have status not only in the UK but worldwide.

Main features of the GCSE

There are four unitary awarding organisations for GCSEs in England (see 'Awarding organisations and examination dates' section, p437). WJEC and CCEA also offer GCSE qualifications in Wales and Northern Ireland. Each examining group designs its own specifications but they are required to conform to set criteria. For some aspects of the qualification system, the exam boards adopt common ways of working. When the exam boards work together in this way they generally do so through the Joint Council of Qualifications (JCQ). The award of a grade is intended to indicate that a candidate has met the required level of skills, knowledge and understanding.

New, reformed GCSEs have been introduced in recent years. Assessment in these reformed GCSEs consists primarily of formal examinations taken at the end of the student's two-year course. Other types of assessment, non-exam assessment (NEA), is used where there are skills and knowledge which cannot be assessed through exams. Ofqual have set the percentage of the total marks that will come from NEA.

The reformed GCSEs feature new and more demanding content, as required by the government and developed by the exam boards. Courses are designed for two years of study (linear assessment) and no longer divided into different modules.

Exams can only be split into 'foundation tier' and 'higher tier' if one exam paper does not give all students the opportunity to show their knowledge and their abilities.

Such tiering is only available in maths, science and modern foreign languages; other subjects do not have tiers. Resit opportunities will only be available each November in English language and maths, and then only for students who have turned 16 by the 31st of August in the year of the November assessment.

Summer 2022 marked the return of GCSE exams for the first time since 2019. Exams in 2020 and 2021 were replaced by alternatives due to constraints imposed following the pandemic. Grades were awarded through teachers' assessments based on mock exams, coursework and other available evidence.

Grading

The basic principle that exam boards follow when setting grade boundaries is that if the group of students (the cohort) taking a qualification in one year is of similar ability to the cohort in the previous year then the overall results (outcomes) should be comparable.

The reformed exams taken in summer 2017 were the first to show a new grading system, with the A* to G grades being phased out.

The grading system is 9 to 1, with 9 being the top grade. Ofqual says this allows greater differentiation between students. It expects that broadly the same proportion of students will achieve a grade 4 and above as those who achieved a grade C and above, that broadly the same proportion of students will achieve a grade 7 and above as those who achieved a grade A and above. There are three anchor points between the new grading system and the old one: the bottom of the new 1 grade is the same as the bottom of the old G grade, the bottom of the new 4 grade is the bottom of the old C grade, and the bottom of the 7 grade is the same as the bottom of the old A grade. Grade 9 will be set using the tailored approach formula in the first award.

Grades 2, 3, 5 and 6 will be awarded arithmetically so that the grade boundaries are equally spaced in terms of marks from neighbouring grades.

The government's definition of a 'strong pass' is set at grade 5 for reformed GCSEs. A grade 4 – or 'standard pass' – will continue to be a level 2 achievement. The DfE does not expect employers, colleges or universities to raise the bar to a grade 5 if a grade 4 would meet their requirements.

Can anyone take GCSE qualifications?

GCSEs are intended mainly for 16-year-old pupils, but are open to anyone of any age, whether studying full-time or part-time at a school, college or privately. There are no formal entry requirements.

Students normally study up to ten subjects over a two-year period. Short course GCSEs are available in some subjects (including PE and religious studies) – these include half the content of a full GCSE, so two short course GCSEs are equivalent to one full GCSE.

The English Baccalaureate

The English Baccalaureate (EBacc) is a school performance measure. It allows people to see how many pupils get a grade C or above (current grading) in the core academic subjects at Key Stage 4 in any government-funded school.

Progress 8 and Attainment 8

Progress 8 aims to capture the progress a pupil makes from the end of primary school to the end of secondary school. It is a type of value added measure, which means that pupils' results are compared to the actual achievements of other pupils with the same prior attainment.

The new performance measures are designed to encourage schools to offer a broad and balanced curriculum with a focus on an academic core at Key Stage 4, and reward schools for the teaching of all their pupils, measuring performance across 8 qualifications. Every increase in every grade a pupil achieves will attract additional points in the performance tables.

Progress 8 will be calculated for individual pupils solely in order to calculate a school's Progress 8 score, and there will be no need for schools to share individual Progress 8 scores with their pupils. Schools should continue to focus on which qualifications are most suitable for individual pupils, as the grades pupils achieve will help them reach their goals for the next stage of their education or training.

Attainment 8 will measure the achievement of a pupil across 8 qualifications including mathematics (double weighted) and English (double weighted), 3 further qualifications that count in the English Baccalaureate (EBacc) measure and 3 further qualifications that can be GCSE qualifications (including EBacc subjects) or any other non-GCSE qualification on the DfE approved list.

General Certificate of Education (GCE) Advanced level (A level)

Typically, A level qualifications are studied over a two-year period. There are no lower or upper age limits. Schools and colleges usually expect students aged 16-18 to have obtained grade 5s (A*-C in the old criteria) in five subjects at GCSE level before taking an advanced level course. This requirement may vary between centres and according to which specific subjects are to be studied. Mature students may be assessed on different criteria as to their suitability to embark on the course.

GCE Qualifications

Over the past few years, AS level and A level qualifications have been in a process of reform. New subjects have been introduced gradually, with the first wave taught from September 2015. Subjects that have not been reformed are no longer be available for teaching.

GCE qualifications are available at two levels: the Advanced Subsidiary (AS), which is generally delivered over one year and is seen as half an A level; and the A level (GCE). Nearly 70 titles are available, covering a wide range of subject areas, including humanities, sciences, language, business, arts, mathematics and technology.

One of the major reforms is that AS level results no longer count towards an A level in England (they previously counted for 50%). The two qualifications are linear, with AS assessments typically taking place after one year and A levels after two.

Some GCE AS and A levels, particularly the practical ones, contain a proportion of coursework. All GCE A levels that contain one or more types of assessment will have an element of synoptic assessment that tests students' understanding of the whole specification. GCE AS are graded A-E and A levels are graded A*-E.

Overall the amount of coursework at A level has been reduced in the reforms. In some subjects, such as the sciences, practical work will not contribute to the final A level but will be reported separately in a certificate of endorsement. In the sciences, students will do at least 12 practical activities, covering apparatus and techniques. Exam questions about practical work will make up at least 15% of the total marks for the qualification and students will be assessed on their knowledge, skills and understanding of practical work.

Summer 2022 marked the return of exams for the first time since 2019. Exams in 2020 and 2021 were replaced by alternatives due to constraints imposed following the pandemic. Grades were awarded through teachers' assessments based on mock exams, coursework and other available evidence

Cambridge International AS & A Level

Cambridge International AS & A Level is an internationally benchmarked qualification, taught in over 130 countries worldwide. It is typically for learners aged 16 to 19 years who need advanced study to prepare for university. It was created specifically for an international audience and the content has been devised to suit the wide variety of schools worldwide and avoid any cultural bias.

Cambridge International A Level is typically a two-year course, and Cambridge International AS Level is typically one year. Some subjects can be started as a Cambridge International AS Level and extended to a Cambridge International A Level. Students can either follow a broad course of study, or specialise in one particular subject area.

Learners use Cambridge International AS & A Levels to gain places at leading universities worldwide, including the UK, Ireland, USA, Canada, Australia, New Zealand, India, Singapore, Egypt, Jordan, South Africa, the Netherlands, Germany and Spain. In places such as the US and Canada, good grades in carefully chosen Cambridge International A Level subjects can result in up to one year of university course credit.

Assessment options:

Cambridge International AS & A Levels have a linear structure with exams at the end of the course. Students can choose from a range of assessment options:

Option 1: take Cambridge International AS Levels only. The Cambridge International AS Level syllabus content is half a Cambridge International A Level.

Option 2: staged assessment, which means taking the Cambridge International AS Level in one exam session and the Cambridge International A Level at a later session. However, this route is not possible in all subjects.

Option 3: take all Cambridge International A Level papers in the same examination session, usually at the end of the course.

Grades and subjects

Cambridge International A Levels are graded from A* to E. Cambridge International AS Levels are graded from A to E.

Subjects: available in 55 subjects including accounting, Afrikaans, Afrikaans – first language (AS only), Afrikaans language (AS only), applied information and communication technology, Arabic, Arabic language (AS only), art and design, biology, business, chemistry, Chinese, Chinese language (AS only), classical studies, computing, design and technology, design and textiles, digital media & design, divinity, economics, English language, English literature, environmental management, food studies, French, French language (AS only), French literature (AS only), general paper, geography, German, German language (AS only), Global Perspectives & Research, Hindi, Hindi language (AS only), Hindi literature (AS only), Hinduism, history, Islamic studies, Japanese language (AS only), English language and literature (AS only), law, Marathi, Marathi language (AS only), marine science, mathematics, further mathematics, media studies, music, physical education, physical science, physics,

Portuguese, Portuguese language (AS only), Portuguese literature (AS only), psychology, sociology, Spanish, Spanish first language (AS only), Spanish language (AS only), Spanish literature (AS only), Tamil, Tamil language (AS only), Telugu, Telugu language (AS only), thinking skills, travel and tourism, Urdu, Urdu language (AS only).
Website: www.cambridgeinternational.org/alevel

Cambridge IGCSE

Cambridge IGCSE is the world's most popular international qualification for 14 to16 year olds. It develops skills in creative thinking, enquiry and problem solving, in preparation for the next stage in a student's education. Cambridge IGCSE is taken in over 150 countries, and is widely recognised by employers and higher education institutions worldwide.

Cambridge IGCSE is graded from A*-G. In the UK, Cambridge IGCSE is accepted as equivalent to the GCSE. It can be used as preparation for Cambridge International A & AS Levels, UK A and AS levels, IB or AP and in some instances entry into university. Cambridge IGCSE First Language English and Cambridge IGCSE English Language qualifications are recognised by a significant number of UK universities as evidence of competence in the language for university entrance.

Subjects: available in over 70 subjects including accounting, Afrikaans – first language, Afrikaans – second language, agriculture, Arabic – first language, Arabic – foreign language, art and design, Baha Indonesia, Bangladesh studies, biology, business studies, chemistry, child development, Chinese – first language, Chinese – second language, Chinese (Mandarin) – foreign language, computer studies, Czech – first language, design and technology, development studies, drama, Dutch – first language, Dutch – foreign language, economics, English – additional language , English – first language, English – literature, English – second language, enterprise, environmental management, food and nutrition, French – first language, French – foreign language, geography, German – first language, German – foreign language, global perspectives, Greek – foreign language, Hindi as a second language, Italian – foreign language, history, India studies, Indonesian – foreign language, information and communication technology, IsiZulu as a second language, Japanese – first language, Japanese – foreign language, Kazakh as a second language, Korean (first language), Latin, Malay – first language, Malay – foreign language, mathematics, mathematics – additional, international mathematics, music, Pakistan studies, physical education, physical science, physics, Portuguese – first language, Portuguese – foreign language, religious studies, Russian – first language, science – combined, sciences – co-ordinated (double), sociology, Spanish – first language, Spanish – foreign language, Spanish – literature, Thai – first language, travel and tourism, Turkish – first language, Urdu – second language, world literature.
Website: www.cambridgeinternational.org/igcse

Edexcel International GCSEs

Pearson's Edexcel International GCSEs are academic qualifications aimed at learners aged 14 to 16. They're equivalent to a UK General Certificate of Secondary Education (GCSE), and are the main requirement for Level 3 studies, including progression to GCE AS or A levels, BTECs or employment. International GCSEs are linear qualifications, meaning that students take all of the exams at the end of the course. They are available at Level 1 (grades 3-1) and Level 2 (grades 9-4). There are currently more than 100,000 learners studying Edexcel International GCSEs, in countries throughout Asia, Africa, Europe, the Middle East and Latin America. Developed by subject specialists and reviewed regularly, many of Pearson's Edexcel International GCSEs include specific international content to make them relevant to students worldwide.

Pearson's Edexcel International GCSEs were initially developed for international schools. They have since become popular among independent schools in the UK, but are not approved for use in UK state schools.

OCR Free Standing Maths Qualifications (FSMQ)

Aimed at those students wishing to acquire further qualifications in maths, specifically additional mathematics and foundations of advanced mathematics (MEI). Further UCAS points can be earned upon completion of the advanced FSMQ in additional mathematics.

AQA Certificate in Mathematical Studies (Core Maths)

This Level 3 qualification has been available since September 2015. It is designed for students who achieved a Grade 4 or above at GCSE and want to continue studying Maths. The qualification carries UCAS points equivalent to an AS level qualification.

AQA Certificate in Further Maths

This level 2 qualification has been designed to provide stretch and challenge to the most able mathematicians. This will be best suited to students who either already have, or are expected to achieve the top grades in GCSE Mathematics and are likely to progress to A level Mathematics and Further Mathematics.

Scottish qualifications

Information supplied by the Scottish Qualifications Authority

In Scotland, qualifications are awarded by the Scottish Qualifications Authority (SQA), the national accreditation and awarding body. A variety of qualifications are offered in schools, including:

- National Qualifications (National Units, National Courses, Skills for Work Courses and Scottish Baccalaureates)
- National Qualification Group Awards (National Certificates and National Progression Awards)
- Awards

National Qualifications cover subjects to suit everyone's interests and skills – from Chemistry to Construction, History to Hospitality, and Computing to Care.

Qualifications in the Scottish qualifications system sit at various levels on the Scottish Credit and Qualifications Framework (SCQF). There are 12 levels on the SCQF and each level represents the difficulty of learning involved. Qualifications in schools span SCQF levels 1 to 7.

National Qualifications (NQ)

National Qualifications are among the most important types of qualification in Scotland.

National Qualifications range from SCQF levels 1 to 7 and include National Units, National Courses, Skills for Work Courses, Scottish Baccalaureates and National Qualification Group Awards.

They are taught in the senior phase of secondary school and they are also offered in colleges, and by some training providers.

They are designed to help young people to demonstrate the skills, knowledge and understanding they have developed at school or college and enable them to prepare for further learning, training and employment.

National Courses

National Courses are available in over 60 subjects, at the following levels: National 2 (SCQF level 2), National 3 (SCQF level 3), National 4 (SCQF level 4), National 5 (SCQF level 5), Higher (SCQF level 6), and Advanced Higher (SCQF level 7).

National 2, National 3 and National 4 courses consist of units and unit assessments, which are internally assessed by teachers and lecturers, and quality assured by SQA. Students complete the unit assessments during class time. National 4 courses also include an Added Value Unit assessment that assesses students' performance across the whole course. This is usually in the form of an assignment, performance, practical activity or class test. National 2 to National 4 courses are not graded but are assessed as pass or fail.

National 5, Higher and Advanced Higher courses do not include units. They involve a course assessment that takes place at the end of the course. For most subjects, the course assessment is a combination of one or more formal exams and one or more coursework assessments (such as an assignment, performance, project or practical activity). SQA marks all exams and the majority of coursework. In some subjects, performances and practical activities are internally assessed by the teacher or lecturer and quality assured by SQA.

National 5, Higher and Advanced Higher courses are graded A to D or 'no award'.

National Units

National Units are the building blocks of National 2 to National 4 Courses and National Qualification Group Awards. They are also qualifications in their own right and can be done on an individual basis — such as National 1 qualifications, which are standalone units. Units are normally designed to take 40 hours of teaching to complete and each one is assessed by completing a unit assessment. Over 3500 National Units are available, including National Literacy and Numeracy Units, which assess students' literacy and numeracy skills.

Freestanding units are also available at SCQF levels 5, 6 and 7 and can be taken on an individual basis.

Skills for Work Courses

Skills for Work courses are designed to introduce students to the demands and expectations of the world of work. They are available in a variety of areas such as construction, hairdressing and hospitality. The courses involve a strong element of learning through involvement in practical and vocational activities, and develop knowledge, skills and experience that are related to employment. They consist of units and unit assessments, which are internally assessed by teachers and lecturers, and quality assured by SQA. Skills for Work courses are not graded but are assessed as pass or fail. They are available at National 4, National 5 and Higher levels (SCQF levels 4 to 6) and are often delivered in partnership between schools and colleges.

Scottish Baccalaureates

Scottish Baccalaureates consist of a coherent group of Higher and Advanced Higher qualifications, with the addition of an interdisciplinary project. They are available in four subject areas: Expressive Arts, Languages, Science and Social Sciences. The interdisciplinary project is marked and awarded at Advanced Higher level (SCQF level 7). It provides students with a platform to apply their knowledge in a realistic context, and to demonstrate initiative, responsibility and independent working. Aimed at high-achieving sixth year students, the Scottish Baccalaureate encourages personalised, in-depth study and interdisciplinary learning in their final year of secondary school.

National Qualification Group Awards

National Certificates (NCs) and National Progression Awards (NPAs) are referred to as National Qualification Group Awards. These qualifications provide students preparing for work with opportunities to develop skills that are sought after by employers. They are available at SCQF levels 2 to 6.

NCs prepare students for employment, career development or progression to more advanced study at HNC/HND level. They are available in a range of subjects, including: Sound Production, Technical Theatre, and Child, Health and Social Care.

NPAs develop specific skills and knowledge in specialist vocational areas, including Journalism, Architecture and Interior Design, and Legal Services. They link to National Occupational Standards, which are the basis of Scottish Vocational Qualifications (SVQs) and are taught in partnership between schools, colleges, employers and training providers.

Awards

SQA Awards provide students with opportunities to acquire skills, recognise achievement and promote confidence through independent thinking and positive attitudes, while motivating them to be successful and participate positively in the wider community.

A variety of different awards are offered at a number of SCQF levels and cover subjects including leadership, employability and enterprise. These awards are designed to recognise the life, learning and work skills that students gain from taking part in activities both in and out of school, such as sports, volunteering and fundraising.

For more information on SQA and its portfolio of qualifications, visit www.sqa.org.uk

SVQs (Scotland)

Scottish Vocational Qualifications (SVQs) are work-based qualifications that demonstrate someone can do their job well and to the national standards for their sector. There are over 500 SVQs that cover many occupations in Scotland – from forestry to IT, management to catering, and from journalism to construction. Experts from industry, commerce and education produce SVQs based on national standards.

Many people study for SVQs in the workplace while carrying out their day-to-day role. Each SVQ unit defines one aspect of a job and what it is to be competent in that aspect of the job. Learners can work through one unit at a time, or gather evidence for several units at the same time. There are no formal written exams, instead learners collect and submit evidence, usually from their own work. They are assessed by an SVQ assessor and the assessment can take place at the learner's place of work, at college or through a training provider.

Find out more at www.sqa.org.uk/svq

Additional and Alternative

Cambridge Early Years

Cambridge Early Years is a new programme for 3-6 year olds. It gives young learners the best start in life, helping them to meet key early milestones and thrive in and outside of school. Cambridge Early Years is the first stage in the Cambridge Pathway, which gives students a clear path for educational success from age 3-19.

The programme is child-centred and play-based and helps young learners to develop at their own pace. It encourages them to act independently, make their own choices and discover feelings of self-worth.

It includes everything schools need for high-quality learning: a holistic, balanced curriculum, engaging classroom resources, professional development and assessment approaches to help measure learners' progress.

The curriculum is made up of six areas:

- communication and literacy
- creative expression
- mathematics
- physical development
- personal, social and emotional development
- understanding the world.

Cambridge Early Years supports learners, whatever their level of English when they begin the programme. Cambridge also help schools offer a bilingual or multilingual approach if learners have a home language other than English
Website: www.cambridgeinternational.org/earlyyears

Cambridge Primary

Cambridge Primary is typically for learners aged 5 to 11 years. It develops learner skills and understanding in 10 subjects: English as a first or second language, mathematics, science, art & design, computing, digital literacy, music, physical education, and Cambridge Global Perspectives. Subjects can be offered in any combination and adapted to suit the school's context, culture and school ethos.

The flexible curriculum frameworks include optional assessment tools to help schools monitor learners' progress and give detailed feedback to parents. At the end of Cambridge Primary, schools can enter students for Cambridge Primary Checkpoint tests which are marked in Cambridge. Website: www.cambridgeinternational.org/primary

Cambridge Lower Secondary

Cambridge Lower Secondary is typically for learners aged 11 to 14 years. It develops learner skills and understanding in 10 subjects: English, English as a second language, mathematics, science, art & design, computing, digital literacy, music, physical education, and Cambridge Global Perspectives. Subjects can be offered in any combination and adapted to suit the school's context, culture and school ethos.

The programme includes a range of optional assessments to help measure students' potential and progress. At the end of Cambridge Lower Secondary, schools can enter students for Cambridge Lower Secondary Checkpoint tests which are marked in Cambridge and provide an external international benchmark for student performance.
Website: www.cambridgeinternational.org/lowersecondary

European Baccalaureate (EB)

Not to be confused with the International Baccalaureate (IB) or the French Baccalaureate, this certificate is available in European schools and recognised in all EU countries.

To obtain the baccalaureate, a student must obtain a minimum score of 50%, which is made up from: course-work, oral participation in class and tests (50%); five written examinations (35%) – mother-tongue, first foreign language and maths are compulsory for all candidates; three oral examinations (15%) – mother tongue and first foreign language are compulsory (history or geography may also be compulsory here, dependant on whether the candidate has taken a written examination in these subjects).

Subjects taught in different languages have the same syllabi, regardless of the language, and the same is valid for examinations – the content is simply translated into different languages. In case of languages, the syllabi vary, but nevertheless, they are harmonized and the examinations have to follow an agreed structure. The EB has been specifically designed to meet, at the very least, the minimum qualification requirements of each member state.

Study for the EB begins at nursery stage (age 4) and progresses through primary (age six) and on into secondary school (age 12).

Syllabus

Languages: Bulgarian, Czech, Danish, Dutch, English, Estonian, Finnish, Finnish as a second national language, French, Gaelic as other national language German, Greek, Hungarian, Italian, Latvian, Lithuanian, Maltese as other national language, Polish, Portuguese, Romanian, Slovak, Slovenian, Spanish, Swedish, Swedish for Finnish pupils.

Literary: art education, non-confessional ethics, geography, ancient Greek, history, human sciences, Latin, music, philosophy, physical education.

Sciences: biology, chemistry, economics, ICT, mathematics, physics.

For more information, contact:
Office of the Secretary-General of the European Schools
Rue de la Science 23, B-1040 Bruxelles
Tel: +32 2295 3745; Fax: +32 2298 6298; Website: www.eursc.eu

The International Baccalaureate (IB)

The International Baccalaureate (IB) offers four challenging and high quality educational programmes for a worldwide community of schools, aiming to develop internationally minded people who, recognizing their common humanity and shared guardianship of the planet, help to create a better, more peaceful world.

The IB works with schools around the world (both state and privately funded) that share the commitment to international education to deliver these programmes.

Schools that have achieved the high standards required for authorization to offer one or more of the IB programmes are known as IB World Schools. There are over half a million students attending almost 5000 IB World Schools in over 150 countries and this number is growing annually.

The Primary Years, Middle Years and Diploma Programmes share a common philosophy and common characteristics. They develop the whole student, helping students to grow intellectually, socially, aesthetically and culturally. They provide a broad and balanced education that includes science and the humanities, languages and mathematics, technology and the arts. The programmes teach students to think critically, and encourage them to draw connections between areas of knowledge and to use problem-solving techniques and concepts from many disciplines. They instil in students a sense of responsibility towards others and towards the environment. Lastly, and perhaps most importantly, the programmes give students an awareness and understanding of their own culture and of other cultures, values and ways of life.

A fourth programme called the IB Career-related Programme (CP) became available to IB World Schools from September 2012. All IB programmes include:

- A written curriculum or curriculum framework
- Student assessment appropriate to the age range
- Professional development and networking opportunities for teachers
- Support, authorization and programme evaluation for the school

The IB Primary Years Programme

The IB Primary Years Programme (PYP), for students aged three to 12, focuses on the development of the whole child as an inquirer, both in the classroom and in the world outside. It is a framework consisting of five essential elements (concepts, knowledge, skills, attitude, action) and guided by six trans-disciplinary themes of global significance, explored using knowledge and skills derived from six subject areas (language, social studies, mathematics, science and technology, arts, and personal, social and physical education) with a powerful emphasis on inquiry-based learning.

The most significant and distinctive feature of the PYP is the six trans-disciplinary themes. These themes are about issues that have meaning for, and are important to, all of us. The programme offers a balance between learning about or through the subject areas, and learning beyond them. The six themes of global significance create a trans-disciplinary framework that allows students to 'step up' beyond the confines of learning within subject areas:

- Who we are
- Where we are in place and time
- How we express ourselves
- How the world works
- How we organize ourselves
- Sharing the planet

The PYP exhibition is the culminating activity of the programme. It requires students to analyse and propose solutions to real-world issues, drawing on what they have learned through the programme. Evidence of student development and records of PYP exhibitions are reviewed by the IB as part of the programme evaluation process.

Assessment is an important part of each unit of inquiry as it both enhances learning and provides opportunities for students to reflect on what they know, understand and can do. The teacher's feedback to the students provides the guidance, the tools and the incentive for them to become more competent, more skilful and better at understanding how to learn.

The IB Middle Years Programme (MYP)

The Middle Years Programme (MYP), for students aged 11 to 16, comprises eight subject groups:

- Language acquisition
- Language and literature
- Individuals and societies
- Sciences
- Mathematics
- Arts
- Physical and health education
- Design

The MYP requires at least 50 hours of teaching time for each subject group in each year of the programme. In years 4 and 5, students have the option to take courses from six of the eight subject groups within certain limits, to provide greater flexibility in meeting local requirements and individual student learning needs.

Each year, students in the MYP also engage in at least one collaboratively planned interdisciplinary unit that involves at least two subject groups.

MYP students also complete a long-term project, where they decide what they want to learn about, identify what they already know, discovering what they will need to know to complete the project, and create a proposal or criteria for completing it

The MYP aims to help students develop their personal understanding, their emerging sense of self and their responsibility in their community.

The MYP allows schools to continue to meet state, provincial or national legal requirements for students with access needs. Schools must develop an inclusion/special educational needs (SEN) policy that explains assessment access arrangements, classroom accommodations and curriculum modification that meet individual student learning needs.

The IB Diploma Programme (IBDP)

The IB Diploma Programme, for students aged 16 to 19, is an academically challenging and motivating curriculum of international education that prepares students for success at university and in life beyond studies.

DP students choose at least one course from six subject groups, thus ensuring depth and breadth of knowledge and experience in languages, social studies, the experimental sciences, mathematics, and the arts. With more than 35 courses to choose from, students have the flexibility to further explore and learn subjects that meet their interest. Out of the six courses required, at least three and not more than four must be taken at higher level (240 teaching hours), the others at standard level (150 teaching hours). Students can take examinations in English, French or Spanish.

In addition, three unique components of the programme – the DP core – aim to broaden students' educational experience and challenge them to apply their knowledge and skills. The DP core – the extended essay (EE), theory of knowledge (TOK) and creativity, activity, service (CAS) – are compulsory and central to the philosophy of the programme.

The IB uses both external and internal assessment to measure student performance in the DP. Student results are determined by performance against set standards, not by each student's position in the overall rank order. DP assessment is unique in the way that it measures the extent to which students have mastered advanced academic skills not what they have memorized. DP assessment also encourages an international outlook and intercultural skills, wherever appropriate.

The IB diploma is awarded to students who gain at least 24 points out of a possible 45 points, subject to certain minimum levels of performance across the whole programme and to satisfactory participation in the creativity, activity, and service requirement.

Recognized and respected by leading universities globally, the DP encourages students to be knowledgeable, inquiring, caring and compassionate, and to develop intercultural understanding, open-mindedness and the attitudes necessary to respect and evaluate a range of viewpoints.

The IB Career Related Programme (IBCP)

The IB Career-related Programme, for students aged 16 to 19, offers an innovative educational framework that combines academic studies with career-related learning. Through the CP, students develop the competencies they need to succeed in the 21st century. More importantly, they have the opportunity to engage with a rigorous study programme that genuinely interests them while gaining transferable and lifelong skills that prepares them to pursue higher education, apprenticeships or direct employment.

CP students complete four core components – language development, personal and professional skills, service learning and a reflective project – in order to receive the International Baccalaureate Career-related Programme Certificate. Designed to enhance critical thinking and intercultural understanding, the CP core helps students develop the communication and personal skills, as well as intellectual habits required for lifelong learning.

Schools that choose to offer the CP can create their own distinctive version of the programme and select career pathways that suit their students and local community needs. The IB works with a variety of CRS providers around the world and schools seeking to develop career pathways with professional communities can benefit from our existing collaborations. All CRS providers undergo a rigorous curriculum evaluation to ensure that their courses align with the CP pedagogy and meet IB quality standards. The flexibility to meet the needs, backgrounds and contexts of learners allows CP schools to offer an education that is relevant and meaningful to their students.

Launched in 2012, there are more than 300 CP schools. Many schools with the IB Diploma Programme (DP) and the Middle Years Programme (MYP) have chosen the CP as an alternative IB pathway to offer students. CP schools often report that the programme has helped them raise student aspiration, increase student engagement and retention and encouraged learners to take responsibility for their own actions, helping them foster high levels of self-esteem through meaningful achievements.

For more information on IB programmes, visit: www.ibo.org
Africa, Europe, Middle East IB Global Centre,
Churchillplein 6, The Hague, 2517JW, The Netherlands
Tel: +31 (0)70 352 6000
Email: support@ibo.org

Pearson Edexcel Mathematics Awards

Pearson's Edexcel Mathematics Awards are small, stand-alone qualifications designed to help students to develop and demonstrate proficiency in different areas of mathematics. These Awards enable students to focus on understanding key concepts and techniques, and are available across three subjects, including: Number and Measure (Levels 1 and 2), Algebra (Levels 2 and 3) and Statistical Methods (Levels 1, 2 and 3).

Designed to build students' confidence and fluency; the Awards can fit into the existing programme of delivery for mathematics in schools and colleges, prepare students for GCSE and/or GCE Mathematics, and to support further study in other subjects, training or the workplace. They offer a choice of levels to match students' abilities, with clear progression between the levels. These small, 60-70 guided learning hour qualifications are assessed through one written paper per level. Each qualification is funded and approved for pre-16 and 16-18 year old students in England and in schools and colleges in Wales.

Projects

Extended Project Qualification (EPQ)

AQA, OCR, Pearson and WJEC offer the Extended Project Qualification, which is a qualification aimed at developing a student's research and independent learning skills. The EPQ can be taken as a stand-alone qualification, and it is equivalent to half an A level in UCAS points (but only a third of performance points).

Students complete a research based written report and may produce an artefact or a practical science experiment as part of their project.

Cambridge International Project Qualification (IPQ)

Cambridge International is offering a new standalone project-based qualification, which can be taken alongside Cambridge International AS & A levels. Students complete a 5000-word research project on a topic of their choice. The qualification is assessed by Cambridge International.

For more information, go to www.cambridgeinternational.org/advanced

Entry level and basic skills

Entry Level Qualifications

If you want to take GCSE or NVQ Level 1 but have not yet reached the standard required, then entry level qualifications are for you as they are designed to get you started on the qualifications ladder.

Entry level qualifications are available in a wide range of areas. You can take an entry level certificate in most subjects where a similar GCSE exists. There are also vocational entry level qualifications – some in specific areas like retail or catering and others where you can take units in different work-related subjects to get a taster of a number of career areas. Also available are entry level certificates in life skills and the basic skills of literacy and numeracy.

Anyone can take an entry level qualification – your school or college will help you decide which qualification is right for you.

Entry level qualifications are flexible programmes so the time it takes to complete will vary according to where you study and how long you need to take the qualification.

Subjects available include: Art and Design, Computer Science, English, Geography, History, Latin, Mathematics, Physical Education and Science.

Functional Skills

Functional Skills are qualifications in English and maths that equip learners with the basic practical skills required in everyday life, education and the workplace. They are available at Entry Level, Level 1 and Level 2. Functional Skills are identified as funded 'stepping stone' qualifications to English and maths GCSE for post-16 learners who haven't previously achieved a grade 3 in these subjects. There are part of apprenticeship completion requirements.

Vocational qualifications

Applied Generals/Level 3 Certificates

Applied General qualifications are available in a wide range of subjects, they are a real alternative to A level support progression to further study or employment aimed at students aged 16-18.

Developed together with teachers, schools, colleges and higher education institutions, they help learners to develop knowledge and skills.

A mixture of assessment types means learners can apply their knowledge in a practical way. An integrated approach creates a realistic and relevant qualification for learners.

BTECs

BTEC Level 2 First qualifications

ie BTEC Level 2 Diplomas, BTEC Level 2 Extended Certificates, BTEC Level 2 Certificates and BTEC Level 2 Award.

BTEC Firsts are Level 2 introductory work-related programmes covering a wide range of vocational areas including business, engineering, information technology, health and social care, media, travel and tourism, and public services.

Programmes may be taken full or part-time. They are practical programmes that provide a foundation for the knowledge and skills you will need in work. Alternatively, you can progress onto a BTEC National qualification, Applied GCE A level or equivalent.

There are no formal entry requirements and they can be studied alongside GCSEs. Subjects available include: Agriculture, Animal Care, Applied Science, Art and Design, Business, Children's Care, Learning and Development, Construction, Countryside and the Environment, Engineering, Fish Husbandry, Floristry, Health and Social care, Horse Care, Horticulture, Hospitality, IT, Land-based Technology, Business, Creative Media Production, Music, Performing Arts, Public Services, Sport, Travel and Tourism, and Vehicle Technology.

BTEC Foundation Diploma in Art and Design (QCF)

For those students preparing to go on to higher education within the field of art and design. This diploma is recognised as one of the best courses of its type in the UK, and is used in preparation for degree programmes. Units offered include researching, recording and responding in art and design, media experimentation, personal experimental studies, and a final major project.

BTEC Nationals

ie BTEC Level 3 Extended Diplomas (QCF), BTEC Level 3 Diplomas (QCF), BTEC Level 3 Subsidiary Diplomas (QCF), BTEC Level 3 Certificates (QCF)

BTEC National programmes are long-established vocational programmes. They are practical programmes that are highly valued by employers. They enable you to gain the knowledge and skills that you will need in work, or give you the choice to progress on to a BTEC Higher National, a Foundation Degree or a degree programme.

BTEC Nationals, which hold UCAS points cover a range of vocationally specialist sectors including child care, children's play, learning and development, construction, art and design, aeronautical engineering, electrical/electronic engineering, IT, business, creative and media production, performing arts, public services, sport, sport and exercise sciences and applied science. The programmes may be taken full- or part-time, and can be taken in conjunction with NVQs and/or functional skills units at an appropriate level.

There are no formal entry requirements, but if you have any of the following you are likely to be at the right level to study a BTEC national qualification.

- a BTEC Level 2 First qualification
- GCSEs – at grades A*-C in several subjects
- Relevant work experience

There are also very specialist BTEC Nationals, such as Pharmaceutical Science and Blacksmithing and Metalworking.

BTEC Higher Nationals

Known as HNDs and HNCs – ie BTEC Level 5 HND Diplomas (QCF) and BTEC Level 4 HNC Diplomas (QCF)

BTEC HNDs and HNCs are further and higher education qualifications that offer a balance of education and vocational training. They are available in over 40 work-related subjects such as Graphic Design, Business, Health and Social Care, Computing and Systems Development, Manufacturing Engineering, Hospitality Management, and Public Services.

BTEC higher national courses combine study with hands-on work experience during your course. Once completed, you can use the skills you learn to begin your career, or continue on to a related degree course.

HNDs are often taken as a full-time course over two years but can also be followed part-time in some cases.

HNCs are often for people who are working and take two years to complete on a part-time study basis by day release, evenings, or a combination of the two. Some HNC courses are done on a full-time basis. There are no formal entry requirements, but if you have any of the following you are likely to be at the right academic level:

- at least one A level
- a BTEC Level 3 National qualification
- level 3 NVQ

BTEC specialist and professional qualifications
These qualifications are designed to prepare students for specific and specialist work activities. These are split into two distinct groups:

- Specialist qualifications (entry to Level 3)
- Professional qualifications (Levels 4-7)

Cambridge Nationals

Cambridge Nationals from exam board OCR are vocational qualifications that take an engaging, practical and inspiring approach to learning and assessment.

They are industry-relevant, geared to key sector requirements and very popular with schools and colleges because they suit such a broad range of learning styles and abilities.

Cambridge Nationals are available in engineering, health and social care, IT, sport, imedia, and child development. They are joint Level 1 and 2 qualifications aimed at students aged 14-16 in full-time study.

Cambridge Technicals

OCR's Cambridge Technicals are practical and flexible vocational qualifications, offering students in-depth study in a wide range of subjects, including business, health and social care, IT, sport, digital media, applied science, performing arts and engineering.

Cambridge Technicals are aimed at young people aged 16-19 who have completed Key Stage 4 of their education and want to study in a more practical, work-related way.

Cambridge Technicals are available at Level 2 and Level 3, and carry UCAS points at Level 3.

NVQs

NVQs reward those who demonstrate skills gained at work. They relate to particular jobs and are usefully taken while you are working. Within reason, NVQs do not have to be completed in a specified amount of time. They can be taken by full-time employees or by school and college students with a work placement or part-time job that enables them to develop the appropriate skills. There are no age limits and no special entry requirements.

NVQs are organised into levels, based on the competencies required. Levels 1-3 are the levels most applicable to learners within the 14-19 phase. Achievement of Level 4 within this age group will be rare.

Occupational Studies (Northern Ireland)

Targeted at learners working towards and at Level 1 and 2 in Key Stage 4 within the Northern Ireland curriculum. For further information see the CCEA website.

SVQs (Scotland)

Scottish Vocational Qualifications (SVQs) are work-based qualifications that demonstrate someone can do their job well and to the national standards for their sector. There are over 500 SVQs that cover many occupations in Scotland – from forestry to IT, management to catering, and from journalism to construction. Experts from industry, commerce and education produce SVQs based on national standards.

Many people study for SVQs in the workplace while carrying out their day-to-day role. Each SVQ unit defines one aspect of a job and what it is to be competent in that aspect of the job. Learners can work through one unit at a time, or gather evidence for several units at the same time. There are no formal written exams, instead learners collect and submit evidence, usually from their own work. They are assessed by an SVQ assessor and the assessment can take place at the learner's place of work, at college or through a training provider.

Find out more at www.sqa.org.uk/svq

Awarding organisations and examination dates

Awarding organisations and examination dates

In England there are four awarding organisations, each offering GCSEs, AS and A levels (Eduqas offers only reformed qualifications in England, whereas WJEC offers in England, Wales, Northern Ireland and independent regions). There are separate awarding organisations in Wales (WJEC) and Northern Ireland (CCEA). The awarding organisation in Scotland (SQA) offers equivalent qualifications.

This information was supplied by the awarding bodies and was accurate at the time of going to press. It is intended as a general guide only for candidates in the United Kingdom. Dates are subject to variation and should be confirmed with the awarding organisation concerned.

AQA

Qualifications offered:
GCSE
AS and A level
Foundation Certificate of Secondary Education (FCSE)
Entry Level Certificate (ELC)
Foundation and Higher Projects
Extended Project Qualification (EPQ)
Applied Generals/AQA Level 3 Certificates and Extended Certificates
Functional Skills
AQA Certificate
Technical Award

Other assessment schemes:
Unit Award Scheme (UAS)

Contact:
Email: eos@aqa.org.uk
Website: www.aqa.org.uk
Tel: 0800 197 7162 (8am–5pm Monday to Friday)
+44 161 696 5995 (Outside the UK)

Devas Street, Manchester M15 6EX
Stag Hill House, Guildford, Surrey GU2 7XJ
Windsor House, Cornwall Road, Harrogate, HG1 2PW
2nd Floor, Lynton House, 7–12 Tavistock Square, London, WC1H 9LT

CCEA – Council for the Curriculum, Examinations and Assessment

Qualifications offered:
GCSE
GCE AS/A level
Key Skills (Levels 1-4)
Entry Level Qualifications
Occupational Studies (Levels 1 & 2)
QCF Qualifications
Applied GCSE and GCE

Contact:
Email: info@ccea.org.uk
Website: www.ccea.org.uk

29 Clarendon Road, Clarendon Dock, Belfast, BT1 3BG
Tel: (028) 9026 1200

Eduqas

Eduqas, part of WJEC, offers Ofqual reformed GCSEs, AS and A levels to secondary schools and colleges. Our qualifications are available in England, Channel Islands, Isle of Man, Northern Ireland and to the independent sector in Wales (restrictions may apply).

Qualifications offered:
GCSE (9-1)
AS
A level
Level 3

Contact:
Email: info@wjec.co.uk
Website: www.eduqas.co.uk

Eduqas (WJEC CBAC Ltd),
245 Western Avenue, Cardiff, CF5 2YX
Telephone: 029 2026 5000

IB – International Baccalaureate

Qualification offered:
IB Diploma
IB Career-related Certificate

Contact:
Email: support@ibo.org
Website: www.ibo.org

IB Global Centre, The Hague, Churchillplein 6, 2517 JW, The Hague, The Netherlands
Tel: +31 70 352 60 00

IB Global Centre, Washington DC, 3950 Wisconsin Avenue, NW Washington, DC 20016, USA
Tel: +1 301 202 3000

IB Global Centre, Singapore, 600 North Bridge Road, #21-01 Parkview Square, Singapore 188778
Tel: +65 6 579 5000

IB Global Centre, Cardiff, Peterson House, Malthouse Avenue, Cardiff Gate, Cardiff, Wales, CF23 8GL, UK
Email: reception@ibo.org
Tel: +44 29 2054 7777

International Baccalaureate Foundation Office, Rue du Pré-de-la-Bichette 1, 1202 Genève, Switzerland
Tel: +41 22 309 2540

OCR – Oxford Cambridge and RSA Examinations – and Cambridge International

Qualifications offered by OCR or sister awarding organisation Cambridge Assessment International Education (Cambridge International) include:
GCSE
GCE AS/A level
IGCSE
International AS/A level
Extended Project
Cambridge International Project Qualification
Cambridge Pre-U
Cambridge Nationals
Cambridge Technicals
FSMQ – Free Standing Maths Qualification

Contact:
OCR
OCR Head Office, The Triangle Building, Shaftesbury Road, Cambridge, CB2 8EA
Website: www.ocr.org.uk
Tel: +44 1223 553998

Cambridge International
Website: www.cambridgeinternational.org
Email: info@cambridgeinternational.org
Tel: +44 1223 553554

Pearson

Qualifications offered:
Pearson's qualifications are offered in the UK but are also available through their international centres across the world. They include:
DiDA, CiDA
GCE A levels
GCSEs
Functional Skills
International GCSEs and Edexcel Certificates
ESOL (Skills for Life)
BTEC Enterprise qualifications
BTEC Entry Level, Level 1 and Level 1 Introductory
BTEC Firsts
BTEC Foundation Diploma in Art and Design
BTEC Industry Skills
BTEC International Level 3
BTEC Level 2 Technicals
BTEC Level 3 Technical Levels in Hospitality
BTEC Nationals
BTEC Specialist and Professional qualifications
BTEC Tech Awards
Higher Nationals
T Levels

Contact:
190 High Holborn, London WC1V 7BH

See website for specific contact details:
qualifications.pearson.com

SQA – Scottish Qualifications Authority

Qualifications offered:
National Qualifications (NQs): National 1 to National 5; Higher; Advanced Higher
Skills for Work; Scottish Baccalaureates
National Certificates (NCs)
National Progression Awards (NPAs)
Awards
Core Skills
Scottish Vocational Qualifications (SVQs)
Higher National Certificates and Higher National Diplomas (HNCs/HNDs)*

*SQA offers HNCs and HNDs to centres in Scotland. Outside of Scotland, the equivalent qualifications are the SQA Advanced Certificate and SQA Advanced Diploma.

Contact:
Email: customer@sqa.org.uk Tel: 0345 279 1000
Website: www.sqa.org.uk
Glasgow – The Optima Building, 58 Robertson Street, Glasgow, G2 8DQ
Dalkeith – Lowden, 24 Wester Shawfair, Dalkeith, Midlothian, EH22 1FD

WJEC

With over 65 years' experience in delivering qualifications, WJEC is the largest provider in Wales and a leading provider in England and Northern Ireland.

Qualifications offered:
GCSE
GCE A/AS
Functional Skills
Entry Level
Welsh Baccalaureate Qualifications
Essential Skills Wales
Wider Key Skills
Project Qualifications Principal Learning
Other general qualifications such as Level 1 and Level 2 Awards and Certificates including English Language, English Literature, Latin Language, Latin Language & Roman Civilisation and Latin Literature
QCF Qualifications

Contact:
Email: info@wjec.co.uk
Website: www.wjec.co.uk

245 Western Avenue, Cardiff, CF5 2YX
Tel: 029 2026 5000

Educational organisations

Educational organisations

Artsmark

Arts Council England's Artsmark was set up in 2001, and rounds are held annually.
All schools in England can apply for an Artsmark – primary, middle, secondary, special and pupil referral units, maintained and independent – on a voluntary basis. An Artsmark award is made to schools showing commitment to the full range of arts – music, dance, drama and art and design.
Tel: 0161 934 4317
Email: artsmark@artscouncil.org.uk
Website: www.artsmark.org.uk

Association for the Education and Guardianship of International Students (AEGIS)

AEGIS brings together schools and guardianship organisations to ensure and promote the welfare of international students. AEGIS provides accreditation for all reputable guardianship organisations.
AEGIS, The Wheelhouse, Bond's Mill Estate, Bristol Road, Stonehouse, Gloucestershire GL10 3RF.
Tel: 01453 821293
Email: info@aegisuk.net
Website: www.aegisuk.net

The Association of American Study Abroad Programmes (AASAP)

Established in 1991 to represent American study abroad programmes in the UK.
Contact: Anna Bermani, AASAP/UK,
First Floor, Templeback, 10 Temple Back, Bristol, England, BS1 6FL
Email: info@aasapuk.org
Website: www.aasapuk.org

The Association of British Riding Schools (ABRS)

An independent body of proprietors and principals of riding establishments, aiming to look after their interests and those of the riding public and to raise standards of management, instruction and animal welfare.
Blenheim Business Centre, Smithers Hill, Shipley, West Sussex RH13 8PP.
Tel: 01403 741188
Email: office@abrs-info.org
Website: www.abrs-info.org

Association of Colleges (AOC)

Created in 1996 to promote the interest of further education colleges in England and Wales.
2-5 Stedham Place, London WC1A 1HU
Tel: 0207 034 9900
Email: enquiries@aoc.co.uk
Website: www.aoc.co.uk

Association of Governing Bodies of Independent Schools (AGBIS)

AGBIS supports and advises governing bodies of schools in the independent sector on all aspects of governance.
Registered charity No. 1108756
Association of Governing Bodies of Independent Schools, 3 Codicote Road, Welwyn, Hertfordshire AL6 9LY
Tel: 01438 840730
Email: enquiries@agbis.org.uk
Website: www.agbis.org.uk

Association of Employment and Learning Providers (AELP)

AELP's purpose is to influence the education and training agenda. They are the voice of independent learning providers throughout England.
Association of Employment and Learning Providers, 2nd Floor, 9 Apex Court, Bradley Stoke, Bristol, BS32 4JT
Tel: 0117 986 5389
Email: enquiries@aelp.org.uk
Website: www.aelp.org.uk

The Association of School and College Leaders (ASCL)

Formerly the Secondary Heads Association, the ASCL is a professional association for secondary school and college leaders.
Association of School and College Leaders, 2nd Floor, Peat House, 1 Waterloo Way, Leicester, LE1 6LP
Tel: 0116 299 1122
Fax: 0116 299 1123
Email: info@ascl.org.uk
Website: www.ascl.org.uk

Boarding Schools' Association (BSA)

For information on the BSA see editorial on page 31

The British Accreditation Council (BAC)

The British Accreditation Council (BAC) has now been the principal accrediting body for the independent further and higher education and training sector for over 30 years. BAC-accredited institutions in the UK now number more than 300, offering everything from website design to yoga to equine dentistry, as well as more standard qualifications in subjects such as business, IT, management and law. As well as our accreditation of institutions offering traditional teaching, BAC has developed a new accreditation scheme for providers offering online, distance and blended learning. Some students may also look to study outside the UK at one of the institutions holding BAC international accreditation.
Wax Chandlers' Hall 1st Floor, 6 Gresham Street, London, EC2V 7AD
Tel: 0300 330 1400
Email: info@the-bac.org
Website: www.the-bac.org

The British Association for Early Childhood Education (BAECE)

Promotes quality provision for all children from birth to eight in whatever setting they are placed. Publishes booklets and organises conferences for those interested in early years education and care. Registered charity Nos. 313082; SC039472
Early Education, Regus offices, 2 Victoria Square, St Albans AL1 3TF
Tel: 01727 884925
Email: office@early-education.org.uk
Website: www.early-education.org.uk

The Choir Schools' Association (CSA)

Represents 44 schools attached to cathedrals, churches and college chapels, which educate cathedral and collegiate choristers.
CSA Information Officer, 39 Bournside Road, Cheltenham, Gloucestershire, GL51 3AL
Tel: 07903 850597
Email: info@choirschools.org.uk
Website: www.choirschools.org.uk

CIFE

CIFE is the professional association for independent sixth form and tutorial colleges accredited by the British Accreditation Council (BAC), the Independent Schools Council or the DfE (Ofsted). Member colleges specialise in preparing students for GCSE and A level (AS and A2) in particular and university entrance in general.
The aim of the association is to provide a forum for the exchange of information and ideas, and for the promotion of best practice, and to safeguard adherence to strict standards of professional conduct and ethical propriety.
Further information can be obtained from CIFE:
Tel: 0208 767 8666
Email: enquiries@cife.org.uk
Website: www.cife.org.uk

Council of British International Schools (COBIS)

COBIS is a membership association of British schools of quality worldwide and is committed to a stringent process of quality assurance for all its member schools. COBIS is a member of the Independent Schools Council (ISC) of the United Kingdom.
COBIS, 55–56 Russell Square, Bloomsbury,
London WC1B 4HP
Tel: 020 3826 7190
Email: pa@cobis.org.uk
Website: www.cobis.org.uk

Council of International Schools (CIS)

CIS is a not-for-profit organisation committed to supporting its member schools and colleges in achieving and delivering the highest standards of international education. CIS provides accreditation to schools, teacher and leader recruitment and best practice development. CIS Higher Education assists member colleges and universities in recruiting a diverse profile of qualified international students.
Schipholweg 113, 2316 XC Leiden, The Netherlands.
Tel: +31 71 524 3300
Email: info@cois.org
Website: www.cois.org

Dyslexia Action (DA)

A registered, educational charity (No. 268502), which has established teaching and assessment centres and conducts teacher-training throughout the UK. The aim of the institute is to help people with dyslexia of all ages to overcome their difficulties in learning to read, write and spell and to achieve their potential.
Dyslexia Action Training and Guild, Centurion House, London Road, Staines-upon-Thames TW18 4AX
Tel: 01784 222 304
Email: trainingcourses@dyslexiaaction.org.uk
Website: www.dyslexiaaction.org.uk

European Association for International Education (EAIE)

A not-for-profit organisation aiming for internationalisation in higher education in Europe. It has a membership of over 1800.
PO Box 11189, 1001 GD Amsterdam, The Netherlands
Tel: +31 20 344 5100
Fax: +31 20 344 5119
Email: info@eaie.org
Website: www.eaie.org

ECIS (European Collaborative for International Schools)

ECIS is a membership organisation which provides services to support professional development, good governance and leadership in international schools.
24 Greville Street,
London, EC1N 8SS
Tel: 020 7824 7040
Email: ecis@ecis.org
Website: www.ecis.org

The Girls' Day School Trust (GDST)

The Girls' Day School Trust (GDST) is one of the largest, longest-established and most successful groups of independent schools in the UK, with 4000 staff and over 20,000 students between the ages of 3 and 18. As a charity that owns and runs a family of 25 schools in England and Wales, it reinvests all its income into its schools for the benefit of the pupils. With a long history of pioneering innovation in the education of girls, the GDST now also educates boys in some of its schools, and has two coeducational sixth form colleges. Registered charity No. 306983
10 Bressenden Place, London, SW1E 5DH
Tel: 020 7393 6666
Email: info@wes.gdst.net
Website: www.gdst.net

Girls' Schools Association (GSA)

For information on the GSA see editorial on page 32

The Headmasters' and Headmistresses' Conference (HMC)

For information on the HMC see editorial on page 33

Human Scale Education (HSE)

An educational reform movement aiming for small education communities based on democracy, fairness and respect. Registered charity No. 1000400
Email: contact@humanscaleeducation.com
Website: www.humanscaleeducation.com

The Independent Association of Prep Schools (IAPS)

For further information about IAPS see editorial on page 34

The Independent Schools Association (ISA)

For further information about ISA see editorial on page 35

The Independent Schools' Bursars Association (ISBA)

Exists to support and advance financial and operational performance in independent schools. The ISBA is a charitable company limited by guarantee. Company No. 6410037; registered charity No. 1121757
167-169 Great Portland Street, 5th Floor, London W1W 5PF
Tel: 01256 330369
Email: isbaoffice@theisba.org.uk
Website: www.theisba.org.uk

The Independent Schools Council (ISC)

The Independent Schools Council exists to promote choice, diversity and excellence in education; the development of talent at all levels of ability; and the widening of opportunity for children from all backgrounds to achieve their potential. Its 1400 member schools educate more than 500,000 children at all levels of ability and from all socioeconomic classes. Nearly a third of children in ISC schools receive help with fees. The Governing Council of ISC contains representatives from each of the eight ISC constituent associations listed below. See also page 30.

Members:
Association of Governing Bodies of Independent Schools (AGBIS)
Girls' Schools Association (GSA)
Headmasters' and Headmistresses' Conference (HMC)
Independent Association of Prep Schools (IAPS)
Independent Schools Association (ISA)
Independent Schools Bursars' Association (ISBA)
The Society of Heads

The council also has close relations with the BSA, COBIS, SCIS and WISC.

First Floor, 27 Queen Anne's Gate,
London, SW1H 9BU
Tel: 020 7766 7070
Fax: 020 7766 7071
Email: research@isc.co.uk
Website: www.isc.co.uk

The Independent Schools Examinations Board (ISEB)

Details of the Common Entrance examinations are obtainable from:
Independent Schools Examinations Board,
Endeavour House, Crow Arch Lane, Ringwood BH24 1HP
Tel: 01425 470555
Email: enquiries@iseb.co.uk
Website: www.iseb.co.uk
Copies of past papers can be purchased from Galore Park: www.galorepark.co.uk

International Baccalaureate (IB)

For full information about the IB see full entry on page 413.

International Schools Theatre Association (ISTA)

International body of teachers and students of theatre, run by teachers for teachers. Registered charity No. 1050103
Lakeside Offices, The Old Cattle Market, Coronation Park, Helston, Cornwall, TR13 0SR
Tel: 01326 560398
Email: office@ista.co.uk
Website: www.ista.co.uk

Maria Montessori Institute (MMI)

Authorised by the Association Montessori Internationale (AMI) to run their training course in the UK. Further information is available from:
26 Lyndhurst Gardens, Hampstead, London NW3 5NW
Tel: 020 7435 3646
Email: info@mariamontessori.org
Website: www.mariamontessori.org

The National Association of Independent Schools & Non-Maintained Schools (NASS)

A membership organisation working with and for special schools in the voluntary and private sectors within the UK. Registered charity No. 1083632
PO Box 705, York YO30 6WW
Tel/Fax: 01904 624446
Email: krippon@nasschools.org.uk
Website: www.nasschools.org.uk

National Day Nurseries Association (NDNA)

A national charity that aims to promote quality in early years. Registered charity No. 1078275
NDNA, National Early Years Enterprise Centre, Longbow Close, Huddersfield, West Yorkshire HD2 1GQ
Tel: 01484 407070
Fax: 01484 407060
Email: info@ndna.org.uk
Website: www.ndna.org.uk

3 Connaught House, Riverside Business Park, Benarth Road, Conwy, LL32 8UB
Tel: 01824 707823
Email: wales@ndna.org.uk

NDNA Scotland, The Mansfield Traquair Centre, 15 Mansfield Place, Edinburgh EH3 6BB
Tel: 0131 516 6967
Email: scotland@ndna.org.uk

National Foundation for Educational Research (NFER)

NFER is the UK's largest independent provider of research, assessment and information services for education, training and children's services. Its clients include UK government departments and agencies at both national and local levels. NFER is a not-for-profit organisation and a registered charity No. 313392
Head Office, The Mere, Upton Park, Slough, Berkshire SL1 2DQ
Tel: 01753 574123
Fax: 01753 691632
Email: enquiries@nfer.ac.uk
Website: www.nfer.ac.uk

Potential Plus UK

Potential Plus UK is an independent charity that supports the social, emotional and learning needs of children with high learning potential of all ages and backgrounds. Registered charity No. 313182
Potential Plus UK, The Open University, Vaughan Harley Building Ground Floor, Walton Hall, Milton Keynes, MK7 6AA
Tel: 01908 646433
Email: amazingchildren@potentialplusuk.org
Website: www.potentialplusuk.org

Round Square

An international group of schools formed in 1967 following the principles of Dr Kurt Hahn, the founder of Salem School in Germany, and Gordonstoun in Scotland. The Round Square, named after Gordonstoun's 17th century circular building in the centre of the school, now has more than 100 member schools. Registered charity No. 327117
Round Square, First Floor, Morgan House, Madeira Walk, Windsor SL4 1EP
Tel: 01474 709843
Website: www.roundsquare.org

Royal National Children's SpringBoard Foundation

On 1 July 2017 the Royal National Children's Foundation (RNCF) merged with The SpringBoard Bursary Foundation to create the Royal National Children's SpringBoard Foundation ('Royal SpringBoard'). The newly merged charity gives life-transforming bursaries to disadvantaged and vulnerable children from across the UK.
6th Floor, Minster House, 42 Mincing Lane, London, EC3R 7AE
Tel: 01932 868622
Email: admin@royalspringboard.org.uk
Website: www.royalspringboard.org.uk

School Fees Independent Advice (SFIA)

For further information about SFIA, see editorial on page 28

Schools Music Association of Great Britain (SMA)

The SMA is a national 'voice' for music in education. It is now part of the Incorporated Society of Musicians
Registered charity No. 313646
Website: www.ism.org/sma

Scottish Council of Independent Schools (SCIS)

Representing more than 70 independent, fee-paying schools in Scotland, the Scottish Council of Independent Schools (SCIS) is the foremost authority on independent schools in Scotland and offers impartial information, advice and guidance to parents. Registered charity No. SC018033
1 St Colme Strret, Edinburgh EH3 6AA
Tel: 0131 556 2316
Email: info@scis.org.uk
Website: www.scis.org.uk

Society of Education Consultants (SEC)

The Society is a professional membership organisation that supports management consultants who specialise in education and children's services. The society's membership includes consultants who work as individuals, in partnerships or in association with larger consultancies.
SEC, Bellamy House, 13 West Street, Cromer NR27 9HZ
Tel: 0330 323 0457
Email: administration@sec.org.uk
Website: www.sec.org.uk

The Society of Heads

For full information see editorial on page 36

State Boarding Forum (SBF)

For full information about the SBF see editorial on page 31

Steiner Waldorf Schools Fellowship (SWSF)

Representing Steiner education in the UK and Ireland, the SWSF has member schools and early years centres in addition to interest groups and other affiliated organisations. Member schools offer education for children within the normal range of ability, aged 3 to 18. Registered charity No. 295104
35 Park Rd, London NW1 6XT
Tel: 020 4524 9933
Email: admin@steinerwaldorf.org
Website: www.steinerwaldorf.org

Support and Training in Prep Schools (SATIPS)

SATIPS aims to support teachers in the independent and maintained sectors of education. Registered charity No. 313688
7 Lakeside, Overstone Park, Northampton, Northamptonshire, NN6 0QS
Website: www.satips.org

The Tutors' Association

The Tutors' Association is the professional body for tutoring and wider supplementary education sector in the UK. Launched in 2013, they have over 1,300 members, including Individual and Corporate Members representing some 50,000 tutors throughout the UK.
Tel: 01628 306108
Email: info@thetutorsassociation.org.uk
Website: www.thetutorsassociation.org.uk

UCAS (Universities and Colleges Admissions Service)

UCAS is the organisation responsible for managing applications to higher education courses in England, Scotland, Wales and Northern Ireland. Registered charity Nos. 1024741 and SC038598
Rosehill, New Barn Lane,
Cheltenham, Gloucestershire GL52 3LZ
Tel: 0371 468 0 468
Website: www.ucas.com

UKCISA – The Council for International Student Affairs

UKCISA is the UK's national advisory body serving the interests of international students and those who work with them. Registered charity No. 1095294
Website: www.ukcisa.org.uk

United World Colleges (UWC)

UWC was founded in 1962 and their philosophy is based on the ideas of Dr Kurt Hahn (see Round Square Schools). Registered charity No. 313690.
UWC International, Third Floor, 55 New Oxford Street, London, WC1A 1BS, UK
Tel: 020 7269 7800
Fax: 020 7405 4374
Email: info@uwcio.uwc.org
Website: www.uwc.org

World-Wide Education Service of CfBT Education Trust (WES)

A leading independent service which provides home education courses worldwide.
Waverley House, Penton,
Carlisle, Cumbria CA6 5QU
Tel: 01228 577123
Email: office@weshome.com
Website: www.weshome.com

Glossary

ACETS	Awards and Certificates in Education
AEA	Advanced Extension Award
AEB	Associated Examining Board for the General Certificate of Education
AEGIS	Association for the Education and Guardianship of International Students
AGBIS	Association of Governing Bodies of Independent Schools
AHIS	Association of Heads of Independent Schools
AJIS	Association of Junior Independent Schools
ALP	Association of Learning Providers
ANTC	The Association of Nursery Training Colleges
AOC	Association of Colleges
AP	Advanced Placement
ASCL	Association of School & College Leaders
ASL	Additional and Specialist Learning
ATI	The Association of Tutors Incorporated
AQA	Assessment and Qualification Alliance/Northern Examinations and Assessment Board
BA	Bachelor of Arts
BAC	British Accreditation Council for Independent Further and Higher Education
BAECE	The British Association for Early Childhood Education
BD	Bachelor of Divinity
BEA	Boarding Educational Alliance
BEd	Bachelor of Education
BLitt	Bachelor of Letters
BPrimEd	Bachelor of Primary Education
BSA	Boarding Schools' Association
BSc	Bachelor of Science
BTEC	Range of work-related, practical programmes leading to qualifications equivalent to GCSEs and A levels awarded by Edexcel
Cantab	Cambridge University
CATSC	Catholic Association of Teachers in Schools and Colleges
CCEA	Council for the Curriculum, Examination and Assessment
CDT	Craft, Design and Technology
CE	Common Entrance Examination
CEAS	Children's Education Advisory Service
CertEd	Certificate of Education
CIE	Cambridge International Examinations
CIFE	Conference for Independent Education
CIS	Council of International Schools
CISC	Catholic Independent Schools' Conference
CLAIT	Computer Literacy and Information Technology
CNED	Centre National d'enseignement (National Centre of long distance learning)
COBIS	Council of British International)

CSA	The Choir Schools' Association
CST	The Christian Schools' Trust
DfE	Department for Education (formerly DfES and DCFS)
DipEd	Diploma of Education
DipTchng	Diploma of Teaching
EAIE	European Association for International Education
ECIS	European Council of International Schools
EdD	Doctor of Education
Edexcel	GCSE Examining group, incorporating Business and Technology Education Council (BTEC) and University of London Examinations and Assessment Council (ULEAC)
EFL	English as a Foreign Language
ELAS	Educational Law Association
EPQ	Extended Project qualification
ESL	English as a Second Language
FCoT	Fellow of the College of Teachers (TESOL)
FEFC	Further Education Funding Council
FRSA	Fellow of the Royal Society of Arts
FSMQ	Free-Standing Mathematics Qualification
GCE	General Certificate of Education
GCSE	General Certificate of Secondary Education
GDST	Girls' Day School Trust
GNVQ	General National Vocational Qualifications
GOML	Graded Objectives in Modern Languages
GSA	Girls' Schools Association
GSVQ	General Scottish Vocational Qualifications
HMC	Headmasters' and Headmistresses' Conference
HMCJ	Headmasters' and Headmistresses' Conference Junior Schools
HNC	Higher National Certificate
HND	Higher National Diploma
IAPS	Independent Association of Prep Schools
IB	International Baccalaureate
ICT	Information and Communication Technology
IFF	Inspiring Futures Foundation (formerly ISCO)
IGCSE	International General Certificate of Secondary Education
INSET	In service training
ISA	Independent Schools Association
ISBA	Independent Schools' Bursars' Association
ISCis	Independent Schools Council information service
ISC	Independent Schools Council
ISEB	Independent Schools Examination Board
ISST	International Schools Sports Tournament
ISTA	International Schools Theatre Association
ITEC	International Examination Council
JET	Joint Educational Trust
LA	Local Authority
LISA	London International Schools Association
MA	Master of Arts
MCIL	Member of the Chartered Institute of Linguists
MEd	Master of Education
MIoD	Member of the Institute of Directors
MLitt	Master of Letters
MSc	Master of Science
MusD	Doctor of Music
MYP	Middle Years Programme
NABSS	National Association of British Schools in Spain
NAGC	National Association for Gifted Children
NAHT	National Association of Head Teachers
NAIS	National Association of Independent Schools
NASS	National Association of Independent Schools & Non-maintained Special Schools
NDNA	National Day Nurseries Association
NEASC	New England Association of Schools and Colleges
NFER	National Federation of Educational Research
NPA	National Progression Award
NQ	National Qualification
NQF	National Qualifications Framework
NQT	Newly Qualified Teacher
NVQ	National Vocational Qualifications
OCR	Oxford, Cambridge and RSA Examinations
OLA	Online Language Assessment for Modern Languages
Oxon	Oxford
PGCE	Post Graduate Certificate in Education
PhD	Doctor of Philosophy
PL	Principal Learning
PNEU	Parents' National Education Union
PYP	Primary Years Programme
QCA	Qualifications and Curriculum Authority
QCF	Qualifications and Credit Framework
RSIS	The Round Square Schools
SAT	Scholastic Aptitude Test
SATIPS	Support & Training in Prep Schools/Society of Assistant Teachers in Prep Schools
SBSA	State Boarding Schools Association
SCE	Service Children's Education
SCIS	Scottish Council of Independent Schools
SCQF	Scottish Credit and Qualifications Framework
SEC	The Society of Educational Consultants
SEN	Special Educational Needs
SFCF	Sixth Form Colleges' Forum
SFIA	School Fees Insurance Agency Limited
SFIAET	SFIA Educational Trust
SMA	Schools Music Association
SoH	The Society of Heads
SQA	Scottish Qualifications Authority
STEP	Second Term Entrance Paper (Cambridge)
SVQ	Scottish Vocational Qualifications
SWSF	Steiner Waldorf Schools Fellowship
TABS	The Association of Boarding Schools
TISCA	The Independent Schools Christian Alliance
TOEFL	Test of English as a Foreign Language
UCAS	Universities and Colleges Admissions Service for the UK
UCST	United Church Schools Trust
UKLA	UK Literacy Association
UKCISA	The UK Council for International Education
UWC	United World Colleges
WISC	World International Studies Committee
WJEC	Welsh Joint Education Committee
WSSA	Welsh Secondary Schools Association

Index